SAP PRESS Books: Always on hand

Print or e-book, Kindle or iPad, workplace or airplane: Choose
where and how to read your SAP PRESS books! You can now get
all our titles as e-books, too:

▸ By download and online access
▸ For all popular devices
▸ And, of course, DRM-free

Convinced? Then go to **www.sap-press.com** and get your
e-book today.

Practical Workflow for SAP®

 **PRESS**

SAP PRESS is a joint initiative of SAP and Galileo Press. The know-how offered by SAP specialists combined with the expertise of the Galileo Press publishing house offers the reader expert books in the field. SAP PRESS features first-hand information and expert advice, and provides useful skills for professional decision-making.

SAP PRESS offers a variety of books on technical and business-related topics for the SAP user. For further information, please visit our website: *www.sap-press.com*.

Ilja-Daniel Werner
ABAP Development for SAP Business Workflow
2011, 194 pp., hardcover
ISBN 978-1-59229-394-0

Rosenberg, Chase, Omar, Taylor, von Rosing
Applying Real-World BPM in an SAP Environment
2011, 698 pp., hardcover
ISBN 978-1-59229-343-8

Mandy Krimmel, Joachim Orb
SAP NetWeaver Process Integration (2nd Edition)
2010, 394 pp., hardcover
ISBN 978-1-59229-344-5

Emmanuel Hadzipetros
Architecting EDI with SAP IDocs (2nd Edition)
2014, app. 825 pp., hardcover
ISBN 978-1-59229-871-6

Jocelyn Dart, Erik Dick, Ginger Gatling, Oliver Hilss,
Somya Kapoor, Silvana Kempf, Susan Keohan, Thomas Kosog,
Paul Médaille, Mike Pokraka, Alan Rickayzen,
Shalini Sabnani, Jörn Sedlmayr, Ted Sohn

Practical Workflow for SAP®

Galileo Press

Bonn • Boston

Galileo Press is named after the Italian physicist, mathematician, and philosopher Galileo Galilei (1564—1642). He is known as one of the founders of modern science and an advocate of our contemporary, heliocentric worldview. His words *Eppur si muove* (And yet it moves) have become legendary. The Galileo Press logo depicts Jupiter orbited by the four Galilean moons, which were discovered by Galileo in 1610.

Editor Stefan Proksch
Copyeditor Julie McNamee
Cover Design Nadine Kohl
Photo Credit Getty Images/Shapeshifters
Layout Design Vera Brauner
Production Iris Warkus
Typesetting SatzPro, Krefeld (Germany)
Printed and bound in the United States of America, on paper from sustainable sources

ISBN 978-1-59229-285-1
© 2013 by Galileo Press Inc., Boston (MA)
2nd Edition 2009, 2nd reprint 2013

All rights reserved. Neither this publication nor any part of it may be copied or reproduced in any form or by any means or translated into another language, without the prior consent of Galileo Press, Rheinwerkallee 4, 53227 Bonn, Germany.

Galileo Press makes no warranties or representations with respect to the content hereof and specifically disclaims any implied warranties of merchantability or fitness for any particular purpose. Galileo Press assumes no responsibility for any errors that may appear in this publication.

"Galileo Press" and the Galileo Press logo are registered trademarks of Galileo Press GmbH, Bonn, Germany, SAP PRESS is an imprint of Galileo Press.

All of the screenshots and graphics reproduced in this book are subject to copyright © SAP AG, Dietmar-Hopp-Allee 16, 69190 Walldorf, Germany.

SAP, the SAP logo, ABAP, BAPI, Duet, mySAP.com, mySAP, SAP ArchiveLink, SAP EarlyWatch, SAP NetWeaver, SAP Business ByDesign, SAP BusinessObjects, SAP Business-Objects Rapid Mart, SAP BusinessObjects Desktop Intelligence, SAP BusinessObjects Explorer, SAP Rapid Marts, SAP BusinessObjects Watchlist Security, SAP BusinessObjects Web Intelligence, SAP Crystal Reports, SAP GoingLive, SAP HANA, SAP MaxAttention, SAP MaxDB, SAP PartnerEdge, SAP R/2, SAP R/3, SAP R/3 Enterprise, SAP Strategic Enterprise Management (SAP SEM), SAP StreamWork, SAP Sybase Adaptive Server Enterprise (SAP Sybase ASE), SAP Sybase IQ, SAP xApps, SAPPHIRE NOW, and Xcelsius are registered or unregistered trademarks of SAP AG, Walldorf, Germany.

All other products mentioned in this book are registered or unregistered trademarks of their respective companies.

Contents at a Glance

Appendices

Contents

7

PART II: Developing Your Own Workflow

10 Business Objects 289

11   ABAP Classes 353

12 Agent Determination Rules 413

13 Using Events and Other Business Interfaces 441

15   Service-Enabling Workflows 501

16   Advanced Diagnostics 535

24 Duet — Microsoft Office Integration 661

PART IV: Using SAP Business Workflow in SAP Business Suite Applications

25 SAP Supplier Relationship Management 679

Foreword

The use of collaboration tools has become increasingly ubiquitous over the past few years. And as we well know, ubiquity does not always provide competitive gain. Advances in technology allow businesses to more easily redesign process management while tool-based human interaction enables access to information across diverse and distributed geographies and landscapes. Flexible, differentiating, and adaptable business process orchestration has become a business imperative. Essential as well, is facilitating faster and better information flow, without borders at times, between organizations and across industries as well as within companies. When using workflow and collaboration tools, the needs of the process step or task workers as well as the information workers must be served.

Although the original preface to the first version of *Practical Workflow for SAP* describes SAP customers as spending "the last seven years quietly automating and improving their business processes with the help of SAP's workflow management tool," we know that presently, in these turbulent economic times, there are few opportunities to engage in "quiet automation and improvement." The more exceptional the events encountered, the more flexibility and, often-frenetic, escalation is needed. But in the present climate where there is often a dearth of resources, and supplies are scarce, getting it right the first time is truly crucial.

This book offers the opportunity to explore using SAP Business Workflow as part of an overall Business Process Management strategy. It challenges you to define, before getting started on a workflow project, exactly what you expect to gain. Is your goal to monitor a particular process to see how long it takes? Is your goal to reduce the cycle time from document creation to approval? Is your goal to ensure quality or see service notifications are handled consistently and in a timely fashion? Companies attempting workflow projects without first accessing anticipated results and those companies refusing to recognize the degree of necessary managerial support needed to reach these ends, normally fail. Successful projects are clearly defined, make proper investments in personnel training, and most importantly have process goals that resonate well with the business users.

This second edition of *Practical Workflow for SAP* evolved as a collaboration process that is provided by the SAP workflow community for the SAP workflow community and for companies who need to increase the value of their SAP implementation investments. Today, SAP Business Workflow is delivered in every SAP NetWeaver Application Server and is tightly coupled to SAP application systems. Simply stated, workflow enables you to get the right work to the right people at the right time for all processes necessary in an SAP application system.

This book can be your starting point to explore the possible options for using workflow. If you choose to start workflow projects, you must be willing to invest a significant amount of time on learning, and you must have senior management support. Workflow can change how people go about their daily tasks, and it can be used to enforce service level agreements on specific processes. It also personifies process optimization. The goal of this book is to get you started in understanding how SAP Business Workflow works and how it fits in with SAP's overall Business Process Management strategy. It is meant to provide an overview of workflow usage in SAP ERP, SAP CRM, SAP ERP HCM, and SAP SRM systems. This book should supply the initial technical knowledge required by the workflow designer and developers, as well as enabling you to understand options for how to ensure each task in the workflow is routing to the correct person.

The creation of this second edition is itself a study in collaborative process improvement as well as community-minded teamwork. The 14 authors hail from 5 countries, 3 continents, and multiple SAP community environments. They span our SAP ecosystem by representing customers, partners, independents, and employees in varied industries and SAP solution areas. The authors' workflow knowledge stems from consulting, development, solution management, education, and most importantly practical and extensive field experience. Knowing as I do the human fabric represented in the author demographics, I dare say the group also is personified by altruistic, supportive behavior, professional as well as social, where sharing knowledge is done generously and munificently by sustaining the work of others in online forum discussions, user groups, customer engagements, and events. Those contributing to the publication of this book exemplify that generosity of spirit and have kindly donated the proceeds of its publication to Doctors Without Borders/Médecins Sans Frontières. An apt gesture from a group of people who see that where uncertainty is greatest, coordination and response know few limits and boundaries.

Marilyn Pratt
Community Evangelist, SAP Community Network
Global Ecosystem and Partner Group
SAP AG

Preface

Welcome to the second edition of *Practical Workflow for SAP*! For those of you who already have experience with SAP Business Workflow, you know that the workflow community really believes in the value of SAP Business Workflow and the real impact it can have on your SAP implementation. The second edition will enable you, the workflow expert and evangelist, to update your workflow skills to SAP NetWeaver with new technical topics such as ABAP classes, user interfaces, inbox options, and new design techniques. For those of you new to workflow, this book is intended for you as well; we hope to have you as an active participant in the workflow community!

Contents of the Book

The first edition of this book was written by SAP workflow experts who are passionate about the topic and about the impact it can have on your business. This second edition of the book stays true to the core goal of providing practical guidance on SAP Business Workflow and expands the first edition with new capabilities and new ways to use SAP Business Workflow.

This book is divided into four parts:

▶ **Part I: Using SAP Business Workflow**
This part of the book starts by introducing SAP Business Workflow, positioning it within the overall SAP Business Process Management strategy. It then discusses what you need to know to get SAP Business Workflow running on your system. It discusses how users get tasks from workflow, how you administer workflow, and the option to use SAP NetWeaver Business Warehouse for workflow reporting.

▶ **Part II: Developing Your Own Workflow**
This part of the book walks you through all of the major areas you need to know when developing your own workflows. You will learn how to design a workflow and where programming comes into play. You do not need to be a professional developer to understand this part, but some basic knowledge,

such as calling function modules, is important. You will learn how workflow communicates with business applications and how you can service enable workflows to call them as part of a broader business context. This part of the book also includes information on debugging, and guidance when preparing for an upgrade.

▶ **Part III: User Interface Technologies and SAP Business Workflow**
SAP applications have seen major user interface changes since the first edition of this book was published. In this part of the book, Web Dynpro ABAP and Web Dynpro Java are discussed for use with SAP Business Workflow. Additionally, Alloy, Duet, Business Server Pages (BSP) and forms are covered as user interface options with SAP Business Workflow.

▶ **Part IV: Using SAP Business Workflow in SAP Business Suite Applications**
This part of the book covers SAP Business Workflow as used by key SAP Business Suite applications. These include SAP Enterprise Resource Planning (SAP ERP), SAP Supplier Relationship Management (SAP SRM), SAP Customer Relationship Management (SAP CRM), and SAP Human Capital Management (SAP ERP HCM).

With the division of the book into four major parts, you can read the different parts as you need them. Part I and Part II are critical for you to understand how workflow works. Part III can be read when you need to integrate one of the discussed user interfaces with your workflow. For Part IV, you can read the chapter that corresponds to the SAP application where you want to use SAP-provided workflows, or you want to know what is unique about workflow on a particular application system.

Target Groups of the Book

This book is intended for business process experts (BPEs) and developers new to the topic of SAP Business Workflow. Although there is some code in this book, the bulk of the "how to build and execute workflows" content requires no programming.

It is also intended for existing workflow experts who are upgrading to SAP NetWeaver 7.0 and need to upgrade their workflow skills. This target group does not need all chapters, but there are new capabilities provided in many chapters (e.g., in the chapters on building workflows and using events), and there are new chapters on ABAP classes and other topics you may not have used on your existing release.

If you are already a workflow expert and are starting a workflow project on SAP SRM, SAP CRM, or SAP ERP HCM, then this book will provide important insight on how to use workflow on these application systems.

Structure of the Book

In detail, the book consists of the following chapters:

▸ **Chapter 1: Introduction**
This chapter provides an introduction into SAP Business Workflow by discussing what SAP Business Workflow is, when to use SAP Business Workflow, its major features, and how SAP Business Workflow fits in with the SAP overall strategy for Business Process Management. If you are an existing workflow expert, we still recommend you read this chapter so you know where workflow fits in the SAP overall Business Process Management strategy.

▸ **Chapter 2: Requirements Gathering Strategy**
Before starting any workflow project, you need to know what is expected when the workflow goes into production. This chapter discusses questions that should be asked before starting a workflow project, how to know if the business problem is a candidate for SAP Business Workflow, and how to measure your results. This chapter is a must read before starting your first workflow project. The content also includes a number of checklists that can be downloaded from the SAP PRESS website (*http://www.sap-press.com*).

▸ **Chapter 3: Configuring the System**
Before you can start using workflow, the system must be configured to use SAP Business Workflow. This chapter discusses how to do the initial required configuration.

▸ **Chapter 4: Work Item Delivery**
Work item delivery discusses the users' experiences with SAP Business Workflow. This chapter discusses the inboxes that exists and the capabilities of the inboxes, and provides recommendations for delivering work items to users.

▸ **Chapter 5: Agents**
When a workflow executes, it is critical that the right person receives the right task. This chapter discusses the role of agents in the design of a workflow.

▶ **Chapter 6: Workflow Administration**

The workflow administration chapter provides information on what reports are available with SAP Business Workflow and discusses how to ensure the workflows and agent assignments are kept updated to meet changing business requirements.

▶ **Chapter 7: Using SAP NetWeaver Business Warehouse for SAP Business Workflow Reporting**

This chapter discusses the option to report on workflow execution from SAP NetWeaver Business Warehouse. This gives the option to provide analytical reports for upper management on how often and how long processes are executing.

▶ **Chapter 8: Creating a Workflow**

Chapter 8 provides concrete examples and guidance when creating your very first workflow. It walks you through each part of workflow creation.

▶ **Chapter 9: Advanced Workflow Design Techniques**

Advanced workflow design goes beyond the most simple workflow design. This chapter discusses more advanced topics such as parallel processing, containers and bindings, and other topics to enhance your workflow skills.

▶ **Chapter 10: Business Objects**

Workflow functionality is based on application functionality. Business objects link the workflow to the application functionality. This chapter discusses how objects work and how to create your own business objects.

▶ **Chapter 11: ABAP Classes**

ABAP classes can be used instead of or in addition to business objects. Classes link workflow to business functionality. This chapter walks you through creating your own ABAP classes for SAP Business Workflow.

▶ **Chapter 12: Agent Determination Rules**

Chapter 5, Agents, discusses how agents work in SAP Business Workflow. This chapter walks through options to determine who should get a specific task at runtime.

▶ **Chapter 13: Using Events and Other Business Interfaces**

After a workflow is created, the application must tell the workflow to start, and possibly when to stop. This chapter walks through how to get the workflow to respond to what is happening in the application.

▸ **Chapter 14: Custom Programs**
This chapter covers the most commonly used workflow application programming interfaces (WAPIs).

▸ **Chapter 15: Service-Enabling Workflows**
After you have a workflow in place, you may need the workflow to be called as a service. This chapter discusses Service-Oriented Architecture (SOA), service-enabling a workflow, and calling the service via SAP NetWeaver Process Integration (SAP NetWeaver PI).

▸ **Chapter 16: Advanced Diagnostics**
Chapter 16 walks through the commonly used tools used to debug and resolve common workflow problems.

▸ **Chapter 17: Upgrading SAP Business Workflow**
This chapter is intended to read as part of preparation when planning an upgrade from SAP R/3 4.6x to SAP NetWeaver 7.0.

▸ **Chapter 18: User Interface Options**
This chapter describes required steps if you want to execute a workflow task using Web Dynpro or Business Server Pages (BSP). This chapter should be read before reading Chapters 19-21.

▸ **Chapter 19: Using Web Dynpro ABAP**
Chapter 19 uses the user decision step type available in SAP Business Workflow to discuss using a Web Dynpro ABAP with SAP Business Workflow.

▸ **Chapter 20: Using Web Dynpro Java**
The Web Dynpro Java chapter covers the major steps required when using Web Dynpro Java to execute a workflow task.

▸ **Chapter 21: Using Business Server Pages**
The BSP chapter walks through an example of executing a BSP as the user interface for a workflow step.

▸ **Chapter 22: Using Forms**
Chapter 22 discusses the form step type in SAP Business Workflow.

▸ **Chapter 23: Alloy — Lotus Notes Integration**
This chapter introduces Alloy and how it works with SAP Business Workflow.

▸ **Chapter 24: Duet — Microsoft Office Integration**
This chapter introduces Duet and the Duet Approval Workflow that is based on SAP Business Workflow.

▶ **Chapter 25: SAP Supplier Relationship Management**
This chapter discusses how workflow is used in SAP SRM 7.0 and SRM 5.0. It describes the workflow frameworks and provides examples of usage.

▶ **Chapter 26: SAP Customer Relationship Management**
This chapter discusses how workflow is used in SAP CRM 2007/7.0. It describes the SAP CRM frameworks, including the SAP CRM UI, and how workflow works in SAP CRM.

▶ **Chapter 27: SAP ERP Human Capital Management — Processes and Forms**
This chapter covers the major use cases for workflow in SAP Human Capital Management (SAP ERP HCM) administrative services. It provides a business and technical overview of form usage in SAP ERP HCM administrative services.

▶ **Chapter 28: Setting Up an SAP-Provided SAP ERP Workflow**
Chapter 28 walks through an example of configuring a workflow template provided by SAP in an ERP system.

▶ **Chapter 29: ArchiveLink**
Chapter 29 finally discusses the use of ArchiveLink for imaging projects with SAP Business Workflow.

▶ **Appendix**
There are several appendices to assist you: **Appendix A** covers common tips and tricks. **Appendix B** gives step-by-step troubleshooting assistance. **Appendix C** is the administrator's first aid guide. **Appendix D** discusses the workflow macros. **Appendix E** walks through setting up your first SAP NetWeaver Application Server Java for Web Dynpro Java. **Appendix F** provides further information for SAP SRM such as delivered Business Configuration Sets (BC Sets), Business Add-Ins (BAdIs), and troubleshooting. In addition to the appendices, there are also ready-to-use checklists for your first workflow project you can download from the SAP PRESS website (*http://www.sap-press.com*).

System Requirements

Although many sections of the book are release independent, the content of this book is based on workflow capabilities available in SAP NetWeaver 7.0. When discussing SAP applications, the SAP Business Suite is generally assumed. Specifically, SAP ERP (ECC 6.0), SAP SRM 5.0, SAP SRM 7.0, and SAP CRM 2007/7.0 are the releases used in the application-focused chapters.

Further Training

If after reading this book you want more information on workflow, SAP Educational Services offers classes on SAP Business Workflow. BIT600 is an introduction class, BIT601 is a class on building workflow, and BIT610 is a class on development with SAP Business Workflow. For further information, visit the SAP Education website at *http://www.sap.com/services/education*.

Acknowledgements

This book could not be possible without the incredible effort done by the authors of the first edition. Alan Rickayzen, Jocelyn Dart, Carsten Brennecke, and Markus Schneider provided a very successful first edition that has been widely used and is greatly appreciated by the workflow community. The effort for the second edition has been complemented with additional workflow developers, consultants, partners, and customers. I would like to say a special thanks to each of the book's authors who participated in the project. Each author made a unique contribution that only he or she could provide. Some of the authors I've known for many years, and others I met during the course of this project. It was a privilege to work with each of them, and I hope you will take the time to read about them in Appendix G.

In addition to the authors, there are several others who played a critical role in this book. From the discussing ideas, to reviewing chapters, to providing content, many people have been instrumental to the second edition. People to thank include Peter Csontos, Sandor Szeman, and Boris Magocsi, for UWL content and guidance; Michael Bonrat and Dagmar Becker, for review of the SAP HCM chapter; Katie Beavers, for her SAP NetWeaver Business Warehouse review and detailed assistance; Sandhya Rani Sahu and Anantharam R, for their help with the ArchiveLink chapter; Michael Hill, for his review of the introduction chapter; Markus Kinateder, for much expert guidance along the way, content, and willingness to share; Carol Thomas, Sky Kimball, and John Villane II, for input and review of the SAP CRM chapter; Thomas Jung, for being the user interface guru that he is and providing timely and helpful feedback; Richard Feco, for providing content, review, and input to the SAP SRM chapter; and Eddie Morris, for content and guidance for upgrading SAP Business Workflow. We also need to say a big thank you to all of the folks who supported us with content and reviews who wish to remain anonymous.

When we started this book project, we all knew it would take time and considerable effort, but the time taken from family was certainly underestimated. We are all very fortunate in life if we can find people who love us, and when those people encourage us and support us during times when work takes front and center, as it did while working on this book, we realize how fortunate we are! So, thank you to our family and friends who provided support, encouragement, and patience throughout this project.

As a final note, I hope you have noticed that all royalties from this book will be donated to Doctors Without Borders/Médecins San Frontières. Each author has individually decided to donate his or her royalties. Your purchase of this book helps us support an international medical humanitarian organization that delivers emergency aid in many countries. Thank you for enabling us to provide support to this important organization.

I hope to see you blogging about workflow on SDN after reading this book!

Ginger Gatling
Senior Product Manager
SAP NetWeaver Solution Management

PART I
Using SAP Business Workflow

This chapter offers a brief overview of SAP Business Workflow and discusses how it fits into the overall Business Process Management offering delivered by SAP. You do not need any previous experience with SAP Business Workflow to read this chapter.

1 Introduction

If you are reading this book, you are interested in getting practical advice on implementing SAP Business Workflow. You won't be disappointed; in these pages, you will find practical instruction from a group of the world's leading experts who collectively have decades worth of experience implementing SAP Business Workflow at dozens of the world's leading companies. But we ask you to take just a moment with us to consider workflow in a broader context.

If you are already an experienced workflow expert looking only for practical advice you may, of course, skip this section. But if you are new to SAP Business Workflow, have broader interests than the subject at hand, or just want to know in which situations SAP Business Workflow is the right tool, then we encourage you to stop for a moment and take a higher level view of the topic.

In this chapter, we introduce the basic concepts of SAP Business Workflow (and workflow in general), and we also consider some related capabilities, namely SAP NetWeaver Business Process Management and how SAP Business Workflow fits in with SAP's overall Business Process Management strategy.

1.1 What Is SAP Business Workflow

SAP Business Workflow is a capability that allows you to automate business processes within your company to improve the efficiency and performance of those processes. Workflows guide the different parts of a process through a company's organization to ensure that the right work reaches the right person at the right time. Essentially, workflows make the SAP system proactive by ensuring each person has his work delivered to him in a timely fashion.

Workflow is a generic term that refers to any definable process flow and to the software that automates that flow. In this book, we will use the terms *workflow* and *SAP Business Workflow* interchangeably whenever the intended meaning is clear from context. The great advantage of SAP Business Workflow is that it is embedded within SAP applications and delivered as part of the application platform, which means that many SAP processes can be automated without any development work. SAP ERP, SAP CRM, and SAP SRM are examples of SAP applications that provide ready-to-use workflows.

Many types of processes are suitable for automating with workflow. These processes include but are not limited to the following:

▶ Approval processes, such as purchase requisition, purchase order, and invoice approval.

▶ Processes that are repeated often and that must follow specific business rules. For example, for each new employee, a specific on-boarding process must be executed.

▶ Processes that could be audited, or areas where you want proof of execution for Sarbanes-Oxley compliance, or other government or corporate policy regulations.

These processes may complete in a matter of a few minutes or may take days to complete. In either case, SAP Business Workflow can be used to ensure that the process takes place as efficiently as possible and within a proscribed timeframe.

Figure 1.1 depicts the way processes may need to involve multiple employees and may cross departments. In this example, a clerk makes a request that could involve a purchasing agent and/or a boss. Based on the content in the request, it may go directly to the boss for approval, or it may need to go to a purchasing agent. The purchasing agent could send it back for a change, and then later accept and approve the document.

The human factor in workflows is one of the most important and interesting aspects of SAP Business Workflow. Workflow is most often used to automate processes that have user involvement (*human-centric processes*) rather than fully automated processes. In subsequent chapters, you will learn how workflows are tied to a company's organizational structure to guide process steps to the appropriate agents.

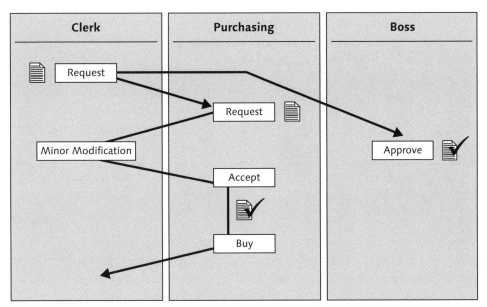

Figure 1.1 Business Processes May Involve Many Different People Across Departments

How users access the workflow process depends on your local installation. Users may access steps in the process via SAP GUI, the Universal Worklist (UWL) of the SAP NetWeaver Portal, or through their normal email client such as Microsoft Outlook or Lotus Notes (see Figure 1.2).

Technically, a business workflow is an executable process that is embedded within SAP applications to automate processes. These executable processes, however, are not coded using a low-level programming language; rather, they are modeled using a graphical modeling tool — the *Workflow Builder*. Because no low-level coding is required, experts in the business process being automated can create, edit, and configure workflows instead of having to rely on software developers.

SAP also delivers hundreds of prebuilt workflows that you can either use as-is out of the box or modify to suit the particular needs of your organization. You can also create your own workflows from scratch, where necessary, to automate any business processes for which there is no workflow delivered from SAP. We will have more to say about both using delivered workflows and creating your own elsewhere in these pages.

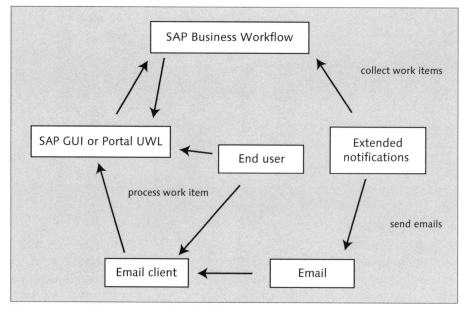

Figure 1.2 Users May Interact with a Workflow Process in Many Different Ways

1.2 What Is SAP NetWeaver Business Process Management

SAP Business Workflow is part of a larger suite of capabilities collectively known as SAP NetWeaver Business Process Management (SAP NetWeaver BPM). Although SAP Business Workflow is a great fit for standardized processes within the SAP Business Suite, SAP NetWeaver BPM enables you to compose processes at the edge of the application core. Edge applications are unique processes to your organization that are not covered by standard application software but interact with and leverage assets from your core processes. These unique processes are often very volatile and differentiating processes that allow you to provide a competitive advantage.

To illustrate the difference, consider an example from purchase order processing. In days past, a company might receive a purchase order in the mail, an employee would then have to enter the data into a sales order transaction, and the order would then proceed through the appropriate approval process until the order had been accepted and filled.

SAP Business Workflow enables automatic approvals of the purchase order based on customized requirements. In fact, purchase order approval is a workflow template delivered with the SAP Business Suite. This means approvers of purchase order do not have to look for purchase orders that need to be approved. Rather, they go to their inbox, and purchase orders requiring approval are provided with key contextual information. The process can include deadlines to ensure proper processing. The approval or rejection of the purchase order pushes the process to the next step, and the process can be monitored to see if it is meeting business expectations.

The next step is to receive purchase orders electronically, for instance, as EDI documents (electronic data interchange) or SOAP messages. If the company has appropriate processes and software (such as SAP NetWeaver and SAP Business Suite) in place, the company can automate the process to the extent that the order is completely processed without, in many cases, any human interaction at all (assuming no human approvals are required). Obviously, this automation both accelerates the process and reduces the cost of running the process.

Now assume the purchase order is automatically received and approved, all within the SAP Business Suite, but before this process starts, the company wants to insert additional steps to the process, for example, to see if any of the master data with the vendor has changed. For this, the process must now include a master data management system. In this situation, SAP NetWeaver BPM can be used to build a process that can connect to any system and can innovate on the existing process without disrupting the core process.

1.3 How Does SAP Business Workflow Fit Into the SAP Overall Business Process Management Strategy

In the following section of this chapter, we will discuss specific situations in which SAP Business Workflow is the right tool for the job. For now, however, we want to make a general recommendation on this point. Because SAP Business Workflow is an embedded capability of SAP applications, it is a natural choice for automating many processes within a single SAP application. Consider the following cases:

▶ **The process is human-centric and runs completely within a SAP application.**
In this case, SAP Business Workflow is most likely the ideal tool for automating such processes. If there is an existing SAP-delivered workflow for the process, then SAP Business Workflow is the right tool.

▶ **The process is human-centric and runs across multiple applications, including web or non-SAP applications.**
In this case, lean toward SAP NetWeaver BPM; this process might call SAP Business Workflow. The overarching process design is in SAP NetWeaver BPM, and SAP Business Workflow is called when required, for example, for approving documents that exist in the SAP Business Suite.

▶ **The process is completely automated, perhaps with allowances for human involvement in exceptional cases.**
In these cases, the preferred approach is to use integration processes in SAP NetWeaver Process Integration (SAP NetWeaver PI). Later in this book, you will see how workflows can be triggered via service (SOAP) calls and how workflows can be linked into such integration processes.

At this point, it should be clear that SAP Business Workflow is a robust, proven technology for automating human-centric core processes within and even across organizations. Because it is embedded in SAP applications, because many processes are workflow-enabled out of the box, and because SAP Business Workflow is a highly capable automation tool, you will likely find dozens of use cases for it in your organization.

1.4   In Which Business Situations Should I Use SAP Business Workflow

In this section, we'll highlight the primary features so that you can decide on the spot (such as during a conversation over lunch) whether or not SAP Business Workflow is likely to be appropriate for the task in hand. Saying "yes, definitely" on the spot does not, however, free you from the more detailed evaluation that will need to follow later.

The primary factors influencing the decision to use workflow are:

▶ Human involvement

▶ Repetition

- ▶ Fruits of success

- ▶ Cost of failure

The following sections describe these points in more detail, but it is worth stressing at this point that many SAP applications rely on SAP Business Workflow to automate their processes. So a significant factor is whether SAP provides a workflow that already covers your needs in this area. Even if the SAP-provided workflow does not exactly match your requirements, you will find that it is a very good starting point because the component is already "workflow-aware."

1.4.1 Factor 1: Human Involvement

One of the key features of all workflow systems is the ability to manage the people involved in a process. The workflow should coax the best out of the participants and compensate for their shortcomings, too. This is the fascination of creating a good business process: Workflow is very people-oriented. Not just in the user interface but also in the way the participants work together in a team. Workflow supports this teamwork.

The people involved in a process are the deciding factor. Although SAP Business Workflow can handle processes that involve no human interaction, most workflows are human-centric. As you will see in Chapter 2, Requirements Gathering Strategy, it is critical to get the right people on board with the workflow project in early stages. You need to have people involved who are willing to change how they perform processes today.

1.4.2 Factor 2: Repetition

The more often a process repeats itself, the better the return on the investment made in modeling the process. It is as simple as that.

This does not mean that there is no point in using workflow if the process does not repeat itself many times a day. If you activate one of the standard workflow templates delivered as part of your SAP component and use it as-is, the cost of automating the process is trivial, so it does not need to run often to give a return on investment. However, if you have a process that runs in a thousand variations, you might think carefully about modeling only the core of the process rather than creating a thousand workflow definitions.

Another exception to the repetition rule is a process that should rarely if ever occur, such as a catastrophe plan. This is related to the fourth factor, cost of failure, but is worth mentioning here. Emergency and exception procedures are good examples of processes worth automating because they have to follow a predefined path, and they have to follow this path as fast as possible, compensating for human nature along the way. A good rule of thumb is that processes that are repeatable are good candidates for workflow.

1.4.3   Factor 3: The Fruits of Success

When starting a workflow process, you need to calculate roughly how much you stand to gain by automating a process. The criteria that you use to measure the success varies from process to process, but these are the critical factors discussed further in this section:

▸ Cost savings that can be realized

▸ How much the speed of the process can be improved

▸ How much the quality of the outcome can be improved

Although you do not want to waste time and money on unnecessary research, it is essential that you get some sort of estimate of the expected savings/results before an implementation gets a go-ahead.

Hint
Before starting a workflow project, you should be able to answer the following questions: ▸ What is expected from this process?   ▸ What should be different?   ▸ How will we know if this process is successful?

Every project is an opportunity to document the usefulness of workflow, but the opportunity is wasted if you don't make a before and after snapshot. Unfortunately, projects often lose sight of this in the rush to go live. The snapshot will be valuable later, when other departments approach you about automating other processes. A quantified measure of success is invaluable to senior management, too. They will be keen to spread the use of a successful technology after they are shown in easy-to-understand terms that it is a success.

In the following section, you will see that to measure the fruits of success, you must ask many questions about the process and conduct research in many different directions. However, don't let the research get out of scope, where you end up trying to design the perfect process, and you find yourself still in the design stage several months into the project. Simply automating the core of the process can often reap the biggest savings.

Cost Savings

Cost savings are influenced by the reduction in time that a participant actively spends in the process. Questions to ask when evaluating the cost savings include the following:

▸ Is the information that participants need provided together with the task when it arrives on their screen, or do they have to do further research?

▸ Can you redistribute parts of a task to unskilled colleagues rather than expecting the skilled (and highly paid) employee to do it all?

▸ Can you automate some of the steps so that the system performs part of the task rather than expecting an employee to do it all?

Replacing complex navigation inside transactions by simple forms-based steps will often create substantial savings on its own.

Speed of the Process

The speed of the process is almost certain to increase dramatically when the workflow goes live. Reducing process time from two weeks to one to two days is typical of most of the workflow projects done using SAP Business Workflow. As well as estimating and comparing the timesaving, you should also prepare a list of intangible benefits. For example: Is a customer served more quickly? Does a new product take less time to reach the market? Is production downtime reduced?

Quality of the Results

The quality of the results of the process is the most difficult to estimate but is becoming increasingly important. Traditionally, workflow is often used for approvals procedures, with approvals being deemed a necessary evil in corporate life. Workflow can, of course, degenerate to an approval process within a hierarchy of rubber-stamping managers, with all applications being approved at some level without question. There is little point in implementing rubber-stamping approvals. Even this, however, must be tempered with the repetition factor. Consider vacation approvals; even though such requests may be approved 99% of the time, it is still convenient to have managers receive such requests in their email inbox via SAP Business Workflow.

However, if the approvers are chosen correctly, and the information brought to them with the task is helpful, the quality of the decisions being made will improve. This is important because good decisions are the single most important factor for a company's success. SAP Business Workflow has been used to improve decision making to reduce waste of materials (e.g., as part of an engineering change), reduce wasting money (e.g., helping to process incoming invoices), and reduce waste of human resources (e.g., during service management).

1.4.4 Factor 4: The Cost of Failure

Strictly speaking, the cost of failure should appear as a by-product when you estimate the "fruits of success." However, because the cost of a process failing is often the most significant cost, and because this factor is often neglected during requirements gathering, it deserves separate attention. How much does it cost to recall a car because an engineering change request has delivered the wrong result? How much damage does it do to a printer company's image if an out-of-date version of the printer driver is delivered to the customers?

The cost of a process failing can be enormous. If it fails to finish in time or delivers the wrong result, you will see lost customers, production standstills, or heavy maintenance bills. You can be sure that it is the failures rather than the successes that make the headlines, so make sure the cost of failure is taken into account when you decide whether or not to automate a process.

In practice, even the best business process stalls or goes wrong occasionally, irrespective of whether or not workflow is being used. However, workflow writes audit logs, making it easier to chase down the sources of errors and correct them as quickly as possible. Workflows can also trigger escalation procedures, for example, when too much time elapses before a participant moves on to the next step. Often this is simply a matter of identifying a user who is sitting on a task too long (maybe due to vacation) and forwarding it elsewhere. Using workflow, it is a matter of a few mouse clicks to identify the holdup. With paper- or email-based scenarios, this can consume a few hours of actual work, spread over several days.

1.5   What Can Be Achieved Using SAP Business Workflow

Irrespective of the process being automated, you will certainly achieve the following general benefits:

▶ The duration of the process is reduced dramatically.

▶ The process definition becomes transparent. Everyone knows what they are doing and why, even when there is high staff turnover.

▶ Each process instance (i.e., each separate run of the process) is transparent. During the process run and afterward, you can track who did what, and when.

▶ The process is under control. You can change the definition on the fly to improve it or to react to sudden changes in the environment.

Of course, in addition to these gains, there are benefits, such as cost savings or fewer failures that are specific to the process you are automating. These will often be the most significant benefits and the reason for automating the process in the first place. However, the four general points mentioned in the previous list are relevant to all processes, and they are supported by features embedded in the tool. In other words, these benefits can be realized with a minimum of effort in the process analysis and a minimum of effort in the implementation. These are the benefits you get for free when you use SAP Business Workflow to automate your process.

Because SAP Business Workflow is integrated directly into the SAP NetWeaver Application Server and because the SAP components mesh with it directly, the administration involved in making sure that the process runs day-in day-out is straightforward and very manageable. We will describe administration in more detail in Chapter 6, Workflow Administration.

1.6   Features of SAP Business Workflow

To meet the large variation in scenario requirements and customer environments, SAP Business Workflow offers a wealth of features and integration possibilities. Providing these in one single tool gives you a consistent approach and allows for future expansion of the process. Hundreds of workflow templates are delivered to kick-start the SAP implementation.

1.6.1 Robust Integration into SAP Applications

The direct integration into SAP application transactions is one of the single biggest advantages of using SAP Business Workflow. For example, an operator can start an ad-hoc workflow process related to the record without having to worry about who is involved in the process or how the process runs. The workflow deals with this automatically. This is useful to avoid the situation where an operator recognizes that something is wrong but does not know how to correct it or who to contact. Without workflow, the user will probably turn a blind eye to the situation and hope that someone else deals with it.

However, if a workflow has been defined, the user simply triggers the workflow and lets the workflow follow a preset routine, correctly notifying the other participants along the way. In addition, many parts of SAP Business Workflow use existing SAP services to perform fundamental duties rather than duplicating these. Examples of this are organizational management; communication services, and security infrastructures.

These are the advantages, but you should also be aware that many applications trigger workflows directly, relying on SAP Business Workflow to drive the processes through the component. In other words, SAP Business Workflow provides an intrinsic part of the SAP component's functionality.

1.6.2 Workflow Builder

The Workflow Builder (see Figure 1.3) allows you to build or enhance a process by simply dragging and dropping the individual tasks (based on transactions, function modules, etc.) into the process definition. A full suite of modeling elements is available to pick and drop into the workflow definition. Different types of branches, loops, and escalation paths can be added with conditions automatically determining which path to follow.

The Workflow Builder links the process to actual functionality, meaning that the process is modeled in a graphical way, activated, and then executed. The Workflow Builder is discussed in more detail in Chapter 8, Creating a Workflow.

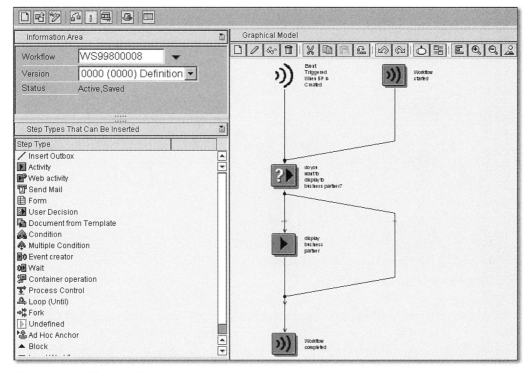

Figure 1.3 Workflow Builder

1.6.3 Graphical Status Visualization

A variety of different process logs can be displayed from the inbox and from various transaction codes (Chapter 4, Work Item Delivery, and Chapter 6, Workflow Administration, discuss how to access the workflow logs):

▸ Graphical (based on the graphic workflow definition)

▸ Summary (used by the operational user to determine what has been done so far by whom)

▸ Chronological (for auditing purposes)

▸ Technical (for debugging a process)

Figure 1.4 shows an example of the graphical workflow log. The book prints in black and white, but the actual graphical log has a bold green line that shows the path taken.

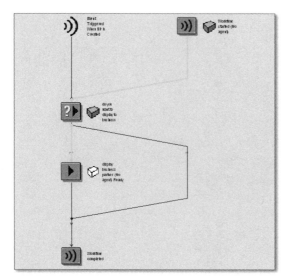

Figure 1.4 Graphical Workflow Log

You can navigate directly to these logs from the application transactions involved in the business process (e.g., while viewing an engineering change request). This is available automatically (providing that the application has enabled this) without the need for customizing, and it has the bonus of providing a useful link between seemingly unrelated business objects within a cross-application business process.

1.6.4 Routing Mechanisms

Routing algorithms can be selected for determining the users performing workflow tasks. A common example is finding a person's direct manager. Other examples include finding the person responsible for the purchasing group, material type, or any other data that are relevant for knowing how you should receive the workflow task. This automatic dispatching is very important when you want to avoid wasting time waiting for a supervisor to manually dispatch a task to someone in his department. The most complex algorithms can be resolved by calling function modules, but most needs are satisfied by simply assigning users or organizational units according to simple criteria without the need for programming.

Organizational Management, which is part of the SAP NetWeaver Application Server, can be used to simplify user administration. Many customers choose to use an organizational chart to define who should be responsible for what tasks.

Other mechanisms, such as custom tables created by the customer (normally known as *Z tables*), office distribution lists, and subscription mechanisms, can be used instead. For customers who decide not to use an organizational chart, custom tables are often used to determine who should be responsible for what tasks.

1.6.5 Deadline/Escalation Management

Deadlines are an important part of process management. They are used to remind users (or supervisors) about tasks that are waiting to be performed. They can also be used to control the process directly. For example, deadline management can specify that if a fourth-level approval is not performed within two days, then the request can automatically be sent through to the final stage of processing, with notifications being sent to the appropriate people. Escalation works in the same way, with corrective action being called automatically when a deadline is missed.

1.6.6 Synchronization Management

Sophisticated event handling allows your process to trigger automatically, based on changes (status, human resources, change documents, etc.) taking place within the SAP component. These events can also be used to synchronize processes with each other. For example, if a supplier is blocked, the engineering change request relying on this supplier can be sent back to the business approval stage before the change goes live.

1.6.7 Integration with Groupware Products

Allowing users to access the task list through their standard email client or user portal (Microsoft Outlook, Lotus Notes, and the SAP NetWeaver Portal) is a major step in getting them to accept the business process. Direct integration is especially important for sporadic but critical processes. SAP Business Workflow provides this integration, seamlessly, without the need to take special steps when creating the workflow.

1.6.8 Ad-hoc Process Enhancers

After the workflow is up and running, the users increase its efficiency by using attachments (to justify a decision, for example) or queries (to get additional information). Other users can view these long after the process has finished. This is clearly an advantage over emails because the emails will be deleted or remain hidden in recipients' inboxes. Attachments and queries (with their answers) can be read directly from the workflow log by anyone with the correct authorization.

In addition, steps or step-sequences (subworkflows) can be added to a workflow while it is running, and these are immediately visible in the graphic workflow log. Reviewers can be added on the fly, and predetermined agents downstream in the process can be replaced (authorization and configuration permitting).

1.6.9   Desktop Integration

Sometimes it is useful to have workflows that produce PC-based documents. For example, a workflow that creates a contract based on a standard Microsoft Word Template can be defined, filling in the details with the data accumulated during the workflow execution. This is particularly useful for creating complicated documents where the formatting as well as the content is important.

In this example, the legal department, which is involved later in the process, still has the chance to add their own changes before the final contract is agreed on. And if you rely on outsourced experts such as translators, lawyers, or writers, think how much time can be saved and how much control can be gained if you integrate them into the process via the Internet.

1.6.10   Analytics with SAP NetWeaver Business Warehouse

Although this is not usually the primary concern when kicking off a project with SAP Business Workflow, workflow reporting with SAP NetWeaver Business Warehouse often becomes significant later on. After your workflow is up and running, the system collects statistics.

SAP Business Workflow provides some standard reports as well as powerful information-gathering technology. The standard reports are of the form:

- ▶ How often does the process run?
- ▶ How long does it take?
- ▶ What is the workload of my department?

You can execute these reports in the SAP application system or use content delivered in SAP NetWeaver Business Warehouse to create reports for analysis on the workflow. For example, you can look at:

▶ How much processing time is involved in failed engineering change requests?

▶ How often does the northern sales division fail to deliver an offer on time?

▶ How often are purchase requisitions under US$20 refused, and how much time is spent processing them?

Often the result of the analysis will simply be to increase or decrease the number of users available for one of the tasks (perhaps on a seasonal basis). Or you might find that some critical information is missing on the FAQ about the workflow procedure on your company's intranet. You do not have to use the reporting, but you are losing a golden opportunity if you do not.

1.6.11 Robust Extensible Architecture

Although the underlying object-oriented methodology used in creating workflow definitions was greeted suspiciously in the first release of SAP Business Workflow in SAP R/3 3.0, this has proved to be one of the biggest assets of the system. Process definitions are quicker to adapt to changes in the business process and changes in the business applications than traditional forms-based workflow management systems. A company's business process must be able to change at very short notice, and existing custom workflows have to adapt automatically to the new features in a new SAP release, so this flexibility and ability to adapt is one of the most prized assets of SAP Business Workflow.

Similarly, the SAP Business Workflow Engine itself has stood the test of time and is equally at home dealing with traditional approval processes as well as being a part of a service-oriented architecture.

1.7 Some Terminology

We have avoided formal terminology in this chapter to make it easier for anyone without workflow experience to read. However, at this stage, it is worth defining a few terms that will crop up through the subsequent chapters, so that you can dip in to them in whatever order you choose but still know what is being discussed. To help visualize this, look at Table 1.1, which also illustrates the terminology with a simple purchase requisition procedure example.

Terminology	Definition
Workflow definition	The workflow definition is the set of rules that determine the path that the process takes. **Example:** How a purchase requisition is processed, from the initial request to the creation of a purchase order.
Workflow	A workflow instance, which is often simply referred to as the workflow, is a single workflow run. **Example:** The processing of a single purchase requisition for an office printer.
Task	The tasks are the steps in the process, which have to be performed either by people or automatically by the software. **Example:** Check that the office does not already have this equipment.
Work item	A work item is the task instance that is performed as a single workflow step. **Example:** Check that there is currently no printer in room I1.29.
Agent	Agents are the people who process the tasks (via the work items). **Example:** Requisitioner, manager, member of the IT deptartment, and a member of the purchasing department.
Participant	Participants are everybody involved in the process, including those who simply receive a notification that something has or has not been done. **Example:** Office colleagues of the requisitioner, who will later receive news of the new printer.
Container content	The container is the place where all data used in the workflow is collected. **Example:** Office (I1.29), Equipment (printer)
Binding	The binding is the set of rules that defines which data is passed to which part of the process. **Example:** The room number of the office and the equipment type is required to perform this task, but *not* the requisitioner's cost center.

Table 1.1 Definitions and Examples to Illustrate Workflow Terminology

More exact definitions will be given in the relevant chapters, but this is enough to keep you going for the moment.

When considering a workflow project, or any project that involves the automation of a business process, you need to ensure you know what is required by the business community and what is expected when the workflow, or process automation, goes live in production. Requirements gathering, the topic of this chapter, is just as critical in a workflow project, as it is in any other IT project.

2 Requirements Gathering Strategy

Gathering requirements for a project involving SAP Business Workflow, as you might expect, is very similar to gathering requirements for a business process. Much the same information would need to be gathered if you were about to write up the business process in a procedures manual. Even if you simply intend to activate one of the workflows delivered in your SAP component, it is worth digesting this chapter to see how even the most mundane things, such as the description that accompanies a work item, can be optimized to increase the success of your project.

> **Note**
>
> In addition to the information in this chapter, you can download checklists you can use when doing your requirements gathering and preparing workflows to move to production. You can find them at *http://www.sap-press.com*.

2.1 Introduction

The key questions behind any business process or workflow can be summarized as follows:

- **Who should?**
  - Who is involved in the process?
  - Who actually does/will do the work; that is, who are the agents?

▶ Who is indirectly involved? This could be people who need to be notified but don't actually participate directly, or people who will do related tasks outside of the workflow that the workflow needs to know about.

▶ **Do What?**

  ▶ What tasks/activities need to be performed?

  ▶ Will the tasks be performed in the same system as the workflow, in another system, or manually?

  ▶ Does someone need to be directly involved in performing the task, or can the task be automated?

▶ **To What?**

  ▶ What entities (objects) and data are involved?

  ▶ If I want someone to perform a task, what data do they need to see and/or use to complete it?

  ▶ If the task is to be automated, what data does the system need to complete it?

▶ **When?**

  ▶ What starts the process?

  ▶ How do we know when a task/activity is complete?

  ▶ How do we know when the process as a whole is finished?

▶ **In What Order?**

  ▶ What is the sequence of tasks?

  ▶ Are tasks dependent on each other?

  ▶ Can they be done in parallel?

  ▶ Do tasks or groups of tasks need to be repeated in certain situations?

As may be evident from these questions, requirements gathering occurs throughout the workflow project, from developing the business case justification to design through to implementation.

One other major question is also relevant:

▶ **Why?**

  ▶ Why are we doing this at all?

  ▶ Why are we doing this with workflow?

Tip

Although a discussion of project management is outside the scope of this book, to give you an idea of what is involved in each stage of a workflow project, some checklists can be downloaded from *http://www.sap-press.com*, regarding:

▶ Gathering Requirements

▶ Evaluating Return on Investment

▶ Quality Assurance Design Review

▶ Building and Testing

▶ Quality Assurance Implementation Review

▶ Going Live

▶ Housekeeping

2.2 Understanding the Business Process

Hopefully the "Why?" question has been asked before you start the workflow, but if not, pose it now. This question goes to the heart of understanding the business drivers for the process and the benefits to be achieved by using workflow on this process. Not only does this help to ensure that you focus on the parts of the workflow likely to give the greatest satisfaction to the workflow sponsors, but it also helps to warn of any problems you may encounter in building the workflow.

2.2.1 Business Drivers for the Process

Knowing the business drivers for the process will help you assess the critical success and failure criteria for the workflow; that is, how do you know when the workflow has achieved its business objective? Some key questions to ask include the following:

▶ Is this process currently performed within the company, or is it a new process?

▶ What does this process achieve for the company?

▶ What would be affected if this process did not happen?

▶ What is the financial impact if this process happens or does not happen?

▶ How often does this process happen?

▶ How many people are or will be involved in a single instance of this process?

- ▶ Are there existing service level agreements that the process must enforce?
- ▶ Is there a requirement to ensure appropriate segregation of duties (e.g., ensuring someone cannot approve their own salary increase)?
- ▶ Is this a self-service process (i.e., do you expect untutored or minimally educated personnel to be involved in the process)?
- ▶ Are there time constraints on the process?
- ▶ Must any legal requirements be met by the process?
- ▶ What else is critical to this process?
- ▶ When was this process last reviewed or re-engineered?

Sometimes the answers are obvious. Take a procurement request process involving procurement requests that are entered, approved, and actioned. Clearly segregation of duties is an issue; you won't want people approving their own purchases. If the procurement requests are entered over the web by the person who wants the goods, then this is also a self-service process that may affect potentially anyone in the company who needs to buy something. The financial impact of not approving the procurement requests can range from revenue lost when goods critical to production are not purchased in time, to expenses for goods that shouldn't have been bought.

When you feel you have a reasonable understanding of the business process, it is time for a reality check. That is, is this business process a good candidate for workflow?

- ▶ Good candidates for workflow usually involve numerous tasks that need to be performed, within given constraints, by numerous people. Often the reasons for implementing the process via workflow revolve around making sure all tasks are performed correctly, all constraints are met, and all relevant people are contacted as efficiently as possible. This is particularly true where communication barriers exist between the people, such as when people are in different locations, different departments, or different companies.
- ▶ If the process is not a good candidate for workflow, take a moment to consider whether there is a better way to accomplish this task. If you are looking at a process where very few people are involved and there is no particular urgency to the process, perhaps a batch job or report is all that is needed. Spending time to build workflows having few benefits does no one any favors.

Understanding the drivers of the process can help you find the factors to concentrate on during workflow design and implementation. For instance, if a process involves time constraints, focus on deadlines. If a process involves segregation of duties, focus on making sure only appropriate personnel can perform a task. If it is a self-service process, focus on making sure that the tasks performed by untutored users are as user-friendly and self-evident as possible.

Lastly, if the process has not been reviewed or re-engineered for some time, workflow may be the catalyst for some business process re-engineering. You should confirm whether process re-engineering is needed or desired. This will give you an idea of how much flexibility there may be in interpreting the business process for workflow. If you know that business re-engineering is a part of your workflow project, there are a few extra questions you should raise:

▶ Is the process still relevant?

▶ Is the process effective?

▶ What improvements do you believe can be made to the process?

2.2.2 Expected Benefits of Workflow

There are three main reasons why companies implement workflows; any or all of these reasons are usually critical success criteria to the workflow project:

▶ **To improve the speed of a business process**
Companies looking to speed up the business process usually want to reduce costs through timesavings or hope to retain and expand their current customer base through improved service. To reach these goals, focus on streamlining the process and making sure that performing the tasks is easy and quick. Aim to automate tasks where possible.

▶ **To improve the consistency of a business process**
Companies concerned with improving the consistency of the business process are usually trying to avoid penalties of some kind, whether financial, legal, or loss of goodwill. If it is important to be able to prove that the correct business process has been followed when examined in retrospect, focus on security, stringent agent determination, and ensuring the workflow is self-auditing.

▶ **To improve the quality of a business process**
Companies concerned with improving the quality of a business process are usually trying to improve the information provided to decision makers,

increase clarity and visibility, reduce errors, and improve acceptance of the process to minimize maverick activity. Focus on ensuring that all tasks are as easy as possible to perform, with good descriptive texts and clear instructions, using attachments to improve communication between people involved in the process, and sending emails to people affected by the process.

If the reason for building the workflow is unclear, try asking the following questions:

▶ What's the expected ROI (return on investment) for this workflow project?

▶ Where does the return come from? Increase in revenue? Savings? Increasing customer base? Reducing time to market? Avoiding legal penalties? Satisfying parent company requirements?

▶ How will this return be measured?

▶ Are there any other critical success criteria for this project? If they are intangibles, how will their success/failure be measured?

> **Tip**
>
> A checklist can be downloaded from *http://www.sap-press.com* to help you evaluate the ROI for workflows.

Knowing the critical success criteria for the workflow helps show where particular care needs to be taken in the workflow design. For instance, if off-site access to the process is critical, then which work item delivery method(s) will be used (i.e., how the task is sent to the agent) needs special consideration.

Consider what metrics will need to be gathered via the workflow to prove whether the success criteria have been met. Some metrics that workflow gathers automatically include process start/end times, task start/end times, task execution versus waiting times, and who was involved in performing a particular task. Start/end times can be used to compute the duration of a process or task. Where additional metrics are required, consider having automated steps in the workflow that gather the appropriate data.

As well as proving whether criteria such as expected total processing time have been met, these metrics are useful to help further improve the process in practice. For instance, if agents are slower than expected in performing a particular task, perhaps more or better information needs to be presented to them. Monitoring can also show whether the tasks are adequately distributed between agents, or help to identify bottlenecks.

2.2.3 How Does the Process Work in Theory

If the process is already defined in a business procedures manual or document, now is the time to look at how the "official" process operates. When is the process triggered? How do we know when the process is complete? If the process currently involves paper or electronic forms, try to obtain copies or printouts because these are often useful when considering what data is needed by the workflow. Look for clues as to which agents are involved, that is, consider whether the task be performed by people in particular positions or with particular skills.

Note any references to related processes that are affected. Check whether the workflow needs to cater for the related processes in any way, such as notifying or passing information on to personnel involved in the related process. Ask whether the related processes currently use workflow or may be implemented with workflow at a future time.

Watch out for parts of the process that are inherent to the way the process is currently being performed. For instance, paper-based processes often require signatures. Ask whether signatures are still needed, or whether we can confirm the correct person is doing the work by checking his user ID and password.

2.2.4 How Does the Process Work in Practice

Sometimes how a process is "suppose" to work, or how it is documented, is different from what people do on a day-to-day basis. It is important that you talk with the people involved in the current process and find out what they really do, as opposed to what they are "supposed" to do.

Another key thing to find out is how the tasks are performed, such as whether tasks are performed in a system or manually. For example, a customer said they wanted to use workflow to automate the approval for invoices. After talking with the customer, we found out the invoice was currently on a piece of paper that was manually routed for approval. After it was approved with physical paper, then the invoice was added to the system. This meant that before we could automate the approval, we first had to get the invoice in the system *before* designing an approval process. After the invoice was in the system, then we could work on automating the invoice using SAP Business Workflow.

When looking at system or manual tasks, consider the following:

▶ How are the tasks performed, manually or on the system?

▶ If on the system, what transactions and reports are used in the process?

▶ Can any of the tasks be automated to improve efficiency and reduce workload on the agents?

▶ Of all the data available on those transactions and reports, which data is critical to performing the task?

▶ Of all the functionality available on those transactions and reports, which functionality is critical to performing the task?

At this stage, you are not restricted to using those same transactions and reports within your workflow. Often routines such as BAPIs (Business Application Programming Interfaces) or user interfaces such as Web Dynpro may be more suitable in the final workflow. However, knowing what functionality is currently used will help make sure all necessary functionality is included and is a starting point in searching for appropriate routines.

The next questions you should ask involved the data that is used for the process. You will want to find out:

▶ How good is the data quality? Poor data quality is usually an issue with paper forms.

▶ What is the cause of any data quality problems? Look for opportunities to improve data quality by providing help or validation for common data mistakes.

Determining who should do each task is a major part of workflow. This book has two chapters devoted to the topic, Chapter 5, Agents, and Chapter 12, Agent Determination Rules. Regarding who will do the work, you should ask:

▶ How easy is it to find out who is responsible for performing each task?

▶ Are there situations where no one is willing to take on a particular task? Why not?

▶ Is the task difficult or unpalatable?

▶ Is there confusion over responsibilities?

- Is lack of training an issue?

- Is it a rote task that could be automated wholly or in part?

- Do all agents have a similar level of skill in performing the tasks?

- What information is needed by an experienced/inexperienced agent to complete the task successfully?

- What information is most critical for an experienced agent to complete the task swiftly?

- Is the work fairly distributed across agents?

- How is the work distributed across agents now?

- Would distributing the work differently help agents to perform tasks quicker and more accurately, for example, by giving an agent related tasks such as all procurement requests for the same material group?

- Are there many delays?

- What causes the delays?

- What happens when an agent is away?

- What happens when an agent changes position or leaves the company?

You also must consider how time relates to the process. Perhaps the company has requirements such as same day ship, which requires all orders to ship on the same day they are received. If this is the case, then timing for a workflow process related to order processing or shipping could be critical. Consider the following to help you know how important time is to the process:

- What are the average, fastest, and slowest times taken to complete the process?

- You want to make sure workflow can improve on the average and fastest times, if possible, and at least not make the process any slower. How is this measured?

- Anecdotal process times are unreliable, so you might want to gather some actual start/finish times to let you show later whether total processing time has been improved or at least made no slower.

You also need to ensure that the users who deal with the process on a daily basis are satisfied with the process. To understand the users' view on the existing process, you should consider:

- What do people complain about most with this process?

- ▸ What is frustrating about the current process? Look for opportunities to improve the process where you can.
- ▸ Try to find quantitative measures for any problem areas so that you can plan to measure, monitor, and compare these against the workflow to show what improvements have been made.

Even if the process is new, and there is little practical experience with it, many of these questions are still relevant. You should at least make sure likely exception situations have been included and potential problems have been considered.

2.2.5 Unions and Workers Councils

If unions or worker's representatives have a say in how work can be organized, they have to be involved right at the very beginning of the planning stages, especially if this is the first time that workflow has been used by the company. There are customizing settings to help you conform to local rules, but this does not mean you can skip a face-to-face consultation. Listen to what they have to say, and make sure that this advice is followed. Because of the positive feedback that the initial users will give, the second workflow is generally far easier to plan and install.

2.3 Gathering Object Data

Gathering the data for a manual business process sometimes seems to be limited to data needed to create paper or electronic forms. Often the data needed is not formally specified in the business procedures manual, and is known only to the people performing the task. With workflow, you need to be much more rigorous about identifying every piece of data because this needs to be explicitly made available to the workflow.

Many individual pieces of data may be used across a workflow, but there are often close relationships among them. In particular, much of the data is related directly to the entities involved in the business process. Using workflow terminology, you would call these entities *business objects*. By knowing the key of the business object, you can derive all sorts of related data.

Take a workflow that controls follow-on processing of a sales order. It is likely that you will need to use a lot of data related to the particular sales order being processed. By knowing that the key field ORDER NUMBER identifies a particular sales order, we can use the order number to derive all sorts of related information about the order.

Tip

Object data includes table-based data, such as the order creation date, who created the order, the customer number on the order, and calculated data such as age of the order.

You can also include extended relationships. By knowing the customer number, which is the key field of the customer business object, you can then access the customer name and customer address.

2.3.1 What Data Is Needed by Workflow

However, before you start collecting your data into business objects, you first need to determine what data is needed by your workflow. Data may be used for a variety of purposes in a workflow including the following:

▶ **Data used in performing tasks**
When a workflow is started, the triggering mechanism usually passes some key information to the workflow, for example, an order number to a workflow dealing with follow-on processing of an order. The workflow can then pass this information on to each task to be performed. For example it can pass the order number to one task that displays order details and another task that updates the order.

▶ **Data used to determine who should perform the task**
If, for example, you decide that the person updating the order is chosen based on the type of sale (retail/wholesale) and the total order value, then you need to make both type of sale *and* total order value available to the workflow.

▶ **Data used to determine escalation times**
For example, if the workflow must be completed within one week after order creation date/time, date *and* time must be made available to the workflow.

▶ **Control data**
Examples are the maximum number of times a subprocess can be repeated before alternative action is taken, or the result of an approval/rejection decision.

▶ **Data used for texts**
Examples are instructions to the person performing the task, for example, the

name of the person who has created the order, and the name of the customer for whom the order was created. These are often not thought about until late in the workflow development, resulting in frantic last-minute development work.

Tip

Encourage early thought about what data should be presented to agents. In particular, make sure that data is meaningful (names not just numbers, descriptions not just codes), and useful (aids quick execution of the task, puts forward salient details necessary for decision making).

This is also a good time to start thinking about how the texts will be worded. Too many instructions created at the last minute or without much thought are abrupt or technical. Encourage prompt action by polite, tactful, and considerate instructions. Ensure the most important information appears toward the start or top of the text so experienced agents can act quickly.

Don't worry about data that is already a part of the transaction (or routine) that is used to execute the task, unless you also need to show this in your instructions to the agent. You do, however, need to make sure that the texts and instructions to the agent, plus whatever is shown by the transaction (or routine), give enough information so that the agent can make decisions and complete the task.

2.3.2   Where to Look for Data

Examine any documents used in the current process, such as paper or electronic forms. These show what information is currently presented to agents, which is a useful starting point. Talk to current and/or potential agents. Ask what data they need to make appropriate decisions and complete tasks. Ask if that data is currently available on the system, for example, as part of a table, transaction, or report. Particularly watch for key data that identifies the entities involved in the process, such as the order number of an order. A lot of data can be derived. For instance, if you know an order number, you can find out who created the order, what was ordered, when it was ordered, and for which customer.

2.3.3   What Data Already Exists

Workflows provide some data by default:

▶ Workflow "system" information (fields on the WFSYST structure, a workflow system structure), such as the workflow initiator, that is, who triggers the process

- Details of tasks just executed, such as who executed it, and start and finish times
- Attachments for emails

Within SAP components, many business objects have already been created, and both table-based data and calculated data are included in them. Existing business objects can be readily reused and extended in an upgrade-friendly manner. Or you can use them as examples for creating your own completely new business objects.

2.3.4 Making the Most of the Data Collected

Collecting data into business objects is more than just a matter of convenience; it is a matter of principle. Many parts of workflow, particularly business objects, are based on object-oriented theory, whose fundamental benefits include consistency and reusability.

When you are planning to put together workflows, consistency and reusability are very important considerations. Throughout a company, business processes tend to mirror one another and work in patterns. Instructions and information are presented in similar formats: Escalation processes tend to operate the same way, email notifications are worded in a similar way, and tasks such as approval/rejection decisions are performed in a similar way.

Workflow tends to emphasize these similarities and often directly contributes to them. From a company's perspective, this is highly desirable. Maintaining similarities results in the following:

- Reduces training requirements and costs
- Simplifies maintenance of data supporting the process
- Improves speed in performing tasks because the agent knows what to expect
- Increases consistency in the way tasks are presented and performed
- Increases consistency in the way outstanding tasks are escalated
- Reduces errors and simplifies troubleshooting

Common Types of Data Needed in a Workflow Process

From a data perspective, consider that when performing a task related to a particular employee, you often want to see not just their user ID or personnel number but their name, address, and contact details. When performing a task for a customer or vendor, you want to see name, contact details, and contact person. Whenever a code or ID is used, you want to see the matching description. When viewing amounts, you want them displayed in the same way, that is, plus or minus sign on the same side, commas and decimal points in a consistent manner, and currency shown in a consistent manner.

Using business objects to collect data helps to encourage consistency and ensures reusability. The more you follow object-oriented rules when collecting your data, the better the consistency and reusability. Again, the important thing to remember is to attach pieces of data to the object with which they have the strongest relationship.

Take a workflow that creates new customer records and assigns them to an appropriate contact person (e.g., an account manager) in your company according to company policy. Two business objects that you want to use are `Customer` and `Employee`. You have discovered you need the following pieces of data for your workflow; to which object will you assign the pieces of data?

▶ Customer ID

▶ Customer name

▶ Customer phone number

▶ Employee ID

▶ Employee name

▶ Employee phone number

▶ Contact person

It is easy to see that customer ID, customer name, customer phone number should be attached to the `Customer` object, and employee ID, employee name, and employee phone number should be attached to the `Employee` object. But what about the contact person? Does it belong with the `Customer` or with the `Employee` object?

At first glance, it could be either or both. After all, the contact person is an employee, but the contact person is assigned to the customer. So which is the stronger relationship? You need to examine the relationship from the point of view of each object:

- ▶ **Employee:**
  - ▶ Is every employee a contact person? – No.
  - ▶ Are most employees assigned as contact persons? – No.
  - ▶ Is every contact person an employee? – Yes.
- ▶ **Customer:**
  - ▶ Does every customer have a contact person? – Yes.

In this case, the `Customer` object has a stronger relationship to the contact person. However the contact person is still an employee. What happens when you want to know the contact person's ID and name? You solve this by attaching the contact person to the customer but not just as a piece of data. Instead, you attach the contact person to the `Customer` object as a relationship to the `Employee` object. Then when you want to find the name of the contact person assigned to the customer, you can reference the employee name via the customer-to-contact relationship.

Understanding the Relationship Between the Data Points Used in a Workflow

What about multiple relationships? For instance, a customer can have multiple sales orders open. You attach a multiline relationship, that is, a list of order relationships to the `Customer` object. This allows your workflow to process all open orders attached to a customer.

What about the relationship between an order and its items? Is "order item" part of the `Order` business object or not? Think of it this way: Do they share the same data? Do you treat them the same way when performing tasks? No, you don't. Take a simple example — quantity and value. An order item has a quantity, a price, and a value derived from them. An order has a total value derived from adding all the item values. Quantity doesn't make sense at an order level because you might have several items in the order dealing with completely different goods or services. This means `Order` and `Order item` are two distinct business objects. Of course, attached to the order, you will probably want a multiline relationship to the matching order items, and attached to the order item, you will probably want a relationship to the matching order so that the two objects can refer to each other.

Each SAP component already provides many business objects with many attached pieces of data, and each upgrade adds to this. All of which you can both use in your workflows and use as a guide to what data should be connected to which business object.

Determining What Data Should Be Included in a Workflow

But not every piece of data needs to be assigned to a business object. Control data such as the number of times a subprocess is repeated before alternative action is taken, or the result of an approve/reject decision, is usually not created against a business object but exist independently within the workflow. However, whenever data has a clear relationship to a business object, and there is any possibility, now or in the future, that this data might be reused by another workflow, you should try to attach it to a suitable business object. Why? Over time, a considerable amount of data will be set up. When you come to build the next workflow, there will be less data to set up and fewer decisions to make about how that data should be attached to existing business objects. This saves time and effort, makes it quicker to implement future workflows, and increases consistency between workflows.

2.4 Determining the Agents

How agents are determined is dealt with in detail in Chapters 5, Agents, and 12, Agent Determination Rules, but we include a summary here because this is an important part of requirements gathering. Determining agents affects directly what can be included in your project and what is out of its scope.

Before you can decide how agents should be found, you need to know and be able to explain to your company how an agent interacts with workflow. For an agent to perform a task, you need to send them a runtime copy of the task that includes the relevant data to be actioned. In workflow terms, you call this a *work item*. To an agent, a work item is superficially similar to an email. It has a title, descriptive information, may contain other documents as attachments, and can be received in the agent's inbox. The big difference between a work item and an email, from an agent's perspective, is that an email can only tell you there is some work to be done, whereas a work item brings the work to you. Depending on how the work item is delivered to the agent, the agent usually only has to click one button or hyperlink to start actioning the data.

From a process or workflow designer's perspective, there is one other important difference between emails and work items to keep in mind. When an email is sent to multiple people, each person receives a separate copy of the email. After they have read the email, it is up to them to remove it from their inbox. When a work item is sent to multiple agents, you usually only want the data to be actioned once, so all agents view the same work item. Once one agent has executed the work item and actioned the data, the work item is automatically removed from all the agents' inboxes. To agents, this means that they know all the work sent to them by a workflow has been completed when they have no work items left in their inboxes. The converse of this is also true — a workflow is held up until the work item is executed, but an email notification allows the process to continue without pausing.

2.4.1 Who Are Your Agents?

Agents include the following persons:

▶ **The person who starts the workflow**
The person who starts the workflow is a special agent, called the workflow initiator. Most workflows include communication between other agents and the initiator throughout the business process. The initiator may not be directly involved in executing work items — in fact, they may only create the trigger for the workflow indirectly — but they are often involved in escalation and usually need to be notified of process milestones or when the process finishes.

▶ **People who perform the tasks**
People who perform the tasks must be able to view relevant texts and instructions as well as to execute work items. They must also have access to the underlying transactions or routines used during execution. The person performing the task should be the person with ownership and responsibility for the work. You want agents to act promptly and that's more likely to happen when they feel ownership for the work involved. Consider the workload on each agent. Are there enough agents to process all the work items created? Keep in mind that executing assigned work items is usually only a small part of a person's daily work.

▶ **People who escalate the process**
People who escalate the process may be able to view outstanding work items but not be able to execute them. It is common for the escalator to be the workflow initiator because they are often the person most interested in having the process completed quickly. This is particularly true of self-service functions such as vacation or purchasing requests.

▶ **People who troubleshoot problems with workflows, particularly those caused by bad or poorly maintained data**
People who troubleshoot problems may be workflow administrators or may be specially trained functional personnel. These are the people who handle document reprocessing when automatic processes have failed, and re-routing outstanding work items where agent determination has failed.

Tip

Try to cut out the "middlemen" of the process because, at best, they lengthen the workflow, and, at worst, they can become bottlenecks. Of each potential agent, ask whether the agent really does anything, and whether what the agent does is critical to the subsequent tasks. Can the agent just be notified by email?

Be aware that all agents must have system access, that is, login and password, so that security can be checked. An important part of any business process is ensuring that only those people who are permitted to do so take part in the process; this is particularly true of approval processes.

People notified throughout the workflow do not need to be agents. This is particularly of interest when dealing with external partners. It is enough to be able to identify an email address, so that an email can be sent to them.

2.4.2 Criteria for Finding Agents

How do you find the agents in a business workflow? People change jobs and positions over time, so you need a reliable way of identifying the current agent(s) responsible for doing the work. This is usually done using attributes or job functions that point to an agent; for example, the material group for an item in a purchase requested is used to identify the buyer responsible for this material group. Of course, both the attributes/criteria and the relationship between the attributes and the agent must already be defined in the system.

Determining the Best Agent for the Task

The possibilities opened by workflow automation present an overwhelming temptation to build complex matrices of criteria for determining agents. This seems to be particularly tempting where approval processes are involved. Resist the temptation! Instead, consider clarity of ownership when deciding how to select agents. Agents need to know why they are doing the work. When they do, they will take more responsibility and be on the lookout for work items they should have received but didn't, and work items they receive erroneously. If it is too hard to understand why they are receiving the work items, agents are likely to react slowly or not at all; but if it is clear why they receive particular work items, they will resolve mistakes and problems effectively.

Clear and appropriate criteria for selecting agents are important for process audits, as well. Auditors need to confirm that the business process is working as expected, and everyone involved in the workflow must have confidence that the business process is working as expected. If the criteria for finding agents are too complex, proving that the business process is working properly will take a long time and confidence in the process will be lowered.

Consider the maintenance burden, both for maintaining the data and for maintaining the programmed rules that select the agent. Both the criteria being used and the relationship between the criteria and the relevant agent(s) need to be maintained. If there is a lot of data to be maintained, this increases the likelihood that no agent will be found or the wrong agent will be selected, due to delayed or neglected maintenance. Each agent determination error results in delays while the error is being found and corrected, and the workflow restarted. It is even worse when the problem is not found; that is, when the system selects the wrong agent to execute the work item, or the work item sits in limbo because no agent could be assigned.

How to Know If You Have a Good Rule to Determine Who the Agent Should Be

A good test of your selection rules is to see if you can work out who will be the agents for a few test cases in your head in a few seconds. If you need to use paper, or it takes longer than a few seconds, the criteria are too complex. A quick way to convince management of this is to show how much maintenance will need to be done if the complex selection criteria are retained. One company had a plan involving four criteria, which worst-case involved 12,000 entries to be maintained, and in the best case was still close to 1,000 entries. Needless to say, a look at the maintenance burden caused a rapid rethink. Usually two to three criteria are more than enough.

Easy ways to determine agents include the following:

- Organization chart evaluation paths
- Distribution lists
- Tables of criteria values matched to agents
- Responsibility rules matching criteria values to agents

Responsibility rules usually have the edge on tables. As well as being able to show abstracted relationships easily — for example, the user ID of the person assigned to a position that is assigned to the criteria — they can also specify priorities on the relationships. For example, if the agent is selected according to the material group, priorities can be set to look for agents assigned to specific material groups. If the material group has not been assigned, however, it falls back to a lower priority, "default" agent. Other options include picking agents dynamically, that is, having a step in the workflow where someone chooses who will be the agent of a subsequent work item.

> **Tip**
>
> Avoid programmed rules if you can because these can add significantly to development time.

Tasks with Multiple Agents

You can have multiple agents for the same task. It is important to recognize the difference between the following:

- Tasks distributed to a pool of agents to spread the workload, so that one work item appears to multiple agents, but only one agent will execute the work item
- Tasks to be executed by multiple agents, where separate work items must be sent to each agent

Forwarding and Substitutes

Consider whether you want to allow work items to be forwarded from the chosen agent to another person. If you do allow forwarding, ask whether the recipient's access privileges need to be checked. Consider substitutes when the current agent is absent or unavailable. Who are acceptable substitutes? Substitutes must have access to execute work items sent to them, even if they are only executing the work items on a backup or temporary basis.

2.5 Determining Work Item Delivery Routes

After you know who the agents will be, you can start to consider how work items will be sent to them. This is an important decision that will be dealt with in more detail in Chapter 4, Work Item Delivery. However, it is an important step in the requirements-gathering process, so a summary of the alternatives is presented here. Your decision will also influence resource planning for rollout, and, in some cases, it will even have repercussions for development planning.

This decision needs serious and in-depth thought for the first workflow implemented at your company. After that, you will most likely use the same work item delivery route in future workflows. However, it is worthwhile to revisit this decision at least briefly in the light of each new workflow design to ensure that the route chosen is still appropriate.

Consider the agent's environment and work habits:

▶ What hardware do they use? PCs? Laptops? PDAs?

▶ What software do they have access to? Web browser? SAP NetWeaver Portal? SAP GUI?

▶ What email system do they use? SAPoffice? Microsoft Outlook? Lotus Notes? Other?

▶ How often do they access their email? This is particularly important when agents belong to higher-level management and may only access email once a day or less.

▶ Do they sit at a desk with permanent access to the network? Or do they work in the field and connect to the network only at certain times? How often do they connect to the network?

▶ Do they regularly access your SAP component for non-workflow needs?

▶ Do they have Intranet, Extranet or Internet access to your network? This is particularly important if the agent is a customer, reseller, vendor or service provider.

▶ What access do they have to training, online help and help desks?

▶ If they are agents of existing workflows, how do they currently receive work items?

Don't forget to factor in the needs of the business process. Such as, how quickly must agents respond for the business process to be successful? Does the business process require any particular type of access, such as web access?

2.6 Confirming the Workflow Design

Workflow design is usually iterative. You start with an initial design, and as you start to gather your requirements, you refine it. As you gather more information, you refine it further; then you gather the answers to more questions, refine it again, and so on. One danger with this approach is that the original success criteria of the workflow can be forgotten. It is worthwhile to go back to your notes on the business drivers for the process and the success/failure criteria for the workflow to make sure the workflow is still on track.

It is helpful to draw up flowcharts showing the workflow design. Most people are visually oriented and can make sense of graphics more quickly than words. The flowchart can be drawn on paper, via a graphics tool, or in the system using the Workflow Builder. The advantage of using the Workflow Builder is that your model then becomes a starting point for the actual workflow implementation. Make sure that the flowchart is easy to read, with clear and meaningful descriptions for each task.

> **Hint**
>
> If you want to build a process in the Workflow Builder as a flow chart only, without adding the specifics of what each step will do, you can use the SAP provided task, TS30100074. This is discussed further in Appendix A, Tips and Tricks.

For complex workflows, consider breaking up the process into multiple flowcharts. For example, you might draw separate flowcharts for before-versus-after approval processes, for the escalation process, for exception processes, and for the main process.

Then it's time for a reality check: Will the workflow achieve the expected benefits? Does the workflow make sense? You should check for the following aspects:

▶ **Consistency**
    Are all tasks equally easy to use? Do different tasks sent to the same user work in a standard way? Is information in tasks or emails displayed in a consistent

manner? Is escalation implemented in a fair and consistent manner throughout the workflow?

▶ **Sequence of steps**

Make sure you are not trying to perform tasks on data that have just been deleted. Watch this particularly with workflows based on human resources employee data. Employee data (stored in infotypes), include the lock indicator in the key; locking or unlocking an infotype results in deletion of the current infotype and creation of a new one.

▶ **Waiting for outside activity**

Make sure the workflow won't hang if something is done outside the control of the workflow. This is particularly important if the initial implementation of your workflow will only cover part of the process or will operate in parallel with a non-workflow version of the process. For example, a "procurement request" process that involves entering, approving, and actioning procurement requests may need to know if the procurement request has been deleted so that the workflow can be cancelled.

▶ **Performance drains**

Is your workflow triggered many times when the business conditions for using this workflows are not met? Will many workflows be closed immediately after they have been started?

Here's a classic scenario suggested by one company: "Create a workflow to notify the goods receiver if an invoice has been received but the goods receipt has not been made within x days of the invoice being entered." Workflows thus need to be started for every invoice with goods receipt outstanding. Most are closed when receipt is done promptly, which is normally the case. That is a lot of workflow activity doing not very much to catch a relatively infrequent exception situation!

A better approach is to create a daily report that first identifies invoices greater than x days old where outstanding goods receipts still exist, and then only trigger workflows for the invoices identified.

Finally, confirm whether the process is still suitable for workflow. It is important to take future plans into account. Many first iteration workflow designs are close to being mere reports, but future plans make workflow clearly the way to go. Remember, business processes change over time, and coping with that change is where workflow shines.

2.7 Workflow Administration

Workflow Administration is discussed in detail in Chapter 6, Workflow Administration. However, we mentioned it here because it is important that you consider building error handling into your workflow to cope with most common errors. Error handling should be included in the first stages of process design. For instance, if the agent determination fails, have the workflow send the work item to an administrator or specially trained personnel with the power to forward it on to the correct agent and get the appropriate data fixed. If a task performed by the system in the background fails, have the workflow retry it some time later; then, if it still fails, send it to be processed manually by specially trained personnel.

It is worthwhile to include your workflow administrator in quality assurance reviews of new workflows. This gives early warning to the workflow administrator of possible problems with the new workflow, and how agent determination works for that workflow.

Tip

At the very least, plan your "escape" routes in advance. What will you do if a background task fails; if an agent has left the company and still has work items outstanding? Can you kill the workflow and complete the process manually if necessary?

2.8 Planning for Production Start

Right from the word "go," you should take into account the infrastructure that will be needed after the project goes live and in the roll-out stage immediately before going live. If this is not the first workflow project in the company, there is probably an infrastructure in place to deal with the following:

▸ Security issues
▸ Naming conventions
▸ Documentation
▸ Workers Councils, unions
▸ Training
▸ Help desk and administration
▸ Archiving

These issues are dealt with in detail in the following chapters, but for your resource planning, consider them right at the beginning. If your company is small or the scope of the project is small, then you may be able to reduce some of these issues to a minimum. If you are breaking new ground in a large company, you may find dealing with the bureaucracy within the company a full-time occupation; however, it will be worth the effort after the project goes live. Even if there is no formal written procedure in place, you may well discover colleagues who have seen how things are done and are willing to share their experiences with you. It is important to learn from other people's mistakes, and every company and every department has it is own culture that cannot be overlooked.

Archiving, in particular, is often ignored until the disks are almost full, and database indexes are clogging up the system. By estimating in advance how often archiving needs to take place and what data needs to be extracted from the workflows before archiving takes place, you will be in a good position to deal with this before a crisis is imminent. It will be much easier to set up the archiving with the same team that blueprints the business processes and develops the workflows than it will be two years down the road, when archiving is necessary, but the skills and know-how have evaporated. For global implementations, it is useful to request and document retention periods for workflow logs while developing the specifications for the workflow, and include business controls in the sign-offs.

This can affect design decisions. For instance, if there are multiple geographies implementing a common workflow solution, but the country requirements dictate variable retention periods due to audit requirements, it may be necessary to create identical workflow templates by geography to allow the necessary flexibility for retention periods when archiving.

2.9 Planning for Future Enhancements

Ensuring your workflows will stand up to future change is essential because being able to change your workflow as your business process changes is one of the key benefits of implementing workflow. Having said that, planning for future enhancements is mostly a matter of common sense.

Build your workflows using patterns, that is, use the same approach to common subprocesses such as escalation, approval/rejection, notification of completion of a process, retry of background processes, and so on. Common patterns make for easier troubleshooting, and reduce development time for new workflows. Wizards are particularly useful in gaining consistency in workflows. When you upgrade, make sure you re-evaluate the patterns to take advantage of new release functionality. Keep the following in mind:

▶ Don't let your current workflows become out of date. Workflow can be an instrument of change.

▶ Regularly review the effectiveness of your current workflows.

▶ Use workflow reports to back up your arguments, for example, arguments about bottlenecks, unreasonable workloads on particular agents, number of workflows in error, types of errors occurring, speed of process.

▶ Have a forum or contact point where agents can make suggestions to improve the process. This may include anything from improved instructions and texts, to suggesting better underlying transactions or routines, to suggesting ways to reduce bottlenecks.

▶ Finally consider change management. When you implement changes to existing workflows, at the very least, create a new workflow version. This allows data currently being processed by the old workflow version to complete using the old process, while any new data triggers the new process. If the workflow or business process has changed significantly, you should create an entirely new workflow and decommission the old workflow. As well as assisting with troubleshooting any issues with the new versus the old process, this also allows you to report the new and old process separately, so that their speed and effectiveness can be compared.

Before you can use SAP Business Workflow, some basic configuration is required. This chapter walks you through the required steps to get your system ready to execute SAP Business Workflow.

3 Configuring the System

Unlike most consultants, workflow consultants actually get a thrill out of visiting a system that has not been set up for workflow. You'll recognize such a system by calling up workflow customizing (Transaction SWU3) and seeing row after row of red crosses, signifying customizing activities that have not yet been performed. Does this sound daunting? Not at all! Click the single button PERFORM AUTOMATIC WORKFLOW CUSTOMIZING (), and presto, a few seconds later, the red crosses in the runtime list have been transformed into green ticks (as shown in Figure 3.1), and it's all systems go.

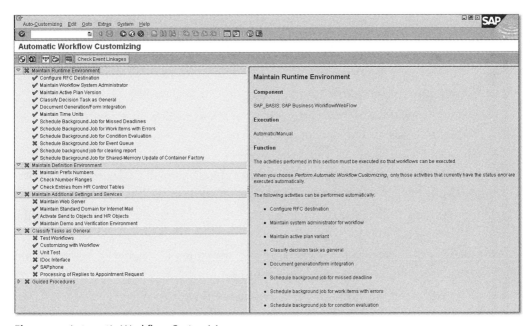

Figure 3.1 Automatic Workflow Customizing

> **Hint**
>
> Normally Transaction SWU3 is done for all workflow customizing. You can also do the customizing in the SAP Implementation Guide (IMG), which is Transaction SPRO. In the IMG, follow the menu path SAP NetWeaver • Application Server • Business Management • SAP Business Workflow.

As you will see in the following section, the list of green ticks shows that your system is now set up well enough to allow workflows to run. However, this is just half the story. Enabling the system to run workflows is just the first step. Not surprisingly, you cannot set up complete workflows or transport them into the production system complete with the user assignments for each step by clicking a single button.

Unfortunately, customers often push the workflow development into the implementation stage of the project, thinking that it is enough to say, "we will use workflow" in the design stage. You should be aware that this is not the case. Apart from the fact that you have to determine the best method for assigning agents to the tasks, there is also a human aspect of workflow management that cannot be underestimated. Getting the users on your side is key to the success of the project, and this is best done if they are involved in the project early on. They can do this on a part-time basis, spending the rest of their time carrying out their normal duties.

The steps necessary to get a successful workflow running are listed here:

1. Configure the workflow system (primarily auto-customizing).

2. Set up workflow-specific customizing for the workflow that you intend to use, assuming it is an SAP-delivered workflow.

3. Create new workflows (only if necessary) or copy and change a SAP-delivered workflow (only if necessary). Workflows are assigned to packages, and this part of your project is development, not customizing.

4. Set up any additional configuration necessary in the SAP IMG, based on the process you want to workflow.

5. Set up the organizational management structures or whatever other method you are using to assign the users to tasks.

6. Transport and perform quality assurance testing.

3.1 Quick Start: Configure the SAP Workflow Engine in Seconds

The SAP Workflow Engine requires certain system settings and system activities, which are carried out on a client-specific basis.

3.1.1 Automatic Workflow Customizing

When you choose PERFORM AUTOMATIC WORKFLOW CUSTOMIZING (), only those activities in the selected branch that currently have not been configured (red crosses) are executed automatically, to prevent overwriting previous customizing activities. Some activities that affect the definition system (used when you want to build your own workflows) can only be carried out manually. However, the runtime engine does not require manual activities.

> **Tip**
>
> It is essential that you have authorization to execute this task and to perform the individual activities such as job planning or creating the required workflow users in the background. To avoid disappointment and to save wasted time when you arrive at a company's site, make sure in advance that either you have the required super-administrator authorization or that you have contacts of a system administrator who can perform this task with you when you arrive.

You can execute all activities manually with the EXECUTE button () as well, if you wish. This way, you can check what the automatic customizing has customized and adjust it as necessary. Some activities can only be executed manually, such as assigning prefix numbers to new custom workflows.

All activities executed, either manually or as part of auto-customizing, are logged under your name. These logs are stored in the database and are very useful when you are in a system where several independent workflow teams are at work, which is often the case. By viewing the logs, you can avoid the typical tugs of war that take place when different teams tweak the settings independently. The logs are displayed in the bottom frame of the screen and can also be read from the database using the menu option EXTRAS • LOGS.

However, the proof of the pudding is in the eating, and at this point, you might be eager to create your own mini-workflow to check that the system really is

85

ready for workflow. However, there is no need to do this because a simple verification workflow is delivered as part of the system.

1. Click the START VERIFICATION WORKFLOW button (🕹). You are prompted for a transport to activate linkages, the workflow is configured (in the background), and the verification workflow starts.

> **Tip**
>
> This is the fastest way of triggering a workflow to demonstrate what a workflow is and how the logs, inbox, and other basic workflow features are used out of the box to improve efficiency. Although there is no business scenario for this example, it is easy for anyone to follow and understand.

2. After you have triggered the workflow, a message confirms that the workflow has been triggered. View the long text of this message to see instructions about what to do next.

3. Go to the SAP Business Workplace by clicking the SAP BUSINESS WORKPLACE button (🕹). You should see a work item here.

4. Execute the work item. You are faced with a decision: EXECUTE BACKGROUND STEP IMMEDIATELY, EXECUTE BACKGROUND STEP IN ONE MINUTE, or CANCEL AND KEEP WORKITEM. Select EXECUTE BACKGROUND STEP IMMEDIATELY.

5. You now receive a mail message that the first work item has been executed successfully and a second mail message confirming that the workflow has completed successfully.

6. Repeat the process, selecting the second option (EXECUTE BACKGROUND STEP A MINUTE), and you again receive two mail messages; however, you have to wait for one minute before the second message is delivered because the workflow uses deadline management to create the second mail.

This verification workflow verifies that several of the more complex parts of the workflow runtime engine have been set up properly:

▶ Work item delivery

▶ Background processing

▶ Event generation

▶ Event linkage

▶ Notifications

If at any time you are worried about what appears to be inconsistent behavior in the Workflow Engine, you can call Transaction SWUI_VERIFY, which triggers other more complex verification workflows. In practice, this transaction is used only by developers at the SAP development laboratories, but it is a useful source of demonstration workflows for understanding a range of workflow techniques.

3.1.2 Specifics of Automatic Customizing

We will now cover the most important parts of the automatic workflow Customizing set up. Automatic customizing quickly configures workflow using defaults so that you are ready to use the system as quickly as possible. You can go back and override the defaults with your own customizing manually later. The most important activities are described next.

Maintain Active Plan Version

The automatic workflow customizing chooses the active plan version, but you can do it manually, too. Only one of the plan versions created in the system can be active. This plan version (with its contents) is seen by the workflow system as the only valid plan version. All SAP Workflows supplied automatically become part of the plan version that has been selected as the active plan version. If you carry out this activity automatically, 01 is set as the active plan version.

> **Note**
>
> If a plan version has already been set, do *not* change it. This has severe repercussions on the workflow definitions that you have created (they will become invisible) as well as on the organizational management structures, including those that are not used in workflow.

Configure RFC Destination

The customizing option to configure the RFC destination is performed as part of the automatic customizing. This setting is required so that the workflow runtime knows how to make required system calls. The workflow runtime system always executes its tRFC calls (transactional Remote Function Call) via the logical destination WORKFLOW_LOCAL_xxx (xxx stands for the three-digit number of the client that you are working in). If this is not configured, the workflows will not run. The workflow runtime system is client-dependent; that is, a single workflow instance normally executes within one client. The naming for the logical destination guarantees that these names are unique across the system.

If you carry out this activity automatically, the logical RFC destination WORKFLOW_LOCAL_xxx is created if it does not yet exist. Background tasks are executed through this RFC destination and performed through the generic user, WF-BATCH, who is assigned to the RFC destination. If the user WF-BATCH does not already exist, it is automatically created as a system user, inheriting the maximum authorization of the current user (SY-UNAME) — no more and no less. However the background user must have the authorization SAP_ALL if the workflow system is to function without problems, so it is essential that the user executing the automatic workflow customization have the SAP_ALL authorization. If necessary, get the system administrator to perform the automatic customizing.

> **Tip**
>
> Some high-volume installations have fine-tuned the RFC settings so that the check returns an error even though the RFC destination works correctly. If this check displays an error but the rest of the settings appear correct, then you should inspect the RFC destination definition first, before deciding whether or not to execute auto-customizing again to correct the apparent error. You might find that the RFC description says that the Transaction SWU3 check will fail, but that this should be ignored. The verification workflow will confirm whether or not the RFC destination is working properly.

You may need to discuss this authorization with your security administrator. WF-BATCH is set as a system user, which means that no dialog login is possible via the SAP GUI. Secondly, special authorizations could be implemented to prevent this RFC destination from being used by programs other than the workflow engine. If you generate the RFC destination and user with automatic workflow customizing (recommended), then the user cannot be used with other RFC destinations because no one knows the password, which was generated randomly.

Automatic execution to create this RFC destination and background user is recommended. A subsequent automatic customizing execution does *not* overwrite this entry after it has been created successfully (assuming that the authorization SAP_ALL has also been assigned successfully). If you carry out this activity manually, you can maintain a different background user (however, in practice, this tends to create problems because every workflow consultant, developer, and administrator will expect you to use the standard WF-BATCH user) or your own predefined password (not recommended for the security reasons described previously). The only manual maintenance of WF-BATCH that is necessary is to assign the user an email address so that emails can be sent in the background (e.g., notifications to external participants). In this case, you might want to maintain the system administrator as an office substitute for WF-BATCH, so that replies to the emails can be periodically scanned.

> **Hint**
>
> SAP Note 1251255 discusses an option to limit security for WF-BATCH. It walks through necessary steps to assign role SAP_BC_BMT_WFM_SERV_USER to WF-BATCH.
>
> However, if this action is taken, WF-BATCH will have no application authorizations; this means no access to execute background tasks. If you chose this option to limit access by WF-BATCH, you must add the application security to WF-BATCH for all background tasks in all workflows.

Maintain the Default Workflow Administrator

The automatic workflow customizing configures the default workflow administrator, naming you as the default workflow administrator. As such, you will automatically receive workflow system error messages, should they arise.

Although it is very convenient to let automatic workflow customizing set this up for you, you should return later and manually re-assign an organizational unit (such as a job or organization) to this setting. This enables several users to act as default administrators at the same time. You should make sure that there is one user for each area where workflow is used, to ensure that a relevant person is notified of errors immediately. If you do not have one central contact person for all workflow issues, then this assignment documents users who need to be informed of any systemwide changes made to the workflow system.

Schedule Background Job for Missed Deadlines

You can schedule the job for missed deadlines to run dynamically, every time a deadline is due instead of at regular intervals. However, this will lead to serious performance degradation in the whole system if many work items with deadlines must be monitored. If in doubt, play safe and use the regular time interval method.

Tip

Deadlines being monitored are not escalated until the deadline job runs.

Prefix Number for Tasks

The three-digit task prefix number must be unique for every client in every system where workflows are developed. This is checked by the global mechanism that manages all number ranges.

Do not try to override this! If two systems have the same prefix, there is a risk that workflows developed in the one system will receive an identical task ID to workflows developed in another system or client. If workflows from both systems are transported into one system, or if two systems are merged, one of the workflows will overwrite the other one. The technical IDs of the workflows developed must be unique. The same applies to the prefix numbers used in organizational management to define the organizational objects, such as positions or jobs.

3.1.3   IMG Activities for Authorization Management

This section covers the following activities:

▶ Assigning roles to users for working with the SAP Workflow Engine

▶ Creating structural authorization profiles with which you can create detailed authorizations for Organizational Management objects

▶ Assigning the structural authorization profiles to users

The specifications you make in this section concern both workflow authorizations and Organizational Management authorizations.

Maintain Roles

Roles contain authorization objects for specific task areas. With this activity, you generate authorization profiles assigned to users based on roles. Refer to the SAP Help Portal (*http://help.sap.com*) for more detail on the workflow roles and authorizations. The roles for the SAP Workflow Engine are listed in Table 3.1. Note that names for your own roles may not begin with the prefix SAP.

Role	Description
SAP_BC_BMT_WFM_ADMIN	Workflow system administrator
SAP_BC_BMT_WFM_CONTROLLER	Process controller (reporting, etc.)
SAP_BC_BMT_WFM_DEVELOPER	Workflow developer
SAP_BC_BMT_WFM_PROCESS	Implementation team
SAP_BC_BMT_WFM_UWL_ADMIN	UWL administrator for workflow
SAP_BC_BMT_WFM_UWL_END_USER	UWL user for workflow
SAP_BC_SRV_USER	User for workflow, communication, and so on

Table 3.1 Workflow Roles

Structural Authorizations

Structural authorization allows you to give users in different organizational units different access rights. You may want to read up about this in the IMG if this sounds relevant to your installation. (The path in the IMG is PERSONNEL MANAGEMENT • PERSONNEL ADMINISTRATION • TOOLS • AUTHORIZATION MANAGEMENT • STRUCTURAL AUTHORIZATIONS FOR ORGANIZATIONAL MANAGEMENT.)

3.2 Task-Specific Customizing

As far as possible in the technical and business sense, the SAP-provided workflows can be run directly without any modifications. However, there are always some settings that must be entered in your system and that cannot be supplied by SAP.

3.2.1 Maintaining the Organizational Plan

The company-specific organizational plan describes the organizational assignment of an employee. This allows the responsibilities of employees for performing individual business activities to be defined in the form of activity profiles. Whether or not you use the organizational plan is up to you. It is included in the SAP NetWeaver Application Server license, so we strongly recommend that you take advantage of it, especially if other teams have already set it up for use elsewhere.

> **Hint**
>
> The organizational plan is maintained in the IMG via SAP NetWeaver • Application Server • Business Management • SAP Business Workflow • Edit organizational plan.

3.2.2 Agent Assignment for Tasks

From an organizational point of view, tasks must *always* be linked to their possible agents. This means that several employees with the same authorization on an organizational basis are offered the same task for execution. One of these employees assumes responsibility for and processes the work item. This assignment principle supports automatic load distribution within work groups with the same activity profile. For a detailed discussion of this, together with the organizational plan, refer to Chapter 5, Agents.

3.2.3 Activating the Triggering Events for a Workflow or a Task

Workflows and tasks can be started via events, as you will see later in Chapter 13, Using Events and Other Business Interfaces. A workflow or a task can have several triggering events. Every time *one* of the triggering events is raised in the system and satisfies the start conditions, then the relevant workflow is started (i.e., it is a logical OR operation between the different start events). The triggering events for a workflow or a task are entered in its definition. If you activate the triggering events, the system automatically activates the associated type-linkage.

If the SAP-provided workflow scenarios are to be started via triggering events, this is mentioned in their online descriptions in the SAP Help Portal (*http://help.sap.com*). If this is the case, the linkage between the triggering event and the workflow (or task) must always be activated to activate the process scenario. The ease with which you can switch the process on and off or use the event activation to swap one process definition for another is a big advantage of using events to trigger workflows. Event activation is usually carried out in the customizing phase.

3.3 Transport and Client Copy

After you have created your tasks and workflows, they will have to be transported from development to production.

3.3.1 Transport of Tasks

Cross-client transport objects, for example, standard tasks (type TS) and workflow templates (type WS), are connected to the transport system. They are automatically included in transport requests, if the client settings allow changes to cross-client objects and if you do not designate the objects as local objects.

3.3.2 Transport of Settings for Tasks and Workflows

You maintain the following settings for tasks on a client-specific basis:

▸ Assignments to their possible agents

▸ The general task attribute or a task or workflow

▸ Type linkages and their activation

▸ Workflow configuration

The system automatically includes these settings in a transport request as long as the system administrator has enable change requests on the client.

Tip
When you have Organizational Management set up in the production system, either via transport, ALE, or customizing, it is a good idea to block the import of agent assignments into the system. Setting this eliminates the risk of overwriting a production organizational model with one that has been set up in the QA (quality assurance) system purely for test purposes. Work with the security administrator on blocking the import of agent assignments when transporting to production.

3.3.3 Transporting a Workflow Definition

The next step is about transporting a workflow definition:

▸ If a workflow definition is transported to another system, only the active version is actually copied.

▸ If a workflow definition exists in the target system, but no executing workflows are based on this version, then the existing definition is simply overwritten by the imported version.

▸ If there are active workflow instances, then the transported workflow definition is imported with a new version number. This allows the existing workflow instances to continue to execute using the old version of the workflow definition, which is necessary to ensure the nonstop operation of the process.

The transported workflow definition becomes the active workflow definition in the target system. The workflows that are started after the import follow the path dictated by this new version of the workflow definition.

3.4 Customizing for the SAP Workflow Engine

Table 3.2 provides a summary of the customizing activities, indicating what is done automatically.

Activity	Automatic	Always Required?	Default Used
Set Active Plan Version	✓	✓	01
Maintain Prefix Numbers	–	✓	
Configure RFC Destination	✓	✓	User WF-BATCH
Maintain the Default Workflow Administrator	✓	✓	▶ SY-UNAME ▶ Your own user ID
Classify Decision Task as General	✓	–	
Maintain Standard Domain for Internet	–	–	
Activate Send to Objects and HR Objects	✓	–	
Maintain Demo and Verification Environment	✓	–	
Schedule Background Job for Missed Deadlines	✓	✓	
Schedule Background Job for Work Items with Errors	✓	✓	
Schedule Background Job for Condition Evaluation	✓	✓	
Schedule Background Job for Event Queue	✓	–	
Schedule Background Job for Clean-up Report	✓	✓	

Table 3.2 Overview of Customizing Activities

After the work item is delivered to the user, the user executes the work item via his inbox. Too often, the users' inbox experience is neglected in project planning and end user training. This chapter helps you understand the various inboxes provided and how they work, and provides guidelines on which inbox is the best choice for your project.

4   Work Item Delivery

After activating a workflow so that the optimum process definition is followed and the best possible agent for the task is selected, it is very easy to lean back and believe that the important work has been done. This is far from the truth. The business user needs an inbox environment that enables him to discover and execute the task in a productive way. When users struggle with the inbox, it has a negative impact on the overall workflow project. The inbox environment and how your users work with tasks must be included in your project plan and definitely in all of your test plans.

4.1   The Human Factor

The benefit of workflow is at its highest when coordinating the work of different people. Humans are doing the job because only they are capable of making the complex decisions or manipulating the data that is involved in the task. Here are some of the features that an inbox can provide to enable your users to successfully work with their tasks:

▶ Easy to access

▶ At-a-glance view of what tasks need to be performed and which tasks need to be tackled first

▶ Clear instructions about how to perform the task

▶ Overview of all of the relevant data that the user needs to know to perform the task well

▶ Mechanisms for letting the user initiate dialogues with other users so that these dialogues are transparent to everyone involved in the process

▶ Alert mechanisms so that a user can pull the emergency cord when he notices that things are not proceeding correctly

▶ Logs to see what has happened and who has participated in the process so far

▶ Graphical overview to show where the process is going next and to make ad-hoc changes

▶ Outbox for researches and to provide positive feedback about the work that an agent has accomplished during the course of the day

This list is long and by no means complete, but it gives you an idea of how critical the human aspect is. In practice, you can distinguish between two different groups of agents:

▶ The occasional workflow participant

▶ The power-agent who concentrates on one set of duties

Usually these two groups of users will mix within a workflow process, so you may have different participants using different inboxes. This is not an issue with the SAP Business Workflow Engine because the workflow definition does not need to be created for one specific inbox. An agent can access the same work item from several different inboxes if he chooses. Making the workflow definition independent of the inboxes used by the agent is part of the tool's philosophy.

There are several options for the users to receive their work items. This chapter will focus on those delivered as part of SAP NetWeaver. In later chapters the other alternatives are described: Alloy for Lotus Notes, Duet for Microsoft Office, SAP CRM, and SAP SRM.

▶ **Business Workplace**
The Business Workplace is the inbox within the SAP GUI. It has the most advanced features. This inbox is recommended if you only have work items in one SAP system, your users do not use the SAP NetWeaver Portal, and your users normally use the SAP GUI.

▶ **Universal Worklist**
UWL is the overall recommended inbox when accessing tasks from multiple systems. It is available in the SAP NetWeaver Portal. UWL can be used for workflow items from many systems (all applications within the SAP Business

Suite) and can receive other tasks, such as alerts, SAPoffice mails, and tasks from SAP NetWeaver Business Process Management, as well as hosting non-SAP tasks.

► **Extended notifications**
Extended notifications enable you to email notifications about tasks to desktop inboxes such as Microsoft Outlook and Lotus Notes. Extended notifications can also link to UWL. The user can receive a link to execute the work item. This is recommended for the occasional workflow user and where the company is not using Alloy or Duet.

► **Business Workflow Workplace**
Business Workflow Workplace is a workflow inbox for the SAP NetWeaver Business Client. This inbox should be used if your company is using the Business Client for the user interface.

► **Microsoft Outlook via Duet**
Duet enables the integration of the SAP Business Suite and Microsoft Outlook. This integration includes SAP Business Workflow. The user is able to execute the task from Outlook, and it includes full integration such as calendar functions, tracking, and delegation.

► **Lotus Notes via Alloy**
Alloy integrates SAP Business Suite with Lotus Notes. This integration includes SAP Business Workflow. The user is able to execute decisions from Lotus Notes, and it enables users more comfortable in Lotus Notes to access SAP information via Lotus Notes.

► **SAP CRM inbox**
SAP CRM does not require the SAP NetWeaver Portal. Therefore, CRM provides an inbox that can be used if you are not using SAP NetWeaver Portal.

► **SRM inbox**
SAP SRM 5.0 has its own inbox. However, with SAP SRM 7.0, UWL is the provided inbox for SAP SRM.

Normally you start with UWL — your power users and regular workflow users will use UWL. You can consider extended notifications and extensions such as Duet and Alloy to increase the reach of your work items to the casual user. In this chapter, we cover the inbox available in the SAP GUI, and then we discuss UWL, extended notifications, and the inbox available in the SAP NetWeaver Business Client. Even if you will use UWL, we recommend you read Section 4.2, SAP Business Workplace, to get an overview of the inbox features provided by SAP.

4.2   SAP Business Workplace

Before describing the inbox features, consider the major differences between a work item and an email:

▶ An email is a text message. You read it, react to the subject of the email, file it, or delete it. In contrast, a work item brings work to you that must be executed. A work item is part of a process and can be monitored for how long it took to execute and who did the work.

▶ If you want to remove an email from your inbox, you simply delete it. The only way for you to remove a work item from your inbox is to complete the work or forward it to another agent.

▶ From the execution point of view, if a workflow sends an email, it immediately continues to the next step. However, if it generates a work item, the workflow will be held up until the work item completes.

▶ Another difference is that an email is usually copied by the mail system when it is sent to several addressees. When one addressee deletes his email, copies of the email remain in the other addressees' inboxes. However, although a work item can be (and usually is) assigned to several agents, as soon as one agent reserves or completes it, it automatically disappears from the other agents' inboxes immediately. It also disappears when an alternative branch makes this step obsolete or the workflow is cancelled. Remember that as a workflow developer, you can have the workflow itself remove the work item from the agent's inbox if it is no longer required (e.g., by using modeled deadline monitoring; refer to Appendix A, Tips and Tricks).

▶ The work item brings with it a host of other information such as the workflow logs.

Figure 4.1 shows the SAP Business Workplace (Transaction SBWP) and some of the common items such as the inbox, which has current work items. Notice the outbox, which shows workflows and work items you have previously executed. The menu bar includes options to reserve, replace, forward, go to the workflow log, and create attachments.

The inbox is how users access their tasks and execute their work. The following sections describe the important parts of the inbox.

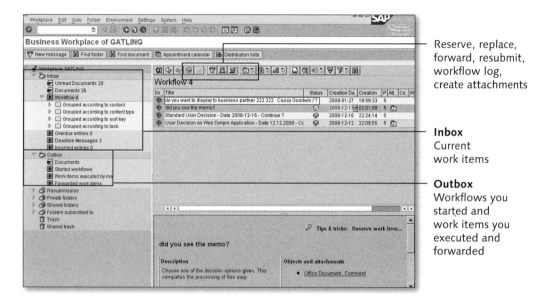

Reserve, replace, forward, resubmit, workflow log, create attachments

Inbox
Current work items

Outbox
Workflows you started and work items you executed and forwarded

Figure 4.1 SAP Business Workplace

4.2.1 Work Item Text

The work item text is easy to set up, and if written carefully, it can have a dramatic influence on the success of the process and on the amount of administration needed to support the users. When a user sees a work item in his inbox, he should know, at a first glance, what the task is for and what is required to execute the task.

The work item text comes in two parts. Both of these texts are maintained in the definition of the standard task (TS). The texts are very important and should be reviewed with your business users as part of the requirements stage.

► **Short text**

The short text is the subject line users see in their inbox. It is recommended that you use variables and key action words the user can use when sorting the inbox. Meaningful variables enable the agent to pick the most important tasks first. The most important variable should appear first. Clear work item text also aids sorting. The variables are also useful when the agent needs to search for a particular work item when someone phones to ask about it. Your business users should be involved when deciding the short text to use for your tasks.

► **Task description**

The task description can always be read, but it is not always displayed as a default. For example, the Business Workplace displays the description in the preview pane, and it can also be transmitted automatically as an email to notify an agent that he has work to do. However, if the information contained in the description makes it easier for the agent to perform the task, he will be interested in viewing the description before executing the task.

A description of what has to be done and how to do it will not be very interesting for an experienced user, but a summary of information relating to the process, which could be obtained otherwise only with complex navigation, is a bonus. If the task is simple to perform, and all of the information that the user needs is displayed when the agent executes the task, then you can assume that the task description will only be used when something goes wrong or when someone new joins the team.

A typical task description contains:

► A description of how to do the task. This includes not just a description of which buttons to click but also a description of how to arrive at a good result. For example, a decision task will describe the important factors that need to be taken into account.

► A summary of the data involved. There is no limit to the number of variables you can use.

► A statement showing why the agent received this work item, for example, "You are responsible for orders issued in plant 1000."

► An address or help desk contact when things go wrong or questions arise.

Texts definitions are maintained by the workflow developer. If you are using tasks provided by SAP, the text can be customized to meet your requirements. Changing the text for a SAP-delivered task is considered a customizing activity, which means the text is transported from development to production.

To get an idea of how the short text can be displayed to the user in the Business Workplace preview pane, take a good look at Figure 4.2. You can see that the first part of the description is the most important part and that typically the attachments and other information are displayed alongside the description.

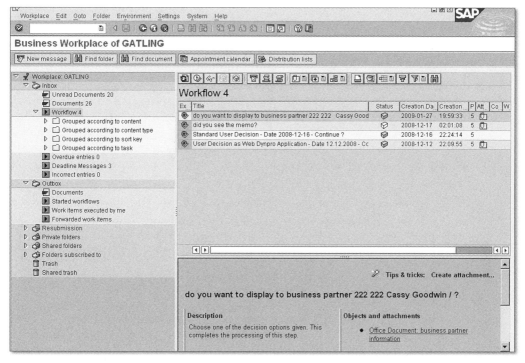

Figure 4.2 SAP Business Workplace Preview

4.2.2 Attachments

Any agent can add attachments to the work item. These attachments are collected after the work item has finished and appended to a list of attachments linked to the workflow. This means that any attachment added is visible to all other agents in the process, even when that particular step of the workflow has finished.

Three types of attachments are generally used:

▸ A text attachment written in an SAP editor by the agent

▸ A digital document uploaded to the workflow

▸ A reference to an SAP Business Object

The text attachments are the most commonly used. The agent creates a new attachment to describe how a particular decision was reached or to include useful information for the agent next in line. Microsoft Office documents as well as Adobe Acrobat documents are common document types to attach. Users may delete attachments they created, but they may not delete other people's attachments.

Tip

The attachments are stored in the workflow element _Attach_Objects. These are always passed to the work item container. When the work item has finished, any new attachments are appended to the workflow container. This means that it is impossible to remove attachments using customer code within a task unless the code simultaneously removes references to the item from the workflow container and deletes the attachments, too.

Attachments are very useful in workflow but are all too often neglected. They can document why a decision was made, especially if a manager wants to explain why he has rejected an employee's request. Try to make sure that the users use attachments because the alternative is often email or telephone. Emails and telephone calls are lost from the audit trail and cannot be referred to later by new participants in the business process.

Of course, a good alternative to attachments is to model the workflow so that it forces the user to create a note as a workflow step. However, this is not always possible or desired. It is a nuisance if the agents are forced to document what they are doing at every step. After the agents are disciplined enough to write and read attachments, you will find that they are thankful for the opportunity to use them.

4.2.3   Reserving and Replacing a Work Item

When an agent reserves a work item via the RESERVE AND REPLACE button (🔲), the work item disappears from everyone else's inbox. This is useful if there are multiple experts in the pool of users. When you start to execute a work item, you will automatically reserve the work item.

Canceling the execution causes the work item to remain reserved in your inbox. Replacing the work item causes the work item to reappear in other people's inboxes. It reappears to all agents who have either received the work item initially or have been forwarded it by someone else. In other words, if you are forwarded a work item that you cannot process, you can simply reserve and replace it so that it reappears in all of the inboxes of the originally selected agents.

Tip

To find out who currently has a work item waiting in their inbox, navigate to SELECTED AGENTS from the workflow log by clicking the WORKFLOW LOG button (☑)

4.2.4   Executing a Work Item

After the agent has executed the work item, he will find himself in the relevant SAP transaction, URL, or whatever else has been configured for this workflow task. By executing a task, the agent automatically reserves the work item so that the work item disappears from all of the other inboxes. If the agent decides to leave the work item for someone else to do, the work item must be released by clicking the REPLACE button (☑) in the inbox. Reserved work items are displayed with a special status symbol (processing started).

It is important that the agents know about this and know how to release work items; otherwise, they will block other users from seeing (or executing) the work item. When an agent leaves the department, all reserved work items must be released; otherwise, the administrator will have to do the clean up.

To make life even more comfortable for the agent, you can provide workflow features that can be called up directly from within the transaction being executed (assuming it is a method executed in an SAP component). This is done by calling the workflow toolbox (shown in Figure 4.3), which allows the user to perform the following functions without having to return to the inbox first:

▶ Forward the work item to someone else.

▶ Read the task description.

▶ Read the work item attachments.

▶ Create a new attachment.

▶ View the workflow log.

▶ Resubmit the work item.

You can learn more about the workflow toolbox in the SAP Help Portal (*http://help.sap.com*) or execute the sample workflow in Transaction SWUI_DEMO. Chapter 14, Custom Programs, also describes in more detail how to develop transactions so that they include the workflow toolbox.

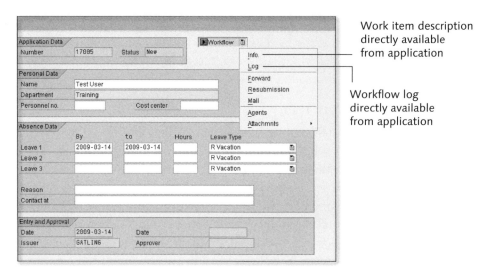

Figure 4.3 Workflow Toolbox

Having executed the work item, the outcome depends on the underlying method and the details in the step definition. If the step has been configured as requiring manual confirmation, then the user must confirm that the step is finished before the workflow continues. Manual confirmation is useful in display or edit tasks where the workflow system cannot determine automatically whether or not the task is finished or whether the agent needs a chance to review what he has done before the workflow finishes. The confirmation button appears as a pop-up dialog after the work item has finished, or alternatively it can be set directly from the work item list.

If the task is asynchronous, there will be a slight delay before the terminating event completes the work item. This delay can be a few seconds at peak times, so if the inbox is refreshed immediately after the work item has been executed, the work item may still be visible. The agents should be aware that there may be a delay (e.g., from training, work item description, or FAQ); otherwise, the help desk will get many unnecessary calls. Asynchronous tasks are described later in this section.

You should also make the agents aware that the work item is completed immediately after it has been executed. Refreshing the inbox simply updates the inbox display and has no effect on the work done by that agent.

4.2.5 Synchronous Dialog Chains

The term *synchronous dialog chain* has nothing to do with the terms *synchronous tasks* and *asynchronous tasks,* which will be explained later in the book. A synchronous dialog chain can be defined in a workflow to allow a user to execute several work items one after the other without returning to the inbox between work items. For example, suppose a manager has to explain why he has rejected a request but does not need to explain why he approved a request. You could use workflow to prompt for the explanation by following the approval/rejection step with an explanation request if the request is rejected. With synchronous dialog chains, each task is executed by the same person, without returning to the inbox between the tasks (as illustrated in Figure 4.4).

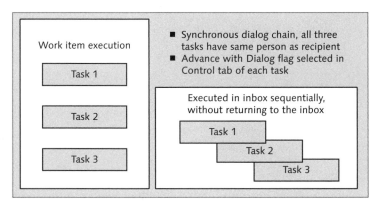

Figure 4.4 Synchronous Dialog Chain Example

Without the synchronous dialog chain, the agent would receive the approval work item in his inbox and select REJECT. The work item is now finished and when the agent refreshes his inbox, he gets a new work item asking for his explanation. This would be cumbersome for the agent because he has to return to the inbox unnecessarily. To avoid this, you define the first step as a synchronous dialog chain using the corresponding flag in the step definition. Now when the agent makes the rejection, the next work item is executed automatically, and he now sees the screen where he can enter the reason for the rejection. In other words, he is taken directly into the next step, which has a number of repercussions:

▶ For the synchronous dialog chain to work this way, the agent must be a recipient for all of the steps in the chain. If he is not the recipient for one of the steps in the chain, then the dialog chain breaks, and the work item lands in someone else's inbox. This is only logical. In fact, any of the steps can be assigned to a pool of agents without breaking the chain, as long as the user is a member of this pool.

▶ This feature is only supported in the Business Workplace inbox, not in UWL.

▶ The agent can at any point interrupt the chain by pressing the [Esc] key. The aborted work item will land in his inbox, ready to execute later.

▶ The agent usually only gets a chance to read the task description of the first work item because all subsequent work items rush past without stopping. Bear this in mind when creating the workflow. You can either include all of the relevant information in the very first task description in the chain, or you can use the workflow toolbox to allow the user to jump to the description from within the transaction that has been called. The same applies to attachments, but the attachments will not change during the chain unless the agent adds attachments.

> **Note**
>
> Synchronous dialog chains are only supported in the SAP Business Workplace in SAP GUI.

4.2.6 Forwarding a Work Item

Forwarding a work item to another agent sends it to that agent's inbox and removes the work item from all other recipients' inboxes. For this reason, the agents should only use this function when either that agent is the only selected agent or that agent wants someone specific to execute the work item.

You can even forward the work item to a user who has already been assigned the work item. This simply removes the work item from everyone else's inbox. If you receive a forwarded work item and replace it, the work item reappears in all inboxes of the originally selected agents (including the agent who forwarded it) and remains in your inbox too, even if you were not one of the originally selected agents. In other words, forwarding also extends the number of selected agents.

You can configure the task so that it can be forwarded to anyone or so that it can only be forwarded to a possible agent (discussed in Chapter 5, Agents). In fact, forwarding the work item does not so much forward it as reassign the selected agents.

> **Note**
>
> When you look at the list of selected agents, you can see who received the work item initially and to whom it was forwarded later.

The principal use of forwarding is in the following situations:

▶ Someone changes position and wants to pass on the work items currently in his inbox to someone else.

▶ The agent determination has failed or is incorrect, and the work item needs to be forwarded to another possible agent.

▶ The agent is new to the job and wants someone with more experience to check the work before releasing it. The freshman agent can create an attachment explaining what needs to be checked, and then he can delete this attachment after receiving it back again.

Make sure that the workflow step is configured as needing manual confirmation in order to work. You may want to encourage this during training. It makes the users much more comfortable.

4.2.7 Priority

Changing the priority of the work item only affects the sorting order in the inbox. It does not affect the priority of the rest of the workflow. The priority can be set in the workflow definition and passed to the workflow dynamically in a binding or be manually changed from the work item display or inbox.

Work items with the highest priority (priority 1) cause an express mail pop-up message to occur if the user is logged into an SAP component, irrespective of which transaction the agent is using but depending on which user interface is being used.

4.2.8 Resubmission

If the agent does not want to deal with a work item immediately, he can resubmit the work item by dispatching it to the resubmission queue for several days (or hours); this is done by clicking the RESUBMISSION button (🗔). The work it automatically pops back in the inbox after the period has expired.

If the agent wants to execute the work item before the resubmission time has elapsed, he can go to the resubmission queue and cancel the resubmission so that it pops back into the inbox queue.

4.2.9   Logs

Many different views of the workflow log are created automatically when the workflow runs. These logs can be referred to while the workflow is running to see what has happened so far or what is about to happen next. They can also be used as an audit trail after the workflow has finished.

Several reports allow you to access the logs, but you can also view the log from the work item inbox, the work item outbox, and usually from the transaction displaying the business object involved in the workflow. All of the details are stored in the logs, but only the technical log displays the complete detailed view. The technical log is useful when developing a workflow and is very useful when tracking down an error. However, the default display is a non-technical view of the log. To get to the logs from the inbox, select a work item, and display the workflow log by clicking the WORKFLOW LOG button ( ).

The user logs show three views of the history of the workflow:

▸ **Chronological view** (VIEW: WF CHRONICLE)
This displays the non-technical steps in the order that they are carried out. You can expand the display to see more details about each step, including the agents who received the work item initially and who added which attachments (see Figure 4.5).

▸ **Agent-oriented view** (VIEW: WORKFLOW AGENTS)
This displays a list of agents who were actively involved in the workflow. You can expand the display to see exactly what each agent did, which steps they were involved in, and which attachments they added.

▸ **Object-oriented view** (VIEW: WORKFLOW OBJECTS)
This displays a list of objects involved in the process, including business objects and the ad-hoc objects such as attachments that have been added. You can display the objects and view where each object was used within the process. This is particularly useful for processes where several basic business objects are used and the agent needs to refer back to a previous object (providing he has the authorization needed to view it).

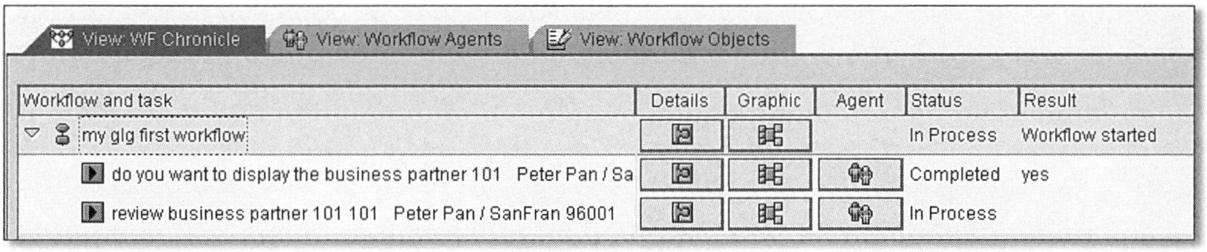

View: WF Chronicle
View: Workflow Agents
View: Workflow Objects
Workflow and task
Details
Graphic
Agent
Status
Result
my glg first workflow
In Process
Workflow started
do you want to display the business partner 101 Peter Pan / Sa
Completed
yes
review business partner 101 101 Peter Pan / SanFran 96001
In Process

Figure 4.5 Workflow Log

The View: WF Chronicle workflow log shows each step, status, result, date, and time (date and time are not shown in Figure 4.5). To get more information, you can select the Details, Graphic, or Agent icons. The graphical log (see Figure 4.6) is especially useful when an agent wants to see where the workflow goes next or wants to debug a workflow that contains many parallel branches or loops. If ad-hoc workflows have been configured, agents can use the graphical log to make on-the-fly changes to the process as it runs.

Display Workflow Log for 'zFirstWorkfl'
Center on selected steps
Graphical workflow log

Figure 4.6 Graphical Workflow Log

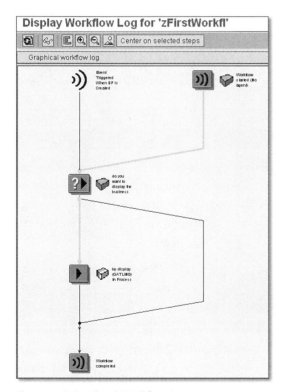

Navigation between a work item and its logs is very flexible, and as you can see, there is a good selection of different views that can be reached. To make life easier for your agents, select the most useful views and include them together with a description of how to reach the view in your FAQ for the process. Spread awareness that there are logs, so that the agents can follow up on common questions such as "What is the workflow doing right now?" (Answer: "Inspect the log from the workflow outbox"). This will drastically reduce the number of help desk calls and bolster the agents' confidence in the system. Bear in mind that the administrator will use more views and has been better trained than the agents.

4.2.10 Outbox

The workflow outbox displays the work items that have already had your involvement. These include the workflows you have started, work items you have executed, and work items you have forwarded elsewhere. The display of the work item varies slightly according to which of these folders you view. You can use the workflow outbox to follow the progress of the workflow; it is just one click to navigate to the workflow log from the work item display.

The workflow outbox is very useful for advanced users. Some users like to look at the workflow outbox at the end of the day to see how many work items they have processed.

4.2.11 Rejecting Work Items

Rejecting work items is not the same as canceling work items. When a work item is aborted by the administrator (not to be confused with simply canceling out of the work item processing), the whole workflow is cancelled. This is usually something that the administrator needs to perform infrequently. Rejecting a work item is much "softer."

Anyone who receives a work item can reject it (if PROCESSING CAN BE REJECTED has been enabled for that step, which is set in the DETAILS tab of the task) if the agent believes that the task is no longer necessary. For example, if the agent recognizes a scanned document as being a duplicate, he can simply reject it.

When the work item is rejected, the process follows a different path from the normal flow. You can add new steps to this path to tie up any loose ends after the rejection. For example, you can force the person rejecting the item to create a note explaining why it was rejected, and you can send notifications to the work-flow initiator or anyone else involved.

The REJECT EXECUTION button (🔳) is only displayed when this option is selected in the workflow step definition.

4.2.12 Substitution

When people are away from work, a substitute should be available to execute the tasks. This might be planned time away, such as vacation, or unplanned time, such as illness. Substitutes are important to ensure the process completes on time to meet the process objectives.

Substitutes can be set up in the inbox using SAP Business Workplace and UWL. Setting up substitutes is discussed in Chapter 5, Agents.

4.3 Universal Worklist

Traditionally, users had to access a variety of inboxes to view and act on impor-tant tasks. From an SAP perspective, this might require a user to access tasks on their SAP ERP, SRM, and CRM systems separately. In addition to SAP, there could be other systems where users must access tasks throughout the day.

Universal Worklist (UWL) is the central task list within SAP NetWeaver. It is not part of SAP Business Workflow, and not a task list specifically for SAP Business Workflow. Rather, it is not tied to any task provider but serves as a central work list for all task types. For example, in addition to SAP Business Workflow tasks, UWL is also used with alerts from the alert framework, collaboration tasks, Guided Procedures actions, and tasks from SAP NetWeaver Business Process Management. Additionally, UWL has an API that can be used to access non-SAP tasks. This could be anything from an RSS feed and Web Services, to tasks from other systems such as custom-developed systems or systems delivered by other software providers.

> **Tip**
>
> In this section, we cover what you need to get started with UWL from a SAP Business Workflow perspective. More details of UWL, such as specifics on customization and all options available, are covered in *Universal Worklist with SAP NetWeaver Portal* (SAP PRESS Essentials, 2008).

4.3.1 Major Features of the Universal Worklist

UWL simplifies the user's work by providing a single consistent interface that delivers tasks from multiple systems into a single location. The user is provided a task list that can be customized, personalized, filtered, and sorted. UWL allows for extensive customization, enabling customers to build a work list that targets their business users' specific requirements.

UWL provides different components out-of-the-box. Figure 4.7 shows the four tabs:

▶ TASKS
The TASKS tab has current work items waiting for processing.

▶ ALERTS
The ALERTS tab has alerts from the alert framework.

▶ NOTIFICATIONS
The NOTIFICATIONS tab contains deadline messages. It can also include email items from SAP Business Workflow if used with the SONiC connector (discussed in Section 4.3.8, Universal Worklist API and the SONiC Connector).

▶ TRACKING
The TRACKING tab displays work items you have completed.

Figure 4.7 Main Tabs in UWL

Tasks are listed in the TASKS tab with the work item text (see Figure 4.8). Notice the line menu at the end of the work item text. The options available from this menu are dependent upon the type of work item in UWL but normally include the ability to FORWARD the work item and to RESUBMIT it.

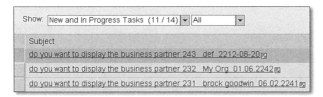

Figure 4.8 Task List in UWL

Figure 4.9 shows the lower pane where you can see the description text for the tasks and the buttons to launch the work item. Also included are options to reserve (Assign To Me), Resubmit, Forward, and any attachments that may be included.

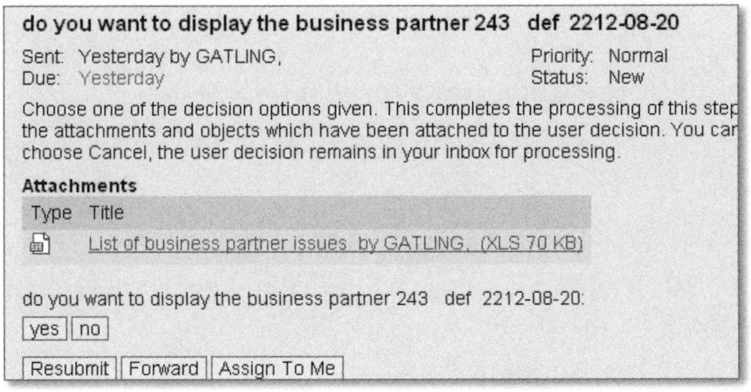
do you want to display the business partner 243 def 2212-08-20
Sent: Yesterday by GATLING,
Priority: Normal
Due: Yesterday
Status: New
Choose one of the decision options given. This completes the processing of this step
the attachments and objects which have been attached to the user decision. You can
choose Cancel, the user decision remains in your inbox for processing.
Attachments
Type Title
List of business partner issues by GATLING, (XLS 70 KB)
do you want to display the business partner 243 def 2212-08-20:
yes
no
Resubmit
Forward
Assign To Me

Figure 4.9 Task Description

The You can also section (in the bottom right of the UWL) enables you to display the details for the work item in the SAP GUI, manage attachments, create an ac-hoc request based on this work item (e.g., you want to ask for a colleague's input before acting on the task), and view the workflow log. The other options in the main UWL display are shown in Figure 4.10. Each user can personalize his own view, manage substitutions, refresh the inbox, and display the connection status for each system providing tasks to UWL.

Create Task
Show Filters
Hide Preview
Refresh
Priority
Personalize View
Normal
Manage Substitution Rules
Normal
Display Connection Status

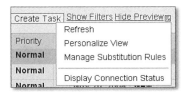

Figure 4.10 Additional User Options

Next to the additional user options, you will see the link Show Filters (in Figure 4.10). When you select Show Filters, you see the filters shown in Figure 4.11. Users can choose to filter on priority, due dates from today to last 90 days, and due dates that will come in the next 90 days. You can also filter on the day the work item was sent, and filter on text in the work item text field.

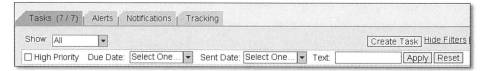

Figure 4.11 Filters in the Universal Worklist

4.3.2 Getting Started with the Universal Worklist

UWL is delivered with the SAP NetWeaver Portal. You must do the following before using UWL:

1. Each system that will be providing tasks to UWL must be added to the system landscape of the SAP NetWeaver Portal, which is normally done by the portal administrator. The addition of the system must include user mapping of the portal users to the SAP Business Workflow system.

2. After the system is added, either the portal administrator or the UWL administrator registers the system for UWL via the portal path System Administration • System Configuration • Universal Worklist & Workflow.

3. Select New to add the system to UWL. The System Alias field must match the alias given to the system when it was added to the portal.

4. Normally, you also set up the delta pull to increase efficiency in the UWL receiving work items from the provider system. When configuring delta pull, you must also set up an RFC destination for the background pull group.

> **Hint**
>
> When configuring UWL, use the delta pull mechanism. This enables the automatic refresh of UWL to occur more frequently. The delta pull requires an RFC destination to be set up, which is discussed in SAP Note 1133821. A search for "delta pull mechanism for UWL" in the SAP Help Portal (*http://help.sap.com*) will provide you with step-by-step configuration.

5. Select Save and Register. You are then ready to use UWL.

6. All of the options for configuration are discussed in the previously mentioned UWL book and in the SAP Help Portal. Search for the phrase "administration and configuration of the UWL", and you will receive the link that walks through the setup in detail.

4.3.3   Working with Tasks in the Universal Worklist

When working with tasks in UWL, you have many of the same features discussed in Section 4.2, SAP Business Workplace. For example, in UWL, you can do the following:

- Access the work item text.
- Add attachments that are available in later workflow steps.
- Reserve, replace, resubmit, and forward work items.
- Execute the work item. Additionally, the developer can substitute an alternative user interface for the task execution (discussed in Chapter 18, User Interface Options).
- Access workflow logs.
- View tasks by status (all, new, in progress, due today, over due).
- Although many of the Business Workplace features are available in UWL, you should be aware that UWL cannot support synchronous dialog chains; this is a specific Business Workplace feature. To use the graphical login UWL, the user needs to use the option DISPLAY DETAILS IN SAP GUI.

4.3.4   Personalization Options in the Universal Worklist

Personalization in UWL refers to what the agents can do. Personalization is accessed via the preview panel shown in Figure 4.12. Personalization includes deciding which columns the user wants and in which order, sorting options, view options, and paging options.

- **Personal attributes and their order**
  When personalizing attributes, you can sort the order of columns, including custom columns as well (e.g., a column with the business partner number, purchasing group, etc.). You can also set how you want the subject to appear (setting the width and justification).

- **Sorting properties**
  For sorting, you can determine prearranged sorting for up to three columns. Additionally, when in the main UWL view, you can sort on any column. Users can also set a filter to say, for example, they want to see items from the last three months.

▶ **Data properties**
In the DATA PROPERTIES area, you can determine how many lines per page to display, how often to refresh the page, when to indicate impending deadlines, and whether to display header and footer properties.

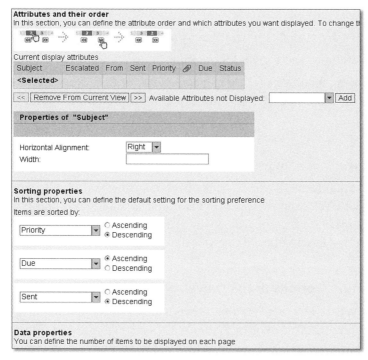

Figure 4.12 Personalization Options

4.3.5 Customizing Options in the Universal Worklist

In addition to the personalization options that can be performed by the business users, there are many customization options that are performed by the UWL administrator. The major options include the following:

▶ **Customize the look of the main UWL page**
For example, which tabs and which actions (RESUBMIT, FORWARD) should be available by default.

▶ **Creating subviews for specific tasks**
For example, create a subview to just see the purchase requisition tasks or the employee expense report tasks.

▸ **Adding custom columns**
For example, business partner number, sales amount.

▸ **Substitute a different UI for a task**
For example, a task by default executes in SAP GUI, but you can use Web Dynpro (ABAP or Java) to launch the task. This customization requires development and is discussed in detail in Chapter 18, User Interface Options.

▸ **Customizing tasks with different features, such as adding the ability to add a memo to a task**
This will be discussed in detail in Chapter 12, Agent Determination Rules.

Customers can do very creative customizing of the inbox. Examples include adding custom columns to bring in attributes such as dollar amount, links to receipts, or other scanned documents; and check boxes to enable mass processing (e.g., selecting APPROVE/REJECT on multiple work items and processing all work items at the same time).

4.3.6 Action Handlers in the Universal Worklist

Action handlers enable you to customize the launch of a work item, substituting a different user interface for the task. Depending upon the customizing handler, development will be required.

For example, your workflow has a task that uses Transaction BP to update a business partner. You want this to be displayed using Web Dynpro. The prerequisite is that you create a Web Dynpro application (ABAP or Java). Web Dynpro-specific code is required to communicate with the workflow container. You must use the workflow APIs (discussed in Chapter 14, Custom Programs) in your Web Dynpro to get data from the workflow container and to push results back to the workflow container.

Here are the most common action handlers:

▸ `SAPWebDynproLauncher`
Launches a Web Dynpro for a Java application.

▸ `SAPWebDynproABAPLauncher`
Launches a Web Dynpro for an ABAP application.

▸ `SAPTransactionLauncher`
Launches an SAP transaction using the SAP GUI for HTML.

▶ `SAPBSPLauncher`
Launches a Business Server Page (BSP).

▶ `URLLauncher`
Launches web locations.

▶ `FunctionModuleActionHandler`
Handles execution of items for which a workflow is executed through a given function module.

▶ `UpdatingContainerHandler`
Handles execution of items that update the workflow container with the specified values.

▶ `UserDecisionHandler`
Handles execution of items of types `UserDecision`.

As your company moves toward UWL, it is important to learn how action handlers work. They are optional but enable greater flexibility in how users work with work items. The Web Dynpro ABAP handler, Web Dynpro Java handler, and BSP handler are discussed in Chapter 18, User Interface Options.

4.3.7 UWL Configuration Wizard

When customizing UWL, there are three options:

▶ Manually create and upload the XML.

▶ Use Transaction SWFVISU for customizing action handlers.

▶ Use the UWL Configuration Wizard.

The UWL Configuration Wizard enables you to customize UWL without having to manually create the XML or use Transaction SWFVISU. You can access the UWL Configuration Wizard from the UWL administration page by navigating to SYSTEM ADMINISTRATION • SYSTEM CONFIGURATION • UNIVERSAL WORKLIST • ADMINISTRATION. Under UNIVERSAL WORKLIST CONTENT CONFIGURATION. Select CLICK to configure item types and customize views using a wizard.

The UWL Configuration Wizard in Figure 4.13 enables you to:

▶ Define custom attributes and customize the corresponding view.

▶ Define and configure what you want to launch when an item is clicked.

▶ Customize attributes and define what you want to launch when an item is clicked (both of the preceding options).

▶ Customize the look of the UWL main page (tabs, etc.).

The UWL Configuration Wizard can help you get started customizing UWL more quickly. It creates XML that you can later download and review if you want to learn how to create your own XML.

Recommendation

When changing the task visualization (customizing what is launched for a particular task), you should use Transaction SWFVISU. SAP applications (e.g. SAP CRM and SAP ERP HCM) deliver content in Transaction SWFVISU out-of-the-box. Maintaining all task visualization changes in Transaction SWFVISU provides a central location to see all launch handlers and is easier to maintain than manual XML changes.

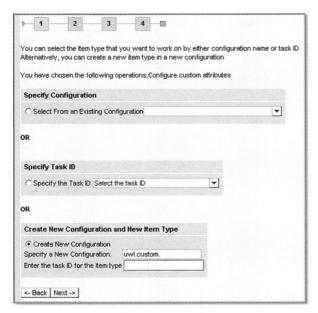

Figure 4.13 UWL Configuration Wizard

Hint

With customized XML, the configuration is evaluated by UWL based on priority given for the uploaded XML. The SAP-provided XML defaults to a low priority. To ensure your XML is used, change the priority to MEDIUM or HIGH.

4.3.8   Universal Worklist API and the SONiC Connector

By default, UWL provides the following connectors to provider systems:

▶ **Workflow**
For SAP Business Workflow items in any SAP system.

▶ **Ad-hoc Workflow**
For collaboration tasks.

▶ **Alerts**
For alerts from the alert framework.

▶ **Action Inbox**
For notifications from the Knowledge Management application.

Universal Worklist API

For tasks from non-SAP systems you can use the UWL API to link the tasks to UWL. To use the API, you need Java skills, including knowledge of the SAP NetWeaver Development Studio (NWDS) and SAP NetWeaver Development Infrastructure (NWDI).

The UWL service API enables you to retrieve items from customer systems or third-party systems, retrieve the navigational model, retrieve additional item attributes (such as description), retrieve attachments, manage attachments, and search, execute, and personalize the view.

The connector API enables the provider to push items to UWL and enables UWL to pull items either when the user is online or in scheduled intervals. The documentation for the Java docs is available in the SAP Help Portal at *http://help.sap.com/javadocs/NW04S/current/uw/index.html*. The SAP Developer Network (SDN, *http://sdn.sap.com*) also has how-to documents for creating your own connector.

SONiC connector

SAP Business Workflow normally creates work items that appear in users' inboxes. However, workflow sometimes generates email as well. For example, you can send an email message to notify someone when a task is completed. There is a task-type that enables workflow to send emails. By default, these emails do not appear in UWL (because they are not a task, but a message). However, SAP provides the SONiC (SAPoffice Notification Connector) to enable email tasks to appear in UWL.

The connector enables SAPoffice mails generated by SAP Business Suite applications or SAP Business Workflow to be accessed in UWL. The code and the installation guide can be downloaded and deployed in project solutions.

The major features of the connector include the following:

▸ Displaying SAPoffice Mail inbox items in UWL

▸ Forwarding SAPoffice Mail items

▸ Retrieval of RAW and URL type attachments

▸ Single Sign-on support with SAP Logon Tickets

The connector can be downloaded from SDN (*http://sdn.sap.com*). In the future, SONiC will be part of UWL releases.

4.4   Examples of Universal Worklist Customizing

The main UWL XML file can be downloaded and uploaded to the SAP NetWeaver Portal via the UWL administration page (SYSTEM ADMINISTRATION • SYSTEM CONFIGURATION • UNIVERSAL WORKLIST • ADMINISTRATION) Because UWL behavior (i.e., custom view, custom columns, custom action handler, etc.) is controlled by the XML file, you can upload your own XML file into the portal for your own UWL customization. The beauty of UWL customization is that your custom XML works as an override on top of the existing default XML. It would be good practice for you to review the existing XML, understand it, and create your own XML to enhance the UWL behavior per your own business needs.

You may want to look at the content in the *uwl_configuration.dtd* file that can also be downloaded from the same UWL administration menu. This DTD file provides the list of elements and attributes used in the UWL XML file, so it will be very helpful for the syntax check of your own UWL XML file. For example, the code in Listing 4.1 is from the DTD file that shows all of the attributes available for the element Action. From that, you can tell immediately that handler is one of the attributes available for the element Action.

```
<!ATTLIST Action
    name CDATA #IMPLIED
```

```
    reference CDATA #IMPLIED
    groupAction (yes|no) "no"
    userDecision CDATA #IMPLIED
    handler CDATA #IMPLIED
    referenceBundle NMTOKEN #IMPLIED
    returnToDetailViewAllowed (yes|no) "yes"
    launchInNewWindow (yes|no|portal) "no"
    launchNewWindowName CDATA #IMPLIED
    launchNewWindowFeatures CDATA #IMPLIED
>
```

Listing 4.1 Element Action in the UWL DTD

4.4.1   How Can I Add/Remove Columns

You can easily add or remove columns from UWL by adding or removing the column definition from the `columnOrder` string in the `View` section. Listing 4.2 shows the original.

```
<Views>
    <View name="DefaultView" selectionMode="SINGLESELECT"
    width="98%" supportedItemTypes="uwl.task"
    columnOrder="subject, isEscalated, createdDate, priority,
    attachmentCount, dueDate, status">
```

Listing 4.2 Original XML for Column Order

Listing 4.3 shows the customized one that does not have the `priority` element. Accordingly, the column PRIORITY won't be showing up in UWL.

```
<Views>
    <View name="DefaultView" selectionMode="SINGLESELECT"
    width="98%" supportedItemTypes="uwl.task"
    columnOrder="subject, isEscalated, createdDate,
    attachmentCount, dueDate, status">
```

Listing 4.3 Customized Column Order, Removing the Priority Column

4.4.2   How Can I Create Custom Columns

Because the dollar amount is typically critical information during the approval process, many users want to have a custom column for it that captures the approver's attention. This requires that you first define the custom column in the view and then populate the custom column with value.

Because this is a custom column, you need to create the definition for the custom column. The element `DisplayAttributes` under the `View` section takes care of the column definition. The XML code in Listing 4.4 defines a column called Total Value. Notice that this section should be placed between the `<View>` and `</View>` section because the `View` is the parent element of `DisplayAttributes`. You can see the hierarchy for these elements in the *uwl_configuration.dtd* file.

```
<DisplayAttributes>
    <DisplayAttribute name="ZTOTALVALUE" type="string" width=""
    sortable="yes" format="medium" hAlign="RIGHT"
    vAlign="BASELINE" maxTextWidth="0" headerVisible="yes">
        <Descriptions default="Total Value">
            <ShortDescriptions>
                <Description Language="en"
                Description="Total Value"/>
            </ShortDescriptions>
        </Descriptions>
    </DisplayAttribute>
```

Listing 4.4 Adding Custom Column ZTOTAL VALUE to UWL XML

The next task is how to populate the values for the custom column. The value can be from a workflow object or from a workflow container; UWL can handle both and can get the values from an ABAP BOR object (Business Object Repository) as well as from the workflow container.

As an example, let's say the workflow object type is `BUS2121` (Shopping Cart) that has a custom object attribute called `ZTOTALVALUE`, and we want to display the value in the custom column. Listing 4.5 shows the corresponding XML code if the source is the workflow object type. Note that the `id` of the `CustomAttribute-Source` must be `ABAP_BOR` to declare that the source is of workflow object type. Also, this section should be placed between the `<ItemType>` and `</ItemType>` because the `ItemType` is the parent element of `CustomAttributes`. Again, you can see the hierarchy for these elements in the *uwl_configuration.dtd* file.

```
<CustomAttributes>
    <CustomAttributeSource id="ABAP_BOR"
    objectIdHolder="externalObjectId"
    objectType="BUS2121" cacheValidity="final">
        <Attribute name="ZTOTALVALUE" type="double"
        displayName="Total Value"/>
```

```
    </CustomAttributeSource>
</CustomAttributes>
```

Listing 4.5 Z TOTALVALUE Referring to Business Object Repository Object

This time, let's say that the workflow has a container element called ZTOTALVALUE, and we want to display the value in the custom column. Listing 4.6 shows the corresponding XML code if the source is a workflow container. Note that the id of the CustomAttributeSource must be WEBFLOW_CONTAINER to specify the workflow container as the source where the value should come from. This section should be placed between the <ItemType> and </ItemType> because the ItemType is the parent element of CustomAttributes.

```
<CustomAttributes>
    <CustomAttributeSource id="WEBFLOW_CONTAINER"
    objectIdHolder="externalId" objectType="WebflowContainer"
    cacheValidity="final">
        <Attribute name="ZTOTALVALUE" type="double"
        displayName="Total Value"/>
    </CustomAttributeSource>
</CustomAttributes>
```

Listing 4.6 ZTOTALVALUE Referring to Workflow Container

Figure 4.14 shows the customized column for the amount. This amount is from Listing 4.5 or Listing 4.6, whichever was used to provide the amount to the UWL.

Figure 4.14 Customized Amount Column

4.4.3   How Can I Make a Mandatory Rejection Memo

When a work item is rejected, it is beneficial to make the rejection remarks mandatory. This can be done easily by using the property `UserDecisionNote` that belongs to `Action`. Listing 4.7 of the XML code creates a memo text box in the preview area of the item and makes it mandatory. UWL forces the user to enter text before submitting a decision alternative corresponding to the decision key. Entering a text in the box and submitting the decision alternative results in a memo upload to the work item. This section should be placed between the `<ItemType>` and `</ItemType>` because the `ItemType` is the parent element of `Action`.

```
<Action name="Reject" groupAction="yes"
        handler="UserDecisionHandler">
    <Properties>
        <Property name="decisionKey" value="2"/>
        <Property name="UserDecisionNote" value="mandatory"/>
    </Properties>
</Action>
```

Listing 4.7 User Decision, Making the Reason for Rejection Mandatory

Another example of the mandatory user decision will be shown in Chapter 19, Using Web Dynpro ABAP.

4.5   Extended Notifications

Extended notifications notify users by email or SMS (Short Message Service) about work items they need to process. The notification can contain links to work items that are launched via SAP GUI. The notification may also contain a URL to launch a Web Dynpro, BSP, or other URLs.

4.5.1   Types of Notifications

Users can receive email notifications or SMS notifications:

▶ **Email notification**
  An email notification can be a simple text that informs the user of work items in his inbox. In this case, the user needs to log on to the system to process the work items. The email notification can also include a descriptive text with links

that enable the user to display or execute the work item directly or display the workflow inbox.

Email notifications can be configured to send one email per work item or to group multiple work items in a single email message. The email message then contains links to the various work items.

► **SMS notification**
An SMS notification can be a general text that informs the user about work items in his SAP Workflow inbox that require processing (including system and client details). It can also include the work item short text (system and client details).

4.5.2   Features of Extended Notifications

With extended notifications, you can notify users of work they need to execute, providing hyperlinks to UWL. You can also provide links to execute the work item directly in SAP GUI. Figure 4.15 shows an example of an extended notification in the Microsoft Outlook inbox.

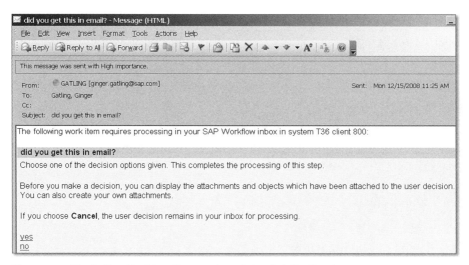

Figure 4.15 Single User Decision Message from Extended Notifications

You can also set reminders for outstanding work. For example, you can set a reminder for two or three days if the work is not completed. You can change the email layout by creating your own copy of the email template (copy the BSP application /SAP/BC/BSP/SAP/SWN_MESSAGE1/MAIN.DO).

4.5.3 Configuration Required for Extended Notifications

Extended notification configuration depends on the setup to send emails from SAP in general. Business communication from SAP to email systems must be configured before you can use extended notifications. The configuration for extended notifications is discussed in the SAP Help Portal (*http://help.sap.com*). In this section, we discuss the major pieces of configuration that must be completed for extended notifications:

1. The primary transaction to configure extended notifications is SWNCONFIG. In this transaction, you can manage the following:

   ▶ Create a delivery schedule.

   ▶ Add a subscription to scenario WORKFLOW, category STANDARD.

   ▶ Create a schedule selection with a filter to get ALL_DELTA that will give you all work items and then the deltas.

   ▶ Adjust the general settings to adjust sender name and provide a link to UWL.

2. After the settings are made, execute program SWN_SELEN to select and send the work items.

Figure 4.16 shows Transaction SWNCONFIG used to configure extended notifications. Use this transaction to set the subscription for which tasks should be included, if there should be one work item per email or multiple work items per emails, and to set the general settings.

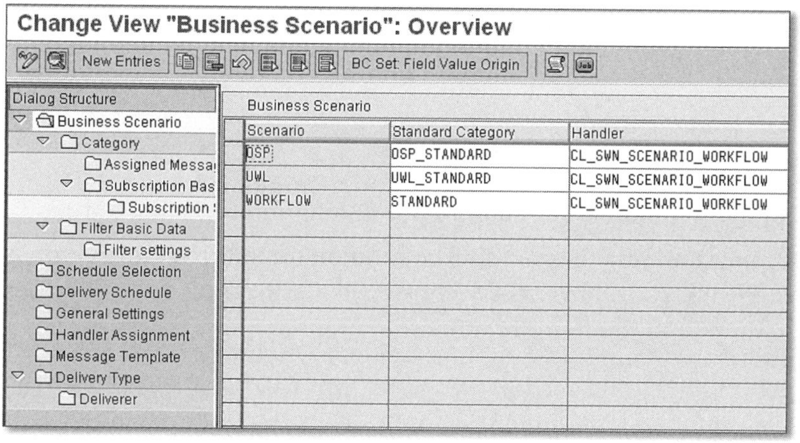

Figure 4.16 Transaction SWNCONFIG

Figure 4.17 shows the minimum changes you should make to the basic configuration of the extended notifications. This includes a link to the UWL and inclusion of a system/client in the sender information.

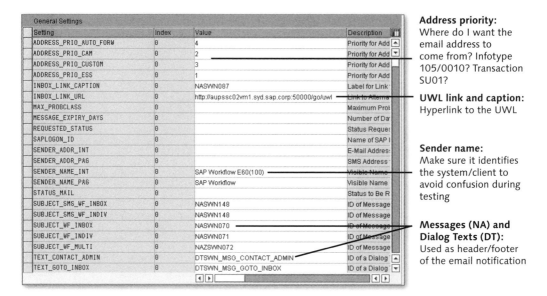

Figure 4.17 Minimum Changes You Should Make to the General Settings in SWNCONFIG

> **Note**
>
> Transaction SWNADMIN can be used instead of SWNCONFIG. The interface is simplified from SWNCONFIG. SWNADMIN supports all required configuration functions for extended notifications, but it does not support transport requests.

4.6 Business Workflow Workplace

Business Workflow Workplace (see Figure 4.18) is a workflow inbox available in the SAP NetWeaver Business Client. From a workflow perspective, this inbox is used if your company is using the SAP NetWeaver Business Client as the user interface.

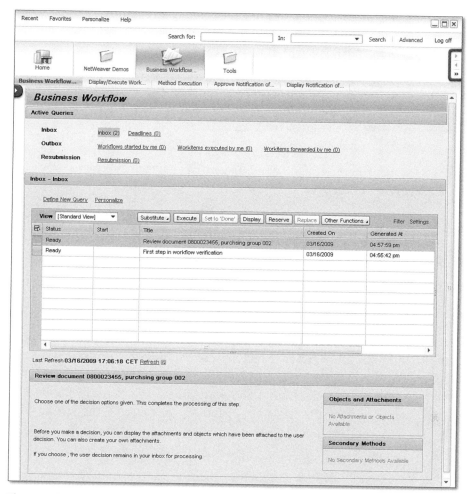

Figure 4.18 Business Workflow Workplace in SAP NetWeaver Business Client

Note

The SAP NetWeaver Business Client (NWBC) is a rich desktop client, using the latest smart client technology. It offers a unified environment for and a single point of entry to Web Dynpro applications and other SAP business applications and technologies. You can get information on the SAP NetWeaver Business Client at SDN (*http://sdn.sap.com*) and at SAP Help Portal (*http://help.sap.com*).

Business Workflow Workplace is written in Web Dynpro ABAP and supports all ABAP tasks (Java tasks are not supported at this time). This new inbox can only be accessed from the SAP NetWeaver Business Client. You can access all your work items, execute, and forward the work items. Additionally, personal substitutes are supported in the Business Workflow Workplace.

> **Hint**
>
> SAP Note 1149144 discusses the SAP Business Workflow Workplace. It is kept updated with all issues related to this new inbox.

4.7 External Users

External users are partners, customers, or vendors who your company works with on a regular basis. Examples of such collaboration include an external supplier in a Supply Chain Management (SCM) process or an engineering process.

The integration of partners into the workflows is often a crucial factor for the speed of the process. There is not a lot to be gained in automating a process if the internal portion of the process runs through in one day, only to be held up for several weeks waiting for a response from a partner. Worse still, if the partner is not integrated by workflow, all of the ad-hoc communications that take place are lost. Contrast this with a workflow-enabled process where all of the attachments are visible to everyone downstream, so anyone can see at a glance what the rest of the people involved have done so far, including, for example, the justification of why they have reached their decisions.

External users will need an SAP user ID to participate in the process. The user ID is written to the workflow logs and used to check the authorizations. Make sure that they switch passwords frequently and check regularly that they still exist. You can even build your own workflow to verify the user and security setup.

The best solution for your partners will be an external facing portal with UWL so that no local installation is necessary. The users can set up substitutes using this inbox and access all of the facilities that they would normally need to use to get the most out of the workflow automation.

You have to make sure that the agents receive email notifications with the URL to the inbox. You cannot expect them to check the inboxes on a regular basis without prompting.

4.8   Other Considerations

Just because your main "customers" are the agents involved in the workflow, do not neglect other employees who are not integrated into the workflow definition but whom the process affects. No workflow definition will ever cover everything, so rather than spending years implementing the perfect workflow, make sure you reach all of the affected users at least indirectly.

For example, some colleagues will be very grateful to be notified when a phase of the process has been reached (as opposed to being at the requested stage). Similarly, other colleagues will be grateful to know when the part of the workflow that affects them has been completed, even if the complete process is still progressing. In both cases, you can do your colleagues a favor by setting up the workflow to send notifications when the relevant stage has been reached.

Even though such employees have not been included directly in the workflow definition, they will still have the advantage of getting the timing right, so that they can proceed with their work using traditional methods. For example, if an order exceeds a certain amount, the key account manager would be only too glad to hear when it has reached the transportation stage because this gives him the opportunity to phone the customer, confirming personally that the goods are about to ship.

Do not overdo the messaging. Often enough during your reality check, you will find that some notifications can be eliminated or implemented on a subscription basis.

When designing your workflows, one major consideration is who should do the work. It is important to understand how to get work items to the correct agent. You also need a strategy to keep this working, despite organizational changes and personnel fluctuation. This chapter shows you the path to success in this area.

5 Agents

Every work item must be processed by one of the following:

▶ The Workflow Engine, using the system user ID `WF-BATCH`

▶ An agent, using a person to execute a dialog task

Agents are the people who do the work within the workflow. They do the work that cannot be done (or that you do not want done) automatically by the Workflow Engine. Agents are the *decision makers* in your business process, which is why finding the right agent for a particular work item is so important. You want the right person to make the decision, the person who understands the impact of the decision on the company — especially if that decision is going to have financial or legal implications, such as approving the purchase of new equipment or hiring a new employee.

One of the most interesting and often time-consuming parts of workflow design is deciding how to determine and assign the correct agent(s) — whether for one particular workflow — or, better yet, an overall strategy for all your proposed workflows. From a business perspective, this is a not a trivial issue, particularly if the process is new, and no one has done this sort of work before. After the business issues have been resolved, you need to decide how much configuration and development needs to be done to determine the agents. If you cannot automatically determine the agents, you can still use your workflow to help someone dynamically choose the correct agent for a subsequent step of your workflow (e.g., by using the Choose Agent wizard described in Appendix A, Tips and Tricks).

But before you can do any of that, you need to understand:

▶ How an agent receives, views, and completes work items

▶ The different ways in which workflow assigns agents to a work item

▶ How agents are identified in the system, via user IDs and organizational objects

▶ The different techniques that can be used to determine the correct agent for a work item, that is, the right person for the job

5.1 Understanding Agent Assignment

The main function of all agents is to complete the work items sent to their workflow inbox by the workflow as quickly and accurately as possible. Clearly, a lot of care must be given to ensure that the correct agents receive the work items. For each work item, the rival claims of several groups of agents may need to be considered by the Workflow Engine to select the correct agents. When you are designing, implementing, and maintaining your workflow and related data, you need to understand how the workflow views these different groups of agents if you are to ensure that the workflow comes to the correct decision.

The groups of agents include the following:

▶ **Possible agents**
Who is allowed to do the work?

▶ **Responsible agents**
Who should do the work in this case?

▶ **Excluded agents**
Who should *not* do the work in this case?

These three groups can overlap and intersect for each work item, as you can see in Figure 5.1. The recipients can only be determined correctly by evaluating all three (assuming all three are required).

Selected agents (also known as the *recipients*) are the agents who actually receive work items in their workflow inbox automatically; they are the initial recipients. You can see the selected agents in the workflow log by selecting the AGENTS icon ( ). If they are permitted to do so, recipients can opt to forward work to other possible agents. So the system needs to check both possible and excluded agents for a work item before it decides whether a particular agent is able to do the work. Finally, the person who has actually executed and completed the work is called the *actual agent*.

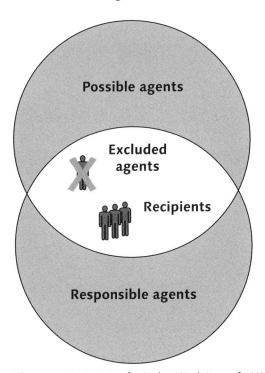

Figure 5.1 Recipients of a Dialog Work Item of a Workflow

Every agent must have a user ID, even when accessing the work item via an external workflow inbox, such as Microsoft Outlook or Lotus Notes. As well as identifying who is executing or has executed a work item, the user ID controls the access the agent has to the work item and, of course, to your system generally (via Security Authorizations).

5.1.1 Possible Agents

Possible agents are the people who are allowed to execute work items based on a particular underlying task. Possible agents are always assigned to a task on which many work items may be based, not to the work item itself. Another way of looking at this is to think of possible agent assignment as a way of securing runtime access to particular tasks. In fact, usually the best way of assigning possible agents is to tie tasks directly to *security roles*.

> **Tip**
>
> Making someone a possible agent of a task does not automatically give that agent access to any data or routine (e.g., transaction or report) called by the task. You still need to ensure the agent has sufficient authorization to complete the work. For example, you need to ensure that the users responsible for posting invoices have the security authorizations to run that transaction. That is why it makes so much sense to use security roles to keep the task access, data access, and routine access synchronized.

If you are not a possible agent of the work item, you cannot execute it. Likewise, if no possible agents have been assigned to a task, no one can execute any work items based on that task.

> **Tip**
>
> There is one exception to this, namely the *workflow administrator*, who is able to execute any work item in an emergency via the EXECUTE WITHOUT AGENT CHECK function (found in Transaction SWIA or menu path TOOLS • BUSINESS WORKFLOW • ADMINISTRATION • WORKFLOW RUNTIME • EXECUTE WORK ITEMS WITHOUT AGENT CHECK). This can be done to fix problems where possible agent assignment has been forgotten or neglected. Refer to Chapter 6, Workflow Administration, for more details.

You can also mark a task with the attribute GENERAL TASK instead of assigning specific possible agents.

> **Hint**
>
> Defining a task as a GENERAL TASK will be discussed in the next section, Assigning Possible Agents.

A general task effectively has *no* security over it; that is, anyone can execute the task. Be *very* careful when marking a task as a general task. People who are new (and sometimes not so new) to workflow sometimes set a task as a general task to simplify the agent determination. That is okay in a development environment, but if you do the same thing in a production environment, you can create performance problems as well as a serious security breach. Consider the following example:

1. An employee requests some items to be purchased, which starts a workflow.

2. The workflow sends a work item requesting approval of the purchase to the employee's manager.

3. The manager needs more details before a decision can be made, so he adds an attachment to the work item asking for more details and forwards the work item to the employee.

4. If the approval task has been marked as a general task, the employee is then able to approve his own purchase (assuming he has the security to approve purchases)!

If the task had been properly assigned to possible agents, the manager would have been warned on attempting to forward the work item that the employee is not allowed to execute it, and, depending on the task attributes, may also be prevented from forwarding it. You should make sure that you only mark tasks as general if you really want anybody to be able to execute work items based on that task. Good examples of general tasks include the following:

▶ **Edit rejected purchases**
You might want anyone to be able change and resubmit any purchases they requested that have been rejected.

▶ **Respond to proposal**
You might want anyone to be able to respond to a proposal that has been sent to him.

▶ **Tasks where you can only determine the possible agents by user ID**
The user who created the purchase order, for instance. However, this approach also has drawbacks; what actions will the workflow take if the holder of that user ID is no longer at your company?

Assigning Possible Agents

Possible agents can be assigned to a task in a number of places:

▶ **In the IMG (Implementation Guide)**
In the relevant workflow configuration section.

▶ **Via a menu option**
When displaying a task via the menu option ADDITIONAL DATA • AGENT ASSIGNMENT • MAINTAIN (Transaction PFTC_DIS), the attributes of the task, such as general task, can also be assigned.

▶ **From an organization plan**
From the TASK PROFILE section of an organizational plan.

▶ **From the Workflow Builder**
The step definition has an AGENT ASSIGNMENT TO TASK icon (📛) to assign possible agents (i.e., for dialog tasks), and basic data allows you to assign possible agents to the workflow itself to enable the agents to start the workflow manually.

> **Tip**
>
> No possible agents are assigned initially to tasks or workflows supplied by SAP. You must always do the possible agent assignment yourself, for example, using *task-specific customizing*.

For each task, the list of possible agents assigned can be quite long. You need to assign everyone who might need to execute work items based on that task. You use responsible agents and excluded agents to narrow down the list of all possible agents to those you want to receive a particular work item.

5.1.2 Responsible Agents

Responsible agents are the people you want to execute this particular work item; they are seen in the workflow log using the AGENTS icon (👥). The responsible agent is the person who is responsible for doing the work in this particular case. You can understand the difference between possible and responsible agents with a simple example:

▶ **Possible agents**
All managers approve requests from employees to attend training courses.

▶ **Responsible agents**
Your manager is responsible for approving requests to attend training courses that have been submitted by you.

Responsible agents are usually assigned at the workflow step level, but they can also be assigned at the task level via the default AGENT DETERMINATION RULE tab in the task definition.

> **Tip**
>
> The default rule is only used if no responsible agents have been entered at the workflow step level or if the step's agent determination rule fails. It is also used if a task is executed without a parent workflow, that is, as a standalone single step task.

It is possible to assign organizational objects (such as an organizational unit, job, or position) as responsible agents, but this option is rarely used in production systems. In most cases, an expression or rule is the best way to determine agents. You can also assign SAP Organizational Objects to identify possible agents in your organization. This allows you the flexibility to have a list of possible agents, where they may not hold the same position, job, or security rule. For more information, see Chapter 12, Agent Determination Rules.

With an *expression*, the agents (responsible, deadline, or notification depending on the context) are predetermined. For instance, if you want to send rejected requests back to the person who created the request, you save the person who created the request (the initiator) to a container element at the start of the workflow. Later you can use an expression to assign the value in the container element to the agent assignment of the workflow step for sending the rejected request. That way, the rejected request is returned to the same person who created it. (Don't forget to check that the creator is still valid in the SAP system.)

With a rule, the agents are calculated dynamically when the work item is created. You can bind data from the workflow to the rule, and the rule will then calculate the agents based on that data. For instance, you might have a rule to calculate the manager of an employee using the employee's user ID and the organizational hierarchy. By passing your user ID at runtime, the rule will find your manager. If you do not assign responsible agents explicitly, by default, all possible agents are assumed to also be the responsible agents, unless a default rule has been linked to the task itself.

Note that the responsible agents should also be possible agents. If you identify responsible agents who are not possible agents, the workflow will not send these work items to them. There's no point in doing so because they do not have proper access to do the work. If the organizational object, expression, or rule includes some agents who are possible agents and some who are not, only the responsible agents who are also possible agents will receive the work items. A thorough treatment of how to calculate responsible agents is given in Chapter 12, Agent Determination Rules.

5.1.3 Excluded Agents

Excluded agents are the people that you do *not* want to execute this particular work item, even though they are a possible or responsible agent. You can see the list of excluded agents in the workflow log. First you select the AGENT icon (![icon]), and then you select EXCLUDED AGENTS. For instance, all agents in a shared services center can approve requests for payment of employee expenses. Normally employees outside the shared services center enter the requests for payment. However, if one of the employees within the shared services center has requested payment of his own expenses, he should not be able to approve his own payment request. Otherwise, he could (deliberately or accidentally) defraud the company by receiving payments to which he is not entitled.

Excluded agents are also useful for segregating duties within business processes. Consider, for instance, a proposal that has to be reviewed by at least two agents within a proposal review team. You send the first "review proposal" work item to all agents in the review team. After the first work item is completed, you set the actual agent of the first work item as the excluded agent of the second work item. That is, the second "review proposal" work item is sent to all agents of the review team except the agent who has already reviewed the proposal. Because the first reviewer is an excluded agent of the second work item, he is not able to review the proposal twice.

Excluded agents are always assigned by an expression to the workflow step. That is, you put all agents to be excluded in a list (a multiline container element) and then use an expression to assign the list to the workflow step.

> **Tip**
>
> An excluded agent does not have to be a possible or responsible agent. This covers the situation where the person who needs to be excluded is acting as a substitute for another agent.

5.1.4 Recipients

Recipients are the people who automatically receive a work item in their inbox when the work item is created by the workflow. They are also known as *selected agents*. Recipients are:

- The possible agents of the task
- Restricted to the list of responsible agents for the work item
- Not members of the list of excluded agents

You should, however, note the following:

▶ If there are no possible agents, no one receives the work item!

▶ If no responsible agents are defined for a step, the system checks for a default agent-determination rule in the task definition. If there is none, all of the possible agents, barring excluded agents, are recipients of the work item.

Hint

If there are no responsible agents, and the task routes to all possible agents, and if you made the task a general task, then *everyone* will receive the task. For example, the task to process inbound error IDocs (Intermediate Documents) is a general task. If the default agent resolution at the task does not exist, the task routes to all possible agents, which is everyone. If you received a few thousand IDocs, then all your users will have thousands of items in their inbox. This is not an uncommon event with new workflow projects, so don't let it happen to you!

Recipients can forward work items to other agents if allowed. However, only possible (but not excluded) agents can execute a forwarded work item. The agent who is forwarding the work item is warned if the new agent is not a possible agent.

Whether a work item can be forwarded is determined by the attributes of the underlying task, which can be defined or viewed from ADDITIONAL DATA • AGENT ASSIGNMENT • MAINTAIN (Transaction PFTC_DIS). Relevant options are:

▶ **General task**
Work items can be forwarded to any user (and executed by any user).

▶ **General forwarding**
Work items can be forwarded to any user.

▶ **No general forwarding**
Work items can only be forwarded to possible users.

▶ **No forwarding**
No forwarding allowed.

5.1.5 Actual Agents

While the work item is still being processed, the actual agent is the user currently processing the work item. After the work item has been completed, the actual agent is the user who last processed the work item.

Knowing who was the actual agent of a completed work item is often helpful. Not only can you tell who made a particular decision in a subsequent step of your workflow, but you can also evaluate who is actually making the decisions in your company.

5.1.6 Assigning Multiple Agents per Work Item

Many agents can be assigned to a single work item. If you send an email to more than one person, every person receives a copy of the email; they can view and delete their own copy of the email whenever they like. That is fine for emails because they simply bring information to the recipients. However, when you send a *work item* to many agents, you are sending work along with the information. Usually the work only needs to be done once. As soon as one of the assigned agents executes and completes the piece of work (or simply reserves it), the work item is no longer needed, and the Workflow Engine removes it from all agents' inboxes.

Another way of understanding how work items appear to several assigned agents is to think of all of the work to be done being collected in a huge pile, each piece of work being represented by a work item. Agent determination is simply a way of sharing out the pile of work to be done.

Sometimes there is only one suitable person to do a piece of work, and therefore only one agent for the work item. In this case, the work will not be completed until the single assigned agent has done it. If that person is sick or attending a training course, the work waits until the agent returns. In other cases, there are several people who can do the same work. They might even work together, such as at a helpdesk or shared services center. The work items that can be done by these people are given to all of the agents. Each agent selects a piece of work and does it. Because the work to be done is shared out, it is completed much more quickly than it could be by a single person. If one agent is sick or attending a training course, the rest of the agents will still be getting the work done in that agent's absence. No single process will be held up until the agent returns.

Sometimes you really *do* want more than one person to act on the same piece of work. For instance, you might want several people involved in deciding whether an expensive piece of equipment can be purchased. To do this, you simply create one work item per agent. There are many ways you can create multiple work items without complicating your workflow. For instance, you can use a list (a multiline container element) assigned to a step in your workflow to create multiple work items, one for each item in the list. This approach is called dynamic parallel processing. In Chapter 9, Advanced Workflow Design Techniques, you will find more information on dynamic parallel processing.

If you want to make sure all agents are doing their fair share, you can track how many work items each agent processes and how much time is spent on the items. You could use this to inspire and reward agents to be even more productive, depending on your company's culture and customizing settings. For suggestions on how to measure and report on work items, turn to Chapter 6, Workflow Administration, and Chapter 14, Custom Programs.

5.1.7 Deadline and Notification Agents

In most workflows, agents are the people assigned to actually perform tasks via work items. However, as a workflow developer, you may also want to assign the following:

► **Deadline agents**
People who receive escalation work items when a deadline has been exceeded. Deadline agents are usually entered on the relevant deadline tab (LATEST START, REQUESTED END, or LATEST END) of the workflow step.

► **Notification agents**
People who are notified via an email when a work item has been completed. Notification agents are usually entered on the NOTIFICATION tab of the workflow step.

Deadline agents may receive deadline work items, which consist of a reminder to escalate a task and a DONE IT button. If they fail to act, the workflow can still continue. Often you do not even need to send them a work item; a simple email may be enough.

Note that deadline agents are recipients of work items just like the agents who actually perform the task, but it can be helpful to think of them separately. Of course, you are not limited to simply notifying agents. As you will see in Chapter 8, Creating a Workflow, you can introduce deadline and escalation procedures into your workflow that are far more sophisticated than simple notifications.

5.2   Agent Assignment Using the Organizational Structure

Every workflow agent must have a user ID. So when you are assigning agents to a work item, whether via possible agents, responsible agents, or excluded agents, you are essentially assigning user IDs.

Unfortunately, assigning user IDs directly is very maintenance intensive. People join, change positions and roles, transfer between departments, and leave your organization continuously. Keeping up with the current agent assignment is hard enough. As you add more workflows, the task becomes nearly impossible. There is a better way of identifying agents, which is called the *organizational plan*.

> **Tip**
>
> The organizational plan is sometimes used for possible agent assignment but can also be used for assigning responsible agents either directly or in conjunction with agent-determination rules.

People often make the mistake of thinking that the organizational plan is only part of SAP ERP HCM (Human Capital Management) and is therefore only available if you are implementing HCM applications. Actually, every SAP NetWeaver Application Server also includes a basic organizational plan that has everything you need for workflow. If you do have SAP ERP HCM, you have access not just to the basic plan, but also to the extended plan. The *extended organizational plan* still has everything needed for workflow, but it includes many more features. Some of the extended features can also be used in your workflows, for example, assigning agents to perform a task based on their formal qualifications to do the job.

5.2.1   The Basic Organizational Plan

The basic organizational plan consists of relationships, represented as a hierarchical organizational structure, between different organizational objects such as:

▶ **Organizational units (▢)**
Each unit represents a group of people, such as a team, section, department, work area, laboratory, helpdesk, or shared services center.

▶ **Jobs (▦)**
Each job describes a functional role within the organization. They equate to a job description. They may represent a full-time or part-time role in your organization.

▶ **Positions (🔒)**
Each position represents a headcount placement, for example, a physical desk or vacancy.

▶ **Users (🗂)**
Each user is the actual user ID of a person in your organization.

> **Tip**
>
> You can build an organizational hierarchy without using jobs, which makes it easier to deploy in SAP ERP HCM where jobs are used for more specific purposes (e.g., where jobs are directly associated with a salaries scale).

Most organizational objects and relationships have validity periods. By default, the validity period is usually set to start on the date on which the organizational object or relationship is created and finish on December 31, 9999; however, the validity period can be changed. Restricting the validity period is useful to indicate temporary relationships, for example, when a user holds a position on a temporary basis such as "acting supervisor," or to show that a person no longer holds that position.

Organizational objects and relationships are maintained via Organizational Management transactions such as PPOM (Organization and Staffing), PPOMW (Organization and Staffing — Workflow View), or in an SAP SRM/CRM system PPOMA_CRM or PPOMA_BBP (Organization, Staffing, and Attributes). Use of these transactions is described in detail in the SAP Help Portal (*http://help.sap.com*).

Within these transactions, you can find organizational objects by ID, description, hierarchical structure, or relationship to other organizational objects. For instance, by finding a position, you can view all users assigned to that position. Several views of the organizational plan can be displayed. For example, you can display both top-down hierarchies (organizational unit to positions to users) and bottom-up hierarchies (users to positions to organizational units), depending on your starting point. You can also create new objects and relationships (also known as *assignments*), edit, copy, move, reposition, delimit, and delete them.

You can display and maintain details of objects (e.g., organizational units have addresses) as shown in Figure 5.2. You can start the display and maintenance of organizational objects at any part of the organizational plan.

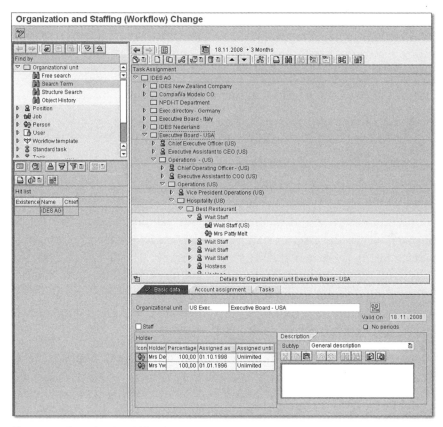

Figure 5.2 Organizational Plan Maintenance

Common relationships between the different parts of the organizational plan include the following (note the icons from Figure 5.2):

▶ *Organizational units* (☐) can be hierarchically linked to other *organizational units* (☐), giving you an organizational hierarchy, for example, teams within sections within departments.

▶ An *organizational unit* (☐) may be linked to several *positions* (🔒), where the positions represent employees belonging to the team, section, department, and so on. Note that these relationships are inherited by hierarchically higher organizational units. For instance, the positions within a department include all positions assigned directly to the department's organizational unit, plus all positions assigned to the organizational units of sections and teams hierarchically below the department.

- A *position* (🧑) may be linked to *jobs* (🏭), where the job describes what the person in the position does. One job may be linked to several positions, for example, when several people perform similar activities.

- A *user* (🧑) may be linked to a *position* (🧑), where the user ID is that of the person currently holding the position. One user may hold several positions (hopefully, each on a part-time basis).

- Workflow tasks may be linked to one or more *organizational units* (▢), *positions* (🧑), *jobs* (🏭), or *users* (🧑).

- This is the standard SAP approach to HR organizations. Your implementation may be different. For example, you may have a *position* (🧑) linked to a *job* (🏭), where the job describes what the positions do. One position may be linked to a single person.

> **Tip**
>
> You need to work closely and collaboratively with the designers of the HR organization structure and its components.

By assigning a workflow task to a job, you are specifying all of the users who are linked to all of the positions linked to that job as agents for that task. For example, if "manager" is a job, and "approve leave request" is a task, then assigning the task "approve leave request" to the job "manager" means all managers are able to approve leave requests. You can change the users and positions linked to that job and know that all users/positions currently linked to the job will be able to execute the tasks assigned. By assigning a task to a position, you are making the user or user(s) who are linked to that position the agents of the task. For example, if "Financial Business Process Owner" is a position, and "approve changes to financial processes" is a task, then the user or users holding that position are able to approve changes to financial processes. You can change the users linked to the position and know that all users currently linked to it could perform the tasks assigned.

If in doubt, assign a task to a job or to a task group, which is in turn assigned to a job or organizational unit as shown in Figure 5.3. This is a logical extension to the organizational management model. Looking at it the other way round, the job is a collection of tasks. As a bonus, using this strategy, you can see online which tasks are assigned to a job, which makes the job description transparent in the system and hence easier to maintain.

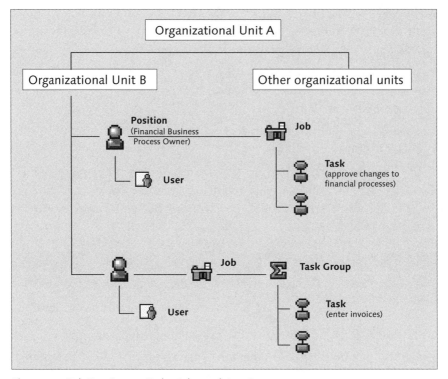

Figure 5.3 Relation Among Tasks, Jobs, and Agents

You can create several organizational plans in different plan versions. This lets you depict different views of your organization in different plan versions. In one plan version, you depict your currently valid organizational plan, that is, the one you use for your current business processes (evaluations, workflow, personnel planning, for example). In additional plan versions, you can depict organizational plans as planning scenarios (for reorganizations, for example).

> **Note**
>
> Workflow *always* uses the current plan version.

5.2.2 The Extended Organizational Plan

If your system includes SAP ERP HCM, then you can use the extended organizational plan. In this case, you have access to additional features above and beyond the basic organizational plan. The most obvious difference between the basic and extended organizational plans is that the extended organizational plan includes *personnel numbers*:

▶ A *person* (👥) represents the personnel number assigned to an employee.

▶ A *person* (👥) may be assigned to one or more positions.

▶ A *user* (🗄) is assigned to a *person* (👥) by setting up a "communication" relationship (otherwise known as infotype 105).

Whenever you assign a *user* (🗄) to a position, job, task, or organizational unit in a system with an extended organizational plan, by default the system will replace the object to *user* (🗄) relationship with an object to *person* (👥) to *user* (🗄) relationship. So if your company is using personnel numbers, and you assign a user ID in the organizational plan, the system automatically maps the user ID to the personnel number. For example, the system knows that user ID PPARKER is mapped to personnel number I007112.

From a workflow perspective, apart from the additional *person* organizational object, using SAP ERP HCM provides the following benefits:

▶ Much more data is held describing organizational objects and relationships that can be used in workflows. For example, if the qualifications (infotype 0024) held by employees are stored, a rule can be built to identify the responsible agents of a work item as those agents with current qualifications to perform the work.

▶ Evaluation paths can be custom built and used as rules for determining responsible agents. Evaluation paths describe a way of moving across the organizational plan to find organizational objects. For instance, the evaluation path SAP_TAGT describes how to find workflow agents belonging to any organizational object, that is, how to find users from an organizational unit, job, position, or person. (Note that some evaluation paths, such as SAP_TAGT exist even in systems without SAP ERP HCM, but there is usually no reason for building custom evaluation paths unless you use SAP ERP HCM.)

▶ Additional security can be provided over tasks using structural authorizations.

> **Tip**
>
> If your system includes SAP ERP HCM, be careful that your use of the organizational plan in your workflow fits with your overall Organizational Management strategy driven by the HR department.

5.2.3 Doing Without an Organizational Plan

Maintaining an organizational plan can be a burden, particularly if there is no specific section or department dedicated to its maintenance. So, do you need to use an organizational plan for workflow?

In fact, you do not. There are alternatives as long as you keep your agent assignments simple using responsibilities built into the SAP component, office distribution lists, or your own custom tables and function modules as described in Chapter 12, Agent Determination Rules. However if you want to build sophisticated relationships between tasks and agents, particularly for possible agent assignments, then an organizational plan will give you significantly greater flexibility and choice.

The alternatives to using an organizational plan for possible agent assignment include the following:

▶ **Setting tasks as general tasks in the task attributes**
This allows all users to execute work items based on the task. Remember, however, that this effectively means you have *no* security on your tasks.

▶ **Assigning security roles as possible agents of tasks**
This allows all users with the security role to execute work items based on that task. Task to security role assignment can be made either via the usual task agent assignment, for example, via ADDITIONAL DATA • AGENT ASSIGNMENT • MAINTAIN (Transaction PFTC_DIS) or via the profile generator (Transaction PFCG).

Any of the responsible agent determination options such as responsibility rules or evaluation paths can also be linked directly to user IDs rather than to organizational objects if you wish.

5.3 Agent Assignment Using Task Groups

Task groups are literally that — a way of grouping workflow tasks together. They are found in the workflow view of the organizational chart and in the Workflow Builder by the TASK GROUP icon (Σ). You can choose how you group tasks into task groups. One task can be assigned to many task groups. You can create a task group using Transaction PFTC, just like any other task. You enter a description for the task group, and list the tasks assigned to the task group:

▶ One option is to use task groups to group together tasks based on similar content, for example, all tasks based on the same business objects, so that you can quickly find all tasks concerned with the same business object. You can use task groups to delimit the search range when calling the Workflow Explorer or within the My workflows and tasks area of the Workflow Builder. You can also use the Where-used list option in the Business Object Repository (Transaction SWO1) to do this.

▶ Another option is to collect all tasks involved in the same or similar business processes into the one task group, again to simplify searching for related tasks. Of course, you can also use the Diagnosis Utility (Transaction SWUD) to get a quick overview of all tasks in a workflow.

▶ However, you can also assign task groups to organizational objects such as organizational units, jobs, or positions, using the usual agent assignment options. This means you can also collect tasks into task groups for the purpose of agent assignment. For instance, you could create a task group called "common management tasks," assign all tasks that all managers need to perform to it, and then assign the task group to the manager job or security role. Then, any time a new task for managers is created, you can add it to the task group, thus assigning all managers as possible agents of the new task (from Transaction PFTC, go to Extras • Agent Assignment • Maintain).

▶ You can also collect task groups into other task groups. So you could create task groups for different job functions and add them together to create a task group for a specific job. For example, you might combine the "common management tasks" task group with a "senior management tasks" task group for a senior manager.

5.4   Implementing and Maintaining the Structure in Practice

This section discusses a few strategies and tips when creating and maintaining your organizational plan.

5.4.1   Strategies for Organization Plan Maintenance

Often the most contentious issue for organizational plan maintenance is deciding who will be responsible for updating the organizational plan. The basic rules for this determination follow:

- If you have an HR section responsible for updating the organizational plan for other reasons, they should also update the organizational plan for workflow requirements.

- If the organizational plan is only used for workflow, persons in the workflow team, for example, business process owners, should be responsible for updating the organizational plan.

Of course, if you start by using the organizational plan only for workflow and then decide to use it for other purposes, you can reassign who is responsible for keeping the organizational plan current. Another option is to have the HR section maintain the organizational plan, but have workflow personnel update rules, such as responsibility rules. However, this requires good communication between the HR section and the workflow personnel to ensure that changes to the organizational plan and the rule data are adequately synchronized.

Regardless of who actually maintains the organizational plan, it is important that the people doing the maintenance are aware of the following:

- Understand the potential impact of their changes and any delay in making those changes on your workflows.

- Communicate with the relevant workflow people, especially the workflow administrator.

- Allow relevant workflow people, especially the workflow administrator and business process owners, the ability to check and review *at any time* what has been done, in case of problems. The ability to check at any time is essential because problems often do not appear immediately.

> **Tip**
>
> If a user is to be removed from the system, to ensure that work items being generated do not end up orphaned (e.g., with no valid agent), it is usually best to assign the new user to the workflow, and then delimit the old user assignment so that it is no longer valid from this date. It is also good practice to check the user to be delimited to ensure that he does not have any workflow tasks in process, which could result in workflows remaining "in process" until it becomes a high priority (and very visible) issue.

> **Caution**
>
> Do not delete the old user because you will lose valuable auditing and reporting information. And remember, if your process requires that a user ID be "valid" (i.e., the creation date of the work item falls within the begin and end dates of your user ID), then you must develop a plan to ensure this happens. SAP does not prohibit the delivery of work items to delimited user IDs.

5.4.2 Transporting Organization Plans

It is possible but potentially problematic to transport organizational plans. You need to be clear about exactly what part(s) of the organizational plan you will transport and what part(s) will be maintained directly in the production environment. Keeping an organizational plan clean, that is, well structured, in a development environment is difficult because configurers and developers often need to change the organizational plan to test their settings and programs. Because of this, the organizational plan may not be ready to transport to a production environment. One way of keeping the organizational plan clean is to create it in a separate client set aside for this purpose, for example, a configuration master client. Even if the organizational units, jobs, or positions are transportable, often the relationship between position and user can only be created in the production environment because most users will not exist in a development environment.

Similar complications ensue when transporting organizational plans across different SAP components, for example, an SAP ERP system and an SAP SRM system. A user may not exist in the SAP ERP system but does exist in the SAP SRM system or vice versa.

Usually, only the organizational plan is transported (or the units within the organizational plan), and not the assignments to actual user IDs. However, if you do want to transport user IDs also, then the Central User Administration (CUA) is one option for keeping the user IDs synchronized across multiple systems. Some systems, such as SAP SRM, also provide mass user creation programs to help assign user IDs to the transported organizational plan.

> **Hint**
>
> CUA is a capability provided with SAP security to centrally manage users in multiple SAP systems. You must work with your security administrator on all transport issues related to user IDs.

Your security person will be aware of the options for transporting the organizational plan. A few of them are listed here, but to learn the details, you need to get with your security administrator.

There are a number of options for transporting the organizational plan. However, they must be discussed with your security and system administrator:

▶ Automatic transport of all organizational plan changes. Table T77S0, entry TRSP.CORR is set to SPACE.

▶ Manual transport of organizational plan changes, by manually selecting what part of the organizational plan is to be transported. Table T77S0, entry TRSP.CORR is set to X. Program RHMOVE30 performs the transport.

▶ Transport via an object lock by using a change request. Table T77S0, entry TRSP.CORR is set to T. Program RHMOVE50 performs the transport.

Regardless of the method chosen to transport the organizational chart, all options require an ALE (Application Link Enabling) distribution model to be created for the HR master data. The model allows IDocs of type HRMD_A to be transported from one system to another. Within the model, you then specify filters determining which infotypes will be transported. Within the organizational plan transactions, change pointers are used to detect what objects have changed in the source system and, therefore, what objects are suitable for transport. Entries in Table T77TR (Transport Lock for Infotype and Subtypes per Object) in the target system can be used to block objects from being transported into the target system. This prevents locally maintained objects and relationships from being overwritten by incoming transports. Customer exits for IDoc HRMD_A allow outgoing and incoming data to be adjusted if necessary. Further documentation on this topic can be found in the SAP Help Portal (*http://help.sap.com*).

5.4.3 Reassigning Work Items from One User to Another

If a user changes jobs or positions, there may be existing work items assigned to that user that need to be reassigned to the person taking over the user's old job or position. This is particularly necessary where changes in the job or position include changes in a user's security, so that they are no longer able to execute the work items assigned to them. Reassigning work items is usually only necessary where work items have been reserved by the user — in other words selected but not completed — or where the user is the only recipient. If other recipients exist, and a work item is still in READY status, there is no need to reassign it.

Users should be encouraged as much as possible to replace "reserved work items," which returns the work item to READY status prior to the move:

► You can find outstanding work items for a user by using the Workload Analysis (Transaction SWI5) report with the TO BE PROCESSED BY option. This report should be run *before* moving the user.

► To find orphaned work items after the move, report Work Items Without Agents (Transaction SWI2_ADM1) is helpful.

Substitution can be used to reassign the work items to a new user either when an agent moves to a new position and has new responsibilities, or when the person has left the company and his user ID is no longer valid (i.e., locked and delimited). You can also, as workflow administrator, forward the work item to an appropriate agent. Generally speaking, having the workflow administrator forward work items should be limited to emergencies; most companies would prefer an audit trail that does not require answering the question "Why was this approval task forwarded to so-and-so?"

5.4.4   Substituting Users

If you want to substitute agents on a temporary basis, for example, while the original agent is ill or attending a course, there are two options:

► **The HR Substitution Relationship A210**
  Substitutes are maintained in the organization chart by creating a relationship between the employee and the substitute. You can create a substitute for a position by creating an A210 relationship between the position and the substitute, for example, another position, person, or user ID. All work items assigned to the original agent *based on that position* are then made available to the substitute. You can further refine which work items are assigned to particular substitutes by specifying a task classification.

  By default, the classifications DISCIPLINARY, PROFESSIONAL, and PERSONAL exist. If you do use classifications, they need to be defined both against the task underlying the work items to be assigned and against the A210 relationship.

This approach can be used if you are deriving the possible agents based on HR positions. It will not work if you are using other methods of agent determination (as described next).

▶ **User substitutions — Table HRUS_D2**
When a substitute is created in the inbox, an entry is made in Table HRUS_D2. Usually the HRUS_D2 entry is created by the original agents via their inbox, such as from the Business Workplace (Transaction SBWP) or from the Universal Worklist (UWL). However, if you want to maintain this table centrally, this is one of the few cases where the table is sufficiently straightforward and independent of other tables that creating your own maintenance view of the table is a reasonably safe option. You can create a substitute for a user by creating an entry in Table HRUS_D2 that identifies another user to act as the substitute. All work items assigned to that user ID are then made available to the substitute. Be aware though, that work items created prior to the begin date of the substitution assignment will *not* be available to the substitute. For this reason, you may need to pre-date the assignment of substitutes.

Maintaining substitutes in this manner also allows the users to be proactive about ensuring their work gets done if they will be out of the office, and reduces the central maintenance burden.

Make sure when creating substitutes that you create a *workflow* substitute, not an inbox substitute because an inbox substitute simply receives the original agent's emails, not their work items. Substitutions can be *active* or *passive*:

▶ **Active substitutions**
Active substitutions are similar to auto-forwarding — all work items sent to the original agent *automatically* appear in the substitute agent's inbox. Active substitution is more suitable when someone is absent.

▶ **Passive substitutions**
Passive substitutions (requiring that the substitute executes SETTINGS • WORK-FLOW SETTINGS • ADOPT SUBSTITUTIONS from their Business Workplace) require the substitute to explicitly choose to see the original agent's work items via the appropriate inbox option. Passive substitutions can be useful when someone is a regular backup for the original agent. The substitution can then exist for a long time but is only used when the substitute is acting as a backup.

Workflow substitution gives the substitute the permissions to view and execute the work item, but it does not give the substitute permission to access underlying transactions and routines used by the work item. So it is usually best to encourage substitution at the same level of the organization, for example, substitute from one manager to another, rather than from a manager to subordinates.

There are a number of APIs (application programming interfaces) available to help manage substitutions according to your business rules. They can be found using Transaction SE37, and entering "SAP_WAPI_SUBSTITUT*".

Users can also do work for agents who are out of the office by using Workflow Views. From the inbox, the menu path for this functionality is SETTINGS • WORK-FLOW SETTINGS • ADOPT VIEW. From here, a user can choose an appropriate evaluation path, and, if they have the authorizations to do so, they can see what is in a colleague's workflow inbox.

In either case, whether using substitutions or adopting views, users need to be reminded to make sure they exit the substitution or the view. Otherwise, they may be concerned that they seem to be getting someone else's work. It's also a good practice for your users to use the REFRESH icon from the inbox, immediately after adopting, or exiting, a substitution or view.

5.4.5 When Do You Choose to Refresh the Organizational Environment

A continual issue with maintaining an organizational plan is buffering. Buffering means that the system holds temporary views of the organizational plan for use at runtime. Even if you change the organizational plan, it will not be used at runtime until the relevant buffer is updated.

The main benefit of buffering is improved performance. However the delay between the time when an update to the organizational plan is made and the time when the changes take effect can be very confusing and cause unusual problems, especially when some buffers may be updated before others. This is particularly relevant in development systems, where frequent changes are made for testing purposes.

Under normal operation, all of the buffers relevant to the organizational plan are updated at midnight system time. So, one strategy for avoiding buffering problems is simply to update the organizational plan the day before the changes will be used. Bear in mind that workflow objects are also refreshed when you run this transaction. As noted in Chapter 6, Workflow Administration, this is commonly referred to as the Cinderella effect.

Another way to prevent buffering problems is to manually trigger the refreshing of buffers. Transaction SWU_OBUF is provided specifically for this purpose. It provides a REFRESH option that resets the timestamp on the HR buffers, thereby invalidating existing buffers, so that all organizational plan data is read from the database and the buffers refilled with this fresh data. You can refresh as often as you wish, remembering that the system will perform a little slower when buffers are being refilled.

If you want to create your own program to refresh the buffers, for example, so that only those objects changed are refreshed, then the following function modules are worth knowing:

▶ RH_WF_OM_INDICES_TIMESTAMP_RFS
Resets the timestamp on all HR buffers.

▶ RH_TASK_INBOX_VIEW_REFRESH
Refreshes the buffer for the current user only.

▶ RH_TASK_AGENTS_INDEX_REFRESH
Refreshes the buffer for a particular task ID only.

Note that it is not a good idea to refresh the buffers if no changes have been made because this degrades system performance for no benefit. For example, creating a background job to reset the buffer timestamp every hour is counter-productive because the benefits of buffering are lost.

5.4.6 Training and Encouraging Agents

Agents are generally very sympathetic toward workflow if it is presented to them properly. They see it as a helping hand, making sure that they know what to do and are presented with their tasks rather than having to fetch the tasks themselves. Usually you will not have a chance to train all of the agents, so make sure that you have power users or change advocates to support the rest of the agents, and make sure you have a good roll-out (e.g., by having power users train each other in a snowball effect) so that everyone feels comfortable. Emphasize the benefits the individual agents will see rather than stressing the advantages to the corporation, and allow the agents to monitor their own performance so that they can see how they improve (e.g., via the outbox). Make it clear that these statistics will not be used to compare individual users with each other.

One of the often-overlooked parts of empowering users is to ensure they have adequate training on the functionality in the SAP Business Workplace. There are many powerful tools that will enable your users to take full advantage of workflow and its capabilities. For example, as mentioned previously in Chapter 4, Work Item Delivery, users can check the status of workflows that they have initiated or participated in via the outbox. They can often find out key information about the object that they are working on by checking the lower-right pane of the workplace for OBJECTS AND ATTACHMENTS, as well as reading any documentation that has been sent along with the workflow.

Try to anticipate the problems that the agents will have (e.g., the workflow appears to have disappeared), and provide solutions. Often these problems will become apparent during train-the-trainers sessions, so be especially careful to take notes when an exception occurs. You may find that you can significantly improve the users' experiences with workflow by adding or reformatting what is contained within the work item description — the one line text that is shown in their workflow inbox.

Make sure all agents understand the difference between an email (copy delivered to every recipient) and a work item (shared by the recipients), and make sure that they do not see the Workflow Engine as an infinitely powerful mechanism that can do everything on its own. The fact that the workflow can have limited embedded intelligence and can perform some actions in background steps does not mean that it can compensate for users' mistakes. It helps if the agents have a rough idea of the complete process in which they are involved. Not only does this heighten their awareness of what is going on in the company they work for, but it also helps them understand why the quality of their work is as important as the speed with which they complete it. Many a user has been surprised when shown the scope of the process and the number of people involved even after they have finished doing their bit.

The administrator plays a key role in the success of the workflow and on publishing this success to the stakeholders. Although very little time needs to be spent on these duties, awareness of these duties is important, and they must be taken seriously. If a problem does arise, the administrator needs to resolve it quickly and confidently. This chapter shows the major reports and tools you can use to administer and maintain your workflows.

6   Workflow Administration

The role of the workflow administrator is to ensure workflows are executing, transported workflows are enabled, and the Workflow Engine is monitored. There is no getting round this simple rule of thumb: If you use a system, you need a system administrator. If you use a workflow, you need a workflow administrator.

After a workflow is activated, experience has shown that any problems with any part of the business process are likely to be blamed on the workflow, whether or not this is justified. This is a very natural reaction on the part of people involved with the business process because the workflow:

▶ Controls their view of the business process

▶ Controls their access to the business process

▶ Controls the flow of the business process between them and other users

▶ Automatically performs parts of the business process that they are not able or not expecting to have to perform manually

Great benefits can be achieved when a process that is critical, essential, or high volume is automated. As a workflow administrator, one of your tasks may be to develop and execute reports to:

▶ Prove that benefits have been achieved

▶ Justify workflow implementation and support costs

▶ Prove the business case for changing the business process or the workflow design

▶ Prove that changes in the workflow have had the desired effect

▶ Prove that users are performing tasks efficiently and promptly

6.1 Reporting on Workflows

Many reports are provided standard with SAP Business Workflow, and many more can be created with tools such as SAP NetWeaver Business Warehouse (SAP NetWeaver BW). Workflow reporting with SAP NetWeaver BW is discussed in Chapter 7, Using SAP NetWeaver Business Warehouse for SAP Business Workflow Reporting. If there is no standard report available in the system, you can, of course, create your own. Refer to Chapter 14, Custom Programs, for more details on custom reporting. You should find the reports listed here a useful starting point, but look around for other reports. Often where standard workflow templates have been built around particular transactions or data, special workflow reports exist for them.

All standard reports lead to the workflow log. You can access the workflow log anywhere you see the WORKFLOW LOG icon (). The reports provide common reporting functions such as sorting, filtering, layout changes, and so on. When selecting a workflow instance, most reports show the major steps executed so far and their agents, and the major object instances used so far. Most standard reports include selection criteria to restrict the list to a particular task, task group, component, and selection period (today, last week, last month, last year, all), as well as by active or completed instances.

Caution
There is the capability to "hide" tasks from representation in the non-technical workflow logs, so the workflow administrator must be aware of which steps the workflow developer has chosen to "hide." Steps may be hidden because they cause visual congestion to the workflow logs.

When you are assessing workflows, it is useful to know what the different workflow and work item statuses mean. A complete list is shown in Chapter 14, Custom Programs, but Table 6.1 lists the statuses that you are most likely to see.

Technical Status	Meaning
READY	This status usually applies to work items. The work item has been created and is activated but has not been executed yet. For example, it is sitting in a user's inbox, but the user has not opened it yet.
SELECTED	This status appears in the work item display as IN PROCESS and usually applies to work items. The work item has been opened or reserved by a user but has not yet been executed.
COMMITTED	This status appears in the work item display as EXECUTED and usually applies to work items. The work item has been executed but is waiting for the user to manually confirm the end of processing, for example, via a SET TO DONE option.
COMPLETED	This status shows that the workflow or work item is completed. No further changes can be made once completed.

Table 6.1 The Most Significant Work Item Statuses

6.1.1 Reporting on Workflow Progress

Usually the most interesting question for anyone involved in a business process is "Who's got the workflow?" Useful reports answering this question include the following:

▶ **Workflows for Object**
Choose RUNTIME TOOLS • WORKFLOWS FOR OBJECT (Transaction SWI6). This report shows all workflow instances linked to a particular object instance, such as a particular purchase order.

Tip
This is one of the most useful reports for general tracking, not just by the administrator but also by all other users of the workflow. However, in newer SAP components, such as SAP SRM, the object keys will be in GUID format (i.e., a 32-character internal identifier). You may find that it is easier to report on all Workflows for Object Type (see next bullet point) and select the specific instance as opposed to entering a 32-character GUID.

▶ **Workflows for Object Type**
Choose RUNTIME TOOLS • WORKFLOWS FOR OBJECT TYPE (Transaction SWI14). This report shows all work items and workflow instances for all object

instances of a business object type, for example, workflows related to all purchase orders.

▶ **Diagnosis of Workflows with Errors**
Choose ADMINISTRATION • WORKFLOW RUNTIME • DIAGNOSIS OF WORKFLOWS WITH ERRORS (Transaction SWI2_DIAG). This report shows all workflows initiated during a specified timeframe that have been set to an error status. You can also narrow the selection to a specific workflow, task, or background task. This transaction also allows the administrator to restart the workflow by clicking the RESTART WORKFLOW button.

6.1.2 Reporting on Workflow Performance

When you are reporting on workflow performance, you need to look at both the frequency of work items/workflow instances as well as the time taken to realistically assess the behavior of the workflow over time. Every workflow instance and work item records the creation time, start time (when the work item was first opened), and end time (when the work item was completed). If deadline monitoring is used, the relevant deadline times for the work item are also recorded.

When evaluating performance time, it is important to consider not just total elapsed time but also the wait and process times. For instance, the workflow may have taken five days from start to finish, but four days may have been spent just waiting for the first agent to act. If you need to speed the process further, you need to know whether you should focus your efforts on improving the workflow design or improving user behavior.

Wait times can result from a number of factors such as:

▶ The agent was sick, taking a course, in a meeting, or on vacation, and there was no substitute.

▶ The agent was not aware of the work item (perhaps the user checks his inbox infrequently).

▶ The agent wasn't sure how to execute the work item.

▶ The agent needed to consult with others before completing the work item.

You should never assume that a long wait time means that the user is acting inappropriately but always investigate the cause of the delay.

However, if the duration report indicates that your background tasks are taking a long time to complete, then you will need to do some serious analysis. Chapter 16, Advanced Diagnostics, provides more detail, but several common causes for delays in background tasks are:

▶ The Transaction RFC queue (tRFC) may have a broken connection to an SAP partner system (i.e., from SAP ERP to SAP SRM or vice-versa). This will cause any transactions or functions that reach across SAP systems to "hang." You can view the tRFC queue by using Transaction SM58.

▶ The business object method being processed by the background task encountered some sort of error that was not coded for appropriately. Perhaps the method relies on the contents of a business object attribute for processing, yet at runtime, the actual attribute is not filled. For this type of issue, it helps to re-create the actual data being used and debug through the method.

▶ The password for user WF-BATCH has inadvertently been changed. Check with your Basis team to ensure that this password is synchronized with the RFC user WF-BATCH.

▶ The background job for deadline monitoring may not be running as it should. This job, SWWDHEX, should have been set up as part of the normal workflow customizing; it resubmits itself for execution after a predefined time period. If you have deadlines on your work items, more detailed analyses can be made, for instance, by using the standard report Work Items with Monitored Deadlines (Transaction SWI2_DEAD).

▶ If you want to know the number of work items processed per period, use report Work Items by Task (Transaction SWI2_FREQ).

6.1.3　Work Items by Processing Duration

When you choose REPORTING • WORK ITEM ANALYSIS • WORK ITEMS BY PROCESSING DURATION (Transaction SWI2_DURA), the report started gives information on the processing duration of work items of the specified type or for the specified tasks that ended in the period, sorted by task. Provided there are appropriate work items, the current period is compared with a prior period of the same length to show the variances and differences.

The process duration of all work items for one task is displayed as standard with threshold values (10 % threshold, 50 % threshold, 90 % threshold). The threshold values should be interpreted as follows: The process duration for the x% threshold means that x% of all work items for this task were processed within this period or a shorter period. You can switch the mode to show the WAIT TIME (i.e., wasted time), PROCESSING TIME, or TOTAL TIME, which is often more useful than the threshold times. You can also look at times for particular work items. For example, if most work items were completed in seconds, but a few work items took several days, you might want to look at the work item, find out who the agent was, and discuss with the agent why the task took so long.

6.1.4 Work Items with Monitored Deadlines

When choosing REPORTING • WORK ITEM ANALYSIS • WORK ITEMS WITH MONITORED DEADLINES (Transaction SWI2_DEAD), the report started shows work items that are subject to deadline monitoring. This report is especially useful for seeing whether deadlines are being met or exceeded because all missed deadlines are shown, whether or not the work item has now been completed. For each missed deadline, the current status of the work item is also shown.

Because the missed deadlines are shown grouped by task, you can quickly see whether any tasks are repeat offenders. This may indicate that the deadline time is unrealistic, or that further training, online help, and so on is needed.

6.1.5 Reporting on Agent Behavior

Apart from monitoring how quickly agents act on their work items, it is worthwhile evaluating the workload on your agents, especially if the agents complain that they are receiving too many work items. You can analyze both past workload, that is what the agent has processed over a given time period, and future workload, that is, what the agent currently has in his inbox that has not yet been processed.

To call Workload Analysis, choose REPORTING • WORKLOAD ANALYSIS (Transaction SWI5). In Transaction SWI5, you can see the Workload Analysis for what has happened and what work items are waiting for execution.

Workload Analysis for the Past

This report is particularly useful for assessing workload over particular time periods, such as end of month or end of financial year. To determine the past workload, select the option COMPLETED SINCE on the selection screen WORKLOAD ANAL-YSIS. The report lists work items completed before the specified date. Only completed dialog work items are shown, and the work items must have an actual agent who is a user assigned directly or indirectly to the organizational object specified in the selection criteria.

You can also opt to see further statistics on the number of work items completed by employees linked to an organizational unit, agent, task, or completion date.

Workload Analysis for the Future

This report is particularly useful for reporting on the type and frequency of tasks being sent to an agent. To determine the future workload, select the option WORK ITEMS TO BE COMPLETED. You must use a date that is in the future for this option. The selection produces a list of work items that must be processed by the members of the organizational object by the date entered.

This transaction is also useful if a workflow agent unexpectedly leaves the office; the workflow administrator can report back to the business process owners of any "work in process" that needs to be handled by other agents.

> **Tip**
>
> When no date is specified, a user's workload is the contents of the workflow inbox. Work items in error are not shown.

The list of work items is grouped according to actual agents and tasks. At the end of the list, the work items and tasks for which no actual user exists are displayed under the header NOT RESERVED BY AN AGENT.

6.1.6 Identifying and Justifying Potential Improvements

When analyzing how to improve the business process, you need to consider not just the workflow but also the process as a whole. Although much can be done in the workflow to help improve the business process, simple considerations such as checking that all agents have received workflow training, sending email notifications to agents of outstanding work items, or an intranet-based FAQ list can be used to improve the process without changing the workflow itself.

The most useful tools for justifying potential improvements are the Error Overview and Performance reports:

▶ **Error Overview**

The Error Overview (Transaction SWI2_DIAG) can be used to show which errors are recurring frequently if you collect the relevant data over a period of time. In particular, frequent failures in determining agents can lead to more robust rules for agent determination, or to tightening of procedures for agent maintenance by HR and security personnel.

▶ **Performance reports**

Workflow Performance reports may show tasks that have long wait and process times. Common ways to improve process times include the following:

▷ Improving the online help

▷ Making the most important details for the decision more prominent when displaying and executing the work item

▷ Improving training and checking that all agents have received training

▷ Sending email notifications of outstanding work items to the agent

▷ Setting up substitutes

▷ Improving the escalation process by notifying someone when an agent has not performed a task in time, or by automatically redirecting work items to a new agent after a deadline has passed

It is a good idea to give agents and others involved or affected by the process an opportunity to provide suggestions for improving the workflow, for example, via an online suggestion box. If many agents are asking for similar improvements, that in itself may be sufficient justification for changing the workflow.

6.2 Error Resolution

When a critical process fails, the organization suffers. Prompt error resolution is vital if confidence in both the business process and the workflow are to be maintained. As a workflow administrator, the worst mistake you can make is to fail to plan for failures.

The most likely time for failures to occur is immediately after the workflow is activated or after changes to the workflow are activated. This is also the most critical time for building confidence in the workflow and the business process. You need to make sure that as a workflow administrator you know how important the process is, who will be impacted by the failure (so you can reassure them that the problem is being handled), what to do, and who to contact to make sure any errors are resolved quickly and confidently. This is particularly true of the very first workflow activated in your organization!

There are three parts to any error-resolution process:

1. Diagnose the problem.
2. Fix the problem.
3. Prevent the problem from happening again.

The workflow administrator also must be able to distinguish between workflows that are actually in an ERROR status and those workflows that have "gone astray" (e.g., they did not reach the expected recipient). This chapter is focused on resolving the errors, not necessarily the workflows that have behaved in an unexpected manner.

A considerable number of tools are provided to help you diagnose errors. These tools range from simple reports to detailed technical traces to complex graphical displays. These error diagnosis tools are heavily used by workflow developers testing their workflows, and as needed by workflow administrators diagnosing errors. Due to the large number and variety of tools, diagnosis is a separate topic covered in Chapter 16, Advanced Diagnostics. If workflow administration is new to you, you may want to get some assistance from your workflow developers in diagnosing errors. Watching a developer solve a workflow problem can be a very effective way to learn how to diagnose workflow errors.

However, when workflow developers diagnose a problem, they usually just abandon the failed workflow instance, make some changes, and start a new workflow instance. In a production environment, you do not usually have the luxury of ignoring failed workflow instances. You actually have to fix the problem. So in this chapter, the focus is on how to resolve the error after you have diagnosed it, that is, determining how to fix it and stop it from happening again.

The possible runtime problems can be grouped into the following categories:

▶ **Agent determination errors**
The wrong agent or no agent was found for a dialog work item.

▶ **Buffering errors**
Buffering errors usually manifest themselves as an inability to access work

items despite the maintenance of the agent determination and security being up to date.

▸ **Work item errors**
Work item errors are usually caused by an incorrectly modeled workflow or rushed transport. For example, the workflow does not take into account incomplete data extracted from legacy systems, or exceptions in object methods are not trapped.

▸ **Event linkage errors**
These are usually caused by changes in the application customizing or incorrectly modeled workflows. Symptoms are that the workflow did not start at all because the triggering event was not raised or failed to start the workflow, or the workflow hangs in the middle of the process waiting on a terminating event that never happens.

As you can see, the majority of errors are preventable by good workflow design and thorough testing (e.g., are the exceptions trapped?). However, despite the best efforts of developers, some errors always occur unexpectedly because of time pressures, inexperience, or changes made by personnel who do not understand their impact on workflow.

Make sure that people involved in the business process are aware that problems need to be reported promptly. Anecdotal evidence that a process has failed is often very hard to match with the offending work item. So encourage people to report object keys (e.g., if the work item was based on a financial document, give the company code/document number/fiscal year of the document) and dates the process started or when they first noticed the problem. As stated earlier, processes that have been put into workflows are nearly always critical, essential, or high volume. So if an error does occur, you need to act promptly and fix it fast!

Tip

It is very useful to keep a running log file of all workflow errors that have occurred, which steps they occur on, and the resolution. This log file can quickly become your FAQ for error resolution and is also a good tool for mentoring additional workflow administrative resources. A simple spreadsheet identifying the Date, System, Object Type, Object Key, Step, Error, and Resolution can also be a powerful tool for shaping the improvements that may be needed or spotting patterns that may be otherwise hard to identify.

6.3   General Techniques for Resolving Runtime Errors

In this section, you will find the basic settings used to assist error monitoring, as well as some generic techniques for finding and diagnosing work items or workflows that are in error. Some of the more specific diagnosis techniques require you to be familiar with some general workflow transactions. In particular, you should know:

▶ How to access and read a workflow log

▶ How to access, read, and change a work item

Reading Tip

Although the information in this chapter is invaluable for a workflow administrator, if you are not yet at the stage of delivering workflows in your production environment, you may find this section dry reading. You will also find that some of the error analysis assumes knowledge that is not described in detail until later in this book. For this reason, you might want to skip forward now to Section 6.4, Working with the Work Item Display, and return later when you need more detailed support.

6.3.1   Basic Settings for Error Monitoring

A few workflow runtime environment settings are particularly important for runtime error monitoring. Most are mentioned in Chapter 3, Configuring the System, but you can refer to the Implementation Guide (IMG) for more details (SAP NETWEAVER • APPLICATION SERVER • BUSINESS MANAGEMENT • SAP BUSINESS WORKFLOW).

The most important configuration setting determines who is a workflow administrator so that erroneous work items can be proactively dispatched to the administrator's inbox. If you are a workflow administrator, you must check your inbox regularly, or, better yet, ensure that your settings are correct to have notification of errors auto-forwarded to you on a regular basis. This includes setting a correct email address (BUSINESS WORKPLACE SETTINGS • OFFICE SETTINGS, choose the AUTOMATIC FORWARDING tab, and enter your email address) and the regular scheduling and execution of an automatic forwarding job (use program RSWUWFML2 in SAP releases below SAP ERP 5.0; use EXTENDED NOTIFICATIONS, discussed in Chapter 4, Work Item Delivery, in newer releases).

6.3.2 Finding and Fixing Work Items

When fixing work items, workflow experts may differ as to which workflow tools are the best, so three of the most powerful are described in detail in the next few sections:

▶ **SWI2_DIAG**
Diagnosis of workflows with errors.

▶ **SWI1**
Work item selection.

▶ **SWI2_FREQ**
Work item frequency.

6.3.3 Diagnosis of Workflows with Errors

Choosing Administration • Workflow Runtime • Diagnosis of Workflows with Errors (Transaction SWI2_DIAG) is probably the quickest report to execute if you already know you have a workflow that is in error. This function displays all workflows with errors and groups them according to error cause (agent, deadlines, binding, or other). This report helps you to assess whether particular types of errors are reoccurring across many workflows, or whether the problem is specific to just a particular work item. You can also fix and restart the workflow from this report.

> **Tip**
>
> The system determines highest-level work items with errors; that is, if a work item is in Error status, the work item shown belongs to the highest workflow in error hierarchically above it.

This report attempts to categorize the errors on all workflows that have an Error status. Some of the categories are:

▶ **Agents**
If you see an agent error, it is a clear indicator that dialog tasks were unable to be delivered to agents. If you drill into any single line on the report by double-clicking, details of the error are displayed. Figure 6.1 shows an example where an error is due to not being able to find any agents.

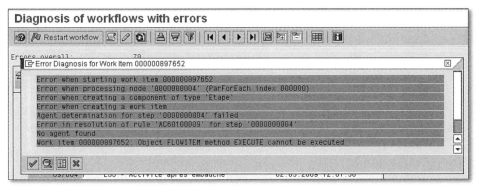

Figure 6.1 Example of No Agent Found

▸ **Binding from workflow to work item**
This type of error indicates that your workflow has been incorrectly modeled. Perhaps some import parameters were marked as mandatory and yet not filled at runtime.

▸ **Miscellaneous**
When the diagnosis report cannot determine the nature of the error, the errors are categorized as MISCELLANEOUS.

In any case, the workflow administrator can use various tools to manipulate the list (filter, sort) as well as workflow-specific tools (restart workflow, view the workflow log, change the workflow).

6.3.4 Work Item Selection

Use the menu path UTILITIES • WORK ITEM SELECTION for reviewing the status of workflows; this is the Work Item Selection report (Transaction SWI1). It lets you select and display work items of all types according to various criteria. In particular, you can use this function for "lost" work items that do not appear in the expected inbox. After you have found your work item, this report also gives you a number of options for fixing work items in trouble.

This report is also useful if you want to get a quick overview of certain types of work items, for instance, to examine background work items (enter work item type B) to check that they are all completing promptly. You can select work items either by criteria such as TYPE, STATUS, TASK/TASK GROUP ID, or DATE/TIME CREATED.

> **Tip**
>
> The task ID must be appropriate to the work item type selected. Work item type W represents tasks (TS types — TSxxxxxxxx); work item type F represents workflows (WS types — WSxxxxxxxx).

By default, the selection criterion is set to show all work items that have occurred in the past hour. When specifying intervals, ensure that the second entry is later than the first. For example, do not use intervals such as "from 13:05:00 to 00:00:00," instead use "from 13:05:00 to 23:59:59." You can also select a single work item by its ID number.

> **Tip**
>
> If you enter a work item ID as a selection criterion, the system ignores all other selection criteria.

It is important to understand the various work item types for effective reporting using Transaction SWI1. Table 6.2 shows the most commonly used work item types. You can see the work item type any time you look at the list of work items in Transaction SWI1.

Work Item Type	Meaning
W	Dialog work item, or a task that requires a user to complete it
B	A background task that is completed by the Workflow Engine
F	Workflow or subworkflow that show you the process flow, as opposed to a single step
D	Deadline work item (e.g., a user had 2 days to complete the task, and the 2 days has past, so the work item is overdue)

Table 6.2 Work Item Types

> **Note**
>
> From the resulting list of work items, you can navigate to the work item display if the entry is *not* type F, or you can go to the workflow log if the entry is type F.

6.3.5 Work Item Frequency

If you choose REPORTING • WORK ITEM ANALYSIS • WORK ITEMS PER TASK (Transaction SWI2_FREQ), the report started can show all workflows initiated during a specified timeframe. You can also narrow the selection to a specific workflow, task, or background task. This report can also be useful to demonstrate the real volume of workflows processes.

When some companies embark on a workflow project, much of the information related to the business process may be anecdotal; these reports give the real facts:

▸ Number of workflows initiated against a specific business object type

▸ Total number of workflows initiated during a time period

▸ Number of dialog tasks that your business users are processing

To fix work items in trouble, a number of options are available under EDIT • WORK ITEM or through the administration reports, which are available in the administration menu:

▸ **Restart after error/Execute without check**
With these reports, you can execute a work item.

  ▹ If the work item is in error, use RESTART AFTER ERROR.

  ▹ If the work item has no valid agent, and you still need to execute it, use EXECUTE WITHOUT CHECK. This option allows you to execute work items unhindered by access restrictions, so authorization to use this option should only be given to the workflow administrator in a production environment. However, the workflow administrator will be logged as the actual agent (i.e., the business approver), so for data governance and security purposes, it is best to reserve this functionality for emergency cases.

▸ **Complete manually**
With this option, you can complete a work item without re-executing it. This function is most useful if a background work item had been hung up, and the workflow administrator made the necessary container corrections to allow the process to continue.

▸ **Replace manually**
If a work item has been reserved by a particular agent, you can use this option to unreserve it, that is, to allow all recipients to see the work item in their inboxes. This function is probably used the most when workflow is first imple-

mented — before users understand that by "touching" a work item, they remove it from ever other agents' queue.

Tip

If you are restarting a work item after error, make sure you restart using the administration report named Restart After Error (Transaction SWPR) to ensure that both the work item and the top-level workflow are restarted. You should always check that the workflow has restarted correctly in case an error occurs (it could even be a new error) before the workflow has a chance to continue.

6.4   Working with the Work Item Display

In this section, we discuss the *work item display* as opposed to the *workflow log*. The distinction is that you can delve into the details of one specific task from the work item display; the workflow log gives you the overview of the entire workflow process. You can access the work item display from most workflow reports, including Work Item Selection. The work item display shows detailed information about the work item and also lets you fix certain problems. Normally the work item display is accessed via a GOTO link in the menu.

It's important to recognize that both the workflow log and the work item display can be shown in several different formats, depending on the user's parameters. It is helpful for the workflow administrator to understand these other views for better communication with users. The user view is, of course, primarily for users; the technical display has some extra options for developers and administrators. You can preset which display variant you want to use in your personal workflow settings, or use the menu options, for example, GOTO • TECHNICAL WORK ITEM DISPLAY to move from the standard display to the technical display. You will be presented with a pop-up screen, which enables you to choose several different formats. Your technical workflow view will vary based on the SAP release you are on.

In particular in the technical display (see Section 6.4.2 as well), you can:

▸ Forward, that is, send the work item to another agent.

▸ Replace work items that are held by one selected agent so that other recipients can see them in their inboxes.

▸ Reject the work item (the workflow follows the reject path that has been defined in the workflow builder).

▸ Change deadlines.

▸ Add attachments, for example, you might want to explain why it was necessary to execute a work item without agent check for the benefit of future audits.

> **Hint**
>
> WORKFLOW LOG DISPLAY flags can be set (and should be set for your users) in Transaction SU01 under the PARAMETERS tab for the parameter WLC. The parameter has positional flags, which are either X (on) or blank (off). The value of these positions is as follows:
>
> ▸ Position 1: Always set.
> ▸ Position 2: Double-clicking on an object opens a new window.
> ▸ Position 3: Work item technical view/user view without ActiveX.
> ▸ Position 4: Enable forwarding to several users.
> ▸ Position 5: Always set.
> ▸ Position 6: Display work item texts in logon language.
> ▸ Position 7: Workflow Log Technical view/user view without ActiveX.
> ▸ Position 8: Workflow Log user view with ActiveX.
> ▸ Position 9: Work Item user view with ActiveX.
> ▸ Position 10: No Tips and Tricks in the workplace.
> ▸ Position 11: No HTML in execution of decision tasks.

6.4.1 Work Item Display — Standard View

The standard work item display shown in Figure 6.2 shows the information about dialog work items concisely. It contains details about deadlines, statuses, agents, attachments, and linked objects for a work item. Be sure to familiarize yourself with all of the features available in the work item display. If the work item execution has failed, the ERRORS function (EXTRAS • TECHNICAL DATA) displays the error message or return codes for executed work items.

All objects that are related to the work item, including the formal process objects and the ad-hoc attachments, are displayed in the list of available objects on the AVAILABLE OBJECTS tab. Of particular interest are:

▸ The object currently being processed (container element _WI_Object_ID of the task container)

▸ The object added for grouping purposes (container element _WI_Group_ID of the task container)

▸ Attachment objects, that is, any additional information that has been added as an attachment to the work item

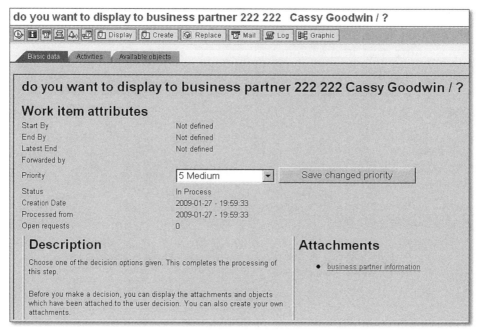

Figure 6.2 Work Item Display Standard View

You can display each object referenced in the work item container with its default attribute. If no default attribute was defined for the object type, the key fields of the object are displayed. The default method of each object can be executed upon request.

> **Tip**
>
> Most objects set the `Display` method as the default method. So when you want to check on the details of the object, for example, to help diagnose an error, you usually do not have to worry about finding the transaction needed to view it. Additionally, if your business rules need to prohibit the use of the default method (to protect data visibility, for example), you can accomplish this by redefining the default method from with the Business Object Repository (BOR).

You can extend and process the list of objects, that is, create, display, and remove them. The main purpose of this is to make extra information available to the agents of the subsequent steps in the workflow, such as why you have forwarded this work item. When you are trying to resolve agent determination problems or just trying to find who has a particular work item, GOTO • AGENT is the most useful work item function. You can see the different categories of agents. The INBOX (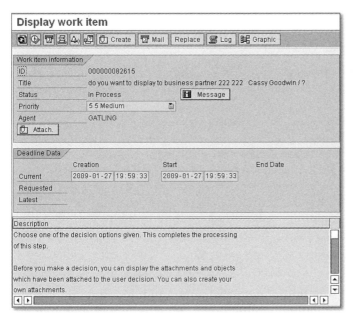) is used to highlight the users that have the work item in their inboxes.

6.4.2 Work Item Display — Technical View

As well as the functions available in the standard view of the work item display, there are additional functions available via the technical view (GOTO • TECHNICAL WORK ITEM DISPLAY). All information from the displayed work item is shown in the technical work item display (see Figure 6.3). The technical work item display is particularly aimed at workflow administrators.

Figure 6.3 Work Item Display with Technical View

The following specifications are displayed depending on the work item type:

▶ Work item ID

▶ Work item status

▶ Actual agent of a dialog work item (after it has been executed)

Additionally, attachments and mails are displayed for the work item. If an error message was generated when the method was executed, you can display this by choosing the MESSAGE button or EXTRAS • DISPLAY RETURN VALUE.

You can find the current dates/times as well as the deadlines that are monitored by the runtime system (requested and latest start and end deadlines). Table 6.3 shows the corresponding work item timestamps.

Current Date/Time	Meaning
Creation date	Date when the work item was created by the Workflow Engine with the status READY or WAITING (if a requested start was used)
Start date/time	Date and time when the status of the work item changes from READY to SELECTED or STARTED for the first time, for example, when a recipient executes the work item
End date/time	Date and time when the status of the work item changes to COMPLETED or CANCELLED
Requested start	Date when the Workflow Engine changed the status of the work item from WAITING to READY (if a requested start deadline was used)

Table 6.3 Work Item Timestamps

A highlighted monitored deadline shows that it has been missed. If the ringing bell symbol (🔔) is displayed as well, an escalation action was triggered by the deadline background job.

You can go to the definition of the instance linkage for terminating events or wait step work items by choosing EXTRAS • INSTANCE LINKAGE. There you can see which event (identified using an object type and event name) is expected by which object (identified using an object reference). This is useful if the work item has been executed but is waiting on a terminating event because this function lets you see exactly what terminating event and event values are expected. Choose EXTRAS • CONTAINER to display the content of the work item container.

The EDIT • CHANGE option lets you:

▶ Change the work item container (e.g., if binding errors caused the wrong data or incomplete data to be passed).

▶ Change the work item text or language.

▶ Change the work item priority.

▶ Logically delete the work item (i.e., mark it as canceled, no longer required).

- Manually complete the work item without re-executing it.

- Lock/unlock the work item to prevent someone from executing it or to give him access to it.

In the following work item types, you can display additional details by choosing Goto • Type specific data:

- For work queue work items, the objects and tasks contained in the work queue are listed.

- For wait step work items, the system specifies how many events are expected and how many events have already been received.

6.4.3 How to Work with the Work Item Container Display

The contents of the container for the relevant work item are displayed in an overall view. You can see the current, runtime-specific data on the specific work item. If you are looking at a dialog or background work item, the container belongs only to that work item. If you are looking at a *workflow* work item, the container belongs to the whole workflow instance. Figure 6.4 shows the work item container, which contains all data available to the task at runtime.

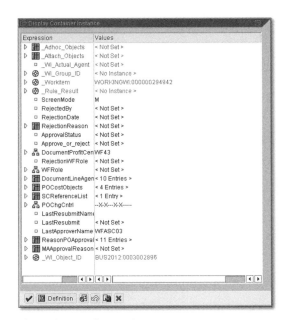

Figure 6.4 Work Item Container

The container holds:

- System fields relevant to the workflow
- ABAP Dictionary-based container elements
- Object-based container elements, that is, object references

Object references are always prefixed with the logical system ID. This is followed by the ID of the object type and the concatenated key of the object. If you need to change an object reference, always use the input help on the object reference field. This enables you to fill in the object key correctly, works out the appropriate system/client references for you, and checks that the object exists.

6.5 Working with the Workflow Log

At runtime, a workflow has its own work item (of type F) that represents the workflow instance. You can use Work Item Selection and similar reports to find the workflow work item for your workflow. However, the work item display will only show you limited information about the workflow instance. The best way to look at the workflow instance is via the workflow log.

The workflow log formats all of the information created or collected during the execution of the business process (i.e., the workflow instance) in one place, as shown in Chapter 4, Work Item Delivery. The workflow log is available in several formats. Two of them are geared toward the agents and process owners who want to get an overview of the steps processed so far. The formats are:

- User view
- Classic user view
- Workflow log — chronicle in the user view

For brevity, we will show only the user view and discuss what options are available to end users. All three views provide essentially the same information in slightly different formats; for most workflow administrators, more time should be spent getting to know the workflow technical log.

6.5.1 User View

Only data for the most significant step types is shown in the user view (see Figure 6.5). In the workflow definition, you can exclude steps with the above step types from being displayed in the workflow log if you wish. If you want to see the complete log, you should switch to the technical view of the log by clicking the list with the Technical Details icon (▦). The workflow log contains the following tab pages:

▶ **WF Chronicle** (What was processed when?)

The WF Chronicle tab (✹) shows a hierarchical display of all steps in the workflow that have been processed so far or are currently able to be processed. If the workflow has a subworkflow structure, the subworkflows are also displayed.

The Details function (▣ symbol) lists the following information about each step in the lower part of the screen:

▷ Who carried out what detailed actions for these work items and with what results

▷ When this action was carried out

▷ The objects involved

The Agents function (✹ symbol) displays the selected/possible/excluded agents of a step.

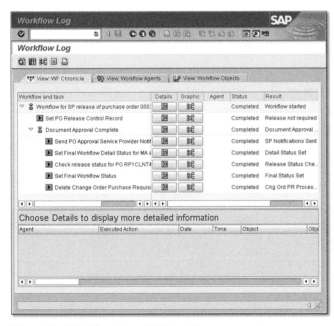

Figure 6.5 Workflow Log with User View

▶ **Workflow Agents** (Who processed what?)
The WORKFLOW AGENTS tab (🐾) shows the agents involved in the workflow up to now. The following is displayed for each agent:

  ▶ What action was carried out in what step

  ▶ When this action was carried out

  ▶ The objects involved

> **Tip**
>
> To hide agent names (e.g., for legal/union requirements) set the customizing switch in Transaction SWPA (Customizing workflow runtime system).

▶ **Workflow Objects** (What was processed?)
The WORKFLOW OBJECTS tab (📝) lists the objects related to the workflow or addressed up to now in the execution of the workflow. This view shows what objects were created and processed, and how. These objects include the following:

  ▶ The main object of the workflow

  ▶ Any attachments and objects added in individual steps of the workflow

The following is displayed for each object:

  ▶ Who carried out what detailed action for what task

  ▶ When this action was carried out

In addition, you can navigate to the graphical workflow log (see Figure 6.6), which displays the workflow steps already processed (✔) in a graphical representation of the workflow definition.

The main benefit of the graphical workflow log is that you can see at a glance which route a workflow instance has taken and which activities are processed in parallel to your own within a business process. Unlike the text version of the workflow log, the graphical workflow log also shows the subsequent flow of a workflow instance. This view also allows you to make ad-hoc changes to this single workflow instance.

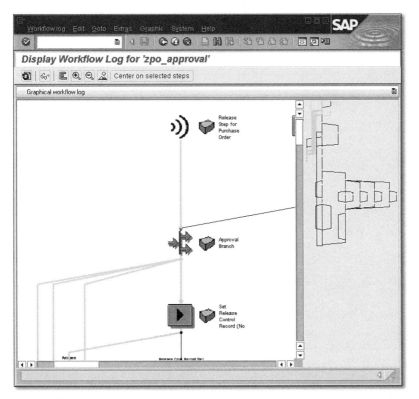

Figure 6.6 Graphical Workflow Log

6.5.2   Technical View

The technical view (see Figure 6.7) shows technical control information and is therefore aimed particularly at workflow administrators. For a workflow with errors, it allows you to see at a glance where the error has occurred and all messages (including warning messages) generated by the workflow. However, it is also a very useful display for determining exactly what happened during the workflow.

The workflow log is displayed as a two-level, hierarchical list. You can adapt the appearance of the list to suit your requirements using layouts. The technical view shows technical nodes and control structures, and makes additional data available, such as container elements (📲), agent data (🎰), and workflow data (🍡). The status of each work item is also displayed.

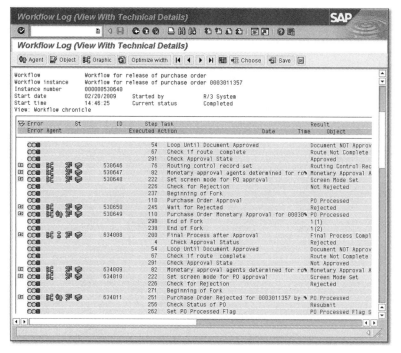

Figure 6.7 Workflow Log — Technical View

If the workflow is in status ERROR, the workflow log may contain a hierarchical list of underlying Workflow Engine function modules that indicate exactly where the error was detected, helping to localize particularly obscure errors.

If you choose VIEWS • OTHER VIEWS • WITH SUBWORKFLOW STRUCTURE, you can decide whether or not to display any subworkflows and their structure. Depending on your personalization, you may have to choose VIEWS • OTHER VIEW • WITH ERROR INDICATORS to view the errors, which are marked in the log with the red traffic symbol (⬤OO). The standard indicator for work items that are not in error is the green traffic symbol (OO⬤). This is useful for identifying at a glance work items with errors, particularly in more complex workflows where many work items are displayed in the log.

> **Tip**
>
> By clicking on the error symbol associated with the parent workflow item (at the top of the list — CURRENT STATUS), you are presented with a complete error analysis of the workflow, showing the probable root of the problem.

Just as with the standard view, you can display a chronicle, agent, or object view.

Since SAP NetWeaver 2004, the technical log has a new appearance. Try to get accustomed to this view, which is shown in Figure 6.8, but if you still need to look at the "old" technical view of the workflow log, you should be able to switch the display by pressing [Ctrl]-[P].

The main difference with the newer technical log is that the process flow can be expanded by clicking on the right arrows (▷), and the details for individual tasks are show in tabbed screens on the lower portion of the log display. The tabbed display on the lower portion of the screen allows you to see critical information in fewer clicks.

The administrative tasks (change a work item status, change a work item container) can be accessed via the new technical log by selecting the work item that is in question, and selecting GOTO • WORK ITEM, or right-clicking the work item and choosing DISPLAY WORK ITEM.

Figure 6.8 New Technical Log

6.6 Resolving Agent Determination Errors

The most probable workflow problem that you are likely to encounter in a production environment is an agent determination problem. That is, a work item is sent to the wrong agents or to no agents at all.

> **Tip**
>
> The Workflow Engine cannot alert you if the wrong agent receives a work item (e.g., agent determination data out-of-date). This is where a good work item description comes to the rescue.

After a workflow is developed and transported to production, it may not need to be changed for some time, and even changes can be planned. With good design and thorough testing, you can prevent most workflow problems. However, agent determination relies on data that is usually maintained directly in the production environment and may need to be changed at short notice. Even a relatively minor delay in updating agent determination rules or agent authorizations can have an immediate negative impact on a workflow.

The most common cause of agent determination errors is inadequate maintenance of the agent determination rule or the authorities given to agents. Ensuring timely maintenance of agent determination rules and workflow security can prevent the majority of agent determination errors. Problems can also occur because an agent has left the company or is absent for some other reason and has no substitute, or has reserved the work item so that none of the alternative agents can access it.

The good news is that implementing simple strategies such as substitution or default agents can help alleviate agent determination problems. For more details on these and other strategies, refer to Chapter 5, Agents.

6.6.1 Fixing Work Items with No Agents or Wrong Agents

As a workflow administrator, it is usually your responsibility to redirect any work items that were sent to the wrong agent or have no agent at all. You will probably also need to diagnose why the problem occurred and follow up any maintenance issues with the relevant personnel; otherwise, the same problem will boomerang back to you on future work items.

Before you fix a work item with an agent problem, always check that you have identified the correct agent; for example, check with the business process owner. Do not just take someone's word for it that they are the correct agent; otherwise, you may inadvertently cause a security breach.

The other point to remember about fixing work items with the wrong agent is that you cannot send a work item to a new agent if it has already been completed. So if the wrong agent has already completed the work item, the most you can do is stop the problem from happening again and discuss the situation with the agents and business process owners involved. It is also a good idea to keep a log of what occurred for the benefit of auditors, or add an attachment to the workflow explaining why the wrong agent executed the work item.

Diagnosing why agent determination has failed is a topic in itself. Chapter 16, Advanced Diagnostics, walks you through a plan of attack for diagnosing agent determination problems. Knowing the cause will help you solve the problem. Table 6.4 shows common problems and recommended solutions.

Problem	Solutions
An agent lacks authorization to execute the work item; that is, the desired agent is not a possible agent of the work item.	▶ After the agent's authorization has been corrected, forward the work item to the desired agent. ▶ If the agent's authorization is correct, but the agent is still unable to execute the work item, it may be a buffering problem. ▶ Determine if the agent's substitute has the correct authorizations, and encourage the substitute to execute the work item. ▶ If the work item needs to be executed before security can be corrected, discuss the data with the desired agent, and use EXECUTE WITHOUT AGENT CHECK to execute and complete the work item.
The wrong agent or no agent was found, even though the desired agent has sufficient authority, that is, the agent determination rule has failed.	▶ If the agent is already a possible agent but was not excluded or selected, forward the work item to the desired agent.

Table 6.4 Common Problems and Recommended Solutions

Problem	Solutions
The desired agent cannot execute the work item because he is an excluded agent; that is, he has been specifically excluded from executing the work item.	▸ If the agent is excluded, he cannot execute the work item, so you need to forward the work item to someone else. The business process owner should be able to suggest an appropriate agent. Before you forward the work item, make sure the new agent is a possible agent of the task and not an excluded agent. ▸ Alternatively, discuss the data with the appropriate agent, and use EXECUTE WITHOUT AGENT CHECK to execute and complete the work item.
The work item cannot be accessed from any agent's inbox.	▸ If an absent agent has reserved the work item, but there are other recipients available, replace the work item. This will allow other agents to view it. The same is true of work items in someone's resubmission queue. ▸ If an absent agent has reserved the work item, and your agents are used to working with workflow substitution, create a substitute for the absent agent. After the workflow administrator replaces the work item, the substitute agent can then execute the work item. Remember that the substitute must still have sufficient authorization to do this. ▸ If there are no alternative agents in the selected agent list, and you do not want to use substitution, forward the work item to the appropriate (possible) agent suggested by the business process owner.

Table 6.4 Common Problems and Recommended Solutions (cont.)

Tip

Due to more stringent Separation of Duties regulations, the workflow administrator's best approach to getting work items to agents may be to set up substitutions for the agents who are absent. An appropriate email or authorization request for this substitution should also be maintained. In this way, the workflow administrator's "fingerprints" are not part of the audit log — the powers-that-be can look at the log and see valid business process agents at all points in the process.

6.6.2 Preventing Agent Determination Problems from Recurring

When you are confident that the immediate problem is solved, you need to ensure that this does not happen again. This may mean:

▶ Ensuring that administration of security and agent determination is done promptly. If you cannot do this yourself, you may need to call on the business process owner and the relevant managers to improve the situation.

▶ Ensuring that personnel who are able to change values related to the workflow are aware of their impact on the workflow. You may need the assistance of the business process owner to improve the situation.

▶ Changing the workflow design or the rule determination design. For instance, if you are using a responsibility rule, you may want to turn on secondary priorities so that a default agent is determined when no specific agent is found.

▶ You may also want to ensure that the workflow design or rule determination design takes into account certain business related criteria in the future. For example, is it valid to send a work item to a person whose validity dates are either not yet active, or expired? Whose personnel status is inactive? Whose user ID is locked or delimited?

By correctly modeling your agent determination rules, you can often avoid the most overlooked scenarios. The fact is, people do move around an organization a lot, and any workflow design that does not take this into consideration is going to be a headache for the workflow administrator.

6.6.3 Support Tools for Agent Determination Problems

The following are reports you can use as support tools for resolving agent determination problems:

▶ **Execute Rules for Work Items**
ADMINISTRATION WORKFLOW RUNTIME • EXECUTE RULES FOR WORK ITEMS (Transaction SWI1_RULE).

You can use this function to repeat the step of defining the recipients for a work item. If a rule was used to determine the recipients, the rule will be re-executed.

▶ **Work Items Without Agents**

ADMINISTRATION • WORKFLOW RUNTIME • WORK ITEMS WITHOUT AGENTS (Transaction SWI2_ADM1).

This report finds all work items that have no agent at all, that is, orphaned work items, for a particular selection period. The list displayed is similar to the work item selection report, and you have the same options available for examining or correcting work items.

▶ **Execute Work Items Without Agent Check**

ADMINISTRATION • WORKFLOW RUNTIME • EXECUTE WORK ITEM WITHOUT AGENT CHECK (Transaction SWIA).

This report enables you to execute work items for which you are not a possible agent. This very powerful tool should be given only to the administrators in production environments. Using the work item selection, you can select the necessary work items and then execute them, complete them, or make them available again to the recipients (i.e., replace them).

If you need to use EXECUTE WITHOUT AGENT CHECK to fix a problem, consider adding an attachment to the work item explaining why this action was necessary and who advised what action should be taken. This can help answer and avoid awkward questions made by auditors or managers who are reviewing business processes retrospectively, long after the problem was solved.

▶ **Mass Deletion of Work Items**

ADMINISTRATION • WORKFLOW RUNTIME • EXECUTE WORK ITEM WITHOUT AGENT CHECK (Transaction SWIA).

A newer feature that has been added to this transaction (see SAP Note 1286336) is the ability to do mass cancellations of workflows. In prior releases, the workflow administrator had to manually delete workflows individually, write a program to cancel them, or run program RSWWWIDE, which is not recommended. By implementing this note, the workflow administrator will have a very valuable — and powerful — tool to use.

6.6.4 Resolving Buffering Errors

Buffering simply means that the system keeps a copy of certain data in memory rather than reading it from the database. This is done to improve overall system performance and is particularly prevalent in Organizational Management entities such as organizational units, jobs, positions, agents, tasks, and relationships between them. Because there are so many buffers used for Organizational Management entities, most of these buffers are normally only refreshed at midnight (system time). Unfortunately, out-of-date buffers can have some curious effects on a workflow.

The majority of buffering errors can be prevented by ensuring buffers are updated whenever new agents are added, or when agent determination rules or workflow-related security is changed. One way to avoid buffering problems is to habitually set up agent assignments and security at least the day before they are going to be used.

Buffering problems result in apparently impossible situations:

▶ The work item may appear in the agent's inbox, but the agent is unable to execute it.

▶ All of the agent administration and security is correct, but the agent determination still does not work.

Most frustratingly, you can spend all day trying to resolve this problem, come in the next morning, and find that everything is working fine. You could call this *Midnight Magic* or the *Cinderella Effect*; that is, everything's back to normal after midnight.

6.6.5   Fixing Work Items with Buffering Problems

You can fix buffering problems by refreshing buffers. This can be done by:

▶ Using the SYNCHRONIZE RUNTIME BUFFER option (Transaction SWU_OBUF) This refreshes the majority of organizational management buffers.

▶ Using the REFRESH INDEX option when assigning agents to tasks. This updates buffering of the agent assignment to a task.

▶ Using the REFRESH ORGANIZATIONAL ENVIRONMENT option in the Business Workplace or in the START WORKFLOW function (Transaction SWUS). This refreshes buffers for the current user ID.

If buffering has stopped an agent from accessing a work item, it is enough to refresh the buffers. However, if buffering has caused an agent determination problem, that is, the work item was not sent to the correct agent, you will still need to fix the agent determination problem on work items created before the buffers were refreshed.

Sometimes security problems can appear to be buffering problems. For instance, if you are in an SAP ERP system, using the Human Capital Management (HCM) capabilities and implementing structural authorizations, a lack of appropriate authorizations will result in agents not being able to access their work items. The error messages that appear when attempting to execute the work item are the same or similar to error messages that appear with buffering problems.

6.6.6 Preventing Buffering Problems from Recurring

You can prevent buffering problems in the longer term by:

▶ Encouraging updates of relevant security, Organizational Management data, and workflow data the day before it will be used.

▶ Synchronizing the runtime buffer after emergency changes to workflow-related security if it needs to be used straight away.

▶ Making agents aware of buffering problem symptoms (e.g., via an intranet) and, where possible, giving them access to the REFRESH ORGANIZATIONAL ENVIRONMENT option so they can refresh their own buffers.

6.6.7 Support Tools for Buffering Problems

You can use the function ADMINISTRATION • WORKFLOW RUNTIME • SYNCHRONIZE RUNTIME BUFFER (Transaction SWU_OBUF) to initialize the main memory buffers used by the Workflow Engine. You can set the current time as the new buffering start time. After the new buffering start time has been set, the system reads the values from the database instead of from the buffer so that the current data is used. As the data is read from the database, it is added to the buffers once more.

> **Tip**
>
> You should always refresh the runtime buffer when you have made a change in a task definition or after transporting new workflows or versions of workflows that are to be used on the day of transport.

After executing this function, some workflow functions will initially have lower than optimal performance. This applies until the main memory rebuilds the buffers up to optimal levels.

6.7   Other Support Tools

In the following list, you can find some more reports and functions that you may find useful in dealing with work item errors:

▶ **Workflow Restart After Error**

ADMINISTRATION • WORKFLOW RUNTIME • WORKFLOW RESTART AFTER ERROR (Transaction SWPR).

This report can be used to display a list of workflows with errors for a particular selection period and then restart those workflows. The benefit of this report is that it allows you to perform a mass restart of workflows.

▶ **Deadline Monitoring for Work Items**

ADMINISTRATION • WORKFLOW RUNTIME • WORK ITEM DEADLINE MONITORING.

Tasks with deadlines also have deadline monitoring based on a background job. You can change the period duration of the background job, and change, schedule, display, or execute it manually (Transaction SWWA). Typically, the workflow administrator schedules this job during the initial workflow runtime configuration, but it may be necessary to tweak the job parameters based on production workloads.

▶ **Work Item Rule Monitoring**

ADMINISTRATION • WORKFLOW RUNTIME • WORK ITEM RULE MONITORING.

If conditions are defined for the work item start or work item end for steps in the workflow, these conditions must be regularly checked. This task is performed by a report that is controlled by a background job.

You can schedule or display the background job. You can also start the report manually using EXECUTE WORK ITEM RULE MONITORING (Report RSWWCOND). Normally the scheduling of this report should be carried out via Transaction SWU3 (Verify Workflow Customizing).

▶ **Continue Workflow After System Crash**

ADMINISTRATION • WORKFLOW RUNTIME • CONTINUE WORKFLOW AFTER SYSTEM CRASH (Transaction SWPC).

You can use this report to select and continue workflows that have had the status STARTED for longer than a day. This means that workflows that have come to a halt after system errors can be continued.

6.8 Help Desk in the Intranet

As you have seen so far, being prepared is the best way of ensuring smooth and efficient processing. However, by distributing responsibility to the workflow agents, you will make the whole process transparent to them and less of a mystery. This allows agents to react faster to exceptional circumstances (such as another agent sitting for too long on a work item) and proactively support other agents downstream in the process.

Take a multipronged approach:

- ▶ Use a help desk to distribute information and provide generic support.

- ▶ Use the agents to help report and diagnose problems promptly. Give the agents enough information to avoid confusion over what is or is not a problem. Many initial perceptions of problems with workflows can be resolved by providing intelligent work item descriptions.

- ▶ Use workflow administrators to deal with problems before they become noticeable to the agents.

6.8.1 Web-Based Help Desks

It is helpful to provide a web-accessible (intranet/extranet) help desk support site that provides:

- ▶ Contact numbers for problem resolution

- ▶ Frequently asked question lists (FAQs) to increase understanding and help users diagnose and resolve their own problems

- ▶ Access to generic training material

- ▶ Access to tips and tricks for dealing with inboxes, attachments, performing tasks, and so on

- ▶ Reference documents explaining the business process and workflow, for example, in the form of a graphical flowchart

- ▶ Highlights of new and soon-to-be-provided workflows

- ▶ Interesting results such as time taken to complete the process before versus after the workflow was implemented, and number and frequency of workflows

- ▶ A "suggestion box" for ways to improve the workflow

- Acknowledgement for users who have contributed to improving workflow
- A Wiki for your user community to collect issues, post surveys, obtain suggestions for improvement, and share information

In addition, when the business process changes, the help desk is the ideal place to publish information to:

- Announce that the workflow process definition has changed.
- Explain why the workflow has been changed and what benefit the changes will give.
- Explain the differences between the new and old process.
- Explain what if any affect this will have on users.

6.8.2 Self Help

Encourage agents to understand where they fit into the business process. One way to do this is to give them a copy of the workflow flowchart with the tasks they perform highlighted. Another way is to hand out "survival packs" or newsletters explaining the workflow flowchart to all users, the expected benefits of the new workflow, and how to access their work items, updating any last minute training information, and showing who to contact if they have any problems.

Send clear, concise, and complete instructions with the work item. If possible, have some of the agents read the instructions prior to the workflow being activated, to check that they make sense. Give the agent enough information to help identify, diagnose, and fix problems. As well as speeding error resolution, this also helps to build the agent's acceptance of the process.

In each work item, tell the agent why they have received it and who to contact if they believe they should not have received it or if they are having problems completing it. Thus, your agents will see:

- "You have received this work item because..."
- "Please contact ... if you believe you should not have received this work item."
- "Please contact ... if you are unable to complete this work item/access this hyperlink."

Encourage prompt reporting of any problems. Anecdotal problems are often difficult to substantiate because the work item is often completed and the evidence lost before any diagnosis can be attempted.

Make reporting problems easy by using a simple workflow. For instance, let the agent enter a text describing a problem, a code for the type of problem found (wrong agent, missing information, cannot execute work item), a code for the process to which it belongs (purchasing request, vacation request, etc.), and user ID/contact details. Have the workflow route the problem reported to an appropriate agent based on the type of problem found and the process to which it belongs. Include an email response directed back to the initiator confirming that the problem has been fixed.

6.9   A Day in the Life of a Workflow Administrator

The title of this section is perhaps a little misleading because, thanks to the high degree of integration of the SAP Business Workflow Engine with the rest of the SAP software, the time spent purely administrating (as opposed to development) is about an hour a week, even in large organizations with high workflow volume. Most of this time is devoted to updating the organizational model to deal with staff fluctuation and organizational changes or helping review workflows currently being developed.

However, if you have been nominated as a workflow administrator, or you are responsible for resourcing workflow administrators, then you will want to take this responsibility seriously, and it helps to have some idea of what a workflow administrator does on a day-to-day basis. You need to consider:

▸ **Who should be the workflow administrator?**
What sort of skills does a workflow administrator need? Are they technical skills, business knowledge, or both? Can the system administrator be the workflow administrator, too? Is it a full-time or part-time position?

▸ **Who makes the business decisions in the event of failure?**
Given that workflows are business processes in action, how does the business interact with the workflow administrator if the workflow fails? Whatever the skill level of the workflow administrator, the individual business owners need to ensure that there is a clear line of responsibility for the most rapid and effective error resolution.

▸ **Crisis response**
When a workflow fails, the business process fails. If the process was important enough to be implemented as a workflow, then any failure is equally critical.

What does the workflow administrator do in the event of such a crisis? Will the business need to rely on paper-based approvals?

▶ **Day-to-day monitoring**
What does a workflow administrator need to do on a day-to-day basis, even when there isn't a crisis? One workflow administrator does a morning check of all short dumps, background jobs (related to workflow), and the tRFC queue. Because the workflow administrator is notified on an as-needed basis about any periodic failures, this is generally sufficient.

▶ **Periodic reality checks**
Are the business users executing the work items in their inbox daily? Are they printing the work items or doing other research before executing the task?

▶ **Housekeeping**
How does a workflow administrator help maintain optimal efficiency of your workflow environment? Here the workflow administrator should be working closely with the Basis team to ensure that performance is optimized.

▶ **Making the most of a precious resource**
How can you make the most of the workflow administrator in your organization?

6.9.1 Who Should be the Workflow Administrator

Workflow administration usually involves both technical activities and business activities, so it makes sense to have both technical and business personnel as administrators. It is rare to find someone with all of the technical and business skills needed to support your workflows, so consider having either a team of administrators who work together, or setting up a contact sequence for support.

Both the technical and business people need to have a good understanding of workflow. Bear in mind that there will not be enough workflow administration duties to perform to keep a single person fully occupied, let alone a whole team. So the administrator will pursue other duties too.

There are a number of possible team structures:

▶ A centralized, dedicated team of technical and business administrators

▶ A centralized, dedicated technical administrator and a decentralized part-time business administrator on an as-needed basis

- Regional teams of technical and business administrators on a part-time basis
- Centralized system administrators who are part-time workflow administrators, with nominated business contacts for each business process
- Workflow administrators who are also workflow developers

The team structure that is right for your organization depends on:

- The number and frequency of workflows you are running. The more workflows you run, and the more you have in the development pipeline, the more likely administration will become a full-time activity.
- The number of people affected by the workflow. This includes not just the agents but also people who are relying on the workflow to complete processes for them. The more people affected, the more business administrators will be needed to help educate and explain the workflow behavior. You can reduce this activity by using a web site to help educate and explain workflow behavior.
- The availability of workflow resources. If you have only a few people skilled in workflow, they may act as workflow developers and workflow administrators. As the number and frequency of workflows grow, you will probably need to separate these roles.
- How extensively workflow is being used, that is, whether workflow is regarded as continuous business improvement, where the administrator plays an ongoing role in the development of new scenarios, or whether only a few limited processes have been activated.

The basic rules of thumb are:

- Set up a help desk or a website as the first point of contact for queries about how the process works and for "what do I do now?" questions.
- Name a technical administrator available to solve deeper problems.
- Assign business process owners who can be contacted to make business decisions in case of failure. Make sure you have backup contacts as well; in a crisis, you may need to contact someone within a few minutes of finding the problem.
- Make sure the workflow developer is available to help solve problems especially in the first couple of weeks after a new or changed workflow is activated in production.

The workflow administrator is on the front line when workflow problems happen. Usually it is your critical, essential, and high-volume business processes that have been worth the cost of implementation as workflows. Therefore, it is vital that your workflow administrator be capable of handling problems as they arise from the very first time a workflow is run in your production environment. Remember that most problems are likely to occur in the first few instances of a new or changed workflow.

Above all, it is not realistic to give workflow administration to a system administrator and expect him to be able to diagnose or resolve problems without any workflow training. Workflow administrators need the following:

▶ An understanding of workflow basics

▶ An understanding of the particular workflows they are supporting

▶ Access to the SAP online support system

▶ Practice in using the various diagnosis and error resolution support tools

▶ Names of persons to contact when a workflow fails and a business decision needs to be made

---

Tip

Pick an administrator with good *people* skills (e.g., communication and tact) and preferably with hotline experience too.

6.9.2   Who Makes the Business Decisions in the Event of Failure

Whatever the cause of a failure, correcting workflows in error is much more than a technical activity. Remember always that the workflow represents the business process, and when you make decisions about how to deal with failed processes, you are literally affecting business operations. You need to have a business process owner (and backup — in a crisis you often have to be able to contact people rapidly) who can be contacted to help manage and resolve the failure by assessing:

▶ How serious is the failure from a business viewpoint?

▶ How critical is this particular failure? If it is not critical now, will it become critical if it is not resolved in the next hour, day, week, and so on?

▶ Who needs to be notified of the failure?

▶ If the fault in your workflow affects a customer directly, you may need to notify the customer. If the fault hinders issuing a payment, this may mean notifying a supplier.

▶ Is there a workaround? For example can someone do the work manually until the problem is resolved?

▶ When the crisis is over, how can you prevent it from happening again? Should the workflow be enhanced to cope with this problem? Should procedures (e.g., for maintaining agent data) be updated? Should the help desk or website include instructions to agents to encourage better and faster reporting of similar problems in the future?

Even if the workflow administrator knows the answers to these questions, most organizations cannot afford for these decisions to be made by one person alone. Your organization will usually need to be able to show that the correct process has still been followed and that the relevant personnel have been involved in deciding on the actions to be taken. On the other hand, you don't want to delay resolving workflow problems while meetings are being held to evaluate possible remedial actions. As much as possible, do the following:

▶ Make sure workflows are designed so that they can be easily restarted in the event of an error.

▶ Build workflows that listen for manual action so that corrective action taken outside of the workflow will not leave the workflow hanging.

▶ Have a plan of action *before* problems happen. Anticipate potential failures and how they will be resolved as part of the workflow design.

▶ After every problem, and particularly after recurring problems, do post-mortems and evaluate what was the root cause of the error and how the process can be improved to prevent the error.

▶ Make sure that problems in the workflow will be quickly highlighted so corrective action can be taken. This means making sure that the workflow reports errors effectively (e.g., by using the standard error monitoring program to notify the administrator).

No matter how well designed your workflow, in the event of a failure, it is the business process owner who ultimately must decide what corrective action should be taken and whether fixing the failed workflow is enough to fix the process from a business perspective.

Real-World Examples

Here is one real-world example of a workflow designed to handle errors effectively:

▶ At one point in a workflow, a background work item updates some data. Because other personnel may also be working on the data, locking conflicts can arise. The background work item is designed to report any errors, including locking errors. If you designate the error as temporary, the Workflow Engine repeats the method execution whenever the locking problem occurs.

▶ If the background work item encounters locked data, the Workflow Engine automatically retries the operation several times after a predefined wait (e.g., 10 minutes).

▶ If the retry count is exhausted so that the work item is sent into an error state, the workflow definition sends a dialog work item to a designated agent, asking the agent to complete the activity manually.

Here is another example:

▶ At one point in a workflow, a work item asking for an approve/reject decision is sent to an agent. Maintenance of the agent determination rules is a problem, and frequently no agent is found. The agent determination rules are maintained using a responsibility rule.

▶ The SECONDARY PRIORITIES option is turned on for the responsibility rule. This allows specific agents to be maintained at high priority and default agents to be maintained on a lower priority setting. Thus, when the work item is assigned, the workflow examines the specific agents first, and uses the default agents only if no specific agent is found. The default agents are trained to determine the correct agent, forward the work item to the correct agent, and update the responsibility rule.

Your workflow developer and technical workflow administrators will probably be able to describe many more examples, but it is the business process owner who must decide what suits your organization best.

6.9.3 Crisis Response

Crisis response is the most important part of any workflow administrator's job. When a process fails, the pain felt by the business, and thus by the head of the workflow administrator, can be considerable. It is helpful to have a plan of attack for those panic calls. Most of the following plan is common sense:

▶ Gather the symptoms of the problem from the person reporting it.

▶ Use these symptoms to identify the workflow.

▶ Check whether the workflow is functioning as designed or not.

- If the workflow is working as designed and there is no error, notify the person reporting the problem and the business process owner. Get the business process owner involved in explaining the designed process to the person reporting the error. If appropriate, ask the business process owner to discuss with the person reporting whether the workflow needs to be altered.

- If the workflow is working as designed, but poor data maintenance is affecting it, notify the business process owner. Get the business process owner to help organize corrections to the data and discuss whether corrective action needs to be taken until the data has been fixed. Notify the person reporting the problem of what caused the problem and what is happening to resolve the issue. Avoid laying blame.

- If there is an error, diagnose the error. Notify the business process owner of the problem, and discuss possible resolutions. Notify the person reporting the problem of what caused the problem and what is happening to resolve the issue. Avoid laying blame. Resolve the problem. Notify the person reporting and the business process owner that the problem has been resolved.

- Keep a log of reported errors. For example, note which workflow, what type of error (education issue, process gap, bad data maintenance, error), who reported it, and which business process owner was involved in resolving it.

- Hold a post-mortem with the business process owner. This may be a quick chat or a formal meeting, depending on the nature of the problem. Discuss whether the problem could have been better handled, and whether it is appropriate to change the workflow to help.

- Use the log of reported errors to demonstrate to management which workflows are causing problems so that corrective action can be taken.

Of course, you can additionally create a special workflow to let users report problems. This will help you find and notify the business process owner, and finally update a reported errors log. If the log is kept on the system, then you can easily summarize the data for management.

Often it is not the workflow itself that causes a problem, but an underlying transaction or routine that has failed in a way not anticipated by the workflow. This could be due to any number of causes, such as:

- Changes that were made to the configuration of transactions or routines without considering possible effects on the workflow. This can include seemingly harmless changes, such as adding a new value for a code.

- Changes in values, including master data, used by the transaction or routine for determining agents for follow-on steps in the workflow. This may have the effect that no agent can be determined from the new values.

- Users operating transactions or routines in an unexpected way, possibly due to inadequate or ineffective training in the process.

- Users involved in the process failing to act in a timely manner, especially where underlying transactions/routines use perishable data.

It is normal for many of the reported "workflow" errors to not be workflow errors at all. Remember that the workflow is some person's view of the business process, and even if the problem is not the workflow itself, make sure you at least help coordinate a response. Thus, the workflow administrator's job is not just diagnosing and resolving errors but also acting as an intermediary to ensure that the process as a whole is running smoothly. This part of the job can easily be split between the administrator and the business process owner. You should decide who will be responsible for what before the workflow is activated in the production environment.

6.9.4 Day-to-Day Monitoring

Even when everything is running smoothly, there are still a few things for the workflow administrator to do. The following are mostly "health checks" that should be carried out at least once a day. If you are running a large number of workflows, you should, of course, make these checks more frequently:

- Regularly check your inbox for workflow errors. The error-monitoring job (SWWERRE) will report severe errors such as event linkage errors, binding errors, and rule resolution errors directly to your inbox. This way you may be able to fix a problem before the agents notice it.

- Execute the Error Overview report (Diagnosis of Workflows with Errors, Transaction SWI2_DIAG) to see what errors, if any, are outstanding.

- Check that the workflow background jobs (set up in Transaction SWU3, Workflow Customizing) are running as expected. Transaction SM37 (SYSTEM • SERVICES • JOBS • JOB OVERVIEW) allows you to view the scheduled and processed background jobs.

You normally want to see the following jobs:

- SWWCLEAR
- SWWCOND
- SWWDHEX
- SWWERRE

Caution

If you notice that a background job listed here has ended or is not scheduled to run, do not immediately submit the job. This can have potentially unpleasant consequences. Instead, identify the workflow instances that might be affected by, for example, the job SWWDHEX not running (all workflow instances with monitored deadlines). Then, working with the business process owners, evaluate the impact of restarting workflows that may actually have exceeded their expected deadlines.

At one customer site, it is common practice for the workflow administrator to begin every workday by performing the following tasks:

- Run Transaction ST22 to see if there have been any short dumps for the past 24 hours. In particular, look for any that have the username WF-BATCH.

- Run Transaction SM37 to confirm the proper processing of the workflow background jobs (typically, these jobs are prefaced with SWW*).

- Run Transaction SM58 to see if there are any transactional RFC errors. Pay particular attention to those where the function module is related to workflow (SWW*, for example) or the target system is Workflow_Local. By drilling down on the transaction ID, you should be able to retrieve the work item ID. If so, look for background tasks that might be hanging due to locking or connectivity issues.

- Run Transaction SWI2_DIAG. Of course, if the workflow administrator is already set up to receive these messages in his email client, he will already be proactively working to resolve any issues.

6.9.5 Periodic Reality Checks

We cannot stress enough how important the human role is in squeezing maximum success out of workflow automation. Having a workflow definition that defines the optimum process is half the story — helping the users to support this process is the other half.

Make sure you periodically check all of your different user groups to see that they are using the workflow the way you had intended, especially in the period immediately after going live. Do not be depressed if the users are not following your guidelines — work with the users to improve things. Typical things that go wrong, and the appropriate solutions, are listed in Table 6.5.

Problem	Solution
Agents print out work items on paper, asking other colleagues to fill in the details on paper. The original agent then types the paper input into the relevant transaction.	Check the business logic of your agent determination rules.
Agents are not completing the work on time because they need to research additional information before completing the task.	Try to retrieve this information up front. You could include it in the work item description.
Agents are not completing the work on time because they are being held up by other processes that are not synchronized with this task.	You can synchronize one process with another by using events.
The agent simply does not understand what has to be done (work item description may be missing).	Update the work item description, and provide more background information on the web.
Deadline notifications are going to the managers, but the managers never log on to the system.	It is often more effective sending deadline notifications to the agents themselves rather than the managers.
Authorization problems are preventing an agent from performing a task in the way it was intended.	Authorization needs to be changed or an alternative method used (such as a form).

Table 6.5 Common Agent Problems and Possible Solutions

Luckily, problems like these are more the exception than the rule, but they highlight the importance of performing these reality checks *after* going live. Most of the common problems are easily resolved, but if they are not resolved, they have a big effect on the overall performance of the workflow. Planning one reality check for the period after going live is just as important as planning the user acceptance before going live — there is no excuse for skipping either.

6.9.6 Housekeeping and Archiving

The workflow administrator is also responsible for the health of the Workflow Engine in the long term. An important part of this job is to ensure that old work items and workflow logs are regularly cleared from the system. If you use data from the work items or workflow logs to create reports via the standard workflow reports or SAP NetWeaver Business Warehouse or similar, make sure you run your reports and summarize the relevant data before the work items and logs are deleted.

▸ **Clearing Tasks**

ADMINISTRATION • WORKFLOW RUNTIME • CLEARING TASKS.

The background jobs of the Workflow Engine create job logs that need to be regularly deleted. This task is performed by a report that is controlled by a background job. You can schedule or display the background job. You can also execute the report Execute Clearing Tasks manually.

▸ **Archiving and Reorganization**

ADMINISTRATION WORKFLOW RUNTIME • REORGANIZATION.

These functions include reports for archiving and deleting work items:

▹ **Archive Work Item**

The archive object for work items is called WORK ITEM. Archiving is performed using the standard archiving utilities. Only completed or cancelled work items are archived. If the work item refers to a workflow instance, dependent work items are also archived. If the work item is part of a higher-level work item (i.e., if the work item is a step of a workflow), it cannot be archived until the higher-level work item is completed or cancelled. Both work item data and matching log data are archived.

Container references are archived, but the objects they represent are not affected. For example, if a work item has an object reference to a material master, the reference will be archived, but the material master data will be unaffected.

During archiving, data that is no longer required in the system is checked using application-specific criteria and put in an archive file. The data is not removed from the database. After the files to be archived have been completely copied to the archive file, they can be deleted from the database in a separate program run.

All actions or programs are processed in the background. You can schedule the necessary background jobs in archive management.

▶ **Display Workflows from Archive**
You can use this report to display a workflow for an application object. After the workflow work item determined by the selection criteria is read from the archive, the system displays the workflow log. The functions of the workflow log are not fully available, however.

▶ **Delete Work Item**
This report deletes work items from tables without archiving. It simply deletes whatever work items you ask it to delete without checking; in other words, you could delete work items from an active workflow! It is primarily designed for clearing abandoned work items from development systems. If you do not set the indicator DELETE IMMEDIATELY, the report is executed only on a test basis.
In a production system, you must use archive management to archive and delete work items to ensure data consistency.

> **Caution**
>
> This report should not be used in a production system. Not only does it run slower than the archiving report, but if used incorrectly, it jeopardizes the good working relationship you have built up with your colleagues! Authorization controls should prevent its accidental execution, other than with a tested report variant.

▶ **Delete Work Item History**
This report deletes all workflow log entries relevant to work items (work item history) without archiving. If you do not set the indicator DELETE IMMEDIATELY, the report is only executed on a test basis.

6.9.7 Making the Most of a Precious Resource

You will want to make the most of your workflow administrator and keep the job interesting so that you retain your administrator for as long as possible. Apart from administration itself, your workflow administrator can:

▶ Develop new workflows.

▶ Enhance existing workflows.

▶ Review new and enhanced workflows (quality assurance).

- ▸ Train agents in using their workflows.
- ▸ Educate personnel responsible for data maintenance, particularly maintenance of agent determination rules and workflow-related security.
- ▸ Educate new business process owners in how their workflows work and the sorts of problems/error resolutions that can or have occurred for their workflows.
- ▸ Evangelize workflow to the organization. It helps to use quantitative data produced by reports to show the benefits of workflow. It may also be useful to show how workflows operate in practice, how the various workflow logs and reports show what is happening, and what sort of information can be evaluated after the process has completed.

Once your workflows are in production, you need to know how they are performing. If you want to provide reports to management on workflow execution, you may want to use SAP NetWeaver Business Warehouse as the provider of your workflow reporting data. In this chapter, we introduce SAP NetWeaver Business Warehouse and describe the content delivered in it for workflow reporting.

7 Using SAP NetWeaver Business Warehouse for SAP Business Workflow Reporting

As you begin to use workflows, you will be drawn to questions such as these: How many workflows were executed for purchase requisition approval? How long, on average, did they take? If too long, why, where is the bottleneck? What is the average process time in each person's inbox? If there are long running workflows, where is the time elapse happening? How often does the process exceed deadlines? These questions can all be answered with existing workflow reports. Many of these reports are discussed in Chapter 6, Workflow Administration. However, you may also want to create management-focused reports for workflow execution and how it fits in with your overall process metrics.

To accomplish this, you can use SAP NetWeaver Business Warehouse (SAP NetWeaver BW). SAP NetWeaver BW delivers out-of-the-box content ready to be used for workflow reporting. This content begins with the tools of release SAP NetWeaver 7.0.

This chapter covers the very basics of SAP NetWeaver BW for the workflow person and then focuses on the workflow content for this area. The knowledge provided should be shared with the SAP NetWeaver BW expert. After the SAP NetWeaver BW experts know the content delivered, they will be able to assist in getting the relevant workflow data to the SAP NetWeaver BW system for reporting.

Throughout this chapter, we focus on the actual objects related to workflow that are available in business intelligence (BI) content (see Section 7.2, Standard Workflow Analysis with SAP NetWeaver Business Warehouse). When it comes to building the actual reports you want, we will discuss what is delivered, but we will not cover how to build your own reports; we will leave the building of new reports to the reporting experts.

7.1 SAP NetWeaver Business Warehouse Basics for the Workflow Expert

Before starting, we will assume you are already aware of SAP NetWeaver Business Warehouse. You should already know that this component, in conjunction with the frontend tools of the SAP Business Explorer (SAP BEx), brings together powerful analysis tools, planning and simulation capabilities, and data warehousing functionality. The BI capabilities of SAP NetWeaver are used to integrate data and transform it into practical, timely business information to drive sound decision making, targeted action, and solid business results. We hope your company already has SAP NetWeaver BW in place or an implementation is currently in progress!

> **Note**
>
> If you are the SAP NetWeaver BW expert reading this chapter, everything you need is in Section 7.2, Standard Workflow Analysis with SAP NetWeaver Business Warehouse. This section discusses the content provided by SAP for workflow.

As a workflow person, there are a few basic terms you need to know to more easily communicate with the SAP NetWeaver BW person. To use SAP NetWeaver BW for reporting on workflow, the workflow data needs to exist there. SAP NetWeaver BW uses specific terminology to relate to the data stored there.

The most basic term to understand is *InfoObjects*. Think of InfoObjects as the fields from workflow that we need for reporting. For example, an InfoObject could be a division, product, business unit, company, or even the net sales, revenue total, or sales overhead. InfoObjects include data fields and calculated fields. Important terms to understand include characteristics and key figures:

▶ **Characteristics**

Characteristics are InfoObjects that are based on known data. Characteristics are business evaluation groupings that specify classification options such as purchasing group, division, product, and company.

If we use workflow terms, then InfoObjects characteristics can be work item ID, workflow number, business object, or agent.

▶ **Key figures**

Key figures are InfoObjects based on calculated data. Key figures are values, quantities, or derived data such as net sales, revenue total, and sales overhead.

If we use workflow terms, InfoObject key figures can be total number of work items, time elapsed, or the total number of deadlines.

The other term you should be aware of is *InfoProvider*. InfoProvider is a generic term for objects where data is stored.

▶ **InfoCube**

An example of an InfoProvider is an InfoCube. InfoCubes are containers that hold summarized transaction data in terms of business dimensions. The various dimensions mean users can analyze information from various business perspectives, such as geographic region or type of sales channel.

▶ **Data Store Object**

Another example of an InfoProvider is a Data Store Object (DSO). DSOs also store transaction data, but DSOs store data in flat, transparent database tables.

As a workflow person, why do you care? Because, SAP provides InfoProviders, including InfoCubes, DSOs, InfoSets (InfoSets are joins of other InfoProviders), queries, workbooks, update rules (rules that specify how the data is updated to the InfoProvider), and other items out-of-the-box to use for workflow reporting.

The overall dataflow of getting data from workflow to SAP NetWeaver BW is as follows:

1. A source system provides data (SAP or non-SAP systems).

2. The data are moved to a data source within SAP NetWeaver BW, which is a temporary staging area for the data.

3. A transformation process begins that moves the data to the InfoProviders (could be InfoCube, DSO, or InfoSet).

4. After the data is in the InfoProvider, queries and research against the workflow data can be executed.

7.2 Standard Workflow Analysis with SAP NetWeaver Business Warehouse

Fortunately, SAP NetWeaver BW delivers a rich set of BI content. This content provides predefined, role-based, and task-oriented information models within SAP NetWeaver BW. The objective of BI content is to make relevant information available to specific roles within an enterprise to provide these users with exactly the information they need to fulfill their daily business tasks.

The following are the objects provided as BI content:

▶ Roles and tasks

▶ Global views, workbooks

▶ Queries, web templates

▶ InfoProviders

▶ Extractors and InfoSources

Standard content for SAP Business Workflow and SAP NetWeaver Process Integration (SAP NetWeaver PI) is delivered with SAP NetWeaver 7.0 BI Content Add-On 2. You can use this out-of-box content to analyze process-related information.

> **Note**
>
> SAP NetWeaver PI enables integration between heterogeneous applications and is discussed more in Chapter 15, Service-Enabling Workflows.

The following are examples of questions you can answer with the provided content:

▶ How many processes of type XYZ were executed?

▶ What is the average processing time for a process or a specific step?

▶ How many steps of type XYZ were executed by org unit ABC?

▶ How many approval processes are in status ABC?

▶ How many processes are concerned with purchase orders of value > $10,000?

7.2.1 Data Flow and Overview of Provided Content

Figure 7.1 shows the data flow and some of the workflow content provided in SAP NetWeaver BW. DSOs, update rules, and the data are stored in InfoCubes with aggregated data. There is a cube for the workflow data, and one for the alert data. Notice there are data sources for work item header information, work item history, work item relationship to business object, deadline data, and alert data.

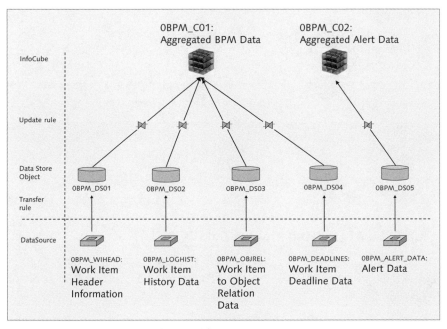

Figure 7.1 Data Flow and Provided Workflow Content

Note
This content was originally created for workflows that execute in SAP NetWeaver PI, commonly referred to as ccBPM processes (cross-component Business Process Management). Therefore, the content includes containers for both work items and alerts because the ccBPM process may trigger the alert framework.

7.2.2 Aggregation Layer

The provided InfoCube is also linked with the employee information, creating the ability to query on the workflow data, including the employee details of the agent.

In Figure 7.2, the InfoCube 0BPM_C01 is combined with the InfoObject 0EMPLOYEE to create an InfoSet combining workflow and agent employee information. Info-Sets are joins, normally between DSOs and InfoObjects. Several queries are provided out-of-the-box.

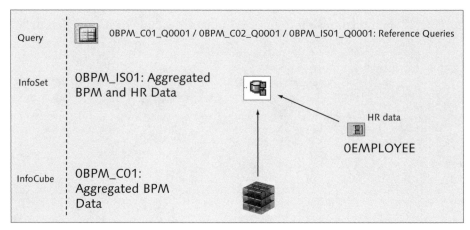

Query	0BPM_C01_Q0001 / 0BPM_C02_Q0001 / 0BPM_IS01_Q0001: Reference Queries
InfoSet	0BPM_IS01: Aggregated BPM and HR Data
	HR data 0EMPLOYEE
InfoCube	0BPM_C01: Aggregated BPM Data

Figure 7.2 Aggregation Layer

7.2.3 InfoCube Aggregated Process Data

The provided InfoCube with the aggregated workflow data contains a great amount of detail on the workflow execution. The following is a sample of some of the data provided:

- **Key Figures** (calculated information)
  - Number of processes (frequency of processes and steps)
  - Number of work items
  - Workflow execution in days (working versus waiting time)
  - Number of deadlines
  - Forwarding history of a work item
- **Characteristics**
  - Object category (e.g., ABAP class or BOR object)
  - Object type (e.g., BUS1006)
  - Business Object instance ID (Business partner number 1234)
  - Parent work item (work item number of WS workflow)

- ▷ Work item ID (work item number of TS task)
- ▷ Work item type (deadline, normal, background, etc.)
- ▷ Agents (actual, forwarded by)
- ▷ Deadline data

- ▶ **Time Characteristics**
  - ▷ Calendar day, month, quarter, year

With this information, you can answer questions such as:

- ▶ How many processes (steps) of a given task type have been executed?
- ▶ How many subprocesses (steps) of a given task type have been executed for a given process?
- ▶ How long does it take (min, mean, max) to execute a step of type X? What is the wait time?
- ▶ How many exceptions are raised during execution of a given step type?
- ▶ Are deadlines due during the execution of a given process (step)?
- ▶ How often was a given step forwarded?
- ▶ How many work items did a given agent create?

7.2.4   Using Standard BI Content

When using the standard BI content, the SAP NetWeaver BW administrator and developer will know what to do to get everything setup. The general outline of what is required includes the following:

- ▶ **Basic settings for source system and SAP NetWeaver BW system**
  The connection between the SAP NetWeaver BW system and the workflow system must be established.

- ▶ **Create SAP source system**
  The workflow system must be defined as an SAP source system in the SAP NetWeaver BW workbench area (Transaction RSA1).

- ▶ **Activate BI Content**
  The SAP NetWeaver BW expert will use Transaction RSOR to install the business content. After the content has been installed, then the workflow data can be loaded into the SAP NetWeaver BW system.

Figure 7.3 shows the content in the SAP NetWeaver BW system for the workflow, so the InfoProviders are included in the content. You can see they start with 0BPM and include the aggregated process data and work item data.

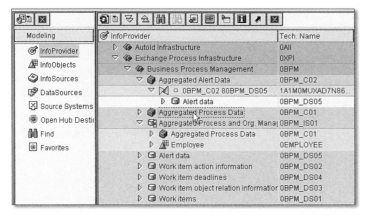

Figure 7.3 BI Content for SAP Business Workflow

PART II
Developing Your Own Workflow

Whether you are building a new workflow from scratch or using an SAP supplied workflow, it is important that you understand the Workflow Builder tool. This chapter gets you started by enabling you to create your first workflow, enhance your workflow, understand data flow, understand types of steps you can use when building a workflow, and get a workflow to production.

8 Creating a Workflow

The central tool for creating, displaying, and processing a workflow is the Workflow Builder. The Workflow Builder is accessed through Transaction SWDD. Alternatively, you can use the menu path TOOLS • BUSINESS WORKFLOW • DEVELOPMENT • DEFINITION TOOLS • WORKFLOW BUILDER • WORKFLOW BUILDER. Within the Workflow Builder, you can create all components of a workflow, including the process flow, the details for each step, and the data flow between steps.

This chapter describes the main features of the Workflow Builder, giving a good foundation to start your own development. To introduce the Workflow Builder, we will explain how to create a simple workflow. We will build upon the simple workflow, enhancing it to show additional features. However, this is not an exhaustive description of all workflow features. When you need more information, the SAP Help Portal (*http://help.sap.com*) describes all of the Workflow Builder features in detail.

Most workflows are started by an *event* (e.g., when a sales order is created, when a quote is entered, when an email arrives, when an error occurs, when a document is printed) that happens in a business application. You define which data from this event needs to be passed to the workflow via *binding*. Events are described in Chapter 13, Using Events and Other Business Interfaces, and Chapter 14, Custom Programs. You can also start any workflow directly, for example, through a transaction code, user interface, or a concept called generic object services (refer to Chapter 13 as well). Because events are a major topic on their own and to keep the focus on the basics of the Workflow Builder, this chapter starts the workflow directly using test tools.

The *workflow container* is used to hold all of the data needed by the workflow. Each workflow has a number of *steps* that execute activities or control the workflow. Data may be passed from one step to another. The activities are handled within *tasks*. You can use the same task in several steps of a workflow (or even in the steps of several different workflows) if you wish. A task has a *task container* that holds all of the data necessary for that task. As described previously, *binding* is the term used to pass data from the workflow container to the task container or from the task container back to the workflow container. Every step has one or more possible *outcomes* depending on the step type, the task, and what the step is doing. For example, for an approval step, possible outcomes might be APPROVE or REJECT.

Expressions are variables used in the workflow to control the workflow (e.g., branches) or to deliver a result (e.g., the agent ID for executing a step). Examples of expressions are simple container elements or the attributes of objects (objects are discussed in Chapter 10, Business Objects, and Chapter 11, ABAP Classes). *Basic data* controls global aspects of the workflow, such as constructor and destructor methods and defaults for the workflow steps. One part of this basic data is version-dependent; the other part applies to all versions. Lastly, the workflow will have one *end point.* There are no hidden exit points.

8.1 Workflow Builder Basics

This section helps you get familiar with the Workflow Builder tool.

8.1.1 Look and Feel of the Workflow Builder

The Workflow Builder provides a graphical view of the workflow definition. The Workflow Builder screen is divided into the following frames (see Figure 8.1 as well); each of the frames can be resized:

▶ **Workflow**
Here you can insert new steps into the workflow definition and process existing ones. Double-clicking on a step displays the associated step definition.

▶ **Overview**
The overview graphic shows all steps in a workflow. The part of the workflow graphic displayed in the Workflow frame is marked with a green rectangle.

Changing the size or position of the rectangle changes the display in the Workflow frame.

▶ **Step types**

STEP TYPE is the default view when you enter a workflow. It lists all of the types of steps you can insert into your process. To insert a new step into the workflow, drag the desired step to the workflow panel, and drop it on the location where you want the step. When dragging in new step types, you will see a plus icon (+) in the appropriate locations to add steps. In Figure 8.1, you can also see a limited list of step options. By resizing the frame, you can see more step options as shown in Figure 8.2.

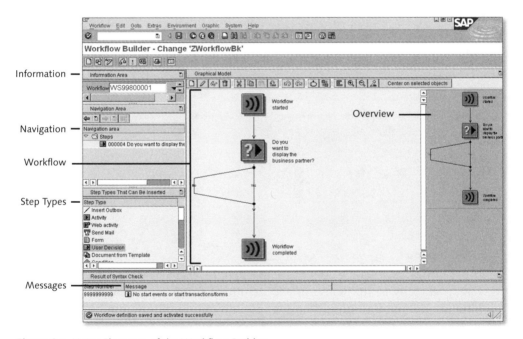

Figure 8.1 Major Elements of the Workflow Builder

▶ **Information**

The information frame (see Figure 8.3) displays which workflow is loaded, the status of the workflow, and the version number of the workflow in the original system. To load a different version, select the version. To load a different workflow, enter the workflow number in the format WS<number> and press [↵]. If you do not know the workflow number, select the arrow and you can search for the workflow.

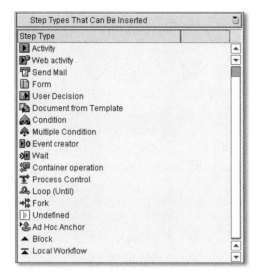

Figure 8.2 More Step Options

Figure 8.3 Information Area

► **Navigation**

The navigation frame contains a list of all of the steps in the workflow. You can jump directly to the relevant step definition from the list. As with all of the frames in the Workflow Builder, you can resize this frame to display the amount of information that you require. The step number corresponds to the number in the workflow technical log (logs are discussed in Chapter 6, Workflow Administration).

► **Messages**

This area contains messages, including general messages and results from where-used lists, syntax checks, and searches.

► **Optional information to display**

In addition to the frames you see in Figure 8.1, you can optionally switch the STEP TYPES to one of the items in Figure 8.4.

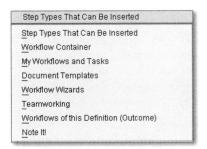

Figure 8.4 Optional Information to Display

▶ **Workflow Container**
The workflow container holds all elements required during the life of the workflow. Container elements will be created automatically, but you can also create your own workflow container elements.

▶ **My Workflows and Tasks**
This frame enables you to quickly see all workflows you have edited. Additionally, you can search for tasks to add to the list. Your choice also determines what is displayed in the Workflow Explorer, which is a separate transaction (SWDM).

▶ **Document Templates**
Document templates add digital documents to a workflow. All of the workflow's document templates that can be used in the step type DOCUMENT FROM TEMPLATE are displayed here. You can generate a where-used list to find the steps in which a document template is used.

▶ **Workflow Wizards**
All Workflow wizards available for the definition of your workflow are displayed here.

▶ **Teamworking**
Here you can search for steps by selected criteria such as who last edited the step in the definition or which steps are grouped together. The result is displayed graphically in the Workflow frame.

▶ **Workflows of this Definition (Outcome)**
Your workflow outbox is displayed here, which displays all currently running workflows for this definition.

▶ **Note It!**
You can create notes and documentation about the workflow in this space.

8.1.2 Building Your First Workflow

In this section, you will build a simple workflow, adding to it step by step. In the end, you will have a workflow with different types of workflow steps:

▶ The first user interaction step asks the user to make a decision: "Do you want to display the business partner?"

▶ If the answer is yes, the business partner is displayed.

▶ If the answer is no, an email is sent to the user, telling the user that he did not choose to display a business partner.

This is a simple scenario that should demonstrate how easy it is to build and execute your first workflow process. Eventually, we will link this workflow to a business partner creation in the application that triggers the workflow, so someone will create a business partner, the workflow will notify that a new business partner has been created, and give the user the option to review the business partner. In this chapter, we focus on creating the basic workflow.

We start by creating the workflow and creating a decision step. To keep it simple, you will be the agent. If you have a test system, you may want to build this process yourself. By following a simple example that becomes more sophisticated as the chapter progresses, you will get a good idea of what workflow can achieve.

Starting the Workflow Builder

When the Workflow Builder is called for the first time or you opt to create a new workflow, a newly created initial workflow definition appears (see Figure 8.5).

This initial workflow has the following parts:

▶ The start of the workflow definition is indicated by WORKFLOW STARTED (▣).

▶ The end of the workflow definition is indicated by WORKFLOW COMPLETED (▣).

▶ The area in which you insert the new workflow definition is indicated by an undefined step with one outcome (▶). Steps are represented by symbols. The name of the outcome is displayed on the arrow leading to the next step in the standard view.

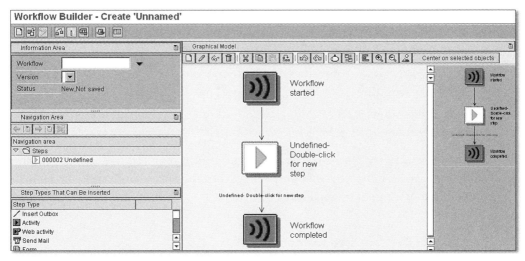

Figure 8.5 Initial Workflow

Create and Save Your First Workflow

Now you are ready to create your first workflow:

1. If you haven't done so yet, navigate to the Workflow Builder by entering Transaction SWDD or using the menu path TOOLS • BUSINESS WORKFLOW • DEVELOPMENT • DEFINITION TOOLS • WORKFLOW BUILDER • WORKFLOW BUILDER.

2. If you do not see an initial workflow similar to Figure 8.5, select WORKFLOW • NEW or click on the CREATE NEW WORKFLOW icon (▯).

3. The workflow now has the title "Unnamed" and has a status, NEW, NOT SAVED.

4. Save your workflow by providing an abbreviation and a name. This is discussed in more detail in Section 8.1.3, Saving, Activating, and Testing. For now, enter a name you will remember later, such as "zFirstWorkfl". You will also need to provide transport information. Assuming this work is being done on a sandbox, select LOCAL OBJECT.

5. Congratulations, you have just created and saved your first workflow.

Your first step illustrates how a user decision works. *User decisions* have their own step type and symbol that looks like this: �}. When a user decision executes, a question together with a predefined list of answers (the possible outcomes) is displayed to the recipients. User decisions are useful in the following situations:

▶ Only *one of several* possible alternatives should be processed in the workflow at execution time. An agent needs to make a business decision about which alternative is appropriate.

▶ An *instruction* (e.g., a user decision with only one outcome) is required to continue the workflow.

▶ For *approval*, *release*, or *status change* steps, the recipient needs to choose whether to approve or reject.

On the DECISION tab, you can make all of the entries required to define an executable user decision. At runtime, the user will see the DECISION TITLE as the SUBJECT text of the work item in his inbox.

Add a User Decision Step to Your Workflow

In the next step of our example, you create a workflow that request a decision about displaying a business partner. The decision will let the user respond "Yes" or "No."

1. In the Workflow Builder, locate the USER DECISION step type in the STEPS THAT CAN BE INSERTED frame.

2. Drag the USER DECISION icon (🔲) to the UNDEFINED step. The step definition of the user decision is now displayed.

3. Enter the title "Do you want to display the business partner?"

4. Enter the decision texts "Yes" and "No." The outcome names default to the decision texts, but you can specify your own names if you prefer.

5. Select EXPRESSION in the AGENTS area of the screen. You will see a dropdown box. Set the agent to the expression to WORKFLOW INITIATOR.

   The workflow initiator is always the person who started the workflow. There are many other options when determining an agent, as discussed in Chapter 5, Agents. However, to keep the first workflow simple, we will route all steps to the workflow initiator.

6. Complete the step by choosing the TRANSFER TO GRAPHIC button (✔).

You have now defined a workflow with a user decision step. However, it must be saved and activated before you can use it.

8.1.3 Saving, Activating, and Testing

When you choose SAVE (🖫) for a new workflow, you must enter an abbreviation and a name for the workflow. You can change both at any time in the basic data of the workflow. You also have to choose a package for transporting the workflow to other systems. If you are in your sandbox environment, then you can select LOCAL OBJECT, which denotes it will not be moved to any other system. The status in the title bar of the Workflow Builder is always visible. After you save your workflow, notice your workflow has a WS name and a number. Workflow templates are saved on the database with a WS and a number. The number range is from the settings you made in Chapter 3, Configuring the System.

To execute your workflow, activate it by choosing ACTIVATE (⚡), which compiles the definition so that the SAP Business Workflow Engine can interpret the workflow for execution. Before activating, the workflow definition is subjected to a syntax check. If you only want to check the syntax of the workflow definition, you can choose SYNTAX CHECK (🔒). All recognized problems are classified as errors or warnings and are output in the message area, together with other useful information. You can process the step in which the error occurs by clicking on the message.

The workflow will only be activated if no syntax errors are found. The status of the workflow is now ACTIVE, SAVED. You can now test your workflow by choosing TEST (🖳).

> **Tip**
>
> When you choose TEST, the workflow is automatically saved, checked, and activated if it is in the *inactive* state and you are in change mode of the Workflow Builder. There is no need to check and activate separately.

Test One

In this example, you will save, activate, and test your workflow:

1. SAVE your new workflow.

2. ACTIVATE the workflow.

3. Test the workflow by choosing TEST (🖳).

4. In the test environment, choose EXECUTE (🕹) to start the workflow.

5. Execute the user decision. Notice the text "Do you want to display the business partner?" and the choices available. Choose YES or NO.

6. Now return to the Workflow Builder (by using the BACK arrow in the TEST screen). Toggle the STEPS THAT CAN BE INSERTED to the WORKFLOWS OF THIS DEFINITION frame.

7. You can double-click on the new entry to see the matching workflow log. Notice the status of the workflow is COMPLETED, and the result of the decision step is displayed in the Result column.

Test Two

In the previous test, you executed the workflow immediately, without navigating to the inbox. In this example, you will test the workflow again but also use the inbox:

1. Test the workflow again, selecting TEST and then EXECUTE as you did in the previous test. The workflow executes immediately.

2. When the decision appears, notice you have three options: YES, NO, and CANCEL AND KEEP WORK ITEM IN INBOX.

3. Select the option CANCEL AND KEEP WORK ITEM IN INBOX.

4. Select BUSINESS WORKPLACE.

5. Select INBOX • WORKFLOW. You will see your work item. Double-click the work item, and select either YES or NO.

6. Use the BACK arrow to return from the inbox to the workflow definition.

7. Notice both times when you execute the workflow, there is only one step, the step to make a decision. Later in this chapter, you will add the step to display a business partner if the choice is YES and to send an email if the choice is NO.

If you tried this example in a test system, you may be surprised that when testing the workflow, you are presented with the decision straight away without having to look in your workflow inbox first. This is because the step is configured as part of the synchronous dialog chain by default (described in Chapter 4, Work Item Delivery). Because the person starting the workflow (you) is identical to the person assigned to perform the first step in the workflow (you), you are presented with the task straight away. To change this behavior, follow these steps:

1. Double-click on the USER DECISION step in your workflow.

2. Select the DETAILS tab.

3. Deselect the checkbox ADVANCE WITH DIALOG.

4. Return to your workflow, and ACTIVATE and TEST it.

5. This time when you test, you receive a message at the bottom of your screen that says *Task started under work item ID ##### (current status: In Process)*. The work item number you receive is the process id. Your workflow has the status IN PROCESS and is in the inbox.

6. To execute the work item, select BUSINESS WORKPLACE.

Congratulations on executing your very first workflow!

8.2 Enhancing Your Workflow

Now that you have created your first workflow, it is time to enhance it. This section covers many topics needed to create workflows. You will add a simple deadline to ensure work is performed on time according to process regulations. You will also add the step to display a business partner, which requires you to create new tasks and understand how objects are used in workflow, including how data is accessed and managed. You will also learn about ad-hoc activities for workflows and the use of review workflows so key or sensitive processes can be closely monitored.

8.2.1 Deadline Monitoring

A major advantage of workflow is the ability to monitor workflow steps according to a predefined schedule. This can be very useful if you want to monitor service level agreements or other process controls that ensure timeframes are enforced in the process. You can monitor a number of different date/time deadlines against each workflow step: requested start, latest start, requested end, and latest end:

▶ If a *requested start* deadline is active for a work item, then the work item only becomes visible to the recipients after the date/time specified. Background work items are started (executed) when the start deadline is reached.

▶ If a *latest start*, *requested end*, or *latest end* deadline is active, then the workflow reacts to the deadline when the specified date/time is reached.

The standard reaction of the workflow system is to send an escalation email. However, you can perform more complex escalation procedures by specifying a deadline outcome name. This lets you add steps to your workflow, which are executed after the deadline fails. This is called a *modeled deadline*.

You define deadlines with respect to a *reference date/time*. The system offers the following reference date/times:

▶ **The creation date/time of the work item**
For example, assume a workflow has 10 steps. Step 6 must be executed within three hours of its start time. The 3-hour clock starts when Step 6 is initiated.

▶ **The creation date/time of the workflow to which the monitored work item belongs**
In this example, assume Step 6 of the 10-step workflow must be completed within 2 days of the workflow starting. The clock for the deadline starts from the moment the workflow was initiated, not from when Step 6 was initiated.

▶ **A date in the form of an expression, which is derived from the context of the application during execution of the workflow**
In this example, assume the step must be completed according to a specific business guideline. Perhaps you have 2 days for a priority B service complaint but only 1 day for a priority A service complaint. Another example would be within 3 days of an invoice posting date. The work item must read the invoice posting date and start the deadline based on the date.

To see the deadline options, double-click on the USER DECISION task in your workflow, and notice the tabs: LATEST END, REQUESTED START, LATEST START, and REQUESTED END. You can activate monitoring of the relevant deadline by selecting one of the deadline tabs, selecting the reference date/time for the deadline, and providing the time details. Activated deadlines are marked with a ringing bell icon (🔔) in the tab index.

If you choose EXPRESSION, you must define the reference date/time by specifying expressions for the date or time. Use the value help (F4) for entering expressions. In the example mentioned previously, of a deadline within three days of a posting date, you need to have the posting date in the workflow container. You then use EXPRESSION to select the posting date variable from the container, and select three days for the time. We will discuss more about how to get the posting date (and other fields) in the container in Section 8.3, Basics of Containers and Bindings.

Tip

The value referenced using the expression must be of data type D for the date and data type T for the time. If you specify a date but *no time*, the system sets the time to 00:00:01 (requested and latest start) or 23:59:59 (requested and latest end).

Specify the deadline by entering duration and an appropriate time unit (e.g., minutes, hours, days). Negative durations can only be used if you define the reference date/time via an expression.

When specifying the type of deadline, the date/time threshold, you can also specify who to notify and what text to send. The text is stored in the details of the task being monitored. For example, if the deadline is on a step to approve purchase requisitions, the task to approve the purchase requisitions holds the text that will be used in case of a deadline. Each task can have its own deadline text.

Tip

With the standard deadline reaction, the status of the monitored work item is unchanged. The work item still has to be executed by one of its recipients before the workflow can continue. If the monitored work item is to be aborted when the deadline is exceeded, you need to use the modeled deadline reaction. Refer to Chapter 9, Advanced Workflow Design Techniques, and to Appendix A, Tips and Tricks, for more details.

Add a Deadline to Your Process

In the following example, you add a deadline to your user decision step and test the deadline:

1. Return to your workflow definition in the Workflow Builder.

2. Double-click on the USER DECISION step. In your user decision step, choose the LATEST END tab.

3. For the reference date and time, select WORK ITEM CREATION.

4. For the TIME field, select MINUTES and enter "2". This means the user will have two minutes from the moment the work item is created to complete the work item.

5. For the RECIPIENT OF MESSAGE WHEN LATEST END MISSED, select EXPRESSION and then select WORKFLOW INITIATOR from the dropdown menu.

6. Test your changed workflow (remember, saving and activating is performed automatically when you choose the TEST option from the Workflow Builder). This time, do not execute the decision step (cancel out of it if you have not removed the ADVANCE WITH DIALOG checkbox).

7. Navigate to the Business Workplace.

8. Wait for the deadline to be exceeded, and you will receive a deadline message in the Business Workplace: The DEADLINE MESSAGES folder contains a message that the deadline was missed. The OVERDUE ENTRIES folder displays all work items that have an overdue deadline.

Tip

The background job for deadline monitoring must be scheduled so that the Workflow Engine can monitor and escalate deadlines. This job is explained in Chapter 3, Configuring the System. When the deadline job runs, all exceeded deadlines are escalated. If you are running this job periodically, then the actual time of escalation is delayed until the job next executes. Use Transaction SWWB to have the job run immediately.

8.2.2 How to Create and Use Tasks

In this section, you add more tasks to our workflow. You will learn how to create a task to display a business partner and how to create a task to send an email. Most steps in your workflow will be tied to business functions: updating a business partner, posting an invoice, approving a purchasing document, updating employee data, and so on. To execute business functions, you use the ACTIVITY steps (▶).

Activity steps are related to tasks, which start with TS. Workflows are created with WS and a number. The number range is determined from the settings you made in Chapter 3, Configuring the System. Those same number ranges are used for TS steps within your workflow.

The user decision step you used earlier is based on a generic decision task (TS00008267) as standard. If you double-click on the user decision step in your workflow, select the CONTROL tab, and you will see the task number. After a TS task is created, it can be reused in multiple workflows.

In this section, you create tasks from within the workflow. However, you can also create tasks independent of the Workflow Builder using Transaction PFTC.

Regardless of how you call the task definition, the same screen for editing the task definition is displayed.

Explanation of Standard Task (TS): Create Screen

Before creating a task to display a business partner, a discussion of the options available when creating a task is needed. Figure 8.6 shows the fields available when creating a new task.

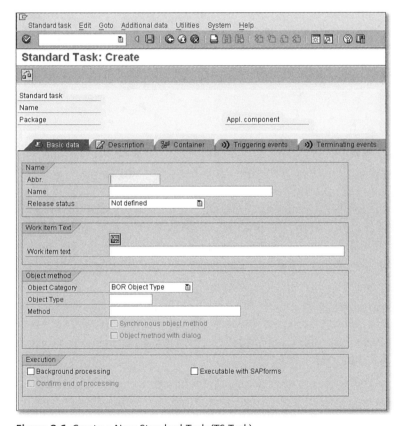

Figure 8.6 Create a New Standard Task (TS Task)

Every task must answer two major questions:

▸ *What* should the task do (*display* a business partner, *update* a business partner, *approve* employee leave)?

▸ *Who* can do the task?

As the options in Figure 8.6 are discussed, keep in mind that the task must always be able to address the "what" and "who" questions:

▶ ABBR. is the abbreviated name of the task. You use this name when searching for the task. You should have a naming convention for creating both TS tasks and WS tasks.

> **Tip**
>
> It is a good idea to decide on a naming convention for task abbreviations to make tasks easier to find, such as a specific prefix for all tasks in the project. Customers normally define their own naming conventions. Some customers may start all of their workflows with Z. Others may use the first two letters as functional area, then an underscore, and nine characters of text. An example might be HR_DisplPern for display personnel work-flow that is part of the HR area, or ZHR_DisplPern if you want to start all workflows with a Z to indicate they are custom built.

▶ NAME is the full name of the task.

▶ WORK ITEM TEXT is the description that will appear in the inbox at runtime. The work item text is very important because it is the first thing the user will see, and it should describe the task for the user. You can pass variables (such as business partner number, invoice amount, etc.) into the work item text to give the item more meaning. Keep in mind that users may have hundreds of work items in their inbox, so the text should be meaningful. During your design phase, you should work with the business users to determine brief but meaningful text to use.

▶ OBJECT CATEGORY describes how you link this task to actual business data. The options available are Business Object Repository (BOR) objects and ABAP classes. BOR objects are discussed in detail in Chapter 10, Business Objects; ABAP Classes are discussed in Chapter 11.

▶ OBJECT TYPE is where you enter the actual object name. The trick to this field is you need to know which object to use. Over time, you will become familiar with the objects provided by SAP, and you will become very familiar with the ones you create yourself. Common BOR objects include: BUS1006 (Business Partner), BUS2032 (Sales Order), and PERSDATA (Employee Personal Data).

▶ METHOD is the action you want to execute for the task. Examples of methods include create, display, update, block, remove block, approve, and release.

The combination of the OBJECT and METHOD fields answers the "what" question. You need both an object type and method to know what the task can do. When you insert the method, the system takes the following from the definition of the object method, as applicable:

- Synchronous or asynchronous object method
- Object method with or without dialog

You cannot change these. If method parameters are defined for the object method, the system gives you the option of creating matching container elements automatically in the task container. The names of these container elements are then identical in the task container and the method container.

> **Tip**
>
> Methods that you execute with a task may be synchronous or asynchronous methods. Section 8.2.3, Using Asynchronous Tasks, explains the differences and their effect on modeling.

- To answer the "who" question, from Figure 8.6, follow the menu path ADDITIONAL DATA • AGENT ASSIGNMENT • MAINTAIN. You are assigning all of the agents who could ever possibly do this task. (Agents are discussed in detail in Chapter 5, Agents, and Chapter 12, Agent Determination Rules.) For example, if the task is displaying a business partner, who are all of the people who would ever need to display a business partner, or approve a purchase requisition, or enter an expense report. The "who" assigned here is who in the broadest sense of the term. In our examples, we will normally make the task a GENERAL task, which means everyone is a possible agent. To make a task a general task, select ATTRIBUTES • GENERAL TASK.

In addition to the fields in Figure 8.6, also notice the following tabs:

- The DESCRIPTION tab enables you to add a longer task description. This *task description* appears in the users' inbox at runtime. The *work item text* is the one liner that appears in the inbox, and the task description is the long description the user will see after selecting the work item. The *task description* can also have variables to better describe to the user what the task is and what is required for the task.

  The DESCRIPTION tab also enables you to add texts for the deadlines. This is the text the user will see when a deadline has passed. For example, if a user has two days to update a business partner, after the deadline has passed, a note is sent to the manager that the deadline has passed. The note sent to the manager contains the text entered in the deadline task description. There is text for each type of deadline: Latest end text, Requested end text, and Latest start text. Additionally, there is also Completion text, which is used for notifications (discussed in Section 8.2.5, Notifications).

▶ The Container tab contains data in the task container. The task container holds all required runtime data. The container always contains what object is used and who is executing the task.

▶ The Triggering events and Terminating events tabs contain events that can be used to stop and start this specific task. This topic is a bit more advanced and is discussed in Chapter 13, Using Events and Other Business Interfaces.

▶ The Default rules tab is used when the task will execute outside of the workflow template (WS task).

An example is a task that starts due to an inbound IDoc (Intermediate Document). Inbound IDocs normally execute a single TS task, not a full WS workflow. In that case, you must know who should get this task at runtime. For example, if an inbound sales order IDoc fails, you may want to route it to the sales area manager for the sales organization. You would use a rule to find the correct sales area manager as discussed in Chapter 12, Agent Determination Rules.

Creating a Task to Display the Business Partner

Now you will create the task to display the business partner. In this example, you add a step to display a business partner if the result from the user decision step is Yes.

1. Return to your workflow in the Workflow Builder.

2. Drag an Activity step (▶) to the Yes branch of your user decision.

3. Select the Create task option from the button list on the button next to Task as shown in Figure 8.7.

4. Enter appropriate texts for the abbreviation and name. For example:

   ▶ Abbr: zbp_display

   ▶ Name: Display business partner

5. Enter the following for the business object fields:

- ▶ OBJECT CATEGORY: BOR Object type

- ▶ OBJECT TYPE: BUS1006

- ▶ METHOD: Display

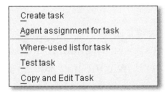

Figure 8.7 Dropdown to Create a Task from the Workflow Builder

Tip

When entering the method, you can see a list of all methods for the object by selecting the dropdown.

6. If you see a message *Transfer missing elements from the object method?*, answer YES (the system is helping you set up the task container; more on this later in Section 8.3, Basics of Containers and Bindings).

7. Provide a work item text. Remember, this is the text the user will see at runtime. To give the text more meaning, we will pass in variables from the business object. Enter the text "Review business partner".

8. Select the INSERT VARIABLES icon (). Select BUS1006 • BUSINESS PARTNER NUMBER. Notice your work item text now has the following variable: &_WI_OBJECT_ID.BUSINESSPARTNER&. Place your cursor at the end of the text, and select the description for the business partner by inserting the variable BUS1006 • DESCRIPTION.

9. Your work item text should now read *Review business partner &_WI_OBJECT_ID.BUSINESSPARTNER& &_WI_OBJECT_ID.DESCRIPTION&.*

10. SAVE (💾) the task. (You need to select LOCAL OBJECT or a development class.)

11. Set up the security for this task by selecting ADDITIONAL DATA • AGENT ASSIGNMENT • MAINTAIN. Normally you would assign the appropriate security role or organizational objects here, but for simplicity, make this a general task by selecting ATTRIBUTES • GENERAL TASK.

12. Return to the workflow. The workflow suggests a binding between the workflow and the task. Accept the binding by choosing ENTER (✔). Set the agent of

the activity step to the workflow initiator expression using the dropdown help.

13. When you return to your workflow, you should see your new task as part of the YES branch from the user decision task. Now when the workflow executes, you can display a business partner.

14. For testing purposes, you need to provide this business partner number when the workflow starts. To do this, toggle the STEPS THAT CAN BE INSERTED frame to WORKFLOW CONTAINER, and double-click on the workflow container element BUS1006.

15. Select the PROPERTIES tab, and select the IMPORT parameter setting. This means the business partner can be imported when the workflow starts. Normally, this is set so that the application can pass the business partner to the workflow container. If the flag is not set, then the business partner is solely contained in the context of the workflow.

16. Test your workflow. To do so, you must enter an object instance of your business partner object type. Select BUS1006. At the bottom of the screen, you see the OBJECT TYPE and a KEY. Select the dropdown in the KEY field, and enter a valid business partner number. (If you do not have a business partner and are on a sandbox system, you can use Transaction BP to create a business partner. When creating a business partner, it is easiest if you create a person and just provide first name and last name.)

17. After you enter a valid business partner number, select SAVE in the TEST DATA area of the screen. This enables you to select LOAD in subsequent tests to use the same business partner number, instead of entering the business partner number for each test.

18. After you start your workflow, you should execute two tests. In the first test, select YES to the user decision. When you select YES, a business partner should display. In the other test, select NO to the user decision, and the workflow should end.

19. Remember, you can see each execution in the WORKFLOWS OF THIS DEFINITION (OUTCOME) frame.

Hint

When testing the workflow, the first step may or may not start automatically depending on the setting of the ADVANCE WITH DIALOG flag in the DETAILS tab of the task.

> **Tip**
>
> The basic data is used to identify a task. Each task is identified by the object identifier TS (for standard task) and an eight-digit task number automatically allocated by the system during creation.

You must specify a package when saving the task in the same way that you specified a package when saving the workflow definition. The transport object in this case is PDTS. If you use LOCAL OBJECT, this means the workflow cannot be transported to another system.

> **Tip**
>
> If you also assign your tasks and workflows to a task group, you can use the task group as a logical package for the complete scenario. This is not only useful for documenting which workflows are the active valid workflows (as opposed to test workflows or scrapped versions) but also makes navigation in the Workflow Builder and Workflow Explorer easier.

Remember the importance of the work item text for your task. The work item text is displayed in the inbox, in the work item selection reports, and in the workflow log. If a work item text is not specified, the name of the task is used instead. You can use expressions within the work item text. They are replaced at execution time with the current values from the task container.

Note that container elements used in the work item text must be filled using a binding. To use expressions in the work item text, position the cursor at the relevant point in the text, and choose EXPRESSION ( ).

> **Tip**
>
> If you are looking at an SAP task or a task imported from another system in display mode, you can redefine the task description (which appears in the inbox as the work item text). Choose the REFIND WORK ITEM TEXT icon ( ), and enter a new text to replace the original text. Using the REDEFINE option overlays your version over the original task description as an extension rather than as a modification.

8.2.3 Using Asynchronous Tasks

A full description of the reasons for using asynchronous methods and the consequences is given in Chapter 10, Business Objects, but for the time being, just think of them as methods that are not completed until the application itself confirms completion by sending an event to the workflow. For an example, think of a step that deletes something: An employee requests vacation and then later decides he does not want the vacation. The original request is deleted.

Deleting is a natively asynchronous activity. You do not want the task completed until the deletion is completed, so a delete task is normally an asynchronous task. From the Workflow Builder point of view, an asynchronous task requires the terminating events to be activated as outcomes of your step. When modeling an activity step, you can bind the results of a synchronous method to a workflow when the method is completed. However, the asynchronous method cannot return information to the workflow via the bindings from method to task, task to workflow. Instead, you define at least one terminating event. You can bind data from the terminating event to the task.

The *terminating events* of a task express the possible end statuses of the task. A terminating event always refers to the specific object for which the event must be triggered. For example, if the work item deletes document 123456, then the work item should only be completed when the event "document 123456 is deleted" occurs and not when any other document is deleted.

When the work item is created, the Workflow Engine automatically registers that this specific work item is waiting for a terminating event for the specific object involved. This is called an *event instance linkage* (refer to Chapter 13, Using Events and Other Business Interfaces, for more details). You define the object for which the event must be triggered in the terminating event definition using a container element, referenced to the event's object type, in the task container.

Example

For example, the event DELETED of object type BUS2032 (Sales Order) is defined as a terminating event for a task. At runtime, the sales order 123456 is passed via the task container. The work item is now only terminated if the sales order 123456 is deleted and the event BUS2032.DELETED is triggered for that sales order. If another sales order is deleted, the work item is not terminated.

If a work item is terminated by an event, the execution of the workflow is continued by a matching outcome. You must activate this outcome, or the terminating event will be ignored. The method does not necessarily have to have been executed before the event occurs. If a work item is aborted, or undefined processing statuses arise, the work item is not terminated because no event is created. Only when the terminating event is received will the work item finish and the workflow continue.

Within a TS task, you maintain the terminating events on the TERMINATING EVENTS tab. You specify a container element of the task container that at runtime will contain a reference to the relevant object. This is generally the task container element _WI_Object_ID. The fields OBJECT TYPE CATEGORY and OBJECT TYPE are filled automatically.

You identify the event by specifying its event name. The event must be defined for this object type. The workflow system creates the event instance linkage required at runtime and activates it. To check the properties of the terminating event, choose the SETTINGS icon (). The properties of the instance linkage are displayed and can be changed.

8.2.4 How to Access Data and Activities

To access data, activities, and events within your workflows, they need to be defined as parts of an object. The object could be part of the Business Object Repository (BOR) (discussed in Chapter 10, Business Objects) or an ABAP class (discussed in Chapter 11, ABAP Classes). Objects can be used in many different workflows, tasks, and rules. SAP components contain many predefined business object types and ABAP classes. These predefined data, activities, or events can be used as is, or you can create your own:

▶ Objects describe, for a particular business entity, the data (attributes), functions (methods), and events used in a workflow. In our example, we used business object type BUS1006, representing a business partner.

▶ Data relating to a business entity needs to be defined as an *attribute* of a business object type before it can be used in a workflow. Attributes are defined as part of the object type to which they are most closely related. For example, the attributes Material name and Material number are defined within the Material object type, but Order number and Order value are defined as part of the Order object type. In other words, the attributes describe data related to the business object.

▶ Activities to be performed on or by using a business entity are defined as *methods* of a business object type before they can be used in a workflow. Every object has methods that define activities that can be executed on that object or its data (e.g., "create business partner" or "update business partner"). Within the method, you can call SAP functions, your own functions, or other external applications.

► Events are another important component of an object. The events describe the status changes that an object can undergo (e.g., "business partner deleted" or "business partner changed"). A workflow can be started, canceled, or resumed (wait step) when an event of this kind is raised. Just like attributes and methods, events need to be defined as part of a business object before they can be used in a workflow. Events are discussed in Chapter 13, Using Events and Other Business Interfaces.

If you want to use workflow to implement a business process, this is a rough picture of what is involved in accessing the relevant data and functions:

1. Identify all business entities involved in your business process. You sort out which business functions and events you want to map in your scenario and which data you want to access.

2. Check whether the relevant business object types with their methods, attributes, and events are defined in the BOR or as an ABAP class. The grouping of object types in the application component hierarchy, and the option of searching generically for parts of a name, help when looking for existing object types:

   ► If you find an object type whose definition meets your requirements, you can use it without making any modifications.

   ► If you find an object type whose definition does not quite meet your requirements, you can extend its definition.

   ► If you do not find a suitable object type, you can define your own object type.

3. Use the methods, attributes, and events of the object type in the relevant parts of your workflow.

Further information on how to create your own object types or extend existing object types can be found in Chapter 10, Business Objects, and Chapter 11, ABAP Classes.

Adding an Attribute of a Business Partner Object to a User Decision Step

In this example, you add an attribute of the business partner object BUS1006 to your user decision step:

1. Return to your workflow, and double-click on the user decision step.

2. Add a variable in your user decision title, for example, *Do you want to display business partner &1?*, and set PARAMETER 1 to the description of your business partner (&BUS1006.Description&) using the input help.

3. TEST your workflow. If you saved the data from a previous test, select LOAD. Otherwise, you must enter an object key of your business object type before executing the workflow test. You can reuse your test data for each execution by selecting SAVE in the TEST DATA area after you select a business partner from the dropdown. On subsequent tests, select LOAD from the TEST DATA area to load your business partner number.

Now that you have tested the workflow a couple of times, you know that after you start the test, you can go to the Business Workplace to see the work item. This time, notice the parameters in the work item text for the user decision task.

8.2.5 Notifications

You have the option to notify someone when a step is completed. It is a simple notification that sends a text note (not a work item) to a specified user when a step completes. Normally it is used to inform someone when a critical step has completed.

Adding a Notification to the Business Partner Display Step

Follow these steps to add a notification so someone will be notified when the business partner display step is completed:

1. Return to your workflow in the Workflow Builder.

2. Double-click on your step to display the business partner (in the YES branch of the user decision step).

3. Select the NOTIFICATION tab. Notice in this tab you update *who* to send the notification to and *what* the notification text should say.

4. Currently there is no specific NOTIFICATION (COMPLETION) text. Double-click on the link to add a notification text.

5. Ensure you are in change mode for the task (using the DISPLAY – CHANGE icon to toggle between change and display mode).

6. Select the DESCRIPTION tab. For the TEXT TYPE, select COMPLETION TEXT. Select the CHANGE TEXT icon so you can update the text.

7. After you have added a COMPLETION TEXT, save your task, and use the BACK arrow to return to the workflow.

8. Update the MESSAGE RECIPIENT FOR COMPLETION to be the WORKFLOW INITIATOR.

9. TEST the workflow again. Be sure to follow the path to display the business partner. After the workflow completes, go to the Business Workplace. You will see the notification text in the DOCUMENTS folder of the inbox.

8.3 Basics of Containers and Bindings

Containers and bindings are a bit tricky when first learning workflow, but as you understand the stability, flexibility, and scalability they provide, you will soon come to appreciate the powerful use of binding between containers. Here are a few of the advantages:

▶ You can reuse elements in your workflow.

▶ You can make major changes to activities within the process without jeopardizing the process as a whole (or vice versa).

▶ Even when the applications that trigger the workflows are changed from release to release, your workflow is sheltered from these changes.

▶ You can use parallel activities within the workflow without worrying about data reconciliation problems or interference between the activities.

Containers and bindings are explained in more detail in Chapter 9, Advanced Workflow Design Techniques. This section provides an introduction to how they are used by first focusing on the task container and then focusing on the workflow container.

All of the data needed to execute the method or to display in the task text must be available in the task container. Container elements for the task container are generated automatically when you enter a method in the task. The container elements needed for the execution are recognized by the workflow system, and the workflow system prompts you to automatically insert these container elements in the task container. In addition to what is automatically provided in the containers, you may want to create your own container elements in the task container and define a binding between the task and the workflow so that these container elements are filled at runtime.

8.3.1 How to Create Containers and Bindings for Tasks

The task container is edited on the CONTAINER tab page (refer to Figure 8.6 as well). To enable the method to process the data, you may (optionally) define a binding from the task container to the method container. The task object itself is automatically bound to the method container. For other method parameters, the system makes a proposal for the binding that can be reviewed on the BASIC DATA tab of the task by selecting the BINDING OBJECT METHOD icon.

However, not defining any binding between task and method is simpler and offers a performance gain, provided the container element names are the same in both containers. In this case, the contents of the task container are matched by element name and automatically copied to the method container (for all elements defined in the method). The same applies to the reverse binding.

Variables used in your work item texts and descriptions are also bound from the task container. In the "Creating a Task to Display the Business Partner" example in Section 8.2.2, How to Create and Use Tasks, you added a task to your workflow and bound the business partner number and description to the work item text. As a reminder, to add variables while editing your description, choose INSERT EXPRESSION to choose a variable from the task container. You can add as many variables to the text as you want (up to the limit of the text field).

8.3.2 Creating Container Elements in the Workflow Container

The work item text of the user decision can display current runtime values from the workflow. You can integrate these values by including variables relevant to the decision directly in the work item text. The variables are replaced at runtime with values from the matching workflow container elements.

Of course, this is just one example of how container elements are used in the workflow, but it is very easy for you to try yourself. (Using the workflow container to link variables for the user decision work item text was done in an example provided in Section 8.2.4, How to Access Data and Activities.)

1. Create container elements by selecting the WORKFLOW CONTAINER frame and double-clicking on the <DOUBLE-CLICK TO CREATE> line in the workflow container tray.

2. Enter the technical name of the container element in the ELEMENT field.

3. Give each container element a technical name (minimum of two characters) that can be used to identify it uniquely. The technical name is not case sensitive and must begin with a letter, but it can be followed by letters, underscores, or digits. Because the technical name is not translated, it is conventional to use English words in multilanguage environments.

4. Under TEXTS, maintain the NAME and the DESCRIPTION (OPTIONAL). Both of these can be translated in multilanguage environments.

5. According to the data type reference of the container element, make the following entries on the DATA TYPE tab: First check whether your container element is modeled on one of the predefined types. Choose the SELECTION OF PRE-DEFINED TYPES icon (🎲), and double-click to choose the predefined type. The system carries out the necessary entries for the data type. If you want to create a container element that is not predefined, make the following entries, depending on the data type:

   ▶ **Object type**
   Choose OBJECT TYPE, select an object type category, and enter the name of the object type. Examples include a specific BOR object (such as BUS1006) or a specific ABAP class.

   ▶ **ABAP Dictionary Reference**
   Choose STRUCTURE and FIELD. In this case, you enter a table/structure and field that the container data should be based on. This reserves space in the container equivalent to the field you enter. It works as a "like" statement.

   ▶ **ABAP Dictionary Data Type**
   Choose ABAP DICTIONARY REFERENCE, and enter the table or structure in the field TYPE NAME. Use this to provide a data type to describe the field in the workflow container.

Tip
The specification of an object type is not mandatory. If no object type is specified, the container element can be assigned a reference to any object type at runtime. However, binding restrictions may limit its use later in the workflow.

Tip

A common misconception of workflow is that only one business object can be used per workflow. This is *not* the case. Often cross-application workflows use several different business objects, and the flow itself forms the link between them. A simple example of such a scenario is the link between a scanned document (e.g., the object type IMAGE) and the invoice record that is posted to the database (e.g., the object type BUS2081).

On the PROPERTIES tab, select whether the new element is to be an IMPORT and/or an EXPORT element. Mark an import element as MANDATORY if applicable. Import means this field will be passed from the application to the workflow. For example, a document is created, triggering an event that starts a workflow. For workflow to receive the document information from the application, the receiving element in the workflow container must be marked as IMPORT.

8.3.3 Changing Container Elements

For any workflow container element you add, it is your responsibility to bind data to the workflow element; otherwise, the element will be empty. There are several ways to get data into your custom workflow container elements:

▶ **By initial values**
You can assign an initial constant value to a container element. When the workflow is executed, the container element is initially filled with this value. Any changes made to the contents of the container element will overwrite this value.

▶ **By a container operation step**
A container operation step lets you fill a container element with a constant or another container element.

▶ **By bindings in a workflow step**
From any workflow step that can output data to the workflow (such as activity steps, user decision steps, document from template steps, etc.), you can transfer data from the task container of the workflow step to the workflow container (or vice versa) via container bindings. Think of bindings as the rules for parameter passing within your workflow.

▶ **By bindings from an event**
Whenever your workflow responds to an event — for example when it is started by a triggering event — data can be passed from the event container to the workflow container. If you want to pass data from a triggering event to

start your workflow, the workflow container elements to be filled from the event container need the IMPORT flag turned on before the bindings can be defined. Refer to Chapter 13, Using Events and Other Business Interfaces, for more details.

Adding a Custom Workflow Container Element and Binding Data to the Element

In this example, you experiment with adding workflow container elements and manipulating them. This example shows how to add and use your own container elements. In this example, you add a container element to represent a date, add another date to this date, and use the new date in the user decision. (Normally you do not add two dates together, so this is not something you would probably use in production, but it will get you familiar with working with container elements.)

1. Toggle to the WORKFLOW CONTAINER frame, and create a new container element by double-clicking on the <DOUBLE-CLICK TO CREATE> line. Provide the following information:
   - ELEMENT: NewDate
   - NAME: MyNewDate
   - SHORT DESCRIPTION: My first try with containers

2. Select the ABAP DICTIONARY REFERENCE:
   - STRUCTURE: SYST
   - FIELD: DATLO

   You can now see the new field in your workflow container.

3. Switch from the WORKFLOW CONTAINER frame to the STEPS THAT CAN BE INSERTED FRAME. Drag the step type CONTAINER OPERATION to the line before the USER DECISION step, and enter the following information:
   - STEP NAME: AddDates
   - OUTCOME NAME: two dates added
   - RESULT ELEMENT: Use the dropdown to select NEWDATE.
   - EXPRESSION: Use the dropdown to see all of the options in the workflow container. Select the object BUS1006, and select CREATEDON.
   - OPERATOR: Use the dropdown to select ADD.
   - EXPRESSION: Use the dropdown to select SYSTEM FIELDS. Then select TIMLO.

4. In your Workflow Builder, you now have an ADDDATES step before the user decision step. You will display the result of the container operation step in the user decision step.

5. Double-click on the user decision step. Set PARAMETER 2 to your NEWDATE container element. Use the dropdown help to do this.

6. Use the variable in your work item text by writing &1 in the text where you want the value to appear, for example, *Do you want to display the business partner &1 &2?*

Tip

The &2 declares this to be a reference to parameter 2 of this step definition. It is optional — you can just use &. However, in a multilingual environment, specifying the number is very useful because the variables often appear in a different order in the translation.

---

7. SAVE, ACTIVATE, and TEST your workflow. Notice the date you see in the work item text. It should be a date far in the future. (Keep in mind the only point for this example was to show how to add a workflow container element and use the container operation step type.)

A Word About the Task Description on the User Decision Step

Although the short text in the generic decision is part of the step definition (to make things simpler), the long text is part of the task. To create your own long text, you can copy task TS00008267 to a new task and write a suitable task description for this new task. You may select your own variables and add these to the task container. After you have created your task, substitute it into the step's CONTROL tab in place of task TS00008267. Do not forget that you need to assign possible agents to your new task.

8.4 Steps

As well as the step types USER DECISION, CONTAINER OPERATION, and ACTIVITY shown earlier, there are other step types available for modeling a workflow. Although ACTIVITY is the main step type to link the workflow to the application, there are many other step types needed to control the workflow process.

8.4.1 What Other Step Types Exist

Table 8.1 shows all step types available in SAP NetWeaver 7.0. The step types cover all of the functions you need to control the workflow process, from what business functions to call, to looping, conditions, container manipulation, using multiple branches, and many other functions.

Step Type	Icon	Runtime Function
ACTIVITY		Execution of a task or subworkflow. At runtime, data is passed from the task or subworkflow to the workflow container on creation of the matching work item, and vice versa on work item completion.
AD HOC ANCHOR		In the definition, you specify workflows that can replace this step. At runtime, an authorized user can select one of the specified workflows. The steps of this workflow then dynamically replace the AD HOC ANCHOR.
CONDITION		Depending on the result of the CONDITION, either the true or the false path is followed. In the condition editor, you can simulate the results of the condition to make the testing of complex conditions easier.
CONTAINER OPERATION		The CONTAINER OPERATION is used to perform arithmetic operations or value assignments to workflow container elements using constants and data in the workflow container. This includes operations on multiline container elements, for example, appending to a list.
DOCUMENT FROM TEMPLATE		A digital document is created from a document template using variables in the text that are filled during workflow execution using the workflow container elements. The workflow container receives a new container element that contains the document ID.
EVENT CREATOR		An event is raised. You fill the event container from the workflow container.
FORK		A FORK is used for parallel processing. You can define how many parallel branches exist and how many branches must be completed for the fork to terminate and the workflow to continue. Alternatively, simply define an end condition.

Table 8.1 Step Types

Step Type	Icon	Runtime Function
FORM		A structure-based container element can be displayed, processed, or approved as a FORM. The data is transferred directly from the workflow container and back again.
LOOP (UNTIL)		A sequence of steps is processed at least once and then repeatedly until the defined termination condition occurs.
MULTIPLE CONDITION		Based on the value of a workflow container element, one of several branches defined in the workflow definition is processed. Any value not specifically assigned to a branch can be processed in an OTHER VALUES branch.
PROCESS CONTROL		This can be used to cancel the execution of a work item or workflow or set a work item to obsolete, so that alternative steps can be taken in the PROCESSING OBSOLETE branch.
SEND MAIL		The text entered in this step type is sent as an email. The task required and the necessary bindings are automatically created by the workflow system.
BLOCK		A BLOCK is a modeling construct that enables you to model a group of steps together. The block has a data interface. Additionally, you can add deadlines to a block, ensuring the entire block must be completed in a certain timeframe. Blocks are discussed in more detail in Chapter 9, Advanced Workflow Design Techniques.
LOCAL WORKFLOW		A LOCAL WORKFLOW is a "free-floating" block that is not connected to the main workflow. Local workflows are triggered by events and enable a design element to be incorporated into the workflow. They may need to execute multiple times during a workflow execution, or may not be executed at all during a workflow execution. Local workflows are discussed in more detail in Chapter 9, Advanced Workflow Design Techniques.
UNDEFINED STEP		An UNDEFINED STEP can be used as a placeholder during development. These steps are ignored at runtime.
USER DECISION		The agent is asked a question and given a predefined list of answers. Each predefined answer is a separate branch in the workflow.

Table 8.1 Step Types (cont.)

Step Type	Icon	Runtime Function
WAIT FOR EVENT		The system waits for a specific event. The work item is only completed if the expected event occurs. Data from the event container can be sent to the workflow container using a binding.
WEB ACTIVITY		The selected container elements are posted using HTTP in an XML or SOAP message. This step can also wait for a message reply.

Table 8.1 Step Types (cont.)

8.4.2 How to Insert New Steps

When inserting new steps, you drag and drop the step type to the location where you want the step. You can insert steps before or after an existing step. Table 8.2 provides an overview of how to insert steps into a workflow.

Where Do You Want to Insert the Step?	What Do You Have to Select?
After a step	Drag and drop on the outcome of the preceding step.
Before a step	Drag and drop on a step to insert before the step.
As a new branch of a fork	Drag and drop on the FORK symbol (⇒) at the start of the fork.

Table 8.2 Insert Steps Into a Workflow

The MY WORKFLOWS AND TASKS frame provides an efficient way of inserting tasks as activities in your workflow. MY WORKFLOWS AND TASKS displays tasks and workflows that you have selected or previously edited. The selection is made using a search area that provides diverse selection criteria. If you frequently need a group of tasks to define your workflows, you can put these tasks together in a task group and insert the group into your search area.

Display the contents of the task group in the tray, select the position in your workflow where you want to insert the task, and choose the task by double-clicking on it. An activity step is then automatically created in your workflow that refers to this task.

Insert a Send Mail Step

In this example, you insert a send mail step if the user decides not to display the material:

1. Return to your workflow, and drag the SEND MAIL step to the No branch of the USER DECISION step.

2. Enter the following information:

   ▷ SEND EXPRESS: Select the checkbox

   ▷ SUBJECT:
   Part 1: You chose not to display business partner.
   Part 2: Select the INSERT EXPRESSION icon, and select BUS1006 • BUSINESS PARTNER.

3. In the large text box, enter text for the email.

4. Select the green checkmark (TRANSFER AND TO GRAPHIC). You are asked for an abbreviation and name, which creates a new task. Enter appropriate values for the name and the description. You also need to provide a development class or have the task be a LOCAL OBJECT.

At this point, your process should look like Figure 8.8. The user decision step is followed by two steps: review of the business partner and send email.

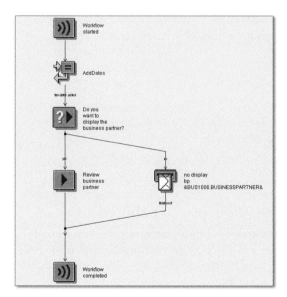

Figure 8.8 Example Process Built in This Section

8.4.3 What Kinds of Outcomes Exist

Outcomes are what the calling step/function can return. Certain outcomes appear in the workflow modeler by default. Outcomes are important because the workflow process branches are based on outcomes. There are different outcomes available according to the step type chosen. To see the possible outcomes of a step, follow these steps:

1. Double-click on a step, and select the OUTCOMES tab.

2. In the workflow from Figure 8.8, if you double-click on the USER DECISION step (*Do you want to display the business partner?*) and select the OUTCOMES tab, you will see three outcomes: YES, NO, and PROCESSING OBSOLETE.

3. If you double-click on the ACTIVITY step (Review business partner) and select the OUTCOMES tab, you see two outcomes: STEP EXECUTED and PROCESSING OBSOLETE.

Notice in the USER DECISION step, the outcome PROCESSING OBSOLETE does not appear in the workflow modeler. Normally, the only outcomes that are displayed are ones that require the workflow to react. Some outcomes are optional, and others are only displayed by the system if they are necessary as a result of specific settings. Table 8.3 shows all possible outcomes.

The Outcome Is ...	The Outcome Exists If ...	Notes and Comments
Event name (terminating event of task)	The task was defined with terminating events.	If the underlying method is an asynchronous method, you must activate at least one event as an outcome.
Value name (possible value of method result)	The synchronous object method is defined with a result for which fixed values are maintained in the ABAP Dictionary.	If you deactivate all values of the results, the system activates the STEP EXECUTED outcome instead.
Exception name (method exception)	The object method is defined with exceptions.	Refer to Chapter 10, Business Objects.
System outcome: DOCUMENT COULD NOT BE CREATED	The step is a document from template step.	This outcome is triggered if document creation fails.

Table 8.3 Step Outcomes

The Outcome Is ...	The Outcome Exists If ...	Notes and Comments
System outcome: TASK EXECUTED SYNCHRONOUSLY	The step is a document from template step.	Normal completion of a document from template step.
System outcome: STEP EXECUTED	▶ The activity refers to a synchronous object method without result. ▶ The activity refers to a synchronous object method with result, but no result is selected.	Normal completion of a step.
System outcome: PROCESSING REJECTED	The indicator PROCESSING CAN BE REJECTED is set.	If processing of the relevant work item is rejected at runtime (e.g., using REJECT EXECUTION in the Business Workplace), the steps defined after this outcome are executed.
System outcome: PROCESSING OBSOLETE	The work item can be set to obsolete using a PROCESS CONTROL step.	▶ The steps defined after this outcome are executed. ▶ This outcome is used to skip steps when modeled deadlines are missed.
System outcome: REQUESTED END, LATEST END, LATEST START	The relevant deadline monitoring is activated and a modeled reaction required. This applies to the workflow wizard MODEL DEADLINE MONITORING.	▶ Within these branches, you model steps to be executed when the deadline is missed. For example, you can model a PROCESS CONTROL step that sets the work item of this step to obsolete. ▶ You cannot deactivate these outcomes.

Table 8.3 Step Outcomes (cont.)

8.4.4 Which Task and Step Attributes Impact Work Item Execution

When setting up a task, there are certain options that impact how the task behaves at runtime. Attributes that influence the execution of work items can be found in both the task definition (when creating the TS task) and the step definition (when inserting the task into a workflow). The following settings reside in the task definition (refer to Figure 8.6):

▸ **Background processing**
Set this checkbox if you want the workflow system (i.e., user WF-BATCH) to execute the work item automatically in the background without user involvement. This flag is only available if the underlying method is non-dialog, meaning that it does not require user involvement. The work item will not appear in any inbox, but you can view it via the work item reports or workflow logs.

▸ **Confirm end of processing**
Set this checkbox if you want the user to decide when the work item is complete. As long as this confirmation has not taken place, the relevant work item remains in the inbox of the agent even if the work item has already been executed. The agent can execute the work item again or forward it. You *cannot* assign this indicator for tasks that are to be executed in the background.

Tip

CONFIRM END OF PROCESSING forces the user to indicate that he is done with the task, in addition to completing the work for the task. Only use this flag if you want additional confirmation before completing the work item. This setting also enables the user to add an attachment with the confirmation completion.

The following settings are allowed in the step definition (in the Workflow Builder, double-click on a task, and select the DETAILS tab):

▸ **Processing can be rejected**
Set this checkbox if the user can opt to skip this step. You can model alternative steps to be taken against the matching REJECTED outcome.

▸ **Step not in workflow log**
Work items for this step do not appear in the standard logs, but they are always displayed in the technical workflow log. The graphical log filters out not only these steps but also the outcomes. If a step with several outcomes is filtered out, all of the outcome branches and the steps included in these branches are

filtered out of the graphical log, until the point is reached where the paths merge together again.

▶ **Advance with dialog (Synchronous dialog chain)**
If the agent of the previous step is also an agent of this step, this step is executed immediately on completion of the previous step as described in Chapter 4, Work Item Delivery.

8.5 Documenting, Translating, Transporting, and Team Development

This section covers topics that should be included in your workflow design, including documenting your workflows, translation, moving your workflow from development to production, and options for collaborative team workflow development.

8.5.1 Documenting Workflow Definitions

Your project should have certain guidelines and expectations around workflow documentation. A workflow definition can be documented in several parts. First of all, you can describe the purpose of the workflow, how it is started, and which subworkflows it calls in the description of the workflow definition. This documentation is found in the Workflow Builder by selecting GOTO • BASIC DATA. Then select the DESCRIPTION tab. You can document using the NOTE IT! link. Additionally, at the task level, you can provide detailed task descriptions that will be available at runtime. Objects can be documented at the object level.

> **Note**
> The task description for dialog steps is displayed in the work item preview, so for dialog steps, only instructions to the user should be entered here. Only add technical documentation to the task description if the step is to be executed in the background.

Obviously, there is a lot more needed to document a workflow project than simply the workflow definition. Checklists can be downloaded from *http://www.sap-press.com* to help you with this.

8.5.2 Translating a Workflow into Other Languages

You can translate all language-dependent texts that appear in the workflow definition. This applies to:

▶ The names of steps and outcomes

▶ Decision texts and titles

▶ Container element names

A user can use personal settings to specify whether work item texts and the work item preview are to be displayed in the original language of the workflow or in the logon language (if the text is available in this language).

To get a complete translation, you have to translate the steps in the Workflow Builder and also translate all of the tasks used in the workflow in the translation transaction (SE63). Finally use the compare translation function in the Workflow Builder to import the changes into the current workflow version; otherwise, the changes will only be visible when the workflow is imported into the next system downstream.

8.5.3 Transporting New Versions of a Workflow

A new workflow always has one version with the number 0000. This version is overwritten by default every time you save your workflow. If you do not want the system to do this, you can generate a new version by choosing WORKFLOW • GENERATE VERSION. The workflow definition is set to status NEW, SAVED.

To avoid increasing the disk space requirements for workflow definitions excessively, only generate a new version under the following circumstances:

▶ If you have made incompatible changes

▶ If there are production workflows running that refer to the current version

The system manages several versions of a workflow definition. Only one of the versions of a workflow is the active version. Select the active version by activating the appropriate version.

> **Tip**
>
> The import and export parameters of the workflow container are not subject to any versioning.

The information tray displays the version you are processing and whether an active version is involved. To display an overview of all versions, choose the BASIC DATA symbol (🔳) in the Workflow Builder. The version number is displayed on the VERSION OVERVIEW tab in the version-independent basic data. An overview of all versions of the workflow definition can be found on the VERSIONS tab in the version-dependent basic data.

> **Tip**
>
> A running workflow always refers to the version of the workflow active at the time it started. Even if subsequently a new version of the workflow becomes the active version, workflows still running continue to refer to the version active when they were started. If you overwrite this version while there are still active workflows, for example, by making changes directly in the production system, unexpected errors can occur.

If a workflow definition is transported into another system, only the active version is transported. If the workflow definition exists in the target system with the same version number, it is overwritten by the transported version if it has no workflows running. Otherwise, the transported workflow definition is saved with a new, free version number. The transported workflow definition becomes the active workflow definition in the target system.

8.5.4 How Do You Share Workflow Development Within a Team

The Workflow Builder offers teamworking functions that support workflow development by a team of developers. It also offers the option to assign a self-defined grouping characteristic to each step. In the optionally displayable TEAMWORKING frame, you can search for steps that have a particular grouping characteristic or particular change data. The Workflow Builder options can also graphically highlight the steps according to the grouping characteristics or according to the last user to make a change. The last user can be seen on the CHANGE DATA tab of the step definition. You define the grouping characteristic of each step on the CHANGE DATA tab page in the step definition.

A grouping name can be assigned to every step. Using this grouping name, you can structure the graphical representation of the workflow. The selection field displays all of the group descriptions previously defined. One of the group descriptions just entered is automatically entered in the selection field and is also available as a selection for all other steps. You can use this to mark steps that need rework or that are to be transferred to a subworkflow, or you can use this to demarcate the different logical parts of a large workflow.

Advanced workflow building covers topics that go beyond the creation of your first few workflows. If you are an existing workflow expert, this chapter provides insight into newer workflow functions and describes the best use of the new features.

9   Advanced Workflow Design Techniques

This chapter moves beyond the creation of your initial workflows. In this chapter, we cover a wide variety of topics, from subworkflows and step conditions, to forks and parallel processing. We also look in detail at workflow containers: what they are, how they work, and why they are important.

When you begin creating workflows, binding can be one of the trickiest concepts to understand. This chapter looks in detail at binding and discusses new options available in the latest SAP releases. Additionally, blocks and local workflows are described and demonstrated. After reading this chapter, you will be ready to take your workflow design to the next level!

9.1   Step Conditions

Conditions have not yet been discussed in detail. Let us start by examining the types of conditions available when building a workflow. They are described in Table 9.1.

This section focuses on the step condition. Step conditions can be based on three condition types: CREATE WORK ITEM, COMPLETE WORK ITEM, and COMPLETION EXECUTION. To configure conditions for a step type, double-click on an activity step in your workflow, and select the tab CONDITIONS (see Figure 9.1).

Type of Condition	Description	Example of Use
Step type: CONDITION	Checks a specific value and returns a Boolean (true or false) result. The step type is modeled in the Workflow Builder. The condition is created from data available in the workflow container.	Sales orders over a certain dollar amount need additional processing. Use a condition step to see if the sales order amount exceeds the threshold.
Step type: MULTIPLE CONDITION	Checks a value comparing to multiple values. The comparison is based on a case (comparison based on container element, system, or constant field) or switch (each possible outcome based on condition to test the value) statement.	When creating a business partner, there is processing specific to certain countries. Use a multiple condition to test the country to know which branch to follow.
Step type: STEP CONDITION	Places a condition based on a specific step in the workflow, not included as part of the process flow.	You only want to complete the work item if a specific condition is true; for example, all of the fields on a form are completed.

Table 9.1 Types of Conditions

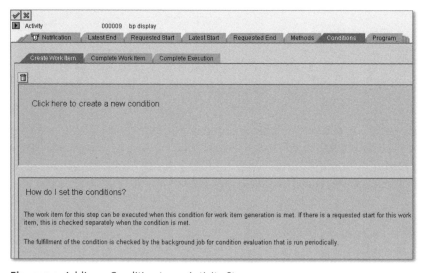

Figure 9.1 Adding a Condition to an Activity Step

> **Tip**
>
> When a condition is added to an activity step, it is done within the step, meaning there is no visual indicator in the Workflow Builder that a condition exists on the step. When you double-click on the step, there is an icon on the CONDITION tab indicating that a condition was set.
>
> Because of this, it is important that you document the condition either in the naming of the step or in the NOTE IT! area. It should be in some place where future workflow developers can easily recognize that a condition was set on a specific step.

Figure 9.2 shows the types of conditions you can create on an activity step. They include create work item condition, complete execution condition, and complete work item condition. We will now look at these in more detail.

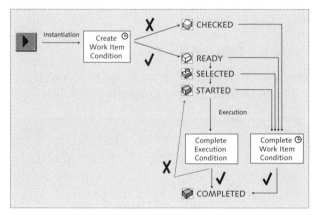

Figure 9.2 Types of Conditions You Can Place on an Activity Step

9.1.1 Step Condition: Create Work Item

The CREATE WORK ITEM condition evaluates a condition before *creating* the work item. At the point in the workflow when the activity step is launched, the work item moves to WAITING state until the condition evaluates to true. The work item cannot move to READY until the condition is fulfilled. The condition is executed by the background job SWWCOND.

9.1.2 Step Condition: Complete Work Item

The COMPLETE WORK ITEM condition evaluates a condition before *completing* the work item. The work item is not completed until the condition evaluates to true.

Both the CREATE WORK ITEM condition and the COMPLETE WORK ITEM condition are evaluated by the background job SWWCOND or by a workflow event defined in the basic data of the workflow. Events for the step conditions can been seen from the BASIC DATA screen.

1. From the Workflow Builder, use the path GOTO • BASIC DATA.

2. Select the VERSION-DEPENDENT tab, and then select the EVENTS tab.

3. In the EVENTS tab, notice the column RECEIVER TYPE. One of the options in the dropdown is EVALUATE PRECONDITIONS AND POSTCONDITIONS.

> **Tip**
>
> SWWCOND must execute for conditions to be evaluated. The condition time depends on the job executing. This job was discussed in Chapter 3, Configuring the System.

9.1.3   Step Condition: Completion Execution

The COMPLETION EXECUTION condition is evaluated *after* the work item executes. If the condition evaluates to true, the work item is set to COMPLETED.

So, now that we have defined step conditions, we still need to explain why to use step conditions; that is, under what conditions does it makes sense to use them. Most of the reasons we have seen for using step conditions are technical reasons. For example, before starting a work item, you want to ensure the object has the specific status, the object was instantiated, or whatever else must be ready *before* the step executes. In this case, a CREATE WORK ITEM condition can ensure the object has technically what should be there before the step executes. Another reason to use the conditions is if the condition is based on an event. For example, you need an event to occur before the step executes, or when an event occurs, you need a specific step to complete.

The COMPLETION EXECUTION condition can be an alternative to a validation loop. For example, a loop executes until data on a master record is completed correctly. With a COMPLETION EXECUTION condition, the work item does not complete until the data is completed according to the condition requirements. In this case, you need very explicit work item text to describe what is required to complete the work item.

9.2 How to Implement Parallel Processing

Assume your workflow needs to execute a step for every line in a sales order, purchase requisition, or purchase order. Parallel processing enables you to have one step in the workflow that creates work items for each line item, routing each item to the appropriate agent.

There also might be a situation where the workflow needs to execute two branches simultaneously. The workflow needs to fork into multiple parallel branches that execute at the same time. One common example of this processing is the workflow to approve invoices: One branch executes the approval branch, while the other branch monitors events that might impact the approval process (e.g., if someone in the application cancels the invoice, it should cancel the approval branch).

SAP Business Workflow supports both types of parallel processing: executing a step for multiple line items and executing multiple branches in parallel. Table 9.2 compares two parallel processing techniques to help you decide which best suits your workflow.

Table-Driven Dynamic Parallel Processing	Fork
The objects to be processed must all be of the same type.	The objects to be processed can be of different types.
All objects are processed with the same task. This task can be a task with or without dialog, or even a subworkflow.	Each object is processed in a separate branch. Different steps, tasks, and even subworkflows can be used in each branch.
All of the objects must be processed before the next step in the workflow can be executed.	Not all branches have to be processed (n-of-m logic or condition logic) before the workflow continues. For example, you can say two out of three branches must complete for the process to continue.
The number of objects to be processed is not known until runtime, for example, the purchase requisition line items to the sales order line items.	The number of objects to be processed is known at definition time.

Table 9.2 Comparison of Parallel Processing Techniques

Table-Driven Dynamic Parallel Processing	Fork
The list of objects is available at runtime in a multiline container element.	The objects are available at runtime in separate container elements of the workflow container.
At runtime, a dialog, background, or workflow work item is created for each object in the list. This work item is processed in the normal manner.	At runtime, an appropriate work item is created for each step within the fork. This work item is processed in the normal manner.
Deadline monitoring, rules for agent determination, and binding can be defined once and then applied equally to each work item created.	Deadline monitoring, rules for agent determination, and binding are defined individually in the normal manner.

Table 9.2 Comparison of Parallel Processing Techniques (cont.)

9.2.1 How to Implement Table-Driven Dynamic Parallel Processing

Suppose you have defined a multiline container element in the workflow container that contains a list of values of the same type at runtime. The exact number of values is not known until runtime. For each value in this list, the same task (or subworkflow) is executed as a step in the workflow. For example, the materials connected with an order are stored in a multiline container element in the workflow container. Stock is checked for each material.

Tip
Another example is a list of agents needing to approve an object. All approvals are made in parallel. The number of approvers is not known until runtime. (There is a selection of wizards in the Workflow Builder to help you build robust approval processes.)

A multiline container element is created with one data type reference and can therefore only include a list of values that refer to the same data type reference. This might be a list of object references. The multiline container element can be filled with a list of values by:

▶ **Binding from an event**
  For example, from triggering event to the multiline import container element in the workflow container when the workflow is started.

▶ **Binding from a task**

For example, from a multiline container element in a task container (result or return parameter of a method) to the multiline container element in the workflow container.

▶ **Repeated binding**

For example, in a loop, from single value container elements to the multiline container element in the workflow container.

In the step definition, enter the multiline workflow container element on the MISCELLANEOUS tab. The number of parallel work items depends on the multiline element entered on the tab page. One work item is created for each value in the container element. If the table is empty, this step is skipped.

> **Caution**
>
> The multiline container element may have a maximum of 99 values.

The data passed to each work item depends on the workflow-to-task binding definition. The multiline container element values do not need to be passed to the task at all. Usually you process the list via one of the following mutually exclusive techniques:

▶ You use a list of objects with the same object type as the task definition in the MISCELLANEOUS tab, binding the relevant current object to the task, and thus processing each object exactly once.

▶ You use a list of values (or objects of a different type to the task definition) in the MISCELLANEOUS tab, binding the same object and the relevant current value to the task in the workflow/task binding, and thus processing the same object multiple times, once for each value.

If you want to pass the relevant current value of the container element to the work item, in the CONTROL tab, define a binding from the multiline container element in the workflow container to a single value container element in the task container. The single value container element in the task container must have the same data type reference as the multiline container element. You can use the Value Help (⌕F4⌗) for the binding definition by choosing the entry <SOURCE_ELEMENT> WITH INDEX.

Tip

You sometimes need a table-driven dynamic loop where different agents process the different work items. For example, you may want different agents to enter the data for different views of a master record. If this is the case, you should start a subworkflow rather than a task in the dynamic loop.

Use the dynamic loop binding to pass the subworkflow both the object and the agent involved in the processing so that the agent can be specified in the subworkflow's step via an expression, for example:

```
TargetAgent <== &MultilineElement [_WF_PARFOREACH_INDEX].agent&
```

Technical Requirements to Implement a Parallel Dynamic Step

The purpose of this example is to demonstrate what must be done to implement a parallel dynamic step. The example is based on a workflow receiving a multiline list of sales orders, and each order must be displayed. The business object used for demonstration purposes is BUS2032.

1. The object that is used for the parallel step must be designated as multiline in the workflow container. Select the item in the workflow container, and update the PROPERTIES to be MULTILINE (see Figure 9.3).

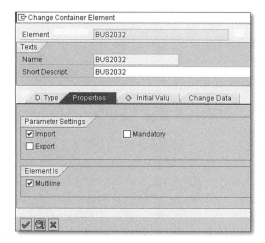

Figure 9.3 Business Object as Multiline

2. The step that executes as multiline must be linked to the multiline container element via the MISCELLANEOUS tab (see Figure 9.4) in the step definition. Double-click on the step and select the MISCELLANEOUS tab (❶).

3. In the MULTILINE ELEMENT field, select the dropdown to view the workflow container (**2**).

4. Select the MULTILINE ELEMENT BUS2032 from the workflow container (**3**).

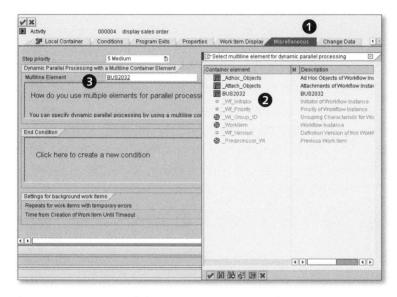

Figure 9.4 Dynamic Parallel Processing Based on Multiline Container Element

5. To test your workflow, navigate to the test area, enter two sales orders as input data, and TEST. Figure 9.5 shows how the testing screen will appear.

Figure 9.5 Testing a Workflow with a Multiline Container Element

9.2.2 How to Implement a Fork

A fork is used in a workflow definition when several different subprocesses can be executed in parallel. You can configure the fork definition to decide whether all branches have to be completed before the workflow can continue.

In the workflow definition, the start (⇥) and the end (⇤) of a fork are shown with the respective symbols. You can create any number of branches in a fork. All branches of the fork end in a JOIN OPERATOR (⇤). As each branch of a fork reaches this join operator at runtime, the end conditions are checked.

To define a fork, specify the number of parallel branches required and the step name. The fork, consisting of the START OPERATOR, the branches (initially each with an undefined step), and the JOIN OPERATOR, is inserted into the workflow definition. To define the termination of the fork, you enter the number of branches required (n-of-m logic) or an end condition.

> **Tip**
>
> You can transfer an existing modeled block into a fork as a new branch by copying or cutting the block, choosing the fork icon (⇤), and then choosing PASTE BLOCK in the context menu.

You can state that all branches must be completed, 1 of 3 branches, 2 of 3, 2 of 5, or whatever combination you require. This is referred to as *n-of-m logic*. If the n-of-m logic has been specified in the fork definition, the system checks whether the number of branches processed agrees with the number of branches required, as specified in the definition. If an end condition has been specified in the fork definition, the system then checks whether the end condition is true.

After the n-of-m logic or end condition has been satisfied, any uncompleted work items of the fork are set to the status LOGICALLY DELETED, and the workflow is continued after the join operator.

> **Tip**
>
> The individual branches of a fork should be functionally independent.

The n-of-m branch is particularly useful for prematurely ending part of a process and moving on to the next stage when further processing is unnecessary. For example, if a decision is final when either two out of three users have approved or when one has rejected, you can model the process using a fork. This speeds up the process because you do not have to wait for the third decision before analyzing the result. If you do not enter an end condition or restrict the number of branches required, the system assumes all branches are required before the workflow can continue.

9.3   Reusing Workflows as Subworkflows

Subworkflows can be used to structure a workflow. They are workflows in their own right but usually do not have triggering events because they are only started by another workflow. You can have a workflow call a subworkflow by using an activity step and specifying the subworkflow instead of a standard task. Use the workflow-to-workflow binding in the activity step to pass data between the workflow and subworkflow. You can only bind subworkflow container elements marked as IMPORT or EXPORT.

To insert the steps from subworkflows directly in your workflow, you can expand a subworkflow. If there are naming conflicts between the container elements of the existing workflow container and the container elements to be inserted, the system informs you and provides the opportunity to rename these container elements.

If you have a large workflow that you want to split into several subworkflows to make maintenance easier, consider carefully what parts of the workflow will be split into subworkflows. Remembering that subworkflows can be reused in other workflows or multiple times in the same workflow, try to break out logical sections of the workflow that can make the most of this ability. Good candidates for subworkflows include the following:

▶ Exception handling

▶ Retry handling for background processes

▶ Pre-decision and post-decision processing

For example, an approvals process might contain one subworkflow defining the process for making the approve/reject decision, and another subworkflow defining the processing that happens after the decision has been made. If you need to change the approve/reject decision subworkflow you do not have to worry about affecting the post-decision handling and vice versa. Also you may later want to reuse the post-decision handling in a new workflow that uses a different approve/ reject decision process.

One very useful technique, which stabilizes maintenance, is to create a main workflow that simply consists of a call to a subworkflow with parallel branches to take care of exception handling. The branches contain WAIT FOR EVENTS steps so that they are only processed when an event representing the exception is raised, for example, by a CREATE EVENT step elsewhere in the workflow definition.

Figure 9.6 shows a workflow that uses a fork to execute a subworkflow, while at the same time, waiting for either the order changed or order deleted events to occur in the application.

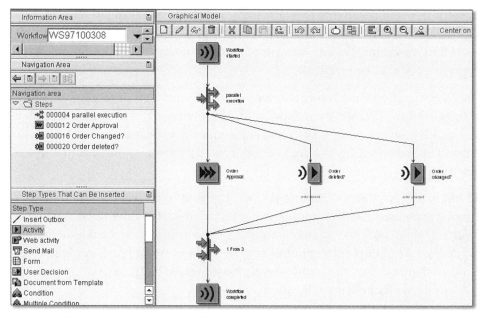

Figure 9.6 Fork Workflow with Parallel Branches Waiting for a Change or Deletion of the Order

9.4   Modeled Deadlines

The defaults discussed in Chapter 8, Creating a Workflow, were simple deadlines. When the deadline occurs, a text notification is sent to the selected agent. Modeled deadlines involve more active deadline monitoring. With a modeled deadline, you can take action when the deadline occurs.

If you choose the modeled variation as the response to a missed deadline, you get a new outcome, where processing starts as soon as the deadline is missed. In contrast to all other branches of workflow, deadline branches are not joined with the actual workflow. Therefore, it is best only to insert steps here that should be executed for exactly this missed deadline (you can have separate branches for the latest end, requested end, and latest start deadlines).

> **Tip**
>
> The time data within the deadline definition normally refers to the time data in the standard calendar, and neither weekends nor public holidays are considered. If you want to use time data that refers to the factory calendar, you use expressions when defining the deadline that refer to a calendar-checking object type that you have created. You can find one way of doing this in Appendix A, Tips and Tricks.

The two most important examples for modeled deadline monitoring are explained next.

9.4.1 Notify Recipients Via Email That a Deadline Has Been Missed

If the notification of the recipients cannot or is not to be implemented as a work item, a missed deadline notification can also be sent as an email or an external document:

1. Maintain the reference date/time, and enter a name on the MODELED tab.
2. Model a send mail step in the newly created branch.

> **Tip**
>
> Keep in mind that the work item being monitored does *not* yet have the status COMPLETED. The status and agent assignment of the monitored work item are not changed by the missed deadline and notification.

9.4.2 Skip the Work Item If Deadline Has Been Missed

You can terminate the execution of the work item (i.e., mark it as obsolete) if a deadline is missed. This may be necessary if the activity to be executed no longer needs to be carried out or the activity must be redirected to other agents. To do this, insert a PROCESS CONTROL step in the new branch.

> **Tip**
>
> You can use the Workflow Wizard MODEL DEADLINE MONITORING to assist you in the creation of modeled deadline monitoring. Select the step that you want to monitor, and choose the Workflow Wizard by double-clicking.

1. The following settings are required in the step definition of the step for which deadlines are to be monitored:

   ▶ On the OUTCOMES tab, activate the outcome PROCESSING OBSOLETE.

   ▶ On the relevant DEADLINE tab, enter the deadline reference date/time/offset, and enter a name for your deadline outcome, for example, "Deadline missed," on the MODELED tab.

2. Insert a PROCESS CONTROL step in the new branch after the outcome DEADLINE MISSED.

3. In its step definition, specify that the work item of the deadline-triggering step is to be set to obsolete.

4. In the PROCESSING OBSOLETE branch, you can model alternative steps that are to be executed when the deadline is missed.

> **Tip**
>
> A new branch is created in the workflow definition for each missed deadline type activated with a modeled response. Model all steps that are to be executed when this particular deadline type is missed in the matching branch. Model all steps that are to be executed, regardless of the deadline type missed, in the branch PROCESSING OBSOLETE.

Note that when you use modeled deadlines, the recipient for missed deadline is *not* notified automatically. If you want a notification to be sent, you model this in the branch after the relevant DEADLINE MISSED outcome using the SEND MAIL step type.

9.5   Containers

Containers store data required during the life of the workflow. A workflow could complete in one to two days, one to two weeks, or even one to two months. During this time, the workflow must always keep track of the process and the key data required to execute the process. You use containers to interface data between different parts of a workflow and between the workflow and business applications.

9.5.1 Containers and Bindings in Depth

The principal containers used in the SAP Business Workflow Engine are the following:

- **A workflow container for each workflow and subworkflow**
  Only the container elements classified as IMPORT can be filled when the workflow is started (e.g., from an event container or the test Transaction SWUS).

- **A task container for each task**
  IMPORT container elements are filled from the workflow container, and EXPORT container elements are transferred back.

- **A method container for each method**
  IMPORT container elements are filled from the task container, and EXPORT container elements are transferred back.

- **An event container for each event**
  All event containers are EXPORT container elements only.

- **A rule container for each rule**
  The IMPORT container elements are filled from the workflow container (or task container in the case of a task's default rule). The _RULE_RESULT element is the only EXPORT parameter, and this is optional (see Chapter 12, Agent Determination Rules).

Figure 9.7 shows how the data flows among the different containers in a workflow as a workflow progresses. The *bindings* simply control which data are needed from the source container and how it is mapped to a target element in the target container.

As you look at Figure 9.7, consider a process that starts when a business partner is created. Based on the region, the business partner is sent to the correct agent to set up information required for business-to-business XML communication with the business partner:

- A business partner creation creates an *event*. The *event container* is populated with the business partner number and the user ID of the person who created the business partner. The event container always contains *who* created the event and *what* object was involved.

▶ This *event container* is passed to the *workflow container*. The person who created the business partner becomes the workflow initiator (WF_INITIATOR). The business partner number is used to instantiate the *object* (WI_OBJECT_ID).

▶ After the workflow executes, the workflow container must pass the object and other relevant information to the task container. The task container then passes the object to the method container, which invokes the functionality (transaction code, program, whatever needs to execute).

▶ When the method and task complete, they pass back information to the workflow container.

▶ The second step needs to be executed by the agent who is responsible for the region of the business partner. The country field from the business partner object is *bound* to the *rule container*. The *rule container* uses the imported region to find the correct agent, and the result is *bound* back to the workflow container. The step is the update of the business partner, which executes a change business partner transaction.

▶ The business partner is sent to the *task container,* which sends the business partner to the *method container.* The method and task then return the outcome, such as business partner successfully updated.

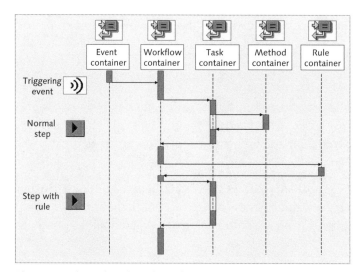

Figure 9.7 Flow of Binding Through Containers

The container holds all data used during execution. The workflow container holds all data values used in control steps (such as container operation, condition, loop steps, etc.) and passed from each step to any subsequent steps. The task container holds all data used in work item texts, descriptions, and passed to/from the method. The method container holds the parameters of the function to be executed, including the results of the function. The rule container holds the criteria used, for example, to determine agents. The event container holds data passed from a business application, so that it can be passed to the workflow.

Containers hold named data and object references known as *elements*. Container elements may hold a single value (including structures) or an object reference, or they can be multiline elements. A multiline element holds multiple values or object references, that is, a list of values or object references. For instance, the workflow container includes a multiline element for attachments. When an agent creates an attachment, it is appended to the attachment element, so that the list of all attachments created so far can be passed to the next agent in the workflow.

Most containers have standard system elements. For instance, the workflow container has the workflow initiator element. You can also add your own container elements to the container. Single-value container elements can be based on complex data types containing embedded structures and hierarchies of structures.

Data can be passed from one type of container to another using bindings. These bindings appear whenever two different types of containers meet. For instance, the workflow to/from task binding appears in the activity step definition that links the task to the workflow. At runtime, the bindings are executed at the appropriate point in the workflow. For instance, for a synchronous task, the workflow-to-task binding is executed as part of work item creation, and the task-to-workflow binding is executed as part of work item completion.

> **Note**
>
> If you assign the agents of an activity step to a rule, the binding is between the workflow and the rule (not the underlying task and the rule), and the binding is executed just before work item creation. If the rule fails, the workflow can stop and inform the administrator without leaving a half-finished work item in limbo. When the problem has been fixed, the administrator can restart the workflow, and the binding is executed again.

Depending on the types of containers involved, you may only be permitted to bind container elements with an IMPORT or EXPORT flag. For instance, to bind data from an event to a workflow, event container elements can only be passed to workflow container elements marked with the IMPORT flag. If binding is permitted in both directions (e.g., workflow-to-task and task-to-workflow), make sure you are binding in the correct direction.

Some binding is automatic. For instance, the system container element `_WI_Object_ID` in the task container automatically determines the object on which the method is to be applied. Often container elements with the same name in both types of container are automatically passed during workflow execution. However, to avoid confusion, you should explicitly define any bindings you need as much as possible.

> **Tip**
>
> Often the system proposes bindings for you. You should *always* check these.

For clarity and efficiency, you should only define the minimum bindings that you need. For example, for an ACTIVITY step linking your workflow to a *Review Business Partner* task, bind only the container element holding the BUS1006 object reference from the workflow to the task. There is no need to bind the Business Partner container element back from the task to the workflow because even if you are changing the business partner details, you are not changing which business partner is being processed (the object key does not change).

9.5.2 Reimplementation of the Container

In releases previous to SAP R/3 4.7, which executes on SAP Web Application Server 6.20, the container implementation relied on two database tables: SWW_CONT and SWW_CONTOB. For customers who use workflow heavily, these two tables experienced rapid monthly growth. The container technology was completely reimplemented in release SAP R/3 4.7. The storage format of the container was changed to XML by default (although the previous format is still supported for compatibility reasons). This change has several advantages:

▶ One major advantage is no restrictions concerning data types. All Data Dictionary types are supported, including binary data, structures with arbitrary lengths and complexity, ABAP object references. With the storage of the container data as an XML document, it facilitates the diversity of supported data types.

▶ Another advantage is saving storage space. This is especially true for large containers and structures. Previously, each structured field required a database entry, but this is no longer the case.

When using the new XML container, Table `SWW_WI2OBJ` holds the relation between business object instances and work items. If you want to evaluate relations between work items and business object instances, use the function modules `SAP_WAPI_OBJECTS_IN_WORKITEM` and `SAP_WAPI_WORKITEMS_TO_OBJECT` instead of using the database Table `SWW_CONTOB` directly.

> **Tip**
>
> When you create new workflows, the persistence defaults to XML, which is the recommended persistence. However, you can switch to the old storage mechanism as well. The old mechanism is still supported for compatibility reasons for existing workflows. As you create new workflows, you should use the "new" XML persistence.

In Figure 9.8, you can see that within the Workflow Builder, you can update the XML persistence by following five steps:

❶ Select BASIC DATA.

❷ Select the VERSION DEPENDENT tab.

❸ Select the CONTROL tab.

❹ Select the PROFILE PERSISTENCE tab.

❺ Select XML PERSISTENCE.

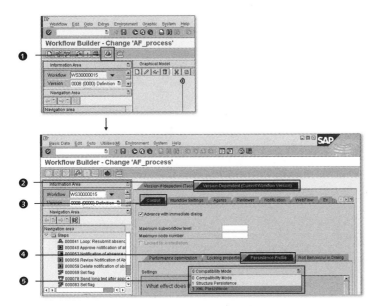

Figure 9.8 Configuring Persistence of the Workflow Container

9.6 Binding

Binding is how the data is passed between the various containers. For example, when an event triggers a workflow, the event container contains *who* triggered the event and *what* object was involved. This is passed to the workflow container via binding. The workflow container then binds data to the work item container. The work item container can also be used to bind from a step execution back to the workflow container.

9.6.1 Binding Editor

Figure 9.9 shows the binding editor, highlighting the major areas of the container, including the source, target, and dragging and dropping to indicate import and export bindings. The source and the target of a binding instruction are *expressions*. A source expression is based on the source container; a target expression is based on the target container.

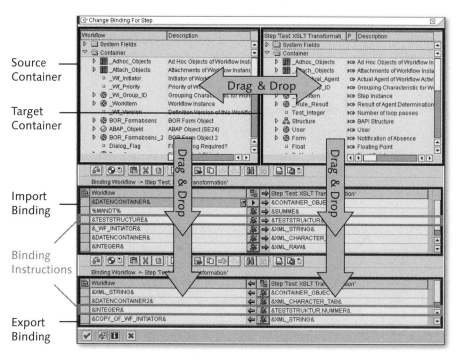

Figure 9.9 Binding Editor

For binding operations, you have many options:

- Assign a value
- Append to a table
- Initialize a value
- Perform XSLT transformation
- Merge elements
- Programmed binding (execute custom code to do the binding)

Besides pure assignment, several interesting binding operators are available, including calls to display methods, functional methods (discussed in Chapter 10, Business Objects), initializing values, and appending to tables.

Binding is a powerful tool, and you should explore binding as you need it. Start with the default bindings, and as you encounter problems you cannot solve, consider binding to help with the solution.

9.6.2 Expressions

When you first begin to build workflows, you bind objects between containers. However, the expressions used in binding can now provide index access to multi-line elements. You can access an entire table line, a particular column in a line, an entire column, or other specific information. Table 9.3 shows common expressions used to access data in a table. You can access the entire table, a column, or a row.

Expression	Description
&table[index]&	Access to an entire table line
&table[index].columnName&	Access to a component of a table line
&table[].columnName&	Projection to a single column
&customers[1].orders[2]&	Second order of first customer

Table 9.3 Expression Options

Expressions can contain functional method calls to BOR or ABAP objects. The expression evaluates to the result value of the method. You can pass parameters to the methods. When using expressions to execute methods, the methods must be read only, and there can be no database changes.

9.7   Blocks and Local Workflows

Blocks are modeling elements that can contain other modeling elements. They represent a data subcontext, have a data interface, have one start and end mode, and can be monitored with deadlines. Block items introduce new levels in work item hierarchies. They are seen in the workflow log as folders. A block is completed only if dependent work items are completed. If a block is cancelled, all its dependent work items are cancelled.

9.7.1   Local Workflows as a Practical Example of Block Implementation

Local workflows use blocks and are an excellent example of the practical use of a block. Local workflows are free-floating blocks; that is, they are not directly connected to the main flow. They are represented by work items of type BLOCK and share most of the features normal blocks support.

One example of a local workflow is for exceptions: You want to catch an exception in the process and execute alternative processing. The exception might occur at various times throughout the workflow, so the exception process is handled outside of the normal workflow process.

Figure 9.10 shows an example of a local workflow. First notice the workflow has a block. Inside the block an exception is raised (❶). The exception is tied to the block (❷) and triggers a local event (❸). The local workflow is triggered (❹) based on the local event.

There is no deadline handling and no exception handling for local workflows. Local workflows can only be started by local events (data binding can be defined). Local events are triggered either directly via an EVENT TRIGGER step or indirectly by connecting a global event to a local event in the BASIC DATA of the workflow. Local workflows belong to the main workflow; they cannot be reused in multiple workflows.

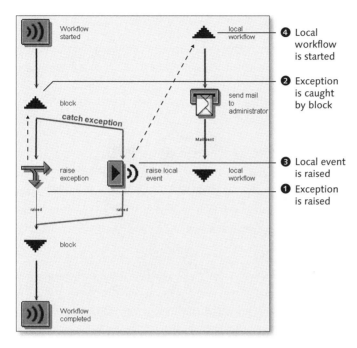

Figure 9.10 Local Workflows

9.7.2 Local Workflows and Other SAP-Provided Example Workflows

Many example workflows are provided for you in all SAP systems. To see the example workflows, use Transaction SWDD, and select workflows that start with WF_Verify*. WF_Verify042 is the example for using blocks and local workflows.

9.7.3 When to Use Local Workflows Versus Subworkflows

In this chapter, we have discussed both subworkflows and local workflows. Subworkflows should be used when you want to reuse workflow steps in multiple workflows.

For example, you have a generic approval workflow that can be called in several workflows. Subworkflows are modeled in the main workflow and must be inserted in each place the subworkflow can be called. Local workflows are used within a single workflow; the local workflow cannot be reused in other workflows. However, the local workflow can be called as many times as required. A local event is called to start the local workflow.

9.8 Ad-hoc Features and Review Workflows

You should also be aware of the ad-hoc features available with workflow and how you can have a reviewer involved in a workflow process. This is of particular interest if you have workflow in SAP Supplier Relationship Management (covered in Chapter 25, SAP Supplier Relationship Management).

9.8.1 Ad-Hoc Features to Change Workflows on the Fly

There are times when you need to enable users, at runtime, to decide what agents to use and what steps to execute. Within SAP Business Workflow, there is the ability to do user-driven agent selection for deciding which steps to execute in the workflow. The following summarizes these features:

▸ **Modeled ad-hoc agent assignment**
You can insert a dialog step in your workflow through which you determine responsible agents for a subsequent step. The recipient of the work item has the opportunity to select the responsible agent from the possible agents of the subsequent step. The chosen agent then receives the work item.

The Workflow Wizard INCLUDE "SELECT EDITOR" can help you model this step. It makes sense to use this step if the agent must be chosen by a person, and there is not a rule that can determine the agent. For example, the workflow is for managing a project. There is a step that assigns an agent to execute a project step. Assume the project step is one that interacts with a customer, such as detailing requirements with a customer. You may want to hand-select the agent to work with a specific customer, so you may want a step in the workflow where the agent is selected by a person, instead of by a routing rule.

▸ **General ad-hoc agent assignment**
When starting the workflow, the workflow system determines the responsible agents for the steps using ad-hoc agent objects. To use general ad-hoc agent assignment, first remove the responsible agent assignment from the relevant steps.

Ad-hoc agent assignment is then activated for all steps without responsible agents by choosing EXTRAS • AD HOC FUNCTIONS • ENABLE AD HOC AGENT ASSIGNMENT from the Workflow Builder, and replacing the default ad-hoc agent object AGENT with your desired ad-hoc agent objects in the generated container elements.

The responsible agents of work items that have not yet been completed (or started) can be specified (e.g., by the workflow administrator) during execution of the workflow.

▶ **Ad-hoc extension of a workflow**

At runtime, you can extend a workflow at predefined places using an AD HOC ANCHOR step (). This step can be replaced by a subworkflow at runtime. The container definition of the subworkflow must be identical to that of the ad-hoc anchor. This subworkflow can itself contain ad-hoc anchors. At definition time, you specify which workflows can be chosen to replace the ad-hoc anchor.

At runtime, an authorized user viewing the graphical log can replace the ad-hoc anchor with one of the designated workflows. The workflow being executed is then extended by incorporating the steps of the selected workflow. This is immediately visible in the log. If the anchor is not replaced, the ad-hoc anchor is ignored when the workflow is executed.

For example, you want the user to have the option to add an additional approver step on the fly. You model the additional approver step as a subworkflow. The ad-hoc anchor step then points to the subworkflow. At runtime, an authorized user can decide to engage the additional approver step, which instantiates the subworkflow.

> **Hint**
>
> Appendix A, Tips and Tricks, describes in detail how to use the ad-hoc anchor step.

9.8.2 Review Workflows

Review workflows enable you to monitor a process and add documentation to the process. They are useful when expert opinions are needed (such as in a workflow controlling the transport of dangerous goods), or when several users have a vested interest in the outcome of a workflow and want to be able to follow and influence its progress.

Normally, only recipients of workflows and system administrators can influence the flow of the workflow, and other users can only view the workflow log. With a review workflow, however, this is different. The review workflow should include a task based on object type `REVIEW` and method `EXECUTE` (passing the workflow ID in the binding). This review workflow's ID is entered in the basic data of the workflow to be monitored.

As a result, the graphical workflow log of the workflow to be monitored receives an additional column. From here, the authorized user can start the review workflow. When the review workflow is started, data from the workflow to be monitored is automatically transferred to the review workflow. As well as receiving notification of the workflow to be reviewed, the reviewer can add attachments that can be seen in the workflow being monitored.

Hint
Appendix A, Tips and Tricks, provides an example of a review workflow.

Business objects integrate the data and functions of business applications into your workflows. They enable SAP Business Workflow to communicate with business applications with all of the flexibility and robustness required for a production environment. Whether you are extending existing SAP objects or creating your own, you will quickly come to appreciate the power that business objects give you. This chapter walks you through the major capabilities available in the Business Object Repository and provides examples of how business objects are used by customers.

10   Business Objects

The purpose of most workflows is to bring together related business applications into a cohesive business process. Given the vast number of existing business applications in SAP components, the SAP Business Workflow Engine needs to readily communicate with business applications to minimize development and maximize return on the investment you have already made in implementing your SAP component.

Business objects are an important interface between workflow and the business applications in SAP components. This chapter describes the interface and how workflows use it to influence business applications. In Chapter 13, Using Events and Other Business Interfaces, you will see the complementary side, namely, how business applications in SAP components use business objects to influence workflows.

At the time SAP Business Workflow was introduced, object-oriented programming was still more of an idea than a reality within ABAP; however, it was clear that object-oriented techniques were the way of the future and critical to underpin workflow if workflow were to provide efficient and effective services. Consequently, SAP Business Workflow was delivered with an approximation of object-oriented programming called the *Business Object Repository* (BOR).

The aim of BOR is to provide object-oriented style techniques and services. Major strengths of the BOR is in how well it provided object-oriented capabilities —

such as inheritance, delegation, association, and polymorphism — to such an extent that it wasn't until SAP R/3 4.6C that a similar depth of object-oriented capabilities was available in ABAP classes, and not until SAP Web Application Server 6.20 that ABAP classes were able to be integrated with SAP Business Workflow to the similar degree as BOR.

> **Note**
>
> SAP equally supports the use of BOR objects and ABAP classes within SAP Business Workflow. This chapter covers BOR objects; Chapter 11 covers ABAP Classes.

This chapter describes the main features of business objects, giving you a good foundation to use them in your workflows or even to develop your own objects. However, in the interests of space, we had to leave out many features. If you find you need more information, the SAP Help Portal (*http://help.sap.com*) describes all of the business object features, fields, and buttons.

The following section on Business Object Basics will help you understand basic business object terminology and concepts that are referenced throughout the rest of the chapter. It will also help you to find, view, and understand existing business objects that you want to use in your workflows, and to identify whether you need to extend them or even create new objects.

To give you a better idea of how the business objects are defined, the following sections guide you through the most important transactions and features of business objects. If you have access to a system where you can follow the examples, you will find it even easier to understand the underlying concepts. If you are the functional analyst or workflow developer responsible for extending or creating business objects, the sections on creating your own business object types and creating object type components are particularly helpful for you. If you are a workflow developer, the section on business object type programming is invaluable.

Finally, the section on useful predefined business objects lists some of the more useful utility functions that will save you precious implementation time and provide examples when creating your own business objects.

10.1   Business Object Basics

Business objects provide the link between SAP Business Workflow and the data and functions in business applications. Business data can be used:

▶ In control steps (including conditions, loops, container operations)

▶ In bindings (including event to workflow, workflow to task, task to method, workflow to rule)

▶ In texts (including work item texts and user instructions)

▶ In start conditions used to determine which workflow will be started and whether a workflow will be started (more on these in Chapter 13, Using Events and Other Business Interfaces)

Business functions can be used:

▶ In methods, within tasks, within workflows

▶ In agent determination rules (within programmed rules; refer to Chapter 12, Agent Determination Rules)

▶ In event linkages within start conditions, check function modules, or receiver type function modules (refer to Chapter 14, Custom Programs)

▶ In secondary, before and after methods (refer to Appendix A, Tips and Tricks) within the workflow step definition

---

Tip

SAP delivers many standard business object types — over 2,000 in SAP ERP. Some contain considerable quantities of data and functions; others only contain a few. Most are based on business entities, for example, `Customer`, `SalesOrder`, `ParkedDocument`, `Material`, and `Invoice`. However, there are also some utility objects, including `WF_TASK` (representing the workflow or task) and `SELFITEM` (representing the work item).

Business objects provide you with an *object-oriented* view of business applications. That is, they organize the business data and business functions into reusable components that can be accessed throughout the Workflow Engine. From a workflow perspective, the main advantages of object-orientation are:

▶ **Reusability**
Each piece of business data and each business function defined are potentially available to all workflows. More importantly each piece of data is available in

the same way, using an *attribute* of an object, regardless of whether data is from the database or is calculated, a single value or a list of multiple values. Equally each business function is available in the same way, using a *method* of an object, regardless of whether the function is based on transactions, reports, programs, function modules, BAPIs (Business Application Programming Interfaces), RFCs (Remote Function Calls) to external system routines, and so on.

▶ **Encapsulation**
Each piece of business data and each business function is defined once and only once for the most relevant business object. For example, the name of the customer is defined for the Customer object. Any workflow wanting to know the customer name accesses the Name attribute of the Customer object. If how the customer name is formatted or derived needs to be changed, it can be changed once for the Customer object and is then immediately and automatically available in the new format to all workflows.

▶ **Inheritance**
SAP provides many business objects with data and functions already made accessible to the Workflow Engine. If you need to extend these objects (e.g., to add data and functions to them) instead of starting from scratch, you can inherit the SAP-provided business objects to your own business objects. That way, your objects can immediately use all of the existing data and functions, supplement the business object with more data and functions, and even replace provided data and functions with your own. When your object inherits from an SAP business object, it does not lose the existing SAP objects, so upgrades are not affected, and any new data or functions added by an upgrade are automatically inherited by your objects as well.

▶ **Polymorphism**
Business objects allow generic programming. This is not necessarily important for your own workflows, but it is vitally important for the tools provided to help you monitor and control them. For instance, from the workflow log, you can execute the Display method of any object related to the log in the same way, regardless of which business object is involved.

Note
In fact, the method executed is the default method of the object. In practice, this should always be a display method. If your object supports several display views, you should choose the most appropriate as the default method.

Tip

For object-oriented buffs, it is worth noting that, for historical reasons, business objects only approximate true object-oriented functionality. Notably they do not have any true constructor/deconstructor methods, and they use an object key to uniquely identify each object instance. However, the general object-oriented concepts of reusability, inheritance, encapsulation, and polymorphism still hold true, and so do their benefits.

10.1.1 Business Objects: Some Basic Terminology

When discussing business objects, you may be referring to either the *object type* or the *object instance* (depending on the context):

▶ The *object type* is the design and implementation of the access to data and functions; that is, the object type contains the program that reads or calculates data and calls business functions. For example, the `Customer` object defines the access to all customer-related data, including customer ID and name, and all customer-related functions, including "Change customer master."

▶ Each *object instance* is a single runtime copy of its object type that holds the data or accesses the functions relevant to that particular instance of the object. For example, the `Customer` object instance for customer ID `ACMYC` is used at runtime to access the customer name "Acme Incorporated" and the customer function to change customer master `ACMYC`.

▶ An *object reference* holds the technical ID of the object type, the object key, and other technical information needed by the system to access an object instance.

Here's a quick overview of a business object type. Each object has the following components:

▶ **Key**
The key defines each object instance uniquely. For example, for the `Customer` object type, the key is the customer ID.

▶ **Attributes**
Attributes provide access to business data. This may be data extracted from the database or calculated values. Attributes may reference a single value or multiple values. Attributes can in themselves be references to other business objects, letting you set up relationships between objects.

▶ **Methods**

Methods provide access to business functions. The underlying code can be based on any business functions, including but not limited to, transactions, reports, programs, function modules, and BAPIs. You can even include your own code (e.g., to update custom tables).

▶ **Events**

Events transmit the status change of an object (e.g., `Created`, `Changed`). They provide the hooks for business applications to influence the workflow. The event names are simply defined against the object type; the implementation is found in the relevant business application (refer to Chapter 13, Using Events and Other Business Interfaces).

Object types have an additional component, called *interfaces*, which are only relevant to design and implementation, and are not used at runtime. These are not interfaces to other systems or applications; instead they refer to the object-oriented concept of interfaces. Essentially, interfaces allow generic programming, partly by helping you to standardize the names used for attributes, methods, and events.

10.1.2 Relationships Between Business Objects

A business object type can have various relationships to other business object types. Relationships between attributes are extremely useful throughout workflow. For instance, in a "Fulfill Sales Order" workflow, you might want to send some work item instructions that include the name and contact details of the sales person responsible for the customer. If the `SalesOrder` object has an attribute `Customer`, referring to the `Customer` object, and the `Customer` object has an attribute `PersonResponsible`, referring to the `User` object, and the `User` object has attributes `Name` and `PhoneNumber`, you can then refer to `SalesOrder.Customer.PersonResponsible.Name` and `SalesOrder.Customer.PersonResponsible.PhoneNumber` in your work item instructions.

It helps to have a basic understanding of what relationships are possible and how they are implemented in the business object type so that you can make the most of them in your workflows. This is especially true if you need to create or extend business object types.

This section describes the major relationships between business object types including the following:

- Inheritance
- Composition
- Association
- Interfaces

None of these relationships is mandatory (apart from the relationship to the interface IFSAP, which is required to implement object-oriented features in each business object), but using them greatly improves the consistency, flexibility, and reusability of your business object types and minimizes development effort.

Inheritance

Inheritance is the most important and general relationship between two objects. The object type from which attributes and methods are inherited is called the *supertype*. The *subtype* inherits components from the supertype. The subtype has the same key fields as its supertype but has extended functionality.

For instance, using inheritance, you can take a generic object type, such as Material, and create from it a more specific subtype, such as StockMaterial. The subtype StockMaterial inherits all of the components of the supertype Material, but you can add new components and redefine existing components to tailor them for the more specific object. This maximizes the use of existing access to business data and functions, and minimizes development and upgrade issues because the supertype program is referenced and no coding is needed for these components in your subtype when using any inherited components. The chance of errors occurring is reduced because common data and functions only need to be defined once in the supertype.

Inheritance is implemented by creating a subtype of an existing business object type. Usually the supertype/subtype relationship is defined when the subtype is created; however, it is possible to change it later. When creating an object, you need to carefully choose its supertype to avoid reworking your object later. If there is no appropriate supertype, you can create a business object without any supertype; that is, you can create a new business object type from scratch.

You can also use inheritance to extend existing SAP objects to your own subtype. You can then effectively replace the standard SAP object with your own by *delegation*, that is, by telling the system to use your subtype whenever the standard SAP supertype is referenced.

Composition

Composition is the "is part of" relationship between object types. For instance, the object type `OrderItem` "is part of" the object type `Order`. The object type `Order` is called the *aggregate* type of the object type `OrderItem`.

In composition, the "is part of" object type usually has an extended key when compared to the aggregate type (e.g., object type `Order` has an order number, whereas object type `OrderItem` has an order number plus an item number) and a completely different functionality.

Composition relationships are implemented by creating an attribute that links one object to another. For instance, the object `Order` has an attribute `OrderItems` that links the order objects to a list of related order item objects. Conversely, the `OrderItem` object has an attribute `Order` that links the order item object back to the order to which it belongs.

Association

Association is a relationship between object types in which an attribute references another object type via an object reference. The object type `Customer` is referenced in the attribute `OrderingParty` of the object type `SalesOrder`. An object may have many of these relationships via its attributes. In many ways, composition is just a special case of the association relationship.

Interfaces

Interfaces are used to ensure consistency and to enable generic programming. For instance, many objects have a method for changing the object. The interface `IFEDIT` ensures that all change methods are called `Edit` regardless of whether the object being changed is `Customer`, `SalesOrder`, `User`, `Invoice`, `Contract`, `Material`, or `Service`. You can then create programs that execute the method `Edit` for any object and choose the object dynamically at runtime from all objects that have implemented the `IFEDIT` interface. This is clearly much better than ending up with every object using a different method name for the same action, for example, `Change`, `Update`, `Alter`, `Modify`, and `Adjust`.

Interfaces are combinations of attributes, methods, and events either without an implementation or with only a default implementation. SAP provides approximately 60 of these interfaces in SAP components.

You implement an interface in a business object type by including the interface as a component of your business object type. To make generic programming possible, it is important that you create an implementation (i.e., underlying code) for all attributes and methods included in the interface if you do not want to use the interface's default implementation. This is often easy to do because interfaces usually contain only one or two components at most.

> **Note**
>
> Every business object supports the `IFSAP` interface.

10.1.3 Business Object Tools

There are two main tools that you can use to work with business objects: the Business Object Builder and the Business Object Repository Browser.

Business Object Builder

You start the Business Object Builder by calling Transaction SWO1 or via the menu path TOOLS • BUSINESS WORKFLOW • DEVELOPMENT • DEFINITION TOOLS • APPLICATION INTEGRATION • BUSINESS OBJECT BUILDER. Use the Business Object Builder (see Figure 10.1) to display, test, create, generate, change, delete, delegate, and change the status of business objects. You can see all relationships between object types using UTILITIES • RELATIONSHIPS on the initial screen. You can also run a where-used list on the object type to find where it has been used in tasks and workflows.

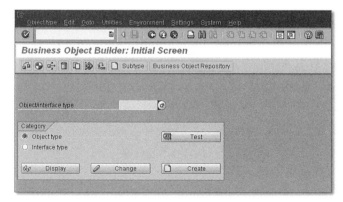

Figure 10.1 Initial Business Object Builder

To access a business object type in the Business Object Builder, you use its technical ID. SAP provides search helps to help you find the technical ID from the object name or description, or you can use the Business Object Repository Browser.

Business Object Repository Browser

Transaction SWO3 is the Business Object Repository Browser, shown in Figure 10.2. This repository browser presents a hierarchical view of all of the business objects available, by SAP application module. Each object type is assigned to an SAP application module indirectly via its package.

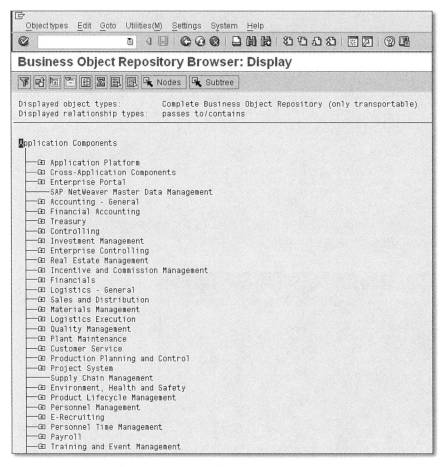

Figure 10.2 Business Object Repository with Business Object Hierarchy

Note

You can inspect the definition of existing object types, but you cannot create new object types in BOR.

10.1.4 Viewing Existing Business Object Types

To use a particular business object type in your workflow, or just understand what it does, it helps to start by having a quick look at it via the Business Object Builder. To give you some idea of what you will see, we will use a business object type that already exists in the BOR throughout this section. This object type is called SBOOK and represents an airline booking reference. This is a training object type that exists in all SAP components. It contains some good examples if you are creating or extending object types, but we simply use it here to demonstrate how to view object types because this object type exists in all SAP components.

If you go to the Business Object Builder (Transaction SWO1), enter object/interface type SBOOK, and choose DISPLAY, you will see a screen similar to Figure 10.3.

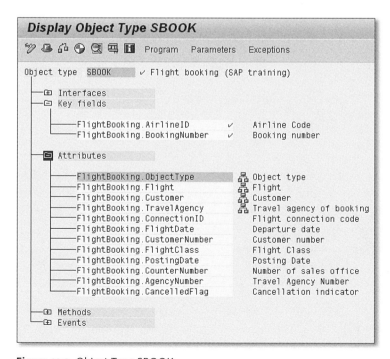

Figure 10.3 Object Type SBOOK

Here you can view all of the components of the object type, including interfaces, keys, attributes, methods, and events. You can expand each node to see the individual components. The individual components are color-coded. Red components are inherited from a supertype or interface; white components are local to this object type.

If you click on the BASIC DATA icon (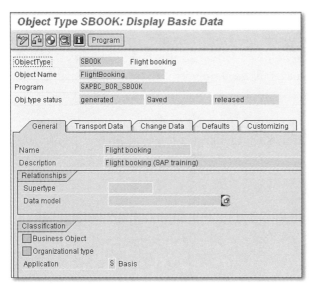), you will see the BASIC DATA for the business object. The BASIC DATA shows you the immediate supertype. You can see there is no supertype for SBOOK in Figure 10.4.

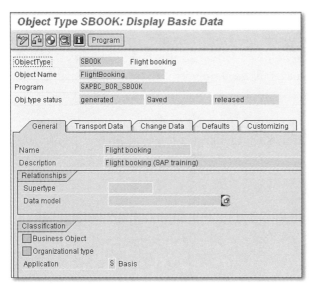

Figure 10.4 Basic Data Information

You can see the details of each individual component by choosing (double-clicking) the component name. Individual components can be local to this object type or come from higher supertypes (including but not limited to "parent," "grandparent," and "great-grandparent" object types) or interfaces. You can see which object type or interface the component is inherited from in the details of the component (field Object Type). For local components, the Object Type field shows the current object type.

If you look at the details of a key field, you can see its data type definition via the REFERENCE TABLE and REFERENCE FIELD settings. By choosing (double-clicking) the field, you can inspect the ABAP Dictionary data type definition of the field. In Figure 10.5, you can see that the key field `AirlineID` of business object `SBOOK` has a reference to Table `SBOOK` field `CARRID` (which defines it as a three-character field).

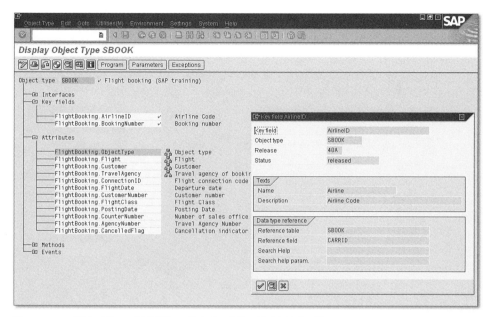

Figure 10.5 Object Type SBOOK — Details of Key Field AirlineID

If you look at the details of an attribute, you can see if it is sourced from a DATA-BASE FIELD or if it is a VIRTUAL attribute (i.e., calculated). Workflow does not need to know where the data comes from, but, of course, the object type needs to know this so that it can determine the attribute value. If the MULTILINE checkbox is switched off, the attribute holds one value only; if it is switched on, the attribute holds multiple values. The DATA TYPE REFERENCE shows you the definition of each attribute value, which may be based on an ABAP Dictionary table/field or refer to another object type.

In Figure 10.6, you can see that the attribute `ConnectionID` of business object `SBOOK` is sourced from the database and is a single value of data type `SBOOK-CONNID` (a four-byte numeric text field). In Figure 10.7, looking at attribute `TravelAgency` shows you a virtual (virtual means calculated) single-value attribute based on object type `SAGENCY`. If you have access to a system, you can choose (double-click) `SAGENCY` to see the `SAGENCY` object type.

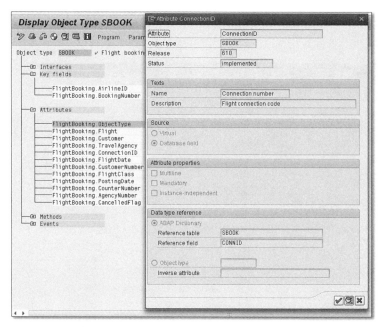

Figure 10.6 Object Type SBOOK — Details of Attribute ConnectionID

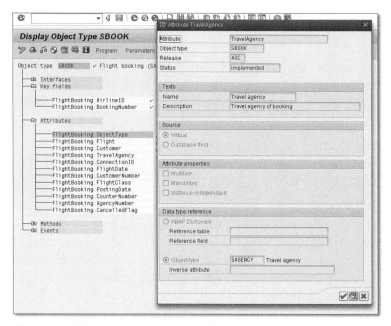

Figure 10.7 Object Type SBOOK — Details of Attribute TravelAgency

Now look at the details of a method:

- If the DIALOG checkbox is switched on, the method requires user interaction. If it is switched off, the method can be executed in the background.

- If the SYNCHRONOUS checkbox is switched off, the method is asynchronous. Asynchronous does *not* mean that the method is launched and the workflow continues without waiting for it to finish. It simply specifies what mechanism is used for confirming that the method has finished, so that the workflow can continue. This is described in detail in Chapter 8, Creating a Workflow.

- If the RESULT PARAMETER checkbox is switched on, you will see that a result type has been specified in the RESULT TYPE tab.

If you choose (single-click) the method name and then choose PARAMETERS, you can see the parameters used by the method. You can see that parameters can be IMPORT or EXPORT. Import parameters are input criteria used to execute the method; export parameters are additional results that can be returned from the method. If you choose (single-click) the method name and select EXCEPTIONS, you can see the possible exceptions (errors) that the method may return. The error type determines how the Workflow Engine responds to the error.

In Figure 10.8, you can see that the method `Edit` of business object SBOOK requires user involvement, is executed synchronously, and has no result. If you have access to a system, you will see it has no parameters and one exception. If you look at the details of an event definition, you can see its name. Business applications that want to communicate with the Workflow Engine can use this name, for example, to trigger the execution of a workflow. In Figure 10.9, you can see the event `Created` of object type SBOOK.

> **Note**
>
> To see the documentation of any component, click the component, and choose the DOCUMENTATION icon (🛈). It is up to the object type programmer to complete the documentation. Not surprisingly, some programmers are more diligent than others. You do not need to read the object type program to work out what each attribute or method does. The name, the documentation, and a little testing (in some cases) are sufficient.

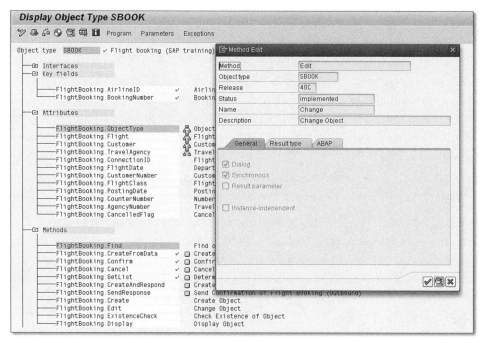

Figure 10.8 Object Type SBOOK — Details of Method EDIT

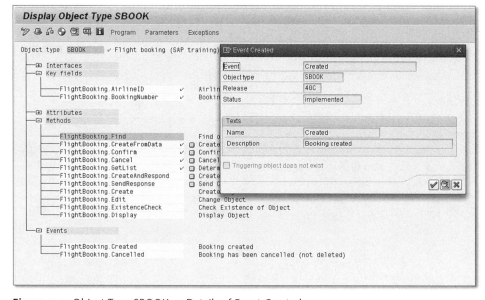

Figure 10.9 Object Type SBOOK — Details of Event Created

To see the program code related to each individual component, click the component, and choose Program. This will take you to the object type program, positioned on the line where the code for that component starts. If you do not choose an individual component before choosing Program, the top of the object type program will be displayed.

Key fields and events do not have any program code associated with them. Key fields are simply declared within the object and are filled when an object is instantiated. The event implementation is coded in the business application and not the business object definition (explained in further detail in Chapter 13, Using Events and Other Business Interfaces).

You can use the Test/execute option () to test the business object type. Here you can create an object instance by entering an appropriate key. All attributes will be extracted from the database or calculated once so that you can check their contents. You can use the Refresh option to recalculate virtual attributes. You can execute methods to verify that they behave the way you expect.

If you have access to a system and want to try this with object type SBOOK, go to the Test/execute option of business object SBOOK (see Figure 10.10). Use the Create Instance option ( ) to choose an existing flight booking. If you do not have any existing flight bookings, use Transaction BC_DATA_GEN to add the training data. Make sure you read the documentation first. When you create an instance, you can either enter the key if you know it, or you can use the input help or the Find option to retrieve the appropriate key.

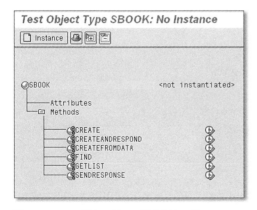

Figure 10.10 Object Type SBOOK — Test

Now all of the attributes are displayed (see Figure 10.11). Database attributes, for example, AGENCYNUMBER, are simply displayed. Virtual attributes, for example, TRAVELAGENCY, have a REFRESH option (🔄) so you can recalculate them. Multiline attributes show you the number of values held. You can expand the list by clicking the MULTILINE icon (🔲) to see the individual values. For any object references shown, clicking the OBJECT icon (⊙) shows the related object instance.

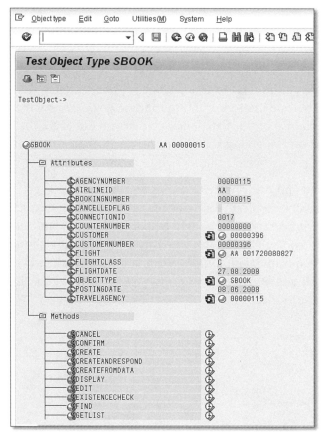

Figure 10.11 Object Type SBOOK — Object Instance Screen

Try choosing the OBJECT icon (⊙) to see the details of TRAVELAGENCY. This displays attributes of the travel agency (e.g., the multiline attribute CustomerList) and test methods of the TRAVELAGENCY object (e.g., method Display to show the name and address of the travel agency).

Each method has an Execute method option (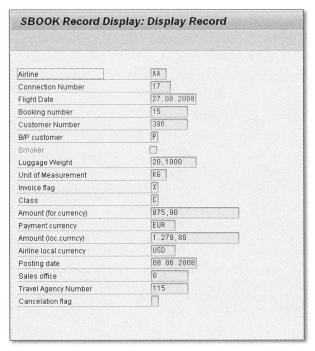) that you can use to start the method. Try executing the `Display` method of your SBOOK object instance (see Figure 10.12). When you execute the method, you will see your flight booking displayed.

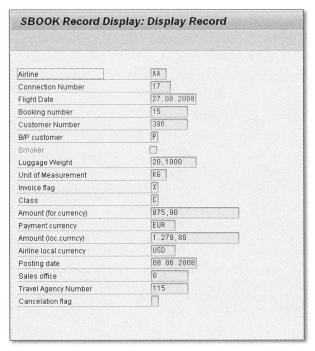

SBOOK Record Display: Display Record

Airline	AA
Connection Number	17
Flight Date	27.08.2008
Booking number	15
Customer Number	396
B/P customer	P
Smoker	☐
Luggage Weight	20,1000
Unit of Measurement	KG
Invoice flag	X
Class	C
Amount (for.currency)	875,90
Payment currency	EUR
Amount (loc.currncy)	1.279,80
Airline local currency	USD
Posting date	08.06.2008
Sales office	0
Travel Agency Number	115
Cancelation flag	☐

Figure 10.12 Object Type SBOOK — Execute Method Screen

10.2   Creating Your Own Business Object Types

Before you create your own business object type, use the Business Object Builder and the BOR to try and find an appropriate existing object type that is close to what you want. Remember that you are trying to minimize development and maximize return on investment, so it is better if you can use or extend an existing object type rather than creating your own from scratch. At the very least, looking at similar object types will give you ideas and examples for creating your own object type. Think carefully about:

▶ What object types do you need for your workflow? For example, `SalesOrder`, `Customer`, `ParkedDocument`?

▶ What attributes do you need for your workflow? To which object will they belong? It helps to know a little object-oriented theory here, but a simple way is to think about what is the strongest relationship. For instance, the name of a customer clearly belongs to the customer object. What about a sales order? We might want to know the customer name on the sales order. Simple! Create a customer attribute on the sales order object that links to the customer object. Then you can not only access customer name but also other attributes of the customer object, including address and credit limit.

▶ What methods do you need for your workflow? To which object will they belong? Remember that each method usually performs one activity, so you might need several methods within your workflow. Rather than creating a huge comprehensive method specific to your workflow, it is better to separate the individual activities, so that they can be used in different combinations by different workflows. It also makes it easier if you later want to change your workflow to add additional activities or adjust the sequence of activities.

▶ What events do you need for your workflow? To which object will they belong? When will you need the business application to let the workflow know that the object has changed its state?

▶ Are there any relevant interfaces? For example, if you want to include a change method, use interface `IFEDIT`. If you want to include a print method, use `IFPRINT`.

There are two ways of creating a new object type:

▶ To create your own object type from scratch, you can create a completely new object type, using the CREATE option on the initial screen of the Business Object Builder. A newly created object type only has the object type components that it inherits from the standard interface `IFSAP`, which is supported by every object type.

▶ To extend an existing object type, you create an object type as a subtype of the existing object type, by entering the existing object type and using the CREATE SUBTYPE option on the initial screen of the Business Object Builder. The keys, attributes, methods, and events of the supertype are immediately inherited by the subtype. All inherited components are marked in red.

When you create a new object type (see Figure 10.13), you specify:

▶ **Supertype**
If any. This field is optional.

▶ **Object Type**
This is the technical ID of the object. Like most technical IDs, it must not have any spaces and must start with an alphabetic character. You do not have to start it with a Z, but it is a good idea to use the usual SAP naming conventions so that you can quickly identify your own object types from SAP object types.

▶ **Object Name**
This describes the object type. Make it meaningful because the name is displayed in monitoring tools throughout the workflow.

▶ **Name**
A short description of the object type useful for finding the object type.

▶ **Description**
A longer description of the object type useful for finding the object type.

▶ **Program**
Each object type has its own program. Like any other program in the SAP system, it must be activated before it can be used at all and activated again after changes have been made. Activating the object type activates the object type program and vice versa.

▶ **Application**
A component, for example, S for Basis, M for Logistics.

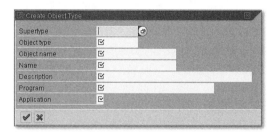

Figure 10.13 Creating a New Object Type

The name, description, and application can be changed later in the BASIC DATA of the object type. If you forget to enter the supertype or want to change it later, you can change it using the menu option OBJECT TYPE • INHERITANCE • CHANGE SUPERTYPE on the initial screen of the Business Object Builder.

The initial status of your object type is MODELED. A modeled object type is designed but not implemented; that is, you cannot use it yet. When an object type has the status MODELED, you can change the status to IMPLEMENTED. After you GENERATE (⊕) the object, you can then use and test the object type. If the tests are successful, you can then change the status to RELEASED.

> **Tip**
>
> Any new components you add or any existing components you change will revert to status MODELED, even though the object type itself is released. There are similar restrictions on using individual components in statuses other than RELEASED.

> **Tip**
>
> There are restrictions on using object types in statuses other than RELEASED. For instance, you cannot use an object type that has merely the status MODELED in tasks or workflows.

10.2.1 Creating New Business Objects

In this example, you will create a new object type representing a "widget," which is a particular type of material. In SAP ERP, SAP delivers a business object type BUS1001 representing a material that has many delivered attributes and methods. By using it in this and the following examples, you will see why it is usually best to use or extend existing object types instead of creating your own from scratch.

> **Caution**
>
> We have chosen object type BUS1001 for use in the following examples. Using an object type that represents a real business entity gives you a better idea of the benefits of extending SAP-delivered object types. However, you should be aware of the following:
>
> ▶ Most SAP-delivered object types representing real business entities have been created and updated over many releases, and their implementation reflects changes in best practice. When you create or extend object types, the *current best practice* for your SAP component release level is shown in training object types such as SBOOK, SAGENCY, or SCUSTOMER.
>
> ▶ Any business object type that you prefer can be used in these examples. For instance, you might want to use LFA1 (Vendor). Make sure that if the object type has a multipart key, you declare all key fields in the example on creating key fields.

▶ If you are in a SAP component that does not include object type BUS1001 or has no material masters, you will need to choose an existing object type from your SAP component instead. For instance, in an SAP SRM or SAP CRM system, you could use object type BUS1178 representing a product or BUS1006 representing a business partner.

▶ You can also execute these examples using the training object type SBOOK in any SAP component if you prefer.

▶ Make sure that whatever object type you use, you have first tested it so that you understand its key, attributes, and methods.

▶ Make sure you have suitable test data available. For example, for BUS1001, you need a valid material ID; for LFA1, you need a valid vendor ID; for BUS1178, you need a valid product GUID; for BUS1006, you need a business partner ID; and for SBOOK, you need a valid booking number.

Finally, SAP delivers tutorials in the SAP Help Portal (*http://help.sap.com*), using the delivered training object types that you can execute in any SAP component. We strongly recommend that you use these tutorials to improve your understanding of the Workflow Engine.

Create a New Business Object from Scratch

The following steps describe how to create a new business object:

1. In Transaction SWO1, enter ZWIDGET1 (or Z and any name), and select CREATE.

2. Leave the SUPERTYPE field blank. This object will not have a parent object.

3. Enter ZWIDGET1 for all other fields, and S for the APPLICATION field.

4. When you select the green check mark to continue (✅), you are asked to provide a PACKAGE for the transport system.

> **Hint**
>
> You should provide a development class for your object and not leave it as a local object. Even if you do not plan to transport your test object, it is still recommended to provide a development class and a transport request.

Create a New Business Object as a Subtype

The following steps describe how to create a new object and how to relate it to a parent object. In this test, ZIDGET2 has object type BUS1001 (material) as its parent.

You will notice the difference between an object with inheritance (ZWIDGET2) and an object where you must create everything from scratch (ZWIDGET1).

1. In Transaction SWO1, enter ZWIDGET2, and select CREATE.

2. Enter BUS1001 as the SUPERTYPE field blank.

3. Enter ZWIDGET2 for all other fields, and S for the APPLICATION field.

4. Compare the two object types. Notice that you have a lot more functionality and much less to develop with ZWIDGET2. On the other hand, you have a lot more freedom, although much more work ahead of you with ZWIDGET1.

5. Look at the object type programs for your two objects by choosing PROGRAM. Compare them, and you will notice the programs are very similar. When you inherit from a parent object, the code remains in the supertype (parent) object. You only see the code in the child (subobject) that was created specifically for that object.

6. Change the status of your object type to IMPLEMENTED using menu option EDIT • CHANGE RELESE STATUS • OBJECT TYPE • TO IMPLEMENTED. Look at the BASIC DATA of your objects to confirm that the status is now IMPLEMENTED.

7. GENERATE your objects.

8. Use the TEST option to test your new objects. This is where you really start to understand the benefits of inheritance because you can access a lot of data and functions via ZWIDGET2 but not much at all with ZWIDGET1.

10.2.2 Extending Existing Object Types Via Delegation

If you create a subtype of an object type, you can choose to *delegate* the supertype to the subtype. Delegation means that wherever the supertype is referenced throughout workflow, the subtype will actually be used instead. This is particularly useful when you find an SAP object type that has most of the attributes, methods, and events that you need and is already used in SAP tasks and workflows. By creating a subtype, you can extend the SAP object type with any additional attributes, methods, or events that you need.

Delegation lets you use all of the existing tasks and workflows based on the SAP object type as if they were using your own subtype. That is, delegation effectively lets you replace parts of the original object type with your own but retain all other parts of the original object type so that you can still profit from any enhancements that SAP delivers when you upgrade to future releases.

For instance, you might delegate the standard SAP object for a customer, KNA1, to a subtype ZCUSTOMER. You have added a new method IncreaseCreditLimit to ZCUSTOMER. This method does not exist in object type KNA1. Delegation lets you create a standard task that refers to method KNA1.IncreaseCreditLimit.

As another example, suppose you want to extend the work item description of a standard SAP task. Here you can use a delegated object type to provide additional information (via attributes). If you use the redefine text option (mentioned in Chapter 8, Creating a Workflow) in the task to add the new attributes, no modification in the business object, task, or workflow is necessary.

You can only delegate to an immediate subtype. Each object type can only be delegated to one subtype. To delegate a supertype to a subtype, from the initial screen of the Business Object Builder, choose menu option SETTINGS • DELEGATE. Enter the original object type as the OBJECT TYPE and the subtype to which it is delegated as the DELEGATION TYPE.

10.3 Creating Business Object Type Components

Before creating any object type components, first check to see if there is a suitable interface that you can use to determine the component name. Using interfaces helps standardize the definition of the object type components and allows generic object type programming. Because many of the monitoring tools use generic programming, using interfaces makes the most of the monitoring tools.

You can use the Business Object Builder to look at suitable interfaces in the same way that you look at object types. All SAP-provided interfaces start with IF. You can create your own interfaces; however, there is no particular need to do so. When you use an interface, you publish to the system that the object type fully supports the methods (with all parameters and all exceptions), attributes, and events defined in the interface. Most interfaces contain only a very few attributes, methods, or events. For instance, the IFEDIT interface contains only one method, Edit.

To add an interface to your object type, choose the component title Interfaces, and choose the CREATE icon (). You can then choose the interface you want to add to your object type by using the search help to find the interface if necessary.

10.3.1 Adding an Interface

The following steps walk you through adding an interface to your new object:

1. Add the interface IFDISPLAY to your object ZWIDGET1. Notice how the method Display has now been added to your object.

2. Choose the method, and then choose PROGRAM to see the default implementation of the method from the interface.

3. If you want to create a new object type component from scratch, choose the component title, for example, Attributes, and then choose CREATE. The technical name of a component follows the usual rules of SAP technical names; that is, it must start with an alphabetic character and must not contain any spaces.

4. If you have an existing component that you have inherited and want to redefine, for example, to change the underlying code, choose the component name and then choose REDEFINE (▧). The component then changes from red (inherited) to white (local), and you can make your changes.

There are some restrictions on what you can change on a redefined component. For example, you can add new parameters but not delete or change the inherited parameters of a redefined method. What happens next depends on the type of component being created.

10.3.2 Creating Key Fields

The key of an object type is not calculated or sourced from the database. Instead, it is provided (usually via an object reference) by the calling workflow, task, method, attribute, or event whenever the object is used. The object instance, instantiated from the object type and key (i.e., as a runtime copy of the object type created), gives you access to all of the attributes and methods of that object.

The key fields of an object type uniquely identify a single object instance of that object type. For instance, the key of the customer object is customer ID. However, keys can also be multipart. For instance, the key of the parked document object is company, document number, and fiscal year. Never include the client (SY-MANDT) within the object key. The assumption is that you are always working in the current SAP client.

Each key field must have a reference to an ABAP Dictionary table/field. This is used to define the data type and length of the key field. Each key field must be based on a single value, not a structure or complex data type. There is an arbitrary limit of 70 characters on the sum of the length of all key fields of an object type.

If you are creating a subtype of an existing object type, you cannot change the key of the object. If you find that you need to change the key of a subtype, then there is probably an error in your design, and you should create a separate business object instead. For instance, SalesOrder might be a subtype of the generic object type Order because both share the same key, namely, order number. However, OrderItem, which has the multipart key order number and order item number, is not a subtype of Order because it has a different key.

Adding a Key Field

In this example, you will add the Material ID as a key field of your ZWIDGET1 object. If you are not using BUS1001 as your example object type, create the same key fields with the same data type references as your example object type.

1. Change your object ZWIDGET1 to add a key field by choosing the component title "Key" and choosing CREATE.
2. Base the key field on the dictionary Table MARA field MATNR.
3. After the key field has been created, go back to the object type program and see that the object declaration has changed.

> **Tip**
>
> Just take note of the program code at this stage; you will see how the object type program is coded later in this chapter.

4. Regenerate and test your new changed object.
5. Attempt to add a new key field to ZWIDGET2. You will not be able to do this because ZWIDGET2 is a subtype. Compare the key and object declaration of ZWIDGET1 to ZWIDGET2.

10.3.3 Creating Attributes

An *attribute* lets you access business data based on the object instance. If you want to use business data in a workflow, for example, in a work item text or a binding, it must first be defined as an attribute of an object. An attribute is something that is known or can be derived from simply knowing the key of the object, or using other attributes of the same object. For example, the customer `Name` is an attribute of the `Customer` object. The customer ID is the key of the `Customer` object. By knowing the customer ID, the name of the customer can be read from the database. Similarly, the `DaysSinceLastOrderPlaced` is an attribute of customer that can be derived by reading the creation date of the last sales order linked to the customer ID.

Attributes can also be instance-independent. Such attributes do not even need an object key. For instance, the total value of all orders placed by customers can be calculated without referring to any particular customer. Attributes do not have parameters and do not return results other than their own value. The name of an attribute is a noun, for example, `TotalValue`, `Name`, `DateCreated`, `CreatedBy`, and `Currency`.

When you create an attribute (see Figure 10.14), you must set the appropriate options to indicate whether the attribute is:

▶ Sourced from a database table/field (default) or virtual, that is, calculated, or an object status.

Database and object status attributes are calculated when the object is instantiated. Virtual attributes are calculated only when and if they are used and are recalculated each time they are used.

▶ Single (default) or multiline (multiple value). Multiple value attributes are nearly always virtual attributes.

▶ Instance-dependent (default) or instance-independent.

You also specify whether the attribute is based on a data type definition (based on an ABAP Dictionary table/field) or an object-type reference.

> **Tip**
>
> You will only be able to choose object status if you have implemented the interface `IFSTATUS` in your object type. An object status attribute is a flag indicating whether or not the object is in that status (according to the SAP central status management).

Usually this is an either/or decision; however, there is one special case where you enter both. If the database field also happens to be the key of another object type, then you can define an object reference using a database attribute. You enter both the data type table/field and the object-type reference by choosing the OBJECT

TYPE REFERENCE option. When the database is read, and the field value returned, the system automatically instantiates an object based on the object-type reference using the field value as the key. This avoids having to code the conversion from field value to object instance. However, this only works when the object-type reference refers to an object type with one and only one key field. Apart from this special case, attributes based on an object-type reference are nearly always virtual attributes.

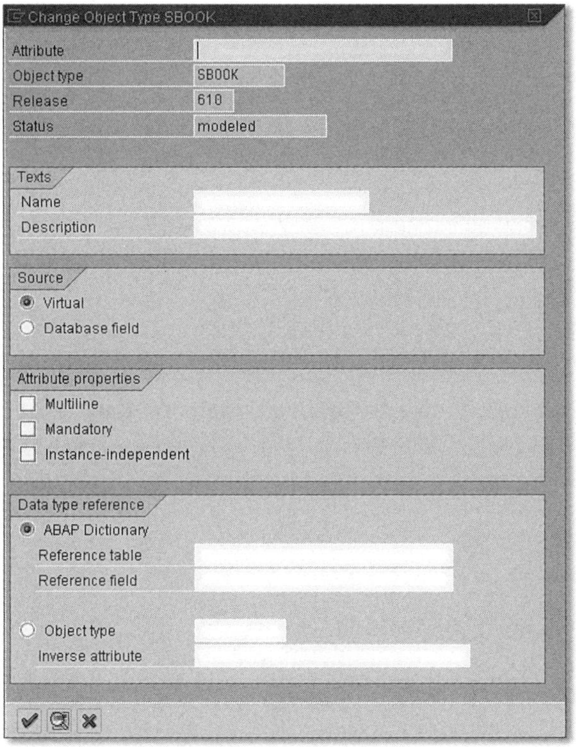

Figure 10.14 Create New Attribute

Because database attributes are the most popular, when you create an attribute from scratch, the system prompts you to see if you are creating a database attribute. The system provides some help in finding the appropriate table/field if you answer YES to the question "Create with ABAP Dictionary field proposals?". Then the system suggests defaults for the NAME, DESCRIPTION, and DATA TYPE REFERENCE.

If you want to create an object status attribute or virtual attribute, or you already know the appropriate table/field, it is best to answer No to the question "Create with ABAP Dictionary field proposals?" Then, go straight to the attribute details screen, and fill in all of the details manually. Object status attributes are always based on the Table SWCEDITOR field OBJSTATUS. At runtime, the status attribute returns X if the status is set, and blank if not.

Each local attribute has a matching implementation in the object type program. Attributes inherited from a supertype have a matching implementation in the supertype program. Within the implementation, the attribute can be buffered to prevent unnecessary recalculations.

> **Tip**
>
> Always fill in the definition's attribute details *before* creating the implementation because the system can then propose an implementation for you.

Database attributes that refer to different fields of the same table share an implementation, so the table is only read once. If you create a local database attribute based on a field from the same table as an inherited database attribute, the supertype implementation is shared. You can declare one attribute as the default attribute in the Basic Data of the object type. This is then used to describe the object in all workflow monitoring reports.

Adding a Database Attribute

In this example, you will add a new attribute for "Material Type" to your ZWIDGET1 object. If you are not using BUS1001 as your example object type, choose a single value ABAP Dictionary-based attribute from your example object type, and create the same attribute in your ZWIDGET1 object.

1. Change your object ZWIDGET1 to add a new attribute by choosing the component title "Attributes" and clicking CREATE.

2. Answer YES to the question "Create with ABAP Dictionary field proposals?" Base your new component on dictionary Table MARA field MTART (material type). Accept the system's proposal for names and descriptions of the attribute. (If you are in an SAP component that does not include field MARA-MTART, use any other field that is relevant to your object.)

3. Notice what checkboxes and values have been set for you in the attribute details screen. You will see that the attribute ID, NAME, DESCRIPTION, DATABASE flag, and DATA TYPE REFERENCE have all been set for you. Notice that the attribute is only in modeled status.

4. Save your object, and regenerate it. Try testing your object. Can you use the new attribute in modeled status? No.

5. Go back to your object, choose your new attribute, and choose PROGRAM. The system asks you if you want it to create an implementation for your attribute. Answer YES.

6. Do not change the code generated at this stage; just inspect it. Note that the status of your attribute has automatically changed to IMPLEMENTED.

7. Regenerate your object, and test it again with a valid material number. Your new attribute shows the material type of the material chosen.

10.3.4 Creating Methods

A method is an activity that can be performed on an object; that is, it lets you access business functions relevant to an object instance. If you want to use a function in a workflow, for example, in a task, it must first be defined as a method of an object. A method is usually a single activity that can be performed on an object instance. The method may include parameters to pass additional criteria from and results to the workflow, and also exceptions to report any errors to workflow.

> **Tip**
>
> All BAPIs, which are standard encapsulated routines provided by SAP that are accessible from inside or outside SAP components, are defined as methods of business object types delivered by SAP. These can be used without changes in workflow, although, in practice, you may want to create your own method as a wrapper around a BAPI to limit its comprehensive functionality. BAPIs are stable, efficient business functions.

A method can be based on any business function or program code you wish, including but not limited to transactions, BAPIs, function modules, RFCs to external system routines, and so on. A method may involve a combination of business functions or even call other methods within its program code. A method name is a verb, for example, `Display`, `Change`, `Create`, `Delete`, or `Post`.

When you create a method, the system prompts you to use a function module as the basis of your method. If you are not using a function module, it is best to answer No to the question "Create with function module as template?" and go straight to the method details. If you choose Yes, the system creates parameters for the method based on the parameters of the function module, and places a call to the function module in the method implementation. As for any generated code, make sure you check it and adjust it (if necessary).

When you create a method (see Figure 10.15), you must specify, via checkboxes, whether the method is:

▶ **Dialog or non-dialog**
Dialog (checkbox is on) indicates that the method requires user involvement. Non-dialog (checkbox is off) indicates that the method can be executed in the background. The Workflow Engine uses this to check if an agent determination is required and whether background processing is possible.

▶ **Synchronous or asynchronous**
Synchronous (checkbox is on) indicates that the activity is complete when the method execution is finished. Asynchronous (checkbox is off) indicates that the activity is not complete until a terminating event is received (e.g., from a business application).

▶ **Returning a result in the standard Result parameter**
If the RESULT PARAMETER checkbox is on, the RESULT TYPE tab must be used to enter the data type definition or object reference for the result. The result can be single or multiline. Results are only relevant for synchronous methods. If the result is a single value based on an ABAP Dictionary data type that has fixed values, then the workflow automatically makes each fixed value a possible outcome of the relevant step. This is in addition to passing back the result value itself.

▶ **Instance-dependent or instance-independent**
Most methods are instance-dependent (checkbox is off); that is, they need an object instance before they can be executed. For example, before a `Display` method of a `Customer` object can be executed, the method needs to know which customer to display. Instance-independent (checkbox is on) methods can be called without an object instance and may be used to create an object instance. For example, a `Create` method does not need an object instance before it is executed but can return the newly created object instance to the workflow.

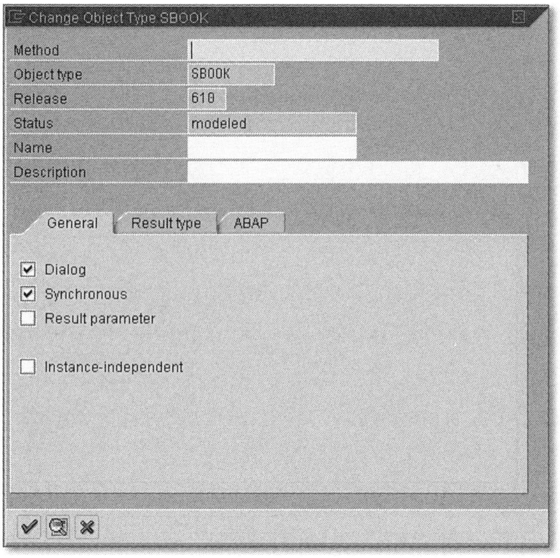

Figure 10.15 Create New Method

You can also use the ABAP tab to enter the main transaction, BAPI, function module, or report to be used in the method. This setting is used to help the system propose an implementation for you but merely provides information after the initial implementation has been proposed.

You can declare one object type method as the default method in the Basic Data of the object. The default method is usually `Display`. It is used when viewing objects from workflow logs and monitoring reports.

Adding a Method to Your Object Type

In this example, you will add a new method "Display" to your ZWIDGET1 object. If you are not using BUS1001 as your example object type, choose a dialog, synchronous method from your example object type, and create the same method in your ZWIDGET1 object. Try to choose a method without parameters based on a simple transaction call. If there is none available, you may need to copy the program code and parameters from your example object type.

1. Change your object ZWIDGET1 to add a new method by choosing the component title Methods and choosing Create.

2. Answer No to the question "Create with function module as template?".

3. Give your method an ID, name, and description. Make it a dialog, synchronous method.

4. In the ABAP tab, choose the TRANSACTION radio button, and enter the transaction ID "MM03" in the field NAME.

5. Notice that your method is only in MODELED status.

6. Generate your object, and test it again. Can you use a method in MODELED status? No.

7. Go back to your object, choose the method, and click PROGRAM. The system asks you if you want it to create an implementation for your method. Answer YES.

8. Do not change the code generated at this stage; just look at it. Note that the status of your method has automatically changed to IMPLEMENTED.

9. Regenerate your object, and test it again with a valid material number. EXECUTE your new method to display the material master of the material you have chosen.

When Do You Define Synchronous Methods

Synchronous methods are called, execute, complete, and return results as an uninterrupted sequence from workflow to task to method and back again. This means the activity performed by the method must be complete when the method execution ends, including any database updates. The following are possible reasons for defining a synchronous method:

▶ The function within the method updates the data in dialog mode; that is, it does not use an update task.

▶ The method is simply to be executed and does not affect the database, as in for example, the method Display for displaying an object.

▶ The user may need to call the method several times while the work item is being processed, and the user manually confirms when the activity is complete.

▶ There is no event that can be used to determine when the activity is complete. In this case, you may need to add completion conditions or subsequent steps to your workflow to check that the activity has been completed, and re-execute the method if not.

When Do You Define Asynchronous Methods

When asynchronous methods are executed, the workflow does not continue to the next step until it receives an acknowledgement that the method has finished. This acknowledgement is returned using a terminating event, which is usually raised by the business application being called from the method.

For example, if you have an asynchronous method `IncreaseCreditLimit` for an object `Customer`, the workflow does not continue until the event `Customer.CreditLimitIncreased` is received. If the agent executing the method (via a work item) only looks at the credit limit or decreases the credit limit, the event is not raised, and the work item remains in the agent's inbox. This also helps agents to confirm they have completed the work correctly.

> **Tip**
>
> If you want to spawn another process to run independently of the current process, instead of creating an asynchronous method in your workflow, simply use an EVENT CREATOR workflow step to trigger another workflow.

Results are not passed from method to task to workflow but from the terminating event to the task to the workflow. By waiting for a terminating event, you ensure that the system is in a consistent state before continuing the workflow, in particular, that any database changes have been committed to the database.

The following are possible reasons for defining an asynchronous method:

▸ The business functions in the method use the update task to change the database.

> **Tip**
>
> Although updates to the database are delayed only slightly by the update task, they can have catastrophic consequences if the workflow continues to the next step before waiting for the updates to be committed. For example, when an object is created in the database in update mode, the next step will terminate with an error if it attempts to query the database reference to the object before the database entry has been written. An asynchronous method ensures that the next step is not started until the database has been committed.

▶ The business function in the method can also be called outside the workflow. You need to know that the activity has been completed regardless of whether it was executed via the work item or directly via a business application.

▶ The business function called in the method has lots of navigation possibilities, in addition to allowing the task in hand to be performed. The only way you can tell that the specific activity has been completed is by receiving the specific terminating event. For example, the `RemoveBillingBlock` method calls a transaction to change a sales order, where many changes can be made. You can only be sure that the billing block was removed when the `BillingBlockDeleted` event is received.

Parameters and Exceptions

You can also define parameters and exceptions for each method. Synchronous methods can accept import parameters and return a result, and export parameters and exceptions. Asynchronous methods can only accept import parameters; they cannot return any results to the workflow directly. However, results can be returned indirectly via terminating events.

> **Note**
>
> Most methods do not need any parameters — knowing the object instance is enough.

Parameters (see Figure 10.16) can be single or multiline, based on an ABAP Dictionary data type definition or an object reference. They can even be untyped. For example, the method `GenericInstantiate` of object type `SYSTEM` returns an export parameter `ObjectInstance`, which is an object instance. However, the object referenced is not known until runtime (in this case, based on the value of import parameter `ObjectType`).

You define method parameters for a method under the following circumstances:

▶ **Import**
Import parameters to pass runtime data, apart from the object instance itself, to the method. These are then used in the method to perform the activity.

▶ **Result**
Result parameter to pass results from the method. This is used for the main result of a method (e.g., the `Result` of an approve method might be the approved/rejected status).

▶ **Export**

Export parameters to pass results, other than the `Result` parameter, from the method (e.g., the rejection reason from an approve method).

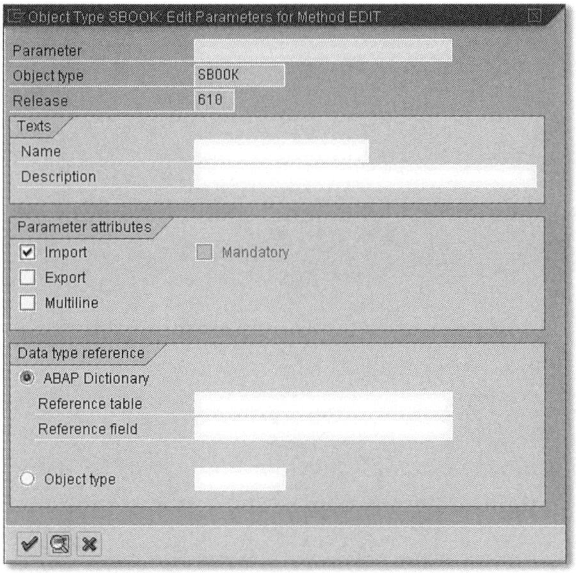

Figure 10.16 Create a New Parameter for a Method

Exceptions (see Figure 10.17) are used to report errors. These are useful both so that the workflow can react to error situations, for example, by steps that help correct the error, and so that the workflow knows if the method has failed to complete the activity successfully. If errors are reported as exceptions, the task and workflow calling the method can take appropriate action, for example, by going into ERROR status.

> **Caution**
>
> If the errors are not reported, the method, work item, and workflow will appear to complete successfully even when the activity fails! This can cause very serious problems in a production environment (refer to Chapter 6, Workflow Administration).

Each exception has a four-digit ID. Your own exceptions can be created in the number range `9000-9999`. SAP also provides many standard exceptions including the following:

▶ 0001-1000

Exceptions defined for interfaces.

▶ 1001-7999

Application-specific exceptions, reserved for SAP development.

▶ 8000-8999

Exceptions triggered by the object manager.

▶ 9000-9999

Customer-defined exceptions, reserved for customers.

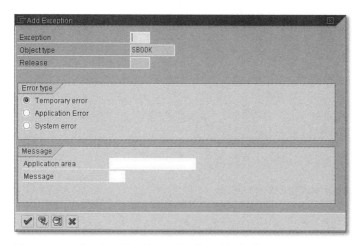

Figure 10.17 Create a New Exception for a Method

> **Tip**
>
> The exceptions are not visible in the task definition, but you will see them again when you inspect the workflow step's outcomes.

For each exception, you specify the class and number of the message to be displayed if the exception occurs. Exceptions are further classified according to error types. The error type determines the default workflow response to be used if the exception is *not* modeled in the workflow. Here are the error types that you can declare:

▶ **Temporary error**
An error where retries can be made to rectify the problem. Suppose, for example, another user has locked the object or canceled execution of the work item.

The default workflow response is to leave a dialog work item in the inbox so it can be retried later. If a background error fails with a temporary error, the Workflow Engine retries the method several times, waiting for several minutes between each attempt (the number of retries and the interval between them is configurable).

▶ **Application error**

An error reported by a business application when, for example, insufficient data are passed to the business function. The default workflow response is to put the work item and workflow into ERROR status.

▶ **System error**

This error type shows incorrect configuration of the Workflow Engine or an inconsistency between object type definition and method call. Missing mandatory method parameters when calling a method is an example of a system error. The default workflow response is to put the work item and workflow into ERROR status.

Each local method has a matching implementation in the object type program. Methods inherited from a supertype have a matching implementation in the supertype program. If you redefine an inherited method, you cannot change or delete the inherited parameters and exceptions that define the interface of the method. You can, however, add further parameters and exceptions.

> **Tip**
>
> Always fill in the method details and parameters *before* creating the implementation so that the system can propose an implementation for you.

Background Method Versus Virtual Attributes

If you have a method that fulfills the following aspects, it is best to convert the method to a virtual attribute:

▶ The method can be run in the background.

▶ The method returns a result.

▶ The method has no other parameters.

▶ The method has no exceptions.

▶ The method does not perform write operations (e.g., update the database).

This is better for overall system performance because an attribute uses fewer resources than a method, and it also minimizes development. To execute a method, you usually require an activity step in your workflow, but a virtual attribute can be accessed directly, for example, in a container operation. Like methods, virtual attributes are only executed when they are used in your workflow.

10.3.5 Creating Events

Events announce a change of state of a business object. Business applications change the state of business objects, so the appropriate business application must include the event-raising implementation and not the object type itself. The object type merely defines the event name so that if several business applications change the state of an object, they will all use the same events consistently and notify the Workflow Engine of the changes in state.

An event name is typically a verb, usually in the past tense. For example, the customer object may have the events Created, indicating a customer object instance has just been created, and Changed, indicating a customer object instance has just been changed.

Creating an Event

The following steps describe how to add an event to an object:

1. Change your object ZWIDGET1 to add an event by choosing the component title EVENTS and then choosing CREATE.

2. Give your event a name.

3. Regenerate your object.

All events automatically include certain parameters within the event implementation, including the object instance and the event initiator (the user executing the business application when the event was triggered).

Events can have additional parameters, which are defined similarly to parameters of a method. When you define additional parameters for an event, you must make sure that the event implementation can fill those parameters. This usually means coding your own event implementation, rather than using generic SAP event implementations (refer to Chapter 13, Using Events and Other Business

Interfaces, and Chapter 14, Custom Programs). Because the implementation is not part of the object type, make sure the event documentation (choose the DOCU-MENTATION icon **i**) explains how the event is triggered for the benefit of other workflow developers.

> **Tip**
>
> Make sure that you document exactly which mechanism raises the event. If it is raised by a program or transaction directly, include the name of the program in your documentation. If your event is raised from outside the SAP component, this documentation is even more important.

10.4 Business Object Type Programming

The access to business data and the calls to business functions are implemented in ABAP code in the business object type program. You have seen in the previous sections that the system can help generate some code for your object type program, but usually you will need to adjust or add your own code to what has been generated.

It is important that you only edit the object type program via the object type in the Business Object Builder because the relationship between the object type and its program is very tight. Avoid using the standard program editor Transactions SE38 (ABAP Editor) and SE80 (Object Navigator) to minimize the risk of synchronization problems between the object type and its program.

> **Caution**
>
> The ABAP editor in the Business Object Builder is more restrictive than some of the other ABAP editors, so you need to take a little more care when creating object type program code.

When you generate a business object type, the system performs a syntax check before generating the object type program. The object type cannot be generated until all syntax errors have been corrected.

If you have examined the code generated by the attribute and method examples, you probably noticed that the object type programs use *macros* extensively. Macros are fragments of code encapsulated in pseudo-ABAP commands. They are used to short-cut development. It is important that you use the macros provided for workflow, particularly when working within the object type program, to ensure consistency and to avoid problems on upgrade.

All macros used within the object type program are included in the INCLUDE program <OBJECT>. This program is automatically included in your object type program when the object type is first created at the very top of the program using the following statement:

```
INCLUDE <OBJECT>.
```

Workflow macros that can be used outside of the object type program, for example, by business applications sending events to workflow or by programmed agent determination rules, are included in the INCLUDE program <CNTN01>. Program <OBJECT> always includes program <CNTN01>.

10.4.1 Key Fields and the Object Declaration

At the top of each object type program is the object declaration bounded by the macros BEGIN_DATA and END_DATA. The object declaration is a complex structure that includes the key fields and the attribute buffer. There is also a private attribute data area where you can buffer intermediate calculation fields that are used by more than one attribute.

Listing 10.1 shows the object declaration that is used in many of the examples in the rest of this chapter. The Table ZWIDGETS is an imaginary ABAP Dictionary table that contains a number of fields, including MANDT (client), ID, Widget_Type, Price, and Quantity. This is presented as a model example of object type programming, showing current best practice at time of printing. However, if you want to recreate this programming in your SAP component, training object types such as SBOOK, SAGENCY, SCUSTOMER, and so on can be used as a guide instead.

```
BEGIN_DATA OBJECT. " Do not change.. DATA is generated.
* only private members may be inserted into structure private
DATA:
  begin of private,
"    to declare private attributes remove comments and
"    insert private attributes here ...
     accountlist type standard table of zwidget_account,
```

```
  end of private,
   BEGIN OF KEY,
       ID LIKE ZWIDGETS-ID,
   END OF KEY,
       TOTAL LIKE ZWIDGETS-PRICE,
       COSTCENTERLIST LIKE ZWIDGET_ACCOUNT-COST_CENTER OCCURS 0,
       OWNER TYPE SWC_OBJECT,
       _ZWIDGETS LIKE ZWIDGETS.
END_DATA OBJECT. " Do not change.. DATA is generated
```

Listing 10.1 Object Declaration in Implementation Program

Provided the object has been instantiated, the key fields will always be filled. You can refer to the key fields in any attribute or method of the object type directly. For example, in Listing 10.1, you can refer to the key field ID as `object-key-id`.

The attribute buffer is used to minimize recalculations. When the implementation of each attribute is executed, it fills the attribute buffer. When the attribute is called again, instead of re-executing all of the code in the attribute implementation, it can retrieve the previously calculated value from the attribute buffer.

Because you do not have full control over when attribute implementations are executed, never retrieve the attribute buffer value of an attribute directly anywhere other than in that particular attribute. If you want to retrieve an attribute value from another attribute implementation or from a method implementation, always use the appropriate macros:

▸ For a single-value attribute, use the macro `SWC_GET_PROPERTY`:

```
SWC_GET_PROPERTY <Object> <Attribute> <AttributeValue>.
```

For example, to retrieve the value of attribute `Name` of the same object, use:

```
SWC_GET_PROPERTY self 'Name' namevalue
```

Make sure that the variable `namevalue` has the same data type definition as the `Name` attribute. `Self` is a special object reference back to the same object instance.

▸ For a multiple value attribute, use the macro `SWC_GET_TABLE_PROPERTY`:

```
SWC_GET_TABLE_PROPERTY <Object> <Attribute> <AttributeValue>.
```

For example, to retrieve the value of attribute `SalesOrderList` (i.e., all sales orders placed by a customer) from a reference to object `Customer`, use:

```
SWC_GET_TABLE_PROPERTY Customer 'SalesOrderList' salesordertab.
```

Make sure that the variable `salesordertab` is an internal table with each row having the same data type definition as the `SalesOrderList` attribute. `Customer` is an object reference pointing to the customer object instance.

▶ All object references, regardless of object type, have the data type definition `SWC_OBJECT`. In the preceding example, `Customer` would have previously been declared using the statement:

```
DATA: Customer TYPE SWC_OBJECT.
```

▶ To fill the object reference, you can instantiate the object using macro `SWC_CREATE_OBJECT`:

```
SWC_CREATE_OBJECT <Object> <ObjectType> <ObjectKey>.
```

To do this, you need to know the technical ID of the order object, in this case, KNA1 (standard object for a customer), and the key of the object instance. In this scenario, the customer ID is held in the field `customer_number`, which has the same data type definition as the key field of object KNA1:

```
SWC_CREATE_OBJECT Customer 'KNA1' customer_number.
```

10.4.2 Programming Attributes

Virtual attributes are implemented with program code. The start of a virtual attribute is the `BEGIN_PROPERTY` macro, and the end is an `END_PROPERTY` macro. The begin/end property macros effectively create a subroutine in which the value of the attribute can be calculated. You can use code and workflow macros to help calculate the value. The usual rules of subroutines apply to your code. Virtual attribute implementations are executed only if and when they are used in the workflow.

The final statement of a single-value virtual attribute implementation is a `SWC_SET_ELEMENT` macro to put the calculated value into the object container under the attribute ID. The Workflow Engine reads the attribute value from the object container.

Tip

The container of an object holds all data accessible to the workflow for that object and is *always* called CONTAINER. The object container's contents include all attributes requested by the workflow and all parameters passed to and from methods.

The basic code of a single-value virtual attribute looks like this:

```
GET_PROPERTY <AttributeID> CHANGING CONTAINER.
  SWC_SET_ELEMENT CONTAINER <AttributeID> <Value>.
END_PROPERTY.
```

Between the `GET_PROPERTY` and the `SWC_SET_ELEMENT` macros, you do whatever you need to do to calculate the attribute value. For example, Listing 10.2 shows the coding of a single-value data type attribute `Total`, which calculates and returns the price multiplied by the quantity. `Price` and `Quantity` are database attributes of the same object; you will see how they are implemented a little later in this section.

```
GET_PROPERTY Total CHANGING CONTAINER.
DATA: price type zwidgets-price,
      quantity type zwidgets-quantity.
  If object-total is initial.
    SWC_GET_PROPERTY self 'Price' price.
    SWC_GET_PROPERTY self 'Quantity' quantity.
    Object-total = price * quantity.
  Endif.
  SWC_SET_ELEMENT CONTAINER 'Total' object-total.
END_PROPERTY.
```

Listing 10.2 Example of a Single-Value Virtual Attribute

Notice how the attribute buffer field `OBJECT-TOTAL` is used. You do not declare it in this code fragment because it has automatically been declared in the object declaration when the attribute details were created. This is evident in the preceding object declaration. Also, notice that before you calculate the value, you check to see if it has been previously calculated by checking whether the attribute buffer field is empty. That way, you only calculate it the minimum number of times and save system resources.

Notice that you only work with the attribute buffer of the current attribute — any other attribute is retrieved using the `SWC_GET_PROPERTY` macro. You cannot retrieve any other attribute directly from the buffer because you cannot guarantee that the implementation for the other attribute has been executed yet. Using `SWC_GET_PROPERTY` ensures that the implementation of the other attribute is executed at least once before you use it.

Multiline Attributes

Multiline attributes are nearly always virtual attributes. The implementation of a multiline attribute is similar to a single-value attribute. The main difference is that the attribute buffer field will be an internal table with each row having the data type reference you specified in the attribute details. Any workflow you create can access the list of values. To write the table to the container, use the macro SWC_SET_TABLE.

The basic code of a multiline virtual attribute looks like this:

```
GET_PROPERTY <AttributeID> CHANGING CONTAINER.
  SWC_SET_TABLE CONTAINER <AttributeID> <InternalTable>.
END_PROPERTY.
```

Between the GET_PROPERTY and the SWC_SET_TABLE macros, you do whatever you need to do to calculate the list of attribute values. For example, Listing 10.3 shows the coding of a multiline data type attribute CostCenterList that calculates and returns a list of cost centers retrieved from Table ZWIDGET_ACCOUNT.

```
GET_PROPERTY CostCenterList CHANGING CONTAINER.
DATA: account_tab TYPE STANDARD TABLE OF zwidget_account,
      w_account_line TYPE zwidget_account.
  If object-costcenterlist[] is initial.
    SELECT id, account_line, cost_center FROM ZWIDGET_ACCOUNT
     INTO CORRESPONDING FIELDS OF TABLE w_account_tab
     WHERE ID = object-key-id.
    LOOP AT account_tab INTO w_account_line
     WHERE NOT cost_center IS INITIAL.
     Append w_account_line-cost_center to object-costcenterlist.
    ENDLOOP.
  Endif.
  SWC_SET_TABLE CONTAINER 'CostCenterList' object-costcenterlist.
END_PROPERTY.
```

Listing 10.3 Example of a Multiline Virtual Attribute

For the sake of the example, the key of ZWIDGET_ACCOUNT is ZWIDGET-ID and ZWID-GET-ACCOUNT_LINE. One ZWIDGET-ID may have multiple ZWIDGET_ACCOUNT entries containing the account assignment split for the ZWIDGET-ID. Not every account assignment line contains a cost center, but the purpose of the CostCenterList attribute is to return all cost centers relevant to the particular ZWIDGET-ID. ZWID-GET-ID is the key of the current object.

Notice the reference to the object key using OBJECT-KEY-ID. Unlike the attribute buffer fields, the key fields of an object are always available, provided the object has been instantiated, because the key fields are filled during instantiation. Notice also that you can use any ABAP code in your attribute implementation, including SELECT, CALL FUNCTION, and so on. You just do whatever you need to do to calculate the list of values.

Of course, if you had several virtual attributes that needed to read data from the ZWIDGET_ACCOUNT table, and they were all used within the same workflow, you could end up calling the database many times to get the same data. There are a few ways you can improve resource usage:

▶ In the ABAP Dictionary, buffer ZWIDGET_ACCOUNT to minimize the direct reads from the database.

▶ Use database attributes instead of virtual attributes because database attributes share the implementation (a SELECT from the database). Of course, this is usually useful only when the attributes are single-value and are taken directly from fields on the table.

▶ Use a subroutine to read the data once and store it in the private object buffer. This way, every subsequent read of the data retrieves the data from the private object buffer.

You will read more on database attribute implementations shortly, so in Listing 10.4, the CostCenterList example is recorded so that other attributes can also use the same ZWIDGET_ACCOUNT data from the private object buffer.

```
GET_PROPERTY CostCenterList CHANGING CONTAINER.
DATA: account_tab TYPE STANDARD TABLE OF zwidget_account,
      w_account_line TYPE zwidget_account.
  If object-costcenterlist[] is initial.
    Perform get_zwidget_account using account_tab.
    LOOP AT account_tab INTO w_account_line
      WHERE NOT cost_center IS INITIAL.
      Append w_account_line-cost_center to object-costcenterlist.
    ENDLOOP.
  Endif.
  SWC_SET_TABLE CONTAINER 'CostCenterList' object-costcenterlist.
```

```
END_PROPERTY.
FORM GET_ZWIDGET_ACCOUNT USING P_ACCOUNT_TAB.
  If object-private-accountlist[] is initial.
   SELECT * FROM ZWIDGET_ACCOUNT
    INTO TABLE object-private-accountlist
    WHERE ID = object-key-id.
  Endif.
  P_account_tab = object-private-accountlist.
ENDFORM.
```

Listing 10.4 Example of Using the Private Object Buffer

Attributes Based on Object References

The single and multiline examples so far have shown how to implement attributes with ABAP Dictionary data type references, but you can also have an attribute that contains an object reference. The code used to implement an attribute based on an object reference is essentially the same, except that the data type of the object reference is always SWC_OBJECT (you can see the automatically generated declaration of owner in the preceding object declaration), and the object reference is filled with a reference to an object instance instead of a value. The object instance can be created using macro SWC_CREATE_OBJECT.

The example in Listing 10.5 shows how to implement an attribute Owner holding a single object reference to the object type User. The owner is the user responsible for widgets of a particular type and price. The key of User is a user ID with data type USR01-BNAME.

```
GET_PROPERTY Owner CHANGING CONTAINER.
DATA: widget_type type zwidgets-widget_type,
      price type zwidgets-price,
      owner type usr01-bname.
  If object-owner is initial.
    SWC_GET_PROPERTY self 'Price' price.
    SWC_GET_PROPERTY self 'Widget_Type' widget_type.
    CALL FUNCTION 'Z_FIND_OWNER'
      EXPORTING
        Price = price
        Type  = widget_type
      IMPORTING
        Owner = owner
      EXCEPTIONS
```

```
      Others = 1.
   If sy-subrc eq 0.
     SWC_CREATE_OBJECT object-owner 'User' owner.
   Endif.
 Endif.
 SWC_SET_ELEMENT CONTAINER 'Owner' object-owner.
END_PROPERTY.
```

Listing 10.5 Example of an Object Reference Virtual Attribute

Notice that the main difference between this and the `Total` attribute implementation is simply the creation of the object reference. In a multiline attribute based on an object reference, each row of the attribute's internal table is an object reference, and the object reference is created in the same way. Notice also that you call a function module from an attribute in exactly the same way as you would in any other ABAP program.

Database attributes whose data type reference shows they belong to the same table share an implementation; that is, there is one implementation per table rather than one implementation per field. This is to minimize resource usage so that each of these tables is read only once when an object is instantiated. The start of the shared database attribute implementation is the `GET_TABLE_PROPERTY` macro, and the end is the `END_PROPERTY` macro:

```
GET_TABLE_PROPERTY <Tablename>.
END_PROPERTY.
```

The begin/end table property macros effectively create a subroutine in which the value of all database attributes using the same table can be calculated. When you create the database attribute details and choose PROGRAM, something like the following implementation is generated (or will be displayed if it has already been generated). Listing 10.6 shows the implementation you would create to implement the `Type`, `Price`, and `Quantity` database attributes that come from Table ZWIDGETS.

```
TABLES: zwidgets.
*
GET_TABLE_PROPERTY ZWIDGETS.
DATA subrc LIKE sy-subrc.
PERFORM select_table_zwidgets USING subrc.
```

```
IF sy-subrc ne 0.
  Exit_object_not_found.
Endif.
END_PROPERTY.
*
FORM select_table_zwidgets USING subrc LIKE sy-subrc.
  If object-_zwidgets-mandt is initial
  And object-_zwidgets-id is initial.
      SELECT SINGLE * FROM ZWIDGETS CLIENT SPECIFIED
        WHERE mandt = sy-mandt
          AND id = object-key-id.
      Subrc = sy-subrc.
      If subrc ne 0. exit. Endif.
      Object-_zwidgets = zwidgets.
  Else.
      Subrc = 0.
      Zwidgets = object-_zwidgets.
  Endif.
ENDFORM.
```

Listing 10.6 Example Implementation of Database Attributes

The macro EXIT_OBJECT_NOT_FOUND sends an exception, that is, an error message "Object does not exist," to the workflow. This tells the workflow that the ID of the widget is invalid or that something is seriously wrong or inconsistent in the database.

Notice the special use of the TABLES statement (remember the TABLES statement is mostly deprecated throughout other ABAP code). Instead of putting the attributes into the container, you fill the TABLES work area ZWIDGETS with the data, and the Workflow Engine retrieves it from here. This is unique to database attributes. Otherwise, the use of the attribute buffer and the calculation of the values is much the same as any other attribute.

> **Tip**
>
> You can replace the generated code with your own, but you must make sure when implementing database attributes that all table fields used in the data type reference of all database attributes in this object *and* its subtypes are filled. You saw when creating attribute details that a database attribute created in a subtype shares the database attribute implementation in the supertype if the supertype already has a database attribute implementation for the relevant table.

10.4.3 Programming Methods

Methods have one implementation per method. The start of a method implementation is the macro BEGIN_METHOD, and the end is macro END_METHOD. The begin/end method macros create, in effect, a subroutine in which the appropriate business functions can be called. The basic implementation of a method looks like this:

```
BEGIN_METHOD <MethodID> CHANGING CONTAINER.
END_METHOD.
```

Between the begin/end method macros, you do whatever you need to do to call the desired business functions.

> **Tip**
>
> Make sure you define the method details and any parameters and exceptions before you create the method implementation. This enables the Business Object Builder to generate not just the start and end of the method but also the macro code to read import parameters from the container at the start of the method. In addition, it copies the result/export parameters into the container at the end of the method.

Listing 10.7 shows an example of a dialog-type (i.e., requiring user involvement), synchronous method called Display that calls a transaction ZWIDGET_DIS. The method is synchronous because it does not involve any database changes. This method does not use any parameters or exceptions.

```
BEGIN_METHOD display CHANGING CONTAINER.
  SET PARAMETER ID 'ZWIDGET' FIELD object-key-id.
  CALL TRANSACTION 'ZWIDGET_DIS' AND SKIP FIRST SCREEN.
END_METHOD.
```

Listing 10.7 Dialog Synchronous Method Calling a Transaction

Notice in Listing 10.7 that methods access attributes in the same way that attributes access other attributes, either using the attribute buffer for the key fields, for example, OBJECT-KEY-ID, or using the SWC_GET_PROPERTY macro for any other attribute. The call to the transaction is made with a CALL TRANSACTION statement exactly the same way you would call a transaction from any other program.

Dialog, Asynchronous Method Calls

Listing 10.8 shows an example of a dialog-type, asynchronous method called `Edit` that calls a transaction `ZWIDGET_CHG`. The method is asynchronous because `ZWIDGET_CHG`, like most SAP transactions, uses `UPDATE TASK` to update the database. This method does not use any parameters or exceptions.

```
BEGIN_METHOD edit CHANGING CONTAINER.
  SET PARAMETER ID 'ZWIDGET' FIELD object-key-id.
  CALL TRANSACTION 'ZWIDGET_CHG' AND SKIP FIRST SCREEN.
END_METHOD.
```
Listing 10.8 Dialog Asynchronous Method Calling a Transaction

Notice in Listing 10.8 that marking a method as synchronous or asynchronous does not necessarily affect the code you use to implement a method; it simply affects how the work item that calls the method will be completed. In Listing 10.8, the transaction `ZWIDGET_CHG` is responsible for sending a terminating event `ZWIDGET.Changed` to the task calling this method when the database update is complete, for instance, by using change document event creation. You will see how business applications send events in Chapter 13, Using Events and Other Business Interfaces. The work item does not complete until the terminating event is received. Calling transactions is usually reserved for dialog methods, where essentially all the workflow needs to do is take the agent to the transaction where the user can complete the business activity.

Background Methods

Background methods usually call function modules or BAPIs where the business activity is performed automatically without any user involvement. Usually, function modules require some sort of parameter input to complete the activity. You use macro `SWC_GET_ELEMENT` to retrieve single-value parameters from the container, and you use macro `SWC_GET_TABLE` for multiline parameters:

```
SWC_GET_ELEMENT <Container> <ParameterID> <Value>.
SWC_GET_TABLE CONTAINER <ParameterID> <InternalTable>.
```

Listing 10.9 shows an example of a background, synchronous method `Delete` that uses a BAPI to perform the deletion. The BAPI requires an import parameter `AuthorizedBy` to receive (via bindings from workflow to task and task to method) the name of the person who authorized the deletion, as well as the ZWIDGET-ID to be deleted.

```
BEGIN_METHOD delete CHANGING CONTAINER.
Data: authagent type usr01-bname,
      authorizer type swc_object,
      authname type addr3_val-name_text.
  SWC_GET_ELEMEMT CONTAINER 'AuthAgent' authagent.
  SWC_CREATE_OBJECT authorizer 'User' authagent.
  SWC_GET_PROPERTY authorizer 'Name' authname.
  CALL FUNCTION 'BAPI_ZWIDGET_DELETE'
  EXPORTING
    ID = object-key-id
    AuthorizedBy = authname
  EXCEPTIONS
    Others = 1.
END_METHOD.
```

Listing 10.9 Background Synchronous Method Using a BAPI

Workflow passes the user ID of the person who authorized the deletion in the import parameter AuthAgent, a single-value parameter with data type reference USR01-BNAME. The method finds the name of the authorizing agent from the attribute Name of object type User, instantiated using the user ID passed in the AuthAgent parameter.

> **Note**
>
> Notice that methods create object references and retrieve attribute values just as you saw in the attribute implementations, and they call function modules in the same way that they are called in any other ABAP program.

Working with Exceptions

There is one major problem with the preceding method. If anything goes wrong with the activity, the Workflow Engine is not notified. It completes normally because everything was apparently successful. Methods that do not return errors can cause a very serious problem from a business perspective. Not only do they let a business process abort in midstream, but they also make it extremely difficult to find out what went wrong when everything in the workflow log states that the method has been successful. Thus, it is important to have some way of detecting these errors within your method, for example, by using the exceptions returned by function modules or the MESSAGES option of a CALL TRANSACTION USING statement. Alternatively, you can make the method asynchronous and use a terminating event to confirm that the business function called was successful.

You can improve this method by reporting any errors. Two major errors might occur:

▶ The AuthAgent might not be a valid user.

▶ The deletion itself may have failed, for example, due to someone locking the ZWIDGETS table entry.

The exceptions need to be defined within the method details, in the EXCEPTIONS section of the method, before they can be used.

Each exception has a four-digit number, such as 9001, which is linked to the message class and message number to be displayed, and also an error type (TEMPORARY, APPLICATION, or SYSTEM error) that helps the workflow to decide how to handle the error. To send an exception to workflow, you use the macro EXIT_RETURN, specifying the exception number and the parameters for the message. Messages have a maximum of four parameters (SY-MSGV1 to SY-MSGV4), and the macro requires that you always send four parameters. So for any unused parameter, you simply use the reserved word SPACE:

```
EXIT_RETURN <Exception> <Var1> <Var2> <Var3> <Var4>.
```

In the example in Listing 10.10, you are reporting system exception 9001 (AuthAgent &1 does not exist) and temporary exception 9002 (Widget &1 could not be deleted). Notice that the error type of the exception does not affect the implementation.

```
BEGIN_METHOD delete CHANGING CONTAINER.
Data: authagent type usr01-bname,
      authorizer type swc_object,
      authname type addr3_val-name_text.
  SWC_GET_ELEMEMT CONTAINER 'AuthAgent' authagent.
  SWC_CREATE_OBJECT authorizer 'User' authagent.
  If sy-subrc ne 0.
    EXIT_RETURN 9001 authagent SPACE SPACE SPACE.
  Endif.
  SWC_GET_PROPERTY authorizer 'Name' authname.
```

```
CALL FUNCTION 'BAPI_ZWIDGET_DELETE'
EXPORTING
  ID = object-key-id
  AuthorizedBy = authname
EXCEPTIONS
  Others = 1.
  If sy-subrc ne 0.
    EXIT_RETURN 9002 object-key-id SPACE SPACE SPACE.
  Endif.
END_METHOD.
```

Listing 10.10 Implementation of Exceptions

As with function module exceptions, when you send a method exception, no result or export parameters are sent, so use exceptions only for error or abort situations. Workflow can respond to the error by either retrying the work item at a later time, putting the work item into ERROR status, or performing alternative steps in the workflow, depending on the error type and whether the exception has been modeled in the workflow.

Methods can also return results in export parameters or in the special Result parameter. The result parameter and any export parameters must be defined in the method details before using them in the method. To return results to the container, you use macro SWC_SET_ELEMENT for single values and SWC_SET_TABLE for multiline parameters:

```
SWC_SET_ELEMENT <Container> <ParameterID> <Value>.
SWC_SET_TABLE CONTAINER <ParameterID> <InternalTable>.
```

Listing 10.11 shows an example of a dialog, synchronous ApproveDeletion method that returns a result of 0 "approved" or 1 "rejected." If rejected, it also returns an export parameter RejectionReason. The special variable RESULT ensures that the result is returned with the special predefined parameter name _RESULT.

```
BEGIN_METHOD approvedeletion CHANGING CONTAINER.
Data: approvalstate type syst-index,
      rejreason type zwidget-text.
  Clear rejreason.
  CALL FUNCTION 'BAPI_ZWIDGET_APPROVEDELETE'
  EXPORTING
```

```
    ID = object-key-id
  IMPORTING
    Approvalstate = approvalstate
    Rejection_text = rejreason
  EXCEPTIONS
    Cancelled = 1
    Others = 2.
  Case sy-subrc.
    When 0.
      SWC_SET_ELEMENT CONTAINER RESULT approvalstate.
      SWC_SET_ELEMEMT CONTAINER 'RejectionReason' rejreason.
    When 1.
      EXIT_CANCELLED.
    Others.
* Send exception "approval failed"
      EXIT_RETURN 9003 object-key-id SPACE SPACE SPACE.
  Endcase.
END_METHOD.
```
Listing 10.11 Dialog Synchronous Method with Result

Notice the special exception EXIT_CANCELLED, which is used to tell workflow that the user has opted not to complete the activity at this time. By default, the work-flow keeps the work item in the agent's inbox in IN PROCESS status so that the agent can complete the activity later. Like any other exception, you can also model alternative steps to be taken if this exception is received.

If you are implementing an instance-independent method that returns an object reference to an instance of the current object type instead of a parameter, you use macro SWC_SET_OBJECTKEY:

SWC_SET_OBJECTKEY <ObjectKey>.

Sometimes you might want to call a method to help calculate an attribute or within another method. To do this, you use the macro SWC_CALL_METHOD:

SWC_CALL_METHOD <Object> <Method> <Container>.

You can use the macros SWC_SET_ELEMENT and SWC_SET_TABLE to fill the import parameters of the method to be called in the container, and the macros SWC_GET_ELEMENT and SWC_GET_TABLE to read export parameters and results after the method is executed. If you want to create a separate temporary container just for calling the method to avoid putting stray data in the current object container, you can use macro SWC_CONTAINER to declare it and SWC_CREATE_CONTAINER to initialize it.

You will find a list of common workflow macros in Appendix D, Workflow Macros.

10.5 Some Useful Predefined Object Types

Next, we will discuss several predefined object types that can be very useful.

10.5.1 Object Type SELFITEM

The object type SELFITEM provides methods that operate on a work item that represents its own task. When you execute the work item, the object on which the method operates is this work item itself. This is chiefly useful when you want to send an email using the method SendTaskDescription or for manipulating attachments. All attachments must be objects of the type SOFM. Useful methods of SELF-ITEM include the following:

▶ SendTaskDescription
The task description is sent as a mail in the background. If the mail cannot be sent, the method reports this with an exception.

▶ PrintTaskDescrBatch
Printing a task description in the background to a nominated printer.

▶ PrintTaskDescrDialog
Printing a task description in dialog. The agent is asked to supply the print parameters, including the printer to be used.

▶ Note_Create
A document is created and then added to the work item as an attachment. The agent is prompted either to create the document or to import it from a document on his local file system or from an SAPoffice folder.

▶ Note_Display
This method is used for displaying an attachment. Most inboxes allow you to optionally display attachments. You can use this method to force the display of an attachment to an agent.

▶ Note_Change

This method is used for changing an attachment.

Tip

The SELFITEM object cannot be delegated. This is the only object type in the system that is prevented by the system from being delegated.

10.5.2 Object Type WF_TASK

The object type WF_TASK provides methods for finding and assigning agents for steps in the workflow. An object of the type WF_TASK is a task specified with type (e.g., TS for standard task) and number (eight digits):

▶ The most useful attribute of WF_TASK is AllAgentsOfTask. This returns a list of all possible agents assigned to a task.

▶ The most useful method of WF_TASK is AllAgentsOfTaskGetAndDispatch. This lets an agent dynamically decide who will be the agent for a subsequent step from a list of all possible agents of the task underlying the subsequent step. The Workflow Builder Wizard CHOOSE AGENT uses this method.

10.5.3 Object Type SYSTEM

Object type SYSTEM holds a few useful utility methods, including GenericInstantiate. This creates an object reference from an object type and its matching key. The parameters are untyped, so you can use this to create any object reference.

10.5.4 Object Type FORMABSENC

This object type provides an absence notification example of a business application object. It is also used in the many SAP-supplied demonstration workflows and in the SAP Help Portal workflow tutorials. Just do a search for "workflow tutorial" at *http://help.sap.com*.

10.5.5 Object Type USR01

Object type USR01 represents a user and includes a very useful method FindUserFromAgentStructure. This is an agent and converts it to a user object (object type

USR01). You can then access attributes of the user, including name and contact details.

Tip

This object type is often included as an attribute in other object types, for example, Dialog Item. So by delegating to extend it, you automatically make your extensions (e.g., you might add the email address of the user) available to all other object types and workflows within the system without even editing them. Even the SAP-supplied workflows will have access to your extension.

10.6 Real-World Examples for Business Object Customizing

As previously mentioned, you should extend an object type rather than create a new object type when you want to create additional components for an object or augment additional components for an object type that are not provided in the standard version and at the same time need to ensure that standard scenarios with the original SAP object type remain operational.

You can create a new object type as the subtype of the original object type, which will then inherit its components and the related implementations. You can then augment this object type and make it the delegation type of the supertype. All calls to the "old" object type (supertype) are redirected to the delegated "new" object type (subtype) so that its definition is read and executed (delegation).

Now let's look at some real-world business scenarios that required the augmentation of a SAP-delivered business object.

10.6.1 Custom Attribute

This section provides examples of custom attributes that were developed by customers.

Object Type BUS2121 — Shopping Cart Approval (SRM)

In SAP Supplier Relationship Management (SAP SRM), the business object for approval of a shopping cart BUS2121 is used by various workflows. The customer's business requirement was to trigger a custom workflow for a shopping cart that is out of the requisitioning limit. The business process must send an email to the requisitioner to inform him that the shopping cart he just created is out of his requisition limit.

SAP does not deliver an approval workflow that meets this requirement, therefore, the customer had to build a custom workflow and wanted to reuse as much of the SAP-delivered components as possible. Additionally, before any approval workflow is triggered, start conditions needed to be evaluated to compare the value of the shopping cart with the users' requisition limit. In order to do this, the customer:

▶ Created a subtype ZBUS2121 for object BUS2121 and performed delegation.

▶ Created a new virtual attribute called ZOutOfLimit in the subtype ZBUS2121. The program for this new attribute determined the requisition limit assigned to this user and compared it with the value of shopping, which is already available when you instantiate the business object.

▶ Set ZOutOfLimit to 1 if the shopping cart exceeded the requisition limit. If the shopping cart did not exceed the limit, then it was set to 0.

After the changes in the business object, the customer was able to use the newly defined attribute in the custom workflow. Additionally, this could be used to evaluate your start conditions and determine if a normal approval workflow should be triggered for a newly created shopping cart or a custom "out of requisition limit" workflow.

Object Type BUS2089 — Employee Trip

In this scenario, the customer required a design in which an employee travel request with an advance should have a two-tier approval process. Initial approval is obtained from the employee's immediate supervisor, and the second tier approval is from the accounts payable manager.

To facilitate this customer requirement, a subtype ZBUS2089 was created for business object BUS2089. An attribute CashAdvance was introduced in business object ZBUS2089, which is really a flag that is set true when a trip has some advance in PTRV_SHDR-SUM_ADVANC, and false when this field has no value.

The attribute CashAdvance can now be used within the workflow template in a condition step to decide if workflow needs to pursue approval from the accounts payable manager for the trip.

Object Type BUS7026 — Appraisal

The customer has implemented workflow for performance appraisal with some enhancements to incorporate their processes. The supervisor of an employee creates an appraisal. When the appraisal is completed and saved, a workflow is triggered with a work item sent to the employee for review. The employee can review the appraisal, update it with comments, and save the document. After the employee saves the appraisal and completes the work item, the workflow should go back to supervisor for final comments. However, because the triggering event for this workflow is CompletedAppraisal, when the employee saves the appraisal, another workflow is triggered for the same appraisal. To avoid duplicate workflows, the customer:

- Created a subtype ZBUS7026 for object BUS7026 and performed delegation.
- Created a new virtual attribute called ZWorkflowStarted in the subtype ZBUS7026. The program for this new attribute used function SAP_WAPI_WORKITEMS_TO_OBJECT to determine if there were active workflows for the appraisal object in question.
- Set ZWorkflowStarted to S if there was an active workflow already in process, and X if there were no workflows in process.
- Created a start condition for business object BUS7026 (Template WS#########) to check that ZWorkflowStarted is X before triggering a new workflow. This ensured that at any given time only one workflow was triggered for an Appraisal Object.

10.6.2 Custom Method

Custom methods enable you to extend the object to include additional functionality and capabilities of the object type. Here we outline three examples that were required by a customer.

Object Type FLA1 — Vendor Master

In this situation, the customer needed to design an approval process for changes made to specific data in vendor master. In this specific case, it was the bank account number (LFBK-BANKN). The bank account number on the vender master can have a change marker attached to it. When the change marker is enacted, a given event is triggered and workflow starts.

The workflow checks certain conditions:

- If they are met, then a work item is sent to the authorized individuals requesting their approval of the change. The custom method was used to unblock the vendor account.

- If the conditions are not met, no approval is required; workflow then executes the task that calls the custom method to automatically release the block on the account.

Object Type BUS2089 — Employee Trip

This scenario is based on approval of a travel expense for an employee. Normally, approval processes automatically go to the employee's direct manager. For this customer, a policy required all expenses created by the CEO to be approved by the CFO. This approval requirement was in conflict with the HR organization chart, which has the CFO reporting to the CEO. This meant an exception is required in the workflow approval process to ensure that only if the expense is created by the CEO should it be sent to this specific position occupied by the CFO.

The customer handled this by creating a custom method to determine if the expense was created by the CEO. This was done in a subtype of BUS2089 that was delegated to the SAP object type. The method was then called as an initial step in the workflow to determine the approval path for the expense claim.

Object Type BUS2014 — Purchase Contract

The customer needed to create an approval process for all contracts that were considerably amended. Criteria for considerable amendment of a contract were if the value, quantity, or validity date of a contract was modified. In the event that a contract was amended, an approval workflow was triggered and sent to the supervisor for approval. Deadline rules were implemented so that the supervisor was given two business days to complete this approval. After the deadlines expired, a work item was sent to the contract amender informing him of the same and allowing him to select an appropriate approver who occupied a position above his in the HR organizational structure.

The following steps outline the custom work that was required for this scenario:

▶ The customer extended business object BUS2014 to ZBUS2014.

▶ A custom dialog, synchronous method was created. The new method had to read the "level" of the current user and build an internal table for all possible approvers, navigating up the reporting chain to the director level.

▶ A pop-up screen was also shown to the user, with a list of possible approvers, within this method.

▶ Certain validations were performed on the selection of approver made in the preceding step.

▶ The final selection was passed back as the agent to the next step, which was approval of contract amendment in a work item.

Thus, the users were given an option of selecting an ad-hoc approver to review the amended contracts.

ABAP classes are the modern-day evolution of ABAP into an object-oriented language. Whereas Business Object Repository objects require specialist programming skills, ABAP classes in workflow use regular object-oriented ABAP, making workflow development more accessible to anyone with up-to-date ABAP development skills, as well as facilitating reuse of objects in workflow and other applications. This chapter demonstrates the techniques required to effectively build and use ABAP classes in workflow.

11 ABAP Classes

Many of the reasons for using object orientation in workflow development have already been discussed in Chapter 10, Business Objects. Therefore, this chapter focuses on what is new with ABAP classes, how using ABAP classes in workflow differs from using BOR objects (Business Object Repository) in workflow, and some advanced techniques only possible by using ABAP classes in workflow.

> **Note**
>
> Although the formal term is in fact is "ABAP objects," we use the term "ABAP classes" throughout this book to accentuate the difference between BOR objects and ABAP objects.
>
> In the BOR world, the term "object" is often generalized to mean both *object instances* and *object types*. In the ABAP objects world, this distinction is emphasized through the use of separate terms for the two concepts, namely *objects* (instances) and *classes* (object types).

This chapter starts by explaining the background behind the different technologies, and then — using practical examples — gradually builds up to implementing a fully fledged business object as an ABAP class in workflow.

Because you are likely to be either an experienced developer already familiar with classes or a workflow developer moving to classes for the first time, this chapter takes on the format of a practical real-world approach rather than repeat the theory contained in Chapter 10, Business Objects. Therefore, if you are new to workflow *and* ABAP objects and skipped Chapter 10, we strongly recommend going back to it because it will greatly enhance your understanding of this chapter. Most object-orientation fundamentals are discussed there, and BOR remains very important because many SAP-delivered workflows are based on BOR.

We have used two example scenarios, both of which can also be built on a SAP NetWeaver trial system (available from SDN, *http://sdn.sap.com*). We start off with a very simple utility class and then a simple business class to implement the equivalent of the USR01 BOR object. The SAP NetWeaver system also includes a great workflow-enabled ABAP class example CL_SWF_FORMABSENC, which uses techniques similar to those described in this chapter.

11.1   ABAP Classes Basics

A relatively new feature within SAP Business Workflow is the possibility to use ABAP objects instead of BOR objects. For the most part, they behave in exactly the same manner when viewed within the Workflow Builder as traditional BOR objects.

11.1.1   History

So the question arises: Why have two completely different technologies to accomplish exactly the same thing? To answer this, we need to look at a little bit of history first:

▶ SAP Business Workflow was introduced into SAP R/3 back in release 3.0C. At that time ABAP was completely procedural — modularity was achieved by the use of PERFORM and CALL FUNCTION. The design philosophy of workflow required features that only object orientation could offer, such as abstraction and encapsulation (as discussed in Section 10.1, Business Object Basics). To overcome the limitations of ABAP, the Business Object Repository (BOR) was developed to emulate object orientation in a procedural language. The BOR objects' emulation of object orientation is of a high standard, but it is not natively object-oriented and therefore lacks certain features found in fully fledged object-oriented languages.

▶ In release 4.6, ABAP became an object-oriented language in its own right, supporting classes natively. However, workflow had already grown into a mature technology firmly rooted in BOR objects and did not support classes.

▶ As of Basis release 6.20 (SAP R/3 4.7 Enterprise Edition), workflow could make use of ABAP objects; however, there were limitations, and their use by customers was not officially supported by SAP. By this stage, the BOR content had grown to more than 1,000 object types.

▶ As of release 6.40, ABAP objects are fully usable in workflow, and their use by customers is also supported by SAP. It is in SAP ERP (ECC 6.0) — based on SAP NetWeaver 7.0 — that we see SAP-delivered workflows using ABAP classes.

Figure 11.1 summarizes this timeline of object-oriented technologies in workflow history.

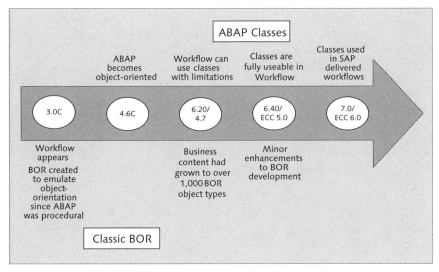

Figure 11.1 Timeline of Object-Oriented Technologies in Workflow

11.1.2 Why Use Classes

Given that there is such a large repository of BOR objects available, you might wonder why you would want to use classes. Obviously, they are new and therefore a more modern technology, but newer does not always mean better. Table 11.1 lists some of the advantages and disadvantages of both ABAP classes and BOR objects.

BOR Objects	ABAP Classes
Advantages	
► More than 1,000 BOR object types exist, and almost all of the existing workflow functionality delivered by SAP uses them. ► BOR objects are used heavily in the SAP Business Suite. SAP Business Suite applications such as SAP ERP, SAP CRM, and SAP SRM use BOR objects. ► There are many events associated with BOR objects that happen natively in the SAP system. These are systemwide events.	► ABAP objects use the newer ABAP Editor and enforce improved coding standards by only allowing the use of object-oriented ABAP standards and syntax. ► Functional methods present great new opportunities to do clever things in bindings. ► After a class is in place, it is very easy to add additional components or functionality. ► The usage of ABAP classes is not limited to workflow. ► ABAP classes can be maintained by developers without any specialist workflow knowledge. ► SAP Business Suite applications use ABAP classes in workflow. SAP SRM, SAP CRM, and SAP ERP HCM ESS/MSS use ABAP classes in addition to BOR objects.
Disadvantages	
► The use of macros to simulate the "object-oriented" constructs are specific to BOR and workflow programming and thus require specialist knowledge for workflow developers above and beyond regular ABAP skills. ► Although BOR provides most components of an object-oriented paradigm, some object-oriented principles such as inheritance and polymorphism are only partly supported (to a lesser extent this is still the case for classes in workflow).	► There is a little more work required upfront to create a new class. This is, however, only a short-term overhead; classes are well worth the effort in the long run as the reduced maintenance costs pays off very quickly. ► Many customers are still on older SAP versions where classes are not yet supported. ► The concept of delegation does not exist. In object orientation, it is not necessary because the same objective can be achieved using interfaces. However, these are not supported by the Workflow Engine.

Table 11.1 Advantages and Disadvantages of BOR Objects and ABAP Classes

BOR Objects	ABAP Classes
	▶ For developers experienced with BOR development but with no knowledge of ABAP objects, there will be a learning curve involved in learning the object-oriented syntax, which is not actually a bad thing because almost all of SAP's internal workflow code is object-oriented!

Table 11.1 Advantages and Disadvantages of BOR Objects and ABAP Classes (cont.)

Note

Varying opinions exist on whether to use ABAP classes or BOR objects for a workflow project. There are expert workflow consultants who use ABAP classes that consider them to be an improvement over BOR objects and tend to use them as much as possible. SAP supports both ABAP classes and BOR objects equally for workflow development.

ABAP objects are integral to the ABAP language, so there is nothing special about developing business objects for use in workflow as far as language is concerned. This means that in projects where an ABAP class is used for workflow and non-workflow development, it is much easier to reuse a class developed for workflow elsewhere or vice versa. More importantly, it also makes workflow programming accessible to many more developers.

To use functionality developed inside a BOR object, you always need to use BOR macros to, for example, call a method or read an attribute of the object, making it unsuitable for use by developers who are not familiar with workflow.

There is also a bonus for readers who do not come from a development background and find the prospect of learning a new style of programming a little daunting. ABAP classes make the learning curve easier because you can ask your friendly ABAP developer for help if you get stuck!

11.1.3 More Resources

The transition from SAP R/3 to SAP NetWeaver was far more than just a change of name. The ABAP language itself underwent a major transformation from a procedural into an object-oriented language, and ABAP objects now form the basis of

ABAP in modern SAP NetWeaver ABAP systems. One reason that BOR objects and ABAP classes in workflow are quite different is that BOR was designed specifically with workflow in mind, whereas ABAP objects are native ABAP language constructs that were later made compatible with workflow.

For this reason, this chapter does not go in-depth on object-oriented ABAP but instead focuses on the workflow-specific aspects. Many resources are available that cover ABAP objects: the SAP Help Portal (*http://help.sap.com*), SDN content (*http://sdn.sap.com*), and various books — ranging from introductory to advanced. To name a few: *Object-Oriented Programming with ABAP Objects* (SAP PRESS, 2009), *ABAP Objects: ABAP Programming in SAP NetWeaver* (SAP PRESS, 2007), *ABAP Objects: Application Development from Scratch* (SAP PRESS, 2008), and *Next Generation ABAP Development* (SAP PRESS, 2007).

If you are into serious development, we particularly recommend the last title. Although it doesn't provide much guidance on the object-oriented language itself, it provides short overviews on several diverse technologies and concepts often used in conjunction with workflow, including data persistence and persistent classes, business classes, Web Dynpro ABAP, Business Server Pages (BSP); SAP Interactive Forms by Adobe, and the SAP NetWeaver Portal.

11.2 Comparing ABAP Classes and BOR Objects

There are a multitude of differences between the two technologies, and this section aims to provide a high-level overview of the key differences necessary to understand before creating your first class. We will also present some of the most important new or changed terminology.

11.2.1 Interfaces

You will see a difference in interface usage between BOR objects and ABAP classes:

▶ **BOR objects**
BOR objects all implement the standard `IFOBJECT` interface, which provides most of the object-oriented functionality. Everything is generated automatically, and developers rarely need to concern themselves with it.

Other interfaces are also available but are also not that commonly used among developers. This is in part due to the limited scope of the object-oriented emulation that BOR provides in this area: The greatest use for interfaces is the object-oriented concept of polymorphism (the ability to substitute one object type for another at runtime without affecting the application that uses it), which only functions in certain scenarios. You cannot, for example, define a container element of type IFAPPROVE for a generic approval workflow for different object types. To some extent, this is also still the case with ABAP classes.

► **ABAP classes**
In contrast, ABAP classes rely heavily on interfaces. The first major difference you will encounter between BOR objects and ABAP classes is that you need to implement the object instantiation yourself in the persistency interface — something done for you when using BOR objects. Although this may seem like additional work, it provides greater flexibility in developing with classes.

11.2.2 Object Identification

Workflow identifies different instances of a business object by means of a key. Where an object represents a business document, this is usually the document number or ID. This key forms part of a *Local Persistent Object Reference* (LPOR), which forms the basis of persistence management of objects in workflow:

► **BOR objects**
BOR object keys consist of one or more fields and can have a maximum length of 70 characters in total.

In the case of BOR objects, this was once again made simple: Everything is handled transparently within the generated BOR code. It was only in rare cases (e.g., programmed binding) that a developer needed to work with persistence using the swc_object_to_persistent and swc_object_from_persistent macros.

► **ABAP classes**
ABAP class keys can also consist of one or more fields; however, their combined length is limited to 32 characters. This can be overcome by the use of GUIDs as described later in this chapter.

With ABAP classes, you need to implement instance and persistence management yourself in the BI_PERSISTENT interface. Although this may seem like more work, it does give you a lot more control.

11.2.3 Class/Component Level

Although the concept of *instantiated* and *instance independent* objects and components is identical in the BOR and class worlds, terminology is different:

► **BOR objects**

In the context of BOR objects, everything either refers to an instance or was specifically termed *instance independent;* that is, it was uncommon to use a specific term for instance-specific objects or components.

► **ABAP classes**

In an ABAP class context, we talk about *levels,* and what BOR called instance specific is now at *instance level,* and instance-independent components are known as *static.* A third level — *constant* — exists, which behaves exactly like a constant declaration in regular ABAP code.

11.2.4 Attributes

With attributes, there is a significant conceptual difference between BOR objects and ABAP classes:

► **BOR objects**

In object-oriented development, methods are functions to be executed, and attributes represent values associated with an object. With attributes, BOR objects deviate from this philosophy because attributes are pieces of code that are executed every time a program queries an attribute. This is exactly how a virtual attribute works, and a database attribute simply generates the code for you.

An advantage of this design over traditional object orientation is the ability to calculate values on the fly in virtual attributes, and a disadvantage is that all attributes are read-only (i.e., it is not possible to assign a value to an attribute from outside the object).

► **ABAP classes**

With ABAP classes, attributes behave in a more intuitive manner: They represent variables that belong to an object. This means that virtual attributes are no longer possible; however, *functional methods* (covered later on in this chapter) provide a superior alternative.

11.2.5 Methods

Methods also have significant differences between BOR objects and ABAP classes:

▶ **BOR objects**
BOR methods have three types of parameters: import, export, and result. They also have additional properties that influence the task that they are used in — namely, the dialog/background and synchronous/asynchronous settings.

▶ **ABAP classes**
ABAP class methods do not have a result parameter, but they do have a returning parameter that is used in functional methods. They also contain no workflow-specific information. Dialog/background and synchronous/asynchronous behaviors are controlled entirely by the task.

11.2.6 Events

There are two sides to events: raising events and consuming or responding to them. Consuming events is identical for both BOR and ABAP classes, however, there are differences when raising events:

▶ **BOR objects**
As you will see in Chapter 13, Using Events and Other Business Interfaces, there are many different ways to raise events. Events are systemwide and can be used for workflows, events, and any other receiver that needs to respond to an event.

▶ **ABAP classes**
A weakness is the fact that not many of the event mechanisms support ABAP classes. The several possible workarounds are presented in this chapter.

11.3 Utility Classes

The simplest object types in workflows are utility objects. These are objects that often do not have to be instantiated and usually contain cross-application functionality. Typical examples within standard SAP are decisions, forms, and Web Services. You may need to develop your own utility classes for things such as dummy background steps, performing calculations, evaluating rules, or more complex objects such as factory calendar deadlines.

The IF_WORKFLOW Interface

There are thousands of ABAP classes in the standard SAP system that have nothing to do with workflow. The key to enabling a class to be used in workflow is the IF_WORKFLOW interface. Simply defining it in a class makes it available to use in the Workflow Builder and task editors.

This interface contains two more interfaces: BI_PERSISTENT and BI_OBJECT, which are added to the class automatically:

▶ **BI_PERSISTENT**
This interface defines methods required for the persistency service. In other words, managing instantiation of objects:

▷ FIND_BY_LPOR returns an instance of an object.

▷ LPOR determines an object's key.

▷ REFRESH reloads an object from the database.

▶ **BI_OBJECT**
This interface defines methods used to manage an object:

▷ DEFAULT_ATTRIBUTE_VALUE returns the default attribute.

▷ EXECUTE_DEFAULT_METHOD implements the default action for the object.

▷ RELEASE performs any actions when an object is no longer needed.

Both of these interfaces are described in more detail later in this chapter.

11.3.1 Creating a Utility Class

The first example we will implement is the simplest possible utility: an empty method to create a dummy step. Some scenarios where a dummy method is commonly used are:

▶ Wait step used in combination with a requested start deadline to pause a workflow

▶ Context switch forcing a switch to the workflow system user

▶ Placeholders for applications that are only executed from the Universal Worklist (UWL), for example, a Web Dynpro ABAP application to fill in an Adobe form

▶ Information/notification popup

The last scenario is useful when mail is unsuitable, perhaps because you need to track when a user has read the information for audit or dependency reasons (i.e., a process shouldn't continue until someone has been notified). We will use this scenario for our first example.

Example Scenario

A new SAP user is presented with a welcome notification containing various pieces of information as well as a link to the terms of use for the corporate SAP system that they need to agree to.

To build this, we will use a simple trick: Create a dialog step with an empty method, and switch on the CONFIRM END OF PROCESSING setting. When the user executes the work item from his Business Workplace, the empty method does nothing, and the CONFIRM END OF PROCESSING dialog pops up immediately. Because it contains the work item text in a simple, uncluttered interface, this is both easy to build and very user friendly.

Note

A similar notification can also be done using a decision task with a single outcome, but when using the SAP Business Workplace, the screen layout of a popup is simpler and has the work item text as the main focus rather than the decision buttons. If using UWL, a decision would look better.

The workflow and resulting execution are shown in Figure 11.2.

To build this, start by creating a new class `ZCL_WF_UTIL` in Transaction SE24, and attach the `IF_WORKFLOW` interface to it by entering it in the INTERFACES tab. As soon as the interface is added, two further interfaces appear: `BI_OBJECT` and `BI_PERSISTENT` (see Figure 11.3).

If you now go back to the METHODS tab, you will see the interface methods that have been added. At this point, they have merely been *defined* but no *implementation* (i.e., source code) exists. Although you may not need to use these methods for a utility class, they must be implemented. Otherwise, the workflow system may try to call a non-existent method, which results in a dump. Implementing methods is also very simple: Double-click on each method to generate the necessary `method` and `endmethod` statements and then activate the class.

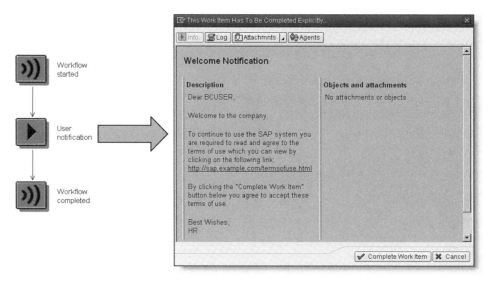

Figure 11.2 Confirm End of Processing Used to Create a Pop-up Notification

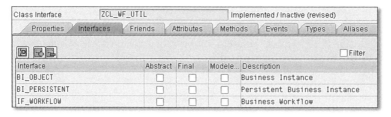

Figure 11.3 Interfaces Used by Workflow

11.3.2 Component Visibility

Before adding further components to the class, we need to explain the visibility of components. In ABAP objects, there are three levels of visibility for attributes, methods, and events:

▶ **Private**
Can only be used in the methods of the class.

▶ **Protected**
Only visible to a class and its subclasses.

▶ **Public**
Visible to the outside world, that is, useable in workflow.

It is considered good practice to only make things as visible as they need to be. The major benefit is that modifications to private components are much easier to carry out and test because you know exactly where and how they are used.

After something is public on the other hand, it can be used anywhere by anyone, and you have less control and less scope for future modifications. Therefore, you should only make compatible changes to anything that is public (i.e., do not delete public components or rename public method or event parameters). This is especially the case if a class has already been used in a productive workflow because even viewing the log of a completed workflow requires the use of the class to display a container object and its attributes.

Unlike workflows, classes and BOR objects are not version-specific and will always behave per the current coding. You may end up with a situation where an old version of a workflow refers to an attribute or method that is no longer present or functions differently, and accessing it via the log results in an error.

11.3.3 Methods

As with the other component types, you can create public or private methods. Private methods are well suited to implement support functions or subroutines, and only public methods can be used in workflow. Any parameters you define for public methods are also automatically recognized by the task builder and added as container elements when creating a workflow task based on the class method.

Take note that the OPTIONAL setting for parameters is automatically applied to task container elements when creating a new task based on the method. Unless you mark a parameter as optional, it will be mandatory in the task container definition (although you can change it afterwards).

Note for BOR Developers

The BOR concept of a result parameter _RESULT is not available in ABAP classes. The equivalent is easy enough to implement by using a regular parameter and evaluating it in a subsequent condition step.

By implementing the IF_WORKFLOW interface, your class is now recognized by the workflow system. The only thing left to do is create a method so that you can create a task. To do this, enter your method name NOTIFY, and enter STATIC for level (no instance required), enter PUBLIC for visibility (to use it in workflow), and add a description (see Figure 11.4).

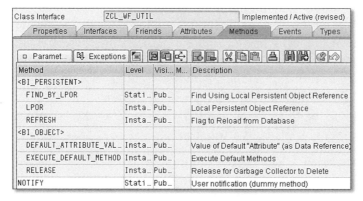

Figure 11.4 A Simple Workflow-Enabled Class

As with the interface methods, we have now only created the definition of the method. Once again, you have to double-click on it to generate an empty code template. You may want to add a comment to note that your method is deliberately empty. Then save and activate your class.

> **Note for BOR Developers**
>
> For BOR methods, you could define methods as being background/dialog or synchronous/asynchronous. However, you can set these properties individually for each task in which a class method is used.

You have just created a workflow-enabled class without writing a single line of ABAP! That, however, will soon change.

11.3.4 Using a Utility Class in a Task

Using classes in workflow tasks is very straightforward. You create a new task either from within the Workflow Builder (Transaction SWDD) or by using Transaction PFTC, setting the object category to CL ABAP CLASS, and entering the class name and method (see Figure 11.5). Note that the SYNCHRONOUS OBJECT METHOD setting is grayed out until a task has been saved for the first time.

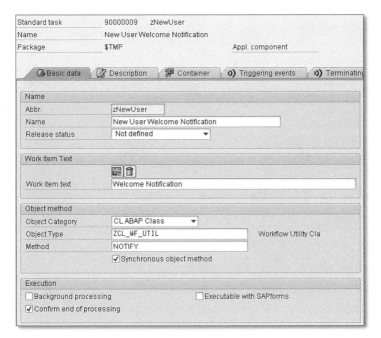

Figure 11.5 Task Based on an ABAP Class

Note

If you are in a release 6.20 system and cannot see the OBJECT CATEGORY choice ABAP CLASS, then you first need to execute Report SWF_CATID to enable ABAP classes as an available object category. Releases 6.40 and higher already have this enabled.

In the task text, you can add a short welcoming note to a new user. The last thing left to do is to create a new workflow, add your new task, and — for ease of testing — go to the possible agents definition and mark it as a general task. Then, assign the workflow initiator as the agent.

Start your workflow using the test facility. You should receive a CONFIRM END OF PROCESSING popup that doubles as a user notification.

Tip

On newer SAP NetWeaver systems, the workflow test environment includes the option to start the workflow without automatically executing the first dialog step — along with several other useful options (see Figure 11.6). This can be handy if you want to test execution from the inbox rather than launching the work item straight away.

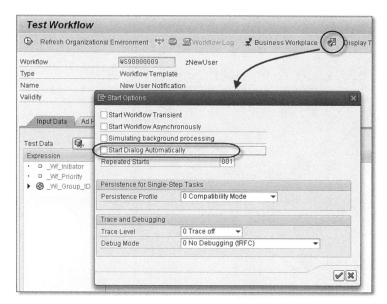

Figure 11.6 Workflow Test Options

11.3.5 Attributes

An attribute is conceptually the same as a variable in a program. This means you can assign values to it, although it is not usually advisable to do this in workflow because — unlike container elements — these values only exist in memory and are lost when the currently executing process completes.

Public attributes are not used very often in utility classes because functional methods are generally more suitable and performance-friendly. For this reason, they will be covered in further detail in Section 11.4, Business Classes.

Attribute Naming Convention

Naming conventions are documented in the SAP Help Portal (*http://help.sap.com*) under "Naming Conventions in ABAP Objects." In keeping with these, all *public* components use proper English names.

However, with *private* and *protected* components, things are a little more flexible, and we find variances in different areas of SAP-delivered code. Most workflow-related classes use the C++/Hungarian Notation style prefix M_ to denote private and protected attributes (short for "Member" attribute), similarly MT_ for tables, MS_ for static, and so on. We find this to be a helpful visual indicator in code to distinguish what is and is not exposed to workflow and have adopted the same convention in this book.

Turning back to our example, the next step is to add a URL into the work item text for the user to click on to read the terms and conditions that he is required to agree to. Because a URL is typically something that can change or be used in different tasks, you can create an attribute to hold it. The easiest way is to create a "Constant" attribute (see Figure 11.7); constants are always instance-independent and can be accessed just like statics.

Attribute	Level	Visibility	Key ...	Re...	Typing	Associated Type		Description	Initial value
TC_URL	Constant	Public	☐	☐	Type	URL	⇨	T&C URL	'http://sap.example.com/terms...

Figure 11.7 Constant Attribute to Hold a URL

This is a great way to define constant text values that need to be used both inside an object and in workflow. However, URLs tend to be more variable, and, in this case, it's not much better than hard-coding it directly into the task text, especially because URLs can point to different portals as the workflow is transported through the SAP landscape. A more flexible approach in this case is to use a STATIC ATTRIBUTE as shown in Figure 11.8.

Attribute	Level	Visibility	Key ...	Re...	Typing	Associated Type		Description	Initial value
TC_URL	Static Attri...	Public	☐	☐	Type	URL	⇨	T&C URL	

Figure 11.8 Static Attribute to Hold a URL

So how is this value populated? ABAP classes always have two special *constructor* methods, which are automatically executed the first time a class is used:

► The CLASS_CONSTRUCTOR method is always executed the first time a class is used in an application — whether it is instantiated or not.

► The CONSTRUCTOR method is similarly executed by each instance when it is created.

Because the utility class is static, you need to use the CLASS-CONSTRUCTOR to populate any static attributes (see Figure 11.9). To create it, choose EDIT • CREATE CLASS CONSTRUCTOR, or click on the CLASS CONSTRUCTOR button to create the class constructor method.

Method	Level	Visi...	M...	Description
CLASS_CONSTRUCTOR	Stati...	Pub...	🔧	CLASS_CONSTRUCTOR

Figure 11.9 Class Constructor

Edit it to add code to assign a value to our Terms & Conditions URL as shown in Listing 11.1.

```
method CLASS_CONSTRUCTOR.
* Populate static attributes
  concatenate 'http://' sy-host '.example.com/termsofuse.html'
       into tc_url.
endmethod.
```
Listing 11.1 Code for Class Constructor to Create URL

This sample code generates a URL that always refers to the current host. If it is transported, the URL still points to whichever system it's running on. If you are following this example in your system, you would obviously need to adapt the code according to your environment.

Using an attribute in a workflow is very simple for instantiated objects (as you will see later in this chapter); however, for static (instance-independent) class attributes such as the URL example used here, there are some limitations:

▶ First, static class attributes cannot be directly used in a work item description. This is not a workflow limitation; the work item description is generated using SAPscript, which is an older technology (it has been superseded by SAP Smart Forms and SAP Interactive Forms by Adobe technologies). SAPscript does not support static classes, and therefore it is not possible to use static attributes directly in a work item text unless the class has been instantiated and is thus accessible via a container element. One workaround for this restriction is to create a singleton instance with a dummy key for use in the task.

▶ Second, you cannot access static class attributes in workflow bindings without an instance.

In practice, the use of static attributes in workflow is rare; they are more likely to be used in an ABAP context rather than in workflow.

11.3.6 Functional Methods

A *functional method* is a method that returns a single result, that is, a method that has a *returning* parameter. Note that the use of functional methods in workflow is only possible from SAP NetWeaver Application Server 6.40 onward.

Typically, a functional method calculates a value, for example, you might use a functional method to return the number of entries in a table or the formatted name of an employee. Unlike static attributes, static functional methods can be used in workflow expressions such as binding (but not in work item descriptions because these use SAPscript), and, in many cases, they are more efficient because only the requested value is calculated (as opposed to several static attributes being calculated in the class constructor when just one is requested).

The method can have *importing* parameters, must have one *returning* parameter, and cannot have any other *exporting* parameters. You should also avoid modifying data and be aware that exceptions are ignored in workflow expressions (a blank value is returned instead). The Class Builder lets you add exceptions, and, of course, you can always modify data wherever you write ABAP code.

Functional method is not just a technical term; it also describes the purpose of the method, namely a small service function to provide a piece of data within an expression. Modifying data in a method that is called during binding or in an ABAP assignment operation can lead to unpredictable results. On the other hand, it is perfectly acceptable to add a returning parameter to a regular method that updates a document and raises exceptions. However, when we speak of *functional methods*, we normally refer to the former usage. One huge benefit of functional methods is that they can be used directly in ABAP expressions and also in workflow bindings and container operations. In code, it look like this:

```
lv_email = lo_user->get_email_address( ).
```

The naming standard recommended and used by SAP is to use GET_ for methods that retrieve or calculate a value, and SET_ for methods to update an attribute value. The Workflow Builder recognizes this naming convention and displays a GET_... functional method as if it were an attribute. Figure 11.10 shows how the preceding example of an email address would look in a binding. Note how the system strips the GET_ and just shows EMAIL_ADDRESS as if it were an attribute.

To continue with our example, we will add a functional method to our utility class to implement a simple deadline based on a factory calendar. Start by creating a static public method get_fc_date, and then add the following parameters as shown in Figure 11.11:

▶ IM_OFFSET type SWD_TIME_O

Importing parameter to specify the required period in days.

▶ RE_DATE type SWF_DLDATE

Returning parameter giving the deadline due date.

Functional method displayed as method ...

... and as an attribute (without the GET_prefix)

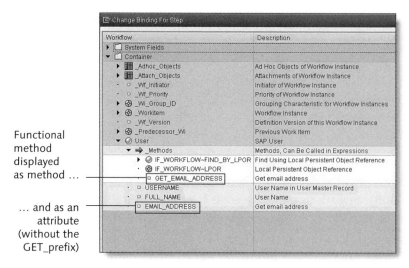

Figure 11.10 Binding for Functional Methods

Parameter	Type	Pa..	O..	Typing..	Associated Type	Default ..	Description
IM_OFFSET	Importing	☐	☐	Type	SWD_TIME_O		Workflow Definition: Offset for Deadlines
RE_DATE	Returning	☑	☐	Type	SWF_DLDATE		WF: Deadline Date

Figure 11.11 Parameters for Deadline Calculation

Inside the method, add the code to calculate the date according to the factory calendar (see Listing 11.2) Note that this is a simple example that uses the international factory calendar.

```
method GET_FC_DATE.
* Calculate a date from today based on factory calendar
  call function 'END_TIME_DETERMINE'
    EXPORTING
      DURATION                        = im_offset
      UNIT                            = 'TAG'
      FACTORY_CALENDAR                = '99'   " International
    IMPORTING
      END_DATE                        = re_date
```

```
   EXCEPTIONS
     OTHERS                                = 1.
   if sy-subrc <> 0.
*    Return default date without calendar
     re_date = sy-datum + im_offset.
   endif.
endmethod.
```

Listing 11.2 Method to Calculate Date Based on Factory Calendar

One minor inconvenience that exists with static methods is that there is no container element to use as a base in bindings and expressions; therefore, you cannot use the Expression dialog box but must type it out directly. Also, because there is no container element, you cannot use the container syntax of enclosing expressions with ampersands (&). Instead, static class methods should be treated as system elements and be specified directly using the class name and enclosed with percentage signs (%). Thus, you need to type the expression directly as:

```
%zcl_wf_util.get_fc_date( im_offset = 3 )%
```

If there is only a single importing parameter, the system allows you to leave out the parameter name, so you can further abbreviate it to:

```
%zcl_wf_util.get_fc_date( 3 )%
```

You can enter this directly in the workflow step under the LATEST END tab as shown in Figure 11.12.

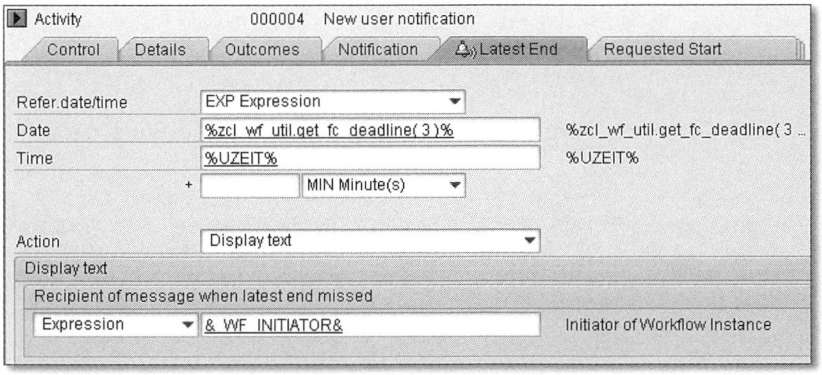

Figure 11.12 Latest End Deadline Based on Factory Calendar

In a real-world scenario, you would probably have different deadline scenarios and therefore use a separate class for implementing different types of deadlines. You may also use different factory calendars, thus requiring two variables. Multiple parameters are added sequentially:

```
%zcl_wf_util.get_fc_date( im_offset = 3 im_calid = 'GB' )%
```

11.4 Business Classes

There is no real technical difference between a utility class and a business class; we use the two terms to differentiate between the way in which they are designed and used. Whereas utility classes tend to be quite simple and often do not need to be instantiated, a business class typically is based on a business document or similar object in the SAP database, for example, a purchase order, SAP user, invoice, employee, and so on. It is instantiated using a key, usually the document number/ID of the document that the business class instance represents.

For our example, we will create a class-based implementation of the USR01 BOR object, which many workflow developers should be familiar with. To start, create a new class ZCL_USER per the ZCL_WF_UTIL example, and add the IF_WORKFLOW interface (remember to make a habit of double-clicking through all of the interface methods to generate the empty code templates). Go to the ATTRIBUTES tab, add an instance attribute USERNAME of type XUBNAME, make it public, and tick the KEY ATTRIBUTE and READ-ONLY boxes (see Figure 11.13).

Attribute	Level	Visibility	Key...	Read-Only	Typing	Associated Type		Description
USERNAME	Instance.	Public	☑	☑	Type	XUBNAME	⇨	User Name in User Master Record

Figure 11.13 Instance Attribute for Username

It is a good practice for key fields' data types to match the underlying database table key.

> **Tip**
>
> It is a good idea to make public attributes read-only, particularly when they represent database fields. Because it is possible to assign values to class attributes, it would otherwise be possible to have an attribute value that does not correspond with the underlying data.

Because you are not in control of when the workflow system will instantiate a class, and there is no way to tell whether an attribute has been changed, it might be difficult to implement an effective update mechanism to write any changed data back to the database. For this reason, any updates should always be performed using methods.

In a pure object-oriented sense, an instance is anonymous and does not require a key; its existence is purely controlled by the variable that references it. To turn a regular object-oriented class into a business class, you need to build the "business" part, and the key is the main differentiator.

Technically, the KEY ATTRIBUTE setting for attributes does not impact the operation of the class in any way. The main use for it is to mark key attributes for external applications to identify the correct data type/structure and associated validation for your object's key. For example, the test tool SWUS uses the KEY ATTRIBUTE indicator to determine which fields can be entered to set up a test instance.

After defining the key, the next job is to make sure a class can only ever be instantiated with it and that the key attribute(s) contain our key value. To do this, you need to implement a CONSTRUCTOR method and add a mandatory importing parameter for the key. Because constructor methods are automatically called whenever a class is instantiated, and the importing parameter is not optional, it will no longer be possible to instantiate the class without supplying a key.

Choose EDIT • CREATE CONSTRUCTOR, or click on the CONSTRUCTOR button to create the constructor method. Click on the PARAMETERS button to add an importing parameter IM_USERNAME of type XUBNAME. Because you are dealing with a piece of business data, you should also validate it and raise an exception if there is a problem. Raising an exception in a constructor has the effect that a class fails to instantiate. For this, you need to add an exception CX_BO_INSTANCE_NOT_FOUND to the constructor using the EXCEPTIONS button. Lastly, add the code to the constructor (see Listing 11.3) to populate your USERNAME attribute and verify that the key is valid.

```
method CONSTRUCTOR.
* Validate key and populate key attribute
  select single bname into username from usr01
      where bname = im_username.
  if sy-subrc ne 0.
    raise exception type cx_bo_instance_not_found.
```

```
    endif.
endmethod.
```

Listing 11.3 Constructor Method to Get the Key

You can activate, test, and verify that this class will only instantiate with a valid username, and then fill the USERNAME attribute with the username. Note that the Workflow Engine will never instantiate a class directly; it will always work via the BI_PERSISTENT interface, described in the remainder of this section.

> **Tip**
>
> In this example, we used a SELECT statement for simplicity, which is perfectly adequate. However, if a BAPI or other interface is available, that is the preferred approach. For example, in a real-world scenario, a user class could make use of BAPI_ USER_GET_DETAIL instead.

11.4.1 Local Persistent Object Reference

To be used in workflow, an object's key must be structured in a specific format known as the *Local Persistent Object Reference* (LPOR). This can be regarded as an "extended key" and has to be implemented by the developer, so it is important to understand how the workflow system manages object references.

There are two persistence states an object will assume:

▶ **Transient**
This is the runtime state in which an instantiated object exists in the memory of an executing application such as the workflow system or the business workplace. As the name suggests, it is temporary, and the object ceases to exist when the application exits. Runtime objects can be manipulated and executed but are not stored anywhere.

▶ **Persistent**
This is a permanent state that does not need any active application. It is a state in which an object is stored in the database.

During the lifetime of a workflow, objects alternate between the two states of persistence. When it needs to be stored in the container, the workflow system *only* stores the LPOR, nothing else. When it needs to work with the object, it instantiates the object. Binding is always performed using LPORs because it is a container operation, and containers are stored in the database, so even if two subsequent tasks for the same user use the same object, the system still converts it back to LPOR and re-instantiates it for the second task.

The workflow system accomplishes this by calling an object's `BI_PERSISTENT~LPOR` and `BI_PERSISTENT~FIND_BY_LPOR` methods.

> **Note**
>
> Where it is obvious, this book drops the interface name from the component, shortening these to `FIND_BY_LPOR` and `LPOR`. One is the reversal of the other:
>
> ► **FIND_BY_LPOR**
> Have key, need object instance.
>
> ► **LPOR**
> Object instantiated, need its key.

Figure 11.14 shows how work item execution works using `FIND_BY_LPOR` to get the instance and using `LPOR` to get the key from an instantiated object.

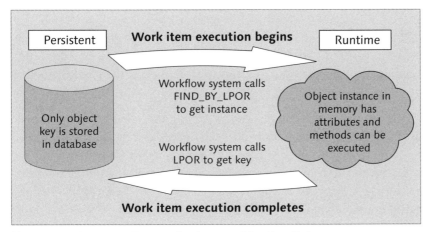

Figure 11.14 Conversion Between Persistent and Runtime States

Implementing simple instance management is relatively straightforward. An `LPOR` always has the Data Dictionary type `SIBFLPOR`, which is a structure made up of three fields:

► `CATID`
A two-character code indicating the object category. This is always `CL` for ABAP Classes. Other values currently used are `BO` for BOR objects and `NN` for undefined (can be used as a placeholder for dynamic object types).

▶ `TYPEID`

This holds the technical name of the object type (ABAP class or BOR object type).

▶ `INSTID`

This is a 32-character field holding the unique instance ID (what we normally consider to be a business object's key). The instance ID can be made up of one of two things:

- ▶ The underlying table's key field(s) if the total length is less than 32 characters. This is the recommended way for classes that are modeled to extend or replace a BOR object — especially if you intend to combine BOR and class functionality.

- ▶ A GUID (Globally Unique Identifier), which may be more suitable for a variety of design reasons, such as: a key is longer than 32 characters, the underlying object has a GUID, the object is not stored in a table, or it is accessed via a persistent class.

Structured Keys and GUIDs

Two scenarios not covered with examples in this chapter are keys based on multiple fields and keys longer than the 32 characters defined in the LPOR structure:

▶ **Structured keys**

Multiple-field keys can be implemented in exactly the same manner as single fields, just by defining them as such in the attributes and by adding additional importing parameters to the constructor and other methods that use the key fields. It may be useful to also create a private type to map the individual fields into a structure. For example, if you have a class with key fields `PO_NUMBER` and `ITEM_NUMBER`, define a type `T_KEY` as shown in Listing 11.4.

```
types:
  begin of t_key,
    po_number   type ebeln,
    item_number type ebelp,
  end of t_key .
```

Listing 11.4 Defining a Key for a Purchase Order Item

In your code, you would then always use this data type when working with the instance ID.

▶ **GUID**

A GUID is a unique identifier throughout the entire SAP system, As mentioned earlier, there are several scenarios where a GUID is to be used as a key — one of which is a key longer than 32 characters.

Some newer SAP-delivered solutions already use GUIDs as their primary key, so you can use that. If this is not the case, you need to do some modifications to the application that create new documents/objects to ensure that any new records include a GUID key. To obtain a new GUID for a new record in the database, you can use class CL_SYSTEM_UUID from release 7.10 onward, or function module GUID_CREATE in earlier versions. To relate a GUID back to the original document key, there are two possibilities:

▷ Extend/modify the existing table to add a GUID reference.

▷ Create a mapping table to cross-reference the GUID to the key fields in the main table.

If you are working with a completely custom development with its own tables, it will be easier because you can incorporate a GUID key from the initial design.

After a GUID has been implemented at the database and application levels, using them in workflow is straightforward because they behave like any other key. You can also instantiate objects using a variety of different reference fields, for example, using the document number or other lookup data. See Section 11.4.5, Alternate Ways to Instantiate Objects, for an example that can be easily adapted to instantiating a GUID-keyed object from a document number or a structured key.

11.4.2 Implementing FIND_BY_LPOR

The FIND_BY_LPOR method is static and is called with an object key. Your job as a developer is to supply an object instance back to the caller (see Listing 11.5).

```
method BI_PERSISTENT~FIND_BY_LPOR.
* Called by workflow to request an object instance
  data: lv_user type ref to zcl_user,
        lv_id   type xubname.
  lv_id = lpor-instid.
  try.
      create object lv_user
```

```
      exporting
          im_username = lv_id.
   catch cx_bo_error.
 endtry.
 result = lv_user.
endmethod.
```

Listing 11.5 BI_PERSISTENT~FIND_BY_LPOR

Tip

In the Class Builder, you can change the way that interface/method names are displayed by going to UTILITIES • SETTINGS and switching on GROUP BY INTERFACES AND SUPERCLASSES.

11.4.3 Implementing LPOR

In theory, the code provided in Listing 11.6 is all that is necessary in our LPOR method.

```
method BI_PERSISTENT~LPOR.
* Called by workflow requesting an instance's key
   result-catid  = 'CL'.
   result-typeid = 'ZCL_USER'.
   result-instid = username.
endmethod.
```

Listing 11.6 BI_PERSISTENT~ LPOR

However, in practice, you may have further uses for the LPOR in your class, so you should typically create a corresponding private attribute and refer to it in the LPOR method as shown in Figure 11.15.

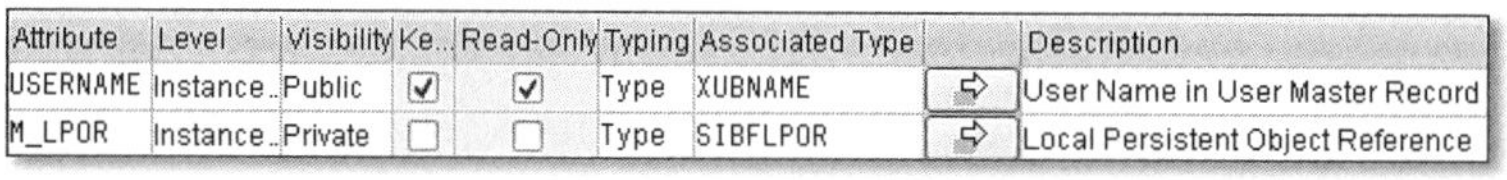

Attribute	Level	Visibility	Ke..	Read-Only	Typing	Associated Type		Description
USERNAME	Instance.	Public	☑	☑	Type	XUBNAME	⇨	User Name in User Master Record
M_LPOR	Instance.	Private	☐	☐	Type	SIBFLPOR	⇨	Local Persistent Object Reference

Figure 11.15 Private Attribute for LPOR

We can then populate it in the constructor (see Listing 11.7), and the LPOR method can then be reduced to the code shown in Listing 11.8.

```
method CONSTRUCTOR.
* Validate key and initialize object
```

```
select single bname into username from usr01
    where bname = im_username.
if sy-subrc ne 0.
  raise exception type cx_bo_error.
endif.
* Populate LPOR
  m_lpor-catid = 'CL'.
  m_lpor-typeid = 'ZCL_USER'.
  m_lpor-instid = username.
endmethod.
```

Listing 11.7 CONSTRUCTOR

```
method BI_PERSISTENT~LPOR.
* Called by workflow requesting an instance's key
  result = m_lpor.
endmethod.
```

Listing 11.8 BI_PERSISTENT~LPOR

11.4.4 Instantiating ABAP Class Objects

We have covered how the workflow system manages switching between the two different instance formats. However, the question still remains of how to get an instance into the workflow in the first place. One way is through events and as a result of methods. But what about when you only have a key of an object that needs to be instantiated?

A simple and robust approach is to use a functional method. To do this, create a method GET_INSTANCE. Because you do not have an instance and will be calling it from outside the class, it needs to be *static* and *public*. Being a functional method, it needs to have exactly one returning parameter for the object instance (if successful). Also, because exceptions in functional methods are ignored in workflow expressions, it is up to the caller to validate that an instance has been returned. Create a GET_INSTANCE method and add an importing parameter for the username and a returning parameter of the type ref to the ZCL_USER class (see Figure 11.16).

Parameter	Type	Pa..	O...	Typing Method	Associated Type	Default value	Description
IM_USERNAME	Importing	☐	☐	Type	XUBNAME		User Name in User Master ...
RE_USER	Returning	☑	☐	Type Ref To	ZCL_USER		SAP User

Figure 11.16 GET_INSTANCE Parameters

The code to return an instance looks something like the code in Listing 11.9.

```
method GET_INSTANCE.
* Return object instance based on key
  try.
     create object re_user
       exporting
         im_username = im_username.
   catch cx_bo_error.
     return.   " simply exit without returning anything
  endtry.
endmethod.
```

Listing 11.9 Method to Instantiate the Object Directly

You may have noticed that this is similar to FIND_BY_LPOR. It makes perfect sense to call FIND_BY_LPOR from GET_INSTANCE (see Listing 11.10).

```
method get_instance.
* Called by workflow to request an object instance
  data: ls_lpor type sibflpor.
  ls_lpor-catid  = 'CL'.
  ls_lpor-typeid = 'ZCL_USER'.
  ls_lpor-instid = im_username.
  re_user ?= zcl_user=>bi_persistent~find_by_lpor( ls_lpor ).
endmethod.
```

Listing 11.10 Method to Instantiate the Object Using FIND_BY_LPOR

In Section 11.8.1, Performance and Instance Management, you will see why this is a good thing. You may also notice the use of ?= to perform the assignment. This is because a narrowing cast is not permitted by default and must be explicitly specified in this manner, or you will get a syntax error because the returned object is declared as type ref to BI_PERSISTENT.

You might wonder why we have two methods for instantiating the object. The reason is simplicity: FIND_BY_LPOR requires a specific importing parameter structure that wouldn't necessarily be used outside of workflow, whereas GET_INSTANCE only requires the object key. Within workflow, we would typically be working with just the object key or document number, as would be the case for another developer using the class for non-workflow purposes.

11.4.5 Alternate Ways to Instantiate Objects

To demonstrate how quickly the initial effort in creating a class can pay off, we will add another common scenario to the user class: instantiating an object from a workflow agent structure (e.g., workflow initiator, last agent, result of rule resolution, etc.). This can already be done with the BOR method USR01.FindUserFrom-AgentStructure, but this requires its own workflow activity step, whereas functional methods can be used in bindings or container operation steps.

As you know, this is a structure containing a two-character object type identification ('US' for User, 'P' for Person, etc.), followed by the object ID. For the user class, all you need to do is add a functional method to convert the agent to a user ID and call GET_INSTANCE. Start by creating a new static public method GET_INSTANCE_FROM_WFAGENT, with an importing parameter IM_WFAGENT of type SWHACTOR and a returning parameter of type ref to zcl_user.

The code here is quite simple (see Listing 11.11). You can easily extend this to cater to other organizational object types.

```
method GET_INSTANCE_FROM_WFAGENT.
* Create instance using WF agent structure.
  data: lv_userid type xubname.
* Handle different org object types
  case im_wfagent-otype.
    when 'US'.             " SAP User
      lv_userid = im_wfagent-objid.
      re_user = zcl_user=>get_instance( lv_userid ).
  endcase.
endmethod.
```

Listing 11.11 Instantiate Object from Workflow Agent

> **Tip**
>
> You can declare type groups on the PROPERTIES tab of an ABAP class. If you find yourself using the same constants in many classes, consider creating a type group that you can then maintain for all your workflow classes.
>
> Look at SAP type group SWFCO for an example that contains many workflow-related constants. For example, the when statement from Listing 11.11 could be expressed with constants rather than literals:
>
> ```
> when swfco_org_user.     " SAP User
> ```

Using this method is also very easy. To instantiate the user object, you can create a container operation step. Or if you want to get an object instance for the actual agent who executed a step, you can use this directly in the binding.

In your example workflow, add a container element `Actual_Agent` of type class `ZCL_USER` to represent the actual agent who executed a step. Then in the binding of a step, return an instance of the user class to workflow by using the system element `_WI_Actual_Agent` as input to your new method (see Figure 11.17). To test this, execute the task, and check the container in the workflow log to verify whether the `Actual_Agent` element contains an instance.

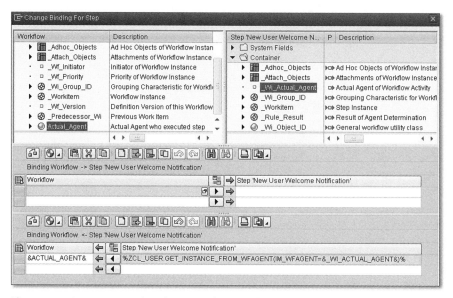

Figure 11.17 Instantiate and Bind a User Object to the Workflow

Another commonly used method is a display function. First, define the method (see Listing 11.12). To display a specific user, the method must be at the instance level, and to use it in workflow, it must be made public.

```
method DISPLAY.
* Display User
  set parameter id 'XUS' field username.
  call transaction 'SU01D' and skip first screen.
endmethod.
```

Listing 11.12 Display Method

Then, you can populate the EXECUTE_DEFAULT_METHOD method to code the default action for the object, for example, when a user clicks on the object link in the SAP Business Workplace (see Listing 11.13).

```
method BI_OBJECT~EXECUTE_DEFAULT_METHOD.
* Call default method: display user
  display( ).
endmethod.
```

Listing 11.13 Default Action When User Clicks on Object in the SAP Business Workplace

11.4.6 Attributes

Now that you have the basic structure in place for a business class, it is time to add some attributes to be used in workflow. In keeping with the design philosophy of only making public what is required, you should only create public attributes for any fields you want to use in workflow. If you need to use other fields internally, you should create a private attribute — M_USR01 in our example — to hold the database record and then transfer only the needed fields to the public attributes. This also makes the workflow log easier to use if there are fewer elements to scroll through than if the entire database record were visible.

For our example, we will add the language. Create a public attribute LANGUAGE of type XULANGU. Because attributes in classes are simply variables, you need to put the correct values into your attributes in your CONSTRUCTOR. The updated select statement looks like Listing 11.14.

```
select single bname langu from usr01
    into (username, language)
    where bname = im_username.
select single bname langu from usr01
    into (username, language)
    where bname = im_username.
```

Listing 11.14 Select Statement

11.4.7 Attributes Versus Functional Methods

An interesting question is whether to use attributes or functional methods. In object-oriented philosophy, the ideal object does not have any public attributes because they violate the goal of encapsulation by giving the outside world direct access to an object's data. Therefore, you should in theory use functional methods in place of attributes wherever possible.

In practice, however, workflow is not 100 % compatible with functional methods, and there are several cases where you cannot use functional methods. For example, you cannot use functional methods in work item texts because those use SAP-script, which is very limited in its ability to handle variables and programming elements. Also, workflow requires an attribute of specific types to be able to access a BOR object via a class. Finally, it may not be that convenient to use functional methods if you have a lot of data elements that are similar, such as data fields of table.

The following are some loose guidelines, but individual circumstances may differ:

▶ **Use attributes if** ...

  ▶ ... you need several fields all from the same database table (also consider creating a structure to group these — it makes the log easier to use if there are many attributes).

  ▶ ... the value is needed in a work item text (however, an alternative is to bind from a functional method to a container element of the task, which is then used in the text).

  ▶ ... you want to reference a BOR object that does not exist separately in the workflow container. This is because a default value specifying the BOR type is required for the workflow log to be able to expand it in the container view.

▶ **Avoid attributes if** ...

  ▶ ... they are not needed in workflow.

  ▶ ... the value requires a calculation or must be read from the database (unless it is part of the key table) because this adds a performance overhead to each instantiation, regardless of whether it is required.

▶ **Use functional methods if** ...

  ▶ ... it is a calculated value.

  ▶ ... it is only occasionally used.

> **Tip**
>
> The IF_WORKFLOW interface is only needed for storing objects as container elements, or if a task is based on a class's method. Classes used as functional method return parameters, attributes of a workflow-enabled class, or for providing static functional methods in an expression do not need the IF_WORKFLOW interface.

11.5   Exception Classes

Another major enhancement that object-oriented ABAP brought was the use of exception classes. They are more powerful and flexible than exception messages because they allow many of the object-oriented constructs such as inheritance, and you can even add custom code into exception classes (with limitations). As a guide for those of you new to object-oriented programming, exception classes are roughly equivalent to the entities in the previous exception message concept (see Table 11.2).

Exception Messages	Exception Classes
Message Class	Exception class
Message Number	Text ID
Message Variables (up to 4)	Attributes

Table 11.2 Exception Message and Class Comparison

The workflow system makes it really easy to implement exception classes. As a naming convention, all exception classes use the prefix CX (ZCX/YCX for customer-created), and the SAP-delivered classes recognized by workflow use CX_BO (business object — here meaning the generic sense, not BOR objects), although this is not mandatory. At the top level, there is the CX_BO_APPLICATION abstract class, which should not be used other than to catch errors raised using subclasses. It has three subclasses that are recognized by workflow, and these correspond to the three types of errors that a BOR method can return back to workflow: *temporary*, *application*, and *system* errors (see Table 11.3).

BOR Exception Type	Exception Class
Temporary	`CX_BO_TEMPORARY`
Application	`CX_BO_ERROR`
System	`CX_BO_ABORT`

Table 11.3 Exception Classes

Any subclasses of these will be treated according to the class it is descended from; that is, all subclasses of `CX_BO_ERROR` are handled as application errors. Several subclasses are already defined in the standard system, or you can create your own subclasses.

Note that the exception class `CX_BO_TEMPORARY` has two uses:

▶ If used in a background step, it causes the workflow system to retry at predefined intervals until it gives up and becomes a permanent error.

▶ If it is used in a dialog step, it indicates that the action is incomplete — for example, cancelled by the user — and the item remains in process.

For our example, let's assume we want to implement custom functionality for managing substitutions centrally, and we need a method to assign a substitute to a user (e.g., by updating Table `HRUS_D2`). We want to raise an exception if the supplied substitute user ID is not valid.

Start by creating the exception class as a subclass of `CX_BO_ERROR`. You can do this by displaying `CX_BO_ERROR` using Transaction SE24, choosing EDIT • CREATE SUB-CLASS from the menu, and creating a subclass `ZCX_BO_USER` (see Figure 11.18).

You can add public attributes to exception classes, which can be used in error texts or class methods. The obvious piece of information for a user class exception is the username, so add a public attribute `USERNAME` type `XUBNAME`. The Class Builder generates the `CONSTRUCTOR` method for exception classes and automatically adds any additional public attributes as importing parameters. You are now able to pass in a username when raising the exception.

Another feature of exception classes is the addition of message texts, which can be done in the TEXTS tab. Notice that the texts for all superclasses already appear here, and an exception ID with the same name as the current class has been added.

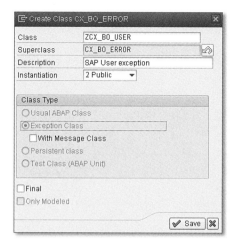

Figure 11.18 Creating an Exception Class

This is the default text that will be used if no specific text ID is supplied when raising the exception. Add a short text to the default exception ID ZCX_BO_USER, and add another exception ID INVALID_USERNAME. Public attributes can be inserted into texts by enclosing them in ampersands (&), so you can use the username as part of the description as shown in Figure 11.19. You can also add long texts if you wish.

Exception ID	Text
CX_ROOT	An exception occurred
CX_BO_APPLICATION	Application business exception raised in business class '&CLASS_NAME&'
CX_BO_ERROR	Error raised in business class '&CLASS_NAME&'
ZCX_BO_USER	SAP User exception
INVALID_USERNAME	The user &USERNAME& is not valid

Figure 11.19 Adding Exception IDs

Note that the Class Builder automatically creates a corresponding public attribute for each exception ID. This public attribute contains the text ID of the associated text in the Online Text Repository (OTR) and should always be used to identify the exception ID when raising an exception (you will see this further on). For your example class, you will see that attributes have been created for ZCX_BO_USER and INVALID_USERNAME similar to Figure 11.20.

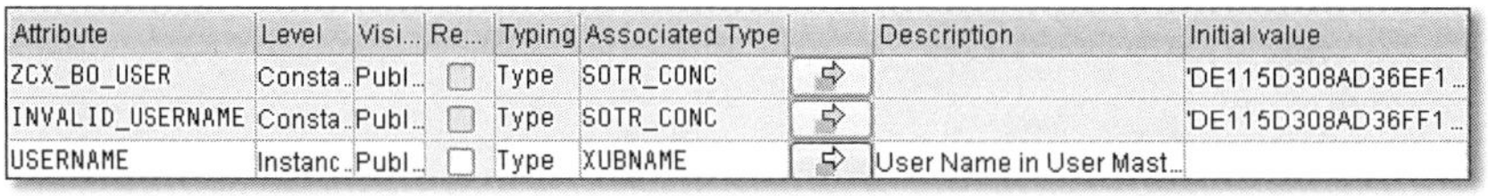

Attribute	Level	Visi...	Re...	Typing	Associated Type		Description	Initial value
ZCX_BO_USER	Consta..Publ..	☐	Type	SOTR_CONC	⇨		'DE115D308AD36EF1 ..
INVALID_USERNAME	Consta..Publ..	☐	Type	SOTR_CONC	⇨		'DE115D308AD36FF1 ..
USERNAME	Instanc..Publ..	☐	Type	XUBNAME	⇨	User Name in User Mast..	

Figure 11.20 Generated Text IDs for Exception IDs

Now that the exception class is complete, you can save and generate it. The next step is to implement the class in a method that will be used in workflow. To continue with our example, edit the ZCL_USER class and create a new method ASSIGN_SUBSTITUTE with importing parameters for the substitute's user ID, a start date, and an end date for the substitution as shown in Figure 11.21. Then, click on the EXCEPTIONS button to add your exception class as shown in Figure 11.22.

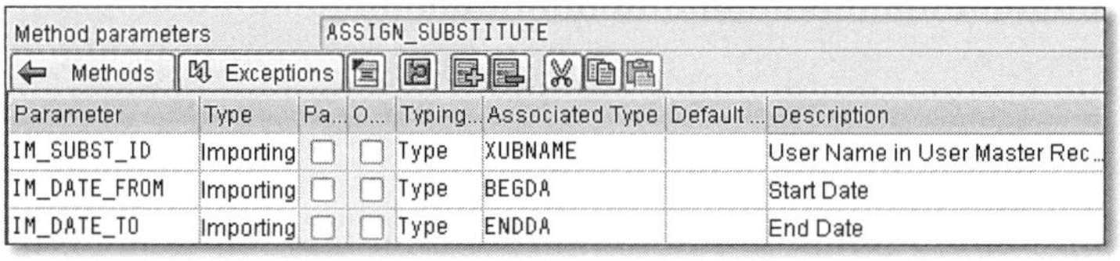

Method parameters				ASSIGN_SUBSTITUTE			
⇐ Methods	🕮 Exceptions 📄 📄 📑📑 ✂📄📄						
Parameter	Type	Pa..	O...	Typing..	Associated Type	Default ...	Description
IM_SUBST_ID	Importing	☐	☐	Type	XUBNAME		User Name in User Master Rec..
IM_DATE_FROM	Importing	☐	☐	Type	BEGDA		Start Date
IM_DATE_TO	Importing	☐	☐	Type	ENDDA		End Date

Figure 11.21 Parameters for ASSIGN_SUBSTITUTE

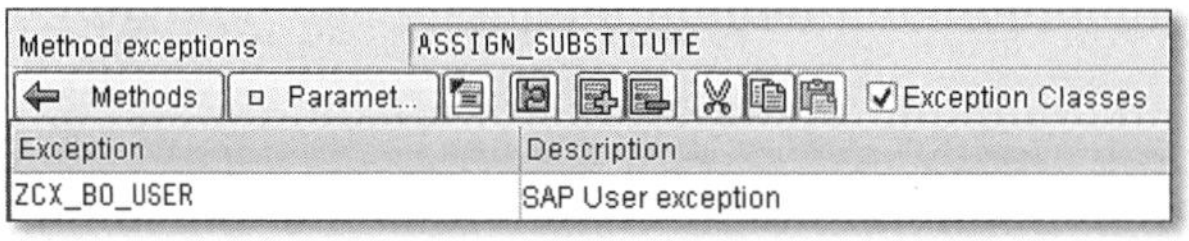

Method exceptions	ASSIGN_SUBSTITUTE	
⇐ Methods ☐ Paramet... 📄 📄 📑📑 ✂📄📄	☑Exception Classes	
Exception	Description	
ZCX_BO_USER	SAP User exception	

Figure 11.22 Adding an Exception to ASSIGN_SUBSTITUTE

The code in Listing 11.15 can be used to raise the exception if the supplied user ID is invalid. For test purposes, we do not need to include the actual code for assigning the substitute in this demonstration. Note the use of the generated public constant INVALID_SUBSTITUTE to supply the text ID for the exception.

```
method assign_substitute.
* Assign substitute for user
  data: lo_substitute type ref to zcl_user,
        ls_subst      type hrus_d2.
* Instantiate the substitute user object
  lo_substitute = zcl_user=>get_instance( im_subst_id ).
  if lo_substitute is not bound.   " UserID is invalid
    raise exception type zcx_bo_user
      exporting
```

```
        textid = zcx_bo_user=>invalid_username
        username = im_subst_id.
  endif.
* ...[code to assign substitute]...
endmethod.
```

Listing 11.15 Assign a Substitute to a User

To test this, create a new workflow containing an instance of the user class (a shortcut for instantiating an object for testing is to specify an ID directly in the INITIAL VALUE tab of the container element), insert a task based on your method, and assign an invalid user ID to the substitute in the binding (see Figure 11.23).

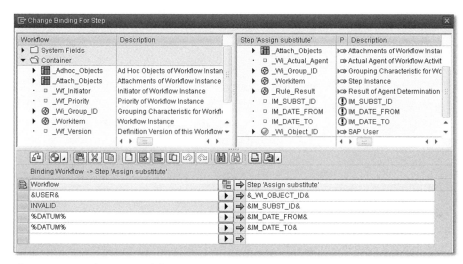

Figure 11.23 Binding an Invalid User ID to Cause an Exception

Generate and test your workflow. Using the user view, an end user can drill down into the log and see a meaningful error message as shown in Figure 11.24. A workflow administrator sees the same message in the technical log as shown in Figure 11.25.

Figure 11.24 User View of an Exception

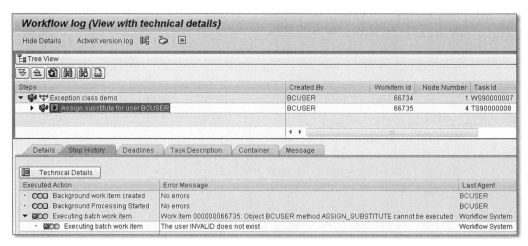

Figure 11.25 Exceptions in the Technical Log

There are several alternative ways to implement exception classes. For example, in a larger project, you can have a top-level exception class representing a business entity (ZCL_USER in this case) and several subclasses for specific scenarios, for example, ZCL_USER_SUBSTITUTION for substitution-related exceptions.

11.6 Events

Events are complex and constitute an area where ABAP classes are the least supported. In a pure ABAP language context, ABAP objects also use a different concept of event as compared to the way we understand it in a workflow context.

11.6.1 Responding to Events

We will deal with the easy part first: responding to events of an ABAP class. This is very straightforward, and the functions are described in Chapter 13, Using Events and Other Business Interfaces.

To use class-based events, you simply set the object category to CL and enter your class event as shown in Figure 11.26. Figure 11.27 shows a wait for event step in a workflow based on an ABAP class event.

Figure 11.26 Workflow Trigger Using Class event

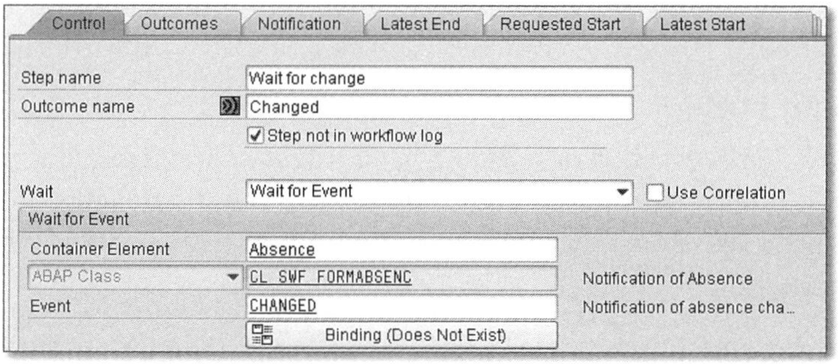

Figure 11.27 Wait Step Using Class Event

11.6.2 Raising Events

The following outlines the major ways to trigger events. For a more detailed discussion on events for SAP Business Workflow, see Chapter 13, Using Events and Other Business Interfaces.

Change Documents

Change documents fully support ABAP class events. All that is required is to set the object category to CL and enter your ABAP class details.

Business Transaction Events

Business transaction events (BTE) are almost exclusively used in the finance area. Because the actual raising of the event is done in ABAP code, this can be done in exactly the same method as will be described a little later. The only difference is that the BTE workflow event wizard does not support classes, so you need to implement the BTE manually.

Status Management

Status management events are only supported with BOR events. A workaround is to replicate BOR events, but this is not for the fainthearted.

Human Resources (HR) Events

As with status management events, the HR event transactions currently do not support ABAP class events. However, instead of an event, you can specify a function module that is to be executed, where you can then raise a class-based workflow event in your own code.

Raising Events Directly in ABAP

If you are already familiar with workflow events, you might come across documentation or examples of an ABAP class and find that the way that events are managed doesn't make sense from a workflow point of view. That's because the two are completely different.

Workflow events are systemwide and used to communicate an object's change in status to the outside world. The event handler is external to the object and to the whole application. Workflow events are managed centrally by the event manager, and receivers are started using RFC in their own logical unit of work (LUW). The question of who will react to an event is defined statically and systemwide using the receivers in the event linkage table. Events can be raised by anyone and do not even need to involve the object.

In contrast, object-oriented ABAP events only exist within a session and constitute part of the interface between an ABAP object and other ABAP objects, or even itself. Events can only be raised within the class in which they are defined or a subclass thereof. They are used for an object to communicate a change of status either internally or to another object that is registered at runtime. This can either be an "inside out" process (an object raising an event for someone else to react to) or a loopback process (an object reacting to its own events). The equivalent to workflow *event receivers* are *event handler* methods that need to register themselves at runtime.

> **Note**
>
> The same definition in the Events tab of Transaction SE24 is used for both types of events (although only public events can be used by workflow).

The easiest option when developing workflow events is to ignore ABAP class events completely and raise your workflow events in code using a utility function or method. In most workflow development projects, this will be sufficient.

For our example, we want to implement custom functionality for managing substitutions centrally, and we need an event to notify workflow when a substitute has been assigned. To demonstrate this, we can continue with the example used in Section 11.5, Exception Classes. Assume in our implementation of custom substitution management, we also want to implement an event to notify workflow when a substitute has been assigned. Start by defining a public instance event SUBSTITUTE_ASSIGNED on the events tab as shown in Figure 11.28.

Figure 11.28 Defining an Event in the ABAP Class

To define the event parameters, use the PARAMETERS button just as you do for methods. You can define a reference to a separate user object to represent the substitute, and a start and end date as shown in Figure 11.29.

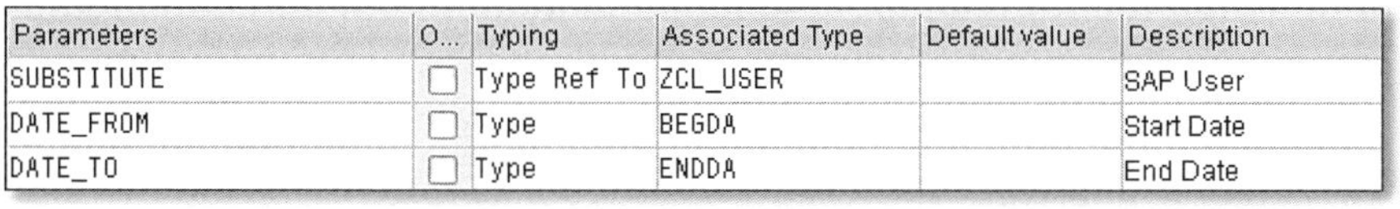

Parameters	O...	Typing	Associated Type	Default value	Description
SUBSTITUTE	☐	Type Ref To	ZCL_USER		SAP User
DATE_FROM	☐	Type	BEGDA		Start Date
DATE_TO	☐	Type	ENDDA		End Date

Figure 11.29 Event Parameters

To raise the event in a workflow sense, you cannot use SAP_WAPI_RAISE_EVENT, so you need to use the event classes (this feature will be implemented in a future support package). A useful technique to standardize things and to make it easier to raise an event with the correct parameters is to create a corresponding "raise" method for raising each event, for example, by defining a method RAISE_SUBSTITUTE_ASSIGNED with the same parameters as the SUBSTITUTE_ASSIGNED event. Once again, if you do not intend to call it from outside the class, it can be private.

Raising the workflow event thus involves three steps:

1. A method performs the action ASSIGN_SUBSTITUTE.

2. On successful completion, the method calls RAISE_SUBSTITUTE_ASSIGNED.

3. RAISE_SUBSTITUTE_ASSIGNED raises the workflow event.

Listing 11.16 shows how the event can be raised.

```
method raise_substitute_assigned.
* Raise workflow event SUBSTITUTE_ASSIGNED
constants: lc_event type sibfevent value 'SUBSTITUTE_ASSIGNED',
           lc_objtype type sibftypeid value 'ZCL_USER'.
  data: lv_objkey     type sibfinstid,
        lo_event      type ref to if_swf_evt_event,
        lo_evt_params type ref to
                      if_swf_ifs_parameter_container.
* Set up the LPOR instance id
  lv_objkey = sy-uname.
  try.
* Get event object
    lo_event = cl_swf_evt_event=>get_instance(
                   im_objcateg =
                    cl_swf_evt_event=>mc_objcateg_cl
                   im_objtype  = lc_objtype
                   im_event    = lc_event
                   im_objkey   = lv_objkey ).
* Get event container
    lo_evt_params = lo_event->get_event_container( ).
* Set Parameters
    lo_evt_params->set( name  = 'SUBSTITUTE'
                        value = substitute ).
    lo_evt_params->set( name  = 'DATE_FROM'
                        value = date_from ).
    lo_evt_params->set( name  = 'DATE_TO'
                        value = date_to ).
* Raise event
    lo_event->raise( ).
  catch cx_swf_evt_exception.
  catch cx_swf_cnt_container .
  endtry.
endmethod.
```

Listing 11.16 Raise Event from ABAP Class

Important Note

Pay particular attention to the fact that a COMMIT WORK statement is required by the caller; otherwise, the event will not be raised. The statement should not automatically be included in the raise event method because it may be called from inside a LUW that has its own COMMIT, for example, during a document save.

An alternative is to add a DO_COMMIT importing parameter to control whether the method should perform a COMMIT WORK.

The last part missing from our example to raise the event is the application code that starts everything off. You can use the ASSIGN_SUBSTITUTE method created in the exceptions section and add a call to the RAISE_SUBSTITUTE_ASSIGNED method followed by a COMMIT WORK (see Listing 11.17). Again, the actual functionality to assign the substitute is not required for this example.

```
method assign_substitute.
* Assign substitute for user
  data: lo_substitute type ref to zcl_user,
        ls_subst      type hrus_d2.
* Instantiate the substitute user object
  lo_substitute = zcl_user=>get_instance( im_subst_id ).
  if lo_substitute is not bound.   " UserID is invalid
    raise exception type zcx_bo_user
      exporting
        textid = zcx_bo_user=>invalid_username
        username = im_subst_id.
  endif.
* ...[code to assign substitute]...
* Raise event
  raise_substitute_assigned( substitute = lo_substitute
                             date_from  = im_date_from
                             date_to    = im_date_to ).
  commit work.
endmethod.
```

Listing 11.17 Method to Raise Event

To test this, you can also reuse or copy the workflow created for the exceptions example. This time, however, bind a valid user ID to the assign substitute task. Test the workflow with the event trace switched on, and you should see the event appear in the event trace similar to Figure 11.30.

Object Type	Event	Current Date	Time	Receiver Type	Info...	Handler/Action
	Trace ON	22.02.2009	01:26:44	BCUSER		
ZCL_USER	SUBSTITUTE_ASSIGNED	22.02.2009	01:32:14		[i]	No receiver entered

Figure 11.30 Event Trace with ABAP Class Event

Combining ABAP Objects and Workflow events

Optional

The content of this section becomes more of an issue on larger, more complex projects, so this may not be relevant or suitable for everyone.

You might argue that the method described so far goes against a benefit of using ABAP classes in workflow in the first place: being able to share development between workflow and non-workflow developers alike. An ABAP developer without the necessary background might not know that he cannot use the "normal" event syntax that he is accustomed to. Also, using a method to raise events in this manner places certain restrictions on more complex object-oriented design concepts where, for example, there may be multiple event handlers, they may be in a different class, or it may be necessary to change/enable/disable the event handlers dynamically — all of which are part of the ABAP events concept.

Fortunately, there is a relatively simple and elegant solution to this apparent dilemma: You can use the ABAP class event handler to raise a workflow event of the same name. In effect, you are "forwarding" an object-oriented ABAP event to a workflow event. First, we need to explain a little bit more about how ABAP objects events work.

In the EVENTS tab of Transaction SE24, it is merely a definition consisting of the event name and any parameters that may be passed along with the event (similar to BOR). In the workflow world, we have an event manager who knows what to do with an event and who is interested in it. In ABAP objects, each event handler is a method that must be registered *at runtime*.

For our example, raising the workflow event now involves the following steps:

1. For the event handler to be called, it must be registered.

2. We need a method that performs the action: `ASSIGN_SUBSTITUTE`.

3. On completion, the method raises the ABAP event `SUBSTITUTE_ASSIGNED`.

4. Event handler `RAISE_SUBSTITUTE_ASSIGNED` raises the workflow event.

For the event handler, we can simply use the RAISE_SUBSTITUTE_ASSIGNED method from our previous example. To designate a method as a handler for a particular event, click on the METHOD PROPERTIES button (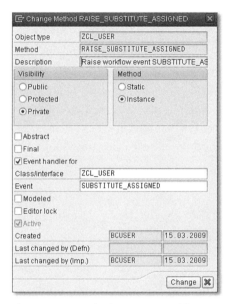) and specify the class and event (see Figure 11.31).

Figure 11.31 Method to Raise Workflow Event

The system asks you to confirm that you want to delete the existing parameters because an event handler can only use parameters defined for the event. You should then notice that the EVENT RECEIVER icon () appears in the METHOD TYPE column. The parameters need to be defined again, and you will see that it is no longer possible to declare the data types, and you can only specify those parameters defined for the event.

The equivalent of event linkage in ABAP Objects is the event handler registration. This is performed at runtime and can occur anywhere in the class. For our example, we will register the event handler in the constructor method as shown in Listing 11.18.

```
method constructor.
* Validate key and initialize object
  select single bname into username from usr01
      where bname = im_username.
```

```
if sy-subrc ne 0.
  raise exception type cx_bo_error.
endif.
* Populate LPOR
m_lpor-catid  = 'CL'.
m_lpor-typeid = 'ZCL_USER'.
m_lpor-instid = username.
  set handler raise_substitute_assigned for me.
endmethod.
```

Listing 11.18 Event Handler Registration

For every instance of the object, raising the `substitute_assigned` event in an object-oriented sense automatically calls the `raise_substitute_assigned` event handler method. The `assign_substitute` method we used earlier now looks like Listing 11.19.

```
method assign_substitute.
* Assign substitute for user
  data: lo_substitute type ref to zcl_user,
        ls_subst       type hrus_d2.
* Instantiate the substitute user object
  lo_substitute = zcl_user=>get_instance( im_subst_id ).
  if lo_substitute is not bound.   " UserID is invalid
    raise exception type zcx_bo_user
      exporting
        textid = zcx_bo_user=>invalid_username
        username = im_subst_id.
  endif.
* ...[code to assign substitute]...
* Raise event
  raise event substitute_assigned
      exporting
        substitute = lo_substitute
        date_from  = im_date_from
        date_to    = im_date_to.
  commit work.
endmethod.
```

Listing 11.19 Raising an Object-Oriented Event to Trigger Workflow

Although ABAP objects events cannot be raised outside the class in which they are defined (or one of its subclasses), implementing an event handler in this way still leaves the possibility of calling the method directly from outside the class. Thus, inside the class, you use `raise event`, and for an outside caller (e.g., in a BAdI), you use an object instance and call `raise_substitute_assigned`. For this reason, we have not followed the ABAP object-oriented naming convention of `ON_<name of event>` for event handlers in this example.

11.7 Using BOR Objects in Classes

Because there is already a large amount of BOR functionality available in the standard system, it makes no sense to reinvent the wheel just for the sake of using ABAP classes — unless the BOR components are really simple. Combining functionality is relatively easy: A class can contain a BOR object as an attribute. However, this is not easily done the other way round.

Note
Remember the following points:
▸ A class can refer to a BOR object.
▸ A BOR object cannot easily refer to a class as one of its attributes.
▸ A BOR object can use a class internally in its code.

Although it is technically possible to create a class-based attribute of a BOR object using similar techniques to those described in this section, you may encounter compatibility issues with older code designed around BOR objects, so we do not recommend this approach.

To promote reuse, a good approach to extending existing BOR functionality is to create any new functionality using ABAP classes and include the BOR object as an attribute of the class. For example, if you have an existing task based on a BOR object, you can bind the attribute directly to the task's main object. In other words, `ZCL_USER.BO_USR01` binds to `_Wi_Object_ID` for a task based on BOR object `USR01`.

To get workflow to recognize an attribute as a BOR object, there is a little trickery involved, namely a specific data type `SIBFLPORB` that must be used. Having to work with persistence and LPORs works to your advantage in this scenario because, as you will see, this is just another LPOR. It is slightly different from `SIBFLPOR` — which we use for the class LPOR — in that the key (`INSTID`) has a maximum length of 70 characters (BOR key length), whereas the standard LPOR key length is 32.

To implement this in our example class, add a public instance attribute BO_USR01 of type SIBFLPORB (see Figure 11.32).

Attribute	Level	Visib...	Key ...	Re...	Typing	Associated Type		Description
BO_USR01	Instance..	Public	☐	☐	Type	SIBFLPORB	⇨	USR01 BOR Object

Figure 11.32 BOR Object Attribute of a Class

In the CONSTRUCTOR method, you can then populate the BOR's LPOR structure. However, there is one more detail to consider. Although it is possible to chain components in bindings if an object is an attribute of another object, this needs a little more work for it to work with BOR attributes of classes. For example:

▶ Class ZCL_PURCHASE_ORDER has an attribute CREATOR of type ZCL_USER.

▶ The expression &PURCHASEORDER.CREATOR.FULLNAME& is perfectly valid. The same goes for BOR objects as attributes of BOR objects.

▶ To mix classes and BOR in this manner, however, the binding editor needs to know the BOR object type upfront. For example, if you have a container element USER of type ZCL_USER with an attribute BO_USR01 representing the USR01 object, you cannot use &USER.BO_USR01.NAMEWITHLEADINGUS& if you only populate the BOR structure in your constructor method. This is because the applications accessing your class need to know the BOR object type *before* it is instantiated. This is easier to visualize if you try to use the BOR attribute of the current example class in a binding. As Figure 11.33 shows, it is not possible to access the attributes of the BOR object.

Figure 11.33 BOR Object Without Type Definition

The important part here is that the category and type portions of the BOR reference (CATID and INSTID) must be prepopulated, even if no BOR object instance exists. The reason for this is that the workflow container displays (e.g., log, binding etc.) use this information to determine what type of BOR object the attribute represents.

Because a BOR object can be used as an attribute of several different classes, it makes sense to store the type definitions separate from our class and make them globally accessible. To do so, create another class ZCL_WF_BOR_TYPES to hold all your BOR definitions in public constant attributes. Go to the ATTRIBUTES tab, and add a public static constant USR01 (type SIBFLPORB) for your BOR object that you want to represent in a class (see Figure 11.34).

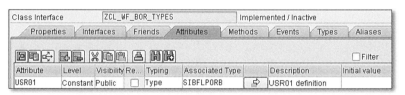

Figure 11.34 BOR Object Type Definition

Because the data type is a structure, we do not want to enter the constant value as a literal but want to assign values to the individual components. Click on the DIRECT TYPE ENTRY button ( ) to assign the value directly. Replace the proposed

```
constants USR01 type SIBFLPORB .
```

with the LPOR of an initial BOR object of type USR01:

```
constants:
    begin of usr01,
      instid type sibflporb-instid value space,
      typeid type sibflporb-typeid value 'USR01',
      catid  type sibflporb-catid  value 'BO',
    end of usr01.
```

Save and activate this class, and return to the ZCL_USER class. In the initial value for your BO_USR01 attribute, you can now specify the constant from your new class as ZCL_WF_BOR_TYPES=>USR01 (see Figure 11.35).

Attribute	Level	Visib...	Key ...	Re...	Typing	Associated ...		Description	Initial value
BO_USR01	Instance.	Public	☐	☐	Type	SIBFLPORB	⇨	USR01 BOR Object	ZCL_WF_BOR_TYPES=>USR01

Figure 11.35 Initial Value That Specifies the Type of a BOR Object Attribute

If you look at the SAP example class CL_SWF_FORMABSENC, you will see the same technique implemented using a static attribute of a global class CL_SWF_BOR_TYPES. This class in turn refers to a type group SWHCL, which contains the default values for various object types, including USR01.

You may ask why use a class to hold a constant and not specify constants from a type group directly? The reason is simply that anything accessing the class from the outside must have the have the same type group declaration to interpret the value. Because this is not realistic, a global class is used that is available anywhere without further declaration.

If you try to use the BO_USR01 attribute in a binding, you will find that the object type is now fully understood by the binding editor. Figure 11.36 shows how the USR01 BOR attribute of the user class can now be expanded to access its attributes.

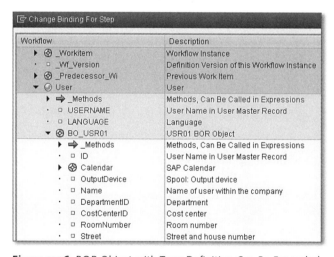

Figure 11.36 BOR Object with Type Definition Can Be Expanded

Using BOR Objects Within a Class

If you need to call methods or evaluate attributes of the BOR object in your own code within the class (e.g., if you need one of its attributes to perform a calculation), you need to enable the BOR macros in your class as well. To do this, click on the MACROS button in the Class Builder and add the following includes:

```
include <cntn03>.    " local types
include <cntn02>.    " BOR macros
```

This enables you to instantiate the BOR object and use the workflow macros such as SWC_GET_PROPERTY and SWC_CALL_METHOD. However, many BOR components are simple enough that it is just as easy to port the BOR code over and implement the equivalent in your class. This has the added advantage of making the BOR components more accessible to other non-workflow applications (e.g., using the same business class as the basis for workflow and for a Web Dynpro ABAP application). There is also a small performance gain from not having to instantiate BOR objects inside your class.

Generic Object Services

A final comment about the interaction between BOR objects and business classes in relation to workflow concerns *Generic Object Services (GOS)*. In most cases, the object type for GOS is hard coded into the application, and it is usually a BOR object.

For example, a purchase order is represented by BOR object BUS2012, and accessing the Workflow Overview from GOS within a purchase order transaction searches for workflows containing a BOR object of type BUS2012 with the key of the current document.

So if you develop a purchase order approval workflow based on a custom ZCL_PURCHASE_ORDER class, for example, your workflow will not be visible from the purchase order display transaction. For this reason, it is often necessary to include both the business class and the corresponding BOR object as container elements of your top-level workflow. This is often the case if your workflow is triggered by a BOR event, and you bind the BOR object to a workflow container element. If, however, your workflows are triggered by a class event, then you need to ensure that the corresponding BOR object is available as an attribute of the class and bind it to a container element in a container operation step.

For example, consider you have a custom business partner credit requested event implemented in a business partner class ZCL_BP, and your workflow is triggered by class event `ZCL_BP.CREDIT_REQUESTED`. If you want the workflow to be visible via GOS, you need to implement the corresponding BOR object `BUS1006` as an attribute of `ZCL_BP` (in many cases, this is done anyway), and you need to perform a container operation to assign `ZCL_BP.BO_BUS1006` to a container element `BO_BP` (you could even do this in the event binding). This element does not have to be used in any way; it just needs to exist.

11.8   Recommendations and Advanced Topics

This section covers recommendations as well as some more advanced techniques for working effectively with ABAP classes in workflow.

11.8.1   Performance and Instance Management

One strong recommendation when using ABAP classes in workflow is to implement some form of instance management. There are several reasons for this:

▶ The workflow alternates between the persistent and runtime representations of an object during the lifetime of the transaction, which means that any database accesses or calculations in the constructor are repeated each time the runtime object is instantiated.

▶ Modular design methodologies such as encapsulation mean that an object is likely to be instantiated several times in a local context. For example, the inbox list, the work item preview, and the work item execution might each instantiate their own local object instance. (In reality, it is even more complex than that.)

▶ When an object is modified, several programs are all instantiating an object. If one instance is modified, all others will immediately be out of date.

On a SAP NetWeaver 7.0 system, a simple business class in a work item, with a work item text that contains attributes of that class, can be instantiated on average 5 to 10 times during the course of a user opening the Business Workplace and selecting and executing the task. Simply clicking on different work items in the work list will cause several new objects to be instantiated.

As you can see, instance management can be quite important because this has the potential to dramatically affect the performance of the Business Workplace if users have many work items (even more so if dynamic columns are used).

Instance management does exactly what the name suggests: It manages the instances of an object to avoid the aforementioned performance and concurrency issues. BOR does this internally; however, with ABAP classes, you need to implement this yourself. Although it may seem like extra work, it is not difficult and gives you greater control and flexibility.

A simple instance management technique is to use a static table for the class to hold all its instances and their associated keys as illustrated by Figure 11.37.

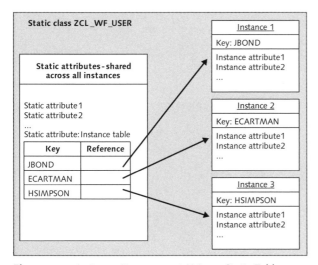

Figure 11.37 Instance Management Using a Static Table

Because an object variable is only a reference (hence, `type ref to`), several programs can simultaneously use the same instance even though the object reference is declared in a program's local `DATA` statement. This can be accomplished at the point a program tries to instantiate the class into an object. The class can do a lookup on the instance table to see if an object with a particular key has already been instantiated. If so, there is no need for a second instance. Instead, the existing instance needs to be returned to the caller.

So how would this look in code? Not as complicated as it sounds: To start with, you need an instance table. Encapsulation means there is no need for it to be visible, so no dictionary structure needs to be defined, and you can create local type declarations instead. Two types are necessary: one to define the instance structure and another for the table. On the TYPES tab, define a private type `T_INSTANCE`, but instead of entering a data type, click on the DIRECT TYPE ENTRY button (⇨)

to declare the data type using regular ABAP. Transaction SE24 generates a stub declaration

```
types T_INSTANCE .
```

which you can extend/overwrite to define your structure consisting of a key and the instance:

```
types:
  begin of t_instance,
    username type xubname,
    instance type ref to zcl_user,
  end of t_instance .
```

Similarly, create a table type T_INSTANCES as a table:

```
types t_instances type standard table of t_instance.
```

Next, define a static private attribute MST_INSTANCES of type T_INSTANCES to hold your instance table. For the "management" part, the FIND_BY_LPOR method needs to implement the process described previously, which can be done per Listing 11.20.

```
method bi_persistent~find_by_lpor.
* Called by workflow to request an object instance
* Instance-managed instantiation.
  data: ls_instance type t_instance,
        lv_username type xubname.
  check lpor-instid is not initial.
  lv_username = lpor-instid.
* Check if an instance already exists
  read table mst_instances with key username =
                       lv_username into ls_instance.
* if not found, instantiate
  if sy-subrc <> 0.
    ls_instance-username = lv_username.
    try.
        create object ls_instance-instance
          exporting
            im_username = lv_username.
```

```
    catch cx_bo_error .
      exit.  " simply exit without returning anything
    endtry.
*   Add new object to the instance table
    append ls_instance to mst_instances.
  endif.
  result = ls_instance-instance.
endmethod.
```

Listing 11.20 Instance Management Using a Static Instance Table

One more thing left to do is to ensure that the object can *only* be instantiated using instance management. In the PROPERTIES tab of the Class Builder, you can change the INSTANTIATION to PRIVATE as shown in Figure 11.38.

Figure 11.38 Private Instantiation

This has the effect that the `create object` statement for this class can only be used inside the class itself. Any other regular ABAP program attempting to instantiate it with a `create object` statement will fail.

11.8.2 Persistent Classes

Another technique for instance management is to make use of existing functionality. *Persistent classes* in ABAP objects can easily be implemented in workflow. Although they can simplify instance management compared to the techniques described in this chapter, they do require a thorough understanding of ABAP objects and ABAP persistent classes, which are outside the scope of this book. You can look at the `LPOR` and `FIND_BY_LPOR` methods of demo class `CL_BOOK_PPF` on a SAP NetWeaver 7.0 system to see how to implement it.

Using persistent objects may not always be suitable if used directly in this way. They tend to work well in scenarios where there is a one-to-one mapping to the underlying data table but can quickly become cumbersome to work with if the underlying data is highly structured such as HR infotypes. In such scenarios, a hybrid approach is also possible: Use persistent classes internally as data sources for your workflow-enabled business class.

11.8.3 Class Design Considerations

As discussed at the beginning of this chapter, shared components between related applications is a design goal that can reduce overall costs of an application. To this end, it is possible to reuse a workflow class in another application. A simplified example is given in Chapter 21, Using Business Server Pages. The example uses the same business partner class in workflow and in a custom BSP application to manage business partners' credit limits.

On the other hand, we also do not want too much functionality in a class that is specific to workflow and will never be used anywhere else. Classes that are too big can become cumbersome and unwieldy. There are no hard rules, and software design is a complex topic on which many books have already been written. However, we want to include some guidelines and ideas for scenarios in which the anticipated use of a business class is shared between workflow and non-workflow applications.

The biggest question in smaller projects or applications will be whether to have a single business class containing all workflow functionality or a separate workflow class. To answer this, consider how many of the planned class components provide business functionality and how many provide services that are unique to the workflow(s) being designed. Bear in mind that the business interface BI_PERSISTENT is not specific to workflow, and instance management is part of good object-oriented design, so these should be disregarded. Also, determining whether a component is workflow-specific or not can be open to interpretation. For example, a method that reads the workflow log for technical purposes inside a workflow could be considered workflow specific, however, a method that reads the workflow log to determine who approved a document can be considered a business function because this might be used in a BSP or Web Dynpro application. Similarly, attributes that represent purchasing item data are business-level components, but a method that returns a table of item information as text lines formatted for a work item text is workflow-specific.

As a rough guideline, if the majority of components are for business functions, you can keep everything in the same class. If, however, you find that more than a quarter of your attributes and methods are dedicated to workflow, you might consider creating separate workflow-specific subclasses or workflow-specific composite classes (classes that have the business class as one of their attributes).

For more complex implementations, a multilayered approach can also be considered:

▶ At the lowest level, ABAP persistent classes provide access to the underlying data. These are only used by business classes.

▶ At the business logic level, business classes provide business functionality. This includes the instance management and object functions provided via the IF_WORKFLOW interface, as well as many of the more business-oriented attributes and methods used in workflow.

▶ At the application level, application classes encapsulate the business classes and provide additional application-specific functions. Examples of these are:

  ▶ Specialized workflow functions only relevant for specific scenarios (e.g., determining if a workflow is already running for a particular document)

  ▶ Model classes in an MVC-based BSP application or Web Dynpro ABAP scenario. These also include many support components that are irrelevant outside the BSP/Web Dynpro context.

The significant advantage of this type of approach is abstraction: The higher-level components do not need to know where the data is stored and how it is retrieved. The entire data store can be moved to another system, and only the persistence layer needs to be changed. In today's world of corporate mergers, splits, and acquisitions, this is not as far-fetched as it sounds.

In some scenarios, you could add an additional layer at the business class level. Consider the case of several subsidiary companies each with their own SAP system. You could maintain a central business class with functions common to all companies and a subclass in each individual system that implements additional company-specific functionality.

Figure 11.39 shows an example of how a large organization with multiple subsidiaries may implement a business object in a complex project that spans workflow and other technologies based on real-world scenarios. Note that this is only one possibility represented as a simplistic design pattern; object modeling and software design are complex topics outside the scope of this book.

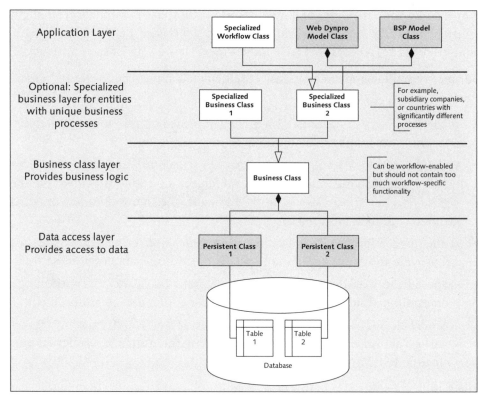

Figure 11.39 Complex Project Scenario UML Diagram (Classes in White Are a Workflow-Enabled Subclass Hierarchy)

It is this sort of big picture thinking and sharing of functionality among multiple developers and projects that makes ABAP classes an excellent basis for workflow development.

Determining the possible and selected agents for a work item is one of the most important and interesting parts of workflow development. Agent determination rules can use a number of different techniques. Some have dedicated maintenance transactions while others require programming. This chapter explains the different techniques that you can use.

12 Agent Determination Rules

You have seen in Chapter 5, Agents, that selected agents are a subset of the possible agents who might be assigned to a task. Assigning possible agents to a task or set of tasks helps provide security by restricting access to the underlying transactions. These are, in essence, relatively *static* lists of everyone who is allowed to execute work items belonging to a particular task.

Selected agents are your company's chosen decision makers for a step in a business process. Because the selected agents will vary for each work item, depending on the data relevant to the particular work item or workflow instance, a static list is not enough. Selected agents are assigned in the workflow definition, as shown in Figure 12.1.

Figure 12.1 uses a rule that finds the appropriate manager. This agent determination rule is a function module that receives an input, for example, the workflow initiator, and reads the organization chart to find his immediate manager. Agent determination rules are needed to assess who should receive the work item according to the criteria you specify.

Another example is the case where all strategic account managers are possible agents of the task "Respond to customer complaint." Suppose, for example, that strategic account manager Sue Kendel has to process the work item "Respond to customer complaint from Igloos Incorporated" because the agent determination rules specify that the strategic account manager for all customers in the Far North region are assigned to Sue Kendel. It is vital that the work item be sent to the correct strategic account manager, that is, the person who understands the current relationship with the customer and can make good decisions when executing the work item, so that the best possible result is achieved.

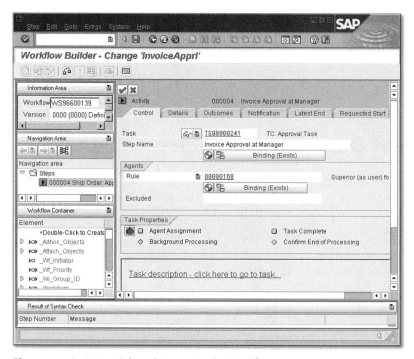

Figure 12.1 Assigning Selected Agents in the Workflow

Making these decisions is not always easy. This chapter deals with the different techniques you can use for agent determination rules. The techniques that you choose affect the development, performance, and maintenance of the rules you create.

12.1 Determining Agents Through Rule Resolution

Determining the responsible agents is one of the most important parts of any workflow. It is also the one area of a workflow that is most likely to fail in practice, so you should make sure your rule resolution is as robust as possible. Where there are many possible agents, rule resolution enables work to be distributed among the possible agents according to the business rules you define in the rule. That is, rule resolution (also known as *Role Resolution*) enables you to push work to the agents who are supposed to do the work. Rule resolution enables you to calculate who is the responsible agent for a particular work item, usually based on runtime criteria. For instance, you might have a rule that calculates the manager of an employee. At runtime, if you pass the rule an employee ID, the rule resolves who that particular employee's manager is.

Within workflow, there are a number of different options for creating standard rules, that is, rules that may be linked directly to a workflow step. You can use:

► Responsibility rules

► Evaluation paths

► Function modules

► SAP Organizational Objects

You can also use techniques such as ad-hoc agent assignment or custom-defined methods if you want to resolve a rule prior to the workflow step in which it is used. This can be helpful if, for example, you want to use the same rule resolution result for multiple steps in your workflow.

A number of rules are provided in each SAP component. These can be used without adjustment or as examples for creating your own rules. All rules have some common features and functions that you need to understand before you create your own rules.

12.2 Rule Basics

You create or edit agent-determination rules with Transaction PFAC. Using the menu path, navigate to TOOLS • BUSINESS WORKFLOW • DEVELOPMENT • DEFINITION TOOLS • RULES FOR AGENT ASSIGNMENT. When saved, the system assigns each rule an eight-digit number created by the system preceded by AC, which is used for identification purposes.

All standard rules contain the following basic parts:

► **ID**
The technical ID for the rule assigned automatically by the system.

► **Abbreviation**
A short free-format text primarily used when searching for rules.

▶ **Description**
A free-format text describing the rule.

▶ **Long Description**
A longer text area where rule documentation can be placed. It is a good idea to use this to explain how the rule works for the benefit of other workflow developers or for those maintaining the rule data.

▶ **Category**
You can define a number of different methods for resolving your rule, including the following:

- ▶ Responsibilities
- ▶ Organizational data
- ▶ Function to be executed
- ▶ Function to be executed asynchronously
- ▶ Organizational model

Hint

The preceding rule categories are further defined later in this chapter.

▶ **Container**
If you click on the CONTAINER symbol (⊞), this is where the criteria on which the rule is based are defined. Any data you need the workflow to pass to the rule to let the rule determine responsible agents must be defined here. Like any other container in the workflow environment, the elements can be simple values (e.g., employee IDs) or object references (e.g., employee object reference). They can be single or multiple values. Defining an object reference as a container element enables easy access to any attribute of that object. However, usually only simple values are used because it is easier to see the true criteria of the rule.

▶ **Terminate on rule resolution failure**
Checking this flag specifies whether the workflow should terminate (i.e., go into ERROR status) if no agents can be found via the rule at runtime. If this flag is set, the default agent determination rule defined in the task is ignored.

12.2.1 Testing and Simulating Rules

Rules can be tested and simulated either by using the SIMULATE RULE RESOLUTION icon (![icon]) provided in Transaction PFAC or by calling function RH_GET_ACTORS from a custom-defined test program.

The standard test facility enables you to enter values against the container elements in the rule. You can also opt to see whether the agents found have related user IDs. This is important: If the agents do not have matching user IDs, no work item can be sent to them. Sometimes it is more convenient to write your own custom-defined program to check rules, for example, by running the rule through a predefined series of tests or by testing whether the responsible agents found are also possible agents.

12.2.2 Rule to Locate the Plant Manager

Listing 12.1 is an example program showing a rule based on a single criterion Plant. This rule finds the plant manager. You don't need to know how the plant manager is found by the rule to test it. It could be found by a rule function module or by responsibility rules. The testing process is the same whatever rule type is used.

```
PROGRAM ZTESTRULE.
Include <CNTN01>.

* Here we have a parameter so that we can test our rule against
* different plants.

Parameters: p_plant type t001w-werks.

data: ev_holders     type standard table of swhactor,
      actor_tab      type standard table of swhactor,
      ac_agents      type standard table of swhactor,
      wa_ac_agents   type swhactor,
      num_lines      type i.


* Here we define our rule container
swc_container ac_container.
swc_clear_container ac_container.
```

```
* Here we fill the container with the plant value entered via
* the parameter
swc_set_element ac_container 'Plant' p_plant.

* Call the rule to find the plant manager
* Note our rule id is number 90000001, so the technical id of
* the rule is AC90000001
* The list of agents will be returned in table ac_agents
  CALL FUNCTION 'RH_GET_ACTORS'
    EXPORTING
      ACT_OBJECT                    = 'AC90000001'
    TABLES
      ACTOR_CONTAINER               = ac_container
      ACTOR_TAB                     = ac_agents
    EXCEPTIONS
      NO_ACTIVE_PLVAR               = 1
      NO_ACTOR_FOUND                = 2
      EXCEPTION_OF_ROLE_RAISED      = 3
      NO_VALID_AGENT_DETERMINED     = 4
      OTHERS                        = 5.
  IF SY-SUBRC <> 0.
* Message ...
  ENDIF.


* Here's an extra step to resolve the agents found to user IDs
* using an evaluation path SAP_TAGT
* This isn't necessary here — Workflow will resolve the agents
* to user IDs at runtime — but it helps us check that valid
* agents were found
 loop at ac_agents into wa_ac_agents.
   if wa_ac_agents-otype = 'US'.
     append wa_ac_agents to actor_tab.
   else.
     clear ev_holders[].
     swc_clear_container ac_container.
     swc_set_element ac_container 'OTYPE' wa_ac_agents-otype.
     swc_set_element ac_container 'OBJID' wa_ac_agents-objid.

     CALL FUNCTION 'RH_GET_STRUCTURE'
       EXPORTING
         ACT_WEGID             = 'SAP_TAGT'
```

```
      TABLES
        ACTOR_TAB               = ev_holders
        AC_CONTAINER            = ac_container
      EXCEPTIONS
        NOBODY_FOUND            = 1
        NO_ACTIVE_PLVAR         = 2
        OTHERS                  = 3.
    IF SY-SUBRC <> 0.
* Message ...
    ENDIF.
    APPEND LINES OF ev_holders TO actor_tab.
  endif.
endloop.

* Reduce the list of agents to user IDs only
delete actor_tab where otype ne 'US'.

* Check for no-one found
describe table actor_tab lines num_lines.
if num_lines is initial.
  Write: 'No agents found'.
endif.

Write: / 'The following agents were found:'.
Loop at actor_tab into wa_ac_agents.
  Write: / wa_ac_agents-otype, wa_ac_agents-objid.
Endloop.
```

Listing 12.1 Rule Based on Single Criterion

As you can see from the test program, the principles of rule resolution are the same regardless of the rule type:

► The contents of the rule container are read.

► The rule is evaluated, based on the data in the rule container and the rule type.

► The list of agents found is returned in an internal table. This table contains the agents as organizational objects (user, person, position, job, organizational unit).

Evaluation Paths

Regardless of whether you use standard rules provided by SAP, or develop your own, it is worthwhile to understand how *evaluation paths* work. There are hundreds of evaluation paths delivered by SAP, and you can also create your own if necessary. You can test and evaluate the results of the various evaluation paths using functions such as RH_STRUC_GET, or RH_GET_STRUCTURE, as shown in the earlier example.

12.3 Agent Determination Rule Resolution in the Workflow Step

To include a rule directly in a workflow step in the Workflow Builder (or as a default rule in a standard task), enter the rule number in the AGENTS section, press ⏎ so that the workflow-to-rule binding button appears, and enter the binding. Check that the binding is correct. For some rules (e.g., AC00000168 – Manager of a user), the system generates bindings automatically when they are first entered against the workflow step. Always examine the generated binding because this usually only compares simple container elements in the workflow to the rule container elements. If, for example, you want to pass an attribute of an object reference, you must do this manually.

> **Caution**
>
> The binding is executed between the workflow container (not the task container) and the rule container. That is, the rule is evaluated *before* the work item is created. If the rule resolution fails, and the TERMINATE-RULE-RESOLUTION flag is set, this means the workflow stops *before* the work item is created. When you restart the workflow, it restarts at the rule evaluation.

When a work item is created, you can see the result of the rule resolution as the recipients (i.e., *selected agents*) listed in the work item display or workflow log. Remember, the recipients are only those agents determined by the rule who are also possible agents. Agents found by the rule (i.e., *responsible agents*), who are not possible agents do not appear. You can also preserve the result of the rule resolution in the standard _RULE_RESULT rule container element, if you define a binding from the rule to an appropriate workflow container element.

After a work item has completed, you normally can only see the actual agent. If you need to see the recipients after the work item has been completed, calculate the recipients in a prior step and store them in a multiline workflow container element of data type `SWHACTOR` or use the `_RULE_RESULT` container element.

To calculate the agents in a prior step, you usually use either the ad-hoc agent assignment technique or create an object attribute or object method and accompanying task to call the relevant rule using function module `RH_GET_ACTORS`. Another option is to use the Choose Agent wizard that allows an agent to dynamically select the agent of a future step from a list of possible agents.

Determining the recipients in advance is a useful technique if you want to do the following:

▶ Use the same list of agents for several steps in the workflow.

▶ Report all agents responsible for the work item who have failed to act when the work item is not completed within deadlines.

▶ Further test the agent list by getting an administrator or business process owner to choose an appropriate agent, rather than letting the workflow fail with a rule resolution error. For example, check that at least one of the agents is a possible agent, and, if not, use the workflow to fix this.

▶ Send an email to all agents identified by a rule resolution.

12.4   What Happens If Rule Resolution Has No Result

Every rule has an indicator that determines how the system reacts if rule resolution fails to produce a result: the TERMINATE IF RULE RESOLUTION HAS NO RESULT flag. Rule resolution failure is defined as when:

▶ A rule resolution based on a function module returns the exception `NOBODY_FOUND`.

▶ An empty agent list is returned.

The advantage of setting the TERMINATE IF RULE RESOLUTION HAS NO RESULT flag is that if no agents are found by the rule, the workflow stops, goes into error status, and the administrator is notified of the error by email. The administrator is then able to correct the rule data or agent assignment (depending on what caused the failure) and restart the workflow from the point of failure, that is, from the rule evaluation. However, the termination only occurs if the rule itself finds no agent. If the rule finds agents, but the agents are not possible agents for the workflow step, no termination occurs. Similarly, if the rule finds agents but none of the agents resolve to user IDs, the termination is not raised.

> **Tip**
>
> You can prevent this to a certain extent by configuration in Table T77S0. By setting the entry WFLOW.ROLE to X, the workflow evaluates both the rule assigned to the workflow step and the possible agents of the underlying task. If there are no responsible agents who are also valid agents, the workflow terminates.

If the responsible agents in the workflow step are based on an expression or an organizational object (job, position, etc.), and the agents are not possible agents, no termination occurs either.

Normally, if no valid responsible agents are found for a workflow step, and the TERMINATE-ON-FAILURE flag is not set, then the work item is either assigned to the workflow administrator or orphaned (i.e., it stays in ready status with no agents assigned).

> **Tip**
>
> If the administrator receives a failed work item, he can forward it to the correct agent. The Work Item Without Agents report (Transaction SWI2_ADM1) lets you view and correct orphaned work items. After you have fixed the rule resolution problem, you can re-execute the rule resolution using this report, too.

Agent determination problems are usually a result of lagging data maintenance, due, for example, to manual paper-based forms being used to trigger update of personnel data after the personnel change has actually occurred. Usually, it is enough to let the administrator fix these problems as described in Chapter 6, Workflow Administration. If you have a particularly critical workflow, where rapid personnel changes and delays in data maintenance cause frequent agent-determination problems, you may want to use default agents instead.

In general, for critical workflows, it is usually best to create rules with default agents rather than let the rule terminate. Relying on the workflow administrator to act on the rule resolution error, fix the problem, and restart the workflow takes time. During that time, the business process is stopped for that workflow instance. A better way is to set up default agents who are also possible agents of the workflow. This is easy to do if you are using responsibility rules (using secondary priorities) or programmed rules.

This not only stops the workflow from going into error, but the default agent can forward the work item to the appropriate agent, or even act on their behalf, keeping the business process moving. The cause of the rule resolution error can be corrected afterwards, rather than having to rush the correction just to keep the workflow working. Making sure the work item text includes some indication of why the agent was chosen can help default agents decide what action to take. For instance, you might end your work item text with "You have been sent this work item because you have been identified as the manager of employee John Doe."

12.5   Responsibility Rules

Responsibility rules are usually the easiest and simplest rules to create and maintain. You can easily see both the rule criteria and how the rule will be evaluated. By using secondary priorities, you can also define default agents as part of your responsibility rule, reducing the likelihood of rule resolution failure. With a responsibility rule, as with any other rule, you create container elements for each of the criteria you want to evaluate. It is worthwhile to keep the number of container elements small because too many criteria become confusing and increase the cost of maintenance of your rule.

12.5.1   Responsibility Rules with Multiple Criteria

If you have a large number of criteria, consider whether you should have more than one rule, rather than create one very confusing rule. For instance, suppose you want to find a manager based on account assignment and value. Possible account assignments are cost center, internal order, and work breakdown structure (WBS) element. So you could create one rule with the following criteria:

- ▶ Cost center
- ▶ Internal order
- ▶ WBS element used in production planning
- ▶ Value

However, in practice, if the assignment is to a cost center, then only the cost center and value are relevant; if the assignment is to an internal order, then only the internal order and value are relevant, and so on. So it is less confusing to create three rules:

▶ **Rule 1:** Cost center, value.

▶ **Rule 2:** Internal order, value.

▶ **Rule 3:** WBS element, value.

If you still want to evaluate all three rules against the same workflow step, you can create a rules based on a function module that determines which of the three rules applies and calls it.

Don't confuse this, however, with using supporting criteria, for instance:

▶ Controlling area

▶ Cost center

▶ Value

▶ Currency

In this case, controlling area helps to further define the cost center, and currency helps to further define the value. So the rule is still based on cost center and value — you are just using controlling area and currency to make sure the cost center and value are accurately depicted.

After you have created your container elements, you create "responsibilities," which are combinations of container element values. Single, multiple, and ranges of values can be specified in one responsibility. The rule definition is a client-independent development object, but the responsibility definitions are client-dependent customizing. For instance, for a rule based on cost center and value, you could create the responsibilities shown in Table 12.1.

Responsibility	Cost Center	Value
Approver A	1000	$0.00
Approver B	1000	$0.01 to $500.00
Approver C	2000, 3000, 4000	$0.00 to $500.00
Approver D	1000, 2000 to 4000	$500.01 to $1000.00

Table 12.1 Responsibilities Defined in a Responsibility Rule

You then assign agents to these responsibilities. You can assign any of the organizational objects, including organizational units, jobs, positions, user IDs, and so on. By default, agents are assigned from the current date until December 31, 9999, but you can restrict the agent assignment to end on an earlier date, for example, when an agent leaves the company.

It is very easy to see who will be chosen as agents by using a few test examples:

▶ If you test the rule with cost center = 1000 and value = $450, the agents assigned to responsibility Approver B are chosen.

▶ If you test the rule with cost center = 3000 and value = $550, the agents assigned to responsibility Approver D are chosen.

Figure 12.2 shows how this rule is configured in practice. Responsibility rules are configured in Transaction PFAC, using the RESPONSIBLITIES tab.

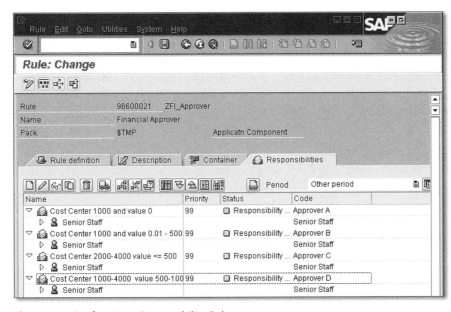

Figure 12.2 Configuring a Responsibility Rule

12.5.2 Secondary Priorities

By using secondary priorities, you can create default agents for your rule. You must specify in your rule that secondary priorities are to be taken into consideration by setting the flag TAKE SECONDARY PRIORITIES INTO ACCOUNT. Priorities take a value of

01 to 99. Higher priorities are evaluated before lower priorities; that is, responsibilities with priority 99 are evaluated before responsibilities with priority 98.

When priorities are used, the highest priority responsibilities are evaluated first at runtime. If a matching responsibility and agents are found, the rule evaluation stops. However, if no matching responsibility is found, then the next highest priority responsibilities are evaluated, and so on until agents are found, or there are no more responsibilities left to evaluate.

To demonstrate how priorities are used, we will add a new responsibility Approver E with priority 01 as shown in Table 12.2. Contrast this with the responsibilities Approver A to Approver D shown in Table 12.1, which have been given priority 99, that is, the highest priority.

Responsibility	Cost Center	Value	Priority
Approver E	*	$0.00 to $9999.99	01

Table 12.2 An Example of a Responsibility Assignment

You can see the asterisk (*) acting as a wildcard. So this responsibility will match any cost center combined with value up to $9999.99. If you then tested the role with cost center = 6000 and value = $600, first the highest priority responsibilities are checked to see if any included this combination. Having failed to find a match, the system then looks at the priority 01 responsibilities, and matches the combination to responsibility Approver E. So the agents assigned to responsibility Approver E are the responsible agents in this case. That is, because there are no specific agents for cost center 6000 and value $600, the system goes to the default agents for all cost centers combined with a value up to $9999.99.

However, if you tested the rule with cost center = 1000 and value = $450, the agents assigned to responsibility Approver B are still chosen. Even though responsibility Approver E matches with all cost centers combined with a value under $9999.99, responsibility Approver E is not evaluated because a match was found with responsibility Approver B, which has a higher priority.

So you can use a high priority to choose agents responsible for particular cost center/value combinations. If, for instance, you have a cost center used to capture expenditure on hardware/software, you might want a specific manager to be responsible for that cost center. Lower priorities can be used to send other cost center/value combinations to default agents. For instance, cost centers used for office equipment and stationery might be managed by a group of default agents, rather than a specific manager.

> **Note**
>
> Although you can have up to 99 levels of priority, generally 2 or 3 priorities are sufficient for most business situations.

Given the flexibility of the responsibility rules, you now understand why it is worth explaining the criteria used in the rule documentation for the benefit of other workflow developers as well as for the people maintaining the rule data. Because responsibility rules involve agent assignment, be careful to watch for buffering problems if you assign agents and then use the rule straight away. Use Transaction SWU_OBUF to refresh the buffers after the agents have been assigned and prior to the rule being used.

12.6 Agent Determination Using SAP Organizational Data

SAP Organization Data allows you to map the responsible agents to business objects. You can use the RULE category of SAP Organizational Data (also known as *SAP Organizational Objects*) to identify the responsible agents with specific data that is related to a business object (either SAP-delivered, or customer defined). A common scenario is the use of purchasing group to identify responsible agents.

In this scenario, the specific values of purchasing group are assigned to various positions, jobs, or persons, depending on your business rules. The definition of which assignments are allowed is created in Table T7791. After this linkage is defined, you can assign the specific values of purchasing group to the organizational object types.

> **Example**
>
> You have members of your purchasing department who may be related to some or many different purchasing groups. You make an entry in Table T7791 to allow linkage between purchasing group and object type S (Position). At this point, you can use Transaction PFOM to assign the defined values for purchasing group to various positions. You can then define the RULE to use SAP Organizational Data, and the corresponding OrgObj-Type is T024.

There is a little more visibility in using this technique than in using a programmed rule; however, it requires the use of special transactions to see the assignments to the organizational plan. And you need to ensure that using the SAP Organizational Object in conjunction with your HR organizational structure is acceptable to your HR department. The basic technique is as follows:

1. Select or create a business object representing the customizing table. This business object must have a key representing the code in the customizing table to be assigned, at least one attribute Description, and one method Existence Check. A special flag ORGANIZATIONAL TYPE in the business object header must also be switched on.

2. Create a rule with type ORGANIZATIONAL DATA, and enter your business object ID.

3. In Table T7791, you can define which organizational objects (organizational unit, job, position, etc.) can be assigned to instances of your business object.

4. Use the special Transactions PFOM (Create assignments to SAP Organizational objects) and PFOS (Display assignments to SAP Organizational objects) to assign the values from the Customizing table, that is, instances of your business object, to the relevant organizational units, jobs, positions, and so on. These transactions use the HR infotype 1208 to define relationships between the business object instances and the organizational plan. If you want to create your own program to update the assignments, you can use function module RH_SAP_ORG_OBJEC_RELATE.

5. When you use the rule in your workflow step, you need to bind an instance of your business object from the workflow container to the rule. You can either create this instance explicitly by using a SYSTEM.GENERICINSTANTIATE task to create an instance from your code value, or implicitly by creating an attribute referring to the customizing table business object in one of the other business objects used in your workflow. For instance, if your workflow is based mainly on business object Material, you might create an attribute Laboratory against the object that links to the organizational type business object for laboratory codes.

A newer variation on this technique is to implement the interface IFSTROBJCT in the business object. This interface includes an attribute Agents, which finds all agents assigned to an instance of the business object; that is, it finds all infotype 1208 relationships to that instance. That way, you don't need to create a rule at all; you can just assign your agents as an expression. For example if you have created an attribute `Laboratory` of your workflow's main business object `Material`, you could define the responsible agents as the expression `&Material.Labora-tory.Agents&`. In other words, the agents are assigned to the laboratory that relates to the material used at runtime in the workflow.

More information on this technique is detailed in the SAP Help Portal (*http://help.sap.com*).

12.7 Function Modules as Rules

Using a function module as a rule gives maximum flexibility but minimum visibility. You can look up data from just about anywhere within the current system and even in external systems to help determine your agents. You can even combine several other rules into one function module. For example, you can try one rule first, and if no agents were found, default to an alternative rule. However, it is very difficult for the agent, process owner, or even other workflow developers to understand how the rule finds the agent, so it is important to make sure that the rule is well documented.

Rules based on function modules are most useful where complex criteria need to be evaluated. If the rule is simple, it is usually better to use one of the other rule types such as responsibility rules or evaluation paths that don't require explicit programming.

12.7.1 Creating a Rule Based on a Function Module

The basic process for creating a rule based on a function module is as follows:

1. Create the function module. At this stage, it is enough to create the interface of the function module, assign it to an appropriate function group, and activate it. For the function module to be used in the rule, you must use the parameters and data type references in Table 12.3 as the interface for your function module. If you do not use this interface, you will not be able to enter your function module against the rule.

2. Create a rule as normal, setting the type FUNCTION TO BE EXECUTED.

3. Enter the function module name. The system checks that the function module interface is correct and returns an error if the interface is invalid.

4. Create the container elements for your rule criteria.

5. Enter the code in your function module using the following algorithm:

  ▸ All of the workflow macros must be made available to the function module by putting an `INCLUDE <CNTN01>.` statement in the global data area of the function group.

  ▸ Workflow macros must be used to read the incoming data from the rule container `AC_CONTAINER`. Use macro `SWC_GET_ELEMENT` to read single values and object references from the container, and macro `SWC_GET_TABLE` to read multiline values and multiline object references.

  ▸ Find the agents. This is where you put your complex criteria. You might be finding agents by reading tables, master data, calling other rules, calling another system, and so on. Do whatever is necessary to find the responsible agents.

  ▸ Convert the agents to agent format. In other words, all user IDs must be preceded by `US`.

  ▸ Fill the outgoing `ACTOR_TAB` with the list of agents.

  ▸ Check whether `ACTOR_TAB` is empty; if so, raise the `NOBODY_FOUND` exception.

Parameter Type	Name	Data Type Reference	Meaning
Table	AC_CONTAINER	SWCONT	This is the incoming rule container.
Table	ACTOR_TAB	SWHACTOR	This is the outgoing list of agents in agent format.
Exception	NOBODY_FOUND		Raising this exception indicates no agents were found.

Table 12.3 Agent Determination Rule Container for a Function Module

Tip

Note that raising any exception other than `NOBODY_FOUND` is not helpful. The various parts of workflow that use rules are only looking for the `NOBODY_FOUND` exception or an empty `ACTOR_TAB` to determine if the rule has failed. Any other exceptions are ignored.

12.7.2 Linking Rule Function Modules from Different SAP Components

In the following example, you can see a realistic example of a rule function module. In this scenario, the rule function module calls another rule in another SAP component to find the relevant agents. This is useful if you are running several SAP components, for example, an SAP ERP system and an SAP SRM system, and you want to share the rules so the data is only set up in one place. In this case, the rule and the data exist in the other SAP component. From the current SAP component, we want to:

1. Get the criteria values from the current system.
2. Fill the rule container with the criteria names from the rule in the other SAP component, matched to the criteria values from the current system.
3. Call the rule in the other system with the prepared rule container.
4. Read the agents returned by the rule in the other system. At this point, the agent list may contain organizational objects, such as positions, that only exist in the other SAP component. A function module is called in the other SAP component to find the holders of those positions in the other SAP component as user IDs.

For this scenario, we have assumed that an agent will have the same user ID in all systems. So we could improve this example by checking that the user IDs found in the other SAP component exist in the current system; that is, the agent exists in the current system. You may also want to check the validity dates of the user ID to ensure that you are using active users (as opposed to locked and delimited).

In the example in Listing 12.2, the <CNTN01> include has already been included in the global data of the function group. The rule container has single value container elements CostCtr, Value, and Destination.

```
FUNCTION Z_FIND_COSTCTR_MGR.
*"----------------------------------------------------------------
*"*"Local interface:
*"  TABLES
*"      ACTOR_TAB STRUCTURE  SWHACTOR
*"      AC_CONTAINER STRUCTURE  SWCONT
*"  EXCEPTIONS
*"      NOBODY_FOUND
*"----------------------------------------------------------------
```

```
data: Costctr          type KOSTL,
      TotalValue       type NETWR,
      Destn            type rfcdes-rfcdest.

data: lt_holders       type standard table of swhactor,
      lt_agents        type standard table of swhactor,
      wa_lt_agents     type swhactor,
      num_lines        type i.

*Read values assigned to the rule criteria in the
*current system
swc_get_element ac_container 'CostCtr'       costctr.
swc_get_element ac_container 'Value'         totalvalue.
swc_Get_element ac_container 'Destination'   destn.

* Call backend rule to determine responsible agents
* Fill container for backend rule - a separate container
* "lt_container" is used to keep the containers for the two
* rules separate

  swc_container lt_container.
  swc_clear_container lt_container.
  swc_set_element lt_container 'CostCenter'     costctr.
  swc_set_element lt_container 'Amount'         totalvalue.

* Call the rule in the other system
  CALL FUNCTION 'RH_GET_ACTORS'
    DESTINATION destn
    EXPORTING
      ACT_OBJECT                  = 'AC90000001'
    TABLES
      ACTOR_CONTAINER             = lt_container
      ACTOR_TAB                   = lt_agents
    EXCEPTIONS
      NO_ACTIVE_PLVAR             = 1
      NO_ACTOR_FOUND              = 2
      EXCEPTION_OF_ROLE_RAISED    = 3
      NO_VALID_AGENT_DETERMINED   = 4
      OTHERS                      = 5.
  IF SY-SUBRC <> 0.
  ENDIF.
```

```
* Return the list of agents in agent format
* As the agents belong to another system, we will need to use
* that other system to convert them to user IDs - if we did
* everything in the current system this step would not be
* necessary.
* Here we have assumed that both systems use the same user IDs

loop at lt_agents into wa_lt_agents.
  if wa_lt_agents-otype = 'US'.
    append wa_lt_agents to actor_tab.
  else.

* Here we call an evaluation path in the other system to find
* the holders of positions/jobs, and so on assigned as agents
    clear lt_holders[].
    swc_clear_container lt_container.
    swc_set_element lt_container 'OTYPE' wa_lt_agents-otype.
    swc_set_element lt_container 'OBJID' wa_lt_agents-objid.

    CALL FUNCTION 'RH_GET_STRUCTURE'
    destination destn
      EXPORTING
        ACT_WEGID            = 'SAP_TAGT'
      TABLES
        ACTOR_TAB            = lt_holders
        AC_CONTAINER         = lt_container
      EXCEPTIONS
        NOBODY_FOUND         = 1
        NO_ACTIVE_PLVAR      = 2
        OTHERS               = 3.
    IF SY-SUBRC <> 0.
    ENDIF.
    APPEND LINES OF lt_holders TO actor_tab.
  endif.
endloop.

* Return list of agents as user IDs only
* Remove all non-user ID agents as the org plans in the two
* systems are different, so any jobs/positions, and so on will
* be meaningless in the current system

delete actor_tab where otype ne 'US'.
```

```
* Check that at least one agent was found
describe table actor_tab lines num_lines.
if num_lines is initial.
  raise nobody_found.
endif.

ENDFUNCTION.
```
Listing 12.2 Rule Function Module That Calls Another Rule in Another SAP Component

You can test your rule using the RULE TESTING option in Transaction PFAC as normal, or by using the FUNCTION MODULE TESTING option in Transaction SE37.

> **Tip**
>
> When building and testing your function modules, save several sets of test data. This is particularly helpful if you are passing multiple values in to the function in your container.

12.8   Evaluation Paths as Rules

Evaluation paths describe how to find one or more organizational objects based on an initial organizational object. For instance, common evaluation paths include those shown in Table 12.4.

Evaluation Path	Description
A003	Belongs to. Identifies the organization to which a position or job belong.
A008	Shows the person who is holding the position or job.
WF_ORGUN	Finds the organizational unit of a user ID or person.
WF_ORGUS	All users of an organizational unit, job, position, and so on.
US_CHEF	Superior of a user.
SAP_HOLD	Holder of a position.

Table 12.4 Useful Standard Evaluation Paths

Evaluation paths exist in all SAP components. Evaluation paths work by using the relationships specified in the organizational plan to move from one organizational object to another. You can create your own evaluation paths. Evaluation paths can be displayed and maintained via Transaction OOAW.

Tip

You can always use the SAP-delivered evaluation paths, and build on them to create your own. You can also insert your own custom relationships for fully flexible evaluation paths. Remember, when creating custom relationships, SAP automatically creates the inverse relationship. In other words, if you create a relationship A01 — Owes Money to, you are also prompted to enter the description of the inverse relationship — Money is ower to. Relationships are maintained with Transaction OOVK.

The evaluation path is described as a sequence of relationships to be tested. For example, when using evaluation path WF_ORGUN to find the organizational unit of a user or person, the following happens:

1. An initial user ID or person ID is supplied as the starting organizational object.

2. If a user ID is supplied, the evaluation path checks whether there is an equivalent person ID (if you are in a system with the HR module within SAP ERP HCM implemented, this is relationship type 208).

3. The evaluation path then looks for any positions held by the user ID or person ID.

4. From the positions found, the evaluation path looks for any organizational units to which the positions belong.

5. The organizational units found are returned.

Figure 12.3 shows an example configuration for evaluation paths.

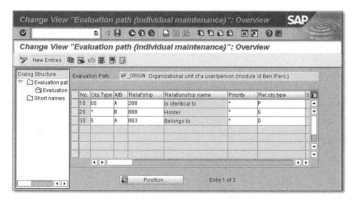

Figure 12.3 Evaluation Path Configuration

You can use Report RHWEGIDO to find suitable evaluation paths based on the initial and result organizational objects desired. To create a rule based on an evaluation path, you do the following:

1. Determine the evaluation path you want to use.

2. Create a rule as normal, setting the type to FUNCTION TO BE EXECUTED; that is, this is a rule based on a function module.

3. Enter the function module RH_GET_STRUCTURE.

4. Automatically (or by pressing ↵), an additional field EVALUATION PATH appears. Enter your evaluation path ID in this field.

5. Create the rule container elements shown in Table 12.5.

Name	ABAP Data Type Reference	Description
OTYPE	OTYPE	Type of the Organizational Management object
OBJID	OBJID	ID of the Organizational Management object
ORG_AGENT	WFSYST-AGENT	Organizational Management object

Table 12.5 Agent Determination Rule Container for an Evaluation Path

These container elements are used to hold the initial organizational object at runtime. You can pass the initial organizational object to the rule by filling in one or the other of the following:

▶ ORG_AGENT with the complete organizational object ID (e.g., USSMITH for user ID SMITH)

▶ OTYPE with the organization object type (e.g., US) and OBJID with the organization object ID (e.g., SMITH).

As evaluation paths evaluate organizational plan relationships, be careful to watch for buffering problems if you change the organizational plan and then use the rule straight away. Use Transaction SWU_OBUF to refresh the buffers after the changes have been made and prior to the rule being used.

12.9   Other Options for Responsible Agent Assignment

A number of rules are provided as-is that are worth examining rather than creating your own rules:

▶ **AC30000012**
Returns all agents assigned to an SAPoffice distribution list. This is perfect when you want a subscription-based agent determination. Agents subscribe and unsubscribe themselves (self-service), so there is zero administration.

▶ **AC00000168**
Returns the chief position of an organizational unit to which a user has been assigned.

There are also a number of rules delivered by SAP that are specifically tailored for SAP workflows. For example, rule AC00000148 (Person responsible for requisition release) reads some customizing tables to determine the responsible agents specifically for SAP-provided workflow WS00000038 (Workflow for requisition release). If you want to use the SAP-provided workflow as-is, you need to use the accompanying rule. However, you can also use these same rules in your own workflows if you wish.

Instead of using a rule, you can assign an expression to a workflow step as the responsible agent. For instance, it is quite common to see the expression &_Workflow_Initiator& (the workflow initiator) used as the responsible agent of a workflow step. An expression refers to a workflow container element or some reference based on a workflow container element, so it is up to you to ensure that the container element is filled correctly prior to the workflow step in which it is used. For instance, &_Workflow_Initiator& is usually filled with the "event creator" as part of the event linkage between the workflow and the triggering event at the start of the workflow.

If you want to make sure the same agent performs a number of steps in your workflow, you can store the actual agent from one step in a workflow container element, and pass it to another step. The actual agent of a work item can be found in the task container element _Work_item. The _Work_item container element contains an instance of business object WorkingWI, which has an attribute Executed-ByUser. So if you want to pick out the agent of the step, in the binding from the task to the workflow (i.e., after the work item has been completed), you could assign the value of &_Work_item.ExecutedByUser.NameWithLeadingUS& to your workflow container element to provide the actual agent in agent format.

Always remember that however your agents are chosen, agents must be passed to the workflow step in agent format (type SWHACTOR), that is, the 2-character agent type (US for user ID, S for position, C for job, etc.), followed by the 12-character agent ID (the user ID, position ID, job ID, etc.).

12.10   Real-World Example of Agent Determination Rules

Creating your own agent determination rules will be an important part of your workflow development. In one real customer scenario, there were multiple workflows that handled a variety of business processes. Some of the processes were related to HR actions and personnel notifications, some were related to procurement (shopping cart, purchase order), and some were related to invoice approvals:

▸ The customer used SAP Organizational Data (see Section 12.6, Agent Determination Using SAP Organizational Data) wherever possible, by defining custom business objects to link to HR organizational object types. Some of the SAP Organizational Objects were more generic for those workflows that routed to diverse areas of the organization, and nothing more specific than "Administrative Secretary" or "Safety Coordinator" was required.

▸ Other rules required more detailed selection criteria. For example, monetary approvals were required with associated clip levels. Some agents are allowed to approve up to $1,000, some up to $10,000, and some agents only want to approve purchases over $100,000. For this SAP Organizational Object, the various "clip levels" were built in as an attribute of the object, so when passing values into the rule container, one of the values would be the approval clip level.

▸ Where the preceding rules required usage of the SAP Organizational Object to identify the agents, function module "wrappers" were written, which essentially bundled calls to the SAP function RH_SAP_ORG_OBJEC_ACTORS_LIST. The data returned from these functions were then evaluated if further restrictions were needed.

▸ Still other workflows required customized relationships to determine who was responsible for approving a certain type of purchase or invoice. A relationship between the possible agents (object type S) and the organization (object type O) was created to identify the persons who were responsible for individual organizational units. This allowed the business to designate approvers in organizations outside of their own. For example, if the administrative secretary for department 100 was not available, the administrative secretary in department 200 had the custom relationship "Approves Invoices for" and could process the invoices for department 100, even though there was no standard relationship between the two. The essential SAP-delivered function for this type of rule resolution is `RH_STRUC_GET`, which returns a wealth of organization information.

The combined usage of these methodologies allows for plenty of flexibility in determining agents, as well as built-in redundancies where business-critical processes are being performed. Groups of approvers are more likely to be found, so there are very few cases where no approver is found. In addition, other applications (including bolt-on and custom developed applications) have used these methodologies, thereby increasing the customer's return on investment in the workflow-based technologies.

This chapter is all about how you connect your workflow with the application. The chapter answers these questions: How do you tell your workflow to start, and what are the options for starting workflows? What if a user does something outside of the workflow that should change what the workflow is doing? This chapter covers events and business interfaces that connect the application with workflow.

13 Using Events and Other Business Interfaces

Because workflows represent business processes, it is vital for business application programs to communicate with workflows. For instance, a business application may need to tell the Workflow Engine the following:

▶ When should a business process start?

▶ When is a business process or activity finished?

▶ When is a business process or activity that has started no longer required?

▶ When do changing circumstances dictate a change in the behavior of the business process?

Chapter 10, Business Objects, discussed how workflow uses business objects to access business data and routines after the workflow has started. Chapter 11, ABAP Classes, demonstrated how you can use ABAP classes to access business data. Now you will see how business application programs can interact with workflow to start workflows, stop workflows and notify workflows when a business application program has changed an object.

The primary business interface between business application programs and workflows is the *event*. In this chapter, we treat events based on BOR objects and events based on ABAP classes the same. When they differ, it is noted in the text.

At the end of this chapter, you will find additional ways of interfacing business application programs with workflows, such as *Generic Object Services* (GOS).

13.1 Understanding Events

Simply put, an *event* is the change in state of a business object instance. An event from a business application program notifies the Workflow Engine of that change in status. For example, if a business application program changes customer master data, then to communicate to the Workflow Engine that the customer master has been changed, the application must raise an event Changed for the business object Customer, passing the customer ID with the event to indicate which customer was changed. The Workflow Engine can then react to this event, for example, by starting a workflow to confirm the changes, which notifies the sales and support personnel who regularly work with that customer.

To use an event as the interface between a business application program and workflow, you need the following:

► **Event definition**
This is a technical name formally defined as part of the business object type. Any special event parameters must also be defined here. By default, events pass the object type, event name, object instance, and the event initiator (i.e., the user ID of the person running the business application program at the time the event was created). In the case of an event for the creation of a business partner, the event passes the following:

   ▸ Object type: BUS1006

   ▸ Event name: Created

   ▸ Object instance: Business partner number 221, for example

   ▸ Event initiator: User ID I001234, for example

   If an event includes parameters, the event parameters have to be filled explicitly by the mechanism generating the event. Not all event-raising mechanisms support this. Similarly, event parameters that can be filled by an event generation mechanism can only be used in the workflow if they are explicitly defined in the event definition. The event definition does not contain information about how the event is raised; instead, it describes the interface of the event (name and parameters) so that it can be used by both the event creator and the event receiver.

► **Event creator**
This is usually a business application program, but it may be a workflow itself using the step type EVENT CREATOR. The event creator is sometimes referred to

as the *event producer, event raiser,* or *event publisher.* The event can be created via a code routine (usually the case in SAP transactions) or as a generic mechanism (useful for raising your own events from SAP transactions). Runtime execution of the event-creation mechanism is called *raising the event.*

▶ **Event receiver**

This is the generic term for whatever reacts to the event. This is sometimes referred to as the *event consumer* or *event subscriber.* You can think of the term event receivers as equivalent to event consumers (as in *producer* and *consumer*) or event subscribers (as in *publish* and *subscribe*). We simply refer to them as receivers to keep things straightforward. Usually the receiver is a workflow, but it may be a task, or a WAIT FOR EVENT step within a workflow. Non-workflow receivers are also allowed, such as a routine that simply creates a mail notifying someone that an event has occurred (refer to Chapter 16, Advanced Diagnostics, for some techniques that do this).

▶ **Event linkage**

Event Linkage specifies the relationship between the event and the event receiver. You must also specify the rules governing the relationship. Rules can be used to determine whether or not the receiver should be notified, what event data should be passed to the receiver, and how. Rules can even dynamically determine the event receiver at runtime. Event linkages may be ACTIVE or INACTIVE. Only active linkages are evaluated at runtime. Linkages may be inactive because they are incomplete, in error, or because you just don't want to use the interface at the moment.

It is worth noting that each event may have none, one or many receivers. This means the event business partner created (`BUS1006.CREATED`) could have no workflows acting as event receiver, or could have several workflows acting as event receiver. For each receiver, a linkage between the event and the receiver must be created.

Tip
The EVENT CREATOR does not need to know whether there are any receivers. It is simply telling the Workflow Engine that the event has occurred. If there are no active event linkages — when, for example, there are no workflows currently interested in the event — nothing happens.

13.2 How to Know What Events Exist

Before discussing how to define new events, it is important to answer a question such as "When a business partner gets created or changed, does an event occur by default?" Whatever your workflow scenario is, you probably need to start the workflow based on some event. How can you know if an event occurs based on a specific action?

13.2.1 Look in the Object

If you know the relevant business object (BOR object) or ABAP class, you can look directly at the object and see the events. For example, if the BOR object is BUS1006, you can navigate to Transaction SWO1, enter BUS1006, and see the events BusinessPartner.Created and BusinessPartner.Changed. However, this does not tell you technically how the event is raised. In this case, it is most likely raised by creating and changing a business partner, but just because the event is listed in Transaction SWO1, it does not confirm technically how the event is raised.

13.2.2 Look in the Event Linkage Table

For SAP-delivered workflows and standard events, you can also look in the event linkage table to see what events are listed. The event linkage table holds the events *and* the workflow associated with the event. To see the event linkage table, navigate to Transaction SWE2 (SWETYPV), or follow the menu path TOOLS • BUSINESS WORKFLOW • DEVELOPMENT • DEFINITION TOOLS • EVENTS • EVENT LINKAGES • TYPE LINKAGES. Here you can see the object event linked to the workflow.

Figure 13.1 shows a listing from the event linkage table of BOR object events to a workflow. For example, the first entry has an object type of ABSENCE, event APPROVED, receiver type WS00400095. The next column TYPE LINKAGE has a checkbox, which means that when the APPROVED event for the ABSENCE object type is created, the workflow WS0040095 should start. The checkbox indicates that the event is active, which means the workflow will start. By looking at the event linkage table, you get an overview of what events linked to what workflows are delivered in your SAP system.

Figure 13.2 shows the same information for ABAP class events.

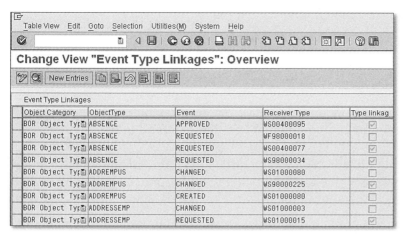

Figure 13.1 BOR Object Events Linked to Workflows

Change View "Event Type Linkages": Overview

Event Type Linkages

Object Category	ObjectType	Event	Receiver Type	Type linkag
ABAP Class	CL_HRASR00_PROCESS_EF OCCURRED		WS17900024	☑
ABAP Class	CL_HRASR00_WF_PROCES COMPLETED			☐
ABAP Class	CL_HRASR00_WF_PROCES COMPLETED		HR ADMINISTRATIVE SER	☑
ABAP Class	CL_HRASR00_WF_PROCES COMPLETED		WS17900015	☑
ABAP Class	CL_HRASR00_WF_PROCES CREATED_BY_XI_MESSAGE WS17900415			☑
ABAP Class	CL_HRASR00_WF_PROCES DRAFT_CREATED		WS17900404	☑
ABAP Class	CL_HRASR00_WF_PROCES DRAFT_TO_ERROR_AGENT	WS17900418		☑
ABAP Class	CL_HRASR00_WF_PROCES TRIGGERED		WS17900011	☑
ABAP Class	CL_HRASR00_WF_PROCES TRIGGERED		WS17900013	☑
ABAP Class	CL_HRASR00_WF_PROCES TRIGGERED		WS17900366	☑
ABAP Class	CL_HRASR00_WF_PROCES TRIGGERED		WS17900367	☑
ABAP Class	CL_HRASR00_WF_PROCES TRIGGERED		WS17900391	☑
ABAP Class	CL_HRASR00_WF_PROCES TRIGGERED		WS17900427	☑

Figure 13.2 ABAP Class Events Linked to Workflows

13.2.3 Remember to Turn the Trace Off When You Are Done

Probably the best way to know if the action you want to trigger your workflow is already an event is to turn on a trace, do the action, and see if an event gets created. This is something you typically do in a sandbox or a development system, *not* in a production system. Wherever you do the test, be sure to turn off the trace when you are done.

Using the Event Trace to Observe Native Events

The next few steps describe how to use the event trace tool:

1. Navigate to Transaction SWELS or follow the menu path TOOLS • BUSINESS WORKFLOW • DEVELOPMENT • UTILITIES • EVENTS • EVENT TRACE • SWITCH EVENT TRACE ON/OFF.

2. Switch the trace ON. Notice there are restrictions available, so you can limit the trace by a user ID or other criteria to limit entries written to the trace.

3. After the trace is switched on, in one session, start Transaction SWEL or follow the menu path TOOLS • BUSINESS WORKFLOW • DEVELOPMENT • UTILITIES • EVENTS • EVENT TRACE • DISPLAY EVENT TRACE.

4. Execute the trace. You should see an entry that indicates the trace has been switched on.

5. Leave the trace up. In a second session, go to the action where you want to know if an event occurs. For example, create a sales order, employee, business partner, or requisition; post an invoice; or take any action. If you are on a sandbox, you can use Transaction BP to create a business partner. You only have to select to create a person, enter a first and last name, and then save.

6. Return to the trace screen, and select REFRESH. If an event was created, you will see a new entry. In our example of creating a business partner, the trace looks like Figure 13.3. The business object is BUS1006; the event is CREATED. The entry NO RECEIVER ENTERED indicates no workflow is listening to the event. So, the event occurs, but no workflow or action is taken when the event occurs.

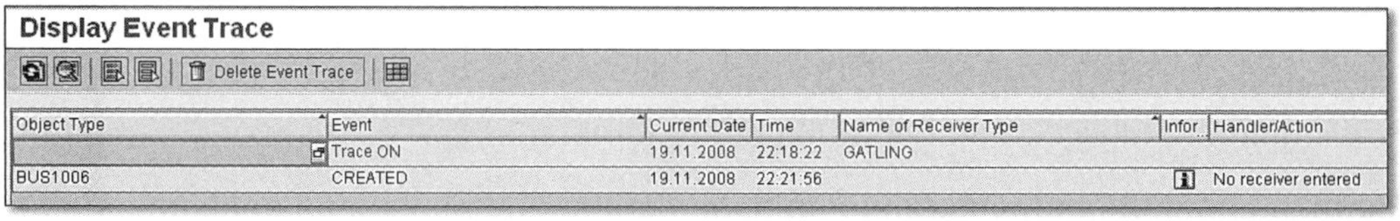

Object Type	Event	Current Date	Time	Name of Receiver Type	Infor.	Handler/Action
	Trace ON	19.11.2008	22:18:22	GATLING		
BUS1006	CREATED	19.11.2008	22:21:56			No receiver entered

Figure 13.3 Trace After Creating a Business Partner

7. Use Transaction SWELS to switch off the trace when you are done. The trace writes to a log file, and there is no need to write to it unless you specifically need to do a trace. Remember, system administrators are our friends!

13.3   Defining Events

You can find existing events in BOR (Transaction SWO1) or in the ABAP Class Builder (Transaction SE24) using the menu path Tools • Business workflow • Development • Definition tools • Application integration • Business Object Builder or Class builder. If no suitable event exists, you can create a new event. Creating new events was discussed in Chapter 10, Business Objects, and Chapter 11, ABAP Classes.

There is never any coding behind an event definition because the coding to create the event is in the business application program itself. Most events do not have special parameters because the standard event container elements suffice. The standard event container elements include the following:

- Event object (e.g., `BUS1006`, `&_EVT_OBJECT&`)
- Event initiator (the person under whose user ID the event was created, `&_EVT_CREATOR&`)
- Event name (e.g., `CREATED`)
- Object key (e.g., business partner number `221`)
- Event creation date/time

You can pass any of the container elements from the event to the event receiver.

Hint
The event must pass the who and what information; that is, who created the event (`&_EVT_CREATOR&`), and what data object was involved (`&_EVT_OBJECT&`). When using events to start workflows, the event creator becomes the workflow initiator, and the event object instantiates the object in the workflow container.

13.4   Raising Events from Business Applications

Before a business application can raise an event, the event creation needs to be coded into the business application program. Fortunately, you will often find that SAP has already done this for you. Usually the event is coded in such a way that you only need to configure what status changes should create events and which events you want to use. For instance, the parked document application programs check a configuration table to see whether the parked document is relevant for workflow before raising events for that document.

Often it is possible to enter new events in the configuration, and the provided event creation coding raises the event for you. Read the configuration documentation to check what needs to be configured and whether you can add your own events. Some of the configuration possibilities are described later in this chapter. However, to add event creation to your own programs, you can implement the event creation code yourself (the APIs are described in Chapter 14, Custom Programs). Business Add-Ins (BAdIs) can provide an appropriate place to add event creation code to existing SAP programs without modifying them, as do the generic mechanisms listed here:

▶ **Change documents** (i.e., audit trail)
Wherever a change document is written, for example, on change of master data, you can configure predefined events or add your own.

▶ **General status management**
Events can be configured to be raised through status changes monitored by status management. Both your own customer-defined statuses and those provided by SAP can be used to raise standard events or your own events.

▶ **Message control**
Events can be raised when a document is created via message control, for example, via output of a sales order. You can configure predefined events or add your own.

▶ **Human resources (HR) master data**
Events can be raised by HR infotype operations. You can configure predefined events or add your own.

▶ **Business transaction events (BTEs)**
Events can be raised by BTEs in financial application programs. You can only use the existing events.

▶ **Application-specific configuration** (e.g., parked documents, requisition release strategy)
Events can be based on the application-specific configuration. Because the configuration is different for each application, you need to read the configuration documentation to see if you can also create your own events. If a business application has special workflow configuration, it appears in the application's configuration, not in the workflow menus.

Wizards can help you set up the event creation configuration. Wizards are available for the following:

- Change documents
- BTEs

The following sections describe the principal mechanisms in detail.

13.4.1 Raising Events Via Change Documents

If the business application program writes a *change document*, the creation of the change document can raise an event. Many business objects are changed frequently. It is often useful and necessary (for audit purposes) to be able to trace the changes made. Many business applications log changes using change documents. This is particularly true of master data maintenance applications. Usually change documents are written when objects are created, changed, or deleted.

To log changes in a change document, an appropriate change document object must be defined in the system. In its definition, a change document object has tables, which represent a business object in the system, and some generated code, which is incorporated into the relevant business application program. You can incorporate change documents into your own programs if you wish.

A change document is written only if a table field designated as *change document-relevant* (in the ABAP Dictionary) has been changed. For example, changes made to the SAP ERP cost center data in the field BUS0012-PersonInCharge (Cost center owner) are automatically logged in a change document for the change document object KOSTL.

> **Tip**
>
> Before configuring events to be raised by changed documents, check that a change document will be written for the table field you want to track. The easiest way to do this is to make the appropriate change via the business application and check that a change document was created via the relevant change document report.

To create an event from a change document, configure the event via Transaction SWEC, menu path Tools • Business Workflow • Development • Definition tools • Events • Event Creation • Change Documents • Linkage. At a minimum, you specify the change document object, the business object type, the event name, and whether the event is to be created for inserted, updated, or deleted data. The event can be restricted further by specifying the old and new values of table fields or a condition (i.e., a logical expression) that must be satisfied before the event is raised. For instance, you might specify that the field MARA-WRKST (Basic material) must be non-blank before the event is created.

The system raises the event whenever a change document is written that satisfies your configuration entries. Change documents are usually written after the change itself has been updated in the database. Using change documents to create the event ensures that the event is only raised when the relevant change has actually been made.

The system fills the event container with information about the change document. You can force the system to write the old and new values of a changed field into the event container by defining the field as a database field attribute for the object type in the Business Object Builder, making sure that the ABAP Data Dictionary reference of the attribute is identical to that of the field in the change document. To transfer these values from the event container to the workflow, you must define event parameters with the same name as the attribute but as multi-line parameters. At runtime, the system writes the old and new values of the attribute as two lines (new value with index 0001, old value with index 0002) in the matching event container element.

> **Tip**
>
> The system also writes the elements CD_OBJECTCLAS (Change object class), CD_OBJECTID (Change object ID), and CD_CHANGENR (Change number) to the event container. You can use these to access the change document from within the workflow. This is particularly useful when the change document object contains line items that you need to analyze. To use these elements in the workflow, you must define them as event parameters so that you can specify them in the event-workflow binding.

Add an Event When a Material Is Changed

The following example adds an event when a material is changed. Changing a material creates a change document. The object is a BOR object, BUS1001006. Transaction MM02 is used to change a material; Transaction MM04 is used to view the change document.

1. Ensure you have an example material you can use, and change the material. You may also want to review the change document for the material. (Use the transaction code just mentioned or the menu path LOGISTICS • MATERIALS MANAGEMENT • MATERIAL MASTER• MATERIAL • DISPLAY CHANGES.)

2. Optionally, look at Table CDHDR to discover the type of change document that was created. The OBJECTCLAS field holds the *type* of change document. You need to know the change document type to link it to an event. The type of change document created when changing a material is MATERIAL.

3. Ensure the event trace is turned on (discussed in Section 13.2.3, Remember to Turn the Trace Off When You Are Done). Change a material, and look at the trace. If you are on a system with no previous workflow development, you will see that *no* event occurred when you changed the material.

4. Navigate to Transaction SWEC, menu path TOOLS • BUSINESS WORKFLOW • DEVELOPMENT • DEFINITION TOOLS • EVENTS • EVENT CREATION • CHANGE DOCUMENTS • LINKAGE, and select NEW ENTRIES.

5. FOR THE CHANGE DOCUMENT OBJECT, enter MATERIAL. The OBJECT TYPE should be BUS1001006. Select the dropdown for the EVENT field. If you are using BUS1001006, you will notice there is no change event. Prior to doing this step, the event must be defined in the object (discussed in Chapter 10, Business Objects, and Chapter 11, ABAP Classes). Select the appropriate event, and select to trigger the event ON CHANGE.

6. Save your event. When saving, you must include a transport request.

7. Return to the application, and change a material. You will now see the event triggered in the event trace (Transaction SWEL).

> **Note**
>
> Change documents can be linked to ABAP Classes as well as BOR objects.

13.4.2 Raising Events Via Status Changes

If a business application uses *general status management*, you can configure event creation according to changes in system statuses. Business applications for internal orders, funds management, projects, production orders, quality inspection, and engineering change requests are among those that use status management. You will know, based on the configuration of the application, if the application uses status management. Status management makes it possible to document the current processing state of an application object using statuses. For instance, you could use status management to track whether all quality inspections have been completed for an object going through the quality inspection process.

A *status object type* identifies the application object being status managed. *Status profiles* are used to link statuses to status object types. If you want to create your own statuses, you need to create an appropriate status profile. For system-set statuses, the relationships are predefined.

Each status is an indicator that is either active or inactive. For instance, the status "inspection close completed" (indicating that all inspections have been completed) is either true (active) or false (inactive). Statuses can be set by the system or by the user, depending on the status type. Both system-set and user-set statuses can be used to create events.

You can configure an event to be raised when a status is changed using Transaction BSVW, menu path TOOLS • BUSINESS WORKFLOW • DEVELOPMENT • DEFINITION TOOLS • EVENTS • EVENT CREATION • STATUS MANAGEMENT. You need to specify the status object type, the business object type, and the event name. You then specify which status changes raise the event by restricting the event creation to a particular status and whether that status is active or inactive.

To learn more about this, you can refer to the tutorial about raising events upon status changes in the SAP Help Portal (*http://help.sap.com*).

> **Note**
>
> Events linked to status changes *cannot* be used for events tied to ABAP classes.

Figure 13.4 shows Transaction BSVX for system settings. You can see the business object, event, and status that is required. These settings only work for SAP applications that natively use status management. So, if this is unclear, then probably your application does not natively use status management. CDM relates to an engineering change management master record change. ECM is the object type, APPROVED is the event, and I0253 is the status for approved.

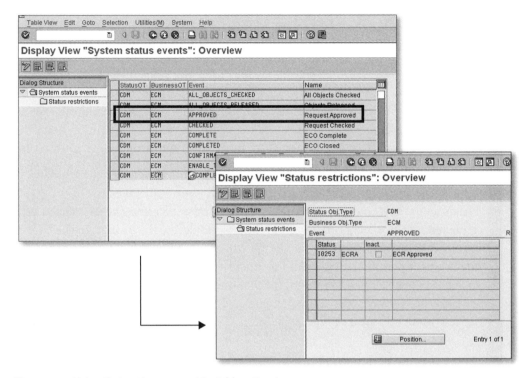

Figure 13.4 Using Status Management to Add an Event

13.4.3 Raising Events Via Message Control

If a business application uses *Message Control* to exchange information between business partners, you can configure raising events as part of message control. Business applications for sales orders and purchase orders are among those that use message control. When message control is executed, any configured events will be raised. For instance, when a sales order is created, message control is executed to output the order to the customer (e.g., by print, email, fax, XML, etc.). You can configure a workflow event (e.g., SALESORDER.CREATED) to be created simultaneously with the order being output to the customer.

An event can be raised whenever message control is executed using Transaction NACE or menu path TOOLS • BUSINESS WORKFLOW • DEVELOPMENT • DEFINITION TOOLS • EVENTS • EVENT CREATION • MESSAGE CONTROL. For the appropriate business application, create a separate output type (e.g., EVENT "Trigger event for workflow"), and designate transmission medium 9 "Events (Workflow)".

> **Tip**
>
> You can alternatively designate transmission medium T "Task (Workflow)" if you merely want to start one and only one workflow without exception. However, using events gives you more flexibility in defining how, which, and whether workflows are affected.

Your new output type requires a processing routine. SAP provides program RVNSWE01 and form routine CREATE_EVENT for this purpose. This routine holds the event creation code. It can be replaced with your own program or routine, for example, to assign values to your own event parameters before the event is raised.

Assign your new output type to an appropriate *access sequence*. The access sequence specifies what *conditions* can be used to define the output. In the case of events, the conditions are used to define which event is created. For instance, you might have a condition based on document type. Then for each document type, you could create a *condition record* for that document type and for the event to be raised. When the message control is executed, the correct event is raised in accordance with the document type.

The access sequence requires appropriate condition records. In the COMMUNICATION section of the condition record, you enter the business object type and event name. Your new output type appears in the CONTROL section of the appropriate message control procedure. The procedure lets you specify what happens when message control is executed, for instance, that it outputs the order by fax and raises a workflow event at the same time. The business application configuration determines which message control procedure is used at runtime.

13.4.4 Raising Events Via Changes to HR Master Data

Changes to HR master data can raise events. Configure an event to be raised when HR data is changed using Transactions SWEHR1, SWEHR2 and SWEHR3 or menu path TOOLS • BUSINESS WORKFLOW • DEVELOPMENT • DEFINITION TOOLS • EVENTS • EVENT CREATION • CHANGE TO HR MASTER DATA. HR *infotypes* and their *subtypes* determine the type of master data being changed.

The HR infotype must be linked to a business object type, which can be restricted to a particular subtype, if appropriate. For example, you might link the infotype 4000, which represents job applicants, to the business object APPLICANT. SAP provides a number of predefined links, and you can add to these.

An infotype operation determines the type of change being made. It must be linked to a business object type and event name. For example, to create an event when a new job applicant is entered into HR, you might want to link the operation "insert" for infotype 4000 to business object type APPLICANT and event CREATED.

SAP provides a number of predefined links between infotype operations and events. You can use these links as is, replace them with your own links, or add completely new links to your own events or those provided by SAP. Instead of linking the infotype operation to one particular event, you can specify a function module, where the event to be raised can be determined dynamically, based on the old and new values of the infotype. SAP provides numerous working examples of these function modules, such as HR_EVENT_RULES_PB4000, which specifies which events are to be created for job applicants.

> **Note**
>
> Only BOR objects can be specified using these transactions; however, it is possible to raise ABAP class events using a custom function module that raises the event dynamically.

13.4.5 Raising Events Via Business Transaction Events

Events can be raised when a *business transaction event* (BTE) occurs. BTEs are not related to business object events. They are triggered from financial applications, such as *G/L Accounting* and *Accounts receivable/payable accounting* in SAP ERP Financials and are used to notify other parts of the system of operations being performed in financial accounting, such as a document being created.

You can link a BTE to a business object event using Transaction SWU_EWBTE or menu path TOOLS • BUSINESS WORKFLOW • DEVELOPMENT • DEFINITION TOOLS • EVENTS • EVENT CREATION • SET UP WITH WIZARD • BUSINESS TRANSACTION EVENTS. If a BTE is linked to a business object event, when a BTE occurs, the system calls a function module containing the event creation code. The function module converts the data from the BTE into workflow event container-elements and creates the business object event.

When you link the BTE to a business object event, the SAP system generates a function module with the appropriate interface and implementation. You have to specify the new function module name and its function group. You can see the existing function modules you have created via the wizard using Transaction BF34. Now assign a new *business product*, which identifies your extensions to the BTE functions, as opposed to system-provided functions. Existing business products can be inspected via Transaction BF24. Only the predefined BTEs and business object events are allowed here. Transaction BF01 displays all BTEs. Table 13.1 lists the predefined event relationships.

Business Transaction Event	Event	
00001030 POST DOCUMENT (on update of standard data)	BKPF Accounting document	CREATED Document created
00001040 REVERSE CLEARING (after standard update)	BKPF Accounting document	CLEARINGREVERSED Clearing reversed
00001050 POST DOCUMENT: FI/CO interface	BKPF Accounting document	CREATED Document created
00001110 CHANGE DOCUMENT (on Save of standard data)	BKPF Accounting document	CHANGED Document changed
00001320 CUSTOMER MASTER DATA (on Save)	BUS3007 Customer account	CREATED Account opened
00001420 VENDOR MASTER DATA (on Save)	BUS3008 Vendor account	CREATED Account opened
00001520 CREDIT MANAGEMENT (on Save)	BUS1010 Customer credit account	CREATED Account opened

Table 13.1 Relationships Between Business Transaction Events and Events

Note
ABAP class events cannot be specified using the wizard, but it is possible to create the BTE function module manually (or to modify a generated function module) to raise an ABAP class event.

13.4.6   Raising Events by Calling a Workflow API

If none of the event configuration options are suitable, or you want to include events in your own programs, you can code the event creation yourself using SAP-provided function modules. For details on how you can do this, read Chapter 14, Custom Programs.

13.5   Using Events in Workflows

Having the business application raise an event is the first step. Your workflow needs to listen for each event, in the context of the business process, and carry out a response to it.

> **Tip**
>
> Just as the event creator does not need to have knowledge about whether there are any active event receivers, the event receiver does not need to know how or in which business application the event was created. This makes the mechanism extremely stable and transparent.

13.5.1   How to Use Events in Workflows

Within your workflow, you can use events to:

▸ Start a workflow or task (i.e., a *triggering event*).

▸ Stop a workflow or task, or complete a WAIT FOR EVENT step (i.e., as a *terminating event*, for example, a workflow executes to approve an invoice. The workflow contains a WAIT FOR EVENT to listen to a significant change to the invoice that may impact the executing workflow.)

▸ Force the workflow to perform an action on itself such as refresh the assignment of agents to work items or restart the workflow. From the point of view of the event linkage, these are identical to terminating events because the event reacts with a workflow instance that is already running.

In addition to this, the workflow itself can raise events via step type EVENT CREATOR. For instance, if an "implement hiring freeze" workflow is started, you may want the workflow to create an event ALLHIRINGFROZEN, which is then used to cancel all currently active "process job application" workflows.

13.5.2 Triggering Events

An event that is used to start a workflow or task is called a *triggering event*. Remember that the same event may also be used as a terminating event in the same or another workflow — it is simply the context in which it is used (or *consumed*) that makes it a triggering event.

When a properly defined triggering event is raised, some other process begins. For example, if an event for "invoice created" is linked to a workflow, then every time an invoice is created, an event will occur and a workflow will start. This might happen a few times a day to a few thousand times a day. Each event triggers a new workflow instance. For this to happen, the event must be:

▶ Linked to a workflow.

▶ Activated in the workflow.

Events can be linked to workflows but not active. If they are not active, then when the event occurs, the workflow will not start.

▶ Any start conditions must be fulfilled.

In the previous example, we said a workflow starts every time an invoice is created. In reality, you may not want to start a workflow *every* time an invoice is created but only when the dollar amount is a certain threshold, or some other criteria. You can put conditions on the events linked to your workflow.

When, in a business application called "create purchasing request," a new request is saved, a "purchasing request created" event is created. The system should then start the "approve purchasing request" workflow automatically. Of course, a workflow (or task) can have several triggering events. If any one of the triggering events is raised, the workflow (or task) is started.

> **Tip**
>
> Linking a triggering event to a task effectively uses the task as a single-step workflow. However, even if you only have a single step in your business process, it is usually better to embed it in a workflow rather than use the task directly because the workflow gives you more control. For instance, you can specify deadlines in the workflow step linked to the task.

Connecting Your Workflow to a Triggering Event

When connecting an event to your workflow, event linkage is the term used to describe linking an event to a workflow.

> **Tip**
>
> The same event can be used as a triggering event (e.g., for one or more workflows) and as a terminating event (e.g., for one or more tasks and wait for event steps), but a separate event linkage is needed for each receiver, and the event linkages will be significantly different.

Link triggering events to a workflow by selecting GOTO • BASIC DATA from within the Workflow Builder. Then select the VERSION-INDEPENDENT tab, and within that, the START EVENTS tab. A triggering event for a task is defined in the TRIGGERING EVENTS tab of the task definition.

To assign the triggering event to your workflow, you must also define a binding between the event container and the workflow container to pass event information to the workflow. Event container elements can be bound only to workflow container elements marked with the IMPORT flag. Usually you want to transfer the event object instance (event container element name _EVT_OBJECT) and the event initiator (event container element name _EVT_CREATOR) as a minimum. The event initiator is usually the user ID of the user indirectly raising the event, preceded by the two characters US to show that this refers to a user ID. If you define *import* elements in your workflow container with the same ABAP Data Dictionary type or object type reference as the elements in the event container before assigning the triggering event to the workflow, the Workflow Builder tries to match up the event and workflow container elements for you.

After the event to be used is designated as a triggering event and the binding is defined, the system automatically creates a type linkage consisting of:

▶ The business object type and event name
▶ The current workflow (or task) as the event receiver

Other linkage settings, such as the receiver function, are created automatically. These are described in detail in Chapter 14, Custom Programs.

> **Tip**
>
> You can change most fields in the event linkage, but be careful not to change the given receiver function module.

Initially, the event linkage is created inactive. Remember to activate the event linkage if you want the system to use it at runtime. Otherwise, it is ignored. If you are still developing your workflow, you can leave the linkage inactive until you are ready for your workflow to start when the event is published.

Event linkages can be transported from one system to another (e.g., from a development system to a production system) using standard SAP transport management.

You can see all triggering event linkages via Transaction SWE2 or menu path TOOLS • BUSINESS WORKFLOW • DEVELOPMENT • DEFINITION TOOLS • EVENTS • EVENT LINKAGES • TYPE LINKAGES. To check that the event linkage has been defined correctly, simulate the event linkage via Transaction SWU0 or menu path TOOLS • BUSINESS WORKFLOW • DEVELOPMENT • UTILITIES • EVENTS • SIMULATE EVENT.

Add an Event to Your Business Partner Workflow

To add an event to your business partner workflow, follow these steps:

1. In Chapter 8, Creating a Workflow, you built a workflow based on business partners. Return to the Workflow Builder (Transaction SWDD), and edit your workflow.

2. Toggle to the WORKFLOW CONTAINER frame, and double-click on your object, BUS1006. Select the PROPERTIES tab. Verify that the IMPORT flag is selected. The IMPORT flag is required for the event to pass information to the workflow container.

3. From within your workflow, select GOTO • BASIC DATA. Ensure you are in the VERSION-INDEPENDENT (TASK) tab, and select the START EVENTS tab.

4. In the OBJECT TYPE CATEGORY field, select BO for business object. In the OBJECT TYPE field, enter BUS1006. Select the dropdown for the EVENT OF THE OBJECT field, and select the event CREATED.

5. There are three other columns. The first is the ACTIVE column. The second is the BINDING column, and the third is the CONDITION column. Select the icon in the BINDING column.

6. The binding should look like Figure 13.5. Notice the &_EVT_OBJECT& is bound to the business object BUS1006, and the &_EVT_CREATOR& is bound to the workflow initiator.

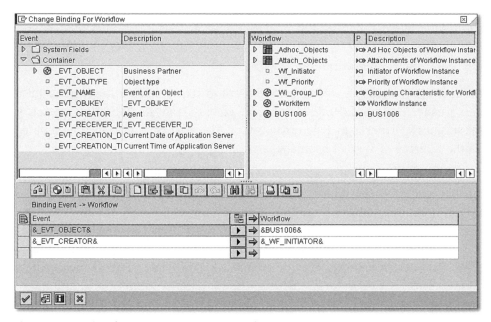

Figure 13.5 Binding from Start Event to the Workflow

7. After selecting the BINDING, the column icon will be green.

8. ACTIVATE the event by clicking on the icon in the ACTIVE column.

9. When you return to the Workflow Builder, notice the EVENT step added to your workflow. SAVE and ACTIVATE your workflow.

10. Create a business partner by using Transaction BP. You can create a person, enter first and last name, and then save. The save creates an event, which starts your workflow. If the event trace is turned on, you can go to Transaction SWEL and see that your event was triggered and your workflow was started.

11. Navigate to the workflow inbox (Transaction SBWP) to see the first step and execute your workflow.

13.5.3 Start Conditions for Workflows

Start conditions specify for a particular event whether or not a workflow should be started. Start conditions are only used for triggering events. There might be many reasons why you want to use a start condition. For example, events always occur when a material is created. However, you only need your workflow to execute for hazardous materials. You could use a start condition to check the material type before starting a workflow.

In the previous example, we added the event to start our workflow when a business partner is created. However, maybe we only want the workflow to start if the business partner is of type organization. The start condition would be based on the category or type of business partner.

The start condition itself is a logical expression that can be based on constants, attributes of the event objects, and system fields. Only if the logical expression is true will the workflow be started. Because start conditions are configuration entries, business analysts, administrators, and super-users can view or change the start condition (i.e., the logical expression) without any programming knowledge. Start conditions may include complex logical expressions, which contain logical AND/OR/NOT operators, existence checks, pattern comparisons, and multi-level parentheses.

Starting a workflow always consumes system resources and processor time, so if you can find an appropriate start condition (or a check function module), you can prevent unnecessary workflows from starting at all, and avoid situations that start a workflow only to have the first step of the workflow cancel it because it is not needed.

Start conditions (or receiver type function modules) are also useful for sending an event to one of a choice of workflows. They are also likely to be more efficient than a monster workflow that simply triggers other workflows. For instance, three alternative approval scenarios for a purchase request (no approval required, one approver required, two approvers required) can be linked to three mutually exclusive start conditions to trigger the appropriate workflow for each purchase request based on, for example, the costs involved in the request and the spending limit of the user who created the request.

Start conditions can be defined from within the workflow. Additionally, all start conditions can be seen via DEFINE START CONDITIONS via TOOLS • BUSINESS WORK-

FLOW • DEVELOPMENT • DEFINITION TOOLS • EVENTS • EVENT LINKAGES • WORKFLOW START CONDITIONS (Transaction SWB_COND) or usually anywhere that you can link a workflow or task to a triggering event.

If you create a start condition for an event, the system automatically adds a pre-defined check function module to the event linkage, such as SWB_ CHECK_FB_START_COND_EVAL. If you change the event linkage later, make sure to keep this check function module, or the start condition will not work.

Adding a Start Condition to Your Workflow

The following steps describe how to add a start condition to your workflow:

1. From within your workflow, select GOTO • BASIC DATA. Ensure you are in the VERSION-INDEPENDENT (TASK) tab, and select the START EVENTS tab.

2. Click on the CONDITION column. A screen appears as shown in Figure 13.6.

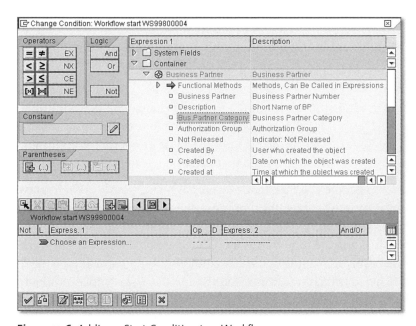

Figure 13.6 Adding a Start Condition to a Workflow

3. Drill into the Business Partner object, and double-click on BUS. PARTNER CATEGORY.

4. Double-click on the CONTAINS PATTERN sign (*).

5. In the CONSTANT field, enter a "1" and press ⏎. The condition should read:

    &Business Partner.Bus Partner Category& = 1.

    Type 1 means the business partner is a person; type 2 means the business partner is an organization.

6. You are asked to associate the condition with a change request. After you are done, the CONDITION column shows the CONDITION icon (🔺) indicating a condition exist.

7. Test the condition by selecting the ENTER TEST DATA icon (📝).

8. Select the Business Partner object, and enter a business partner number. You can drill into the Business Partner object to see the category.

9. Select the EVALUATE CONDITION WITH TEST DATA icon (📟) to test the condition. You can see the results of the evaluation.

10. To remove the condition, highlight the condition line, and select the DELETE ROW icon (📇).

11. Notice that after deleting the row, you must reactivate your event. ACTIVATE your workflow after removing the condition.

13.5.4 Terminating Events

When an event is used to stop a workflow or task, or change the behavior of an already started workflow, it is called a *terminating event*. Remember that the same event may also be used as a triggering event of the same or another workflow — it is simply the context in which it is used that makes it a terminating event.

The most common example is a task that executes asynchronously. When a task executes in an asynchronous mode, the workflow does not know when the task is done, so a terminating event is required to let the workflow know it can continue. One example is task TS 7986 from workflow WS00000038. This is the workflow for purchase requisition approval. The task to release the requisition is asynchronous, and it has terminating events defined for the task. Notice in Figure 13.7, the task has an asynchronous task. You can tell because the SYNCHRONOUS OBJECT METHOD is not selected. When a task has an asynchronous method, it must also have a terminating event; otherwise, workflow will not know when the task is completed.

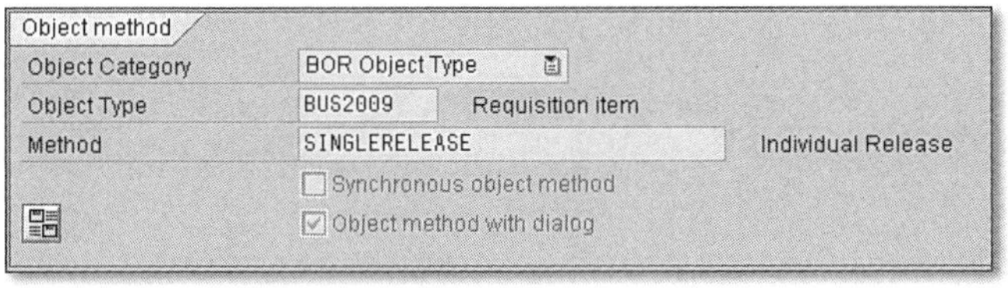

Figure 13.7 Terminating Event on a Task

When the event is created, if the event linkage is active and the linkage rules are satisfied, the status of the work item is set to COMPLETED, and the next step is started. Figure 13.8 demonstrates the terminating events associated with task TS 7986.

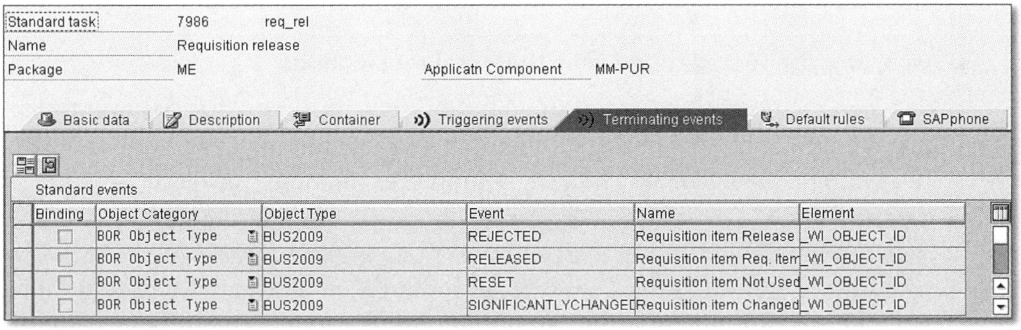

Figure 13.8 Terminating Events Defined on a Task

Linking Workflows to Terminating Events

Whenever a workflow, task, or WAIT FOR EVENT step is to be completed when an event is created, an event linkage is created automatically between the event and the appropriate event receiver. However, whereas a triggering event only needs to know the workflow definition for which a new workflow instance should be started, a terminating event needs to know exactly which workflow instances, work items, or WAIT FOR EVENT step instance should be terminated.

For example, when an event terminates (completes) the workflow step "release engineering change request 103," all of the other engineering change requests that are waiting for release must remain unaffected. For this reason, the linkage for terminating events always consists of two parts:

▶ An *event type linkage* to specify the rules that are the same for all object instances of the event

▶ An *event instance linkage*, which identifies the particular receivers (i.e., work item IDs) per object instance

After the system has processed the terminating event, the instance linkage is automatically deleted.

Note

Define terminating events for a task in the TERMINATING EVENTS tab of the task definition as seen in Figure 13.8.

Define the terminating event for a WAIT FOR EVENT step in the step definition itself.

Assigning the Terminating Event to Container Elements

To assign the terminating event to your workflow, task, or WAIT FOR EVENT step, as well as specifying the business object type and event name, you must also specify a container element that holds a reference to the object instance. This object instance is used to automatically create the event instance linkage at runtime. That is, a workflow, task, or WAIT FOR EVENT step is always waiting for a terminating event for the business object type, event name, and object instance combination. For instance, an "Update customer master data" work item based on object instance "Customer: ABC Pty Ltd" with a terminating event "Customer updated," should only be completed if the event is raised for that particular customer and no other. If more than one work item is waiting on the same terminating event (e.g., two work items waiting for event "Customer updated" for "Customer: ABC Pty Ltd"), then at runtime both receivers will finish when the event is raised.

A binding definition is optional for terminating events. Usually, it is enough to know that the event has occurred for the specified object instance. However, you can define a binding between the event container and the workflow container to pass event information to the workflow if you wish. In fact, this is the only way of passing information back from an asynchronous method to the task that started it.

Caution

You can only bind terminating event container elements to the workflow/task container elements marked with the IMPORT flag.

After you have designated the event to be used as a terminating event and designated the container element that will hold the object instance at runtime, the system creates an event type linkage consisting of:

▸ The business object type and event name

▸ A generic name for the event receiver, for example, WORKITEM for terminating events linked to tasks and workflows or EVENTITEM for terminating events linked to WAIT FOR EVENT steps

▸ A flag indicating that the instance linkage needs to be examined at runtime

> **Note**
>
> The event is automatically activated. Do not deactivate it.

An appropriate receiver function module and the default settings for the other event linkage fields are automatically included in the event linkage. You can change most fields in the event linkage, but be careful not to change the given receiver function module. The type linkage of a terminating event usually does not need to be changed at all. All terminating event linkages can be inspected via Transaction SWEINST or menu path TOOLS • BUSINESS WORKFLOW • DEVELOPMENT • UTILITIES • INSTANCE LINKAGE.

13.5.5 Workflow Header Events

Events defined in the header of the workflow enable the workflow to be a receiver, or event listener, responding to events that can impact the running instance of the workflow. Figure 13.9 shows how workflow header events are defined. Define terminating events for a workflow in the Workflow Builder by choosing the BASIC DATA • VERSION-DEPENDENT tab, and within that, the EVENTS tab. Here you specify whether the event should:

▸ **Cancel the workflow.**
This cancels the entire workflow (e.g., if the sales order or invoice is canceled).

▸ **Evaluate preconditions and post conditions.**
This evaluates any steps on conditions (discussed in Chapter 9, Advanced Workflow Design Techniques).

▶ **Reevaluate rules of active work items**
This executes the rule resolution for active work items; for example, when the cost center owner changes, you want to reevaluate rule resolution.

▶ **Cancel and restart a workflow.**
The workflow is completed, canceled, and restarted with the values in the workflow container.

▶ **Go to the wait step event.**
The event is delivered to a wait step defined in the workflow; if no active event exists (if the wait step was not yet reached), the event is parked. This is discussed in Section 13.5.6, Parked Events.

▶ **Trigger local event.**
Triggers a local event that can be used to start local workflows defined in the workflow or to complete wait steps.

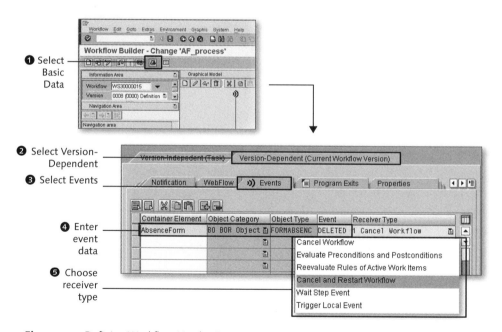

Figure 13.9 Defining Workflow Header Events

13.5.6 Parked Events

Normally, workflow can only react to events if there is a wait step defined to listen to the event, and the workflow is at the point in execution where the wait step has been instantiated. However, if the event comes before the wait step, then the workflow misses the event.

Take the following example: Your workflow has six steps in it. Step 2 executes a task. Step 4 waits for an event (e.g., invoice canceled, form deleted). If the event for Step 4 happens while the workflow is still executing Step 2, the event is lost. To eliminate this problem, workflow now "parks" the events automatically and waits for the event to occur. This means if the event for Step 4 occurs while Step 2 is still executing, the Workflow Engine parks the event for Step 4, and then when the workflow completes Step 2 and Step 3 and gets to Step 4, the workflow processes the event, and the wait step is completed. If there are multiple wait events, the first matching event item created consumes the first parked event.

13.5.7 Event Queues

Event queues can be used to improve overall system performance and manage events in error. Event queues store the results of the event linkage temporarily in a database table after the start conditions and check functions have been evaluated. This means there is a slight delay before the workflows are started, which helps to spread out the system load caused by the creation of workflows.

There are three major steps when working with event queues:

▶ **In the event linkage of the triggering event, enable the event queue.**
To use the event queue to spread system load, you need to set the ENABLE EVENT QUEUE flag in the event linkage. This is found via the menu path TOOLS • BUSINESS WORKFLOW • DEVELOPMENT • UTILITIES • EVENTS • TYPE LINKAGES or Transaction SWETYPV.

▶ **Use the queue administration to activate the event queue and to administer and monitor the event queue.**
The queue administration is found via the menu path TOOLS • BUSINESS WORKFLOW • DEVELOPMENT • ADMINISTRATION • EVENT MANAGER • EVENT QUEUE or Transaction SWEQADM.

The BASIC DATA tab specifies the default error handling for all events. In the BACKGROUND JOB tab, you can schedule and view the background job, SWEQSRV, which periodically processes the event queue. The LINKAGES WITH ERRORS tab shows all events that are currently in error status.

▶ **Use the event browser to see waiting events and their status.**
Examine the event queue via the menu path Tools • Business Workflow • Development • Utilities • Events • Event Queue Browser or Transaction SWEQBROWSER. This transaction shows those events waiting in the event queue that have already been processed along with their status. If processing failed the first time, the event will be automatically retried in the next run. If an event has not yet been delivered, or is in error, you can opt to redeliver it. Optionally, you can deliver events that are waiting in the queue.

The event queue can also store erroneous event linkages, so that they can be restarted later, after the error has been corrected. To send events in error to the event queue, set the Behavior Upon Error Feedback flag in the trigger event linkage to either Mark linkage as having errors or Do not change linkage.

The background job SWEQSRV periodically processes the queued items. This is set up in workflow customizing.

Do not confuse the *event queue* with the *event trace*. Event queue is queuing up events to execute. Event trace is tracing what events are actually occurring in the system, regardless of their association with a workflow. Event trace is commonly used for problem solving and is described in detail in Chapter 16, Advanced Diagnostics.

13.6   Generic Object Services

Generic Object Services (GOS) are a set of business object-based services you can include in business application programs. In many cases, SAP has already built this into the appropriate SAP transactions. Usually GOS is included in the business applications that display or change the business object instance.

For instance, while displaying an engineering change request or a marketing lead, you can access the GOS for the lead. The available services are visible via the menu System • Services for Object, as a button on the screen, or as a floating toolbar, depending on the SAP release and GUI used. Keep in mind that not all business objects support GOS.

Although the list of services varies from release to release, it includes the following:

- Starting new workflows ad-hoc based on the object instance via the Start Workflow service

- Viewing all current and completed workflows involving the object instance via the Workflow Overview service

- Subscribing (or canceling subscriptions) to events based on the object instance via the Subscribe to/Cancel Object service, which simply notifies when an event occurs for that object instance

- Sending an email with this object instance as an attachment via the Send Object with Note service.

- Adding attachments or notes to the business object.

So, for example, you can use GOS to view all current workflows based on the marketing lead selected and track their progress.

> **Note**
>
> You can only reach these services if the transaction has first implemented GOS. To add GOS to your own transactions, consult Chapter 14, Custom Programs.

13.6.1   Starting Workflows Manually

Sometimes it makes sense for business personnel to start workflows manually on an ad-hoc basis. For example, while viewing material master data, someone might notice a value that needs to be updated but may not have the privileges to change it, so instead the user wants to start a workflow to contact the person responsible for that material.

By starting a workflow manually, rather than by sending an email, the user can make sure the correct material is passed (no chance of typing errors), let the workflow find the current person responsible for that material, follow the workflow's progress, and be notified by the workflow automatically when this person has made the changes.

When you start a workflow manually, the workflow begins immediately, and may even take you directly into the first step (see synchronous dialog chains in Chapter 4, Work Item Delivery). If you have defined a start form for the workflow, then this form is displayed. To start a workflow manually, you need to be a possible agent of the workflow.

Tip

In an emergency, all workflows can be started manually by a system administrator, via RUNTIME TOOLS • TEST WORKFLOW (Transaction SWUS). If the administrator is assigned to the workflow as a possible agent, they can use Transaction SWUI (via RUNTIME TOOLS • START WORKFLOW).

As you can see in Figure 13.10, the standard screen for starting workflows has two sections. On the left-hand side, all of the workflows are listed for which you are a possible agent. When you select a workflow, the description of the workflow is displayed on the right. The function START WITH DETAILS is used to add information such as attachments, notes, or deadlines to the workflow via three tab pages. These attachments and notes are made available to all agents of the workflow.

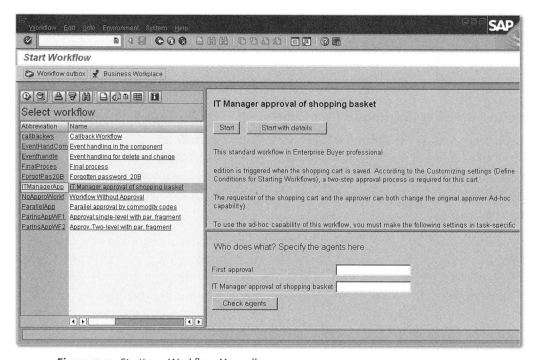

Figure 13.10 Starting a Workflow Manually

13.6.2 Viewing the Logs of Related Workflows

The GOS menu lets you browse the status of all workflows that are processing the displayed business object. A list of workflows that reference this business object instance is shown, and you can navigate to the different logs of each workflow. The list includes ad-hoc workflows, and workflows where the object was added as an attachment rather than part of the workflow definition.

13.6.3 Subscribe to an Object Instance

If you do not need to start a workflow but just want to be notified of particular events related to a particular object instance, then you can subscribe to an object instance using the GOS SUBSCRIBE. This function is useful for users who want to know when events occur that are related to a particular object instance, for example, whenever a particular cost center master is changed.

To make yourself a receiver of the event occurrence mail, in the application that supports GOS for this object, use GOS to subscribe to (or cancel the subscription, if you are already subscribed) events for this object. So that users can subscribe to your own events, create an event linkage (Transaction SWE2) for your event, listing SUBSCRIBE as the receiver type, SGOSSUB_REC_FB_SEND_MAIL as the receiver function module, and SGOSSUB_CHECK_FB as the check function module. The texts of the mail and the specific check function module to be used can be customized in configuration Table SGOSSUB.

13.6.4 Sending an Email

You can use the option to send an email to someone else with this business object instance as an attachment. The object can only be viewed if the receiver receives the email in the Business Workplace. Microsoft Outlook and Lotus Notes may support this feature depending on whether the groupware interface has been installed.

A reference to this email is attached to the object so that anyone who calls up the transaction used to display the object will see that the email has been sent. If you intend to use this feature, make sure that all users are aware of how to use it and for what purposes it should be used. Make sure they realize that they cannot send the email to a user outside the system because the attachment will not be usable.

13.7 Starting Workflows from Messages

Whenever a message (e.g., error message or warning message) is sent to a screen, a user can view the long text of the message. If you create a workflow to be started from the error message, an extra START WORKFLOW button is added to the error message long text screen that users can optionally push to start the workflow.

> **Caution**
>
> Workflows cannot be started automatically when an error message is created.

For instance, if the error message indicates some master data is missing, you might set up a workflow that the user can start to contact the person responsible for the master data.

To create a workflow linked to an error message, use the wizard via Transaction SWUY or menu path TOOLS • BUSINESS WORKFLOW • DEVELOPMENT • DEFINITION TOOLS • EXECUTE THE WIZARD 'CREATE WORKFLOW-MESSAGE LINKAGE.' This creates an entry in Table T100W and generates the stub of a workflow definition with all of the relevant container elements so that the details (including message type, message class, message number, message text, message parameters) of the error message can be evaluated in the workflow.

When your stakeholders require you to enhance the process with your own reports or control mechanisms, then in the interests of robust, stable, future-proofed programs, you are best off keeping to the well-trodden path of public interfaces. These include the workflow open APIs, advanced business interface options, and email (office document) interfaces. This chapter discusses the most commonly used workflow APIs (WAPIs).

14   Custom Programs

After you get some workflows in production and get familiar with SAP Business Workflow, you may need to access workflow from outside the application. For example, you might have a background job that processes data received from a supplier, and you want to start a workflow. Or you might want custom programs you have created to interact with a workflow. To do this, you need to understand the types of work items you can work with and the *workflow application programming interfaces* (WAPIs). This chapter is also useful to the system administrator who wants to understand the Workflow Engine in more depth.

14.1   The Engine

The Workflow Engine provides a number of ways to add your own functionality to a process. Before you create your own custom programs, read this chapter to get an overview of the Workflow Engine.

> **Caution**
>
> The detailed description here is meant to help you understand how the system works. Do not create functions to write to the database tables directly or via internal SAP function modules because you might cause inconsistencies that can have a fatal effect on the workflows currently executing.
>
> Play it safe, stick to the public interfaces, and use these carefully.

14.1.1 Work Items

When a workflow runs, it generates an anchor, the *workflow instance*, which references all of the relevant data of this particular instance. The workflow instance is stored in Table SWWWIHEAD as a work item of type F. The workflow ID is unique in the system and is allocated using a number range that can be customized but uses a default if no customizing is performed.

The major steps in the workflow are given their own anchor, the work item ID. This can be of type W, B, or F, depending on whether or not the step is a dialog task (appearing in a user's inbox), a background task (performed automatically without user intervention), or a subworkflow (a workflow called as a step of a parent workflow), respectively. There are other work item types, which you will see later in this section.

Some technical steps, such as the container operation, are not represented as work items. However, all dialog tasks and background tasks are represented by work items. Even though you can customize a workflow step based on a task so that it does not appear in the chronological and graphical logs, a work item is still created and appears in the technical log. The detailed history of what has happened in each work item is stored in a separate table (SWWLOGHIST).

The agents assigned to a work item are also stored in separate tables. However, this varies from release to release. Some tables are simply transient buffers that are deleted after the work item has been executed, so only use the public interfaces to query the agents assigned to a work item.

Every work item references the task on which it is based and its parent workflow work item (if any) as shown in Figure 14.1. This allows the Workflow Engine to climb from a work item through the tree of parent work items until it reaches the root workflow instance. Workflow work items reference the workflow task (e.g., WS0000001) with the version number.

This is important because when you change the workflow definition, you will have old work instances that need to follow the old workflow process, and new work instances that need to follow the path of the newly activated workflow definition. In some systems where the process duration is long, and the workflow was changed, you will find more than two versions of a workflow definition being followed at any one time, depending on when the workflow instance was started.

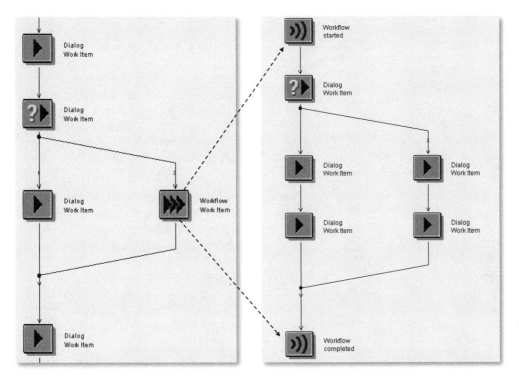

Figure 14.1 Work Item Hierarchy

Hint

Generate a new version in the Workflow Builder, every time you change the process flow or the binding.

The complete list of work item types is shown in Table 14.1. If you look into a system that has been productive for many releases, you might find some of the obsolete work item types shown in the list.

Work Item Type	Purpose	
A	Work queue work item	Used for work queues. In asset management, a work queue is a list of assets handled by the same workflow instance.

Table 14.1 Work Item Types

Work Item Type	Purpose	
B	Background work item	Background work items are executed by the user WF-BATCH in the background. A background task has no agents assigned to it and does not appear in any inbox. Background work items use tasks, which are defined as "background" and are based on a method that does not have the DIALOG flag.
C	Container anchor	Obsolete. Container anchor work items are strictly speaking not workflow items because they are not associated with any workflow. They were used to link IDocs to the business object that is created from the incoming IDoc. To delete these work items, use report RSW-WCIDE as described in SAP Note 153205. These work items are *not* deleted with Transaction SARA, the archiving transaction.
D	Missed deadline work item	Missed deadline work items are created when a (modeled) deadline is missed. These work items are routed to the deadline agents.
E	Wait step work item	Event work items are created when you have wait-for-event steps in your workflow. When the event occurs, and it matches the conditions set in the wait step, then the status of the event item is set to COMPLETED, and the workflow continues the branch that follows this step.
F	Workflow work item	The workflow item represents a single workflow or subworkflow. Assigned to it are work items representing the different steps in the workflow. Double-clicking on a work item in Transaction SWI1 displays the workflow log. If the WORKFLOW INSTANCE has the status COMPLETED, then all its dependent work items are completed or canceled as well.

Table 14.1 Work Item Types (cont.)

Work Item Type	Purpose	
W	Dialog work item	Dialog work items appear in the agent's inbox or Universal Worklist (UWL). The task for such a work item is started when the user launches the work item. This task can call the connected dialog method to start a SAP transaction, or this task can start an associated Business Server Page (BSP) or Web Dynpro application.

Table 14.1 Work Item Types (cont.)

Although you should only access Table SWWWIHEAD via the public interfaces, it is helpful to know some of the principal fields available as shown in Table 14.2 because most public interfaces return these.

Technical Field Name	Meaning
WI_ID	The work item ID
WI_TYPE	An abbreviation to show the type of work item (refer to Table 14.1).
WI_STAT	The status that the work item is in (see Table 14.3).
WI_CHCKWI	The parent work item. If this field is blank, then this work item is a top-level work item.

Table 14.2 SWWWIHEAD Public Interfaces

The data needed by the workflow are stored in containers. These can be standard tables or XML container tables. Every work item has its own container. This includes the workflow work item and every subworkflow, dialog, or background work item beneath it. Although the workflow container is used to fill other work item containers (as shown in Figure 14.2), having their own container allows the tasks to work independently of one another. This is especially important when they are executed in parallel. When the tasks finish, the contents of the work item container are passed back to the workflow container according to the binding rules as described in Chapter 8, Creating a Workflow.

If you want to access the container runtime data from your own programs, then use the function module SAP_WAPI_READ_CONTAINER. This function returns the workflow data, no matter if it is stored in XML format or the older format. Those older workflows, or workflows where the definition has been configured not to use XML, use the Tables SWW_CONT and SWW_CONTOB. SWW_CONTOB contains elements based on object references; whereas SWW_CONT contains structures and simple elements.

The flow of data from one container to another is defined by the binding between them. Figure 14.2 shows the different bindings possible.

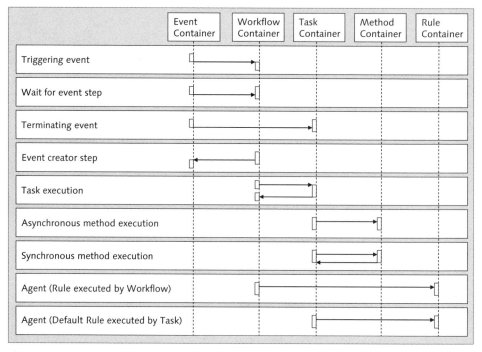

Figure 14.2 Possible Binding Definitions Within a Workflow

Hint

For performance reasons, it is better *not* to define the binding between task and method. When this binding is not defined, then the SAP system just passes the whole task container to the method container and back.

14.1.2 Events

Events are transient. You can capture snapshots of them if you like using the event trace, workflow trace, or event queue, but bear in mind that when the event has finished its job (such as triggering a workflow), it disappears (almost) without a trace. This is also true of the event's container.

14.1.3 Work Item States

You can see at a glance if a workflow is in progress or has completed by examining the state of the workflow work item. There is no need to access the workflow's history unless it is the detailed information (e.g., Who added which attachment when?) that you are interested in.

The parent work item is not completed until all of the steps in the workflow are completed or logically deleted. Each work item may pass through a number of states depending on the steps and techniques used. Table 14.3 gives a summary of all work item states and their causes.

Work Item Status	Short Text and Description
CHECKED (⬡)	IN PREPARATION The work item can be created, but the CREATE WORK ITEM condition for the step is not yet fulfilled.
WAITING (⬡)	WAITING The work item has been scheduled for its *requested start*. A work item has this status: ▶ If it already exists but the *requested start* specified in the workflow definition has not yet been reached ▶ If it has been set to resubmission Dialog work items in the WAITING status are not displayed in the workflow inbox.
READY (⬡)	READY The dialog work item has been released for execution and appears in the workflow inbox of its recipients. The REPLACE option in the inbox also sets a work item to READY status.

Table 14.3 Work Item State

Work Item Status	Short Text and Description
SELECTED (icon)	RESERVED The dialog work item has been reserved (e.g., via the RESERVE option in the inbox) by one of its recipients with the result that its status has changed from READY to SELECTED. A work item in the SELECTED status is then displayed to this recipient only. It is no longer displayed in the workflow inboxes of the other recipients.
STARTED (icon)	IN PROCESS The work item is currently being processed by an agent, or it is in the middle of being executed in the background. A work item also has this status ▶ If the work item is waiting for a terminating event ▶ If the user canceled out of the method ▶ If it is the anchor for a whole (sub) workflow, and this instance is still running
COMMITTED (icon)	EXECUTED The dialog work item has been executed but is awaiting explicit confirmation of its completion. The work item only has this status if it is necessary to confirm that it has been completed. A work item with COMMITTED status can be repeatedly executed or forwarded until it is set to the status COMPLETED.
COMPLETED (icon)	COMPLETED The execution of the work item is completed. Dialog work items in the COMPLETED status are automatically removed from the SAP GUI inbox. In the UWL , they are removed at the next REFRESH.
CANCELLED (icon)	LOGICALLY DELETED Execution of the work item is no longer possible. A work item is changed to the CANCELLED status when: ▶ The required number of processing paths has been executed in a fork, and the work items in the other paths that have not yet reached the COMPLETED status are automatically set to the CANCELLED status. ▶ A process control step sets the status, for example, as part of modeled deadline monitoring.

Table 14.3 Work Item State (cont.)

Work Item Status	Short Text and Description
CANCELLED (⬡) (cont.)	▶ An administrator intervenes; the administrator can only set a work item to the CANCELLED status if it has not yet reached the COMPLETED status and is not part of a higher-level workflow. Work items in the CANCELLED status are not displayed in the inbox. A work item with the CANCELLED status may have caused database changes or other actions (raise event, send email). These changes are not rolled back automatically.
ERROR (⬡)	ERROR Execution of the work item was terminated with an application or system error. When a step in a workflow terminates with an error, the parent workflow itself is assigned the ERROR status. These items appear in the administrator's error report. A WORKFLOW INSTANCE in status ERROR can be restarted via Transaction SWPR, after the cause for the error is cleared. For example, a background method cannot find the agent for the next step in a custom table, so it raises the error exception. After the data is added manually to that table, then the workflow administrator can restart this workflow instance.

Table 14.3 Work Item State (cont.)

Although not all types of work items can be found in all of these states, it is nevertheless a very useful guide as to what is possible. The status changes of dialog work items are shown in Figure 14.3.

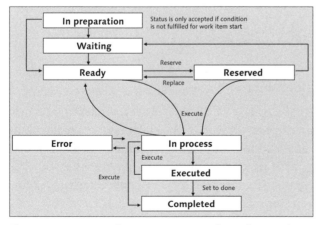

Figure 14.3 Status and Status Transitions of a Dialog Work Item

> **Hint**
>
> The status of a work item can be switched to CANCELLED, as long as the work item does not have the status ERROR or COMPLETED.

14.2 Workflow APIs

The WAPIs allow you to develop your own custom programs, which show workflow data or change the status of work items. For example, a supervisor wants a customized process monitor that displays workflows and their contents at a particular status.

> **Note**
>
> The list of provided functions is growing with every release. Just look for all function modules starting with SAP_WAPI*. Start these functions on a test system by providing an existing work item number or a business object instance.

> **Hint**
>
> Examples for using the WAPI can be found in the chapters for the Web Dynpro and BSP programs, Chapters 19 to 21.

The WAPI function modules are delivered as a part of the SAP NetWeaver Application Server (ABAP). The parameter interface to the function modules has been designed so that it is easy to call the WAPIs from outside the workflow environment. The SAP_WAPI function modules are RFC enabled. The following sections describe how to invoke a workflow with the SAP_WAPI function modules.

14.2.1 The Simple WAPI Container

The simple WAPI container is used by several WAPI calls and differs in structure from the container used within the workflow. The WAPI container is made up of simple name/value pairs. In other words, the container structure SWR_CONT has two fields, ELEMENT and VALUE, each of type string, making them easy to fill. The time format used is hhmmss, and the date format is yyyymmdd (the internal SAP format). The SWC container macros may *not* be used to fill the WAPI container.

Hint

The contents of ELEMENT must be provided in uppercase characters.

14.2.2 SAP_WAPI_CREATE_EVENT

As the name suggests, the SAP_WAPI_CREATE_EVENT call generates an event, which can be used to start a workflow or some other event receiver. The other receivers can be terminating events for task or function modules as defined in the event linkage. In common with all other WAPI calls, this call uses the WAPI container to pass data to the event container, which is in turn transported to the receiver.

Hint

At runtime, the event only occurs after the next COMMIT WORK of the calling program. If you use this function module in a BAdI, then do not add a COMMIT WORK. The calling program issues this command.

14.2.3 SAP_WAPI_START_WORKFLOW

SAP_WAPI_START_WORKFLOW, together with SAP_WAPI_CREATE_EVENT, is the simplest and most useful WAPI call. Simply fill the container with name/value pairs and specify a workflow definition to start. If the return code is zero, the workflow has started properly. For an analysis of whether to start a workflow with an event or whether to start it directly, refer to Section 14.3.1, When Should a Workflow with an Event be Started.

When this API is used to start a workflow, make sure that the user running the program that starts the workflow is assigned to the workflow as a possible agent; otherwise, the user will not have the authority to start it. This is true even if it is a background job that calls the WAPI.

When using SAP_WAPI_START_WORKFLOW, you pass name/value pairs, which means you do not pass an instantiated object. This means that the receiving workflow must instantiate the object in the first step of the workflow. Listing 14.1 shows an example of a function module that starts a workflow using SAP_WAPI_START_WORKFLOW.

```
*-> Prepare import parameters of the workflow

data: RETURN_CODE TYPE  SYSUBRC.
data: WI_CONTAINER TYPE STANDARD TABLE OF swr_cont WITH HEADER LINE.

move 'BusinessPartner' to WI_CONTAINER-element.
move  objkey   to WI_CONTAINER-value.
append WI_CONTAINER.

*-> Start workflow
  CALL FUNCTION 'SAP_WAPI_START_WORKFLOW'
    EXPORTING
      task    = 'WS99800011'
    IMPORTING
      return_code    = RETURN_CODE
      WORKITEM_ID    = WI_ID
    TABLES
      input_container = WI_CONTAINER.

ENDFUNCTION.
```

Listing 14.1 Example of Calling SAP_WAPI_START_WORKFLOW

In Listing 14.1, the business partner is passed to the function module as an import parameter in the field objkey. This function module returns the work item ID of the workflow that was started (WI_ID). This code starts workflow WS99800011. This workflow has a container field called BusinessPartner and a container element for the object type Business_Partner. The very first task in the workflow executes a method to instantiate an object of the Business_Partner as shown in Listing 14.2.

```
BEGIN_METHOD ZGET_BP CHANGING CONTAINER.

swc_get_element container 'BusinessPartner'
  object-key-businesspartner.
swc_set_objectkey object-key-businesspartner.

END_METHOD.
```

Listing 14.2 Method to Instantiate the Business Partner

When using SAP_WAPI_START_WORKFLOW just remember that the object is instantiated in the workflow.

> **Hint**
>
> Another way to instantiate an object in your workflow is to create a task based on object SYSTEM and method GENERICINSTANTIATE. The method receives an object type, a key, and import parameters; it returns an instantiated object type. This is also discussed in Appendix A, Tips and Tricks.

14.2.4 SAP_WAPI_WORKITEMS_TO_OBJECT

The function call SAP_WAPI_WORKITEMS_TO_OBJECT is useful when you are creating your own status reports about the lifecycle of an object. For example, you have a custom workflow for the material master process, where each view is its own dialog step. Now you need a report that shows the creator for each view. By collecting all of the work items related to this material master record and by sorting them chronologically, you can create a simple status report showing who did what when and who is currently working on the material master.

The amount of data collected depends on the input parameters used. You can speed up the call by leaving the TEXT flag blank so that the work item text is not returned with the list of work items. If you simply want to know whether or not running work items exist, use SAP_WAPI_COUNT_WORKITEMS with the appropriate filter.

> **Note**
>
> Be aware of the values for the SELECTION_STATUS_VARIANT variable:
> - 0000 — All instances.
> - 0001 — Active instances (RUNNING, READY, COMMITTED, etc.).
> - 0002 — Finished instances (COMPLETED, CANCELLED).
> - 0003 — Active instances (ALL).

14.2.5 SAP_WAPI_READ_CONTAINER

Use the SAP_WAPI_READ_CONTAINER call to read the current values of the container elements from a work item. This can be very useful when writing your own custom reports to show details of a workflow's progress.

14.3 Advanced Business Interface Techniques

This section discusses advanced options for using the SAP WAPIs in conjunction with events to start workflows.

14.3.1 When Should a Workflow with an Event Be Started

Whenever you want to automatically start a workflow, it is usually best to use an event. It is possible to automatically start a workflow directly from a business application program, for example, by using function module SAP_WAPI_ START_WORKFLOW in the code. However, events are much more flexible, because:

▸ You can start none, one, or many workflows without changing the business application.

▸ You can change the conditions under which the workflow starts and which workflows start without changing the business application.

▸ You can activate/deactivate them whenever you want. For example, you can deactivate an existing workflow and activate a new workflow in its place without changing the business application.

▸ You can use the same event not just to start workflows but also to complete work items, complete workflows, restart workflows, or change the direction of existing workflows.

▸ You can use event queues to spread peak loads for improved system performance.

▸ By starting a workflow by an event, a possible error in the workflow has no impact on the starting program.

The disadvantages of triggering a workflow via an event are:

▸ Events could overrun the RFC queue if triggered thousands of times in a short time interval, typically in overnight background reports.

> **Hint**
>
> In problem cases, activate the event queue via Transaction SWEQADM. This prevents the RFC problem.

▶ There is no handle (work item ID) returned to the calling program.

▶ If you want the first step of the work item to pop up immediately without the user visiting his inbox (synchronous dialog chain), you cannot start the workflow with an event.

Note

UWL does not offer the "dialog chain".

Unless you need to cover one of the exceptional circumstances described previously, it nearly always makes sense to start the workflow by raising an event. Only if you are using a release prior to SAP R/3 4.6C, if you have serious performance problems that cannot be resolved by using the event queue, or if you are triggering large volumes of workflows in background jobs, should you consider starting the workflow directly from your own programs.

Tip

If you are using a SAP R/3 4.6C system or above and are dealing with workflows creating a high volume of work items, you should use the event queue to distribute event creation at peak times. This gives better results than starting the workflow directly. The event queue is described in detail in Chapter 13, Using Events and Other Business Interfaces.

14.3.2 Raising Events by Calling a Function Module

If none of the event configuration options described in Chapter 13, Using Events and Other Business Interfaces, are suitable, or you want to include events in your own programs, you can code the event raising yourself using SAP-provided function modules.

Make sure that the event is raised at the right time. For instance, if you are creating an event to tell the Workflow Engine you have just created a new application object, you must make sure that the event is only raised if the application object is created (i.e., you don't want to raise the event if the user cancels out of the program or the object creation fails). Otherwise, the workflow might start out in error (if the object doesn't yet exist) or look at old instead of new data (if changes have not yet reached the database).

Events notify workflow about object status changes that have already occurred. So make sure the event is not raised until the relevant status change has actually taken place, that is, has updated the database. For this reason, the function module for raising an event should be called in the same *logical unit of work* (LUW) as the one in which the status change is made.

> **Caution**
>
> The event will not be raised until the ABAP command COMMIT WORK is called. A common mistake in custom programs that raise events is that no explicit COMMIT WORK is made following the function module call. If you forget this, the data changes made in the program will still be committed to the database (via an implicit commit when the program finishes), but no event is raised.
>
> If you are using this call in a BAdI, rely on the SAP programs to make the COMMIT WORK call so that the SAP commit logic (the LUW) is not interfered with and the data remains consistent. SAP_WAPI_CREATE_EVENT has a parameter that determines whether or not a commit work should be performed by the WAPI call itself.

It is usually sufficient to raise events by calling the function module SAP_WAPI_CREATE_EVENT. At a minimum, you need to specify the event to be raised, including the object type and object key. If the event is defined with parameters in Transaction SWO1, then you can use the optional event container to pass additional data.

Listing 14.3 shows some sample code that raises the event Cancelled for business object SBOOK when a matching application table is updated. Note that the event is raised only after the database has been successfully updated.

```
PROGRAM ZCREATE_EVENT.

* Change your application object ...
  UPDATE sbook ...
* Check that the change has worked before raising the event
  IF sy-subrc EQ 0.
* If the new data needs to be committed to the database
* for the receiver type function module, check function
* module, or workflow start condition, you can add another
* COMMIT WORK statement at this point
* Fill the container with any event parameters ...
    EVENT_CONT-ELEMENT = 'ELEMENT1NAME'.
```

```
      EVENT_CONT-VALUE    = 'VALUE1'.
      APPEND EVENT_CONT.
* Cast the reservation number to the object key.
      OBJ_KEY = reservation_no.
* Raise the event
      CALL FUNCTION 'SAP_WAPI_CREATE_EVENT'
        EXPORTING
            OBJECT_TYPE             = 'SBOOK'
            OBJECT_KEY              = OBJ_KEY
            EVENT                   = 'Cancelled'
            COMMIT_WORK             = ' '
        IMPORTING
            RETURN_CODE             = rc
        TABLES
            INPUT_CONTAINER         = EVENT_CONT.
        IF rc is not initial.
            MESSAGE ...
        ENDIF.
      ENDIF.
* Perform additional database access
* Save all the work in the one logical unit of work
      COMMIT WORK.
```

Listing 14.3 Example Code to Trigger an Event for a Business Object

For more complicated situations, you must use alternative function modules to ensure the event is raised at the right time. These function modules have the same interface as SWE_EVENT_CREATE.

SWE_EVENT_CREATE_IN_UPD_TASK

The SWE_EVENT_CREATE_IN_UPD_TASK function module makes it possible to raise events in an update task, where the logical unit of work is split between dialog and update processes. In contrast to the function module SWE_EVENT_CREATE, it can be called with the addition of IN UPDATE TASK, so that it is synchronized with the database changes.

Use this function module if your program updates the application object using the update task. Most SAP-provided programs use the update task for making database changes. Make sure the event is created after the application object update in the update sequence but before COMMIT WORK.

Typical situations are when the event is raised within a user exit, BAdI or your own transactions. Make sure the user ID of the person triggering the workflow is added to the event container so that it makes its way through the update task and the RFC queue to the workflow. This ensures that the workflow initiator is set correctly despite the triggering from within the update task. The same applies to the next function module, SWE_EVENT_CREATE_FOR_UPD_TASK.

SWE_EVENT_CREATE_FOR_UPD_TASK

The SWE_EVENT_CREATE_FOR_UPD_TASK function module is for a very specific situation, namely that you have an asynchronous task based on a Create method. In other words, you want the task to be completed when the object is physically created in the database. Normally terminating events need to know the object key when the work item is created, but if you are creating an object, you often will not know the new object key until after the method has completed.

Your own program code that creates a new object should include this function module, which picks up the last work item as the work item requestor before raising the event, so that the terminating event can be correctly matched to the waiting work item. Make sure the call to this function module is made after the application object update in the update sequence but before COMMIT WORK.

> **Caution**
>
> A common cause of synchronization problems in a workflow arises when a terminating event precedes the database changes. Choose your triggering function module correctly to avoid such problems.

Incidentally, the SAP programs that control the general status management or the change document event-raising use these function calls. That is why you must specify explicitly whether or not you are triggering a creation event in these transactions. Remember that regardless of which function module you use, the event creator never knows whether there are none, one, or many receivers, so the function call cannot tell you if any workflows were affected by the event.

Check Function Module

A check function module dynamically determines whether a receiver should be notified of an event being raised, for example, whether the workflow is triggered.

You should use start conditions wherever possible to determine whether or not to trigger a workflow (as described in Chapter 13, Using Events and Other Business Interfaces). Only revert to check function modules for very complex rules. The result of a check function module is either:

▶ **Successful execution**
In which case, the receiver is called. In other words, the workflow is triggered, or the step is terminated properly.

▶ **An exception**
In which case, the receiver is not called. In other words, the event is ignored by this receiver.

In practice, you usually only create a check function module when you want to determine whether a workflow should be started. You can use any of the information in the event container to determine the outcome in the check function module. The interface of the check function module is described in the documentation for the function module SWE_TEMPLATE_CHECK_FB. You must use this interface exactly as specified. There is no naming convention restriction on the name of the function module, and, of course, the code inside the function module is completely up to you.

Listing 14.4 shows an example of a check function module for an SBOOK.CREATED event. Notice that all parameters are information you can use to determine whether the receiver should be notified. The only result is either an exception or successful execution. So that the appropriate workflow macros can be used (such as SWC_GET_ELEMENT), the statement INCLUDE <CNTN01> should be included in the global data area of the matching function group.

```
FUNCTION Z_CHECK_CHANGED_BY_VALID_USER.
*"----------------------------------------------------------
*"*"Local interface:
*"  IMPORTING
*"     VALUE(OBJTYPE) LIKE  SWETYPECOU-OBJTYPE
*"     VALUE(OBJKEY) LIKE  SWEINSTCOU-OBJKEY
*"     VALUE(EVENT) LIKE  SWETYPECOU-EVENT
*"     VALUE(RECTYPE) LIKE  SWETYPECOU-RECTYPE
*"  TABLES
*"     EVENT_CONTAINER STRUCTURE  SWCONT
*"  EXCEPTIONS
*"     INVALID_USER
*"----------------------------------------------------------
```

```
* This check function module checks if the user who created
* the flight booking is a workflow tester. The tester is stored
* in a custom Table ZPILOT_USER. After the test is done, then
* delete this check function module from the event linkage
  DATA: pilot_users LIKE pilot_user_line,
        initiator   LIKE swhactor,
        user        LIKE sy-uname.
* Read the event initiator from the event container
* The standard container element for the event initiator
* is called _EVT_CREATOR and is in agent format
  SWC_GET_ELEMENT event_container '_EVT_CREATOR' initiator.
  SELECT user FROM ZPILOT_USER
   WHERE user = intiator-objid.
  IF sy-subrc NE 0.
    RAISE invalid_user.
  ENDIF.
ENDFUNCTION.
```

Listing 14.4 Check Function Module for Event

To use the check function module, insert it into the appropriate event linkage entry (Transaction SWETYPV) after first activating the event linkage in the Workflow Builder. Before diving in to create your own check function module, remember that if you want to determine whether or not to start the workflow based on event parameters or attributes linked to the event object, then it is easier, quicker, and far more transparent to create a start condition.

14.3.3 Advanced Event Linkage

The event linkages (Transaction SWETYPV) are normally created for you automatically from the Workflow Builder. The only exceptions to this are when you want to:

▶ Raise an event in a remote SAP component, in which case, you have to define the event linkage manually.

▶ Use a check function module.

▶ Create your own receiver type function module to determine which workflow to start dynamically.

▶ Switch on the "event queue" monitoring for this event. So if the event queue program is running (Transaction SWEQADM), then these events are spread out to optimize the system performance.

Processing in the Event Linkage Table

Before discussing how to create your own receiver function module, it is worth looking in to the processing of the event linkage table in a little more detail. At runtime, when an event is raised, the *event manager*:

▶ **Creates the event container**
This includes creating and adding the object instance (based on the object key used when raising the event) and the event initiator (based on the current user). Any special event parameters passed during the event creation are also added.

▶ **Checks to see if a specific work item requestor has been saved**
This is done via function module SWE_EVENT_CREATE_FOR_UPD_TASK.

▶ **Finds all active event linkages for the event**
This involves finding all active linkages, not just for this object and event but also any supertype objects linked to the same event. For instance, if you create an event RetailCustomer.Created and RetailCustomer is a subtype of business object type Customer, the Customer.Created event-linkage is also evaluated.

If the work item requestor has been passed, the work item requestor is used to find the appropriate event linkage.

▶ **Determines the receiver for each event linkage**
If a single receiver is specified in the event linkage, then that receiver is used. If a receiver type function module is specified in the event linkage, then it is called to dynamically determine the receiver.

▶ **Checks whether the receiver should be notified for each event linkage**
If a check function module is specified in the event linkage, this is run to determine whether the receiver should be notified. If the function module is successful, the receiver should be notified. If the function module raises an exception, the receiver should not be notified.

Remember that if you have specified a start condition, the check function module (automatically added by the system when you defined the start condition) checks the start condition. If the start condition is true, the receiver is notified. If the start condition is false, the receiver is ignored.

▶ **Starts the receiver for each event linkage**
Provided that both the receiver type function module and the check function module calls were successful, the receiver is started by calling the receiver

function module or receiver method. Unless you have turned on event debugging, the receiver is started in a separate LUW.

▶ **Writes an entry to the event trace for each event linkage if the trace is active**
If the event trace is switched on (Transaction SWELS), then Transaction SWEL displays the event trace. (For performance reasons, this trace should normally be disabled in the production system.) This trace shows the workflow instance, which was started by the event. If there was a problem, then the trace also shows an error. For error cases, look at Chapter 16, Advanced Diagnostics.

Receiver Type Function Module

A *receiver type function module* dynamically determines the receiver at runtime. Only one receiver can be returned, and this is usually the ID of the workflow or task that is to be started. The SAP Document Management System uses this to determine which process to follow (i.e., which workflow to start), according to the document type. You can use any of the information in the event container to decide which workflow should be started.

The interface of the receiver type function module is described in the documentation for the function module SWE_TEMPLATE_RECTYPE_FB. You must use this interface exactly as specified. There is no naming convention restriction on the name of the function module, and, of course, the code inside the function module is completely up to you.

Listing 14.5 shows an example of a receiver type function module for an SBOOK.CREATED event. Notice that the result is returned in parameter RECTYPE; all other parameters are information you can use to determine the receiver. So that the appropriate workflow macros can be used (such as SWC_GET_PROPERTY), the statement INCLUDE <CNTN01> should be included in the global data area of the matching function group.

```
FUNCTION Z_RECTYPE_BY_FLIGHT_CLASS.
*"----------------------------------------------------------------
*"*"Local interface:
*"  IMPORTING
*"     VALUE(OBJTYPE) LIKE  SWETYPECOU-OBJTYPE
*"     VALUE(OBJKEY) LIKE   SWEINSTCOU-OBJKEY
*"     VALUE(EVENT) LIKE    SWETYPECOU-EVENT
```

```
*"    VALUE(GENERIC_RECTYPE) LIKE  SWETYPECOU-RECTYPE
*"   EXPORTING
*"    VALUE(RECTYPE) LIKE  SWEINSTCOU-RECTYPE
*"   TABLES
*"    EVENT_CONTAINER STRUCTURE  SWCONT
*"   EXCEPTIONS
*"    OBJECT_NOT_FOUND
*"----------------------------------------------------------------
* This receiver type fm determines the workflow to be started
* by flight class of the reservation in the object key
  DATA: OBJECT  TYPE SWC_OBJECT.
  DATA: FCLASS   LIKE SBOOK-CLASS.
* To find the flight class, first instantiate the
* reservation object from the object type and key.
  SWC_CREATE_OBJECT OBJECT OBJTYPE OBJKEY.
  IF SY-SUBRC NE 0.
    RAISE OBJECT_NOT_FOUND.
  ENDIF.
* Then get the flightclass attribute of the reservation
  SWC_GET_PROPERTY OBJECT 'FLIGHTCLASS' FCLASS.
* Set the appropriate receiver based on the class value.
  IF FCLASS EQ 'F' AND ...
    RECTYPE = 'WS96000011'.
  ELSE.
    RECTYPE = 'WS96000012'.
  ENDIF.
ENDFUNCTION.
```

Listing 14.5 Receiver Type Function Module for Event

A receiver type function module lets you pick one of a number of possible receivers using a single event linkage entry. You can achieve the same result by having separate event linkage entries for each of the receivers and using mutually exclusive start conditions to determine which receiver should be started. Whether to use start conditions or whether to develop a function module depends on the number of possible workflows and how the event-linkage configuring is to be performed.

14.3.4 Adding Generic Object Services to Your Own Transactions

Generic Object Services (GOS) are described in detail in Chapter 13, Using Events and Other Business Interfaces, but here is a nutshell description to refresh your memory. GOS is a sort of Swiss army knife of useful functions, two of which are related to workflow. It is a mechanism linking the application transactions to the workflow logs related to the object being displayed. In other words, the user can navigate directly from the record to the logs of the workflows that have processed the record (or are in the middle of processing it).

If you want to add GOS to your own transaction, you should publish the object instance just before it is displayed. In the following examples, you see how to publish an object instance with key 4500000138 and type BUS2105:

▶ In Releases prior to SAP R/3 4.6C, call function module SWU_OBJECT_PUBLISH passing the object type and object key:

```
CALL FUNCTION 'SWU_OBJECT_PUBLISH'
  EXPORTING       objkey  = 'BUS2105'
                  objtype = '4500000138'
  EXCEPTIONS      OTHERS  = 1.
```

▶ In Releases SAP R/3 4.6C and above, instantiate an instance of class CL_GOS_MANAGER, passing your business object instance:

```
DATA:
  borident    TYPE borident,
  gos_manager TYPE REF TO cl_gos_manager.
borident-objtype = 'BUS2105'.
borident-objkey  = '4500000138'.

CREATE OBJECT gos_manager
  EXPORTING    is_object = borident
  EXCEPTIONS   OTHERS    = 1.
```

The result of this simple call is that when your transaction is executed (e.g., display custom record), the GOS toolbar is displayed, and these services are also activated in the system menu. When you consider how many useful features this gives your users, compared with the five minutes spent adding this code to your transaction, there is little excuse for *not* implementing this interface. In terms of ROI, GOS provides unbeatable value.

14.3.5 Implementing the Workflow Toolbox in Your Own Transactions

The workflow toolbox is a set of work-item based services you can use from any appropriate screen in an SAP component while executing a work item. For instance, you may have a task that asks you to update a material master by calling the material master update transaction. If you execute a work item based on that task, while you are in the material master update transaction, the workflow toolbox appears, allowing you to check the work item description, add attachments to the work item, view the workflow log, and so on without returning to the inbox. If the material master update transaction is executed normally in the SAP component without workflow, the workflow toolbox does not appear because it is not relevant.

To include the workflow toolbox in your own transactions and screens, you need to instantiate a toolbox object based on class CL_WAPI_WF_TOOLBOX before the appropriate screen is displayed. The mode parameter controls how the toolbox is displayed, that is, modally or modeless, as buttons or menus, or as a floating toolbar. The example in Listing 14.6 shows how to include the workflow toolbox on your own screen 0900 of your own program called ZMYPROGRAM, passing the relevant work item ID. The variable CC_TOOLBOX refers to an instance of class CL_GUI_CUSTOM_CONTAINER, that is, a custom container specifying where the toolbox will appear on the screen.

```
data: c_toolbox  TYPE REF TO CL_WAPI_WF_TOOLBOX.

CREATE OBJECT c_toolbox
  EXPORTING
    i_container = cc_toolbox
    i_mode      = cl_wapi_wf_toolbox=>c_mode_inplace_with_info
    i_repid     = "ZMYPROGRAM"
    i_dynnr     = "0900"
    i_wi_id     = workitemid
  EXCEPTIONS
    OTHERS      = 1.
```
Listing 14.6 Including the Workflow Toolbox

14.4   Office Document Interfaces

In addition to WAPI function modules to programmatically deal with workflow, there are also function modules to interface with Office documents, such as email with workflow. The mail function modules area is discussed in this section.

14.4.1 Business Communications Services

Business Communications Services (BCS) is a generic way for any application to integrate sending into their applications. It is described in the SAP Help Portal (*http://help.sap.com*). This interface offers very flexible generation of emails and attachments. The discussion of BCS is outside the scope of this book because it is not specific to workflow. BCS includes all of the classes you need to interact with, create, and manage mail documents, express messages in applications, SAP appointments, GOS (already discussed in Section 14.3.4, Adding Generic Object Services to Your Own Transactions), and the postprocessing framework.

14.4.2 SO_*_API1 function modules

These modules are the forerunner of BCS. The function modules are documented. Using the SO_*_API1 function modules as an example, we will show how emails can be generated from the data in the workflow and transmitted as notifications or reminders to the workflow agents. The calls support different types of recipients, including SAPoffice users and Internet mail addresses:

▶ SO_OLD_DOCUMENT_SEND_API1
Sends an existing mail to one or more addressees. This is good for standard replies where the text does not change. The main import parameter is the key of the message that will be sent.

▶ SO_NEW_DOCUMENT_SEND_API1
Creates a new message (the text is passed as a parameter) and sends the message to one or more addressees.

▶ SO_NEW_DOCUMENT_ATT_SEND_API1
Creates a new message together with attachments. The text of the mail and of the attachments is passed as a parameter. The mail is sent in MIME format if it is sent over the Internet so that any email client can read the attachments.

▶ SO_DOCUMENT_READ_API1
Requires the key of an existing mail as an import parameter. The function exports the text of the mail. This is useful if you want to parse incoming messages.

A situation may arise when you want to trigger a workflow externally, as a Web Service. This chapter describes the options and steps for exposing a workflow as a service and calling it externally.

15 Service-Enabling Workflows

By now, you are feeling very comfortable with creating, configuring, and using SAP Business Workflow. Now we will extend this concept to cases where you need to trigger a workflow externally, as part of a larger business process.

15.1 Workflow in the Context of a Business Process

Workflows typically are executed within a single business system and are used to make business processes more efficient. But processes today cross system boundaries and often even organizational boundaries. The explosion of technologies that make cross-system and cross-organizational processes possible have enabled this type of collaboration to become common. In this chapter, we explore ways to make your workflow available externally from one of these collaborative processes.

Specifically, we describe how to trigger a workflow using a Web Service interface as part of a larger collaborative process. For instance, consider the process for creating a business partner; suppose that we want to put this in the context of a collaborative process that is partially executed by an external agent (see Figure 15.1).

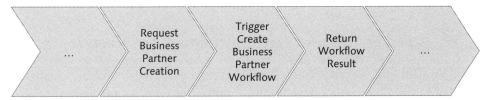

Figure 15.1 Steps of a Collaborative Process

The middle step shown in Figure 15.1 represents an external agent calling into our system to execute our workflow to create a business partner; the next step shows the workflow returning the business partner ID, or a reason for rejecting the business partner, to the external agent.

We should be clear, at this point, that we are treating our workflow as an atomic step in this process. What we are specifically not doing is exposing the individual steps of the process to various agents, some perhaps internal and some perhaps external. For workflow experts who want to explore a broader and deeper application of SOA principles to collaborative processes, especially those that cross system boundaries, we recommend that you research SAP NetWeaver Business Process Management. This application will see extensive growth in the years to come and delivers a model-based engine for building collaborative processes.

This chapter discusses how you can trigger the workflow as a step in this larger process. Workflows can be triggered via a Remote-enabled Function Module (RFM); an RFM can be triggered remotely; hence, the workflow can be triggered as one step in an overall business process. The question, then, is how to call the function module remotely. One way of doing this is to expose the function module as a Web Service. With the rise of Web Services as the reigning methodology for integrating applications, this is the approach we will describe.

We will start with a very brief overview of Web Services and Service-Oriented Architecture (SOA) for the benefit of readers who may not be familiar with these concepts. If you already have at least a basic understanding of these topics, you may skip forward to Section 15.5, Implementing the Service Interface for a Workflow. There we describe two techniques for calling the function remotely. The first is simpler but has narrower uses; the second makes use of the Enterprise Services Repository, outside-in design, and, optionally, SAP NetWeaver SOA middleware (known as SAP NetWeaver Process Integration) to create and call the workflow service.

15.2   Web Services and Service-Oriented Architecture

Web Services and Service-Oriented Architecture (SOA) represent an important new paradigm for designing and building applications and data management services. Because services offer ease of both development and integration, they can help accelerate the pace of adaptation within IT organizations. This, in turn, can help companies become more agile, flexibly adapt to changing environments, and push innovation in their businesses. SAP is a major player in the world of SOA, and customers have been leveraging SAP Enterprise Services for years.

Although a complete discussion of Web Services and SOA are well beyond the scope of this book, we should introduce some basic concepts around these terms. You can find a complete discussion of these topics in the following books: *Enterprise SOA Roadmap* (SAP PRESS, 2008), and *Developing Applications with Enterprise SOA* (SAP PRESS, 2008).

15.2.1 What Are Web Services

Web Services offer a way to both develop and integrate applications based on common standards. A Web Service is a piece of application functionality that has been exposed so that it can be called over a computer network, such as the Internet or a corporate intranet, using standard protocols such as HTTP. There are two entities that participate in a service invocation, namely the *service provider*, the actual system that implements the service-based functionality, and the *service consumer*, which is any entity that calls the service.

The main advantage of exposing applications as Web Services is that such services are accessed via widely adopted standards, and these standards are agnostic with respect to vendor, platform, and language. The consumer thus needs no specific knowledge of the service or the application that is providing it, beyond very basic information that is required to access the service: the structure of the service interface, the address at which it can be called, and certain technical information such as the security required (e.g., basic authentication with username and password, or certificate authorization via the exchange of X.509 certificates). This stands in stark contrast to older service models, where complex programming was required to access low-level APIs of the provider application.

Standards, then, are the drivers that make the whole Web Services edifice possible. Te next section introduces some of the important Web Service standards.

15.2.2 Web Services Description Language

Web Services are described, that is, the abstract and physical parameters that can be used to call them have been detailed, in a standard format known as *Web Services Description Language* (WSDL). WSDL is a standard of the World Wide Web

Consortium (W3C). The standard is fully documented at *http://www.w3.org/TR/wsdl*.

The abstract part of the service definition includes the data types that are used to call a service and the message format for encoding those types. The physical part of the definition includes the *binding*, which describes how the service can be accessed (e.g., via an XML document sent in the body of an HTTP request, or most commonly, via a SOAP call over HTTP — more about SOAP in a minute), and the physical address, expressed as a URI, where the service can be called. Figure 15.2 shows an XML document that describes the parameters for a service interface.

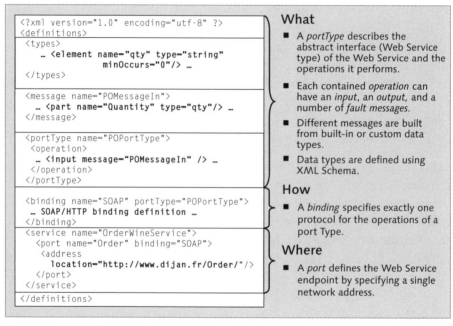

Figure 15.2 WSDL Document

The WSDL description of a service comprises a contract that service providers and consumers use to insure compatibility, regardless of which platform either is running on or the language in which either is written. WSDL documents are typically published to a *service registry*, which is a searchable repository of available services with end point and other information. These registries are usually implemented in (or compatible with) another standard called *Universal Description, Discovery, and Integration* (UDDI). Such registries are usually compared to Yellow Pages, which are directories of providers of physical services in the real world;

service registries allow developers to locate existing Web Services that they can use in whatever process they are developing. By downloading the WSDL from the link in the service registry and feeding it to an intelligent development environment, they can generate the client code for calling the service, leveraging low-code and no-code approaches, thus streamlining the development process and reducing the overall time to create new applications and integrations.

15.2.3 Web Services and SOAP

Although there are different ways to consume Web Services, by far the most common is by sending an HTTP request that has in its body an XML structure in a format known as *SOAP*. SOAP is a standard protocol of the W3C, and the formal definition can be found at *http://www.w3.org/TR/soap*.

What Does SOAP Stand For?

The original version of the standard was Simple Object Access Protocol and given the acronym SOAP. It was felt that this was not a good description of what SOAP was used for, so in subsequent versions of the standard they abandoned the former name and made "SOAP" the name of the protocol, without having the letters stand for anything in particular. Some people today refer to SOAP as the Service-Oriented Architecture Protocol.

A SOAP message is an XML document that has a particular structure. A SOAP message contains a SOAP *envelope*, which has two parts: an optional SOAP *header* and a mandatory SOAP *body*. The SOAP header contains application-specific information such as security information or processing instructions, whereas the SOAP body contains the business data to be passed to the Web Service (or, in the case of a response message, the data to be sent back to the calling application). An example of a SOAP message over HTTP is shown in Figure 15.3 .

The SOAP message is contained within the body of the HTTP request. In our example, the SOAP header contains a transaction code; this would have some meaning to the application that is processing this SOAP request. The SOAP body contains the business data, that is, the account number, currency, and amount of the online transaction. It is up to the implementing application to know how to parse and process this message. Because SOAP is a widely adopted standard, however, there are many messaging systems and even applications that can handle SOAP messages natively.

Figure 15.3 A Simple Example of a Fictional SOAP Request Message

15.2.4 Other Web Service Standards

The basic trio of Web Service standards described previously — WSDL, SOAP, and UDDI — is sufficient to implement and call services in the simplest case, but the real world presents complexities that cannot be handled so easily. Such concerns as security (authentication, encryption, non-repudiation), quality of service (guaranteed delivery, serialization, service level agreements), and governance (policies, semantic interoperability) require a more extensive set of standards.

There are several standards bodies that promote and promulgate Web Service standards, including the W3C, the Organization for the Advancement of Structured Information Standards (OASIS), the United Nations Centre for Trade Facilitation and Electronic Business (UN/CEFACT), and the Open Applications Group (OAGI).

Some of the important standards that these and other bodies promote, together with a brief description of the standards, follows:

▶ **WS-Security (W3C)**
Provides a way of encoding security information, such as authentication, trust, and message security in the SOAP header of a message. WS-Security also allows for encryption of the message using XML encryption.

▶ **WS-ReliableMessaging (OASIS)**
Enforces quality-of-service related functionality in compliant systems, for instance, for sequencing messages that should be processed in a particular order.

▶ **WS-Policy (W3C)**
WS-Policy offers a method of describing the complex parameters of a message exchange, such as security models that are acceptable, qualities of service, and so forth, in the WSDL document that describes the service. By publishing this information with the service description, service consumers have a complete picture of what policies they must adhere to for a successful implementation of a service connection.

▶ **WS-BPEL (Business Process Execution Language, OASIS)**
Business Process Execution Language (BPEL) is a process automation language that allows developers to use modeling tools to implement processing logic in the exchange of Web Service messages. This is not necessary in the case of a simple request/response scenario but may be when complex interactions involving multiple messages, perhaps with multiple partners, and such programmatic features as looping, decisions, and so forth are required. In essence, it provides a stateful processing layer on top of the other Web Services standards.

▶ **CCTS (Core Component Technical Specification, UN/CEFACT)**
CCTS provides a methodology for semantic data modeling, achieving a common understanding of data structures and message types on a syntax independent level, as well as a way to identify, capture, and maximize the reuse of business information to support and enhance information interoperability across multiple business situations. In essence, this allows developers to add semantic quality to purely technical artifacts, thereby increasing interoperability at the business level.

This is by no means a complete list of standards that are extant in Web Service environments today, but hopefully they give some idea of the extent and maturity of standards in the Web Services world.

15.3 What Is Service-Oriented Architecture

A Service-Oriented Architecture (SOA) is just what the name implies: an architecture. When we think of an "architecture" in the classic sense, as in the architecture of buildings, we think in terms of a *design* and a *plan*. Although a whole host of technologies and materials are necessary to implement that plan, such as earth moving equipment, wiring, steel beams, and so forth, the plan stands on its own as a piece of work. SOA is a plan, then, to implement the structures that enable organizations to leverage Web Services in a complete and holistic way.

SOA is not a set of technologies, nor is it a product you can buy from a vendor. This can seem confusing, as we speak of SOA vendors or SOA technology; but although this may be convenient, it is, strictly speaking, a misuse of the term "SOA." Technologies and products are necessary for implementing SOA, but the essence of SOA is still in the plan and the methodology used to approach building applications and integrating business processes.

SOA offers a framework for decomposing processes into discrete units: the Web Services that we discussed earlier. Services can then be combined into complex processes, exposed to trading partners securely, or used to build "edge" applications that enhance the existing functionality of packaged applications.

Some of the goals of an effective SOA are detailed here:

▶ **Reusability**
Too often, when faced with the task of coding a business process, developers must "re-invent the wheel;" that is, implement a full-cycle coding regimen when the functionality, or something very much like it, may already exist within an organization's IT assets. With SOA, however, functionality has been decomposed into services, and the services have been published to a central registry. Developers can discover very quickly whether there is already a service that can be used as is or modified to meet the requirements of a given situation.

▶ **Process-oriented design**
An effective SOA allows processes to be modeled from a business perspective and then implemented using modern coding methodologies (low-code, interface first design). This puts control of the process with the business, where it belongs, and keeps IT in alignment with the needs of the business.

▶ **Rapid development**
Modern tooling allows for a tremendous amount of code generation and simplifies the task of creating applications, allowing developers to focus on core tasks without worrying about peripheral issues such as integration logic.

▶ **Simplified integration**

Loose coupling of systems and shared interface design (based on the WSDL description of a service) make integration between homogeneous systems much simpler. So-called "middleware" (usually in the form of an Enterprise Service Bus or ESB) is used to provide connectivity to non-SOA compliant systems and eases that formerly code-intensive task.

▶ **Agility**

Organizations that have modeled their information assets on an SOA framework are better able to adapt to changing market and regulatory conditions.

Practically speaking, to implement SOA, an organization needs not only to organize development around the principals of SOA, they also need technology and applications that allow them to decompose their business processes into services and to provide and consume those services natively. These technologies are widespread among forward-thinking companies and are starting to become common even among smaller IT organizations. A good SOA backbone provides at least the following:

▶ **Applications and application servers that are SOA standards aware**

Applications can be built as services from the ground up, or existing functionality can be service-enabled if the appropriate technology is in place. Application servers need the ability to, for instance, parse SOAP documents, including headers for different standards such as WS-Security or WS-ReliableMessaging.

▶ **SOA middleware or Enterprise Services Bus (ESB)**

These provide connectivity to legacy applications, managed services, security services, and process automation capabilities. Legacy applications within the data center are not service-enabled, and middleware is used to translate the existing integration capabilities of these applications into Web Service calls, usually without any manual programming. An ESB can provide routing and mapping services, publish/subscribe functionality, and guaranteed delivery and serialization of messages. Often, WS-BPEL process editors and runtime environments are part of the middleware layer.

▶ **Monitoring and governance tools**

These help close the cycle of design, development, and process improvement.

15.4 SOA at SAP

SAP recognized the importance of Web Services and SOA as a next generation computing infrastructure many years ago. Accordingly, SAP started recrafting its infrastructure and applications to take advantage of the opportunities and benefits presented by SOA. SAP now delivers bundles of Enterprise Services to customers worldwide, allowing them to deploy services flexibly and non-disruptively on top of the platform they already use to run their businesses.

SAP started delivering Enterprise Service bundles in 2006. Enterprise Services can be described as follows:

▶ They are technically Web Services; that is, they are described by a WSDL document and are callable via SOAP messaging.

▶ They are semantically harmonized with each other and with the SAP Business Suite.

▶ They are based on global data types, which are modeled on the UN/CEFACT CCTS standard.

▶ They are developed under a strict governance mechanism.

▶ The deliver enterprise-level business value.

▶ They are published in a central UDDI repository for easy discovery.

These Enterprise Services are not just a random decomposition of SAP functionality into WSDL-wrapped services but deliver real business value to customers. SAP consults with customers in specific industry segments to determine which services are most useful and how those services can be most effectively designed to meet the needs of those businesses.

SAP also hosts a collaborative online community, the SAP Developer Network (*http://sdn.sap.com*), which brings together business process experts (BPEs), technical practitioners, and SOA architects to promote knowledge sharing and foster wider expertise in all of these areas.

Enterprise Services run on SAP NetWeaver, the platform for all SAP applications, which offers a strong technical foundation for SOA at SAP and includes the following capabilities:

▶ **Enterprise Services Repository**
A central repository of service metadata that hosts SAP and non-SAP service definitions. This is a design time repository that brings transparency to service modeling and design.

▶ **Services Registry**
A UDDI V.3-compliant service registry, with extended classification and search functions that makes service discovery easier and fosters reuse.

▶ **Enterprise Service bus/SOA middleware**
SAP NetWeaver Process Integration (SAP NetWeaver PI) is a service bus for calling SAP and non-SAP services, and for implementing automated system-to-system processes, integration with legacy applications, and extensive service-monitoring tools.

▶ **SAP NetWeaver Business Process Management**
SAP NetWeaver BPM is a BPMN (Business Process Modeling Notation) based BPM design tool with integrated business rules management.

▶ **Service-enabled data management**
That includes powerful business intelligence and master data management capabilities

▶ **Application server**
An application server that hosts both ABAP and Java applications and includes an integrated Web Services runtime that supports important standards such as WS-Security, SAML, WS-ReliableMessaging, and WS-Policy.

▶ **Application development environment**
An integrated application development environment based on the Eclipse standard that allows building service-enabled applications.

▶ **Framework**
An SOA framework, based on TOGAF (The Open Group Architecture Framework), the leading framework for SOA implementations.

▶ **Modeling and design tools**
Modeling and design tools to bridge the gap between business users and IT implementers.

Customers use these tools and services as needed to implement SOA in SAP environments, and they have found and continue to find, that they represent the shortest route to SOA for SAP-enabled businesses.

15.5 Implementing the Service Interface for a Workflow

As stated earlier, we will trigger our workflow through the agency of a remote-enabled function module exposed as a Web Service call. We have written a simple function module to start the workflow; first, we will discuss this module, and then we will discuss two ways to service-enable it.

15.5.1 The Function Module

Our function module takes a business partner number as input, and then triggers the sample workflow that we have been using in this book. The code looks like Listing 15.1.

```
FUNCTION Z_START_WS99800008.
*"----------------------------------------------------------------
*"*"Local Interface:
*"  IMPORTING
*"     VALUE(OBJKEY) TYPE  BUT000-PARTNER
*"  EXPORTING
*"     VALUE(WI_ID) TYPE  SWWVPUBLIC-WI_ID
*"----------------------------------------------------------------
INCLUDE <CNTN01>. " definition of container and object macros
data: RETURN_CODE TYPE  SYSUBRC.
data: WI_CONTAINER TYPE STANDARD TABLE OF swr_cont
                   WITH HEADER LINE.

move 'BusinessPartner' to WI_CONTAINER-element.
move  objkey   to WI_CONTAINER-value.
append WI_CONTAINER.
*-> Start workflow
  CALL FUNCTION 'SAP_WAPI_START_WORKFLOW'
    EXPORTING
      task   = 'WS99800011'
    IMPORTING
      return_code    = RETURN_CODE
      WORKITEM_ID    = WI_ID
    TABLES
      input_container = WI_CONTAINER.

ENDFUNCTION.
```

Listing 15.1 Example of Function Module Starting a Workflow with SAP_WAPI_START_WORKFLOW

As you can see, we have kept this very simple to keep the intent of our actions clear. We pass name/value pairs to the workflow container. In this case, `Busi-nessPartner` is a field in the workflow container, and `objkey` is the business partner number passed to the function module `Z_START_WS99800008`. `SAP_WAPI_START_WORKFLOW` is called, receiving the name/value pairs. `SAP_WAPI_START_WORKFLOW` starts workflow `WS998000008` with the business partner number as input. The function module returns the work item ID of the instantiated work-flow, as well as the function module return code (which tells us if the function executed successfully). We return a message with the success of the workflow as well.

SAP NetWeaver now offers a unified Web Services runtime; that is, whether the service is called directly from the application server hosting the service, or is a managed service called through SAP NetWeaver PI, there is a single environment and call structure. We will show two ways to service-enable our function module: exposing it directly from the application server ("inside-out"), and creating a proxy interface in SAP NetWeaver PI.

15.5.2 Service-Enabling in the Application (Inside-Out Approach)

You can use the Object Navigator (Transaction SE80) to create the Web Service from the function module:

1. From the SAP menu, choose TOOLS • ABAP WORKBENCH • OVERVIEW • OBJECT NAVIGATOR.

2. In the dropdown box on the left-hand navigation frame, select the FUNCTION GROUP entry. In the data entry field below, enter the name of the function group containing your function module, and press ⏎. The elements of the function group, for instance, function modules, macros, and includes, are organized into folders.

3. Open the FUNCTION MODULES folder, select your function module, right-click, and from the context menu, select CREATE • WEB SERVICE. (see Figure 15.4) A wizard starts.

4. In the first screen of the wizard (see Figure 15.5), enter a name and short description for your service, as well as an ENDPOINT TYPE — in this case, the end point is a function module. This is selected by default because you started the wizard from a function module. (The phrase "Kurzbeschreibung" means "Short Description" and is untranslated in this system.)

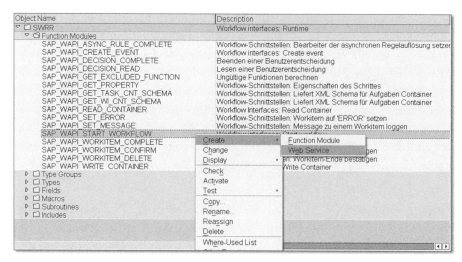

Figure 15.4 The Create Service Wizard Can Be Called Directly from the Function Module in SE80

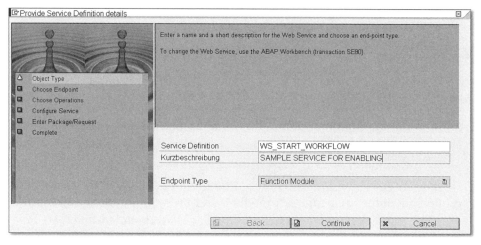

Figure 15.5 The Create Service Wizard

5. In the next screen of the wizard, enter the name of the function module to enable; because you started the wizard from the context menu for the function module, it is selected by default. If you select the NAME MAPPING checkbox (it is selected by default), the wizard selects the existing name for the service end point but removes the underscores and capitalizes initial letters. So, for instance, if the function module name was z_my_function_module, the end point name would be ZMyFunctionModule.

6. If you were configuring a BAPI or a function group, you would see a screen now that would allow you to select which operation, for instance, which function module in a function group, that you want to enable. Because you are enabling a function module, the wizard skips this screen and takes you to a screen where you can configure the service (see Figure 15.6). In this screen, you set a security profile. The following profiles are possible:

▷ PRF_DT_IF_SEC_NO
   No Authentication and No Transport Guarantee

▷ PRF_DT_IF_SEC_MEDIUM
   Authentication with User and Password and Transport Guarantee

▷ PRF_DT_IF_SEC_LOW
   Authentication with User and Password, No Transport Guarantee

▷ PRF_DT_IF_SEC_HIGH
   AUTHENTICATION WITH CERTIFICATES AND TRANSPORT GUARANTEE

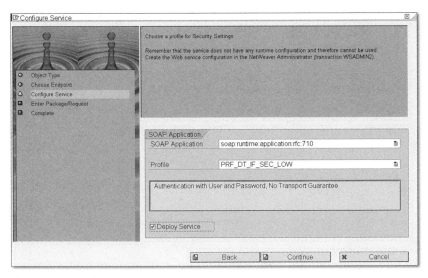

Figure 15.6 Configure the Service

If you want to deploy the service to the service runtime (and you almost certainly do, although it is possible you want to create the service definition now and deploy it later), select the DEPLOY SERVICE checkbox. The SOAP application is selected for you based on the type of entity (in this case, a function module) that you are creating the service from.

7. The next screen of the wizard asks you to assign the service to a package; if you select a transportable package, you also have to furnish (or create) a transport request so the service can be transported through the system landscape. Provide the necessary information, select CONTINUE to move to the last screen, and finally, click the COMPLETE button to create the Web Service. Because you checked the DEPLOY SERVICE checkbox in the wizard, the service has been automatically deployed to the service runtime, and it is ready to use as is.

8. After completing your service, you can view the service, change the configuration, or create additional end points by calling Transaction SOAMANAGER. If you are working with a system based on a SAP NetWeaver release lower than 7.0 SP14, then you use Transaction WSADMIN instead. If you start Transaction SOAMANAGER from Transaction SE80 with your service definition still loaded (you can do this by clicking the ASSOCIATE icon on the toolbar), it opens with your service selected (see Figure 15.7); otherwise, you have to enter the name of your service in the SEARCH PATTERN field and click the GO button.

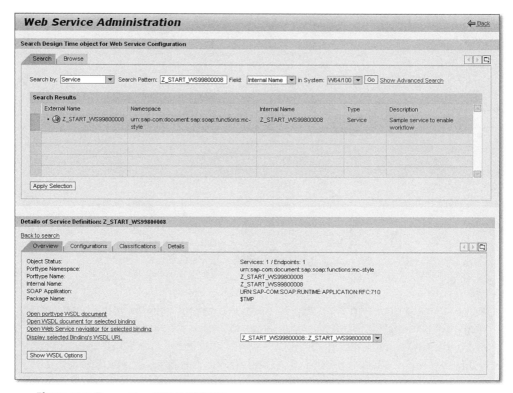

Figure 15.7 Transaction SOAMANAGER

Transaction SOAMANAGER is a Java-based transaction that runs in a browser window. It is used to configure service end points, publish services, and perform other service management tasks.

9. Your service appears in the search results table; click the APPLY SELECTION button to see the details. From here, you can edit the configuration, call the Web Service Navigator to view the WSDL or test the service, and perform other administrative tasks for your service.

Testing the Service

To test the service, follow these steps:

1. Open your service in Transaction SOAMANAGER, display the details, and click the link titled OPEN WEB SERVICE NAVIGATOR FOR SELECTED BINDING from the OVERVIEW tab (see Figure 15.8).

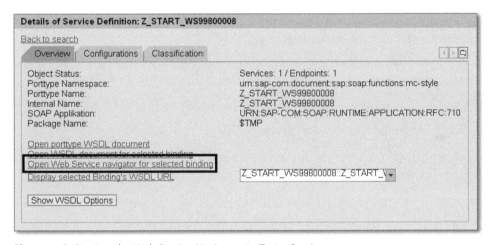

Figure 15.8 Starting the Web Service Navigator to Test a Service

2. The Web Service Navigator appears in a new browser window. To test the service, click the TEST link located on the blue navigation bar. This opens a screen that allows you to select which operation you want to test. Because you have enabled a function module, there is only one operation shown, and you can click this link to launch the test tool.

3. The test tool allows you to enter the input parameters of your service. Enter the business partner number to test, and click the SEND button. You will see the

result in the ensuing screen (see Figure 15.9). If the call was successful, you see the work item ID in the response message.

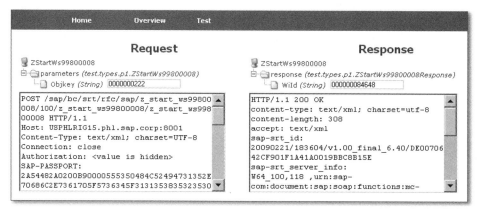

Figure 15.9 A Successful Test in the Web Services Navigator

Publishing the Service to the Registry

To allow a developer to create a consumer application for calling the workflow via the service interface, you can do one of two things:

▶ Give the customer a copy of the associated WSDL document directly.

▶ Publish the interface to your service registry.

A prerequisite for publishing the service interface is that your SAP system administrator had maintained at least one connection to a service registry.

Services can be published automatically to the service registry after an end point has been configured, and the service has been assigned to a policy (there will be some delay because this implicit publication is performed by a background job that runs periodically). A prerequisite for this is that the SAP system administrator has maintained the publication rules for your system, and that a business or service administrator has maintained the policies and assigned your service to a policy.

1. If you want to publish the service explicitly, you can access the service registry and navigate to the PUBLISH tab.

2. Enter the URL of the WSDL document for your service. To find this URL, use Transaction SOAMANAGER, open your service definition, navigate to the

OVERVIEW tab, and click the link labeled DISPLAY SELECTED BINDING'S WSDL URL. You can then copy this URL to the clipboard.

3. Back in the service registry, paste the WSDL URL into the END-POINT WSDL text box, and click the PUBLISH button. You may have to provide a username and password for accessing the application system that holds the WSDL document.

4. If there is a problem with the publication, for instance, if there are features that are not supported, you can edit the service configuration in Transaction SOA-MANAGER before attempting to publish again. If publication is successful, you will see the following message: WSDL PUBLISHED SUCCESSFULLY. You can now search the registry to see your published service (see Figure 15.10).

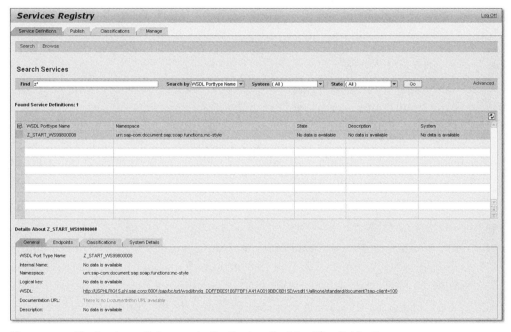

Figure 15.10 The Service as It Appears in the Services Registry After Publication

There are many aspects of service definition and publication that are not described here; we don't discuss classifications, or options for the service, or maintaining configuration profiles and policies, for instance. But our goal is not to give an exhaustive description of the what's and how's of services in SAP NetWeaver; rather, it is to give you a general feel for the service-enablement of a workflow. For more information about creating, editing, and publishing services, see the SAP Help Portal at *http://help.sap.com*.

15.5.3 Service Enabling from the Enterprise Services Repository (Outside-In Approach)

We have shown how to service enable the function module, and therefore the workflow, directly from the application. There is another approach, the *outside-in* approach, which starts in the Enterprise Services Repository and allows you to make mediated as well as direct calls. Mediated calls are Web Service calls that are made from the SOA middleware, known as SAP NetWeaver PI, and allow, in addition to the basic Web Service functionality, the following options:

▶ Calling the service from non-service-enabled applications

▶ Routing service calls to multiple receivers

▶ Mapping (transformation) to or from different interfaces

▶ Including the service call in an automated business process

▶ Centrally configuring a direct call between SAP systems

In addition to these capabilities, when you create the service in this way, you have the service interface defined centrally in the Enterprise Services Repository, which promotes transparency in the service definition and your integration landscape in general. Although a complete discussion of the Enterprise Services Repository, service creation, and using SAP NetWeaver PI is outside the scope of this book, we outline the process here:

1. You start by creating a service interface and the associated data objects in the Enterprise Services Repository.

2. After you activate these objects, you generate a *proxy* in the ABAP development environment. A proxy is simply the dictionary and code objects required to implement a service based on the interface definition.

3. After generating the proxy, you simply complete the coding for your service and configure the service to be executed at runtime.

Data Objects for Service Definition

We will begin this process by describing how to create the service objects in the Enterprise Services Repository. The service objects are described next.

We will create a *service interface* in the Enterprise Services Repository, which is a WSDL document that describes the operations and data structures for a Web Service. This is the abstract part of the WSDL document because at this point, we have no physical systems defined, nor are we limiting ourselves to any particular runtime binding (such as HTTP or SMTP). A service interface includes one or more operations. For instance, if you were defining the service interface for a purchase order service, you might define operations to create a purchase order, query the data of a purchase order, update a purchase order, or delete a purchase order.

The operations themselves are based on *message types*. A message type is an XML Schema that defines the actual messages to be passed at runtime, that is, the business data that makes up the SOAP payload of the service call. A synchronous (request/response) service has a request message type and a response message type defined. Asynchronous services do not have a response message defined because the calling application is not expecting and cannot process a response. In addition to these, *fault* messages may be (and should be, in most cases) assigned to the operation so that the server can return an error message in the case of a failure during the service call. (Obviously, an outbound asynchronous operation would not have a fault message assigned because the application is not expecting any response, not even an error message. An inbound asynchronous operation may have a fault message assigned, however, as it can then register an error with the middleware).

Message types, in turn, are based on *data types*. Data types are XML Schema Definition Language (XSD) compliant data types. Data types can be reused within multiple message types, and they foster reusability. For Enterprise Services, as discussed earlier, these data types are based on the UN/CEFACT Core Component Technical Specification (CCTS), which allows for strong data type governance and a unified data model across SAP applications. For most home-built services, *freestyle* data types are used. These are data types that are not compliant with the CCTS standard.

The service interface has two attributes that must be defined and that apply for all of the operations of the service interface: a *category* and an *interface pattern*. The category can be one of the following:

▶ **Inbound**
Use this category to define a provider service; that is, the request message for this service will be inbound to the application.

▶ **Outbound**
Use this category to define a consumer service; that is, the request message will be sent outbound from the application.

▶ **Abstract**

This category is used for defining interfaces used in BPEL-based processes and need not concern us here.

The interface pattern is used to define how the service will be coded in the back-end, and the details of this are not important to us. Suffice to say that in almost all cases, including our example, the STATELESS pattern is the correct one to use.

Creating the Service Objects in the Enterprise Services Repository

Service-enabled SAP systems are associated with a specific instance of the Enterprise Services Repository. You access the Enterprise Services Repository by running Transaction SXMB_IFR. This opens up a web page in a browser that has links to the Enterprise Services Repository and other functionality (e.g., the Services Registry). The exact links on the page differ depending on whether the Enterprise Services Repository is hosted by an SAP NetWeaver PI system or an SAP NetWeaver Composition Environment system, but in either case, click the link to ENTERPRISE SERVICES REPOSITORY to open UI for creating your objects.

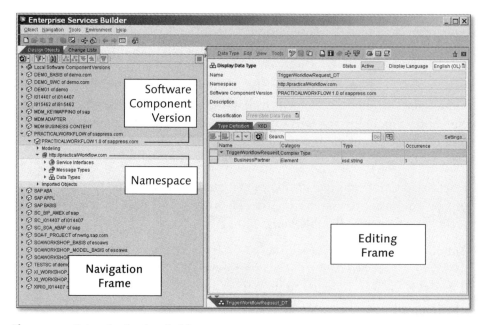

Figure 15.11 Enterprise Services Builder

The Enterprise Services Builder (see Figure 15.11) is a Java-based UI application for creating objects in the Enterprise Services Repository. Content here is organized by Software Component Version (SWCV) and namespace. A prerequisite for development in the Enterprise Services Builder is that an SWCV has been created in the System Landscape Directory (SLD) and has been imported into the Enterprise Services Builder, and furthermore, that a namespace has been created within the development SWCV.

Creating the Data Types

The navigation frame on the left side of the screen allows you to drill down through the SWCV and namespaces for developing your objects. You can select the object type to create from the navigation tree on the left side, and enter header data for the object on the right hand side:

1. Select the correct namespace within your SWCV, right-click on the namespace, and choose NEW.

2. From the list of objects in the popup window, open the interface objects hierarchy, and select DATA TYPE. Enter a NAME and DESCRIPTION (optional), and click the CREATE button (see Figure 15.12).

Figure 15.12 The Create Object Dialog in the Enterprise Services Builder

3. The editing frame includes its own main toolbar and menu bar, a header area, and an editing area. The editing area has its own toolbar. You can add new lines

to your data type by clicking on the INSERT NEW LINES icon on the editing area toolbar. You have the option to add a single element, a single attribute, or multiple rows (of type element or attribute) to the data type definition. Each row of the data type in the editor corresponds to either an XML element or an XML attribute of the final XSD type. Each row, that is each element or attribute, can be assigned the following fields:

▶ **Name (required)**
The name of the attribute or element as it will appear in the instantiated SOAP XML document at runtime.

▶ **Category (automatically assigned)**
Denotes whether the row defines a structure element, a data element, or an attribute.

▶ **Type (required)**
Assign either a built-in XSD data type (string, integer, etc.) or a previously created data type from the Enterprise Services Builder (this allows you to reuse common data types, such as address structures).

▶ **Occurrence (required, but implicit for root elements)**
Describes the number or possible instances of the element or attribute in the XML SOAP document at runtime. Attributes can be either optional or required; elements can be assigned occurrences in accordance with the rules of XSD. For instance, an element can have occurrence 1, meaning required, but only one instance is allowed; 0..n, meaning that the element is optional, but there can be at most *n* instances; or m..n, meaning there must be at least *m* instances but at most *n* instances.

▶ **Default (optional)**
Specify if a default value is to be inserted in the element at runtime even if there is no value for the element in the message at runtime.

▶ **Details (optional)**
Allows you to specify XSD facets, such as minimum or maximum length, a pattern for the field (such as a date format), or whether it is an enumerated type and what the enumerated values are.

▶ **Business Context (optional)**
A business context for the field, such as an industry-specific designation.

▷ **Description (optional)**

A description of the element or attribute.

▷ **UI Text Object (optional)**

Use a UI text object if the data type will be used in a UI application, and you want to assign a text to the field in the UI.

4. When you have created all of the fields for your data type, you must save it before going on.

For our simple interface, we created two simple data types: one for the request message type, called `TriggerWorkflowRequest_DT`, which has a single element for sending the business partner number to the function module; and a data type for the response message type, called `TriggerWorkflowResponse_DT`, which has a single field for receiving the Work Item ID back from the function module (see Figure 15.13).

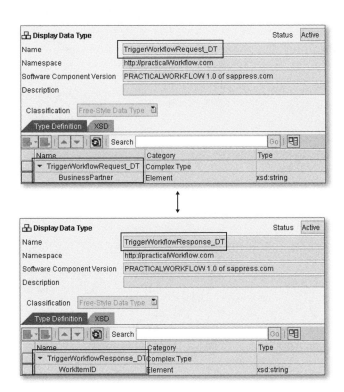

Figure 15.13 Data Types for the Trigger Workflow Service

Creating the Message Types

Creating the message types is even easier than creating the data types:

1. To create a message type, right-click on your namespace, and choose New.

2. From the list of objects in the popup window, open the interface objects hierarchy, and select Message Type. Enter a name and description (optional), and click the Create button.

3. Enter a name and description as before; however, the name for a message type has a significance beyond design time. The name you give the data type must match the name of the root element of the SOAP XML document that will be processed at runtime. So, for instance, if the root element of the SOAP body will be `TriggerWorkflowRequest`, then use this as the name for the message type in the Enterprise Services Builder.

4. After creating a message type, simply assign the correct data type that you have created for the message type. You can do this by dragging and dropping the data type from the navigation frame to the editing frame, or by using the search help in the message type editor. For our service, we created two message types: One called `TriggerWorkflowRequest`, which uses our `TriggerWorkflow Request_DT` data type (see Figure 15.14), and one called `TriggerWorkflow Response`, which uses our `TriggerWorkflowResponse_DT` data type.

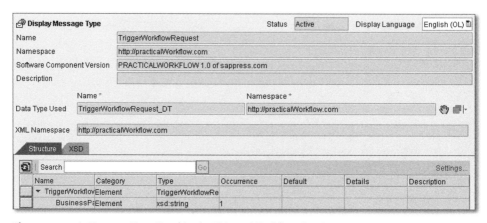

Figure 15.14 A Message Type Used in the Trigger Workflow Service

Creating the Service Interface

To create the service interface, follow these steps:

1. As before, right-click on your namespace, and choose NEW.

2. From the list of objects in the popup window, open the interface objects hierarchy, and select SERVICE INTERFACE. Enter a name and description (optional), and click the CREATE button.

3. In the header area of the editing frame, enter the appropriate attributes for the service interface. Because you are creating the provider service, choose INBOUND for the category, and, as described earlier, choose STATELESS for the INTERFACE PATTERN.

4. When you create the service, it automatically creates an operation for you, with the same name as your service interface. Go ahead and use this operation. You need to set two attributes for the operation: the OPERATION PATTERN and the MODE (see Figure 15.15). For your type of service, and in almost all cases, the only operation pattern available for this service interface type is NORMAL. The mode refers to whether the operation is synchronous or asynchronous, and because you will be sending a partner number and receiving back a work item ID, this is a synchronous operation.

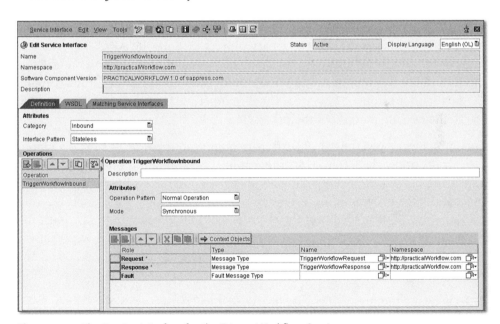

Figure 15.15 The Service Interface for the Trigger Workflow Service

5. Because this is a synchronous operation, you must provide a request message type, a response message type, and, optionally, a fault message type. To keep

this as simple as possible, we will not use a fault message type. For the request and response messages, simply drag and drop the previously created message types, `TriggerWorkflowRequest` and `TriggerWorkflowResponse`, to the appropriate entry fields in the operation editing area. Save the service interface.

6. There is one last task you must perform before leaving the Enterprise Services Builder: activating your objects. In the navigation frame, select the CHANGE LISTS tab, drill down to your SWCV to the change list that has been created automatically, right-click on the change list, and select ACTIVATE. Now you are done in the Enterprise Services Builder.

Generating the Proxy

Generating the proxy is, as we said before, a push-button operation. Proxy generation takes care of creating the object you will need to provide or consume a service (because you created an inbound service interface, you will be creating a provider proxy).

Exactly what objects are created depends somewhat on whether you are generating a provider or a consumer proxy. For a consumer proxy, all of the objects are completely created: the Data Dictionary objects that are the ABAP implementations of the data structures used for the data types and message types of the service interface; the implementing ABAP proxy class for the proxy interface; and the method for calling the service. The developer only needs to write a program to call the execute method of the proxy class.

For a provider proxy, the ABAP Dictionary objects are created, as well as an interface for the proxy class. (This is slightly confusing terminology that requires some explanation. We have been talking about service interfaces; but in the world of object-oriented programming, an interface is an archetype for a class. It is a contract, if you will, that spells out the requirements an object of that class must fulfill when it is created. It is this sense of the word "interface" that we are using here.) In this case, the developer must implement the execute method of the proxy class.

1. To generate the proxy, navigate in SAP GUI to Transaction SPROXY.

2. Your SWCV, namespaces, and other objects from the Enterprise Services Repository appear in a hierarchy in the left navigation pane. Drill down to your SWCV and namespace, and open the SERVICE INTERFACE tree.

3. Locate the service interface for which you want to generate a proxy, and double-click (or right-click, and select CREATE PROXY from the context menu). The proxy generation wizard starts (see Figure 15.16).

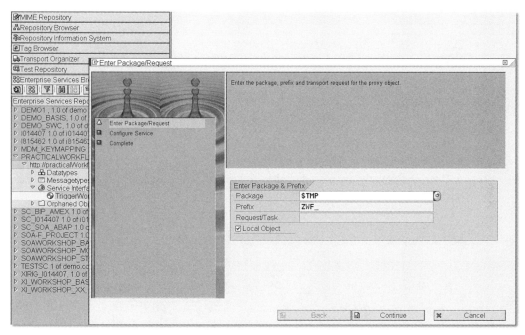

Figure 15.16 Starting the Proxy Generation Wizard

4. In the first screen of the wizard, enter a PACKAGE for your developments, and if you choose a transportable package, you also select or create a change request. You must also enter a PREFIX, and this requirement deserves some explanation.

5. In the Enterprise Services Repository, you have already seen that development objects are organized by SWCV and namespace; the ABAP environment does not have these structures to organize your development. Thus, the prefix is prepended to the names of ABAP structures and objects to insure that they are uniquely named within the ABAP repository.

6. After making the necessary entries, click the CONTINUE button, click the COMPLETE button on the next screen, and the proxy is generated.

Figure 15.17 shows the objects that were created during proxy generation. In this case, these are:

▶ ZWF_II_TRIGGER_WORKFLOW_INBOUN

An ABAP objects interface that represents the foundation for the proxy class.

▶ ZWF_TRIGGER_WORKFLOW_REQUEST

A Data Dictionary structure that is the ABAP implementation of the request message.

▶ ZWF_TRIGGER_WORKFLOW_REQUEST_D

A Data Dictionary structure that is the ABAP implementation of the request data type.

▶ ZWF_TRIGGER_WORKFLOW_RESPONSE

A Data Dictionary structure that is the ABAP implementation of the response message.

▶ ZWF_TRIGGER_WORKFLOW_RESPONSE1

A Data Dictionary structure that is the ABAP implementation of the response data type.

Type	ABAP Name	Prefix	Name	Namespace	Status	Info
⚙	ZWF_II_TRIGGER_WORKFLOW_INBOUN	ZWF_	TriggerWorkflowInbound	http://practicalWorkflow.com	□	
▭	ZWF_TRIGGER_WORKFLOW_REQUEST	ZWF_	TriggerWorkflowRequest	http://practicalWorkflow.com	□	
▭	ZWF_TRIGGER_WORKFLOW_REQUEST_D	ZWF_	TriggerWorkflowRequest_DT	http://practicalWorkflow.com	□	
▭	ZWF_TRIGGER_WORKFLOW_RESPONSE	ZWF_	TriggerWorkflowResponse_DT	http://practicalWorkflow.com	□	
▭	ZWF_TRIGGER_WORKFLOW_RESPONSE1	ZWF_	TriggerWorkflowResponse	http://practicalWorkflow.com	□	

Figure 15.17 Proxy Objects Created by the Proxy Generation Wizard

You will notice a couple of things about the names of these objects: first, they all start with the prefix, ZWF_, that you specified in the proxy generation wizard; second, some of the names are changed from their Enterprise Services Repository names. Some are shortened (1, 3, 5 in Figure 15.17) to comply with the 30-character name limit for ABAP structures, and one has a number appended (5 of the above) to insure that it is uniquely named within the ABAP repository.

Before you can complete the service implementation, you must save and activate the proxy objects that were generated. You can do this by navigating in the menu to PROXY • ACTIVATE.

Completing the Proxy Implementation

Because you have created a provider proxy, you must write the logic for the execute method of the proxy class. The created class name is <Prefix>CL<ABAP name of the service interface>; so, for instance, our class name is ZWF_CL_TRIGGER_WORKFLOW_INBOUN.

1. To access this class, double-click on the class name from the PROPERTIES tab of the proxy definition in Transaction SPROXY (see Figure 15.18), or open it directly in the ABAP Class Builder (Transaction SE24).

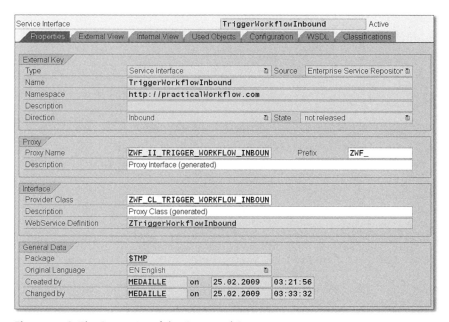

Service Interface		TriggerWorkflowInbound		Active

Properties | External View | Internal View | Used Objects | Configuration | WSDL | Classifications

External Key				
Type	Service Interface		Source	Enterprise Service Repositor
Name	TriggerWorkflowInbound			
Namespace	http://practicalWorkflow.com			
Description				
Direction	Inbound		State	not released

Proxy			
Proxy Name	ZWF_II_TRIGGER_WORKFLOW_INBOUN	Prefix	ZWF_
Description	Proxy Interface (generated)		

Interface	
Provider Class	ZWF_CL_TRIGGER_WORKFLOW_INBOUN
Description	Proxy Class (generated)
WebService Definition	ZTriggerWorkflowInbound

General Data				
Package	$TMP			
Original Language	EN English			
Created by	MEDAILLE	on	25.02.2009	03:21:56
Changed by	MEDAILLE	on	25.02.2009	03:33:32

Figure 15.18 The Properties of the Generated Proxy

2. Every proxy class has an EXECUTE method; the name of this method is given as `<Class Name>~<Operation Name>`. So, in our case, the name of the method is `ZWF_II_TRIGGER_WORKFLOW_INBOUN~TRIGGER_WORKFLOW_INBOUND`.

> **Note**
>
> In earlier releases of SAP NetWeaver PI, also known as SAP NetWeaver Exchange Infrastructure (SAP XI), only a single operation per interface was allowed. In older versions, the name of the execute method will be either `<Class_Name>~EXECUTE_SYNCHRONOUS`, or `<Class_Name>~EXECUTE_ASYNCHRONOUS`.

3. Open the method in the method editor, and enter the implementation code. Listing 15.2 shows the simple method implementation method for the workflow service. As you can see, the basic tasks of implementing the inbound proxy method are quite simple; collect the input data from the inbound message and assign it (through local variables, if necessary) to the input of the func-

tion module; and assign the output of the function module to the response message structure of the service operation.

```
method ZWF_II_TRIGGER_WORKFLOW_INBOUN~TRIGGER_WORKFLOW_INBOUND.

*** **** Simple Execute method for calling a function module **** ***

*" Declare local variables to send and receive FM parameters
data: l_objkey type BUT000-PARTNER,
      l_wi_id  type SWWVPUBLIC-WI_ID.

*" Assign the business partner from the incoming message
*" to the local variable for calling the function module
l_objkey = INPUT-TRIGGER_WORKFLOW_REQUEST-BUSINESS_PARTNER.

*" Call the function module and receive the return parameter
*" In the local variable
Call function 'Z_START_WS99800008'
exporting OBJKEY = l_objkey
IMPORTING WI_ID = l_wi_id.

*" Assign the output of the function module to the
*" output structure of the service operation
OUTPUT-TRIGGER_WORKFLOW_RESPONSE-WORK_ITEM_ID = l_wi_id.

endmethod.
```

Listing 15.2 Simple Example of an Execute Method for Calling a Function Module

4. You must, of course, activate your method before it can actually be used.

In a real proxy application, of course, we would check for valid data, handle any errors returned from the function module, and if an error occurred, send a fault message back to the service consumer. Because we do not want to get bogged down in the details of proxy programming, we omit these here.

Even with these desirable features, the method implementation is still very simple, relatively speaking. This is a *low-code approach* because we did not have to do any tricky message parsing, parameter passing, or create any code to actually handle the HTTP call. All of this is done automatically by the proxy runtime. We only need to focus on the essential tasks of implementing the desired functionality.

Tip

If you want to learn more about using ABAP and Java proxies and proxy programming, an excellent book is *SAP Exchange Infrastructure for Developers* (SAP PRESS, 2007).

Creating the Web Service

Although you are finished with the proxy implementation, you have not actually created a callable service yet. If your proxy is to be used in mediated scenarios, that is, if it will be called from SAP NetWeaver PI, then there is nothing more you need do at this point. You will have to configure the scenarios that use your proxy within the SAP NetWeaver PI configuration tool, but a description of that is outside the scope of this chapter.

If you want to call the service directly from the application server, as in the previous example, you must create an end point for your service:

1. Open Transaction SOAMANAGER, and on the APPLICATION AND SCENARIO COMMUNICATION tab, choose SINGLE SERVICE ADMINISTRATION.

2. Enter a search term for your service (e.g., in this case, you could search on `*trigger*`), click the GO button, select your service in the search results, and click on APPLY SELECTION.

3. In the DETAILS area, choose the CONFIGURATIONS tab, and select CREATE SERVICE. Enter a name for your service, a short description, and a name for the binding. Click APPLY SETTINGS. You may edit the service settings at this point, such as the security or transport settings.

4. After you save the end point, your service is available and can be called from a client application. At this point, you can also publish your service to the Enterprise Services Registry as before.

Overall, this is clearly a lot more work than simply generating a service from the function module itself; but it is also a lot more general. Proxies allow you to service enable arbitrary functionality in the backend, not just function modules. They allow you to make service calls in either a point-to-point or mediated fashion. They put the service metadata in the Enterprise Services Repository, where it can be seen and understood by all stakeholders in a process. And they allow you to build outside-in, interface-first service operations in accordance with good SOA methodology. All in all, the proxy approach is well worth pursuing.

Troubleshooting workflows is not the simplest of activities, but the army of tools provided will help you quickly diagnose and correct derailed workflows. This chapter is particularly useful for anyone creating or extending workflows. Although you rarely have to troubleshoot workflows in a production environment, this chapter is also useful as preparation for the workflow administrator.

16 Advanced Diagnostics

This chapter is a companion to Chapter 6, Workflow Administration, in which recovery procedures for run-of-the-mill production problems are described. Luckily, the Workflow Engine has proven exceptionally stable, so the problem diagnoses in this chapter will primarily be of use in the development environment where anything, from programming errors to inconsistent customizing or authorization problems, is possible.

16.1 The Tools of the Trade

Because workflows implement whole business processes and not just individual activities, workflows involve more dimensions than simple transactions that start, execute, and terminate in one logical unit of work (LUW). A workflow involves different users, is spread over time, and may involve synchronization with other workflows or business transactions as it progresses. All of these factors prevent you from simply stepping through the workflow in the way you can step through a simple program. However, workflow provides a set of diagnostic tools that will make your troubleshooting work much easier, even though you will have to rethink your analysis techniques if you are used to simply debugging programs.

> **Tip**
>
> The better you document your workflows, the easier it will be for you and for anyone else maintaining them to understand and troubleshoot your workflows after you have moved on to your next project. Changes will almost inevitably be asked for by the business process owners, and good documentation can facilitate making these changes. If you are on a workflow project as a consultant, your customers will certainly appreciate your conscientious documentation as part of knowledge transfer.

> **Tip**
>
> Be especially careful to document any part of the workflow that is liable to fail due to neglected or inaccurate data maintenance in the production environment.

To give you an idea of how troubleshooting workflows differs from debugging transactions, here are some examples of the sort of symptoms that can occur:

- The wrong agent receives the work item.
- The workflow disappears (meaning that the expected agent has not received the work item).
- Too many agents receive a work item.
- No one receives the work item.
- The workflow does not trigger automatically.
- Duplicate instances of the workflows are triggered.
- The workflow stalls (suspends operation).
- A background step starts but occasionally does not finish.
- The workflow stops and goes into ERROR status.

As you can see, there are plenty of uncomfortable situations that can occur, although most can be resolved very quickly and are unlikely to appear in the production environment. Some will probably be due to an incorrectly modeled workflow; some result from neglected administration or data maintenance.

You should be very aware that there is only a thin line between the symptoms of a badly modeled workflow definition and the sort of problems that can occur in a typical production environment when master data gets out of sync. It is important to ensure that your administrators are well trained in a variety of troubleshooting techniques so that they can quickly resolve issues.

16.2   The Diagnosis Logs

The diagnosis logs are your best allies when it comes to pinpointing problems, so it is worth taking a moment to learn about each of them in a bit more detail, before going through the list of symptoms and solutions.

16.2.1   The Workflow Log

The *workflow log* charts the progress of the workflow. A new log is written for every workflow started. Everything that takes place while the workflow is running, from system interactions (such as work item created) to user interactions (such as work item forwarded), is logged.

There are different views of this log; the most important one for troubleshooting is the technical log (LIST WITH TECHNICAL DETAILS).

> **Tip**
>
> In any environment, you can set the technical view as your default view in your personal workflow settings. You can even customize your own view as described in Chapter 6, Workflow Administration.

The technical log shows all of the steps in the workflow, including those that have been masked out of the standard logs either because they are too technical in nature or because they have been explicitly excluded in the workflow step definition (refer to Chapter 8, Creating a Workflow).

The technical log shows the steps that are executed and the messages that are generated as it progresses. Some of these are warnings (yellow traffic lights) that can be ignored, but the errors (highlighted with red traffic lights) yield the most significant information when troubleshooting the workflow. When a fatal error is generated, it is logged under the workflow step where it occurred, and it also triggers a new fatal error message at the top level of the workflow, that is, in the work item representing the workflow instance. The workflow step error message is the more significant of the two.

Symptoms worth investigating with the workflow log:

▶ Workflow goes into ERROR status

▶ User does not receive a work item in their inbox

▶ Workflow appears to take the wrong branch

Starting points for investigation:

▶ In which step does the error occur?

▶ Who is a possible agent for this step?

▶ What were the container values just before branching?

16.2.2 The Diagnosis Transaction

The diagnosis transaction (SWUD) is your primary diagnostic tool. When it is called, it analyzes your workflow definition and presents a list of checks to perform based on this analysis, so it is worth getting to know the transaction in a bit more detail. The order in which the tests are listed is based on a pragmatic approach. The tests that determine the most common errors are displayed first, so you should follow the tests in the order they are suggested.

Think of this transaction as your "one-stop shopping" for workflow diagnostics; although all of the subsequent diagnosis tools can be reached via distinct transaction codes, here they are all bundled in logical order for your ready usage. The first screen (see Figure 16.1) is divided into three sections:

▶ The current workflow definition to be analyzed

▶ The list of test options

▶ A list of the last 10 workflow definitions that you have worked on

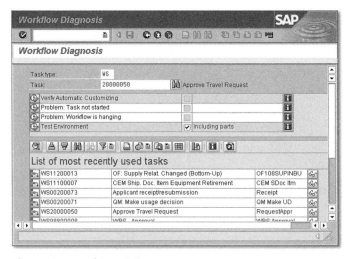

Figure 16.1 Initial SWUD Screen

To diagnose a new workflow definition, simply type in the ID of the workflow or use the search function to find it based on the standard search criteria. The four test options are your main testing paths:

▶ **Verify Automatic Customizing**
A customizing check is the first in the list simply because incomplete customizing is the most frequent source of problems in an unfamiliar system (and the rarest check performed in practice). Always call this when you suddenly discover that the workflow you created and tested last week no longer works today! There is a chance that someone else has changed the customizing settings without your knowledge.

▶ **Problem: Task not started**
When the workflow does not start or cannot be found, then you should call this option to track down why this is happening. It brings you to another list of potential causes to be checked, such as the event trace, the transactional RFC queue (RFC log), and so forth.

▶ **Problem: Workflow is hanging**
When the workflow starts but stops before completion, either with an error or simply by failing to start the next step in the workflow, then this is the path you should follow. You are presented with another screen of options, such as ABAP Dump Analysis, and the transactional RFC queue (RFC log).

▶ **Test Environment**
When you are developing a workflow and want to access the complete suite of test tools from one place, this is the option for you. Not only will you see a list of all of the checks available, tailored to the components used in your workflow, but you will also see a list of all of the components (subworkflows, tasks, business objects, delegated business objects) that are used in the main workflow. You can also see at a glance if possible agents have been assigned to the tasks used, so this is a useful option for the administrator, too.

The last section of the first screen shows you a history of previous workflows you have worked on. To pick one of your previous workflows for analysis, simply choose the RECENTLY USED TASKS icon () to the left. The workflow ID that you have chosen pops into place at the top of the screen, ready for more detailed analysis. After you have investigated it, you will see that this ID has jumped to the top of the history list, and the workflow that you were working on before has slipped down one place.

If you want to display one of the workflows that you had been working on previously, just choose the DISPLAY icon (🖉) on the right of the definition.

16.2.3   The Event Trace

The *event trace* writes a trace for all events raised (as shown in Figure 16.2). Do not confuse this with *event queues*, described in Chapter 13, Using Events and Other Business Interfaces, which smooth the workload of high-volume events at peak times and put failed events in a separate queue for reprocessing later.

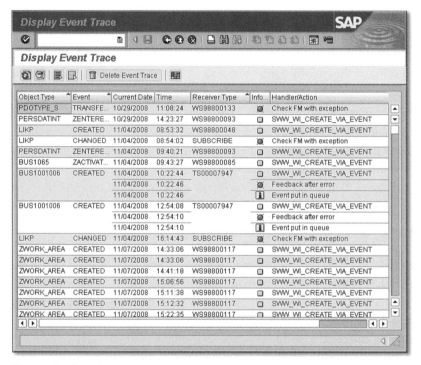

Figure 16.2 Event Trace

Tip

The event trace should be switched off in a production environment because it degrades system performance. If you do switch it on to cope with an emergency, make sure that it is only switched on for as short a time as possible, and use filters so that only the event you are interested in is traced. And don't forget to use Report RSWELOGD to clean up the event log files afterward.

The trace writes an entry for every event raised in the system, even when no workflow has been assigned to this event. Switching the trace on in your development environment enables you to track down errors related to workflows (and their steps) that do not trigger or terminate as expected.

Bear in mind that as the next step after writing the event trace entry, the "start workflow" command is placed in the RFC queue, as shown in Figure 16.3. So an event trace that shows success does not really tell you that the workflow has started. The event still has to work its way through the RFC queue, so this RFC queue is worth checking next via Transaction SM58 or Transaction SWUD.

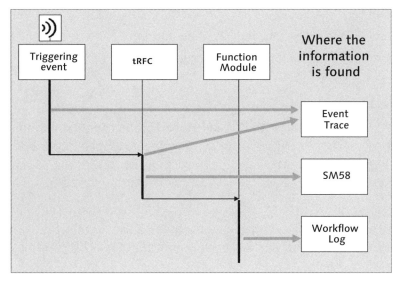

Figure 16.3 Diagram of Sequence of Events (Log, RFC, WF Log)

Symptoms worth investigating with the event trace:

▶ Workflows not triggering

▶ Duplicate workflows triggering

▶ Terminating events failing to stop a workflow step

Starting points for investigation:

▶ Is an event logged at all?

▶ Are start conditions used?

> **Note**
>
> If any object attributes used in the start condition return an exception, such as "object does not exist," this causes the start condition to abort unexpectedly. Also, when using multiple start conditions for the same object, bear in mind that they must be completely mutually exclusive; a particular object must never meet more than one start condition. If this happens, you will get the message "Workflow not unique."

▶ Is a check function module called, and what is the result? If you are unsure, you should be able to replicate the data in the check function module to determine what its outcome should have been.

▶ Is the event duplicated?

▶ Do two different events trigger one workflow definition?

▶ Is the object key correct, including any leading zeros?

16.2.4 The RFC Log

The Workflow Engine makes internal RFC calls for background steps and event-raising. If a workflow stalls without reason or an event fails to trigger a workflow, then there is a chance that the RFC call is still stuck in the RFC queue or has aborted while it was being processed.

Two queues are used; the WORKFLOW_LOCAL_xxx destination and the destination NONE (the queue must be searched according to the user logged in at the time the Workflow Engine made the call). The diagnosis Transaction SWUD will display the relevant queue for you.

Symptoms worth investigating with the RFC log:

▶ Sporadic load-based problems leading to the RFC queue choking (workflow stalls — corrected via customizing)

▶ Incorrectly programmed background methods, which abort or hang in the middle (workflow stalls — corrected by improving the BOR object)

▶ Event to workflow bindings that are erroneous (workflow does not start — correct the workflow definition).

Starting points for investigation:

▶ Is the queue empty? Entries are automatically deleted from the log as they are successfully completed.

▶ Is a background method stuck due to an unexpected need for dialog input? This problem is particularly likely if the method is based on BDC (batch data communication) — batch input — or CATT, especially after an upgrade if the underlying transactions being called have changed.

▶ What error messages are showing for stalled entries?

16.3   Debugging with the ABAP Debugger

The ABAP Debugger has undergone significant visual and functional changes since release 4.6C. If you are working on SAP NetWeaver 7.0, the debugger has two main panes, which allow you to view the source code on the left, and variables of different types (local and global as well) on the right. There are also numerous tabs that allow you to view structures, objects, breakpoints, and so on. It is well worth the time spent to familiarize yourself with the new debugger, even if you feel more comfortable in the older version (which you can revert to by closing the right-hand pane).

Regardless of the debugger version on your systems, occasionally you may want to debug a section of the ABAP code, such as a business object method or the code that precedes an event being raised. When you do this, bear in mind that some calls are made via an internal RFC call, so you will lose control if you do not set a breakpoint where the RFC call is made. Other calls, especially those related to event-raising, are made in the update task, so you need to switch on update task debugging after you are in the *ABAP Debugger* to keep control.

However, you can debug in some situations, particularly if you are working in your development environment. For example, if there is a background task that is going astray, you can always put a breakpoint (*break username*) in the method, generate the object, and switch the task from background processing so that it will be a dialog task. When you instantiate the workflow, you should execute that task (quickly, so as not to annoy your co-workers) and drop it into the ABAP debugger. From there, you can debug the method as you would have from the BOR. ABAP debugging is also handy for finding rule resolution errors if a function module is being used to return agents.

Another method of debugging a task (method) in the context of workflow is to set breakpoints within the Business Object Repository (BOR) code using the the the menu path UTILITIES • BREAKPOINT • SET. When testing, you can set your START OPTIONS (GOTO • OPTIONS) to ASYNCHRONOUS EXECUTION USING aRFC in Transaction SWUS (see Figure 16.4). When you start the workflow, you are taken to the ABAP Debugger when the method executes. This is particularly helpful because your breakpoint will be executed even if the method in question is not the first method in the workflow. You can also set an external breakpoint in a function that is called by the BOR method, and set the start options the same way.

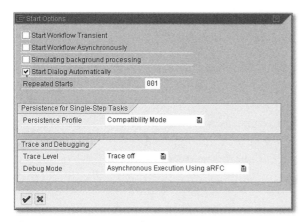

Figure 16.4 Start Options from Transaction SWUS

The Workflow Engine uses RFCs and dynamic function calls extensively, so you will find it hard work trying to debug through the Workflow Engine. Intelligent use of the different workflow logs and traces, together with unit testing of the individual components (such as methods, function modules, and tasks) is the recommended approach.

However, you can debug in some situations, particularly if you are working in your development environment. For example, if there is a background task that is going astray, you can always put a breakpoint (break username) in the method, generate the object, and switch the task from BACKGROUND PROCESSING so that it will be a dialog task. When you instantiate the workflow, you should execute that task (quickly, so as not to annoy your co-workers) and be dropped into the ABAP Debugger. From there, you can debug the method as you would have from the BOR. ABAP debugging is also handy for finding rule resolution errors if a function module is being used to return agents.

When working with SAP Supplier Relationship Management (SAP SRM) or another application where the user interface is not native in the SAP GUI, you can use the ABAP Debugger as well, if you know the starting point. In SAP SRM, you can set an *external breakpoint* in the function BBP_PDH_WFL_DB_UPDATE. Check your IP matching settings as well (UTILITIES • SETTINGS • DEBUGGING). When you execute an approval task from the SAP SRM inbox, the ABAP Debugger pops up for you in the SAP GUI. There are many other points where you could set a breakpoint; the function module listed here is just an example.

16.3.1 The Workflow Trace

The workflow trace used to be known as the "technical trace" and to put it mildly, it *is* technical. Although originally intended for use by developers for all manner of problem analysis (locking, synchronization problems, etc.), its primary use has turned out to be for investigating binding issues. It shows you in detail every single binding operation that takes place for one workflow instance. You can see the containers before the operation and the values that are appended or modified in the target container after the operation.

This trace can be switched on for one particular event or workflow instance and will continue to be written during the complete lifecycle of the workflow, however long it takes and however many users are involved. There is no danger of switching it on globally in the productive environment for workflow.

The main ways of starting the workflow trace are:

▶ **Setting the workflow trace flag in the diagnosis test environment (Transaction SWUD — Start Task or Create Event options)**
This is the simplest method because the trace is automatically switched off after the workflow has started. Back out of the START WORKFLOW screen, and choose the DISPLAY WORKFLOW TRACE option from the initial screen, and the correct log is presented to you straight away.

▶ **Switching on the workflow trace for the session (Transaction SWU9) and then executing the application without switching to another session window**
Switch the trace off (Transaction SWU9 again) or close the session window after executing the transaction, so that no new workflows are traced in the same log file. Even after you switch the session trace off, your workflows started in that session continue to be traced.

> **Tip**
>
> You rarely need to switch a workflow's trace off because only the workflow that is started while the trace is switched on is traced. When the workflow finishes, the trace finishes too. However, the workflow trace makes the execution of the workflow very slow, so you might occasionally want to abort it manually. The same technique can be used to start a workflow trace for a workflow that has already been triggered. If you only want to trace one section of the workflow, switch the trace on for the workflow work item just before the work item that you are interested in is created.

Evaluating the Workflow Trace in SAP Systems Prior to SAP ERP

To analyze bindings, look for the `ContBindExecute` entries (or choose the binding filter from the menu), and double-click on the entries (see Figure 16.5). The log entry preceding the `ContBindExecute` entries shows the type of binding that is being performed (workflow to task, workflow to rule, method to task, etc.).

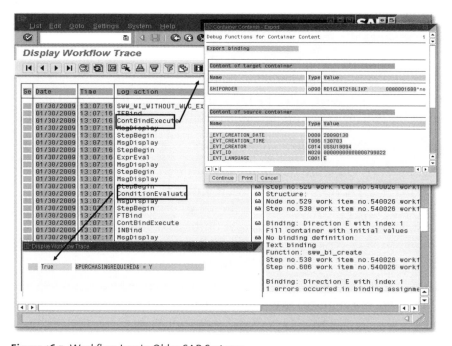

Figure 16.5 Workflow Log in Older SAP Systems

You see the source container and the target container. New entries in the target container are marked `*new*`, and modified entries are shown with their previous value and the value after the binding has executed. Table entries are shown with their index value. Structures are shown one field at a time.

> **Caution**
>
> Complex data types stored in XML format cannot be displayed in the workflow trace.

You can also use the workflow trace to analyze condition evaluation in steps that use logical expressions as part of their step definition (e.g., loop until, loop while, condition, multiple condition, conditional work item start, or completion and start conditions in the event linkage configuration). Double-clicking on Condi-tionEvaluate entries not only shows the result of the condition but also gives detailed information about how this final result was reached. You will see the container used for the condition, together with the final results, partial results of the different expressions in the condition, and any warnings and errors (e.g., "Object does not exist") that occurred during the evaluation.

Evaluating the Workflow Trace in SAP ERP

With SAP ERP (ECC 6.0), using SAP NetWeaver 7.0, the workflow trace functionality has been significantly enhanced. Transaction SWU9 is your starting point for trace initiation and evaluation. In the new release of this transaction, SAP's commitment to moving toward an object-oriented approach is evident; you will see more references to classes and persistence than in previous versions (see Figure 16.6).

To review the bindings that have been performed, look for the package SWF_BND or use the ALV filters. When you want to see the details of the binding executions, click on the DATA EXISTS column. Figure 16.7 shows a trace, with the DATA EXISTS column selected for SWF_BND. Notice the additional popup window showing more details of the binding.

You can see in Figure 16.7, the pop-up window with the binding has the object type (BUS1006) and all of the attributes in the object type. This format enables you to view the containers used for binding in the same format as the workflow logs. This is a far easier interface, after you get used to it, than the more mature SAP releases had. The SWF_BND line gives you the ability to select whether you want to see the import or exported bindings. So, as with the workflow logs, you can open a container element and view the contents in the pane below.

Figure 16.6 Workflow Trace

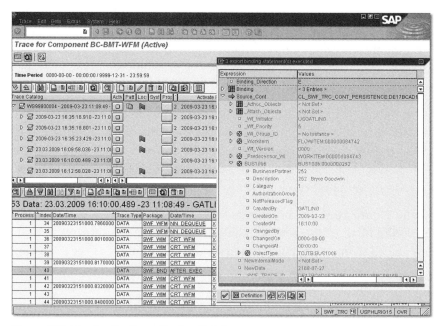

Figure 16.7 Viewing the Trace Binding Details

The new workflow trace also gives you the ability to view conditions and their outcomes via the SWF_RLS package, as opposed to searching the older trace for ConditionEvaluate. With the new workflow trace, the details of the workflow container (called the rule container within the trace) are easily visible.

16.3.2 When to Use the Workflow Trace

Symptoms worth investigating with the workflow trace:

▸ An event fails to trigger a workflow after you have evaluated the event trace for inconsistencies

▸ Inconsistent data in the workflow

▸ A workflow step does not execute after checking for short dumps and RFC errors

Starting points for investigation:

▸ Is the binding performed correctly?

▸ Is the target container being filled as you expected? Watch out for truncation problems if the elements being bound do not use matching data types.

▸ Are warnings recorded when the condition is evaluated?

Workflow trace files are deleted automatically two weeks after the last trace entry is written. The same trace mechanism is used in other parts of the system, such as for communications; so do not be alarmed to see other trace files created that are not related to workflow.

16.4 Preparing a Task to Go to Production

The best way of ensuring a smooth and trouble-free introduction of your new or changed workflow into your production environment is to vigorously test and comprehensively document the development work in advance. This is particularly true of workflow, where troubleshooting is more complicated than traditional programs, as you saw at the beginning of this chapter. And, because workflow crosses many traditional IT/business boundaries, there are usually many pieces that need to be in place for any new workflow or enhancement.

For example, are you sure the master data will be ready? Is the HR team on board with any additional requirements for agent determination? This last section reminds you of some of the duties you need to perform before going live.

There are many test utilities in the Workflow Engine, and you should take advantage of them where you can. This section shows you which tools to use in different types of tests. You can use the following sequence as a general guide for testing a typical, brand-new workflow from scratch:

- **Test the business objects.**
  Use the business object test option (accessible from the Business Object Builder (Transaction SWO1) by choosing the relevant business object) to check that all new and changed attributes are working correctly.

- **Test the methods.**
  Use the business object test option to test any new or changed object methods. This includes testing that exceptions are raised by methods in the appropriate circumstances. Unless you are testing an instance-independent method (such as "Create" or "Find"), you need to create an object instance first. This is simpler than it sounds. You simply create the business object equivalent of the application object you want to test by choosing CREATE INSTANCE from the menu bar and specifying the key of the object. This reads the tables in the SAP database for this object key to build a virtual business object equivalent that you can then test.

  Bear in mind that the methods tested are not simulated; they will really do what they are meant to do. For example, the method `PurchaseOrder.Delete` really deletes the purchase order.

Tip

If you need to debug a method, it is easiest to put a `BREAK-POINT` statement into the method itself, prior to running the test. Do not forget to remove the breakpoint afterwards. Make sure that you turn on the DEBUGGING switch (in the SETTINGS menu) before you start to debug the method.

- **Test the rule and agent determination functions.**
  Using Transaction PFAC, ensure that the rule returns agents. Development environments typically get out-of-sync with production environments, particularly in the area of person/user consistency. Make sure as you promote your

new or enhanced workflow definition, that the rules and other agent determination functions can return valid agents.

▶ **Test task/workflow consistency.**

Perform a consistency test (think of this as similar to a syntax check on a program) on the workflow and all related tasks and events using Transaction SWUD (results shown in Figure 16.8).

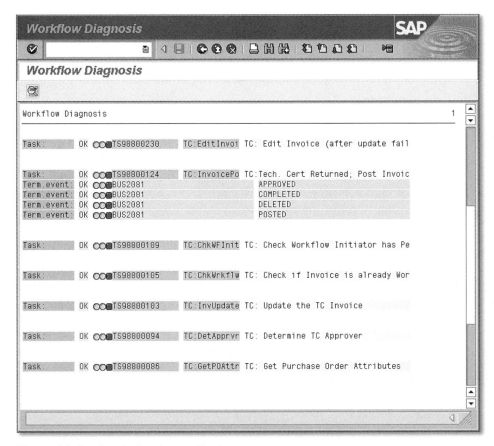

Figure 16.8 Results of a Consistency Check

▶ **Test the tasks.**

Use the START TASK tool to test each new or changed task. Make sure you have assigned yourself as a possible agent of the task first, or you will not be able to execute the task. It is good practice to test even background tasks in this way, but you need to remove the BACKGROUND PROCESSING flag from the task first, so that you can test it in dialog mode. After you are satisfied the task is working, you can replace the background flag, and test it again in background mode to ensure it still behaves correctly. If the task is asynchronous, make sure you also check that the terminating event (e.g., using the CREATE EVENT tool) completes the work item as expected.

▸ **Test the agent determination rules.**
Simulate the agent determination rules used in the workflow by using the rule simulation in the rule editor (Transaction PFAC). You can also check the results in the _RULE_RESULT container element if you have defined a return binding for the agent determination rule. It can be useful to define this binding just so that you can easily track any problems in the productive environment.

▸ **Test the conditions.**
The complex conditions used in the workflow are evaluated according to the mathematical priority of the operators, and if this is difficult for you to resolve, simply use a liberal supply of parentheses to explicitly define the order of evaluation. The rule is parsed when it is saved so the parentheses have no effect on performance. Simulate any conditions used in the workflow. The condition editor includes a powerful simulation tool that is very useful when the conditions are complex.

▸ **Test the workflow and subworkflows.**
Use the START TASK tool to test each subworkflow and then the workflow as a whole. If you are having binding problems, turning on the container monitor or the workflow trace can be useful. Do not forget to turn them off when you are finished.

> **Caution**
>
> If you are developing workflows for SAP SRM (or SAP CRM) you absolutely must make sure the container monitors are switched off. If a workflow task is performed via the web frontend, the system attempts to communicate the contents of the container back to the user. Because there is no context for this, you will get a short dump DYNPRO_SEND_IN_BACKGROUND.

▸ **Test the event linkages.**
Use SIMULATE EVENT to check that the event linkages for triggering and terminating events you are using (see Figure 16.9) are defined correctly and activated.

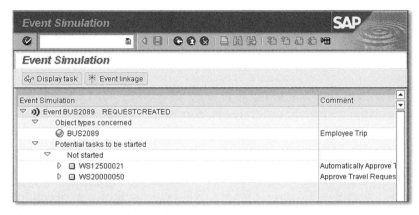

Figure 16.9 Event Simulation Check Menu

▶ **Test the triggering event manually.**
Use Create Event to trigger the events manually and the Event Trace to check that they affect your workflow in the way you expect. Simulate any start conditions (or check function modules or receiver type function modules) used to trigger the workflow. Then you should also check to ensure that no *other* workflows were unexpectedly started or terminated by these events.

▶ **Test the triggering event from the business application.**
Test the workflow by raising the events from the application. Make sure you do this for all triggering and terminating events. Hopefully, the workflow developer has done his due diligence as far as documenting the business transactions that are involved with the workflow; this makes testing and validating the business application easier.

▶ **Test the authorizations.**
Most developers in the development and QA systems have more authorization than the users in the production environment. It is essential that before going live, you test the workflow with the authorization profiles that the operational users will have.

▶ **Test error scenarios.**
After everything is working correctly, do not forget to test all possible workflow paths, including simulating error situations (e.g., by forcing the object method to send an exception) to make sure they behave as expected. You do not need to model a response to every possible error in your workflow, but it is vital that serious errors throw an exception so that if one does occur, the

default Workflow Engine error handling and the administrator can catch the error and resolve it. Be particularly careful to simulate any error situation that might be caused by neglected or incorrect data maintenance.

Ideally, when you run the CONSISTENCY CHECK (see Figure 16.8), you will see only green lights; however, some yellow lights may be acceptable. For example, in a step that sends email, you may have received a consistency check warning "Subject is too long. Maximum of 50 characters permitted." Because we already know that email subjects have a maximum of 50 characters and have used that space appropriately, this warning is of no real concern.

If you need to test deadlines in your workflow, avoid putting short test deadlines in your workflow step, which you may forget to remove later. It is better to put the real deadline times in your workflow steps. You can then check that the correct deadline time is calculated, and change the deadlines (from the work item display, choose WORK ITEM • MORE FUNCTIONS • CHANGE DEADLINES) to verify that the escalation process is working. Do not forget to check that the deadline background job has been activated (refer to Chapter 3, Configuring the System).

Upgrade projects include workflow upgrades, even if the workflow is limited to a technical-only upgrade. This chapter provides recommendations when planning and executing an upgrade.

17 Upgrading SAP Business Workflow

If this is the first chapter you are reading in this book, then you probably have several existing workflows in your production system, are planning an upgrade, and are wondering how the journey will go. This chapter gets your journey started through a discussion of recommended steps to take before your upgrade begins, steps you should take during the upgrade, and what to do after the upgrade completes.

The workflow upgrade will be successful if it has a complete project plan, including a thorough understanding of your existing workflows, setting user expectations for what will happen before and after the upgrade, creating workflow test plans, executing a proof of concept, and performing significant testing.

17.1 First Steps to Upgrading Workflow

Assessing, learning, and planning should be the very first thoughts you have when considering an upgrade and the impact to your existing workflows:

▶ **Your upgrade planning should begin with an inventory of your existing workflows.**
 You should be able to answer the following questions:

  ▷ How many workflows do you have in production?

  ▷ How often do they execute?

  ▷ How many instances of workflow are in error?

  ▷ What custom business objects have you created?

▶ How many custom attributes and methods have you created in a business object?

▶ Have you done any modifications to existing objects or other workflow functions?

▶ Have you created custom copies of SAP provided workflow templates and customized these copies?

▶ **Plan to perform a proof of concept on the upgrade.**
Your full upgrade project will probably include a mock upgrade or proof of concept upgrade on a copy of your production system. Ensure workflow is included in this effort.

Workflow testing should be performed on the most critical workflow processes. This enables you define realistic timelines and user expectations for the project.

▶ **Consider an archiving strategy before your upgrade project.**
If your existing system has been around for many years, you may have completed work items from many years ago. Archiving these work items reduces the amount of time and effort involved in the upgrade.

▶ **Leverage other customers who have already completed an upgrade.**
Your region should have a local SAP user community. Be sure to network with your regional SAP user community to find customers who have already performed their workflow upgrade. Some user groups may have a special interest group focused on workflow. Networking with other customers who have completed an upgrade is normally very insightful.

▶ **Familiarize yourself with new workflow features.**
You want to ensure you leverage what SAP delivers to the fullest extent. There is no need to create a custom feature when the feature is already provided by SAP. Doing your homework on the new workflow features can save development time.

By reading the other chapters in this book, you have started learning the new features! For the upgrade preparation, be sure to read Chapter 9, Advanced Workflow Design Techniques. This chapter covers new container and binding features that you need to understand when testing your workflows after the upgrade.

17.2 Steps to Take Before the Upgrade Begins

Planning, planning, planning is critical to your workflow upgrade. The following steps outline what should be done *before* the upgrade begins. Some steps can be started at the beginning of your planning process. For many of the steps, the earlier they start, the better!

17.2.1 Complete All Running Workflow Instances

Maybe you cannot complete all, but at least complete all of the ones you can *reasonably* complete. Completing all running workflow instances is much easier to recommend than to actually do. Many of the customer issues appearing after an upgrade are due to existing work items in the users' inboxes. You should do an evaluation to know which workflows you can reasonably complete.

Be sure to complete as many workflow instances as you possibly can. If you have long-running workflows, for example, training workflows that could take months to complete, you will not be able to complete all instances. But you should look at each workflow individually and determine which ones can and should be completed before the upgrade begins. Many short-lived approval and EDI (electronic data interchange) workflows should be completed before the upgrade.

17.2.2 Create Workflow Test Plans

Your existing workflows must be fully tested. The test plans should include full executions of each workflow you have in production:

▶ For the critical workflows, ensure you test each process scenario within the workflow (test each branch).

▶ For workflows that must be "in progress" when the upgrade happens, ensure examples of each workflow in progress are included in your test plan.

After the upgrade completes, there should be no surprises when executing a work item that was in a READY status before the upgrade began.

17.2.3 WF and T Tasks Versus WS and TS Tasks

Depending on the release you are upgrading from, you may have created WF and T tasks when creating your own workflows. If you are upgrading from a release where WF and T tasks were used, you should know that SAP recommends all workflows be based on WS and TS tasks. WS and TS tasks types are client-independent objects and recommended by SAP for all custom workflow development.

You are not required to convert your WF and T tasks to WS and TS tasks; it is recommended you do copy the T to TS and WF to WS. However, this does not have to be done before the upgrade; it can be done over time after the upgrade.

17.2.4 Clean Runtime Tables

Cleaning the runtime tables is one of the most important things you can do to help not only with the speed of the upgrade but also to ease debugging after the workflow upgrade completes. Removing the workflow runtime tables of all unnecessary data enables the upgrade to run faster. The best option is to *archive* as much workflow runtime data as possible according to SAP Note 573656.

Anytime the word *archiving* comes up, the conversation normally gets very quiet. Many customers prefer not to archive anything. The tricky part about archiving workflow is that workflow items are normally considered one part of a total archiving project. For example, if you have SAP SRM shopping basket approvals, the archiving strategy could dictate you archive the entire shopping cart and the related purchasing documents. If your company has an archiving strategy, be sure workflow is included. If not, work with your business stakeholders on a possible archiving project for your old work items.

There might also be runtime data you simply do not need any longer, for example, workflow related to EDI processing or other work items where the workflow is not subject to a business or system audit. If you have runtime data that is not needed in the future, consider deleting this data via Report RSWWWIDE (see SAP Note 49545). Be aware that once deleted, the data is no longer available. Various workflow database tables may contain unnecessary entries after you delete the work items. Therefore, it is also a good idea to run Report RSWWWIDE_DEP to remove these unnecessary entries.

SAP Note 1068627 covers all notes you should use when upgrading to SAP NetWeaver Application Server 6.40 or 7.0. Ensure *all notes* listed are applied to your system. Also ensure you review *any recommendations* contained in the notes.

17.3 Steps to Take During and After the Upgrade

This section discusses steps you should take during and after an upgrade.

17.3.1 Conversion of Event Linkage Tables

In release SAP R/3 4.6C, the instance linkage for workflow steps was stored in Table SWEINSTCOU. Beginning with release 4.7 (Basis 6.20) and onward, this information is stored in Table SWFDEVINST. During the upgrade, Report RSWFEVTXPRA moves the entries from the old table into the new table. This conversion can take a very long time. However, if you can delete and archive existing work items, the event linkage tables will be cleaned up as well.

17.3.2 Basis Support Package

After the workflow upgrade, you should apply the latest Basis 7.0 support package. The latest support package has all current fixes, and it is important that you immediately upgrade to the latest support package.

17.3.3 Configure Your System for Workflow

On completion of the workflow upgrade, it is important that you configure the upgrade system by calling up workflow customizing (Transaction SWU3). You have to define the workflow administrator configure RFC destination and schedule the workflow batch jobs. You may choose to PERFORM AUTOMATIC WORKFLOW CUSTOMIZING (🔧) or execute all activities manually with the EXECUTE button (🔧).

For more details on configuring, refer to Chapter 3, Configuring the System.

17.3.4 Workflow Definition and Binding

After you do your upgrade, you may have issues in your workflow definition and in the binding. SAP Note 1060762 discusses container operations with date fields and time fields, providing guidance on container operations that may need adjusting. You might also have Data Dictionary objects in your workflow container that are no longer valid after the upgrade. This is covered in SAP Note 1058159.

Binding checks are stricter in SAP NetWeaver 2004 and SAP NetWeaver 7.0. Binding definitions that did not error or cause problems may result in binding errors. Your workflow template containers may refer to Data Dictionary data types that no longer exist in the upgraded system. SAP Note 939489 covers the issue and recommends that you re-create the missing type ABAP Dictionary element. If this is not possible, the note also provides a program you can execute to resolve the problem.

17.3.5 Tables SWW_CONTOB and SWW_CONT

One major new change from release SAP R/3 4.7 is persistence of the workflow container. This is discussed in Chapter 9, Advanced Workflow Design Techniques. The change is the use of XML persistence. Tables SWW_CONTOB and SWW_CONT only continue to be used if you choose the "old" container persistence. When using XML persistence in your workflow, no entries are written to these tables. You can change the settings for the persistence profile of a workflow. In the Workflow Builder, select GOTO • BASIC DATA • VERSION DEPENDENT • CONTROL. Look in the PERSISTENCE PROFILE tab to change the settings.

Figure 17.1 shows the persistence options for the workflow container. XML PERSISTENCE is the new entry. The other options continue to use the SWW_CONTOB and SWW_CONT tables for container persistence.

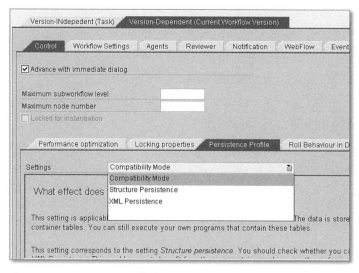

Figure 17.1 Persistence Profile for Container Storage

Entries with XML persistence are stored in Table `SWWCNTP0`. The only issue you will have with the XML persistence is custom code that reads from Tables `SWW_CONTOB` and `SWW_CONT`.

> **Recommendation**
>
> Do not change the persistence profile for existing workflows. Use the XML persistence for new workflows created after the upgrade.

17.3.6 Changed Locking Behavior of Runtime

The locking behavior at runtime has been changed in SAP NetWeaver 7.0 for synchronous dialog chain steps. The change was made to improve throughput.

Figure 17.2 shows the difference between the old and new locking mechanisms. In previous releases, when each step executes in a dialog synchronous chain, the work item ID is locked when the step is executing. The lock is enqueued when the step starts, and dequeued when the stop completes. After the first step completes, then the parent work item ID (work item ID for the WS template) is locked. The parent ID is dequeued when the next step in the chain begins. Throughout the three steps, either the parent work item ID or the TS task ID is locked. For each lock acquired and released, the lock must be enqueued and dequeued.

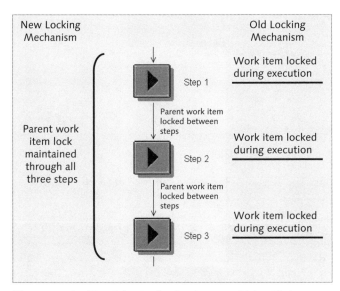

Figure 17.2 Locking Behavior for Synchronous Dialog Chains

For customers who have very high volume and require more throughput, the design was changed so that the parent work item ID is locked throughout the entire synchronous dialog chain.

Locking throughout the entire dialog chain results in faster throughput and fewer system resources consumed. However, when a workflow executes with parallel steps, sometimes the new locking can lead to locking conflicts. When this occurs, the workflow stops until the next scheduled run of the job SWWERRE to fix workflow errors.

You have the option to configure the use of the standard locking or the new locking. You configure it in the workflow definition via the menu path GO TO • BASIC DATA • VERSION DEPENDENT • CONTROL. Then select the LOCKING PROPERTIES tab. The options are shown in Figure 17.3.

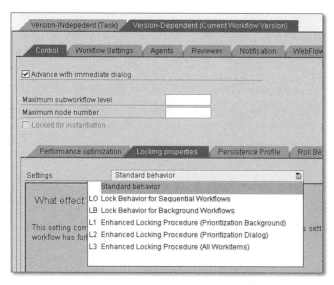

Figure 17.3 Locking Properties for a Workflow Definition

The recommendation is to use the standard behavior, which is the old locking, or the L3, ENHANCED LOCKING PROCEDURE (ALL WORKITEMS).

Recommendation

Use the standard locking unless you have a specific throughput situation where you need the enhanced locking. If enhanced locking is required, use the L3 option. Refer to SAP Note 1122756 for more details.

17.3.7 Other Issues After the Upgrade

After the upgrade completes, there are a few other issues you need to consider:

- If you stay with the SAP GUI, you need to upgrade to the latest SAP GUI release and patch level.

- After upgrade, some users find that they can no longer display the object method by clicking the link in the preview pane of Transaction SBWP (the transaction for the inbox). This also may affect the users' ability to view work item attachments or secondary methods. This is due to missing authorization of Transaction SWO_ASYNC, which is detailed in SAP Note 1006235.

- After the upgrade completes, there might be issues with deadlines, hanging workflows, and transports that were in progress before the upgrade began. Notes to assist in resolving upgrade issues are show in Table 17.1 in the following section.

- After the upgrade, you might find some objects do not work as normal. The solution for this is to generate the object and any subtypes associated with the object via Transaction SWO1.

17.4 Important SAP Notes

Table 17.1 lists important SAP Notes when it comes to upgrading.

SAP Note	Topic
Preparing for the upgrade	
1068627	Composite workflow upgrade note
573656	Collective note for archiving work items
Event linkages	
1019080, 808790	Performance during upgrade
Workflow definition and binding, conditions	
1060762	Container operation with date fields and time fields
1058159, 939489	Missing elements in the workflow container
1228836	Compatibility of conditions with date/time constants

Table 17.1 Important SAP Notes

SAP Note	Topic
Security access for SWO_ASYNC	
1006235	Authorization check for Transaction SWO_ASYNC
Deadlines, transport, and hanging workflow notes	
1092157, 1025249	Deadlines
215753	Old workflows hanging
571302	Collective note for workflow transport issues

Table 17.1 Important SAP Notes (cont.)

PART III
User Interface Technologies and SAP Business Workflow

Most of your time when designing a workflow is focused on the process: "Do I have the process right and the right people involved?" Of course, it is also critical that you consider the experience of the end user. In this chapter, we explore various UI options and discuss common threads found in all of the options.

18   User Interface Options

Normally, a task in a workflow executes specific application functionality. This functionality probably exists with or without the workflow. For example, approving purchasing documents, on-boarding employees, and updating materials all happens even if a workflow does not yet exist. However, after you have decided to use workflow, the user no longer must "find" the task because the task is routed to the right person at the right time.

When using SAP Business Workflow, you can stick with the default user interface (UI) for the function, or you can change the interface. You want to ensure the UI for executing the task is consistent with the application and the users' requirements. For example, approving a purchase requisition can be done via a traditional SAP GUI screen. For your users and your process, this may be exactly what you need. However, you may want to replace the SAP GUI to provide a different look and feel.

> **Note**
>
> This entire part of the book is devoted to the options available when enhancing UIs for SAP Business Workflow – this is *optional*. Before we start this chapter and thus Part III of the book, you should know that changing the look and feel requires *development* effort. If you only have limited development days on the project, then use the default UI of the object method assigned to the workflow task (methods are discussed in Chapter 10, Business Objects, and Chapter 11, ABAP Classes).
>
> Also, if you are new to workflow, you may want to skip to Part IV of the book that discusses how workflow is used in specific SAP Business Suite components, and return to this section when it is relevant for your project.

The major UI options discussed in this part of the book include Web Dynpro ABAP, Web Dynpro Java, Business Server Pages (BSP), SAP Interactive Forms by Adobe, Alloy, and Duet. Alloy and Duet are included in this part because they provide completely different interfaces for users to interact with work items. If you are reading this part of the book with a specific interest in Alloy or Duet, you can skip to Chapter 23, Alloy — Lotus Notes Integration, or Chapter 24, Duet — Microsoft Office Integration, respectively.

This chapter provides a general introduction into what you will see in the subsequent chapters for this part of the book. We recommend you read this chapter, followed by the chapter that best matches the UI you plan to create. However, you should be aware that this section of the book does not provide a "how-to" create Web Dynpro ABAP, Web Dynpro Java, or BSP. It is assumed you have read other books, gone through other tutorials, and already know how to create the UI. Each chapter focuses on the where and how to connect the work item ID, and where to use the workflow APIs in your custom UI.

> **Note**
>
> This part of the book covers several of the workflow APIs. These APIs are discussed in more detail in Chapter 14, Custom Programs. Please read this chapter before exploring this part of the book.

18.1 Inbox and the User Interface

Chapter 4, Work Item Delivery, discussed the inbox options available with SAP Business Workflow. The ones mentioned were Business Workplace, Universal Worklist (UWL), Extended Notifications, Business Workflow Workplace, Alloy, Duet, CRM inbox, and SRM inbox. When discussing the development of custom UIs, the three major inboxes to consider are Business Workplace, UWL, and Business Workflow Workplace.

Table 18.1 shows the three major inboxes and their support for Web Dynpro and BSP. It is important to know the inbox your users will access for work items and the impact that has on your UI choice.

User Interface Technology	Business Workplace (SAP GUI)	Universal Worklist (SAP NetWeaver Portal)	Business Workflow Workplace (SAP NetWeaver Business Client)
Web Dynpro Java	Not supported	Transaction SWFVISU to configure	Not supported
Web Dynpro ABAP	Not supported	Transaction SWFVISU to configure	Transaction SWFVMD1 to configure
BSP	Supported natively (no inbox configuration required)	Transaction SWFVISU to configure	Transaction SWFVMD1 to configure

Table 18.1 Major Inbox Options and Support for Web Dynpro and BSP

This chapter focuses on UWL because it supports Web Dynpro Java, Web Dynpro ABAP, and BSP. UWL supports other UIs as well (URL, portal content), but full coverage of UWL is beyond the scope of this book.

> **Tip**
>
> Full coverage of UWL is available in *Universal Worklist with SAP NetWeaver Portal* (SAP PRESS Essentials, 2008).

For the purposes of SAP Business Workflow, with the inclusion of UWL, workflow tasks can be executed using Web Dynpro, BSP, URLs, and portal content. The inclusion of SAP Interactive Forms by Adobe is done via Web Dynpro. When using SAP Interactive Forms for online usage, there are no specific requirements for workflow to communicate with the Adobe form; Web Dynpro handles the form and the communication with the workflow container.

As you can see in Table 18.1, using Web Dynpro with UWL requires configuration in Transaction SWFVISU. If you go to Transaction SWFVISU on your system, you may see SAP entries. The number of entries will vary by the application and the enhancement package. For the SAP-provided workflows that use Web Dynpro, no configuration is required on your side. When you register the system in UWL, all delivered entries in Transaction SWFVISU will create XML for UWL to ensure that the SAP-delivered task executes with the SAP-delivered Web Dynpro (ABAP or Java).

18.2   Containers, Bindings, and Data Flow

Chapter 8, Creating a Workflow, and Chapter 9, Advanced Workflow Design Techniques, discussed containers and binding between containers. However, it is worth a couple of words to ensure containers and bindings are understood.

Figure 18.1 shows the process flow of a workflow, with Step 1, Step 2, Step 3 (could be either branch or both branches, depending on the design), and then Step 4. As the steps execute, the workflow container holds the global variables for the entire workflow. When a step executes, that step has its own container and holds local variables. If a step returns a value (such as approve or reject) that needs to be used in a later step, the work item container for the step binds the value into the workflow container.

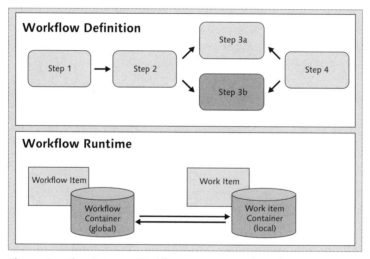

Figure 18.1 Flow Between Workflow Container and Work Item Container

18.2.1   Where the Customized UI Fits in with the Data Flow When Using Universal Worklist

Figure 18.2 shows where your customized UI fits in and how it relates to the containers. This is true for both SAP-delivered workflows that use Web Dynpro and BSP and custom built workflows. The workflow container automatically passes data to the work item container. The task then appears in UWL. UWL is customized to use the appropriate launch handler (e.g., Web Dynpro ABAP or Web Dynpro Java) to launch your UI.

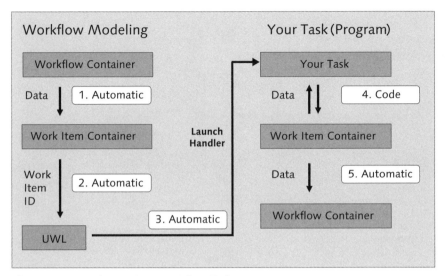

Figure 18.2 Launching a Custom UI for a Task

Figure 18.3 describes the data flow between the workflow container and your UI:

▸ The workflow container *binds* the data from the workflow container to the work item container.

▸ When the task is created, the work item appears in the inbox.

▸ The passing of the data and work item ID to the UWL is done automatically.

▸ The UWL then launches the customized UI for the task. This is done automatically, based on the settings made in Transaction SWFVISU.

▸ After your Web Dynpro or BSP is launched, the work item is received by the UI, and the UI must read the container using the workflow APIs (SAP_WAPI*). This is done via code development.

▸ The workflow APIs must be used to read (and update) the workflow container information, as well as update the work item status when completed. This ensures the workflow knows the step has completed and moves on to the next step in the workflow.

> **Note**
>
> Your UI *must* communicate with the work item container. This is done using the workflow application programming interface (WAPI) as discussed in Chapter 14, Custom Programs. The work item container then automatically updates the workflow container.

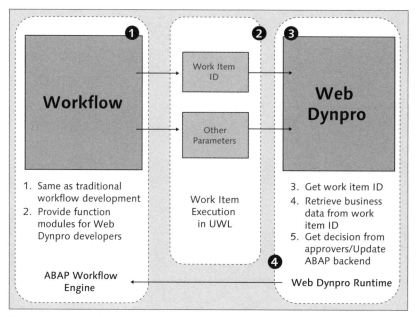

Figure 18.3 Data Flow with Web Dynpro and SAP Business Workflow

Figure 18.3 mentions in Step 2, "Provide function modules for Web Dynpro developers." This could be the case if the Web Dynpro developers require a specific function to call, or if you prefer to have wrapper function modules around the provided workflow APIs. You will see an example of this in Chapter 20, Using Web Dynpro Java.

18.2.2 Common Steps When Using Web Dynpro and Business Server Pages with Universal Worklist

Following are the common steps used when using Web Dynpro and BSP with UWL:

1. The UI must receive the work item identifier, WI_ID, as an input parameter.

2. The UI executes SAP_WAPI_GET_HEADER (or detail), SAP_WAPI_RESERVE_WORK_ITEM, and SAP_WAPI_READ_CONTAINER to retrieve data from the WI_ID.

> **Hint**
>
> You *must* call SAP_WAPI_RESERVE_WORK_ITEM. Normally the Workflow Engine makes sure that only one user can launch a work item. That is not true for Web Dynpro work items from UWL. The results from the RESERVE workflow API must be checked:

▶ If the return is OK, then you can continue.

▶ If the return is not OK, this means someone else is already working on the work item.

3. The UI displays the details, for example, details for an approval into a screen.

4. After the user completes the task in the UI, the UI executes `SAP_WAPI_WORKITEM_COMPLETE` to complete the work item. This includes updating the workflow container with any results or values needed from the UI execution.

> **Hint**
>
> When completing a work item, there are two options: complete the work item via the `SAPI_WAPI` directly, or publish an event that terminates the task. Chapter 13, Using Events and Other Business Interfaces, and Chapter 14, Custom Programs, discuss terminating events.

5. Configure Transaction SWFVISU to map the specific task (`TS`) to the UI. Re-register the system in UWL after this is complete for the UWL to generate the XML required to launch the task.

When linking the UI to the UWL, there are three options to create the required XML:

▶ Transaction SWFVISU.

▶ UWL configuration wizard.

▶ Manually creating the XML.

In the upcoming chapters in this part of the book, you may see some sections refer to Transaction SWFVISU, some refer to manually changing the XML, and others refer to the UWL configuration wizard. All three are valid ways to create the required XML. The UWL configuration wizard, however, is the newest way and is explained briefly in Chapter 4, Work Item Delivery. It is also explained in detail in the SAP Help Portal (*http://help.sap.com*).

> **Recommendation**
>
> When changing the task visualization (customizing what is launched for a particular task), use Transaction SWFVISU. SAP applications (e.g., SAP CRM, SAP SRM, and SAP ERP HCM) deliver content in Transaction SWFVISU out-of-the-box. Maintaining all task visualization changes in Transaction SWFVISU provides a central location to see all launch handlers and is easier to maintain than manual XML changes.

User decision steps are very common in SAP Business Workflow. This chapter discusses options for user decision steps and then shows the major touchpoints that exist between user decisions using Web Dynpro ABAP and the user decision step type in SAP Business Workflow.

19   Using Web Dynpro ABAP

Web Dynpro ABAP usage in the SAP Business Suite and among customers is growing fast. It definitely makes sense to use Web Dynpro ABAP with SAP Business Workflow if you are using an application from the SAP Business Suite that uses Web Dynpro ABAP, or if you are beginning to develop user interfaces with Web Dynpro ABAP.

This chapter uses Universal Worklist (UWL) as the inbox for the work item. The example in this chapter is based on the following workflow process:

1. A requestor enters a request for business partner creation.

2. An approver approves or rejects the new business partner.

3. If the business partner is approved, the business partner is created. In either case, a notification is sent to the requestor.

4. The focus of this chapter is on Step 2, creation of the user decision. This chapter assumes this is the first step being worked on, and the first goal is to get a very basic user decision displayed in Web Dynpro ABAP. For this scenario, we want to provide a simple YES/NO choice with a reason for the choice.

> **Note**
>
> This chapter assumes some basic workflow, UWL, and Web Dynpro ABAP knowledge. You should have already read the chapters on Work Item Delivery (Chapter 4), Creating a Workflow (Chapter 8), and User Interface Options (Chapter 18). Additionally, you should already have some experience creating Web Dynpro ABAP applications. This example does not walk through "how to build" a Web Dynpro ABAP application. Instead, we focus on the link between Web Dynpro ABAP and the workflow.

19.1 Example Based on User Decision

The user decision step is very commonly used in SAP Business Workflow. The workflows you created in the previous chapters of this book included user decisions. The user decision is an ACTIVITY type that is simple to use and has many use cases. Any time you have a process where you require intervention from the user to know what the process should do next, the user decision is the perfect choice. Before showing the required steps to have Web Dynpro ABAP display the user decision, let's look at other options available when using a user decision.

19.1.1 Standard User Decision

One option is to use the standard user decision as it is, out-of-the-box. In this case the entire work item is handled in UWL, using standard functions. You can see how this user decision works by executing your task from the workflow you created in Chapter 8, Creating a Workflow. Chapter 8 walked through all of the necessary steps to build your workflow with a user decision.

When you execute a basic user decision work item in UWL, it looks like Figure 19.1.

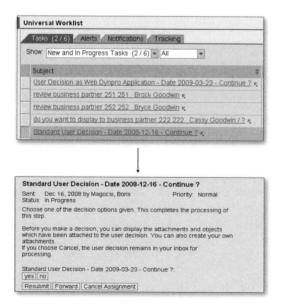

Figure 19.1 Basic User Decision Step in UWL

19.1.2 User Decision with Note in Universal Worklist

With UWL, the USER DECISION WITH NOTE option requires the user to enter a reason for the decision. This option is provided by XML customization with UWL. It is not tied to the decision activity step in SAP Business Workflow or to Web Dynpro. An example of this was also shown in Chapter 4, Work Item Delivery.

> **Hint**
>
> UWL supports two features for adding notes:
> - The first is called ADD MEMO. This action can be added for any step where the user adds comments, and it is passed to subsequent steps.
> - The second is USER DECISION WITH NOTE. This applies specifically to the user decision activity step and can be used to *require* the user to add text (e.g., to enforce a rejection reason).

To implement the USER DECISION WITH NOTE, no change is required in your workflow; you just need to have a workflow with a user decision step. To implement the USER DECISION WITH NOTE, you need to create the XML in Listing 19.1 and load it into UWL using the UWL administration area. This was discussed in Chapter 4, Work Item Delivery.

> **Note**
>
> When you create your XML, be sure to update the `systemId="W64"` to be your system ID.

```xml
<?xml version="1.0" encoding="UTF-8"?>
<!DOCTYPE UWLConfiguration PUBLIC '-//SAP//UWL1.0//EN'
 'uwl_configuration.dtd'>
<UWLConfiguration version="1.0">
<ItemTypes>
  <ItemType name="uwl.task.webflow.decision.TS00008267"
   connector="WebFlowConnector" defaultView="DefaultView"
   defaultAction="viewDetail" executionMode="default">
  <ItemTypeCriteria systemId="W64" externalType="TS00008267"
   connector="WebFlowConnector"/>
  <Actions>
    <Action name="Yes" groupAction="yes"
     handler="UserDecisionHandler"
     returnToDetailViewAllowed="yes"
```

```
        launchInNewWindow="no">
        <Properties>
        <Property name="UserDecisionNote" value="true"/>
        <Property name="decisionKey" value="1"/> </Properties>
        <Descriptions default="Yes"/>
        </Action>
        <Action name="No" groupAction="yes"
         handler="UserDecisionHandler"
         returnToDetailViewAllowed="yes"
         launchInNewWindow="no">
        <Properties>
        <Property name="UserDecisionNote" value="mandatory"/>
        <Property name="decisionKey" value="2"/>
        </Properties>
        <Descriptions default="No"/>
        </Action>
      </Actions>
      </ItemType>
    </ItemTypes>
    </UWLConfiguration>
```

Listing 19.1 Customized XML for User Decision with Note Feature in Universal Worklist

---

Note

The XML listing in Listing 19.1 uses the default user decision task, TS00008267. This means if you load this XML, then *every* user decision in *every* workflow will use this XML to execute a USER DECISION WITH NOTE. If you only need the USER DECISION WITH NOTE implemented for some workflows, then you should copy the SAP user decision task, TS00008267, to your own task and use this customized task in your workflow.

Creating a copy of the standard user decision task is discussed in Appendix A, Tips and Tricks: You just copy the standard task to your own custom task (Transaction PFTC_COP) and assign possible agents. Then in your workflow, insert a user decision step as normal, and switch the TS definition from TS00008267 to your custom task in the CONTROL tab. And don't forget to do agent assignment for the task.

Notice the XML in Listing 19.1 states that when the decisionKey has a value of 2, a note is required. The value 2 relates to the rejection value in the user decision step. Normally, when you enter decision choices in the user decision activity step, the first choice corresponds to a value of 0001, the second value is 0002, and so on.

Figure 19.2 shows a user decision step defined in a workflow. To get the exact values of each decision, you can execute function module SAP_WAPI_DECISION_

READ against any work item based on a user decision task in the relevant work-flow task. You then take those values and use them in your XML.

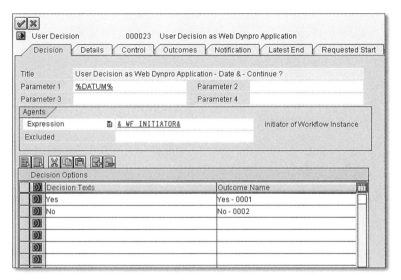

Figure 19.2 User Decision Activity Step

The following steps are what you need to load the customized XML:

1. Navigate to the UWL configuration in the portal by selecting SYSTEM ADMINISTRATION • SYSTEM CONFIGURATION • UNIVERSAL WORKLIST.

2. Select CLICK TO MANAGE ITEM TYPES AND VIEW DEFINITIONS.

3. Upload this XML by selecting the UPLOAD NEW CONFIGURATION tab, entering a name such as UserDecisionMemo, linking to the file you created, selecting HIGH PRIORITY, and selecting UPLOAD.

4. After you upload the XML, you will see it in the CURRENT CONFIGURATION tab.

5. Return to the UWL administration page, and select to CLEAR the UWL cache from the CACHE ADMINISTRATION page.

After you do these steps, when you execute your workflow, the decision step work item in UWL will look like Figure 19.3. The note is added and passed to the next step in that appears in UWL automatically. The subsequent work items in UWL will have an option to look at the note added in previous steps.

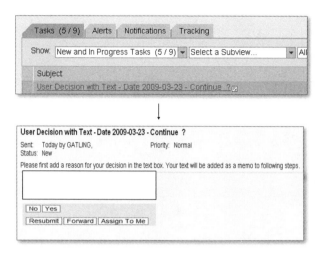

Figure 19.3 User Decision with Note Option

You may be thinking, this is nice, but what does this have to do with Web Dynpro ABAP? It is important for you to understand options with user decisions for several reasons:

▶ User decisions are used in many workflows.

▶ Many times, standard decisions need to be customized.

▶ You can use custom user decisions in UWL without using Web Dynpro.

▶ User decisions provide good context when learning new things to do with workflow.

19.1.3 User Decision with Web Dynpro ABAP

Now we can finally get to implementing the user decision in the workflow with Web Dynpro ABAP. When doing the user decision with Web Dynpro ABAP, you have two options:

▶ Keep the user decision exactly as is in the Business Workflow, using the standard task (TS00008267) as the user decision.

> **Warning**
>
> This means the customization applies to *every* workflow where there is a user decision step.

▸ Create your own copy of the SAP task (TS0008267). This task can be customized to hold the decision text in the workflow container

Recommendation

If you are customizing the user decision task in any way, you should copy the task for use in the specific workflows where you need the customization.

Figure 19.4 shows the user decision executed with Web Dynpro ABAP modification. In this example, the decision includes a reason that is passed back to the workflow container.

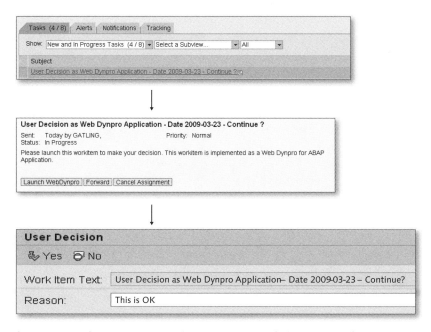

Figure 19.4 Web Dynpro ABAP and User Decision, Including Return of a Reason

Notice Figure 19.4 has the work item in the UWL, the description including the button to launch the Web Dynpro, and the Web Dynpro with the ability to pass back a reason for the decision.

In the previous example, when using the USER DECISION WITH NOTE in UWL, we used the XML configuration in the UWL to save a reason for the decision as a note attachment in the workflow container. The previous example works with UWL, passing the reason to the next step. What if we wanted to save the reason entered in a custom table or the workflow container so we could use it for some other purpose later in the workflow? For example, we want to take the reason to use it in a later Web Dynpro or BSP.

If you want complete flexibility with how to use the reason given for the decision, you need the reason entered in the workflow container. If you want to do this, then you need to copy the standard user decision task, create your own, and enhance the container to save a text reason for the decision. The example we will show you has the user decision task copied with the container extended to hold the reason entered.

Figure 19.5 shows a copy of the user decision task. In this example, notice the REASON added to the work item container. The REASON holds the reason for the decision. The container field is based on a text data type. If you look closely, you will also notice the task object is based on a subtype of the DECISION object type. Most workflow consultants recommend that you create a subtype of the DECISION object provided by SAP and use the subtype for all customizations. The key here is that you can extend the task used by the workflow with additional container elements and pass back information from Web Dynpro to those container elements.

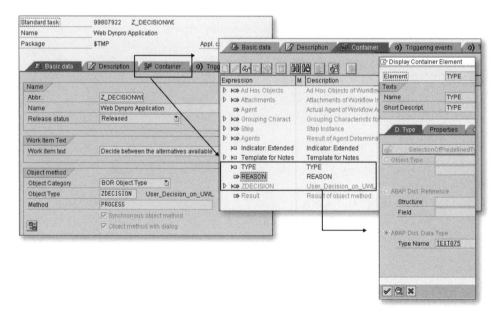

Figure 19.5 Copied User Decision Task with Extended Container to Hold Reason for the Decision

> **Hint**
>
> Do *not* define a systemwide delegation when you create a subtype of `DECISION` to `ZDECISION` because the `DECISION` object is used as the standard user decision that is used in all workflows, and the delegation might have a negative impact on the other workflows.

At this point, you have a workflow with a user decision that is either based on the standard user decision or based on an extension of the SAP-provided user decision.

19.2 Required Settings in Web Dynpro ABAP

In this section, we will look at a Web Dynpro example for the user decision, showing the major changes made to communicate with workflow. As mentioned in Chapter 18, User Interface Options, Web Dynpro has the responsibility to:

▶ Receive the work item identifier, `WI_ID`, as an input parameter.

▶ Execute `SAP_WAPI_GET_HEADER` (or detail), `SAP_WAPI_RESERVE_WORK_ITEM`, and `SAP_WAPI_READ_CONTAINER` to retrieve data from the `WI_ID`.

▶ Display the detail of the task, which is, in this example, a window in the Web Dypro application.

▶ Execute `SAP_WAPI_WORKITEM_COMPLETE` to complete the work item. If the user decision has the ability to pass back the reason, this should also include updating the `REASON` field.

In addition to Web Dynpro, you also need to configure Transaction SWFVISU to map the specific task (`TS`) to the UI. Re-register the system in UWL after this is complete for the UWL to generate the XML required to launch the task.

Let's look at the impact of these requirements on Web Dynpro ABAP. The next sections look at the required settings in various parts of Web Dynpro, including the Web Dynpro application, the Window, the View, and the required Context.

19.2.1 Web Dynpro ABAP Application

When creating the Web Dynpro application, you need to have work item `WI_ID` as an input parameter and have a `START` plug. Figure 19.6 shows an example of a Web Dynpro ABAP application. In this situation, we have the `WI_ID` defined as a string and an input parameter. There is also a START plug for the PLUG NAME. The START plug uses SAP_WAPI_RESERVE_WORKITEM, SAP_WAPI_GET_HEADER, and SAP_WAPI_READ_CONTAINER.

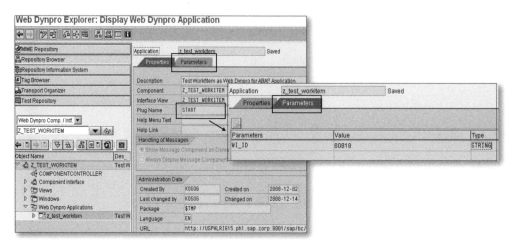

Figure 19.6 WI_ID as Input Parameter and START Plug

The handlestart method for the START plug is show in Listing 19.2. The job of the start plug is to use the work item ID to read data from the work item container and to reserve the work item.

```
METHOD handlestart .
  DATA: lo_node                TYPE REF TO if_wd_context_node,
        lr_current_controller  TYPE REF TO if_wd_controller,
        lr_message_manager     TYPE REF TO if_wd_message_manager.
  DATA lv_wi_id                 TYPE sww_wiid.
  DATA lv_parameter             TYPE symsgv.
  DATA ls_workitem_attributes   TYPE swr_wihdr.
  DATA lv_new_status            TYPE swr_wistat.
  DATA lt_simple_container      TYPE TABLE OF swr_cont.
  DATA lv_container_line        TYPE swr_cont.
  DATA lv_return_code           TYPE syst-subrc.

* When the user launches the work item from the UWL in the
* PORTAL, then the Portal is calling the Web Dynpro Application
* with the Import Parameter WI_ID
  CALL METHOD wd_context->get_child_node
    EXPORTING
```

```
            name        = 'WORKFLOWRAWDATA'
        RECEIVING
          child_node = lo_node.
*   Store this work item in the CONTEXT,
*   so that it is available for the Window and the View
      lo_node->set_attribute( value = wi_id name = 'WI_ID' ).
*   Type transfer of the work item ID for function calls
      lv_wi_id = wi_id.
*   Check that the work item still has the correct status
      CALL FUNCTION 'SAP_WAPI_RESERVE_WORKITEM'
        EXPORTING
          workitem_id = lv_wi_id
        IMPORTING
          new_status  = lv_new_status
          return_code = lv_return_code.
      IF lv_return_code NE 0.
        lr_current_controller ?= wd_this->wd_get_api( ).
        CALL METHOD lr_current_controller->get_message_manager
          RECEIVING
            message_manager = lr_message_manager.
        lv_parameter = lv_wi_id.
        CALL METHOD lr_message_manager->report_t100_message
          EXPORTING
            msgid = 'SWR'
            msgno = '210'
            msgty = 'E'
            p1    = lv_parameter
            p2    = space
            p3    = space
            p4    = space.
      ELSE.
        CALL FUNCTION 'SAP_WAPI_GET_HEADER'
          EXPORTING
            workitem_id         = lv_wi_id
          IMPORTING
            workitem_attributes = ls_workitem_attributes
            return_code         = lv_return_code.
*
        CALL METHOD wd_context->get_child_node
          EXPORTING
            name        = 'WORKITEMDATA'
          RECEIVING
```

```
              child_node = lo_node.
* Store header data in CONTEXT
    lo_node->set_attribute(
            value = ls_workitem_attributes-wi_text
            name = 'WI_TEXT' ).
    lo_node->set_attribute(
            value = ls_workitem_attributes-wi_cd
            name = 'WI_CD' ).
  ENDIF.
* Read work item container
  CLEAR lt_simple_container.
  CLEAR lv_container_line.
  REFRESH lt_simple_container.
  CALL FUNCTION 'SAP_WAPI_READ_CONTAINER'
    EXPORTING
      workitem_id                    = lv_wi_id
    IMPORTING
      return_code                    = lv_return_code
*     IFS_XML_CONTAINER              =
*     IFS_XML_CONTAINER_SCHEMA       =
    TABLES
      simple_container               = lt_simple_container.
  LOOP AT lt_simple_container INTO lv_container_line
    WHERE element = 'TYPE'.
    EXIT.
  ENDLOOP.
  CALL METHOD wd_context->get_child_node
    EXPORTING
      name     = 'CONTAINER'
    RECEIVING
      child_node = lo_node.
* Store in CONTEXT
  lo_node->set_attribute(
          value = lv_container_line-value
          name = 'TYPE' ).
ENDMETHOD.
```

Listing 19.2 Code for the START Plug

19.2.2 Window

In the Window developed in Figure 19.7, you can see the MAIN view and the START plug. The START plug is associated with the handlestart method. As shown in Listing 19.2, the `handlestart` method has the workflow APIs (WAPIs) to read from the workflow container.

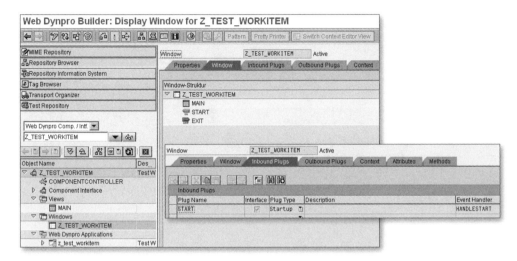

Figure 19.7 Web Dynpro Window

The method depends on the controller context definition and mapping of the context to the window and the view. The critical context is shown in Figure 19.8. Notice the work item ID (`WI_ID`), the work item data (`WI_TEXT`, `WI_CD`), and the reason that will be passed back to the work item container (`TEXT`).

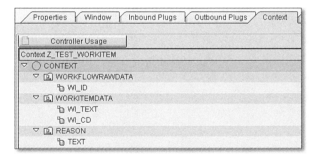

Figure 19.8 Context with the Work Item ID

19.2.3 Main View

The last piece we need to look at is the `MAIN` view, including the layout, actions, and methods. Figure 19.9 shows the most important parts. The Layout tab has the view for how the Web Dynpro will look to the user. The information is from the context where the work item text is passed to the view. The view allows a user to enter a reason, which is passed back to the workflow.

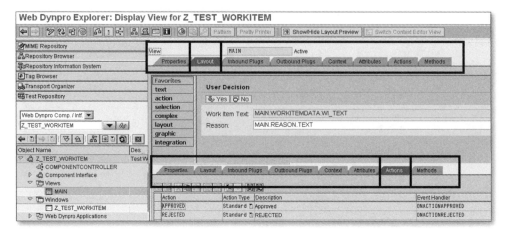

Figure 19.9 View Definition

The important code from this MAIN view is the code related to the actions tied to the YES and No buttons: APPROVED is tied to the YES button; REJECTED to the No button.

The code for the actions approved and rejected look very familiar (see Listing 19.3 and Listing 19.4). The key elements for both include passing the text back and the result from the decision. Notice the approved method passes back 001, and the rejected method passes back 002. The numbers associated with the user decision were discussed in Section 19.1.2, User Decision with Note in Universal Worklist. It mentioned the use of SAP_WAPI_DECISION_READ to know the number associated with each possible decision.

```
METHOD onactionapproved .
  DATA lo_node               TYPE REF TO if_wd_context_node.
  DATA lv_wi_id              TYPE sww_wiid.
  DATA lv_text               TYPE text075.
  DATA lt_simple_container   TYPE TABLE OF swr_cont.
  DATA lv_container_line     TYPE swr_cont.
  DATA lv_new_status         TYPE sww_wistat.
  DATA lv_return_code        TYPE syst-subrc.
```

```abap
* Get work item from Context
  CALL METHOD wd_context->get_child_node
    EXPORTING      name      = 'WORKFLOWRAWDATA'
    RECEIVING      child_node = lo_node.
  lo_node->get_attribute(
          EXPORTING name  = 'WI_ID'
          IMPORTING value = lv_wi_id  ).
* Get reason from Context
  CALL METHOD wd_context->get_child_node
    EXPORTING      name      = 'REASON'
    RECEIVING      child_node = lo_node.
  lo_node->get_attribute(
        EXPORTING name  = 'TEXT'
        IMPORTING value = lv_text  ).
* Prepare work item container
  CLEAR   lt_simple_container. REFRESH lt_simple_container.
* Export text
  lv_container_line-element = 'REASON'.
  lv_container_line-value   = lv_text.
  APPEND lv_container_line TO lt_simple_container.
* Tell workflow to go down the "YES" branch
  lv_container_line-element = '_RESULT'.
  lv_container_line-value   = '0001'.
  APPEND lv_container_line TO lt_simple_container.
  lv_container_line-element = '_WI_RESULT'.
  lv_container_line-value   = '0001'.
  APPEND lv_container_line TO lt_simple_container.
* Change work item status
  CALL FUNCTION 'SAP_WAPI_WORKITEM_COMPLETE'
    EXPORTING
      workitem_id      = lv_wi_id
    IMPORTING
      return_code      = lv_return_code
      new_status       = lv_new_status
    TABLES
      simple_container = lt_simple_container.
* Exit from Web Dynpro
  data: l_ref_exit_plug  type REF TO ig_z_test_workitem.
  l_ref_exit_plug      = wd_this->get_z_test_workitem_ctr( ).
  l_ref_exit_plug->fire_exit_plg( ).
ENDMETHOD.
```

Listing 19.3 Approved Method

The method for the rejection is the same as for the approval. The only difference is the setting of the result value, which is shown in Listing 19.4.

```
* Tell Workflow to go down the "NO" branch
  lv_container_line-element = '_RESULT'.
  lv_container_line-value   = '0002'.
  APPEND lv_container_line TO lt_simple_container.
  lv_container_line-element = '_WI_RESULT'.
  lv_container_line-value   = '0002'.
  APPEND lv_container_line TO lt_simple_container.
```
Listing 19.4 Rejected Method

The Web Dynpro workflow requirements are now in place. You can test the Web Dynpro at this point. The easiest way to do this is to start a workflow with a user decision in it, get the work item ID for the user decision step (from the inbox, discussed in Chapter 4, Work Item Delivery, or the workflow logs, discussed in Chapter 6, Workflow Administration), and manually add it as a hard-coded value in the PARAMETERS tab of the Web Dynpro application. Normally, the work item ID is passed as a variable at runtime, and you launch the Web Dynpro from UWL. However, if you want to test the Web Dynpro from Transaction SE80, then you need to hard code in a work item ID from an existing workflow.

19.3 Configuration for the Universal Worklist

Now that you have a Web Dynpro that can execute a work item, you need to ensure UWL knows to execute the Web Dynpro. To do this, use Transaction SWFVISU. Create a new entry that provides the task, and link it to your web Dynpro (see Figure 19.10). In the UWL administration page, re-register your system, and then clear the cache.

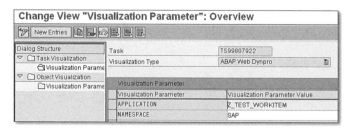

Figure 19.10 Transaction SWFVISU

If you want to see the XML that was generated with the registration reading Transaction SWFVISU, you need to go to the UWL administration area (SYSTEM ADMINISTRATION • SYSTEM CONFIGURATION • UNIVERSAL WORKLIST). You then must select CLICK TO MANAGE ITEM TYPES AND VIEW DEFINITIONS. In the view definitions, you can see all custom views and all XML files. Changes made in Transaction SWFVISU are written to the XML file `uwl.webflow.<SID>`. By looking in the configuration file `uwl.webflow.<SID>`, you can find the XML specific for your task and all tasks updated in Transaction SWFVISU.

Optionally, you can "overwrite" these settings with your own XML file, which then should have a high priority. At runtime, UWL starts searching for work item definitions in the files with a high priority first and stops with the first definition found.

In Listing 19.5, you see the definition for the task that was generated based on the settings in Transaction SWFVISU.

```
<ItemType name="uwl.task.webflow.TS99807922.W64"
 connector="WebFlowConnector" defaultView="DefaultView"
 defaultAction="launchWebDynPro" executionMode="default">
      <ItemTypeCriteria systemId="W64"
       externalType="TS99807922" connector="WebFlowConnector"/>
      <Actions>
        <Action name="launchWebDynPro" groupAction=""
         handler="SAPWebDynproABAPLauncher"
         returnToDetailViewAllowed="yes"
         launchInNewWindow="yes"
         launchNewWindowFeatures="resizable=yes,scrollbars=yes,
         status=yes,toolbar=no,menubar=no,location=no,
         directories=no">
<Properties>
        <Property name="WebDynproApplication"
        value="Z_TEST_WORKITEM"/>
           <Property name="newWindowFeatures"
            value="resizable=yes,scrollbars=yes,status=yes,
            toolbar=no,menubar=no,location=no,
            directories=no"/>
           <Property name="openInNewWindow" value="yes"/>
           <Property name="WebDynproNamespace" value="SAP"/>
           <Property name="display_order_priority" value="5"/>
        </Properties>
        <Descriptions default=""/>
```

```
        </Action>
      </Actions>
    </ItemType>
```

Listing 19.5 UWL XML to Launch Web Dynpro ABAP

The end result is a user decision in UWL, shown back in Figure 19.4, executed with Web Dynpro ABAP. After you know the touchpoints, you can then use Web Dynpro ABAP for many workflow tasks.

19.4 Ensuring the User Only Executes the Work Item in the Universal Worklist

If you are transitioning from using the SAP Business Workplace in the SAP GUI to execute work items to using UWL, then you may want to ensure the users do not execute the user decision from SAP Business Workplace. SAP Business Workplace does not support Web Dynpro ABAP, so to ensure the users execute your Web Dynpro, you might want to stop them from executing it from the SAP GUI.

To do this, insert the following code into your customized user decision task, based on business object ZDECISION. The code in Listing 19.6 should be added to the PROCESS method. This code executes if the task is launched from the Business Workplace in the SAP GUI and asks the user to execute the task from UWL.

```
begin_method process changing container.
call function 'POPUP_TO_INFORM'
  exporting
    titel = 'Warning'
    txt1 = 'Work item may only be launched from Portal UWL.'
    txt2 = 'This work item will stay in your Inbox.'.
* Prevent user from executing this work item from the SAP GUI
exit_return 9001 'Work item may only be launched from Portal UWL'
space space space.
exit_cancelled.
end_method.
```

Listing 19.6 Code to Ensure User Only Executes Decision from the Universal Worklist

> **Note**
>
> When the work item is launched from UWL, this ZDECISION method is never executed at all. UWL launches the Web Dynpro application as it was defined in the XML file.

The Web Dynpro Java option with SAP Business Workflow makes sense if you have Java skills, or if you are working with an application that uses Web Dynpro Java as the major user interface. This chapter discusses the major touchpoints between Web Dynpro Java and SAP Business Workflow.

20 Using Web Dynpro Java

When creating a Web Dynpro Java application to work with SAP Business Workflow, there are three areas to consider:

1. What must be done on the workflow side
2. What must be done on the Java side
3. What must be done for Universal Worklist (UWL) to call Web Dynpro

This chapter walks through each of these areas, focusing on the critical parts in each area.

> **Note**
>
> This chapter assumes some basic workflow, UWL, and Web Dynpro Java knowledge. You should have already read the chapters on Work Item Delivery (Chapter 4), Creating a Workflow (Chapter 8), and User Interface Options (Chapter 18). Additionally, you should already have some experience creating Web Dynpro Java applications. This example does not walk through "how to build" a Web Dynpro Java application. Instead, we focus on the link between Web Dynpro Java and the workflow.

20.1 Real-World Example of Web Dynpro Java and Workflow

This example is based on a business partner approval scenario with Web Dynpro Java. The three major development areas required for this scenario are SAP Business Workflow, Web Dynpro Java, and XML for UWL:

593

1. Requesters create a request for a business partner creation from a custom Web Dynpro Java application.

2. The request is routed to an approver, and the approver executes the work item from UWL to approve or reject the work item.

3. On approval, a business partner is created in the background mode, and a notification is sent out to the requester. If rejected, a notification is sent out to the requester.

Figure 20.1 shows the workflow that will be used for this scenario.

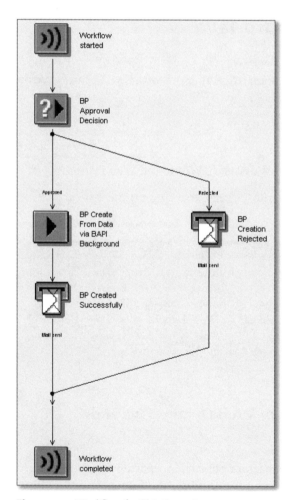

Figure 20.1 Workflow for This Scenario

Web Dynpro Java development might be quite challenging in the beginning if you are new to this area. It requires specific setup and configuration on the Java EE 5 side. If possible, you may want to install the SAP NetWeaver Application Server Java engine on your own desktop so that you can deploy Web Dynpro Java to your local Java engine to perform unit testing. The technical configuration required for a local installation of the Java engine to be able to develop and create with Web Dynpro Java is covered in Appendix E, Preparation for Java Development.

20.2 What Must Be Done on the Workflow Side

In this scenario, a workflow is started from a Web Dynpro Java screen. After a user enters the detail of a business partner to be created, the user clicks on a SUBMIT button in the Web Dynpro Java screen. The SUBMIT button calls the function module SAP_WAPI_START_WORKFLOW that starts the workflow. In this case, the workflow is started, rather than triggered by events.

The SAP_WAPI_START_WORKFLOW function module has the table parameter INPUT_CONTAINER. The detail data (e.g., business partner type, address, etc.) entered for the business partner is passed to the workflow via this parameter.

Often when calling the SAP_WAPI function modules, the workflow developer provides wrapper function modules for the call. This section explains three wrapper function modules created by the workflow developer for the Java developer:

▶ Function module to start the workflow from the initial business partner request screen (SAP_WAPI_START_WORKFLOW)

▶ Function module to read data from the workflow container in the approval step (SAP_WAPI_READ_CONTAINER)

▶ Function module to complete the work item after the approval/rejection (SAP_WAPI_WORK_ITEM_COMPLETE)

Listing 20.1 is the first wrapper function module provided to the Web Dynpro Java developer. The Web Dynpro Java developer creates an RFC model in the Web Dynpro application by using this function module to develop the business partner REQUEST screen. Notice that the metadata in the function module (input, export parameters) is used in the development of the request screen layout in the Web Dynpro.

```
FUNCTION Z_BP_REQUEST.
*"----------------------------------------------------------
*"*"Local Interface:
*"  IMPORTING
*"     VALUE(IV_BPTYPE) TYPE  BAPIBUS1006_HEAD-PARTN_CAT OPTIONAL
*"     VALUE(IV_FIRST_NAME) TYPE  BUT000-NAME_FIRST OPTIONAL
*"     VALUE(IV_LAST_NAME) TYPE  BUT000-NAME_LAST OPTIONAL
*"     VALUE(IV_COMPANY_NAME) TYPE  BUT000-NAME_ORG1 OPTIONAL
*"     VALUE(IV_SEARCH_TERM) TYPE  BUT000-BU_SORT1 OPTIONAL
*"     VALUE(IV_HOUSE_NO) TYPE  BAPIBUS1006_ADDRESS-HOUSE_NO OPTIONAL
*"     VALUE(IV_ADDRESS) TYPE  ADDR1_DATA-STREET OPTIONAL
*"     VALUE(IV_CITY) TYPE  ADDR1_DATA-CITY1 OPTIONAL
*"     VALUE(IV_STATE) TYPE  ADDR1_DATA-REGION OPTIONAL
*"     VALUE(IV_ZIP_CODE) TYPE  ADDR1_DATA-POST_CODE1 OPTIONAL
*"     VALUE(IV_COUNTRY) TYPE  ADDR1_DATA-COUNTRY OPTIONAL
*"  EXPORTING
*"     VALUE(EV_WI_ID) TYPE  SWW_WIID
*"----------------------------------------------------------

  data: lv_work_itemid type SWW_WIID.
  data: lv_retuRN_CODE TYPE  SYSUBRC.
  data: lt_simple_container TYPE STANDARD TABLE OF swr_cont
                            WITH HEADER LINE.

*-> Pass detail to the Container parameter
  move 'BPTYPE' to lt_simple_container-element.
  move IV_BPTYPE to lt_simple_container-value.
  append lt_simple_container.

  IF IV_BPTYPE EQ '1'.  "Person
    move 'FIRST_NAME' to lt_simple_container-element.
    move IV_FIRST_NAME to lt_simple_container-value.
    append lt_simple_container.
    move 'LAST_NAME' to lt_simple_container-element.
    move IV_LAST_NAME to lt_simple_container-value.
    append lt_simple_container.
  ELSEIF IV_BPTYPE EQ '2'. "Organization
    move 'COMPANY_NAME' to lt_simple_container-element.
    move IV_COMPANY_NAME to lt_simple_container-value.
    append lt_simple_container.
  ENDIF.
```

```
move 'SEARCH_TERM' to lt_simple_container-element.
move IV_SEARCH_TERM to lt_simple_container-value.
append lt_simple_container.

move 'HOUSE_NO' to lt_simple_container-element.
move IV_HOUSE_NO to lt_simple_container-value.
append lt_simple_container.

move 'ADDRESS' to lt_simple_container-element.
move IV_ADDRESS to lt_simple_container-value.
append lt_simple_container.

move 'CITY' to lt_simple_container-element.
move IV_CITY to lt_simple_container-value.
append lt_simple_container.

move 'STATE' to lt_simple_container-element.
move IV_STATE to lt_simple_container-value.
append lt_simple_container.

move 'ZIP_CODE' to lt_simple_container-element.
move IV_ZIP_CODE to lt_simple_container-value.
append lt_simple_container.

move 'COUNTRY' to lt_simple_container-element.
move IV_COUNTRY to lt_simple_container-value.
append lt_simple_container.

*-> Start workflow
  CALL FUNCTION 'SAP_WAPI_START_WORKFLOW'
    EXPORTING
      task    = 'WS96000259'   "<- hard coded for this demo
    IMPORTING
      return_code    = lv_return_code
      work_item_id   = lv_work itemid
    TABLES
      input_container = lt_simple_container.

*-> Started workflow ID is returned
  ev_wi_id = lv_work_itemid.
```

Listing 20.1 Wrapper Function Module to Start the Workflow

During runtime, when a user clicks on the SUBMIT button, this function module is executed to start the workflow. Notice that the parameter EV_WI_ID in this wrapper function module is the workflow work item ID that was started from the function module SAP_WAPI_START_WORKFLOW. This workflow work item ID is displayed for the requester for confirmation.

After the workflow is started, the approval agent receives the work item. When the user selects the task in UWL, Web Dynpro Java is launched. At that point, the work item ID is passed from the UWL to Web Dynpro Java. Web Dynpro Java calls the workflow APIs (WAPIs) SAP_WAPI_RESERVE_WORK_ITEM and SAP_WAPI_READ_CONTAINER to retrieve the detail business partner data entered by the requester.

The second wrapper function module (see Listing 20.2) is used to wrap SAP_WAPI_READ_CONTAINER, retrieving the data from the workflow container for the approver. Notice that the metadata in the second wrapper function module (export parameters) is also used in the development of the APPROVAL screen layout in the Web Dynpro application. Also note that IV_WI_ID in the function module is the work item ID that was just executed from UWL, not the workflow work item ID returned from the first wrapper function module (not the work item ID for the entire workflow, but the work item ID for the approval step).

```
FUNCTION Z_BP_GETDATA_FROM_WI.
*"----------------------------------------------------
*"*"Local Interface:
*"  IMPORTING
*"     VALUE(IV_WI_ID) TYPE  SWW_WIID OPTIONAL
*"  EXPORTING
*"     VALUE(EV_BPTYPE) TYPE  BAPIBUS1006_HEAD-PARTN_CAT
*"     VALUE(EV_FIRST_NAME) TYPE  BUT000-NAME_FIRST
*"     VALUE(EV_LAST_NAME) TYPE  BUT000-NAME_LAST
*"     VALUE(EV_COMPANY_NAME) TYPE  BUT000-NAME_ORG1
*"     VALUE(EV_SEARCH_TERM) TYPE  BUT000-BU_SORT1
*"     VALUE(EV_HOUSE_NO) TYPE  BAPIBUS1006_ADDRESS-HOUSE_NO
*"     VALUE(EV_ADDRESS) TYPE  ADDR1_DATA-STREET
*"     VALUE(EV_CITY) TYPE  ADDR1_DATA-CITY1
*"     VALUE(EV_STATE) TYPE  ADDR1_DATA-REGION
*"     VALUE(EV_ZIP_CODE) TYPE  ADDR1_DATA-POST_CODE1
*"     VALUE(EV_COUNTRY) TYPE  ADDR1_DATA-COUNTRY
*"----------------------------------------------------
```

```
*-> get BP detail from work item ID

  DATA: lt_container       TYPE TABLE OF swr_cont.
DATA: ls_container        TYPE swr_cont.
DATA: lv_return_code TYPE SYSUBRC.
DATA: lv_new_status type SWR_WISTAT.

*-> Reserve the work item
  CALL FUNCTION 'SAP_WAPI_RESERVE_WORK_ITEM'
    EXPORTING
      WORK ITEM_ID = iv_wi_id
      DO_COMMIT    = 'X'
    IMPORTING
      NEW_STATUS   = lv_new_status
      RETURN_CODE  = lv_return_code.

  if lv_return_code <> 0.
    EV_return_code = lv_return_code.
    exit.
  endif
  CALL FUNCTION 'SAP_WAPI_READ_CONTAINER'
    EXPORTING
      work item_id      = iv_wi_id
    TABLES
      simple_container = lt_container.

  LOOP AT lt_container INTO ls_container.
    if ls_container-element = 'BPTYPE'.
      EV_BPTYPE = ls_container-value.
    endif.
    if ls_container-element = 'FIRST_NAME'.
      EV_FIRST_NAME = ls_container-value.
    endif.
    if ls_container-element = 'LAST_NAME'.
      EV_LAST_NAME = ls_container-value.
    endif.
    if ls_container-element = 'COMPANY_NAME'.
      EV_COMPANY_NAME = ls_container-value.
    endif.
    if ls_container-element = 'SEARCH_TERM'.
      EV_SEARCH_TERM = ls_container-value.
```

```
    endif.
    if ls_container-element = 'HOUSE_NO'.
      EV_HOUSE_NO = ls_container-value.
    endif.
    if ls_container-element = 'ADDRESS'.
      EV_ADDRESS = ls_container-value.
    endif.
    if ls_container-element = 'CITY'.
      EV_CITY = ls_container-value.
    endif.
    if ls_container-element = 'STATE'.
      EV_STATE = ls_container-value.
    endif.
    if ls_container-element = 'ZIP_CODE'.
      EV_ZIP_CODE = ls_container-value.
    endif.
    if ls_container-element = 'COUNTRY'.
      EV_COUNTRY = ls_container-value.
    endif.

  ENDLOOP.


ENDFUNCTION
```

Listing 20.2 Wrapper Function Module to Read Data from the Workflow Container

Now, say that the approver approved the business partner via UWL by clicking on the SUBMIT APPROVAL button with either an APPROVAL or REJECT radio button selected. As mentioned in the data flow discussed in Chapter 18, User Interface Options, it is the responsibility of Web Dynpro Java to complete the work item.

For this, you need a third wrapper function module (see Listing 20.3). This third wrapper function module is executed by the SUBMIT APPROVAL button in Web Dynpro Java. The third wrapper function module gets the approval decision and executes the function module SAP_WAPI_WORKITEM_COMPLETE.

```
FUNCTION Z_BP_APPROVAL.
*"----------------------------------------------------------
*"*"Local Interface:
*"  IMPORTING
*"     VALUE(IV_WI_ID) TYPE  SWW_WIID OPTIONAL
*"     VALUE(IV_APPROVAL_STATUS) TYPE  SWX_PROCST OPTIONAL
```

```
*"   EXPORTING
*"      VALUE(EV_RETURN_CODE) TYPE   SYSUBRC
*"----------------------------------------------------------

  data: lv_work itemid type SWW_WIID.
  data: lv_retuRN_CODE TYPE   SYSUBRC.
  DATA: lt_simple_container TYPE STANDARD TABLE OF swr_cont
                            WITH HEADER LINE.

*-> Process wi_id
  data: lv_new_status type SWR_WISTAT.
  data: lv_new_status2 type SWW_WISTAT.
  data: ls_cont type swr_cont.
  data: lt_cont type table of swr_cont.

*-> Gets the decision result
  ls_cont-element = '_RESULT'.
  if iv_approval_status = 'A'.   "approved.
    ls_cont-value = '0001'.
  elseif iv_approval_status = 'R'.   "rejected.
    ls_cont-value = '0002'.
  else.
    EV_return_code = 4.   "neither approve, nor reject
    exit.
  endif.



*-> Complete the work item passing the decision result
  clear lv_return_code.
  append ls_cont to lt_cont.
  CALL FUNCTION 'SAP_WAPI_WORKITEM_COMPLETE'
    EXPORTING
      WORK ITEM_ID       = IV_WI_ID
      DO_COMMIT          = 'X'
    IMPORTING
      RETURN_CODE       = lv_return_code
      NEW_STATUS        = lv_new_status2
    TABLES
      SIMPLE_CONTAINER = lt_cont.

  if lv_return_code <> 0.
    ev_return_code = lv_return_code.
```

```
    exit.
  endif.

ENDFUNCTION.
```
Listing 20.3 Wrapper Function Module to Complete the Work Item

Notice that the import parameter IV_WI_ID in this wrapper function module is the work item ID being executed. The user decision made on the Web Dynpro Java screen is being passed as IV_APPROVAL_STATUS in this wrapper function module, and finally goes to the SAP_WAPI_WORKITEM_COMPLETE to complete the work item. You provide this third wrapper function module to the Web Dynpro Java developers so that Web Dynpro Java calls the function module when the SUBMIT APPROVAL button is clicked.

The remainder of the workflow development is the same as the typical approval workflow developments. The remaining steps in the workflow design, shown earlier in Figure 20.1, include the method CreateFromData of object type BUS1006 to create a business partner in the background. Finally, sending a notification to the requester of the successful business partner creation is the last step in the workflow.

One important item to note is the binding in the user decision step, which is shown in Figure 20.2. Because the business partner has not yet been created, there has not yet been an instantiation of any object, so the fields must be passed in individually.

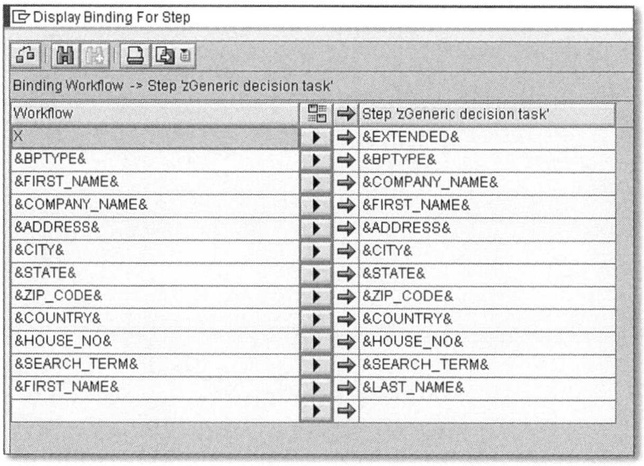

Figure 20.2 Binding in the User Decision Step

20.3   What Must Be Done on the Java Side

Typically, the presentation design is the starting point of Web Dynpro Java development. It means that the screen navigation, data context in the screen, and the triggering point of those screens should be determined early in the development stage. After you know what is needed in the *presentation layer*, then you can move on to the *model layer* to support the presentation. The *controller layer* comes in to integrate the presentation and the model layer together. So let's get started with the presentation layer.

20.3.1   Presentation Layer

First you need at least two screens in this business partner approval scenario, REQUEST and APPROVAL:

▶ The REQUEST screen should allow the user to enter the detail for the business partner that is to be approved. The request screen can be executed from the portal as an iView or as a standalone application.

▶ The APPROVAL screen should display the entered data and allow the approvers to approve or reject. The approval screen should be brought up upon the work item execution from UWL.

These two screens naturally lead to two Web Dynpro Java applications: one for the requester, and one for the approver.

As a Web Dynpro Java developer, you need to work closely with the workflow developer. When designing the business partner request screen, you need the first wrapper function module. Using the function module, you may want to create a screen similar to Figure 20.3. Make sure that all of the fields are rendered in EDIT mode except for the work item ID. The work item ID is populated automatically after selecting the SUBMIT REQUEST button.

Both the second and third wrapper function modules are needed to develop the APPROVAL screen. The second wrapper function module has the detail of the business partner (i.e., business partner type, address, etc.). The third wrapper function module is used to process the decision. Using these function modules, you may want to create a screen similar to Figure 20.4. Make sure that the fields are rendered in DISPLAY ONLY mode except for the radio button for APPROVED/REJECTED.

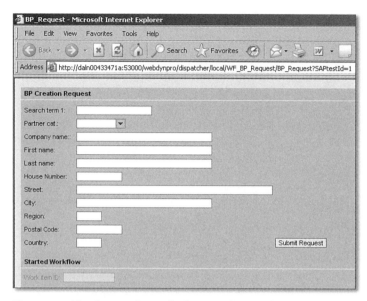

Figure 20.3 The Request Screen for Business Partner Creation

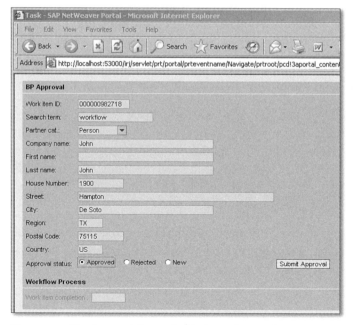

Figure 20.4 The Approval Screen for Business Partner Creation

20.3.2 Model Layer

After you know what is needed in the presentation layer, you can move on to the model layer. A critical part of Web Dynpro Java is the inclusion of the RFC model that links to the wrapper function modules created. This is done by creating a model in Web Dynpro and selecting IMPORT ADAPTIVE RFC MODEL. The model in Web Dynpro is used to specify where the data comes from. Enter the name of the model and the names of the JCo destination. Two JCo destinations must be entered: model instance and metadata. These JCo destinations must be defined in the Web Dynpro Java runtime system. The creation of the model is shown in Figure 20.5.

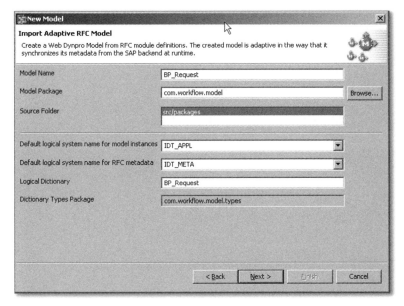

Figure 20.5 Enter JCo Destination for Model Instance and Metadata

When creating the RFC model, you enter the first wrapper function module that is RFC enabled and click on the SEARCH button. Note that only the RFC-enabled function modules can be used. After you select the wrapper function module (see Figure 20.6), it downloads all of the metadata and signatures from the function module, finally creating those Java classes automatically. Figure 20.7 shows the model classes created successfully.

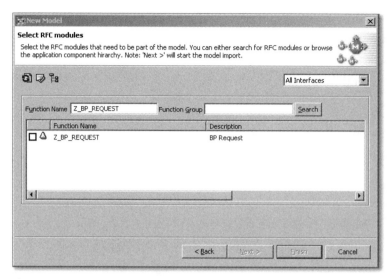

Figure 20.6 Enter Function Module Name and Search

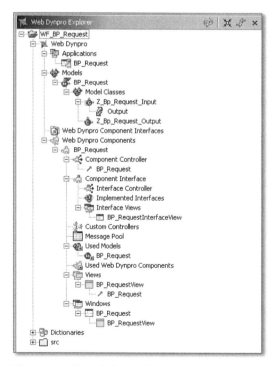

Figure 20.7 Model Classes Created

After the required model is created, you can continue to work on screen layout, data binding/mapping, coding, and so on. Figure 20.8 shows the final screen layout of the request screen.

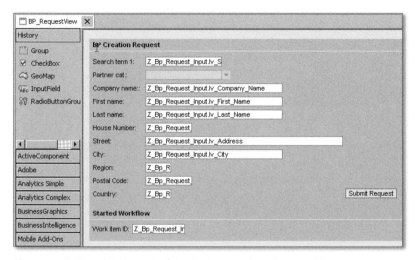

Figure 20.8 Complete Layout of the Business Partner Request View

After the development is complete, you deploy the Web Dynpro Java application to the Java engine for unit testing. Then, you must do the same development for the APPROVAL application, linking to the other two wrapper function modules.

Listing 20.4 is an example of Java code to call the function module when the SUBMIT REQUEST button is clicked. The RFC model bound to the node Z_BP_Request_Input is being executed by the code in Listing 20.4. This code can be manually entered or generated by a Web Dynpro template wizard. The Web Dynpro template wizard can be started from the context menu by right-clicking on the component controller. If you choose to use the wizard, select the SERVICE CONTROLLER from the TEMPLATE menu, do the model binding, and generate the method using the wizard.

```
public void executeZ_Bp_Request_Input( )
{
  //@@begin executeZ_Bp_Request_Input()
  //$$begin Service Controller(717412881)
  IWDMessageManager manager =
      wdComponentAPI.getMessageManager();
```

```
try
{  wdCotext.currentZ_Bp_Request_InputElement().
   modelObject().execute();
    wdContext.nodeOutput().invalidate();
}
catch(WDDynamicRFCExecuteException e)
{
   manager.reportException(e.getMessage(), false);
}
```

Listing 20.4 Java Code to Call Wrapper Function Module

20.4 What Must Be Done in the Universal Worklist

If you are using Web Dynpro Java, then UWL is the inbox requirement. When the work item appears in UWL, there is a preview of the work item that has the task description from the task design. When you link the Web Dynpro application to the task, you want to ensure there is a button in the preview area to launch the Web Dynpro application. The button you create corresponds to an action, and the behavior determined by the button corresponds to an action handler" in XML coding.

For example, if this work item is about invoice approval, you might create a button such as DISPLAY SCANNED INVOICE. Let's say there is a custom Web Dynpro Java application ready that calls a scanned invoice document. Users click on the button from UWL, review the scanned invoice copy displayed from the button, and finally approve or reject the invoice. In this case, the action is Display Scanned Invoice, and the action handler is SAPWebDynproLauncher.

The Web Dynpro Java approval is launched from UWL by the action handler SAP-WebDynproLauncher. The action handler expects the following properties:

▶ WebDynproApplication **(mandatory)**
Application name of the Web Dynpro application to be launched.

▶ WebDynproDeployableObject **(mandatory)**
Namespace of the Web Dynpro application to be launched.

▶ System **(optional)**
A system alias of the system in the portal system landscape, that is, where to launch the Web Dynpro application. Default is the system where the work item originated.

- DynamicParameter **(optional)**

  Dynamic parameters (name/value pairs, separated by &) to be passed to the Web Dynpro application.

- DebugMode **(optional)**

  The values are true and false.

Listing 20.5 is the definition of an action that launches a Web Dynpro application WebDynproConsole.

```
<Action name="launchWebDynPro" handler="WebDynproLauncher">
  <Properties>
    <Property name="WebDynproApplication"
     value="WebDynproConsole"/>
    <Property name="WebDynproDeployableObject"
                    value="sap.com/tc~wd~tools"/>
   <Property name="fruit" value="apple"/>
   <Property name="DynamicParameter" value="vegetable=potato"/>
  </Properties>
 </Action>
```

Listing 20.5 XML to Launch Web Dynpro

Every Web Dynpro application has its own name. The property WebDynproApplication expects to have the name of the application. The property WebDynproDeployableObject means the name space that includes the Web Dynpro project name. In Listing 20.6, the XML code passes the work item ID to the Web Dynpro application with the variable name of param1.

```
<Property name="DynamicParameter"
  value="param1=${item.externalId}"/>
```

Listing 20.6 Passing Work Item ID to Web Dynpro

Listing 20.7 is the complete UWL XML data for the business partner approval process that uses the Web Dynpro Java action handler.

```
<?xml version="1.0" encoding="UTF-8"?>
<!DOCTYPE UWLConfiguration PUBLIC '-//SAP//UWL1.0//EN'
 'uwl_configuration.dtd'  >
<UWLConfiguration version="1.0">
  <ItemTypes>
    <ItemType name="uwl.task.webflow.decision.TS96000171.
```

```
IDTCLNT800" connector="WebFlowConnector"
defaultView="DefaultView" defaultAction="viewDetail"
executionMode="default">
 <ItemTypeCriteria systemId="IDTCLNT800"
                   externalType="TS96000171"
                   connector="WebFlowConnector"/>
  <Actions>
    <Action name="launchWebDynPro"
     handler="SAPWebDynproLauncher"
     launchInNewWindow="yes">
       <Properties>
         <Property name="WebDynproApplication"
          value="BP_Approval"/>
         <Property name="WebDynproDeployableObject"
          value="local/WF_BP_Approval"/>
         <Property name="System" value="SAP_LocalSystem"/>
         <Property name="DynamicParameter"
          value="param1=${item.externalId}"/>
       </Properties>
       <Descriptions default="Call WD Java for
        Workflow book demo"/>
    </Action>
  </Actions>
 </ItemType>
</ItemTypes>
</UWLConfiguration>
```

Listing 20.7 UWL XML to Call Web Dynpro Java

The example in Listing 20.7 states that a Web Dynpro Java application named WF_BP_Approval will be called from the work item task TS96000171. The work item ID is being passed from UWL to the application. After the XML file is complete, you should upload it into the SAP NetWeaver Portal via the UWL ADMINISTRATION menu. Now you are ready for testing. In Figure 20.9, the UWL shows the work item for business partner approval. When the work item is executed, it launches the corresponding Web Dynpro Java application, shown earlier in Figure 20.4.

To summarize, the workflow developer and Web Dynpro developer need to work together in a highly collaborative environment to ensure both the workflow process and the user experience meet the requirements of the end user and the business process.

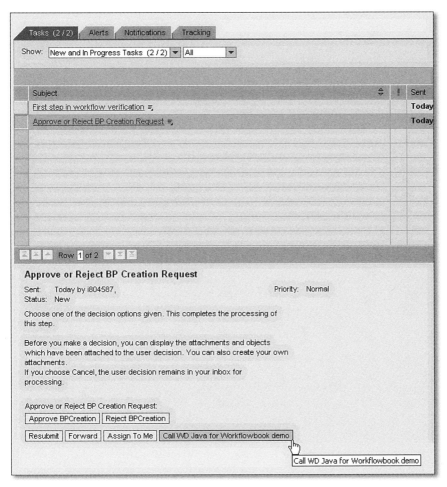

Figure 20.9 Work Item in UWL

Business Server Pages can interact with workflow in a variety of ways. This chapter explores some of the different possibilities to help you choose the right approach for your project. It also demonstrates how a common code base can be shared among workflow and non-workflow applications using ABAP classes.

21   Using Business Server Pages

Although Business Server Pages (BSP) are an older technology than Web Dynpro ABAP, they are by no means deprecated. The two technologies are complementary, suited to different types of applications, and often even coexist in the same environment. In this chapter, we will explore the different techniques of integrating workflow and BSP applications, as well as demonstrating the use of ABAP classes in workflow as part of a bigger application.

21.1   Building the Example BSP and Workflow

In this section, the focus is on building a simple BSP and using it with SAP Business Workflow.

21.1.1   Laying the Groundwork

First, we need to create our BSP application. We assume that you are familiar with BSP, so this example is a very simple flow logic page application using plain HTML. Most BSP projects use HTMLB extensions or similar, and in many cases also a model view controller (MVC) design pattern. The code used in this example will nevertheless function exactly the same when used in other scenarios; it is merely presented here in the simplest possible context.

For the example scenario we will use the following process:

1. A new business partner is created and needs a credit limit assigned.

2. A department manager enters a recommendation for a credit limit.

3. This limit is then approved by Finance.

Step 2 is implemented using a BSP and is the focus of this chapter, and Step 3 has been added to demonstrate how a value can be returned from a BSP application and stored in the container for subsequent use in the workflow.

Because we will explore different techniques for launching and completing BSP work items, we will include them all within the same example. In a real-world scenario, you would only use the technique relevant to your implementation.

Business Class ZCL_BP

You may want to use ABAP classes in your web-based applications that use SAP Business Workflow (this includes Web Dynpro) if the business objects are to be used by the web application. As discussed in Chapter 11, ABAP Classes, this can result in significant timesaving by being able to share developments between workflow and BSP/Web Dynpro, as this chapter will also demonstrate. Start off by creating a business partner class ZCL_BP, and enable it for use in workflow by adding the IF_WORKFLOW interface. This will be an instance managed class, so add two private types, T_INSTANCE and T_INSTANCES, and use the DIRECT TYPE ENTRY button (⇨) to define them as shown in Listing 21.1. Add the attributes as shown in Figure 21.1.

Attribute	Level	Visib...	Key ...	Re...	Typing	Associated Type		Description	Initial value
PARTNER	Instanc...	Public	☑	☑	Type	BU_PARTNER	⇨	Business Partner Numb...	
M_BUT000	Instanc...	Private	☐	☐	Type	BUT000	⇨	BP: General data I	
MC_CATID	Consta...	Private	☐	☐	Type	SIBFCATID	⇨	Category of Objects in Pe...	'CL'
MC_TYPEID	Consta...	Private	☐	☐	Type	SIBFTYPEID	⇨	Type of Objects in Persis...	'ZCL_BP'
MST_INSTANCES	Static A...	Private	☐	☐	Type	T_INSTANCES	⇨	Instance table	
M_LPOR	Instanc...	Private	☐	☐	Type	SIBFLPOR	⇨	Local Persistent Object ...	
M_INSTID	Instanc...	Private	☐	☐	Type	SIBFINSTID	⇨	Instance Identification in ...	

Figure 21.1 Attributes of the Business Partner Class

```
types:
  begin of t_instance,
    partner  type bu_partner,
    instance type ref to zcl_bp,
  end of t_instance .
types:
  t_instances type standard table of t_instance .
```

Listing 21.1 Type Definitions for Instance Management

In addition to the standard methods used for workflow-enabling and instance management as discussed in Chapter 11, ABAP Classes, add another two functional methods (see Figure 21.2):

▶ GET_FULL_NAME
   With returning parameter RE_NAME type BU_NAME1TX

▶ GET_TYPE_DESCRIPTION
   With returning parameter RE_TEXT type STRING

Method	Level	Visi...	M...	Description
CONSTRUCTOR	Insta...	Pub...	🖧	CONSTRUCTOR
GET_FULL_NAME	Insta...	Pub...		Get full name
GET_TYPE_DESCRIPTION	Insta...	Pub...		Get partner type description

Figure 21.2 Additional Methods for Business Partner Class

The barebones code for the various class methods is given in Listing 21.2.

```
method BI_PERSISTENT~FIND_BY_LPOR.
* Return instance using LPOR
  data: ls_instance type t_instance,
        lv_pnum     type bu_partner.
  call function 'CONVERSION_EXIT_ALPHA_INPUT'
    exporting
      input  = lpor-instid
    importing
      output = lv_pnum.
* Check if an instance already exists
  read table mst_instances
      with key partner = lv_pnum
      into ls_instance.
* If not found, create new instance
  if sy-subrc <> 0.
```

```
      ls_instance-partner = lv_pnum.
      try.
          create object ls_instance-instance
            exporting
              im_partner = lv_pnum.
          append ls_instance to mst_instances.
        catch cx_bo_error .
          exit.   " Exit without returning anything
        endtry.
      endif.
      result = ls_instance-instance.
  endmethod.
*-------------------------------------------------------------*
  method BI_PERSISTENT~LPOR.
    result = m_lpor.
  endmethod.
*-------------------------------------------------------------*
  method CONSTRUCTOR.
* Instantiate object
    data: lv_instance type t_instance.
    partner = im_partner.
    read_data( ).
    if m_but000-partner is initial.
      raise exception type cx_bo_instance_not_found.
    endif.
    me->m_lpor-catid  = mc_catid.
    me->m_lpor-typeid = mc_typeid.
    me->m_lpor-instid = im_partner.
  endmethod.
*-------------------------------------------------------------*
  method GET_INSTANCE.
* Return instance of object
    data: ls_lpor    type sibflpor,
          lv_partner type bp_partner.
    call function 'CONVERSION_EXIT_ALPHA_INPUT'
      exporting
        input  = im_key
      importing
        output = lv_partner.
    ls_lpor-catid  = mc_catid.
    ls_lpor-typeid = mc_typeid.
    ls_lpor-instid = lv_partner.
```

```
      re_instance ?= zcl_bp=>bi_persistent~find_by_lpor( ls_lpor ).
endmethod.
*----------------------------------------------------------------*
method GET_FULL_NAME.
* Return full name irrespective of partner type
  case m_but000-type.
    when 1.    " Person
      concatenate m_but000-name_first m_but000-name_last
          into re_name separated by space.
    when 2.    " Organization
      re_name = m_but000-name_org1.
    when 2.    " Group
      re_name = m_but000-name_grp1.
  endcase.
endmethod.
*----------------------------------------------------------------*
method GET_TYPE_DESCRIPTION.
* Return description of partner type
  case m_but000-type.
    when 1.
      re_text = 'Person'.
    when 2.
      re_text = 'Organization'.
    when 2.
      re_text = 'Group'.
  endcase.
endmethod.
*----------------------------------------------------------------*
method READ_DATA.
* Private method to read instance attribute data
* Following could be redesigned using BAPI calls
  select single * from but000 into m_but000
      where partner = partner.
endmethod.
```

Listing 21.2 Business Partner Class Code

BSP Application ZBP_LIMIT

In Transaction SE80, create a BSP application ZBP_LIMIT to create a web-based input form for the credit limit as shown in Figure 21.3.

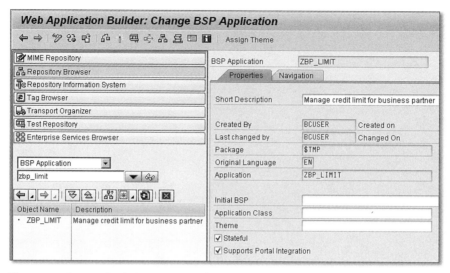

Figure 21.3 Partner Credit Limit BSP Application

Create two pages, `input.htm` to do the main input processing, and `submitted.htm`, which will contain a confirmation for the user that the limit has been submitted for approval. For the input page, the following page attributes will be needed (see Figure 21.4):

► `limit`
The credit limit to be entered by the user.

► `partner`
The business partner object instance.

► `pnum`
The business partner number — needed because object instances cannot be passed as parameters.

► `sapwfcburl`
The callback URL, which is generated by the launch handler when a BSP work item is launched. Defining it as an import parameter allows you to make further use of it as described in Section 21.2, Launching the BSP and Transferring Data, and Section 21.3, Completing Workflow Tasks from BSP Applications.

► `wi_id`
The work item ID. Typically, you would use either the callback URL or the work item ID to identify the associated work item.

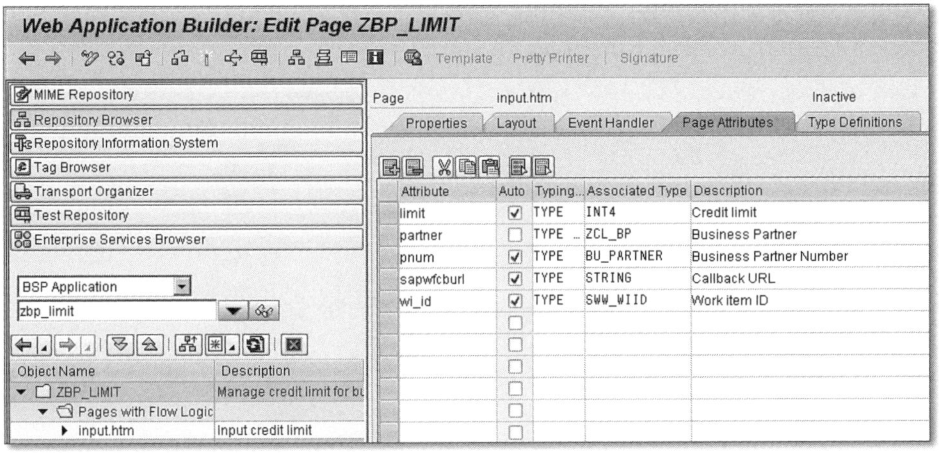

Figure 21.4 Page Attributes for input.htm

Because object instances cannot be passed as a parameter, you need to pass the partner number as a parameter and instantiate it in the `OnInitialization` module. This is also where you retrieve the work item ID from the callback URL. The code in Listing 21.3 caters for both.

```
* event handler for data retrieval
* Get work item ID from callback URL.
  try.
      call method cl_swf_ifs_ws_export=>get_callback_ctx_params
        exporting
          callback_url = sapwfcburl
        importing
          wi_id        = wi_id.
    catch cx_swf_ws_exception.
  endtry.
* Get partner object
  partner = zcl_bp=>get_instance( pnum ).
```

Listing 21.3 OnInitialization Module for imput.htm Page

A typical BSP application uses HTMLB extensions (`<htmlb>`), but for simplicity, we will create the page using plain HTML. The page consists of a short display of partner information, an input box to enter the credit limit, and buttons to submit the form back to workflow using different alternatives discussed later in Section 21.3, Completing Workflow Tasks from BSP Applications. Listing 21.4 shows an example BSP that provides the input from the user on the business partner and enables the user to submit the form.

```
<%@page language="abap" %>
<html>
  <head>
    <title>Enter credit limit for business partner</title>
  </head>
  <body>
    <h3>A new business partner has been created and
        requires your input</h3>
    <table>
      <tr> <td>Type:</td>
           <td><%=partner->get_type_description( )%></td>
      </tr>
      <tr> <td>Name:</td>
           <td><%=partner->get_full_name( )%></td>
      </tr>
    </table>
    <br>
    Please enter the credit limit (if any) to be extended to
    this partner. <br>
    This will be sent to Finance for approval. <br>
    <form method="post">
      <input type  = "TEXT"
             name  = "limit"
             value = "100" />
      <input type  = "SUBMIT"
             name  = "OnInputProcessing(submit_event)"
             value = "Submit via WAPI" />
      <input type  = "SUBMIT"
             name  = "OnInputProcessing(submit_http)"
             value = "Submit via HTTP" />
      <input type    = "SUBMIT"
             value   = "Cancel"
             onclick = "javascript:window.close()" />
    </form>
  </body>
</html>
```

Listing 21.4 input.htm Source

21.1.2 Setting Up the Web Service Handler

Before you can use Web Services in workflow, the Web Service handler must be configured for the SAP system. To do this, start Transaction WF_HANDCUST, and switch to change mode. You should see a dialog box popup asking whether to generate the handler entry automatically. Because automatic generation is the easiest option, click on the AUTOMATICALLY button, and the appropriate entries are generated. Repeat this for the LAUNCH HANDLER, CALLBACK HANDLER, and CALLBACK DIALOG tabs. You can click on the GENERATE URL button to generate a test URL that can then be tested using the TEST URL button as shown in Figure 21.5.

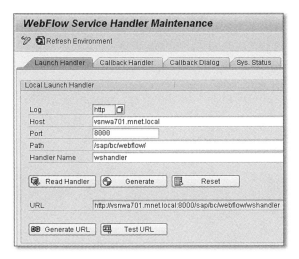

Figure 21.5 Workflow Service Handler Maintenance

If successful, you should receive a message similar to Figure 21.6 in a browser window. Again, repeat this for the other services on the LAUNCH HANDLER, CALLBACK HANDLER, and CALLBACK DIALOG tabs, and save everything when done.

Figure 21.6 Successful Web Service Handler Test

Up to this point, we have successfully created a BSP application based on an ABAP class and have configured the Web Service handler to manage the communication between BSP and SAP Business Workflow.

21.2 Launching the BSP and Transferring Data

This section walks through the steps you need to launch the BSP and to transfer data to and from the workflow.

21.2.1 Defining the Workflow Service and Creating a Task

The easiest way to create a task that launches a BSP application is to use the wizard available in the system. Start Transaction WF_EXTSRV, create an entry for your BSP application, and enter the corresponding service information, such as the service ID, the host used to launch the task, and the port (see Figure 21.7).

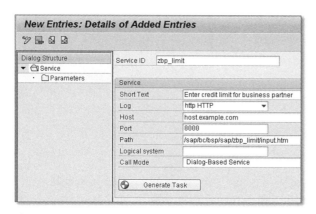

Figure 21.7 Creating a New Web Service for Workflow

Note that although we have used the same name for the service ID as the BSP application, this is not necessary. The service ID is a unique identifier for a service used by workflow. It is possible, for example, to have different service ID entries for different pages or controllers of a single BSP application.

Next, in the PARAMETERS view, you can define the import/export parameters for the BSP application, not unlike binding in a workflow context. For our example, define import and export parameters for the partner number and limit (see Figure 21.8).

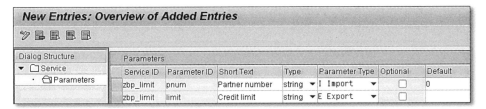

Figure 21.8 Web Service Parameters to Be Exchanged with Workflow

Note

Here, the terms *import* and *export* are from the point of view of the Web Service.

After the entries for the parameters in WF_EXTSRV have been saved, go back to the service details, and click on the GENERATE TASK button to start the wizard, which is mostly self-explanatory. At the end, make a note of the task number that has been generated (see Figure 21.9).

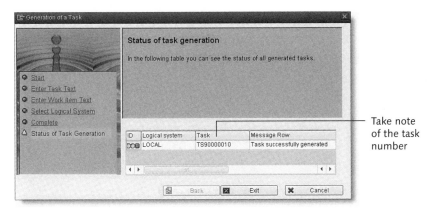

Figure 21.9 Using the Wizard to Generate a Web Service Task

This task will have the appropriate import and export parameters to match the parameters defined earlier.

Note

In Basis release 6.20, the table linking the task and the Web Service is not transported, and there is no way of maintaining this in other systems other than by editing the Table SWLWPTSSID directly using Transaction SE16. SAP Note 746709 talks about this in the context of recruiting.

21.2.2 Creating a Test Workflow

The next step is to insert the task into a workflow. For our example, start by creating a new workflow with container elements:

▶ **Partner**
Type ABAP Class `ZCL_BP`

▶ **Limit**
Type `int4`

Then insert a step based on the task you previously generated, bind just the partner number (not the partner object) to the step, and bind the limit back to the workflow as shown in Figure 21.10. It is not possible to bind anything other than simple data elements to a Web Service parameter.

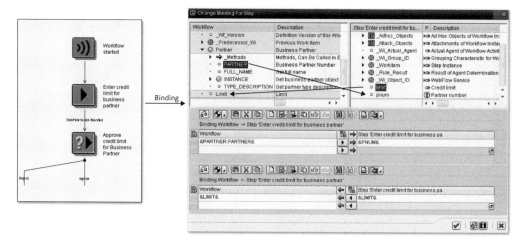

Figure 21.10 Binding for Web Service Step

For testing purposes, you may want to assign an initial value to the business partner (create one using Transaction BP if necessary), or else you can manually enter one as importing parameter when testing. You should also set the task's agent assignment attributes to GENERAL TASK and assign the workflow initiator as agent in the workflow. Figure 21.10 shows the binding for the partner and the limit between the workflow and the BSP.

Add a second decision step that shows the limit as a parameter in the work item text as shown in Figure 21.11; for our test purposes, this will let us view the results of the BSP step.

Figure 21.11 Approve Credit Limit Decision Step

You have now completed a test workflow with which you can launch a BSP application. There are several ways to launch a Web Service task within a workflow, depending on scenario:

▶ From the SAP Business Workplace (Transaction SBWP)

▶ From another web application

▶ From the Universal Worklist (UWL)

We will look at each of these in detail.

21.2.3 Launching a BSP Application from the Business Workplace

When a Web Service work item is executed in the SAP Business Workplace, Transaction SBWP launches a browser on the user's system. However, it does not call the BSP directly but rather does so by calling the Web Service handler service WSHANDLER. This service does two things:

▶ It generates an additional parameter sapwfcburl — the Callback URL — which is a link to call the WSHANDLER service a second time to complete the work item. This is covered in more detail further on in this chapter under Section 21.3, Completing Workflow Tasks from BSP Applications.

▶ The WSHANDLER service then launches the actual web application associated with the task as defined in Transaction WF_EXTSRV.

21.2.4 Launching a BSP Application from Another Web Application

If you want to launch a BSP work item from, for example, another BSP application, the same result as a launch from Transaction SBWP can be achieved using function module SAP_WAPI_LAUNCH_URL_GET. This returns a URL that also launches the target BSP via the WSHANDLER service.

Use the test facility from the Workflow Builder or Transaction SWUS to test your workflow with a business partner instance. You should receive a work item in your inbox, and executing it should launch your BSP as shown in Figure 21.12.

Figure 21.12 Executing the BSP Application

21.2.5 Launching a BSP Application from the Universal Worklist

The BSP work item appears in UWL straight away; however, there is additional work required to get it to function correctly.

Registering the BSP Task

If you attempt to execute the work item, you may notice that the system launches another browser window and asks for a username and password again. What is happening here is that UWL is not aware of the work item's link to a Web Service and tries to execute it using the ABAP layer as a regular business object and method, which in turn launches a completely new browser session. This can also be seen in the work item preview, which looks just like a regular SAP GUI-based task (see Figure 21.13).

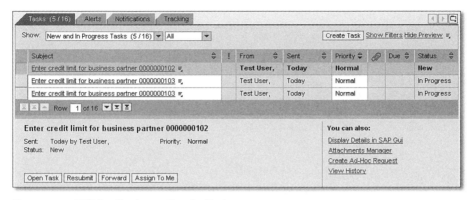

Figure 21.13 BSP Application as Regular Task

What needs to happen is for the work item to be registered in the UWL with the corresponding Web Service that must be executed. This can be done directly by creating an XML configuration file for the UWL (Chapter 19, Using Web Dynpro ABAP, has an example in a Web Dynpro context); however, an easier way is by means of the task visualization configuration using Transaction SWFVISU.

Create a new entry specifying your task ID with a visualization type BSP Standard. You also need to specify the visualization parameters; the minimum required parameters are `Application` to specify which BSP application is used and `Page_ID` to specify the page to be launched. Enter the values for your application as shown in Figure 21.14.

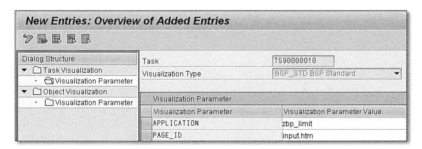

Figure 21.14 Task Visualization Parameters in SWFVISU for UWL

The next step is to register the visualization for your task in the UWL administration page by clicking on your system's Re-Register button and clearing the cache. If you now look at the work item preview, you should see that the Open Task button has changed to Launch BSP (see Figure 21.15).

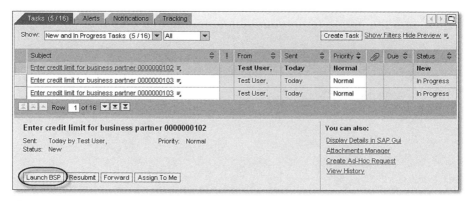

Figure 21.15 BSP Application Correctly Configured in UWL

Importing Parameters

Without the use of the WSHANDLER service to launch the BSP task, the parameters are not automatically supplied to the BSP application. Therefore, it also becomes the BSP developer's responsibility to import the necessary information from the workflow container. For the example scenario, we will demonstrate both methods. Update the code to cater for both as shown in Listing 21.5.

```
* event handler for data retrieval
data: lt_cont type standard table of swr_cont.
field-symbols: <cont> type swr_cont.
* Get work item ID from callback URL if supplied
if wi_id is initial.
  try.
      call method cl_swf_ifs_ws_export=>get_callback_ctx_params
        exporting
          callback_url = sapwfcburl
        importing
          wi_id        = wi_id.
    catch cx_swf_ws_exception.
  endtry.
endif.
* If partner not supplied, read it from the work item container
if pnum is initial.
  call function 'SAP_WAPI_READ_CONTAINER'
    exporting
      workitem_id                        = wi_id
```

```
      tables
        simple_container              = lt_cont.
    read table lt_cont assigning <cont>
      with key element = 'PNUM'.
    if sy-subrc = 0.
      pnum = <cont>-value.
    endif.
  endif.
endif.
* Get partner object
partner = zcl_bp=>get_instance( pnum ).
```

Listing 21.5 Read Work Item Container from BSP

21.3 Completing Workflow Tasks from BSP Applications

The next part to implement is the process of completing execution of the task. Unlike a regular SAP GUI-based task that executes a method of an object, all Web Service tasks are based on one of the methods of the WEBSERVICE object (PROCESS-DIALOG in our example), or the EXTSRV object on older systems. In other words, the method has nothing to do with the actual business activity to be performed as part of this workflow step; instead, it acts as a placeholder to launch the associated business application.

Because the BSP application is completely standalone and not under the control of the workflow runtime, it is the responsibility of the BSP developer to implement the termination of the work item that launched it. There are two ways to accomplish this: by using the callback URL supplied by the WSHANDLER service, or by completing the work item directly using SAP_WAPI API functions. This is illustrated in Figure 21.16.

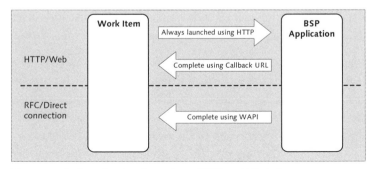

Figure 21.16 Coordinating Execution of BSP and Work Item

The question of which one to use depends on the environment in which it is implemented because there are advantages and disadvantages to using either. The most significant factor is likely to be the extent to which UWL is used because this restricts the use of WSHANDLER and thus a callback URL.

Completion via Callback URL

The Callback URL is generated by the WSHANDLER service and includes an execution GUID (Globally Unique Identifier) unique to each work item. This maps a subsequent request to the WSHANDLER service with the work item that was launched and completes the work item.

Because it uses HTTP, it can be used between different systems and even over the Internet. An added layer of security is provided by the use of the execution GUID because you cannot obtain this in a web-based scenario without executing the work item. In other words, the BSP URL is tamper-resistant because a user cannot complete another work item that they do not have in their inbox simply by changing the work item ID in the URL.

> **Note**
>
> Web application security is a major topic on its own and outside the scope of this book. However, we recommend additional security measures to be put in place wherever workflow routing itself is an aspect of security from a business process perspective. A simple technique is to verify that the user is one of the work item's recipients, which can be determined using the API function SAP_WAPI_WORKITEM_RECIPIENTS.

The use of a callback URL also provides a more standardized interface and can be implemented by a BSP developer without any knowledge of workflow. All that is needed is to receive a callback URL at the start of the application and submit it upon completion with any returning parameters appended. Because this uses HTTP, it also makes this easier to implement in a multisystem landscape.

To implement a callback URL, an importing parameter sapwfcburl needs to be declared to receive this (as has been done in our initial example). Upon completion of the BSP application, this can be submitted by executing the static method cl_swf_ifs_ws_export=>launch_callback. Additional optional parameters can be passed which contain values to be returned to the task. In the following example, we use exp_params_nvp, a simple name-value-pair table with one row per container element.

> **Note**
>
> The use of a Web Service handler is deprecated in a UWL environment. This means the techniques described here are not suitable if you are using UWL as your primary method for launching workflow BSP applications. However, it is also possible to implement both approaches described in this section together to keep using the benefits of the callback URL (most notably passing parameters and a more secure BSP URL) in a non-UWL context.

Completion via Events

The use of events is ideal if a greater level of control is needed such as using different events to continue different branches of the workflow depending on input provided in the BSP. Of course, it is also possible to use both methods together; for example, you can use HTTP callback for the standard process and raise events for any exceptions that should trigger a wait step or alternate branch in the workflow.

To use events, a little additional work may be required in certain circumstances: The generated task based on the WEBSERVICE BOR object is an asynchronous task and uses a terminating event COMPLETED. This is how the callback URL is processed internally. However, a peculiarity of this specific terminating event is that it only becomes active after the task has been launched using the WSHANDLER service. In other words, raising the event while the task is still in READY status has no effect. However, another slightly unusual behavior is that any parameters can be passed back to the task using this event, even though the event has no formal parameters.

This does not work in all scenarios: There are cases where users might access the web application directly and bypass the work item completely, for example if there are multiple entry points to the application: either via a task launched from UWL, or using an integrated management application for the particular business scenario — both of which call up the same BSP. Another example is if multiple terminating events for the business class are required to continue along different branches (similar to a decision). In both cases, you need to add an event to the business class, and the task must include the object in its container to link a terminating event to the correct instance.

Example

Before we implement our termination in the example scenario, we should implement a user-friendly result in the user interface in response to clicking on the button. To do this, add another page `submitted.htm` with a short message for the user as shown in Listing 21.6.

```
<%@page language="abap" %>
<html>
  <head>
    <title>Enter credit limit for business partner</title>
  </head>
  <body>
    <br>
    Credit limit has been submitted for approval.<br>
    You may now close this window.<br>
  </body>
</html>
```
Listing 21.6 submitted.htm

Define a navigation request `TO_END` on the BSP application's Navigation tab as shown in Figure 21.17. This will be called after the button clicks have been processed.

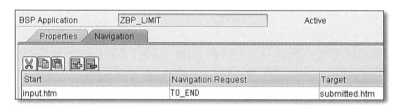

Figure 21.17 Navigation Request to the Completion Notification

For our example, we will implement two methods of termination linked to the two Submit buttons. One will complete the work item using the callback URL, and the other will raise an event. Because the `WEBSERVICE.COMPLETED` terminating event does not work in the standard UWL configuration, we have to create a custom event for our business object and define it as a terminating event for the task.

> **Tip**
>
> Another alternative is to complete the work item directly using `SAP_WAPI_WORKITEM_COMPLETE`. The technique is similar for events and is demonstrated in Chapter 19, Using Web Dynpro ABAP, and Chapter 20, Using Web Dynpro Java. The use of events enables you to implement multiple outcomes to a single task.

We will implement the event for the ZCL_BP class using the techniques described in Chapter 11, ABAP Classes. First, add a public instance event LIMIT_REQUESTED to the ZCL_BP class, with one parameter LIMIT of type INT4. Create a corresponding public instance method RAISE_LIMIT_REQUESTED with an importing parameter IM_LIMIT of type int4. The code for this method is shown in Listing 21.7.

```
method RAISE_LIMIT_REQUESTED.
* Raise workflow event LIMIT_REQUESTED
constants: lc_event type sibfevent value 'LIMIT_REQUESTED',
           lc_objtype type sibftypeid value 'ZCL_BP'.
  data: lv_objkey     type sibfinstid,
        lo_event      type ref to if_swf_evt_event,
        lo_evt_params type ref to
          if_swf_ifs_parameter_container.
* Set up the LPOR instance id
  lv_objkey = partner.
  try.
* Get event object
      lo_event = cl_swf_evt_event=>get_instance(
                     im_objcateg =
                       cl_swf_evt_event=>mc_objcateg_cl
                     im_objtype  = lc_objtype
                     im_event    = lc_event
                     im_objkey   = lv_objkey ).
* Get event container
      lo_evt_params = lo_event->get_event_container( ).
* Set Parameters
      lo_evt_params->set( name  = 'LIMIT'
                          value = im_limit ).
* Raise event
      lo_event->raise( ).
    catch cx_swf_evt_exception.
    catch cx_swf_cnt_container .
  endtry.
endmethod.
```

Listing 21.7 Method to Raise limit_requested Event

Next, edit your BSP task, and add an additional importing container element Partner defining its type as your ZCL_BP class. In the TERMINATING EVENTS tab, the LIMIT_REQUESTED event is based on this parameter as shown in Figure 21.18.

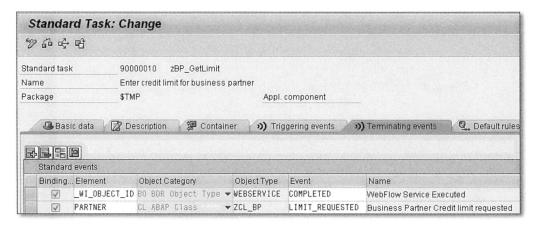

Figure 21.18 Additional Terminating Event for Web Service Task

Select the event, and use the binding button (⊞) to bind to only the limit back to the corresponding container elements as shown in Figure 21.19.

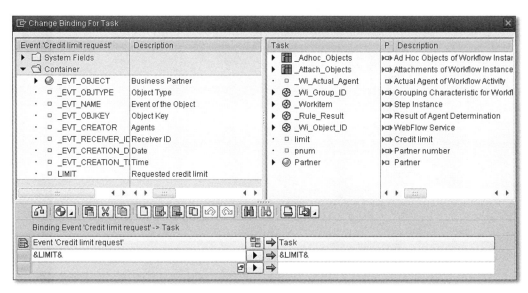

Figure 21.19 Binding the Event Parameter to the Task

The last thing left to do for the workflow portion is to activate the new event as an outcome of the step on the OUTCOMES tab in the Workflow Builder as shown in Figure 21.20. You now have two outcomes to the step corresponding to the two submission buttons of the BSP application.

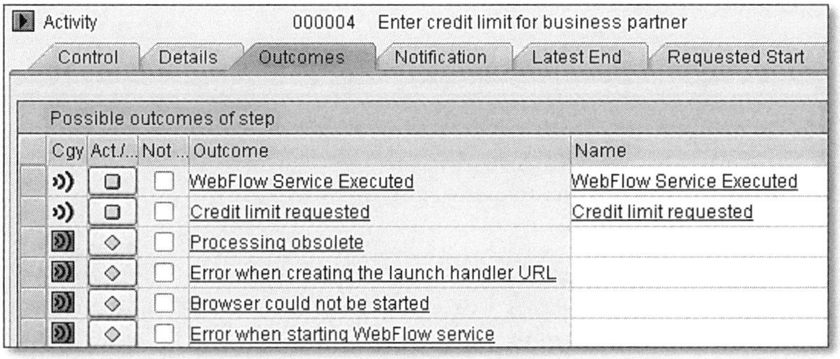

Figure 21.20 Step Outcomes for Different Terminating Events

Terminating the work item is done from the BSP application's `input.htm` page. Both the HTTP and event techniques for completing a work item using the two submission buttons are implemented in the `OnInputProcessing` event. Choose this event in the EVENT HANDLER tab, and enter the code shown in Listing 21.8.

```
* event handler for checking and processing user input and
* for defining navigation
data: lt_params type tihttpnvp,     " Used for HTTP
      lv_key     type swo_typeid,   " Used for event
      lt_cont    type standard table of swr_cont.
field-symbols: <param> type ihttpnvp,
               <cont>  type swr_cont.
case event_id.
* Complete work item processing using http callback
  when 'submit_http'.
* Assign container elements to be passed back
    append initial line to lt_params assigning <param>.
    <param>-name  = 'limit'.
    <param>-value = limit.
    try.
        cl_swf_ifs_ws_export=>launch_callback(
            callback_url   = sapwfcburl
            exp_params_nvp = lt_params
               ).
      catch cx_swf_ws_http_exception .
      catch cx_swf_ifs_exception .
    endtry.
* Complete work item processing using event
  when 'submit_event'.
```

```
* Raise event LIMIT_REQUESTED
    partner->raise_limit_requested( limit ).
    commit work.
endcase.
navigation->next_page( 'TO_END' ).
```
Listing 21.8 OnInputProcessing Event Handler for input.htm

Start two test workflows using Transaction SWUS, and execute the resulting work items by clicking on the different SUBMIT buttons. In both cases, you should see the response page shown in Figure 21.21.

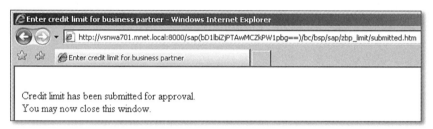

Figure 21.21 Successful Submission Notification

And looking in Transaction SBWP, you should see the value you entered for the limit carried through to the subsequent decision step (see Figure 21.22).

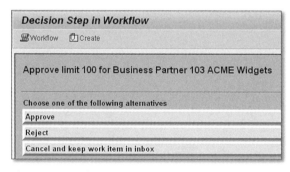

Figure 21.22 Value Entered in BSP Shown in a Subsequent Workflow Step

Note
As this chapter has demonstrated, there are several different methodologies to implementing a BSP workflow scenario. There is no clear "best" way to approach such a project because there are several significant factors such as system architecture and development skills available within your organization that can influence your decisions.

Forms in SAP Business Workflow can be used to create a simple user interface. This chapter discusses the forms options available with SAP Business Workflow.

22   Using Forms

Electronic forms are a great way of integrating occasional users into a workflow process. They are little more than the electronic equivalent of paper forms, displaying existing data and providing simple data entry fields, with no sophisticated controls or navigation to confuse or unsettle the occasional user.

22.1   SAP Interactive Forms by Adobe

SAP Interactive Forms by Adobe are interactive forms delivered via a partnership with SAP and Adobe. SAP and Adobe partnered with the goal of automating and streamlining forms-based communication to support customers who create reusable forms for their business processes. SAP Interactive Forms are integrated into workflow via Web Dynpro. Both Web Dynpro ABAP and Web Dynpro Java support SAP Interactive Forms.

> **Tip**
>
> The book *SAP Interactive Forms by Adobe* (SAP PRESS, 2009) has more detailed information about SAP Interactive Forms.

When using SAP Interactive Forms online and Web Dynpro, there is no impact on the integration with workflow. Web Dynpro manages the form and the `SAP_WAPI*` calls to the workflow container. To use SAP Interactive Forms in your workflow, enhance your Web Dynpro with forms, and they will be available to the workflow with no additional configuration required. The only reason they are mentioned in this chapter is to ensure you understand that SAP Interactive Forms are not integrated into SAP Business Workflow but into Web Dynpro.

22.2   SAP Business Workflow Forms

The most common types of forms supported by the SAP Business Workflow Engine are:

- ▶ Simple forms (FORMS step)
- ▶ PC document forms (DOCUMENT FROM TEMPLATE" step)
- ▶ Email
- ▶ Business Server Pages (BSP)
- ▶ Web Dynpro forms, including SAP Interactive Forms

Forms are easy to create and easy to use. However, you must make sure from the outset that using electronic forms really is the direction you want to take. There is a danger that what starts off as a form will gradually turn into a complex transaction because the requirements from the stakeholders change and grow as they start to realize what can be achieved with workflow. Avoid this trap as best you can because forms that evolve into transactions are difficult to develop and maintain.

Bear in mind when designing a process that where forms can be used, there are probably other steps involving power users who access the data through their standard transactions with all of the navigation and data verification that this supports. So your process should still use business objects and ABAP classes where possible rather than collecting the data in flat container structures. You usually want to transfer from one to another, which can be done via the binding between the steps and the workflow or via your own business methods. A typical example of this type of hybrid forms/transaction process arises when data is initially collected in forms before being written to the database using a BAPI and then processed as a business object in the following steps.

22.2.1   Simple Forms Creation

The simplest way of generating forms is to use the FORMS step. These forms are generated Dynpros. The advantage of these forms is in the simplicity of generation together with the degree of integration with the SAP Business Workflow Engine.

One prerequisite when using forms is that the workflow container must contain a container element that references a structure. A structure and container elements for single data type is not enough because the form requires a container element based on a structure to pass the data into the form and accept the modified data when the form is saved. When the form is generated, a screen is generated containing all of the fields and their descriptions. The information about the data types and descriptions of the fields is taken directly from the ABAP Dictionary to simplify the generation process.

When the work item is executed, the agent will see three tabs as shown in Figure 22.1:

- The primary tab (FORM FIELDS) displays the screen that you have generated.

- A second tab (PROPERTIES) shows a summary of information relating to the work item, such as deadline information and its current status.

- A third tab shows the WORKFLOW TOOLBOX, displaying the task description and attachments, and allowing ad-hoc activities such as forwarding the work item.

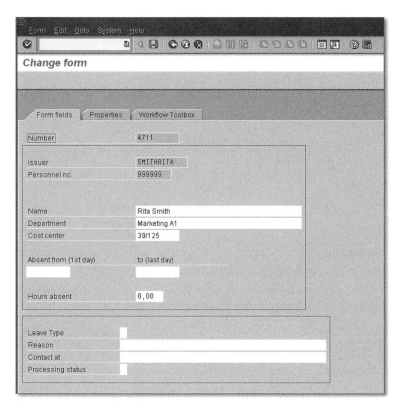

Figure 22.1 Form with Tab Pages

Using the FORMS step is a very powerful technique because the primary tab displaying the form preserves simplicity. But by switching to the other tabs, you can easily access all of the other workflow features, such as the workflow log or attachment handling.

In the STEP DEFINITION (▤), you can decide which type of form handling to use. Your choice determines the buttons that are displayed in the generated form (e.g., APPROVED/REJECTED) as well as the possible outcomes of the step. The combinations are shown in Table 22.1.

Form Type	Buttons (Menus) Available
DISPLAY	EXIT
EDIT	SAVE AND EXIT
APPROVE	APPROVE, REJECT, EXIT
APPROVE WITH QUERY	APPROVE, QUERY, REJECT, EXIT

Table 22.1 Simple-Form Types and Their Buttons

When a form is created by a form creation wizard (see Figure 22.2), a corresponding custom function group is generated (i.e., function group name is like ZWSnnnnnnnn where nnnnnnnn is the workflow template number) behind the scene. The function group is all yours, which gives you full control on the screen. You can add your own screen logic to the form to determine which fields are display only and which fields are open for input. For example, an EDIT form may contain fields that cannot be edited, and an APPROVAL form may well contain fields that can be edited (such as the reason for rejecting the request).

You can even use extra hidden fields to control the display of the form. For example, you can reserve one field in the structure to represent the role of a user and another field for the type of record that is being displayed. You can then use the screen logic to control whether the rest of the fields in the form are displayed or open for input according to both the user's role and the type of record.

The display logic is fully under your control. You can even allow the ABAP Dictionary definition of the relationships between the fields to control the error handling in the form and the input help. Forms can also be generated to trigger a workflow. To generate a triggering form, navigate to the BASIC DATA of the workflow definition (VERSION-INDEPENDENT) and generate the form from the START

FORMS tab. From here, you can generate the accompanying transaction and add it to a favorites list to make life easier for the workflow participants.

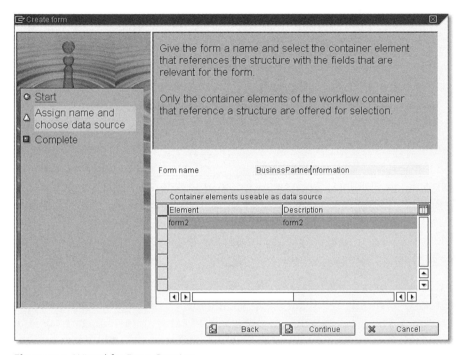

Figure 22.2 Wizard for Form Creation

Note
One final note on the technical side: You may be surprised to see that in the workflow definition, there is no binding between the form and the workflow. This is correct. Data is transferred directly from the workflow container to the form. When SAVE is chosen, the data is written directly back to the workflow container. Because DISPLAY FORMS do not have a SAVE button, they cannot change the contents of the workflow container

22.2.2 Document Templates

Another simple and powerful way of presenting information to the users is to use a form based on a *document template.* This can be used for creating complex documents using the relevant PC applications via workflow. A prerequisite is that the PC application for which you want to create a document must be installed on your PC.

> **Note**
>
> Strictly speaking, these are not forms but they can be used very effectively in many situations where forms are required.

The use of PC documents for forms is very effective because they are so easy to read, and the templates are so easy to create and maintain. The user who creates the document template does not need a technical background, so the users that will be actively involved in the workflow can design the form themselves. The documents are stored centrally in the SAP Knowledge Provider so they are available to everyone with access to the system.

Because the SAP Knowledge Provider is used, different versions of the forms can be deployed. For example, the same form can appear in several languages, or the form can give different views of the same data according to role of the workflow agent. The Business Object that is used to represent the PC document is WF_DOC, but there is no need to call this as an activity because it has been integrated directly into the PC DOCUMENT step type ().

When the work item is executed in the SAP GUI for Windows (such as from the Business Workplace), the relevant PC application is opened with the template for the work item. The user can cancel processing to keep it in the inbox or save the form to enable the workflow to continue to the next step:

1. To create a form, use the DOCUMENT TEMPLATES tray of the Workflow Builder to create a new template. You will be presented with a list of document types that have been configured in your system. Adobe Designer and Microsoft Office tools are supported.

2. Select the appropriate document type, and enter the content that you require, including graphics or whatever else you choose to do to make it easier for your users to digest the data. Add the variables from the workflow by double-clicking on the container elements you want to add.

3. Having designed your template, you can now create a DOCUMENT FROM TEMPLATE step, specifying the template that you have just designed.

4. The PC documents are not suitable for mass printing although mass emailing is supported. To send the document by email, you must convert it to an office document first by calling up the background WF_DOC_CREATE_SOFM method, which creates a PC document in the SAPoffice tables. This SAPoffice document

can be processed further with the methods based on the SOFM object type, such as the SEND method.

5. When the agents execute the work item, they display the form that you have created, with the variables replaced by data in the workflow.

The primary use described here is for the simple display of data, which has been collected during a workflow process. However, the same technique can be used for creating complex documents such as contracts, presentations, marketing collateral, or spreadsheets. By using workflow to support the document creation process you are ensuring that the process follows a predefined path and that all of the attachments and comments are preserved with the process and visible to everyone in the process. All of the standard workflow functions can be integrated into the document step, including deadline management and notifications.

There are obvious benefits to executing the workflow decisions directly in the user's Lotus Notes inbox. Alloy, a joint product from SAP and IBM, enables this as part of the Alloy capabilities. Because it is a joint development, the benefits go well beyond what has been achieved in the past and open the door for new opportunities. This chapter introduces Alloy and discusses how it can be used with SAP Business Workflow.

23 Alloy — Lotus Notes Integration

Different vendors and system integrators have made several attempts at enabling SAP Business Workflow items to appear in the user's Lotus Notes inbox. However, in terms of capabilities, customer support, user interface, and performance, the limitations of these attempts were pretty apparent. That is why, when a joint collaboration between SAP and IBM was investigated, workflow integration was one of the customer requirements that was taken seriously from the word go. The final product developed jointly (and supported jointly) by IBM and SAP is called Alloy 1.0. And sure enough, Alloy does support SAP Business Workflow.

▶ What Alloy is *not*:

  ▷ Alloy is not a merely user interface for SAP Business Workflow.

  Alloy supports SAP Business Workflow decisions, but this is just part of the Alloy capabilities. In addition to decisions, several Human Capital Management (HCM) processes in the SAP Business Suite and SAP reporting (both SAP ERP and SAP Business Explorer) are also supported.

  ▷ Alloy is not a replacement for the standard SAP user interfaces for all SAP users.

  Alloy is aimed at the business users who typically spend very little of their day, if any, in the SAP user interface but feel at home working in Lotus Notes.

▶ What Alloy *does provide*:

  ▷ Alloy provides a native Lotus Notes user interface for SAP decisions.

  Alloy was designed and built with IBM to take into account future capabilities as well as SAP's knowledge of the SAP Business Suite environment.

▶ Alloy provides an ability to enhance decisions spawned from SAP Business Workflow with the Lotus collaborative environment.

▶ Not only does Alloy merge seamlessly into the Lotus user interface, it is completely intuitive using standard Lotus entities such as mail and calendaring.

23.1 The Design Paradigm

The Lotus Notes 8.0 user interface is a quantum jump from previous releases in terms of the capabilities and appearance. Alloy 1.0 makes use of this in four ways:

▶ Sidebar
▶ Mail inbox
▶ Views
▶ Calendar items

23.1.1 Sidebar

The sidebar is the area on the right of the main panel that displays additional information to the user, such as RSS feeds. By and large, users decide what they want to display. In the case of Alloy, after the users have been activated on the server, they receive the invitation to use the Lotus widget framework for adding the Alloy sidebar. After it has been enabled, it provides a launch pad of Alloy capabilities. So the user can, for example, create a travel request or request the latest data in a report from buttons on the sidebar and, of course, call up the view of all pending workflow decisions.

> **Note**
>
> In fact, the manager's sidebar also displays a short list of the latest pending approvals as a reminder and can click on them to execute the decision directly.

One of the most useful features of the sidebar is that it can be context specific so that it displays specific information relevant to a particular decision or other item in the Alloy context. For example, when entering a leave request, the user sees the remaining days/time available for that particular leave type. When viewing a report, it can show the scheduling information about the report. Customers can extend the information displayed by adding new segments (out of scope of this book) so that context information relating to the decision can also be displayed. This not only allows additional context information from the SAP application, such as deadline information or additional business data, but also what is available in the Lotus environment, such as a Lotus Quickr™ room or Lotus Connections™ for locating experts in a particular field.

Figure 23.1 shows an expense approval in Alloy. Notice the sidebar with the Alloy features.

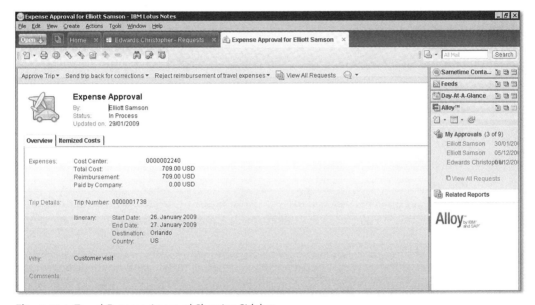

Figure 23.1 Travel Expense Approval Showing Sidebar

23.1.2 Mail Inbox

The mail inbox is the place where the decisions arrive in the manager's Lotus environment, along with other Lotus items such as emails or calendar requests. It is also where status notifications arrive. These notifications are sent when a decision is performed or becomes obsolete (such as when a colleague reserves or forwards a decision).

By delivering the decisions in the manager's inbox, they can be acted on immediately (including offline) and eliminate the need for additional training. The manager can see at a glance that these are decisions by the sender name (otherwise known as FROM column), which is configurable by admin (e.g., RISK APPROVAL). Opening the decision displays the decision buttons if the decision has not been made. Opening a status notification shows the current status at the time the notification was generated, and the manager can select the decision button to navigate to the original decision to show the details.

The details of the decision are shown in the body of the decision itself. So, for example, a trip approval shows the details of the trip (where, when, who, cost center), whereas an expense approval shows the expense details (how much, who) The sky is the limit for what you customized into the body of a customized decision.

One important point about the decisions arriving in the inbox is that even though they can be easily removed from the inbox, the decisions do not disappear and can be accessed from other places, such as the short list in the sidebar or the view of pending decisions.

An even more important point that managers soon recognize and appreciate is that when they perform a decision by selecting one of the decision buttons, it immediately disappears from the inbox. So executing the decisions promptly results in an uncluttered inbox. Difficult decisions can be moved to other folders and can trigger all sorts of collaborative traffic until the decision is made (email, Lotus Sametime™ chat, etc.), but even these disappear as soon as the decision is made.

This enables the manager to work extremely efficiently in his own personalized manner, so the current of business processes will be stronger than the pre-Alloy days, and the results of the decisions will definitely be more reliable.

23.1.3 Decision Views

Irrespective of whether the decision is waiting in the inbox, has been moved to another folder, or has been completed by the manager or a colleague (perhaps in another medium), the decision can be revisited easily from one of the Alloy *request views*. These views can be reached using the VIEWS button in the sidebar or from standard Lotus menu or views navigation. Because many decisions relate to self-service requests, these views are called REQUEST views, and the manager when selecting this view can also see any requests he has created (such as a travel request). Figure 23.2 shows multiple pending decisions in Alloy.

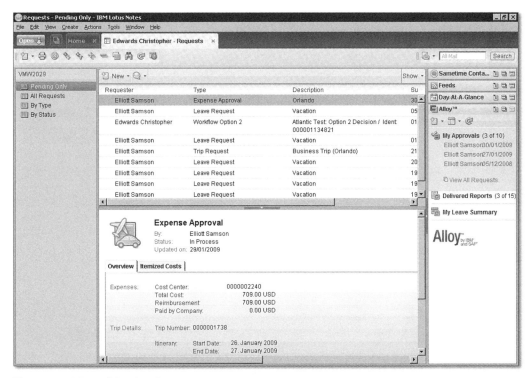

Figure 23.2 View of Pending Decisions

The following views are available in Alloy 1.0:

▶ Pending decisions (only available for users in the manager role)

▶ Decisions by status

▶ Decisions by type

▶ Decisions by user

When a manager selects the requests views, he is taken directly to the last view that he was working in. So if he spends most of his time processing requests from his time or other decisions of any type, he lands in the PENDING view by default. However, if he prefers spending a certain time each day concentrating on decisions of one particular type, then the DECISIONS BY TYPE view is his default. In other words, Alloy adjusts the user interface according to the way the users work.

One final point concerning these views is that the PENDING view shows a filter of all decisions, filtering out the decisions that have already been made or are obsolete. All other views show all items in a tree structure according to the view selected. So the view by status shows a tree of the different statuses with the corresponding list of decisions under each branch.

Figure 23.3 shows a tree view for the pending decisions.

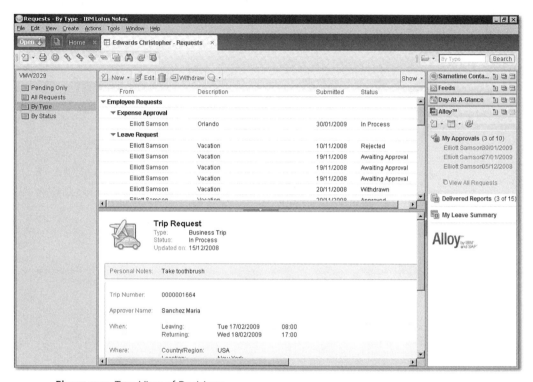

Figure 23.3 Tree View of Decisions

Tip

It is a Lotus specialty that by clicking on a column header, you override the branch category and sort according to the column selected. To return to the tree view, simply click on the column header a second time.

23.1.4 Calendar Items

Calendar items are not strictly related to the decisions themselves. These are generated automatically when an employee makes certain Alloy requests. However, because the request itself is part of a process, the calendar item reflects the decision status, so it is worth describing here. This is not part of the generic decision enablement in Alloy, and you can read more about the Alloy requests and the processes later in this chapter. Figure 23.4 shows a calendar that includes the status of various tasks.

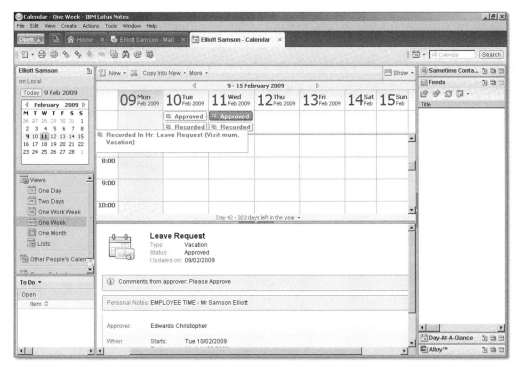

Figure 23.4 Calendar View of a Request Showing Status

However, when a user creates a leave request or a travel request, the status notifications not only arrive in the employee's mail inbox but are also reflected in the calendar entry directly. The status update occurs when the employee opens the notification item.

For example, when a user creates a leave request (in Lotus or the SAP NetWeaver Portal), the leave request is displayed in the employee's Lotus Notes calendar, and the status is shown as PENDING APPROVAL. When the manager approves the request, the employee receives a notification that it has been approved, and the calendar is updated to APPROVED so that when the employee looks at the calendar later, he can see at a glance that it has been approved. The same is true of requests that do not need approval such as jury service leave request.

The SAP software approves automatically without involving any managers, and the notification is generated and the calendar updated. The same is true if the request is declined. To avoid embarrassment or any HR issues, all employee requests are marked as private by default. The requestor can make them public at any time at his discretion, but independent of the privacy flag, any manual approvals are routed to the correct manager and include the necessary details to make the decision.

23.2 Prerequisites for Alloy

Alloy requires both SAP and Lotus software to run, as well as Alloy server software to link up the two and choreograph the Web Services. Lotus Notes is the client software from IBM that is installed on the client PCs, and Lotus Domino is the name given for the Lotus server software. There is no Alloy client software that needs to be deployed because the Domino server replicates the Alloy user interface to any client that is activated for Alloy, and the sidebar plugin can be deployed directly as a widget.

Alloy has the minimum release system prerequisites shown in Table 23.1 based on the information available at the time of publication, but because they are liable to change, verify this on the SAP Service Marketplace (*http://service.sap.com*).

System	Release
IBM Lotus Notes Client	Release 8.02
IBM Domino Server	Release 8.02
SAP ERP	SAP ERP 6.0 SPS 14 running on SAP NetWeaver 7.0 SPS17 with the ECC-SE 602 or higher add-on

Table 23.1 System Requirements for Alloy

Alloy was designed to enable multichannel access so the Business Workplace or Universal Worklist (UWL) can be used in parallel with Alloy. Similarly, you may decide to only give one group of managers access while the others work in another medium; this is supported by Alloy. In fact, if a particular manager prefers working offline in Lotus Notes and online in the Business Workplace then no additional administration, personalization, or customizing is necessary to enable this. Alloy is multichannel.

23.3   Generic Workflow Capabilities

Clearly the ability to make a decision (clicking a button) or view pending or completed decisions is supported by Alloy. In addition, a manager can add ad-hoc comments or view previous ad-hoc comments when making a decision.

Other generic capabilities come with time, so consult your online documentation or the SDN forums to discover what is possible with the Alloy release that you are working in.

23.4   Adding New Decisions to Alloy

The travel approval and expense approvals are based on SAP Business Workflow and are good examples of what you can achieve by adding your own decision steps from existing workflows to Alloy. The customizing principle is simply: Basic decisions can be added with a minimum of effort and can be customized for more effectiveness if needed using existing SAP and Lotus tools.

Table 23.2 shows the basic customizing capabilities that are possible with increasing sophistication as you go down the table.

Goal	Result	Tools
1. Propagate workflow decisions to Lotus Notes. The decision is not restricted to two outcomes.	The decisions are displayed in the Lotus inbox, and views and can be executed from Lotus Notes offline or online. The long description of the task is shown in the body of the decision, so this should contain all of the data that the manager needs to perform the decision. The work item short text is displayed, as are the buttons as defined in the generic decision task of the workflow.	No development tools. Select the workflow steps required in the Alloy (Information Worker) IMG. and specify a name for this type of approval to display in the views.

Table 23.2 Customizing Capabilities

Goal	Result	Tools
2. As above, but design a new user interface for the decision.	Each decision type is rendered using a new custom-built form in Lotus Notes to make it easier and more attractive to use.	As above, but also copy the existing Lotus decision form template and enhance it as you wish. This is done using the easy to use Domino Designer tool for creating user interfaces. The complete contents of the workflow container can be displayed in the decision.
3. Bring in more data from the SAP Business Suite.	One or more user exits (custom handler) can be invoked when a work item is propagated to Lotus Notes to add additional information that is not in the workflow container. This is typically done when the key of an object being transferred needs to be augmented with the detail contained. In addition, context information from other SAP Business Suite sources can be added at this point.	A standard ABAP routine is added to the IMG customizing. ABAP skills are necessary to perform this.
4. An approval step based on an activity (non-generic decision step) is added. This is restricted to the two outcomes APPROVE and REJECT.	Any workflow dialog decision can be propagated to Lotus, even if it is not based on the generic decision task. However, it may only have two outcomes, and no other container data may be modified. The resulting APPROVE or REJECT is the outcome, and these buttons are rendered in Lotus Notes.	An ABAP exit is defined to handle the outcome of the decision. The code may invoke BAPIs or other exits that perform further actions. For example, an APPROVE outcome could trigger ABAP code that releases a purchase requisition if desired.

Table 23.2 Customizing Capabilities (cont.)

Goal	Result	Tools
5. Additional sidebar information and actions.	Because the decisions container is propagated to the Lotus Notes client, the sky is the limit when it comes to what can be done with this data when you develop your own HTML sidebar fragment. Additional data from other Domino applications can be displayed in the sidebar and even additional capabilities, such as online meetings with colleagues or partners involved in the decision in any way. You could even search for experts to help with the decision by leveraging on Lotus Connections.	Lotus Notes development.

Table 23.2 Customizing Capabilities (cont.)

These possibilities can be combined to provide whatever context information you require in the final implementation. The amount of development effort that you invest may very from decision to decision, depending on how important it is. The effort can vary from simply adding the entries to the IMG tables to efforts of several days or weeks to get the user interface for particular decisions just right. This will vary from customer to customer and decision to decision.

23.4.1 Adding New Decision Steps

Follow these steps to add new decisions steps to Alloy:

1. Select workflow and the generic decision in your existing workflow that you want to propagate to Lotus Notes; note the task ID (not necessarily TS00008267) and the step number. To enter this data, you need to specify a new name for this type of decision, which will later be propagated to the Lotus decision/request views. This is called an Alloy "application," and each application may contain several workflow decisions, such as when a hierarchical decision process is involved in completing a decision.

2. Specify the application name in Lotus customizing of Alloy, and register this on the SAP add-on.

3. In Lotus customizing, you may want to specify related links, and similarly in SAP IMG customizing, you may want to specify related reports through the reporting customizing. The related reports enable the decision maker to view the reports from the sidebar after opening a decision.

4. Verify that the long text is appropriate. Because the task description has been used prior to Alloy in other user interfaces such as UWL or the Business Workplace, you may want to check that the text is appropriate for the Lotus client and if necessary correct this.

Figure 23.5 shows the configuration required on the Domino server.

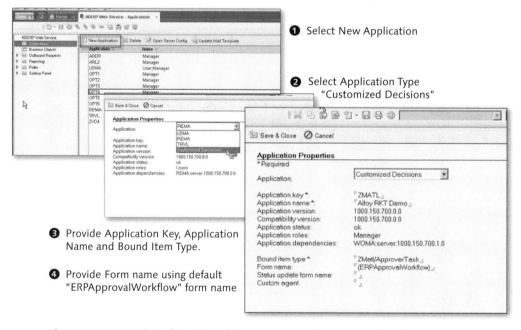

Figure 23.5 Screenshot of Domino Admin Customizing New Application Name

23.4.2 Design a New User Interface for the Decision

A description of how to use Lotus Designer is out of scope of this book, but good tutorials exist on SDN (*http://sdn.sap.com*). Because Lotus Designer is probably new to you, you should reach out to the Domino administrators and developers who are present at most Lotus Notes deployments. This is because historically application development work often goes hand-in-hand with a Notes deployment so the skills to develop new forms based on the existing template to customize the form appearance are already present at Lotus sites. The workflow container data is pre-parsed into XML named pairs to enable it to be incorporated easily into the form. In fact, both the workflow container and the work item container are both transferred to take into account the fact that sometimes the form renders a generic decision and sometimes it renders a dialog task.

Figure 23.6 shows a decision task in Alloy. Notice you can see the container elements in the decision.

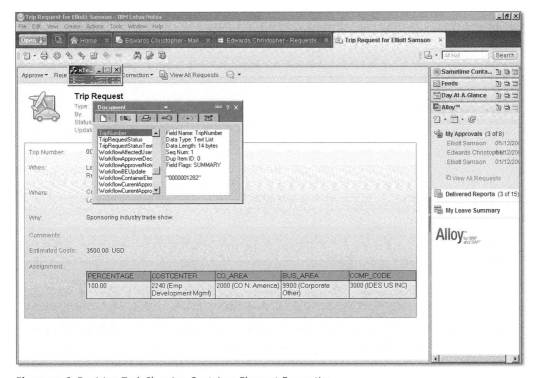

Figure 23.6 Decision Task Showing Container Element Properties

The button text is taken directly from the workflow definition, so there is no need to render the buttons in the form. Figure 23.7 shows collaboration capabilities with a more complex decision. Notice in Figure 23.7 the use of Lotus Sametime integration showing which colleagues are online.

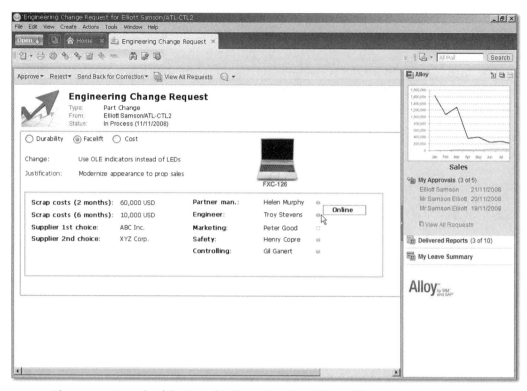

Figure 23.7 Example of the Sort of Collaboration Possibilities Offered in a More Complex Decision

23.4.3 Add Additional Data from the SAP Context

A custom exit (termed custom handler) allows a consultant to define additional SAP data that will be transferred to the form. This may be the case when a lot of attributes, including tabular elements, need to be displayed in the form. In such a case, the key of the business objects in the workflow is not sufficient, and the properties of the objects have to be passed too.

It is bad practice to expand the workflow container with these properties because this diminishes the performance of the SAP workflow; instead, one or more exits (*outbound* custom handlers) can be added to collect the information and add it to the bound item that is transmitted to the Domino Server.

This is done in the IMG customizing. It requires ABAP skills and the creation of a function module that follows a particular interface. After this has been done, the additional data can be incorporated into the Lotus form as if it came from the workflow container itself. So this technique adds no additional complexity to the Lotus customizing. In fact, the colleague designing the form in Domino Designer does not need to worry whether data being rendered comes from the workflow container or the custom handler simplifying his task.

23.4.4 Adding a Dialog Task

The decision does not have to be based on a generic decision, but if it is not, then it is limited to Approve and Reject because these are the two buttons that the Lotus client renders by default. The technique used is very similar to what is done in the UWL. The method of the task is bypassed and replaced with the Lotus approval form and ABAP logic of your own to make sure the result is processed properly.

Use the standard custom handler to terminate the processing of the work item as normal, but add your own *inbound* customer handlers to perform the consequences of approving or rejecting. You need detailed knowledge of the workflow and the business object to do this. In some cases, the workflow is modeled so that the approve or reject handling is taken care of in the next step (in which case, you don't need to perform any development), but in other cases, this is handled in the body of the method that you are bypassing, so you will need to code the consequences in your inbound customer handler.

23.4.5 Sidebar Enhancements

Enhancing the sidebar is out of scope of the book and is something where the possibilities evolve with time through the SDN and Lotus development communities. The possibilities arise because the container data is exposed to the sidebar and can be manipulated and rendered according to what you want to achieve. Suggestions include the following:

▶ Graphically rendering decision context data to display a pie chart (such as budget availability), traffic lights (threshold exceeded), or graph (trend) to highlight the decision context

▶ Sametime integration for people involved in the decision, such as colleagues involved in prior steps in the process or stakeholders not directly involved in the process

▶ Application data extracted from other Lotus Notes databases

Tip

When enhancing, take into account the design paradigm of Alloy. All essential information should be shown in the body of the decision. All secondary information can be shown in the sidebar.

23.5   Standard Alloy Decisions

This section discusses decision steps in Alloy:

▸ **Leave approvals**
Lotus Notes can have the same user interface, regardless if a user decision is based on SAP Business Workflow or some other technology. For example, leave approvals in SAP Manager Self-Service (MSS) are not always based on SAP Business Workflow. The use of workflows in SAP MSS depends on customizing. This illustrates how the Alloy user interface filters out complexity from the users so that they see one user interface, independent of the underlying software details of the automated decision.

With time, it is clear that other SAP workflow and decision engines will have to be enabled within Alloy. But the advantage of this approach is that it is transparent for the users in Lotus Notes, and the behavior is predictable and self-explanatory.

The leave request shows how the body of the decision has been customized so that additional SAP data, such as outstanding leave due, are displayed immediately without the need to research. The body is also sametime enabled so that the manager can chat online with the requestor directly (the same is true for the requestor). Related reports can show the team view of which team member is also scheduled to be absent at the time of the leave request, and the manager can navigate straight to the Lotus calendar to confirm this if he wants to. In addition, the manager may go to his view of pending requests to get an idea of who else is asking for leave at the same time and juggle his decision making accordingly.

▸ **Travel and expense approvals**
Travel and expense approvals are based on SAP Business Workflow. They also show what is possible by designing your own form using the contents of the workflow container.

The Duet software solution from SAP and Microsoft enables users to easily and quickly interact with SAP business processes and data via their familiar Microsoft Office environment. This chapter provides introductory information on using Duet with approval tasks from SAP Business Workflow.

24 Duet — Microsoft Office Integration

Duet provides easy access to information by combining SAP data with Microsoft Outlook. Microsoft Office is a great environment in which to implement specific business scenarios and end user tasks. The focus for Duet is to bring selected SAP business processes into the information worker environment. In Office, the information worker receives emails to stay informed, schedules appointments, works with spreadsheets, works with contact information, and creates documents. All of these tasks can be extended with SAP business functionality as shown in the different Duet scenarios.

Every organization has unique workflow requirements. To accommodate this requirement, specifically release Duet 1.5 offers a Duet Workflow Approval template (see Figure 24.1). The Duet workflow approval template offers a user-friendly approach to workflow approvers by integrating into Microsoft Outlook. Within this well-known environment, approvers can approve or reject a request. While acting upon requests, approvers can view relevant contextual information in the Duet Action Pane to help them make an educated decision. Duet approval functionality is available both online and offline.

The Duet workflow approval template enables you to customize Duet with SAP Business Workflow to create an approval workflow application containing the actions and features approvers need, along with decision supporting information.

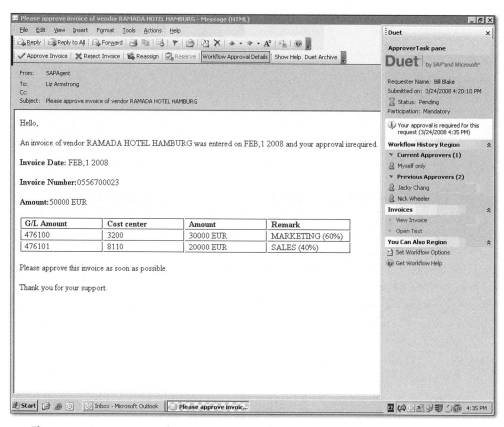

Figure 24.1 Invoice Approval Exposed in Microsoft Outlook Through the Duet Workflow Approval Template

Hint

This chapter provides an overview of the Duet workflow approval template. For details on configuring the Duet workflow approval template, see the guide *Developing a Decision Making Scenario Using Duet Workflow Approval Template* in SDN (*http://www.sdn.sap.com/irj/sdn/duet*).

Business processes require at least one person to complete a series of tasks. Such processes can benefit from approval workflow applications that automate the tasks, thereby reducing costs, removing errors, speeding processes, and tracking the status of the process. An approval workflow application in Duet lets you automate tasks, which often involve automatically sending mail messages such as making a request for a trip or for vacation.

Real-World Scenario

When a manager needs to approve a business event, for example, order of a new laptop or travel request, the business process is controlled by a SAP workflow. With the Duet workflow approval template, any SAP workflow approval step can be handled through Microsoft Outlook. The scenario template gives the developer the right tools and pre-configured objects to connect it into SAP Business Workflow and enrich the message (which shows up in the Outlook inbox of the approver) with the right SAP business information to make the approval decision.

24.1 Design Time Layout

Users are notified of a Duet workflow task either through an email notification or business task. This section discusses the layout of the notification email that is received by the approver.

The email notification is a Duet workflow approval request with actions, such as dynamic links, and contextual information that lets the end user dive further into detailed information to make a decision. For example, for a leave request, the manager can view contextual information, such as vacation days left, accruals, and planned vacation, or even dynamically navigate to a external link containing vacation policy before approving his employee's leave request.

The email notification for a Duet workflow tasks contains the following areas, which are shown in Figure 24.2:

▶ **Duet toolbar/ribbon**
As shown in area ❶ of Figure 24.2, this region is placed on the top of the email body. The Duet toolbar/ribbon includes actions an approver can take on a specific workflow request: APPROVE, REJECT, SUBSTITUTE, and REASSIGN, RESERVE, as well as a SHOW AND HIDE ACTION PANE button and a contextual Duet HELP button.

▶ **Mail header**
The header, which you can see in area ❷ of Figure 24.2, contains the FROM, TO, SUBJECT, and ATTACHMENTS. The FROM is the scenario's name, the TO is the full name of the contact, and the SUBJECT is the application name and full name of the sender. The ATTACHMENTS refer to a text file that includes all comments relevant to this item. Comments can be inserted whenever an approver takes an action.

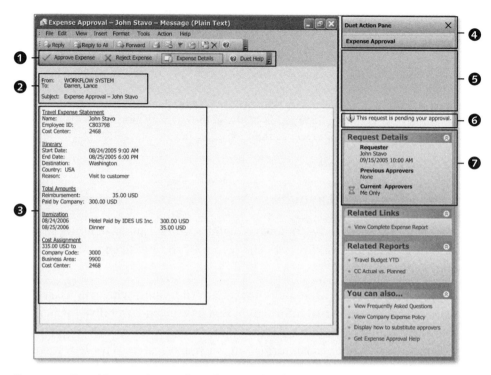

Figure 24.2 Travel Expense Approval Email Received in the Approver's Inbox.

▶ **Email body**

Area ❸ of Figure 24.2 has the email body. All of the details of the request are pushed into the body by the backend and are mostly application specific. So, for example, in Figure 24.2, you can see that the trip approval shows details of the trip (when, where, who, cost center, etc.), whereas the report template shows other details (report name, delivery option, description, frequency). The options are variable and customized into the email body of the scenario template.

▶ **Duet Action Pane**

As shown in area ❹ of Figure 24.2, this is the region on the right side of the main panel. The majority of the contextual information related to the workflow decision is displayed in the sidebar called the *Duet Action Pane*. For example, when entering a leave request, the user sees the remaining days/time available for that particular leave type. When scheduling a report, it can show the scheduling information about the report.

The Duet Action Pane of the approval template primarily is delivered with the following regions: BRANDING, OBJECT IDENTIFICATION (OID), YOU CAN ALSO, plus a workflow specific region called HISTORY. The YOU CAN ALSO region provides the administrator with the option to extend the information displayed by adding new segments in the form of dynamic links to make informed decisions. Data from the approval request can be embedded in links such as company travel policy and company vacation policy to allow navigation to additional relevant information from legacy systems, company portals, and so on.

▸ **Object Identification region (OID)**
Area ❺ of Figure 24.2 shows the object identification region, which is part of the Action Pane and displays the summary of the enterprise context for the opened Duet item. The workflow template provides the following default label/value pairs, which are configurable; that is, you can add or remove the backend fields to this region (out of scope of this book).

  ▸ **Requester name**
  Full name, preceded by a presence control when supported.

  ▸ **Submitted on**
  Time that the request was submitted on. The default should be the short version timestamp.

  ▸ **Status**
  The STATUS is preceded by an icon that describes the different statuses. Both the Business Task (approver side) and the Business Request status (requester side) use the icons shown in Figure 24.3.

Status	Icon
Not started	◇
In process/Awaiting approval	⌛
Approved/Completed	✔
Rejected	▬
Canceled	⊗
Reassigned	🗗
Reserved	🗐
release	TBD

Figure 24.3 Status Icons Available in the Duet Workflow Approval Template

▸ **Dynamic Messages Region (DMR)**
Area ❻ of Figure 24.2 is a mandatory region located at a fixed location under the Object Identification region (OID). The goal of this region is to provide the

user dynamic contextual messages about an object or process within a Duet scenario. DMR supports the display of error messages that occur asynchronously. Messages that can be displayed might come from the backend, client-side validation mechanism, or guidelines for the user, for example, "Please enter your project code to complete the workflow." In Figure 24.2 within the DMR region, the user is alerted to take action to complete the travel request; whereas in reporting the DMR region is used for notification purposes, for example, "This report was triggered on 10/11/2008 at 10:00p.m."

> **Note**
>
> DMR should not be used for activity of detailed messages (i.e., DMR should not be used as an inbox; applications that desire the handling of activities history should create a separate region dedicated to that issue).

▶ **History region/Request details**
Area ❼ of Figure 24.2 is the History region. This region displays the participants in the workflow process. Here the approver is able to see if and who is required to take an action during the current workflow step as well as the approvers of the previous step. The approver may contact participants directly using the presence control (supported in Microsoft Office Communicator 2007 only). The History region is divided into two sections: The CURRENT APPROVERS section and the PREVIOUS APPROVERS section. The CURRENT APPROVERS part is expanded by default, and the PREVIOUS APPROVERS part is collapsed by default.

> **Note**
>
> The PREVIOUS APPROVERS part always refers to the previous step only even if there are more than two steps; this means that not all approvers are necessarily displayed in the region.

24.2 How an Approval Workflow Application Works in Duet

When a request is initiated, the request triggers a process in the SAP system. The SAP system sends an email and a business task to the approver, and the status of the task is set to WAITING FOR APPROVAL. When the approver approves the request, its status changes to APPROVED, and a message with the new status is displayed in the approvers Duet client (in the Action Pane for the user).

The requestor receives a message confirming the approval in the SAP system inbox. When a step in the task is completed, the request moves on to the following step, the SAP system is updated accordingly, and the requester receives a notification and status information. The request is completed when all of the tasks are completed. However, if a request is rejected, then the process is terminated, and all approvers at that stage are informed about the rejection.

For example, you can model a workflow application describing the business rules about how a transaction involving the accounts is approved, rejected, or assigned to another person for approval. The approver is characterized by:

▶ A need for a single place to track, "things I need to process"

▶ A need to contribute and then move on, with less interest in the entire lifecycle of a process

▶ A need to have access to contextual information to support his decision

▶ An occasional need to understand his role in the process, including who else is involved

A business process enabled as an approval workflow application in Duet is initiated by a request. One or more approvers can approve or reject the request, reassign it to someone else, substitute someone else in place of an approver for a period, or reserve a request for a later response. In addition, approvers have access to relevant information in Microsoft Office Outlook to help them make an informed decision.

The Duet workflow approval template supports all types of approver relationships, as defined in the SAP system. Table 24.1 shows the common types of approver relationships.

Type	Description
Single approver	There is only one approver for a request. This is a simple and common workflow.
Parallel approvers	There is an AND relationship between several approvers. This requires all approvers of a particular step to approve a request for the flow to be complete. A rejection by any of the approvers stops and completes this step in the process. For example, both John and Jane must approve a leave request.

Table 24.1 Types of Approver Relationships

Type	Description
Multiple approvers	There is an OR relationship between several approvers. This requires only one of the approvers to approve or reject the request to complete the task. For example, John, Jane, or Bob can approve a leave request.
Combined	A combination of the types of approver relationships is possible in the template. One of the steps can consist of a single approver, while other steps consist of multiple or parallel approvers.

Table 24.1 Types of Approver Relationships (cont.)

The Duet workflow approval template supports the actions shown in Table 24.2.

Decision Type	Description
Reservation	Where one approval is sufficient to complete the step for a multiple approver scenario (any of the current approvers may "reserve" (lock the request for his approval only).
Approve	Upon approval, the STATUS in the OID is updated to APPROVED, and the bound item syncs with the SAP system. The particular approver is not notified of any further steps of the process unless there is a rejection by another approver; as far as he is concerned the request is completed.
Reject	At any stage of the approval process, an approver might decide to reject. In that case, the entire process is terminated, and all people that have participated are notified. The status of the request changes to REJECTED. Approvers of following steps (if any) are not made aware of the request.
Substitution	Permits an end user to assign a supplementary approver to respond on his behalf. This is often used when someone is away on vacation, ill, or on a trip with limited access to mail. Substitutes are designated per a Duet workflow application for a predefined period of time (thus a substitute is not selected for a particular request). The assigned substitute can perform the same actions as the original approver. Both the original approver and the assigned substitute are possible approvers (multiple approvers relationship).

Table 24.2 Types of Actions You Can Take on a Duet Approval Workflow Task

Decision Type	Description
Reassign	An approver may choose to reassign a particular workflow request to another person. Upon reassigning, the original approver is replaced with the newly assigned approver. The original approver may still access the request item, but loses the ability to take further actions upon it.
Add Comments	Approvers may add comments to a particular request upon clicking one of the action buttons; APPROVE, REJECT, RESERVE, or REASSIGN. A dialog allows the user to add his comments and submit the response. Approver's comments are optional by default.

Table 24.2 Types of Actions You Can Take on a Duet Approval Workflow Task (cont.)

24.3 Prerequisites to Use the Duet Workflow Approval Template

The Duet workflow approval template leverages the existing Duet infrastructure that comprises both SAP Business Suite and Microsoft Office Suite. The basic architecture of Duet software consists of the following major elements:

▶ Duet client add-on for the Microsoft Office environment

▶ Duet Server

▶ Duet add-on for SAP software

There are no changes required to the Microsoft Exchange Server; it is purely used for messaging purposes. Duet has the minimum release system prerequisites shown in Table 24.3. The perquisites provided are based on the information available at the time of publication of this book, but they may change, so verify this on the SAP Service Marketplace (*http://service.sap.com*).

System	Prerequisites
Microsoft Office Client	Microsoft Office Outlook 2003 or a later version, Microsoft Visual Studio 2005
Microsoft Windows Server	Release 2003 SP2

Table 24.3 Technical Prerequisites for Using Duet

System	Prerequisites
SAP ERP	SAP ERP 6.0 SPS 14 running on SAP NetWeaver 7.0 SPS17 with the ECC-SE 602 or higher Add-on
Microsoft Exchange	2003 SP2 (Enterprise Edition) 2007 SP1 (Enterprise Edition)

Table 24.3 Technical Prerequisites for Using Duet (cont.)

Duet was designed to enable multichannel access so the SAP Business Workplace or Universal Worklist (UWL) can be used in parallel with Duet. Similarly, you may decide to only give one group of managers access, while the others work in another medium, and this is supported by Duet too. In fact, if a particular manager prefers working offline in Microsoft Outlook and online in the Business Workplace then no additional administration, personalization or customizing is necessary to enable this. Duet is natively multichannel.

24.4 Creating Your Approval Workflow Application

Before you create a Duet approval workflow application, carefully plan the actual workflow. There are workflow approval applications already in use in the SAP system. Using the Duet workflow approval template, you can enable these existing approval workflow applications for use in Microsoft Office Outlook.

To create a completely new approval workflow application for use in Duet, first create the workflow in your SAP system, and then customize and extend it using the Duet workflow approval template. By default, the Duet workflow approval template provides you with mailing features for your workflow approval application; however, you must decide on the type of approver relationship you want to implement. Doing so allows you to identify the various requirements of the application, such as the roles to enable in the application. In addition, you can identify the various steps and tasks associated with a role and can create an outline of the relationship between the roles.

The following is a summary of the sequence of tasks for creating an approval workflow application in Duet:

▶ **Step 1**

Ensure that the approval workflow application (template) you want to create in Duet already exists in the SAP system. The approval is normally based on a USER DECISION task in SAP Business Workflow.

▶ **Step 2**

Configure the SAP system for the Duet workflow approval template. This includes the configuration of extended notifications. Extended notifications (discussed in Chapter 4, Work Item Delivery) are used in Duet approval workflow applications.

Thus, in addition to configuring the SAP Business Workflow, you also need to configure extended notifications. Extended notifications in SAP NetWeaver refer to the interaction point between SAP Business Workflow and Duet approval workflow components. An extended notification takes the instance status of an approval workflow runtime and sends this information to the Duet client. It focuses only on the decision-making tasks. The overall process can be divided into the following two subprocesses:

▷ **Outbound process**

Holds a runtime instance of the workflow triggered by an application in the SAP system and broadcasts the same instance to Duet, enabling the agent of the task to make decisions within the Duet environment.

▷ **Inbound process**

Provides the mechanism for approval decisions from the Duet.

▶ **Step 3**

Install the Duet Approval Workflow Configuration tool on the Duet client (developer laptop). Customize the Duet workflow approval template to enable you to create a model of your approval workflow application for use in Duet. The Duet Approval Workflow Configuration tool is an add-in in Visual Studio 2005, which is a visual designer based on domain-specific language tools. It helps the administrator depict the graphical representation of email or task as seen on the Duet Outlook client.

The add-in can be used to drag and drop Duet client-specific components without writing code. The tasks include the following:

▷ Modify the attributes and properties of the Duet workflow approval template.

> ▶ Configure the attributes and properties of the Duet workflow approval template.

> ▶ Generate and package all of the files for the modeled application.

▶ **Step 4**
Generate and deploy the files for the approval workflow application.

24.4.1 Adding New Decisions to Duet

The travel approvals and expense approvals are based on SAP Business Workflow and are good examples of what you can achieve by adding your own decision steps from existing workflows to Duet. The customizing principle is basically that decisions can be added with a minimum of effort and can be customized for more effectiveness if needed using existing SAP and Visual Studio tools. Table 24.4 shows the basic customizing capabilities that are possible with increasing sophistication as you go down the table.

Goal	Result	Tools
1. Propagate workflow decisions to Outlook. The decision can have multiple outcomes.	The decisions are displayed in Outlook and can be executed from Outlook offline or online. The long-description of the task is shown in the body of the decision, so this should contain all of the data that the manager needs to perform the decision. The work item text is displayed, as are the buttons as defined in the generic decision task of the workflow.	No development tools. Select the workflow steps required in the Duet IMG, and specify a name for this type of approval to display in the views. Note: You must use the standard USER DECISION task for this option.
2. Same as above, but design a new user interface for the decision.	Each decision type is rendered using a new custom-built template in Visual Studio to make it easier and more attractive to use.	As above, but also copy the template and enhance it using the Duet workflow template provided in the Visual Studio. This is the standard tool for creating user interfaces and is simple to use. The complete contents of the workflow container can be displayed in the decision.

Table 24.4 Options to Add New Decisions to Duet

Goal	Result	Tools
3. Bring in more data from the SAP Business Suite.	One or more user exits (custom handlers) can be invoked when a work item is propagated to Outlook to add additional information that is not in the workflow container. This is typically done when the key of an object being transferred needs to be augmented with the details contained. In addition, context information from other SAP Business Suite sources can be added at this point.	A standard ABAP routine is added to the IMG customizing. ABAP skills are necessary to perform this.
4. An approval step based on an activity (non-generic decision step) is added. This is restricted to the two outcomes APPROVE and REJECT or actions on SUBSTITUTE, RESIGN, or RESERVE.	Any workflow dialog decision can be propagated to Outlook, even if it is not based on the generic decision task. However, it may only have two outcomes, and no other container data may be modified. The outcome is APPROVE or REJECT, and these buttons are rendered in Microsoft Outlook.	An ABAP exit is defined to handle the outcome of the decision. The code may invoke BAPIs or other exits that perform further actions. For example, an APPROVE outcome could trigger ABAP code that releases a purchase requisition if desired.
5. Additional sidebar information and actions.	Because the decisions container is propagated to the Microsoft Outlook client, the sky is the limit when it comes to what can be done with this data when you develop your own HTML sidebar fragment. Additional data from other Duet applications can be displayed in the sidebar and even additional capabilities, such as online-meetings with colleagues or partners involved in the decision in any way.	Visual Studio add-in for Duet 1.5 workflow approval template.

Table 24.4 Options to Add New Decisions to Duet (cont.)

These possibilities can be combined to provide whatever context information you require in the final implementation. The amount of development effort that you invest may vary from decision to decision depending on how important it is. The effort can vary from simply adding the entries to the IMG tables to the effort of several days or weeks to get the user-interface for particular decisions just right. This will vary from customer to customer and decision to decision.

24.4.2 Design a New User Interface for the Decision

A description of how to use Visual Studio is out of scope of this book. However, at most Duet installations, there will be administrators and developers with .NET skills to develop new templates based on the existing Duet default template to customize the template form appearance.

The workflow container data is pre-parsed into XML named pairs to enable it to be incorporated easily into the template. In fact, both the workflow container and the work item container are both transferred to take into account that sometimes the template renders a generic decision, and sometimes it renders a dialog task.

Figure 24.4 depicts the Duet template in Visual Studio. The template contains two main entities: the *model data source* and the *workflow item*.

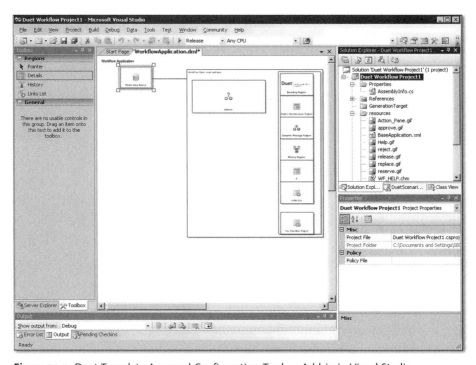

Figure 24.4 Duet Template Approval Configuration Tool — Add-in in Visual Studio.

The model data source, which is shown in the large box in Figure 24.4, represents the SAP system you want to configure for your workflow application. It contains a list of parameters based on the default workflow application. This entity is connected directly to the other major entity, the workflow item (mail and task), denoting a relationship between the two entities.

> **Note**
>
> You cannot delete the model data source entity, but you can edit its contents.

24.4.3 Add Additional Data from the SAP Context

A user exit in Duet allows you to add additional SAP data to the template. This may be the case when a lot of attributes, including tabular elements, need to be displayed in the form. In such a case, the key of the business objects in the workflow are not sufficient, but the properties of the objects have to be passed too.

It is bad practice to expand the workflow container with these properties because this diminishes the performance of the SAP workflow, so instead, one or more exits (*outbound custom handlers*) can be added to collect the information and add it to the bound item that is transmitted to the Duet client. The adding of custom handlers is done in the IMG customizing. It requires ABAP skills and the creation of a function module that follows a particular interface. For example, to obtain detailed information about a trip, such as the cost, the dates, and shipment, you need to develop a custom handler that can retrieve.

After this has been done, the additional data can be incorporated into the Visual Studio Duet template as if it came from the workflow container itself. So this technique adds no additional complexity to the Outlook customizing. In fact the colleague designing the template in Visual Studio designer does not need to worry whether data being rendered comes from the workflow container or the custom handler.

24.4.4 Adding a Dialog Task

Normally, the approval decision is based on the USER DECISION generic decision task (TS8267). However, it does not have to be based on this task. If the decision is not based on the USER DECISION task, then the approval options are limited to APPROVE and REJECT (plus the other options to REASSIGN, RESERVE). The limitation is to two actions because these are the two buttons that the Lotus client renders by default.

The technique used is very similar to what is done in UWL. The method of the task is bypassed and replaced with the Duet workflow approval template and ABAP logic of your own to make sure the result is processed properly. Use the standard custom handler to terminate the processing of the work item as normal, but add your own *inbound customer handlers* to perform the consequences of generic decision type.

You need to have detailed knowledge of the workflow and the business object to do this. In some cases, the workflow is modeled so that the approve or reject handling is taken care of in the next step (in which case, you do not need to perform any development); however, in other cases, this is handled in the body of the method that you are bypassing, so you need to code the consequences in your inbound customer handler.

> **Note**
>
> The default inbound custom handler writes to the work item container elements. If the work item is a GENERIC DECISION task, it calls the appropriate APIs to complete the decision. If the work item is a DIALOG ACTIVITY task, then it sets the status of the work item to complete. If it encounters an error, it constructs an error mail with a link to the approval task.

24.4.5 Sidebar Enhancements

The sidebar is the Action Pane entity in the Duet workflow approval template. All of these fields can be edited as described in Section 24.2, How an Approval Workflow Application Works in Duet. Some of these regions represent activities in the workflow application, such as APPROVE, REJECT, HELP, SHOW ACTION PANE, REASSIGN, RESERVATION, and SUBSTITUTION.

> **Note**
>
> You cannot delete the Action Pane entity; however, you can add regions to it and edit their properties. The possibilities are endless based on the workflow container data configured or customized by the custom handler in the backend.

PART IV
Using SAP Business Workflow in SAP Business Suite Applications

SAP Supplier Relationship Management uses SAP Business Workflow as the central technical infrastructure to do critical tasks such as processing shopping carts, purchase orders, and invoices, as well as confirming goods and service deliveries. This chapter shows how this processing is core to the SAP SRM system.

25 SAP Supplier Relationship Management

SAP Supplier Relationship Management (SAP SRM), including the predecessor product, Enterprise Buyer Professional, has a long history with SAP Business Workflow. Since the first edition of this book, significant growth has occurred in SAP SRM, in particular as it relates to approval processes. The recent release is SAP SRM 7.0.

SAP SRM uses both BOR objects (Business Object Repository) and ABAP classes for workflow processing (see Chapter 10, Business Objects, and Chapter 11, ABAP Classes, for background information you need to understand these objects and classes). Table 25.1 provides an overview of the most commonly used business objects in SAP SRM, and Table 25.2 shows the commonly used ABAP classes with SAP SRM workflow. All classes implement the IF_WORKFLOW interface.

BOR Object Type	BOR Description	SAP SRM Name
BUS2121	EC Requirement Coverage Request	Shopping Cart/Internal Request
BUS2200	Bid Invitation EC	Request for Quotation
BUS2201	EC Purchase Order	Purchase Order (SRM local)
BUS2202	EC Vendor bid	Quotation
BUS2000113	Purchase Contract	Global Outline Agreement, Local Contract, Central Contract

Table 25.1 Major Business Objects Used in SAP SRM

BOR Object Type	BOR Description	SAP SRM Name
BUS2203	EC Confirmation Goods/Services	Confirmation
BUS2205	EC Incoming Invoice	Invoice (SRM local)
BUS2209	EC Purchase Order Response	Purchase Order Response
BBP_PCARD	Procurement Card	Procurement Card

Table 25.1 Major Business Objects Used in SAP SRM (cont.)

ABAP Class	Description
/SAPSRM/CL_WF_PDO	Base class for SAP SRM procurement documents referenced in approval workflows
/SAPSRM/CL_WF_PDO_CONF	Confirmation
/SAPSRM/CL_WF_PDO_CTR	Contract
/SAPSRM/CL_WF_PDO_INV	Invoice
/SAPSRM/CL_WF_PDO_PO	Purchase order
/SAPSRM/CL_WF_PDO_QTE	Quote (Bid)
/SAPSRM/CL_WF_PDO_RFQ	Request for Quotation (Bid Invitation)
/SAPSRM/CL_WF_PDO_SC	Shopping Cart

Table 25.2 ABAP Classes for SAP SRM Workflow

Note
The Purchase Order Response (BUS2209) has been changed between SAP SRM 5.0 and SAP SRM 7.0. In the SAP SRM 5.0 release, this object was supported by workflow templates (WS). With SAP SRM 7.0, the underlying business logic was reworked, and no longer makes use of templates but, instead, uses standard tasks (TS).

Documents based on these object types and classes must be approved or confirmed before SAP SRM processes can continue. This means that workflow plays a critical role in the productive use of SAP SRM. SAP Business Workflow is used for most approval processes supported by SAP SRM.

SAP understands that approval processes are customer specific: considerations such as when to approve and for what dollar limits are specific to each customer. SAP SRM is delivered with the assumption that approval conditions are highly customized, and it enables you to configure your own requirements easily.

SAP SRM's use of SAP Business Workflow is both tightly coupled and very unique to SAP SRM. For processing to work correctly in SAP SRM, it takes both a combination of SAP SRM approval frameworks and related SAP Business Workflow templates. Only this combination enables SAP SRM to offer special features that extend the normal offering in SAP Business Workflow. Major features gained by this unique combination include the following:

▶ The ability to support dynamic adaptation of the process when document changes occur

▶ A visualization of the approvers in an approval process overview, including a preview of who will approve the document

▶ Ad-hoc process extension

This chapter focuses on the unique combination of the SAP SRM framework with SAP Business Workflow. In SAP SRM, there are some standard workflows that do not use the SAP SRM framework, but they are not discussed in this chapter. Instead, this chapter covers the following SAP SRM functions:

▶ Approval processes in SAP SRM, what they are and the requirements they must meet

▶ Overview of the SAP SRM approval frameworks, and usage in SAP SRM 5.0 and SAP SRM 7.0

▶ Details of each SAP SRM framework

25.1 Approval Processes

Requirements for approval processes can be quite complex. In this section, we look at the types of approval processes that exist in SAP SRM.

25.1.1 Simple Approval Processes

If you stick with the strictest definition, then approval is about exposing a document to a decision maker and asking for approval. The selected agent accepts or not; it is as simple as that. To simplify this even more, when people discuss these approval processes, they normally take the positive decision (e.g., we don't call it a rejection or a decision process but an approval process).

The simple approval process is still very effective and continues to be used for a multitude of SAP SRM processes. For example, an employee selects an item from a catalog and orders it. The system forwards the requirement to their responsible line manager for approval. The simplicity of this process can depend on the depth of the company's hierarchical structure or on the complexity of the requirements requested.

25.1.2 Complex Approval Processes

Many customers require either more functionality along the decision path, or more flexibility concerning to whom an approval item is routed. Combinations of these two functional requirements are very common. Examples of customer requirements provided to SAP include the following:

▸ When a user places an order, normally the user selects an item from a catalog. However, if the user cannot find the item he needs, he can describe the item using "free text." A purchasing specialist then gets involved to provide the missing data to turn the request from a text-based only request into something that can be ordered from a supplier. Missing data can be added, or the entire request can be changed to ensure the item can be accurately ordered from a supplier.

▸ The approver requires additional information to make the decision to approve or reject. This might be anything from additional information, such as a product specification provided in a Microsoft Word document, to consulting a user from another department. In the case of adding additional people to the process, the approval process must be sufficiently flexible to update the process based on the approver's request.

▸ The approver approves the item but only if changes are made, such as a price change on a line item of a multiline contract document, an account assignment change on a purchase order item, or a deletion of an invoice line item. In all of these cases, the approver might want to send the changes back to the business document initiator for review, or the approver might need to immediately accept the change to expedite process without notifying the initiator.

▶ For some items ordered, there is a requirement to involve other people in the process to make statements (notes or attachments) about the document to be approved. For example, you are responsible for the purchasing of telecommunication products for your company. Your task is to select and approve the bid for new phones and headsets. Because many headsets are offered as options, you need to involve one of your telecommunication experts to help you pick the right headset type for your company.

As you can see, these requirements suddenly turn from "find my manager and get them to approve" into a much more complex process. A complex approval process is normally referred to as *combined completion and approval* processes. But for the sake of simplicity, we stick with the term *approval processes* throughout this chapter.

25.1.3 Key Concepts and Requirements That Make Up the Foundation of SAP SRM Approval Processing

This section describes the key terms, key concepts, and major customer requirements that drive the approval framework within SAP SRM. The requirements determine how an approval process should work, who should be involved, how a dynamic process should work, how the user should be able to visualize the process, and how to find the appropriate approval agents.

General Rule of Thumb for How an Approval Process Should Work

Throughout all SAP SRM releases, the conceptual idea of approval processes has been consistent:

▶ Approvals happen in consecutive levels (also known as *process depth* or *approval depth*).

▶ To reach the next level, the decision must be complete and final for the entire document at the current approval level.

This has important ramifications:

▶ Individual items of a document cannot pass the complete approval process; either the entire document moves to the next approval level, or none of the document moves to the next level.

▶ Individual items of a document cannot be released to later process/step unless a decision is made for the entire document.

▶ Approval processes in SAP SRM are at a document level. For a document to complete an approval level, the entire document must be approved:

　▷ If specific line items are rejected, the document can be sent back to the requestor for update, or the line item can be removed.

　▷ If a line item is removed, then the entire document can move to the next approval level.

　▷ If a line item is rejected and returned to the requester, then the document cannot move to the next approval level.

All line items in a document must be approved before moving to the next approval level.

Types of Job Roles/Job Functions Involved in an Approval Process

During the approval processes, four job roles are used:

▶ **Requester**
Person who initiated the request.

▶ **Specialist**
Person who is responsible to check the request for correctness or completeness. The role is referred to as *purchasing specialist*.

▶ **Approver**
Person who makes decisions (and potentially changes/corrections to the document).

▶ **Reviewer**
Person inspecting the process, providing comments, and attaching additional information to the process.

What a Dynamic Process Should Be Able to Do

The ability to support dynamic processes is a key customer requirement for the SAP SRM approval processes. Dynamic processing has two dimensions:

▶ The ability to dynamically determine the process based on document content. Different parts of the organization require different processes; for example, approval process differs depending upon the organizational unit or what cost center was entered into the account assignment of a particular line item.

▶ The ability to dynamically alter the process based on actual document content. When a process has been altered, the history of the document should be kept whenever possible. This means that when a document is changed, the process automatically recognizes the change and makes adjustments in the approval chain. A dynamic process change can have the following impact on the executing process:

  ▶ Adjust the number of required approval levels.

  ▶ Restart the current process.

  ▶ Terminate the current process, and start a different process.

Ad-Hoc Process Extension

Ad-hoc process extension is important to the requirement purchasing approval cycles in SAP SRM. The most common situation is that a SAP SRM approver needs to be added to an existing approval chain due to, for example, an exceptional situation or due to an ad-hoc decision by other approvers. However, ad-hoc processing can be used to completely define or refine the entire document approval path. For certain business scenarios, a predefined approval path cannot be designated. In such situations, users can, according to departmental guidelines, define the whole approval path ad-hoc, without a predefined decision template. Bear in mind that in such cases more than technical feasibility should be considered. Other design aspects, for example, legal consideration such as SOX (Sarbanes-Oxley) compliance, should be considered.

To make the approval chain transparent in its entirety, the approval process overview in SAP SRM comprises the determined agents, all added ad-hoc agents, and all other workflow chain extensions.

Approval Process Overview: User-Focused Process Visualization

Due to the possibility of having considerable dynamic in processing and approver determination, it is critical that the requestor and others involved in the process always have access to the actual information. All users should always be able to access the approval process overview displaying the upcoming approvers.

Let's consider an urgent process where approval must be performed within two business days. The requester wants to know the current status after the first day to ensure the purchasing request can be completed on time. The visualization of the approvers enables you to easily recognize who the current approver is so you can, for example, reach out to the person directly. The approval process overview is also critical for ad-hoc approvers. The approval process overview gives a user the opportunity to add ad-hoc approvers to the right spot of the approval chain.

A process overview has to be provided for the user. The overview displays:

▶ The history of the executed process levels and steps, including the agents that were involved

▶ The status and assignment of agents on the current process level

▶ A preview of the expected process levels (including the agent assignment)

Any time the user requests the "approval process overview," the system simulates steps of the corresponding workflow and presents the relevant information to the user; that is, the system determines all necessary and already executed approval steps based on the current procurement document and resolves the agents (users) that will be or were involved on each step. When the user updates the respective procurement document, for example, during the creation phase, the system adapts the preview accordingly.

The system does not simulate all possible process variants but only the one in which all approvers approve. The variants that result from rejecting a part of or the whole document are not simulated. The simulation of this approval process variant ensures that the maximum number of steps is determined.

Determining Who Has What Responsibility, and Why

Responsibility is a central concept for the SAP SRM Approval Frameworks. For each approval level, it must be determined *who* can make the decision for the entire document at that level. The determination of *who* can do *what* level of approval normally relates to the organization structure in your company, but it does not have to be tightly coupled to the organizational structure. Consider the following examples:

▶ Your business rules define that the immediate supervisor be the approver. In this case, the responsible approver can easily be determined by reading your company's organizational structure and finding the manager responsible.

▶ When certain products are ordered that are considered dangerous or hazardous, a "hazmat" expert must approve the order. In this case, a determination of direct line manager does not return the correct values. This particular situation requires that the "hazmat" approver is found dynamically, for example, via hazardous product category responsibility or via referring to a special organizational unit.

Approvers can be set up to have different levels of responsibility for a document. The normal use cases are:

▶ **Single responsibility**
The responsible agent must approval all items in a document. This means for each approval, one person is responsible.

▶ **Split responsibility**
There are multiple responsible agents for a document. For example, a document has multiple line items pointing to different product categories, and each product category has its own responsible approver. In this example, all product category approvers have to approve the document. If one product category approver rejects the document, then the entire document is rejected.

▶ **Shared responsibility**
There are multiple responsible agents for a document, where multiple approvers must approve the same line item. A common example for shared responsibility is cost center splitting, such as a new copier where the cost will be shared by two or more departments. In this situation, all involved cost centers must approve the purchase of the new copier. If just one of the cost centers approvers rejects the purchase order, then the entire order cannot move forward in the process.

The use cases of single split and shared responsibility can be combined when processing a document. Take the example of a new copy machine where the cost is shared between multiple cost centers. The first level of approval requires a shared responsibility where every cost center involved must approve the new copier. The next approval level can be set up as a single responsibility, where one person, for example, the director or vice president, must approve the purchase of a new copier.

Decision Sets

As you can see, for a particular document, there can be one approver or many approvers. From a workflow perspective, each approver requires his own work item. So, if a document has 10 line items, each pointing to different approvers, each approver should receive his own work item for the approval. The items that a single approver receives are referred to as a decision set. The responsible approvers can view all items in a document but only edit and approve the ones they have been assigned to as responsible agents.

A decision set is the list of items that an approver works on in the current approval level. Each work item created is associated with one decision set. For complete responsibility, all items belong to the same decision set. For split and shared responsibility, multiple decision sets are formed. It is easiest to think of a decision set as a work item that has the line items for each approver.

> **Hint**
>
> Chapter 9, Advanced Workflow Design Techniques, discusses how to start multiple work items based on a multiline container element, which is the technique used here. Each decision set corresponds to a subworkflow that is called multiple times.

25.2 SAP SRM Approval Frameworks

Now that we have talked about the requirements for SAP SRM, let's discuss in more detail how those requirements are implemented. SAP SRM has two approval frameworks, show in Figure 25.1:

▶ **Application-controlled workflow**
The application-controlled workflow was introduced several years ago. Application control is based on traditional SAP Business Workflow, where there are different physical workflows for the different approval processes. You can see this in Figure 25.1 where there is one workflow definition for one-step approval workflow and another workflow definition for two-step approval workflow.

▶ **Process-controlled workflow**
The process-controlled workflow was introduced in SAP SRM 7.0. With process-controlled workflow, one generic workflow is used. The configuration for

how the workflow should execute is done in the Business Rules Framework (BRF). With very simple configuration, an approval scenario is ready to execute. The goal is to enable the process to be configured without requiring expert SAP Business Workflow knowledge.

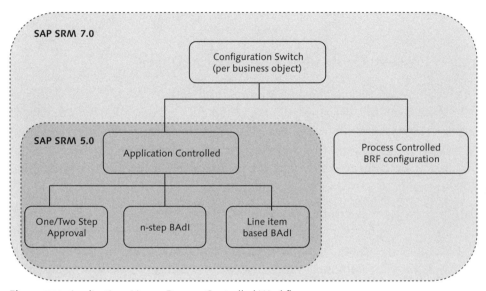

Figure 25.1 Application- Versus Process-Controlled Workflow

Recommendation

Of course, SAP recommends customers use the process-controlled workflow available in SAP SRM 7.0. Process-controlled framework is the basis for future development in SAP SRM. Customers currently on SAP SRM 5.0 (or lower releases) continue to use application-controlled workflow. Customers planning an upgrade to SAP SRM 7.0 can continue to execute their processes using application-controlled workflow without disruption.

An upgrade does *not* require that you switch to process-controlled workflow. *After* you complete your upgrade to SAP SRM 7.0, you have the option to upgrade your logic to process-controlled workflow. SAP SRM 7.0 comes with a set of tools to help migrate the configuration of application-controlled workflow to process-controlled workflow. This is covered in more detail in Section 25.10.1, Upgrading a System.

The use of process-controlled or application-controlled workflow is technically determined by a switch that is maintained in the Implementation Guide (IMG). A couple of important items about the switch:

▶ You can only switch from application-controlled workflow to process-controlled workflow, not the other way around (SAP does not support the switch from process-controlled workflow back to application-controlled workflow).

▶ The switch should only be done after you are ready for the change and are aware of the impact.

25.3 Process-Controlled Workflow in Detail

The process-controlled framework introduced in SAP SRM 7.0 was done to provide more flexibility, offering a configuration-only approach for the majority of customers with simple approval use cases. Process-controlled framework consists of process levels, and each process level is an approval level. A document can require one or many process levels. The process levels are configured in the IMG. You can set up to 999 process levels if required.

Each process level determines the level of responsibility needed (single, shared, or split) and whether the approver can change the document or simply approve or reject the document. When an approver can also change a document during approval, the corresponding process level is called *approval with completion*. When an approver can only approve or reject the document, the process level is called *approval.*

In addition to the process levels, there are rules that determine if a process level should be executed. The rules to determine if a process level should be executed are part of the BRF. Before executing a process level, the associated rule is checked to see if the process level should be executed. A rule can be tied to a dollar limit or some other criteria. Figure 25.2 shows an example of a rule that says this process level should always be executed ("Execute always"). An example of a rule based on dollar amount would have the following in the formula: "Overall value > 1.000".

Process levels are combined into process schemas. A process schema may have multiple process levels. Each of those levels is associated with an approver (or approvers in the case of shared or split responsibility), and each level has a rule associated with it to determine if the level should be executed.

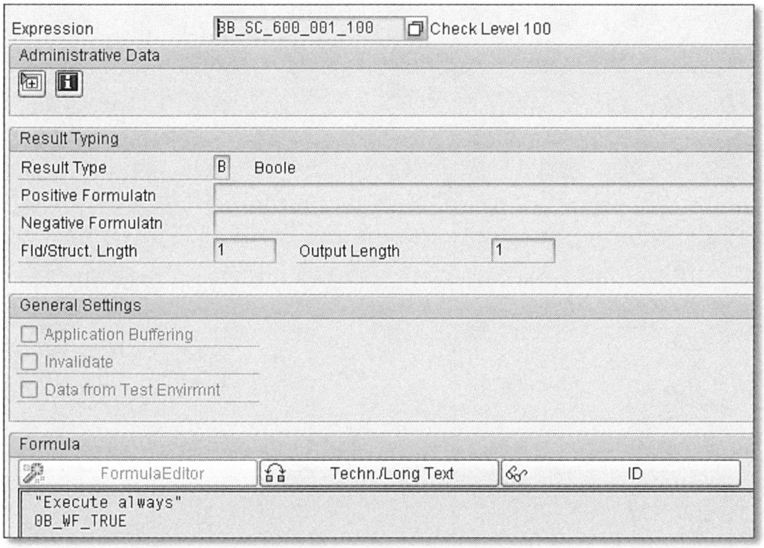

Figure 25.2 Example of a Business Rule, "Execute Always"

Figure 25.3 is an example of a simple process schema. It has LEVEL 100 and LEVEL 999. LEVEL 999 is used if all other levels are skipped. If you look back at Figure 25.2, you see that for LEVEL 100, the rule is to "Execute always".

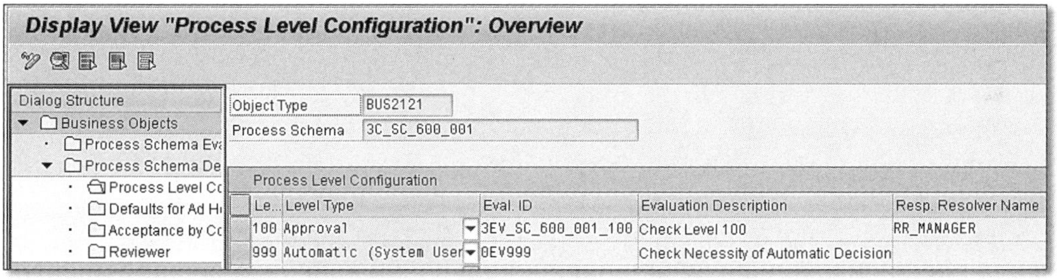

Figure 25.3 Simple Process Schema Definition

The overall flow for all process schemas looks like Figure 25.4. Within a process schema, the first question is "does this process schema have a next process level?" If the answer is yes, then we check the rule associated with the process level, "should we execute this level?" If yes, then the responsible approver(s) is determined and, a work item is assigned.

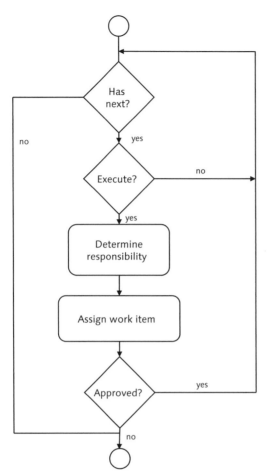

Figure 25.4 Process Schema Flow

Determining the responsibility at each process level is done by the assignment of a responsibility strategy to a process level. The responsibility determined is linked to a very flexible plugin mechanism: Business Add-Ins(BAdIs). These plugins are also called *Responsibility Determination Strategies*. SAP SRM comes with a set of plugins that you can use to define process level responsibility. If the provided implementations do not match your needs, you can also extend the system by coding your own strategy. Assuming that all required strategies are available for your business, you can change the executed process by simply replacing the rules or strategies. No further workflow knowledge is required. Finding the right agent is further discussed in Section 25.3.5, Agent Determination.

25.3.1 Technical Background

Now that you have seen an overview of how the process-controlled workflow works, let's dig a bit deeper into the technical details. Whenever a business document is to be approved, the system first performs a business check to see if the document is ready to be approved. If so, the status of the document is changed to AWAITING APPROVAL, and the framework logic is triggered to identify the process schema and start the process. The identification of which process schema to execute is also determined by business rules. Figure 25.5 shows a process schema definition, with the process levels. In this figure, you can see multiple process levels and multiple evaluation IDs that map to BRF expressions. Evaluation IDs are discussed in more detail in Section 25.3.3, Configuration of Approval Levels.

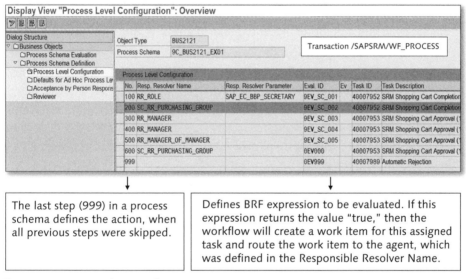

Figure 25.5 Process Schema Definition

If the system could identify a valid schema, the framework copies the process schema from its internal design time/configuration storage to a runtime storage (allowing ad-hoc extensions). After that, it raises the generic event READY_FOR_WORKFLOW to trigger the start of the approval process logic at the SAP Business Workflow. After this is completed, the framework internally switches all SAP SRM logic related to this document into a service mode only. The control for this document lies now with SAP Business Workflow. SAP SRM only allows operation on the document if a corresponding work item exists. Therefore, workflow becomes the only way to interact with the document.

> **Caution**
>
> When a document is handed over to SAP Business Workflow, the Workflow Engine owns and controls the process execution. Any other operation on the underlying data may *potentially endanger* either the consistency of the data or of the process itself.

25.3.2 Basic Assumptions for Document Processing

There are several fundamental aspects of SAP SRM that a user must be familiar with:

▸ **Without a work item, you cannot edit or approve a document.**
  All approvals must be done in the context of an executing work item.

▸ **Users must never approve their own document.**
  From a business perspective, this appears to be obvious. If the user has the necessary authorization, then no approval is required. If not, then the user needs approval by authorized persons. Even when acting as a substitute, users must not approve their own documents. Releasing a document by the document owner at the end of the approval process is not considered as approval and is therefore not supported.

▸ **A document must not allow changes by the approver if the responsibility for approval is split.**
  If a document has line items that require multiple approvers, then the approvers cannot change the document. This is important for compliance; otherwise, an approver could change the document so that he no longer is responsible for the content but still approve it. In addition to this being a compliance and governance issue, this scenario means the stability of the process cannot be guaranteed.

25.3.3 Configuration of Approval Levels

The configuration of process schemas and process levels can be found in the IMG: at SAP SUPPLIER RELATIONSHIP MANAGEMENT • SRM SERVER • CROSS-APPLICATION BASIC SETTINGS • BUSINESS WORKFLOW • PROCESS-CONTROLLED WORKFLOW • BUSINESS PROCESS CONFIGURATION • DEFINE PROCESS LEVELS.

Process Schemas

Process schemas are delivered by SAP and can be defined. Later, we will discuss how to use the schemas provided by SAP, but for now, let's look in more detail at the process schemas.

For each business object, one or more process schemas can be defined. A process schema is defined at design time, specifying all potential process levels a document has to pass before it can be finally approved. For each process level, it is also determined if the approver can change the document (approval with completion) or approve only. Figure 25.6 shows the business objects that are available for process schemas.

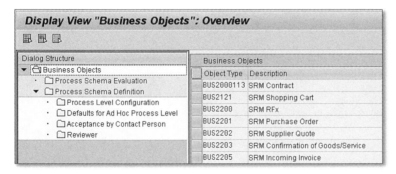

Figure 25.6 Business Objects Available for Process Schemas

Figure 25.7 shows the various process schemas for BUS2121, the shopping cart business object.

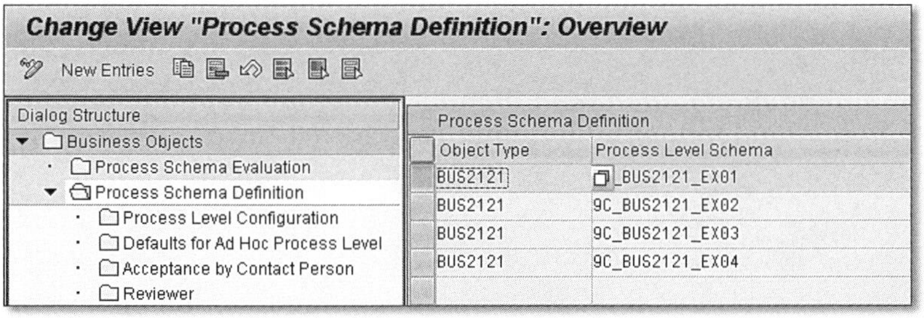

Figure 25.7 Process Schema Definition for BUS2121

Process levels are defined by their type and a condition that must be met to have the level processed. A process level can be either of type completion or type approval. Figure 25.8 shows a process level configuration with multiple process levels. Notice the level type set as APPROVAL WITH COMPLETION or APPROVAL. The EVALUATION ID corresponds to the rule called to determine if the level should be executed. The RESPONSIBLE RESOLVER NAME has the agent determination strategy that is used to find the correct approvers.

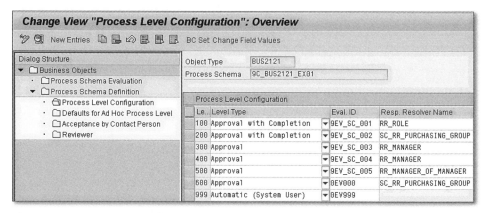

Figure 25.8 Process Level Configuration

As already discussed, APPROVAL WITH COMPLETION means the document can be changed by the approver. When the process level is APPROVAL WITH COMPLETION, there is one work item and one approver, but the approver can approve or reject each item of the document individually. APPROVAL means no changes are allowed. If the process level is APPROVAL, then the document can be split into multiple work items (decision sets) that are sent in parallel for approval to multiple approvers. Each approver receives one task with his document items to approve.

Decision Types

Decision types refer to whether an approver can approve the entire document, or approve each item. There are four decision types:

▶ **Type 1**
Document has one approver, and approval is at the document level.

▶ **Type 2**
Document has one approver, and approval is at the item level. (Approver can approve or reject individual items.)

▶ **Type 3**
Document has multiple approvers, and approval is at the document level.

▶ **Type 4**
Document has multiple approvers, and approval is at the item level.

More information is provided at the SAP Help Portal (*http://help.sap.com*).

Process levels set to APPROVAL WITH COMPLETION can only support decision type 2. Process levels set to APPROVAL support up to decision type 4.

Process Level Activation

Every process level in the process schema may or may not be executed. Rules determine if the process level will execute. The level activation option at design time is provided through events and expressions, supported by the BRF (see next section). At runtime, the rules may be used to decide which of the predefined process levels have to be activated or deactivated, respectively, for one specific process level.

25.3.4 Business Rules Framework

The Business Rule Framework (BRF) is provided by SAP NetWeaver. BRF was designed to evaluate application-specific business rules applying complex logical expressions (rules) to a single value. The result is a unique value, either a Boolean result (true or false) or any other non-multivalue, for example, a string.

Hint

Any other SAP or customer component can make use of the BRF for a variety of purposes. It is not limited to SAP SRM or how SAP SRM uses BRF.

The strengths and weaknesses of the framework are, to some extent, related. Although it can evaluate any (error-free) expression, it does not provide business content or business logic by itself. The business logic has to be provided by the corresponding business application, for example, SAP SRM. So, if new rules are to be evaluated using BRF, all expressions that are required in the business context must be made available explicitly.

Starting from SAP SRM 7.0, BRF is used to control specific aspects of the standards implementation for approval processes. It is not a workflow or a Workflow Engine. The BRF, with its events and expressions, is used for the following:

- To evaluate process schemas
- To evaluate process levels
- To define defaults for ad-hoc process levels
- To determine whether the contact person for a document receives a work item when the approval process is finished
- To define rules based on which reviewers are added to the approval process

Access to document attributes is typically required for evaluation of BRF events. Information about the current approval process is also sometimes necessary. In SAP SRM 7.0, all major attributes that are available when a business object has been instantiated (e.g., a shopping chart) can be accessed via BRF expression.

The following BRF terms are important for you to understand:

- **BRF event**
  A BRF event:

  - Forms a connection between the application and the rules framework
  - Can have multiple rules associated with it
  - Has contextual data associated with it

> **Caution**
>
> The term *event* in BRF event should not be confused with events used by SAP Business Workflow. BRF events are the central entry point to the rules evaluation. Whereas workflow events are used to stop and start workflows, BRF events are called when it is time to evaluate a rule.

- **BRF expression**
  A BRF expression determines if a rule should be executed. BRF expressions return a flat data type (it does not have a structure or a reference to an object). For example, expressions can return a Boolean value, character, date, and other flat data types.

25.3.5 Agent Determination

During the approval process, a document can be split into decision sets. There is one decision set per work item. The created decision sets are then handled in parallel. For each decision set, a new instance of the subworkflow template starts. To execute an approval step, the appropriate agents who receive a work item must be determined. For example, if there are multiple cost centers involved, then there is a decision set for each cost center, sent to the required approver for that cost center. For each process level, the system determines the agents responsible for completing or approving purchasing documents.

Agent determination is carried out using BAdI /SAPSRM/BD_WF_RESP_RESOLVER (Define Agents), which you can use to make your own process level-specific implementations. SAP SRM delivers implementations for the following typical scenarios using the organizational plan:

▸ Purchaser of responsible purchasing group

▸ Line managers (by evaluating the reporting line)

▸ Users with a specific role

▸ Spending limit approval

Hint
Available agent determination strategies are available in Appendix F, Additional Information for SAP SRM.

As you can see, the organization plan is critical in SAP SRM agent determination. The organization plan in SAP SRM contains information such as spending limits, role assignment, reporting lines, and other critical data that is used during agent determination.

The responsible agents are determined in three steps:

1. An area of responsibility is assigned to the items. All items with the same area of responsibility form a decision set. An area of responsibility can be, for example, a department, a product category or a cost center. For each decision set, a new subworkflow is started.

2. For each area of responsibility, the agents for the approval tasks are determined. All agents found in this step get a work item. If the area of responsibility is a department, for example, all employees belonging to that department can be returned as agents. If the area of responsibility is a cost center, the person responsible for the cost center can be returned as agent.

3. If no agent was found for an area of responsibility, fallback agents can be provided to avoid the workflow getting stuck.

There is a standard task (TS) provided in the generic workflow for APPROVAL WITH COMPLETION and APPROVAL that is executed to find the correct agents. This task has a responsibility rule that calls the function module /SAPSRM/WF_CORE_ RESP_RESOLVER. WF_CORE_RESP_RESOLVER determines the responsible agents for the actual decision set. You can see the specific task in the process level configuration. If you look at Figure 25.8, you see the RESPONSIBLE RESOLVER NAME. There are additional columns in the configuration. One of those columns has the specific standard task (TS).

To ensure the flexibility of assigning agents, the actual strategy to find the correct agents is implemented by BAdIs. The BAdIs are filter-dependent. This implies that you can have several BAdI implementations for the same enhancement implementation. At runtime, the system decides, using the filter values, which implementation to call. The evaluation of the filter values has to be unique; that is, only one active BAdI implementation is allowed for a given filter. If more than one implementation is found at runtime, the BAdI is deactivated. The filter values associated with a BAdI are defined in the Object Navigator, along with the implementing class for the BAdI. Fallback agents are also determined in the BAdI. The implementing class for the BAdI definition /SAPSRM/BD_WF_RESP_RESOLVER must be provided in the IMG; the menu path is SAP SUPPLIER RELATIONSHIP MANAGEMENT • SRM SERVER • BUSINESS ADD-INS • BUSINESS WORKFLOW • PROCESS-CONTROLLED WORKFLOW • DEFINE AGENTS.

For each of these enhancement implementations, several BAdI implementations for the determination of agents exist. Refer to Appendix F, Additional Information for SAP SRM, for a list of delivered BAdI implementations. An implementation is assigned to a process level at runtime through the process level configuration using the following level parameters as filter values:

▶ Document type of purchasing document (filter value always required).

▶ Responsibility Resolver Name (filter value always required).

▶ Responsibility Resolver Parameter; the implementations for RR_EMPLOYEE and RR_ROLE use this parameter as required input. Whether a value is needed or not depends on the actual implementing class.

25.3.6 Approval Process Overview: User-Focused Process Visualization

Normally, in an approval process, users want to know who will approve the document. As the approval process executes, the approver list is easily visualized for the user. The approval process overview enables the users to see what is really happening at runtime. The user can see process levels that have been executed, the current process level, and future process levels. Approvers, ad-hoc approvers, manually added reviewers, and rule-based reviewers are also shown.

Figure 25.9 shows an approval process overview. You can see in the HEADER tab, there are three sequences, which relate to three process levels. The STATUS says OPEN, which means no one has started to work on it yet. The PROCESSOR column tells you whose inbox it is in. This includes everyone who has any item that needs approval.

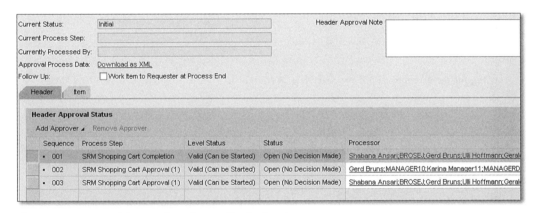

Figure 25.9 Approval Process Overview — Header Level

Figure 25.10 shows the ITEM tab. The ITEM tab has all items an approver needs to approve. Remember that items can require approval by one person, or multiple people. In the ITEM tab, you can see all of the items that you need to approve. Notice Figure 25.10 has the ITEM tab selected and is on the first item, LINE NUMBER 1. The STATUS is still OPEN, which means no one has worked on the item yet. The bottom portion of the screen shows all of the approvers who received this item to approve.

Figure 25.11 shows the second line item of the shopping cart. Notice, however, that the approvers are different for the second line item. The STATUS is still OPEN, so no approvers have started working on it, but this line item only had one selected approver.

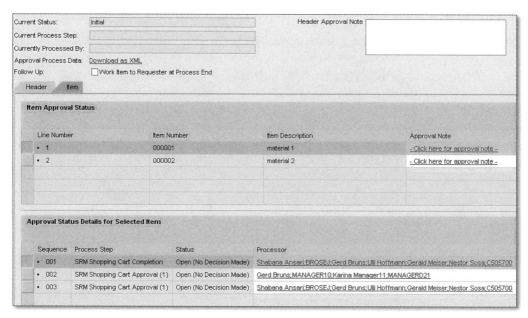

Figure 25.10 Approval Process Overview — Item level

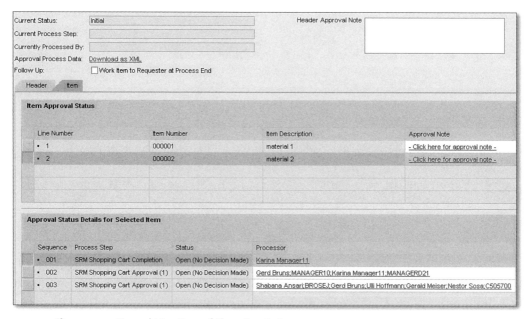

Figure 25.11 Second Line Item of Shopping Cart

In addition to seeing the approvers in the approval process overview, you can also add and remove ad-hoc approvers and add and remove reviewers. Approval notes can be maintained.

Ad-hoc Levels

You can insert ad-hoc agents before or after any process level. If you are at the first process level, you can insert an ad-hoc agent after process level one or before/after any other process level. When inserting ad-hoc levels, you can determine which task should execute for the ad-hoc approver. An example is shown in Figure 25.12. For BUS2121, with the process schema in Figure 25.12, TS40007954 is the default task to be executed for ad-hoc approvers.

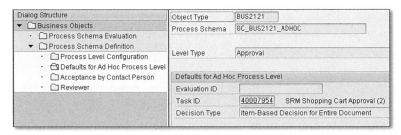

Figure 25.12 Configuration of Default for Ad-Hoc Levels

The configuration for ad-hoc approvers is included with the configuration for the process-controlled workflow: SAP SUPPLIER RELATIONSHIP MANAGEMENT • SRM SERVER • CROSS-APPLICATION BASIC SETTINGS • BUSINESS WORKFLOW • PROCESS-CONTROLLED WORKFLOW • BUSINESS PROCESS CONFIGURATION • DEFINE PROCESS LEVELS.

Reviewer

You can add reviewers to the approval process. Reviewers can follow the entire approval process for a procurement document, independent of which *decision type* applies. In particular, they can do the following:

▸ Display the document.

▸ Display existing attachments or create new ones.

▸ Add notes.

▸ Insert more reviewers.

Reviewers cannot approve or reject the document, and they cannot add more approvers. The system records whether the reviewer has accessed the work item or taken any action. The following options are provided to add reviewers:

▸ **Manually inserted reviewer**
Document creators and approvers who are assigned a work item can add ad-hoc reviewers to the approval process. The BAdI /SAPSRM/BD_WF_REVIEWER_F4 (Adjust Search Help for Reviewer) allows specifying who is authorized to add ad-hoc reviewers and who can be added as an ad-hoc reviewer.

▸ **Rule-based reviewer**
Apart from adding ad-hoc reviewers, it is also possible to configure the system so that reviewers are inserted automatically into the approval process, according to rules. This configuration is done in the process schemas and process levels in the IMG: SAP SUPPLIER RELATIONSHIP MANAGEMENT • SRM SERVER • CROSS-APPLICATION BASIC SETTINGS • BUSINESS WORKFLOW • PROCESS-CONTROLLED WORK-FLOW • BUSINESS PROCESS CONFIGURATION • DEFINE PROCESS LEVELS. The system determines reviewers in the same way that it determines approvers, for instance, by specific document fields, such as product category or accounting type, by business object attributes, or by specific roles or users. The BAdI /SAPSRM/BD_WF_REVIEWER_RULE (Define Reviewers) is supplied to assign documents to groups of agents for review. Figure 25.13 shows this with task TS40007945 being used as the task the approver will execute. The role used is SAP_EC_BBP_SECRETARY, which finds the administrative assistant.

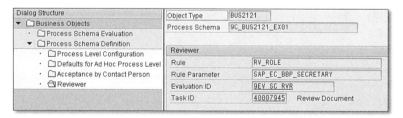

Figure 25.13 Configuration of Rule-Based Reviewer

25.4 Real-World Example of a Process-Controlled Workflow

Now that we've talked about how it works, let's discuss an example to get you started using a process-controlled workflow. The scenario is that every shopping cart has to be approved by the direct manager of the requester. In the second approval level, the users belonging to the purchasing group responsible for a shopping cart item have to approve the respective item. The users of a purchasing group have to approve only those items they are responsible for. The scenario assumes that the organization chart has been setup.

25.4.1 Simplest Scenario, Execute Without Approval

For the first example, assume that approval is not required; the shopping cart should immediately be approved. The status of the document should be transferred to APPROVED without user interaction. By starting with this very simple scenario, we can know the system is correctly configured.

When approving a document immediately, meaning without human interaction, no work item is required, so no workflow is started. For this to work, you need to ensure the event linkage (Transaction SWE2) for the event READY_FOR_RELEASE is switched on.

> **Hint**
>
> Transaction SWE2 and event linkage are discussed in Chapter 13, Using Events and Other Business Interfaces. The event READY_FOR_RELEASE is based on the following:
>
> ▶ Object Category: ABAP class
> ▶ Object Type: /SAPSRM/CL_WF_PRO
> ▶ Event: READY_FOR_RELEASE
> ▶ Receiver type: SRM_PROCESS_START

Process-controlled workflow delivers Business Configuration Sets (BC Sets). BC Sets allow users to record, save, and share customized settings. In the context of SAP SRM, BC Sets are used to enable quick and simple configuration of process schemas.

> **Hint**
>
> SAP SRM delivers many BC Sets. These include shopping cart, purchase order, confirmation, invoice, contract, quote, and RFx. More details are included in Appendix F, Additional Information for SAP SRM.

BC Sets must be activated before our first example can be executed. The configuration of BC Sets is done via Transaction SCPR20. For each of these business objects, there is one BC Set to customize a process without approval and one to customize a process with one-step manager approval. When you activate a BC Set, the system automatically creates a process schema and configures all necessary process levels. For each business object, you can only activate one BC Set.

You should keep in mind that the activation of BC Sets does not delete existing configuration but only changes or completes it. Before activation, you have to make sure that the existing configuration does not interfere with the desired configuration. For preventing interference, the existing configuration should be deleted. This takes place in the IMG via SAP SUPPLIER RELATIONSHIP MANAGEMENT • SRM SERVER • CROSS-APPLICATION BASIC SETTINGS • BUSINESS WORKFLOW • PROCESS-CONTROLLED WORKFLOW • BUSINESS PROCESS CONFIGURATION • DEFINE PROCESS LEVELS.

After the deletion is done, you can activate the BC Set /SAPSRM/C_SC_600_000_SP04 for the process without approval in Transaction SCPR20. After the BC Set is activated, it should be tested by creating a shopping cart. Without user interaction, the status of the shopping cart should be transferred to APPROVED.

> **Hint**
>
> The configuration of zero-step approval without usage of SAP Business Workflow is an option to implement a lightweight automatic approval.

25.4.2 Configuring Two-Step Approval

After successful configuration of the process without workflow interaction, the development of the approval chain can start. For this purpose, the event linkage (Transaction SWE2) for the event READY_FOR_WORKFLOW has to be checked and switched ON.

For one-step approval, BC Sets are delivered as well. As for the configuration without approval, the existing configuration should be checked for interference with the desired configuration and be deleted if necessary. In Transaction SCPR20, the BC Set (/SAPSRM/C_SC_600_001_SP04) that contains the configuration for one-step approval can be activated.

After successful activation, the second approval level should be added. The IMG path is SAP SUPPLIER RELATIONSHIP MANAGEMENT • SRM SERVER • CROSS-APPLICATION BASIC SETTINGS • BUSINESS WORKFLOW • PROCESS-CONTROLLED WORKFLOW • BUSINESS PROCESS CONFIGURATION • DEFINE PROCESS LEVELS. Select the Business Object BUS2121 (SRM Shopping Cart), and in the PROCESS SCHEMA DEFINITION, select the process schema 9C_SC_600_001_SP04 that was created by the BC Set.

Now you have to start process level configuration. After the first approval level, a second approval level should be inserted with the following parameters:

- Sequence Numbers: A number bigger than the sequence number of the first level
- Level Type: APPROVAL
- Evaluation ID: 0EV000 (always true)
- Resp. Resolver Name: SC_RR_PURCHASING_GROUP
- Resp. Resolver Parameter: Blank
- Task ID: 40007953 (SRM Shopping Cart Approval)
- Decision Type: ITEM-BASED DECISION FOR PARTIAL DOCUMENT

That's it! At this point, you can check if the process runs without errors: A shopping cart should be created and ordered. Transaction SLG1 can be used to check BRF processing. Transaction SLG1 shows which process scheme was found and which process levels are active.

> **Note**
>
> For more information on available BAdIs for agent determination, see Appendix F, Additional Information for SAP SRM.

25.4.3 Details on BRF Integration

Let's have a closer look at the entries that were created in process configuration. The IMG path is SAP SUPPLIER RELATIONSHIP MANAGEMENT • SRM SERVER • CROSS-APPLICATION BASIC SETTINGS • BUSINESS WORKFLOW • PROCESS-CONTROLLED WORKFLOW • BUSINESS PROCESS CONFIGURATION • DEFINE PROCESS LEVELS. Look especially for the activation of BC Set /SAPSRM/C_SC_600_001_SP04.

In the configuration, you see an overview of the SAP SRM procurement documents supported by process-controlled workflow. These entries are available already before the activation of BC Sets. When selecting business object BUS2121 (SRM Shopping Cart) and navigating to the process schema definition, you can find available process schemas for the selected business object as shown earlier in Figure 25.7. After the BC Set for one-step approval was activated, you should see here exactly one available process scheme.

However, if two or more process schemes were defined, it has to be decided at runtime which process schema has to be used. That's why there is an Evaluation ID set per business object in the Process Schema Evaluation (see Figure 25.14).

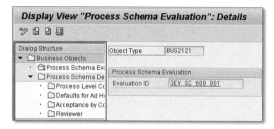

Figure 25.14 Evaluation ID

This Evaluation ID is a business rules event that contains an expression. The expression is evaluated at runtime and returns the valid process schema. This expression can contain a function module, a BAdI, a formula, or even a constant. A constant is normally used when only one process schema for a business object exists.

To find the event 3EV_SC_600_001 from Figure 25.14, you have to start Transaction BRF and select application class SRM_WF to get an overview of the business rules objects. The list of objects is grouped thematically. If you expand navigation node down to Events, you can find the Evaluation ID of the example (see Figure 25.15).

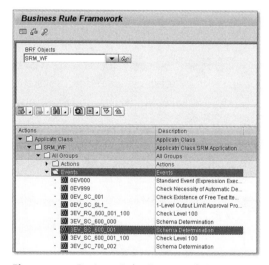

Figure 25.15 Business Rules Framework Event

> **Note**
>
> The BRF objects delivered by SAP SRM follow a naming convention. Objects that start with a number (0 to 9) were created by SAP. Objects that will be created by customers should start with a letter.

When selecting the event, you can see detailed information on the right side (see Figure 25.16). This event contains an expression 3C_SC_600_001.

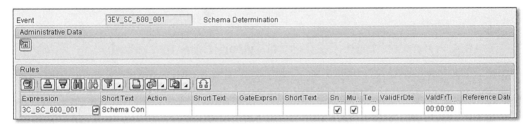

Figure 25.16 Business Rules Framework Event Expression

Double-clicking the expression leads to the expression definition (see Figure 25.17). The expression contains a constant 3C_SC_600_001. That means in case of evaluation of the event, the value 3C_SC_600_001 will be returned. The SAP SRM approval framework knows that the process schema 3C_SC_600_001 has to be executed. You first saw this process schema in Figure 25.3.

Expression	3C_SC_600_001	Schema Constant

Administrative Data

Result Typing

Result Type	C	Characters		
Fld/Struct. Lngth	30	Output Length	30	

General Settings

☑ Application Buffering
☐ Invalidate
☐ Data from Test Envirmnt

Constant

Constant	3C_SC_600_001

Description

Figure 25.17 Expression 3C_SC_600_001

For every process level, an evaluation ID has to be provided. This evaluation ID is an event to determine if the process level step is executed or not. The event is evaluated at runtime. The expression assigned to the event can contain a function module, a BAdI, or a formula. If the result of the expression is `true`, the step is executed. You can find the corresponding rule event in the same way as described for the process schema evaluation ID. For example, the expression `3EV_SC_600_001_100` contains a formula that always returns `true`. So this process level will always be executed. This was shown earlier in Figure 25.2.

25.5 Application-Controlled Workflow in Detail

Now we will focus on the approval framework application-controlled workflow. This is the framework used in SAP SRM 5.0 (and lower releases). The application-controlled workflow includes one- and two-step approvals, the use of n-step BAdIs, and line item BAdIs. This is shown in Figure 25.18.

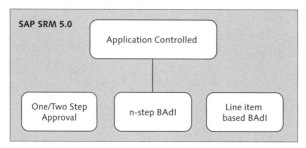

Figure 25.18 SAP SRM 5.0 Application-Controlled Workflow

25.5.1 One-/Two-Step Approval

One- and two-step approvals have a specific workflow template delivered for a specific process. The workflow templates support the ability to change the executed process and the ability to provide a process overview (visualization of approvers). When executing a process, it is determined if another workflow template should execute. If this is the case, the current process is terminated, and the new process is triggered.

This approach works fine as long as the flow model of the workflow template follows certain design rules. SAP delivers workflow templates for the one-step approval (WS10000060) and two-step approval (WS10000129). These templates can be adjusted to a certain degree to meet the requirements of the customer. For example, the agent determination can be adjusted.

In regards to approvers, these templates support an approver for the entire document. The approver can change the document, but the document must always be approved by one approver (no split or shared responsibilities). Ad-hoc approvers are supported.

25.5.2 N-step BAdI

The n-step BAdI is based on generic workflow templates, which are the same workflow templates used to support multiple processes. The generic workflow is used iteratively for different approval levels and assigns work items based on the required approver. Although n-step BAdIs do provide some support for functions such as additional reviewers and ad-hoc approval levels, every customer is required to implement a BAdI to configure the ad-hoc capabilities.

The n-step BAdI works as described in Figure 25.19. If there is a next approver, the responsibility for that approval is determined, and the work item is assigned. If approved, a check is made for another approver.

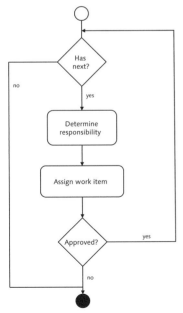

Figure 25.19 Generic Loop to Support N-Step BAdI

With the one-/two-step approval, the process overview is tied to the workflow design. With the n-step BAdI, you enhance the design, but you cannot see the ad-hoc steps in the workflow design. The process overview is provided by calling the BAdI to present the results in the process overview. The n-step BAdI uses text to enter an item, requires a purchasing expert to complete the data, and then sends for approval. Just as with the one- and two-step workflows, the approval must happen by a single approver. Ad-hoc steps are supported.

25.5.3 SAP-Provided BAdIs and Workflow Templates

SAP provides BAdIs and workflows to support application-controlled workflow. Table 25.3 describes the major BAdIs used in application-controlled workflow.

BAdI Definition	Description
BBP_WFL_APPROV_BADI	Determines approval for n-level; Dynamic approval workflow
BBP_WFL_SECUR_BADI	Overwrites the authorization level of the approver

Table 25.3 Provided Business Add-Ins with Application-Controlled Workflow

Sample implementations and descriptions can be found in the technical BAdI documentation: Go to Transaction SE18, and display the BAdI BBP_WFL_ APPROV_BADI. You can select the DOCUMENTATION button to view the documentation for the BAdI. The documentation provides detailed examples. To see the example implementation, select IMPLEMENTATION • OVERVIEW from the menu bar. You will see the following examples:

▶ Example implementation with value limit approval for PO

▶ Example of an implementation of this BAdI

▶ Simple example for BAdI version for item approval

▶ Example for BAdI implementation in line item approval

BBP_WFL_APPROV_BADI is called via background steps using the method NextDy-namicApproverGet of the BOR object BUS4101. Standard task TS14007989 (Determine Next Approver) is the task that uses this BAdI. Table 25.4 shows the provided workflow templates that use the BAdI task TS14007989.

Template ID	Name	Related BOR Object
WS14000109	Approval n-Step Over Value Limit	BUS2121 (Shopping Cart)
WS14000133	Approval Shopping Cart n-Level (BAdI)	BUS2121
WS14500015	Item-Based Main Workflow	BUS2121
WS14000145	Approval n-Step for Purchase Order (BADI)	BUS2201 (Purchase Order)
WS14000148	Approval n-Step for Contract (BADI)	BUS2000113 (Contract)
WS14500028	Main Workflow: n-Step Approval Bid Invitation	BUS2200 (Bid Invitation)
WS14500044	n-Step Approval Vendor Bid	BUS2202 (Vendor Bid)

Table 25.4 Workflow Templates That Use the BAdI

25.5.4 Line Item Based BAdI

This is the same approach as the n-step BAdI (supporting completion of the information, approval, ad-hoc approvers). Additionally, the line item BAdI enables work items based on split and shared responsibility.

25.5.5 Approvers Changing Documents in Application-Controlled Workflow

To determine if an approver can change a document, application-controlled workflow uses a special personalization attribute with the technical name BBP_WFL_SECURITY. You can assign one of several predefined values to roles or to users directly to determine the authorization level and the ability for the approver to change documents. This setting is assigned using the PERSONALIZATION tab in Transaction SU01. This can also be done in role maintenance (Transaction PFCG) using the PERSONALIZATION tab.

> **Hint**
>
> The details of BBP_WFL_SECURITY can be found in the SAP Help Portal (*http://help.sap.com*) by doing a keyword search. Additionally, you can use the BAdI BBP_WFL_SECURE_BADI to override BBP_WFL_SECURITY.

25.5.6 Configuring Approval Processes

In the application-controlled workflow, the configuration of approval process is done primarily with SAP Business Workflow.

Configuration of Start Conditions

Start conditions (Transaction SWB_COND) determine which workflow should be started based on the contents of the document. For example, you may want shopping carts under $500 to be processed via the auto-approval workflow and carts over $500 to be processed via the one-step approval workflow. A general discussion of start conditions can be found in Chapter 13, Using Events and Other Business Interfaces.

When creating or changing start conditions in SAP SRM, it is *crucial* to keep in mind that the criteria being used must exist when the event is raised. For example, shopping cart approval workflows are started when the shopping cart is saved. At this time, we know a lot about the shopping cart such as its total value, whether any free text items exist, the material groups, and the account assignment used. However, we do not know if the shopping cart items will be converted to local or backend purchase orders, backend purchase requisitions, or backend reservations because this decision is not made until approval is finished. So we can create a start condition for a shopping cart approval workflow based on total value and material group but not on the total value together with the backend object type.

> **Hint**
>
> If you always want to use just one approval workflow, assign it to a start condition that is always true.

When setting up start conditions, you can simulate events (Transaction SWU0) to determine if the right workflow will trigger when a particular event is raised (e.g., event SAVED defined at the BOR object type BUS2121). However, if you want to test the events and test the start conditions, you need to pass the object key. To do this, test with Transaction SWUE to actually trigger the event and test the start conditions.

> **Caution**
>
> Normally an event is published, a start condition may be analyzed, and a workflow is started (based on the result of the start condition). However, this is not the case with application-controlled workflow. What really happens is the document is saved (e.g., a shopping cart), the start conditions are evaluated, and then the workflow is started via the workflow APIs (WAPIs). This means you will not see an event in the event trace (Transaction SWEL). The application-controlled workflow is reading the conditions and starting the workflows programmatically, so no events are actually triggered.

Adapting Delivered Scenarios

Delivered approval scenarios include auto-approval, one-step approval, two-step approval, and spending limit approval of procurement requests. A limited choice of approval scenarios is also available for approving confirmations, invoices, and so on. All approval scenarios can be used as is or as patterns for creating your own approval scenarios.

When using the spending limit approval scenario (i.e., approval is only required if the request exceeds the requestor's spending limit), the spending limit can be configured to a default based on the user's role and overridden on an organizational object basis or even on a per-user basis if necessary.

When authorizing approver's change procurement requests during approval, the decision as to whether changes require approval can be configured to a default, based on the approver's role, and they can be overridden on a per-user basis, or according to business rules specified in the BAdI.

> **Note**
>
> All texts in work items and emails sent by SAP Business Workflow can be redefined without modification to suit your company's needs. This is done in the same way work item text in all standard tasks (TS) is refined, via the REFINE WORK ITEM TEXT button (⬚) available in standard tasks delivered by SAP.

Creating Your own Start Condition Criteria

Start conditions are based on attributes of the object in the event linkage. For shopping cart approval workflows, the event used is the shopping cart SAVED event, and the object is the shopping cart (BUS2121).

If you want to create additional criteria to be used as part of the logical expression of a start condition, you need to create additional attributes. To create additional attributes, first create a subtype of BUS2121 (e.g., ZBUS2121), and use systemwide delegation to delegate BUS2121 to ZBUS2121. Additional attributes can then be added to the subtype ZBUS2121, and through delegation, these will be available to all start conditions, event linkages, workflows, and tasks using BUS2121.

When programming your own attributes for start conditions, keep the following points in mind:

▸ Any exception raised by an attribute causes the start condition to fail. Usually if you cannot find a value for an attribute, you want to set the attribute to its empty value (e.g., blank or zero) and return normally.

▸ Every attribute checked should have a valid value (which may be an empty value) for *all* shopping carts. This is particularly important when creating attributes that are only relevant to goods or service items. Make sure your attribute still returns a valid value if the shopping cart contains only goods items, only service items, or a mixture of goods and services items.

▸ When a shopping cart is transferred to a local or backend object, significant data changes may occur (depending on the SAP SRM release). For this reason, when testing your new criteria, always test against parked (held) shopping carts or unapproved shopping carts, which still contain all data in a pre-approved state, and never against carts that have already been transferred.

▸ It is recommended that you do *not* read data directly from database tables; instead, use the routines in the standard business object definition because the relationship between the various shopping cart tables is complex and varies from release to release. A further complication is that data need to be read and returned in a slightly different way when the shopping cart does not yet exist (i.e., for approval preview scenarios). The safest option is to closely examine the standard business object BUS2121 for the code behind similar attributes to make sure your new attributes use a consistent approach.

25.5.7 Agent Determination

Possible agents are usually assigned via security roles to minimize the maintenance burden on the organizational plan. Within certain SAP SRM workflows, such as shopping cart (i.e., procurement request) approval, possible agent assignments not only control who is able to execute work items, but also:

- ▶ Determine whether an employee is allowed to dynamically change the approver.

- ▶ Determine which approvers can be selected via the add/change approver options.

For one- and two-step approvals, the agent determination at runtime is based on dedicated BOR objects, APURMANAG (BOR object to find a default manager for one and two step approvals). For the n-step BAdI and line item BAdI, the agent determination is based on BOR methods that delegate the agent determination to a BAdI implementation.

As mentioned earlier, SAP delivers an example implementation for the BAdI definition BBP_WFL_APPROV_BADI. To leverage the BAdI-based approval workflow, you have to provide your own implementation that covers your specific business rules (see more details in Section 25.5.9, Implementing Dynamic Processes).

25.5.8 Ad-hoc Agent Assignment

Assigning an approver to a shopping cart is done via ad-hoc agent assignment. Ad-hoc agent assignment enables agents to be determined at the start of the workflow via a reference to an ad-hoc agent business object. The agents can then be manipulated generically throughout the workflow, regardless of how the original agents were found.

In SAP SRM, ad-hoc agent assignment is used to enable agents to be determined prior to the approval steps so that they can be displayed in approval previews and status displays. It also enables proactive substitution via the change/replace approver functions. Thus, if authorized, you can dynamically change the agents selected for a particular work item. As a side benefit, you can also see in the workflow log, via the workflow container, all agents that were chosen before *and* after work items have been executed.

> **Hint**
>
> The replace approver function applies to application-controlled workflow. Process-controlled workflow has a REMOVE APPROVER function and an ADD APPROVER function. With application-controlled workflow, you can change approvers that were found automatically. In process-controlled workflow, you can only remove ad-hoc agents.

Ad-hoc Workflows — Additional Approvers

Ad-hoc workflows enable extra steps to be added to an existing workflow dynamically, as shown in Figure 25.20. The ADD APPROVER functionality enables additional approval steps to be included in an existing shopping cart workflow. Both requestors and approvers can be permitted to add approvers via the ADD APPROVER option during shopping cart creation, change, and approval.

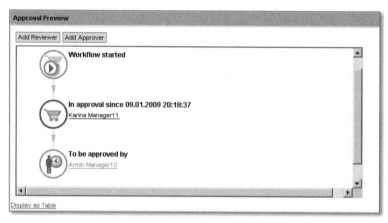

Figure 25.20 Add Approver Dynamically

To enable this, *ad-hoc anchor* steps are included in the workflow design. The ad-hoc anchor steps (also discussed in Chapter 9, Advanced Workflow Design Techniques, and Appendix A, Tips and Tricks) are essentially placeholders to indicate where it makes sense to add another approver. Several ad-hoc anchor steps can exist in one workflow.

The ad-hoc anchor references a subworkflow that holds the steps to be inserted if the ad-hoc functionality is activated at that point. The subworkflow container must be identical to the main workflow (i.e., have the same element names and types). The subworkflow itself can include another ad-hoc anchor to itself, allowing a potentially limitless number of approvers to be added (until memory or the requestor's patience runs out). In SAP SRM, when someone chooses to add an approver, the workflow is extended with the additional steps in the subworkflow.

Ad-hoc Workflows — Add Reviewers

A *reviewer* is someone who can monitor an active workflow instance (e.g., for escalation purposes) and make limited changes (e.g., add attachments). For instance, if you created a shopping cart in SAP SRM but were about to leave for a training course, you might want to make one of your colleagues a reviewer so that he could monitor the approval process on your behalf.

The ADD REVIEWER functionality (discussed in Chapter 9, Advanced Workflow Design Techniques, and Appendix A, Tips and Tricks) enables a reviewer workflow instance to be created. This instance runs in parallel with the original approval workflow. To do this, the review workflow is entered in the version-dependent basic data of the Workflow Builder for the relevant workflow. The workflow has the property "has a review workflow," whereas the workflow that performs the review has the property "review workflow."

When the review workflow is started, data are passed from the current workflow to the review workflow. Container details and the instance number of the main workflow are passed to the review workflow on creation. The review workflow can then use its own steps/tasks/methods to perform the review.

25.5.9 Implementing Dynamic Processes

As mentioned in the introduction, the SAP SRM application offers dynamic processes, especially with respect to the approval workflows. A part of the process flow is fixed by the SAP SRM standard implementation. However, there are numerous dynamic aspects you can define at runtime, including the number of required approval levels, the definition of responsibility areas (i.e., which part of a document has to be approved by whom), and the executing workflow process based on changes made to the underlying procurement document.

Determining Approval Levels (n-Step)

More approval levels can be added to the shopping cart approval workflows by copying the SAP-provided shopping cart workflows and adding additional levels. Be sure to keep the workflow features the same, such as the ability to dynamically add more approvers, to keep the new workflow consistent for approval status displays.

It is important to retain the standard subworkflows for handling change and deletion events and for handling the final processing after the approve/reject decision is made, so that your new workflow does not restrict use of, and operates consistently with, standard SAP SRM functionality.

Note

You need to create your own rules for the additional approval levels.

You need to check that the approval status display in the shopping cart status still shows the approval flow in an acceptable format. A Java applet is used to represent a simplified graphic workflow log (up to SAP SRM 5.0). Complex operations such as "loops" cannot be visualized.

To implement approval processes that are more dynamic at runtime without creating your own templates, you can use one of the BAdI-based workflows delivered by SAP SRM. Several workflow templates are delivered that are designed to incorporate the BAdI `BBP_WFL_APPROV_BADI`. They are listed in Table 24.4. These workflows delegate a significant part of the process definition to your BAdI implementation, which should cover the business rules regarding the required approval process.

This technique has an impact on the plain template-based workflow modeling. Usually the workflow is fully defined at design time by the workflow template you create via the Workflow Builder. The workflow templates incorporating the BAdI, however, do contain a loop whose iterations are determined by the BAdI implementation at runtime!

With one and the same workflow template, you can implement numerous variants of approval processes with respect to determining approval levels and involved approvers. BAdI-based workflows within SAP SRM also have an impact on how the ad-hoc capabilities are supported. In contrast to the ad-hoc anchors used in plain template-based workflows, manually added approvers are written to the main workflow container. They are considered within the loop of approval levels and are involved in the approval process.

Listing 25.1 is from one of the examples provided for `BBP_WFL_APPROV_BADI`. It adds approvers to a list based on the total value in the document header.

```
    IF ls_header-total_value < 490000000.
*** 2-step approval
      CASE actual_approval_index.
        WHEN 0.
          ls_approver-approval_index = 1.
          ls_approver-approval_agent = 'USMANAGER1'.
          ls_approver-name = 'Arthur Manager1'.
          ls_approver-approval_description =
            'First approval step'.
          APPEND ls_approver TO approval_table.
          ls_approver-approval_index = 2.
          ls_approver-approval_agent = 'USMANAGER2'.
          ls_approver-name = 'Arnold Manager2'.
          ls_approver-approval_description =
            'Second approval step'.
          APPEND ls_approver TO approval_table.
          ls_approver-approval_index = 2.
          ls_approver-approval_agent = 'USMANAGER4'.
          ls_approver-name = 'Thomas Manager4'.
          ls_approver-approval_description =
            'Second approval step'.
          APPEND ls_approver TO approval_table.
        WHEN 1.
          ls_approver-approval_index = 1.
          ls_approver-approval_agent = 'USMANAGER1'.
          ls_approver-name = 'Arthur Manager1'.
          ls_approver-approval_description =
            'First approval step'.
          APPEND ls_approver TO approval_table.
          ls_approver-approval_index = 2.
          ls_approver-approval_agent = 'USMANAGER2'.
          ls_approver-name = 'Arnold Manager2'.
          ls_approver-approval_description =
            'Second approval step'.
          APPEND ls_approver TO approval_table.
          ls_approver-approval_index = 2.
          ls_approver-approval_agent = 'USMANAGER4'.
          ls_approver-name = 'Thomas Manager4'.
          ls_approver-approval_description =
            'Second approval step'.
          APPEND ls_approver TO approval_table.
        WHEN 2.
```

```
      ls_approver-approval_index = 2.
      ls_approver-approval_agent = 'USMANAGER2'.
      ls_approver-name = 'Arnold Manager2'.
      ls_approver-approval_description =
        'Second approval step'.
      APPEND ls_approver TO approval_table.
      ls_approver-approval_index = 2.
      ls_approver-approval_agent = 'USMANAGER4'.
      ls_approver-name = 'Thomas Manager4'.
      ls_approver-approval_description =
        'Second approval step'.
      APPEND ls_approver TO approval_table.
    WHEN OTHERS.
      no_further_approval_needed = 'X'.
  ENDCASE.
```

Listing 25.1 Example BAdI SAP_APP_BADI_EXAMPLE

Using Split and Shared Responsibility with Dynamic Processes

When a shopping cart with several items is released, it often makes more sense to select approvers according to several criteria that are determined by the individual items than to have all items approved by each approver. Examples include cost center responsibility (the *shared copier* mentioned earlier in this chapter) and shopping carts with items from different product categories. The advantage of this procedure is the separate determination of approvers for all individual items.

In the case of classic, non-item-based approval, each approval step affects all items. This means that the approver needs to approve or reject each item of the whole shopping cart, even those for which he is not responsible.

With item-based approval, the approver only receives the items for which he is responsible — his "area of responsibility." As in the classic case, the shopping cart is only transferred to further processing (ordered) after the entire approval process has been completed. This means that items that require no approval are not ordered immediately independently of the items requiring approval but wait until the entire approval process has been completed.

> **Hint**
>
> Item-based approval is also described in the SAP Online Help. Do a search for "item-based approval of shopping carts" at *http://help.sap.com*.

You can use workflow WS14500015 to enable approvers to only get the work items assigned to them. This requires an implementation of BAdI BBP_WFL_ APPROVE_BADI. This BAdI includes the approval criteria, their characteristics, and the respective approvers. This workflow template also supports line item BAdIs.

> **Hint**
>
> Before using this item-based n-step BAdI approval process, make sure that you have implemented and tested your process using the normal n-step BAdI approval procedure. From practical experience, the implementation of the item-based n-step BAdI approval process takes more effort.

For more information, see the documentation for this BAdI in Customizing for SAP Supplier Relationship Management under SAP SUPPLIER RELATIONSHIP MANAGEMENT • SRM SERVER • BUSINESS ADD-INS • BUSINESS WORKFLOW • APPLICATION-CONTROLLED WORKFLOW • DETERMINATION OF APPROVER FOR N-STEP DYNAMIC APPROVAL WORKFLOW.

> **Note**
>
> SAP Note 731637 includes more details on how to use the item-based approval.

Implementing Dynamic Process Adaptation

While a procurement document is awaiting approval, it might become necessary to change the document again. The changes can be applied by an approver or by the document's creator. Again, based on the BAdI BBP_WFL_APPROV_BADI, you can provide an implementation that evaluates the latest content of the document and take appropriate measures. In the workflow template design, (workflows listed in Table 25.4), the BAdI is called on each approval step, which allows you an immediate evaluation of the current condition and an adequate dynamic process adaptation.

Assume a shopping cart is awaiting approval by the requester's manager, and the requester decides to order additional items. Provided sufficient authorization, the requester is able to edit the shopping cart and add the missing items. Most likely this will result in an increased total value. Consequently, you may want to consider determining additional approval steps. Even a restart (beginning with the first approval step again) can be an appropriate measure in specific scenarios.

Because the interface of the BAdI definition `BBP_WFL_APPROVE_BADI` always requires a return to the complete list of approval steps, you can dynamically determine a new or updated process definition at runtime. After a certain period of time, new or adapted requirements with respect to your approval process are most likely inevitable. Usually, this will force you to change the ABAP code of your BAdI implementation. To reduce the effort for process adaptations, you may consider defining a configuration table that is evaluated within your BAdI implementation by creating a database table and a corresponding maintenance view in a customer's namespace. One of the major benefits of this technique is that you require neither a workflow expert nor an ABAP developer to activate specific adaptations of the approval process(es). Instead the business expert who is familiar with your internal business rules (e.g., a professional purchaser) can implement the changes on his own.

25.5.10 Tracking Workflow Instances

SAP SRM provides a shopping cart status function for requestors to track their shopping carts, as well as the progress of approval workflows. As a workflow administrator, you can often benefit from more powerful reporting mechanisms. You can use any of the standard workflow reports; however, most of the time, the most useful report is one that shows all work items for a particular object instance, Transaction SWI6.

25.6　Real-World Example of Application-Controlled Workflow

The scenario for this example is that every shopping cart has to be approved by the direct manager of the requester. In the second approval level, the users belonging to the purchasing group responsible for a shopping cart item have to approve the respective item.

25.6.1 Without Approval

SAP SRM delivers a dedicated workflow template that supports releasing a shopping cart without approver involvement (`WS10000060`), that is, automatic approval by the system itself. There are two major steps to be performed to implement this process in your system:

1. Make sure that the corresponding event type linkage is maintained (the mentioned template has to be registered to the event SAVED of the BOR object BUS2121).

2. Define the start conditions according to your needs. This step can be easy depending on the number of different approval processes you want to support. If the automatic approval is the only one you need, you can simply deactivate all start conditions for other workflow templates so that any intersection is prevented.

Now all ordered shopping carts in your system should be processed by the workflow template WS10000060, resulting in immediate release without approver involvement.

25.6.2 Two-Step Approval

The two-step approval example requires the manager of the shopping cart's requester to approve on the first level and the members of the responsible purchasing group (depending on used product categories) to approve on the second level.

To implement this two-step approval scenario, you have two options; for the second option, you must provide the BAdI implementation:

▶ Either you model a corresponding workflow template, ideally by copying a delivered one (e.g., WS10000031).

▶ Or you opt for one of the delivered workflow templates that incorporate the BAdI BBP_WFL_APPROVE_BADI.

In general, you should consider whether one of the existing workflow templates is very close to your required approval process and the required agent determination is covered by one of the delivered BOR-Objects (e.g., ASBPURLIST). If this is the case, and there are no special requirements with respect to dynamic process adaptation at runtime, it is easiest to go for the first option: Copy the workflow template, and incorporate the required changes.

SAP SRM delivers the workflow template WS10000031, which defines a two-step approval process where the requester's manager has to approve on the first level, and the manager's manager is involved on the second level. In our example, we want the second approval to be done by the responsible agent for the purchasing group. This means we need to change the second approval step. Fortunately, there is an existing BOR object, ASBPURLIST, that includes agent determination. If you look in the workflow and select the FIRST APPROVAL step, you will see the agent determination is set to &AGENT_0001.Agents&. AGENT_0001 is a container element based on the object type ASBMANAGER. AGENT_0002 is a container element based on the object type ASBMANOFMA. To make the change for the second approval to be based on the purchasing group, you can change the container or AGENT_002 to be based on ASBPURLIST.

After that, the same steps as described earlier have to be performed, that is, enter the corresponding event type linkage and start conditions for your new workflow template.

Choosing to implement a custom two-step approval with a BAdI workflow typically results in a higher effort at first but might pay off mid-term depending on how your requirements toward approval processes evolve over time. Usually, if new requirements are to be implemented, you do not have to change the underlying workflow template or even create a new one from scratch. Instead, you have to adapt your BAdI implementation accordingly. The most common approach is to create a custom table (*Z table*) to hold the rules that change often.

25.7 Inbox

Up to this point, we have discussed how the approval processes work and how to configure approval processes. Now we turn our attention to the execution of the business processes and the inbox experience for the users.

SAP SRM 5.0 delivers its own inbox for task processing; Figure 25.21 shows the SAP SRM 5.0 inbox. Beginning with SAP SRM 7.0, UWL is used. Chapter 4, Work Item Delivery, discusses the major features available with UWL. SAP SRM processes are highly dynamic and very user-intensive. Therefore, substitution is a very important topic to consider, and it is critical that your users maintain appropriate substitutes. Substitutes can be maintained via the inbox (in both the SAP SRM 5.0 specific inbox and UWL). Substitutes are maintained in database Table HRUS_D2.

Because UWL connects to multiple backends and also supports multiple types of tasks, a UWL substitution rule can apply to all systems. The integrated SAP SRM inbox (up to SAP SRM 5.0) does not connect multiple backends.

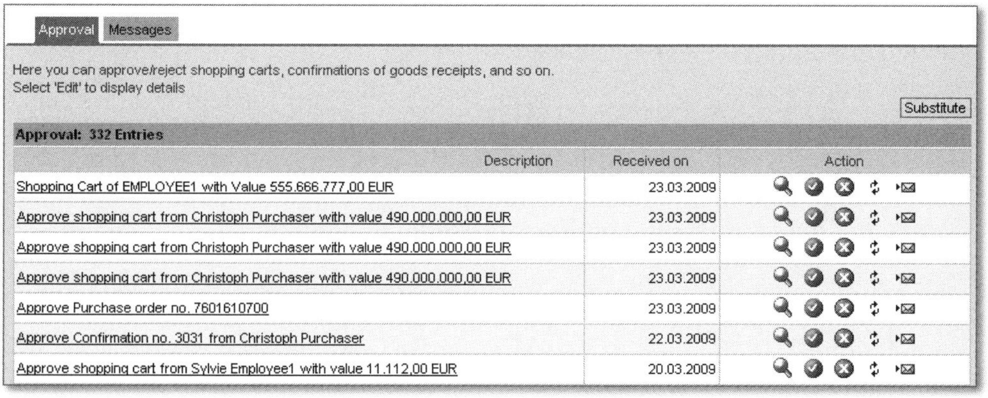

Figure 25.21 SAP SRM inbox

25.8 Offline Functionality

Approvers of SAP SRM procurement documents can process work items without logging on to the system. The system can send work items by email so that users can process them in their Microsoft Outlook mail client. The email formatting was implemented and tested using Microsoft Outlook client. Totally correct email formatting cannot be guaranteed using other email clients. With software-specific small adjustments, the usage of other email clients, for example, handheld applications, should be possible.

The work items that are selected for offline approval remain in the approver's inbox until the reply emails containing the decisions are received and processed by the SAP SRM system. If these work items have been processed online, the system ignores the reply emails.

Hint

Business Communication Services is (BCS) used for sending emails. BCS is part of the SAP NetWeaver Application Server. Detailed information is available in the SAP Online Help (*http://help.sap.com*).

25.8.1 Outbound Processing

In SAP SRM 7.0, use Report /SAPSRM/OFFLINEAPPROVALSEND to create the email settings; in SAP SRM 5.0, use Report RWSUWMLEC. The settings can be specified for certain tasks, business objects, or work items. You can, for example, set the message frequency to be one email per work item.

One required setting is the return address for the emails. The return address must be identical to the recipient address in SAPconnect.

25.8.2 Offline Approval by the Recipient

The approver can use a link to log on to the system directly and process the work item online. Depending on the settings made in Report /SAPSRM/OFFLINEAPPROV-ALSEND or RWSUWMLEC, the email can also contain two pushbuttons used to approve or reject offline. The decision then applies to the entire decision set; that is, the approver cannot decide individually for each item. When the approver chooses one of the pushbuttons, the system sends a reply email.

25.8.3 Inbound Processing

SAPconnect is used for synchronous inbound processing. When the system receives a reply email from an approver, the specified class (CL_BBP_SMTP_INBOUND_OFFAPP up to SAP SRM 5.0; /SAPSRM/CL_OFFLINEAPP_INBOUND for SAP SRM 7.0 and later releases) entered in Transaction SO50 is used for processing. The work item ID, status, and the decision of the approver are evaluated. The system only processes reply emails from a sender that is identical to the recipient of the corresponding notification email. If the document is locked when the email is received or if immediate processing fails for any other reason, the reply email is forwarded to the Business Workplace inbox (Transaction SBWP) of the user who is assigned to the specified address. If you are using UWL, the SONiC connector (discussed in Chapter 4, Work Item Delivery) enables UWL to receive the mail messages.

25.9 Deadline Monitoring

In the standard SAP Business Workflow technology, you can define various time-based events for a work item, which might trigger follow-on activities (deadline monitoring is discussed in Chapter 8, Creating a Workflow, and Chapter 9, Advanced Workflow Design Techniques). Normally the maintenance of the deadlines requires a change to the template by the customer.

Because SAP SRM wants to provide as much functionality as possible by configuration only, it offers deadline maintenance through customizing via SAP SUPPLIER RELATIONSHIP MANAGEMENT • SRM SERVER • CROSS-APPLICATION BASIC SETTINGS • CROSS-APPLICATION BASIC SETTINGS • EVENT AND EVENT SCHEMA FOR ALERT MANAGEMENT • DEFINE EVENT SCHEMA in the IMG.

SAP SRM customizing is available for the following deadlines:

▶ Latest Start Date/Time

▶ Requested End Date/Time

▶ Latest End Date/Time

Additionally, deadlines can be calculated dynamically by implementing the BAdI /SAPSRM/BD_WF_DEADLINES (Define Deadlines for Events). Deadline configuration applies to both application-controlled workflow and process-controlled workflow; however, the use by each one differs:

▶ Deadlines with process-controlled workflow are very close to the standard deadline monitoring. It stores the determined data in the task container of the work item to be executed and uses the information for the modeled deadlines of that step. Thus, the different inbox variants available at SAP are able to display, filter, and sort based also on the deadline data. In addition, process-controlled workflows can support the deadline Requested Start Date/Time, if this data is provided by the BAdI BD_WF_DEADLINES.

▶ Application-controlled workflows do not use modeled deadlines. Rather, the workflow forks a parallel workflow during task instantiation to monitor the execution of the work item. As a consequence, the deadline information is not available in the inboxes; the deadline appears as an additional work item or an email stating that a deadline has been reached.

The reaction on reached deadlines can either be defined in the corresponding workflow templates, or you can use the SAP SRM Alert and Event Framework to create alerts and notifications. By default, the shipped workflow templates use the alert framework when a deadline occurs.

25.10 Recommendations When Getting Started

This section outlines a few recommendations for getting started with SAP SRM workflow.

25.10.1 Upgrading a System

As mentioned in Section 25.2, SAP SRM Approval Frameworks, an upgrade to SAP SRM 7.0 does not mean you must immediate switch to process-controlled workflow. It is recommended that you switch at some point after the upgrade, but it is not required to make the switch with the upgrade. Keep in mind that after you switch to process-controlled workflow, you cannot switch back.

The procedure for upgrading from application-controlled workflow to process-controlled workflow is described in detail in the corresponding upgrade guide (available in the SAP Service Marketplace at *http://service.sap.com/instguides*). However, a short overview is provided here.

Required Configuration When Switching from Application-Controlled Workflow to Process-Controlled Workflow

Analyze your existing workflow configuration of application-controlled workflows. If you use only the standard templates, you can use a migration tool to migrate start conditions. For details, see the IMG path SAP SUPPLIER RELATIONSHIP MANAGER • SRM SERVER • CROSS-APPLICATION BASIC SETTINGS • BUSINESS WORKFLOW • UPGRADE • MIGRATE WORKFLOWS TO BRF.

A manual configuration for process-controlled workflow is also possible. The automatic wizard converts the start conditions to process-controlled workflow. When manually migrating from application-controlled workflow to process-controlled workflow, you must convert your existing start conditions to business rules. This is discussed in the IMG at SAP SUPPLIER RELATIONSHIP MANAGEMENT • SRM SERVER • CROSS-APPLICATION BASIC SETTINGS • BUSINESS WORKFLOW • PROCESS-CONTROLLED WORKFLOW • BUSINESS PROCESS CONFIGURATION.

Required Framework Switch

The switch to the process-controlled workflow framework is available in the IMG at SAP SUPPLIER RELATIONSHIP MANAGEMENT • SRM SERVER • CROSS-APPLICATION BASIC SETTINGS • BUSINESS WORKFLOW • SELECT WORKFLOW FRAMEWORK. The process-controlled workflow framework is configured by system default (on delivery from SAP).

Note

In test systems, it is possible to switch to process-controlled workflows by business object types. This upgrade strategy can help you become familiar with process-controlled workflows before switching to this framework in your production system.

However, if the application-controlled workflow framework was subsequently configured, and you later want to use process-controlled workflows, you must switch back to the process-controlled workflow framework.

Recommendation

We strongly recommend that you use only one workflow framework in your production system. Switch to the process-controlled workflow framework for all business object types in the production system.

Process Migration (Optional)

Before using the process migration tool described next, carry out the configuration of your process-controlled workflows. A migration tool for existing approval processes (application-controlled to process-controlled) is provided in the IMG via SAP SUPPLIER RELATIONSHIP MANAGEMENT • SRM SERVER • CROSS-APPLICATION BASIC SETTINGS • BUSINESS WORKFLOW • UPGRADE • CONVERT WORKFLOWS. Executing this report stops all running approval processes and restarts them using the process-controlled workflow framework.

Recommendation

Depending on the number of running approval processes, the migration process can take some time. SAP recommends that you run the migration process with exclusive system access.

If you do not do the migration, documents processed with application-controlled workflows and documents processed with process-controlled workflows will exist in the system in parallel. Note that the system behaves differently depending on the approval framework being used. You must configure UWL for application-controlled workflows because remaining documents must be listed in the respective approver's UWL.

25.10.2 Archiving

After you have been live for awhile, you may need to consider an archiving project. When taking a closer look at archiving SAP SRM objects, document data as well as process data have to be taken into consideration. If workflow data is archived, the connection of the SAP SRM document with the workflow data gets lost. That's why SAP SRM documents must be archived before archiving workflow data.

SAP Note 1038660 states that when you archive SAP SRM documents, the related workflow data are archived as well. For process-controlled workflow, archiving SAP SRM document data also archives all relevant workflow data.

25.10.3 New Installation

Before configuring SAP Business Workflow, you have to create your organizational structure. Then you need to do the standard workflow configuration (discussed in Chapter 3, Configuring the System).

Application-Controlled Workflow

With the SAP SRM releases, different predefined workflow templates are delivered (e.g., zero-step approval or one-step approval for shopping cart). Before activating event linkage and start conditions, a decision has to be made if the delivered workflow templates meet your business rules with respect to number of approval levels and agent assignment. With SAP SRM 5.0, workflow templates were introduced that use BAdI implementations for agent determination and determination of the number of approval levels.

If no workflow template satisfies the business needs of the customer, workflow templates have to be created by copying a SAP SRM standard workflow template and making the required adaptations. The following tasks must be completed:

▶ Activate the event linkage of those workflows that you want to use.

▶ Assign a processor to the tasks if it is not general task.

▶ Create appropriate start conditions.

> **Caution**
>
> The start conditions have to be maintained in a way that exactly one start condition fits to the attributes of the corresponding business object. If an event is triggered, for example, a shopping cart is ordered, and no start condition satisfies the shopping cart attributes, an error is thrown. If more than one start condition satisfies the shopping cart attributes, an error will also be thrown.

Process-Controlled Workflow

The quickest way to get started with process-controlled workflow is to activate a BC Set. As mentioned earlier, BC Sets are available for shopping carts, purchase orders, confirmations, invoices, contracts, quotes, and RFx (bids). For each of these business objects, there is one BC Set to customize a process without approval and one to customize a process with one-step manager approval. When you activate a BC Set, the system automatically creates a process schema and configures all necessary process levels. For each business object, you can activate one BC Set only:

▶ **BC sets for processes without approval**
The process schema configured when you activate a BC Set for processes without approval contains only one process level, in which the items of the document are approved automatically. In these processes, there are no reviewers, no defaults for ad-hoc approvers, and the contact person does not receive a work item for acceptance when the approval process is finished. If you use only BC Sets for processes without approval, and you have not configured any other process schemas, SAP Business Workflow is not involved, and you do not have to perform any customizing activities for SAP Business Workflow.

BC Sets that configure processes without approval use the naming convention /SAPSRM/C_<BO>_600_**000**_SP04. For enabling processes without approval, activate the event type linkage in Transaction SWE2 of class /SAPSRM/CL_WF_PDO. The event is READY_FOR_WORKFLOW, and the workflow template is WS40000014. BC Sets are activated in Transaction SCPR20.

▶ **BC sets for processes with one-step manager approval**
The process schema configured when you activate a BC Set for processes with one-step manager approval contains one process level for approval by the document creator's manager and one for automatic decision. If the system cannot determine a responsible agent, the document is rejected automatically. In these

processes, there are no reviewers, no defaults for ad-hoc approvers, and the contact person does not receive a work item for acceptance when the approval process is finished.

BC Sets that configure processes with one-step manager approval use the naming convention `/SAPSRM/C_<BO>_600_001_SP04`.

Note

Available BC Sets are listed in Appendix F, Additional Information for SAP SRM.

After activating BC Sets, you can execute an approval process. To adapt the workflow to your business needs, the configuration can be easily maintained in the IMG via SAP Supplier Relationship Management • SRM Server • Cross-Application Basic Settings • Business Workflow • Process-Controlled Workflow • Business Process Configuration • Define Process Levels.

A basic set of agent determination functionality is delivered as BAdI implementations. This enables a high flexibility because the customer can easily implement and use its own specific agent determination. Depending on the business object, the basic agent determination strategies listed in Appendix F, Additional Information for SAP SRM, are delivered.

Customers expect a speedy response on their inquiries. Using workflows in SAP Customer Relationship Management ensures a quick and precise reaction on customer inquiries. At the same time, it guarantees that necessary approval procedures are always maintained and can be easily adapted to new requirements. In this chapter, you will learn important SAP CRM concepts that impact SAP Business Workflow. You will learn what is provided in SAP CRM systems for SAP Business Workflow and how to customize workflows provided by SAP.

26 SAP Customer Relationship Management

SAP Customer Relationship Management (SAP CRM) enables you to fully integrate all internal and external business processes of your customer management. All employees, irrespective of whether they are from marketing, sales, service or call centers, can access the same customer data. Partners can be involved in the business processes and access the same data where applicable and permitted. All customer data, interaction, and information are clearly visible and consistent to all members of your company, and the customer is confident that your company knows and understands his needs.

Consistent workflows across the company play a vital role in this scenario to control and monitor business processes. Especially to support more complex processes, SAP CRM contains SAP standard business workflows that integrate actions from members across the company. Additionally, SAP CRM offers a variety of standard actions that can be easily adapted or even replaced by your own specific actions.

Examples of standard SAP business workflows in SAP CRM are:

▶ Follow-up and approval processes in marketing

▶ Follow-up and approval processes in opportunity and lead management

▶ Sales order processing

▶ Approval processes in pricing

▶ Approval processes in claims and funds management

▶ Routing and processing of incoming emails in the customer interaction center

▶ Follow-up processes in channel management

> **Note**
>
> Many workflow templates are provided in SAP CRM. You can do a search in the SAP Help Portal (*http://help.sap.com*) within SAP CRM on the keyword "workflow," to get links to the workflows. Some examples are explained in detail in Section 26.5, SAP CRM Standard Workflows.

26.1 Introduction

SAP CRM is an independent application that can be integrated into an SAP ERP backend. It contains the SAP NetWeaver Application Server and provides specific technologies on top of the application server:

▶ **One Order framework for all business transactions**
The idea of the one order concept is that any business transaction is based on the same generic business object type. Any business transaction, such as sales order, service order, contracts, opportunity, and so on, is implemented by the same application programming interface (API) of the One Order framework. It also integrates all other data of a business transaction such as partner determination, pricing, billing, and so on.

▶ **Middleware**
This is meant to be for backend integration via exchange of XML Business Documents (BDoc).

▶ **Business Object Layer and Generic Interaction Layer Framework**
The Business Object Layer (BOL) framework offers together with the Generic Interaction Layer (GenIL) an abstraction between the API of the different business applications and the user interface layer (UI). The BOL framework provides functionality to easily build end-user applications and integrate the business applications with each other on the BOL layer by using the respective BOL models. The GenIL layer handles the data transfer between the BOL layer and the API of the underlying business application. Business transactions, marketing objects, or business partners are examples for underlying business applications.

▶ **SAP CRM Web Client User Interface**

The SAP CRM Web Client UI is a web-based UI that runs on the BOL framework. It is highly flexible and configurable for your business needs; for example, it can be configured role specific to adapt to the needs of every business role in your company. The possibilities of configuration reach from adding or removing business applications in the context of a business role down to labeling, removing, and adding single fields on the UI.

All SAP CRM business applications, besides some administrative functions, customizing, and some specific exceptions, have been implemented in the SAP CRM Web Client UI and BOL framework. Thus, a unified look and feel and consistent behavior is ensured across all business applications.

Tip
Note that this chapter deals with the current release SAP CRM 2007 (6.0). The BOL framework as the basis for all SAP CRM business applications was introduced with this release. The same applies for the unified SAP CRM Web Client UI. The PCUI framework and SAP GUI-based applications have been replaced by the BOL framework and the SAP CRM Web Client UI as of release 2007.
SAP Note 1118231 provides further information about the SAP CRM Web Client UI. You can also find additional information at the SAP Help Portal (*http://help.sap.com*) by doing a search on "CRM Web Client UI".

26.1.1 One Order Concept

As mentioned, the one order concept is an integral part of SAP CRM. It implies that all business transactions share the same database tables and API and use the same processing concept. Because all objects are implemented by the same API and reuse the same data structure, the various components of a business transaction, such as pricing, partner processing, and so on, can be reused in different business contexts.

Note
Further details about SAP CRM business transactions are available in the SAP Help Portal (*http://help.sap.com*) under SAP CUSTOMER RELATIONSHIP MANAGEMENT • COMPONENTS AND FUNCTIONS • BASIC FUNCTIONS • BUSINESS TRANSACTION.

The following main function modules are available to read and maintain business transactions:

- Function module `CRM_ORDER_READ` to read all data of any SAP CRM business transaction
- Function module `CRM_ORDER_MAINTAIN` to maintain the data of any SAP CRM business transaction
- Function module `CRM_ORDER_SAVE` to save the data that was changed before by calls of `CRM_ORDER_MAINTAIN`

Another concept of the One Order framework is the event handling for the processing of business transactions and their components. During the processing of `CRM_ORDER_MAINTAIN`, one order events are raised in the One Order framework. If an event callback function module is registered for a one order event, it is called by the One Order framework with the corresponding business transaction and event data. Standard event callback function modules are registered for such events.

> **Hint**
>
> Event handlers and callback function modules are similar to regular workflow events. They are events that are published from the SAP CRM One Order framework. The handlers/callback function modules enable you to configure how you want to react to the event. Instead of using Transaction SWE2 to configure how to respond to the event, you use the Implementation Guide (IMG).

You can also register customer event callback functions for these one order events and react to data changes during the business transaction processing. You can customize your own handler function modules for one order events in the IMG under CUSTOMER RELATIONSHIP MANAGEMENT • TRANSACTIONS • BASIC SETTINGS • EDIT EVENT HANDLER TABLE.

The event handler table for the one order event registration is structured by object type. A registration for `BUS20001` means that the registered event callback function module is called for every business transaction type. This is the case because `BUS20001` is the supertype of all business object types in the One Order framework. This is also reflected in the Business Object Repository (BOR) because `BUS20001` represents the generic supertype of all other BOR object types of a one order business transaction.

For an example and further details about event callback function modules, refer to the IMG documentation.

26.1.2 Business Transaction and SAP CRM Business Objects

As usual, the Business Object Repository (BOR) provides the basis of the business logic for workflow development. The one order concept is technically implemented in the BOR by business object type BUS20001.

Business object type BUS20001 is the common supertype of all other business object types BUS2000xxx in the one order context. This is achieved by the standard inheritance functionality of the BOR. The generic supertype BUS20001 already covers the main methods, attributes, and events for all SAP CRM business transactions and avoids that the same functionality has to be implemented individually for every business object type.

The same principle of one generic supertype has been implemented for the BOR object types of the marketing scenario. In this scenario, BUS20100 is the common supertype.

Table 26.1, Table 26.2, and Table 26.3 provide an overview of the most important business object types within SAP CRM and other common business object types.

Business Object Type	Description
BUS20001	CRM Business Transaction
BUS2000108	CRM Lead
BUS2000109	CRM Contract
BUS2000111	CRM Opportunity
BUS2000115	CRM Sales Transaction
BUS2000116	CRM Service Process
BUS2000117	CRM Service Confirmation
BUS2000120	CRM Complaint
BUS2000125	CRM Task

Table 26.1 Business Object Types of SAP CRM Business Transactions

Business Object Type	Description
BUS2000126	CRM Business Activity
BUS2000311	CRM Claim
BUS2000312	CRM Prepayment Request
BUS2000402	CRM Budget Posting

Table 26.1 Business Object Types of SAP CRM Business Transactions (cont.)

Business Object Type	Description
BUS20100	CRM Marketing Project
BUS2010010	CRM Marketing Project Plan
BUS2010012	CRM Marketing Project Plan Element
BUS2010020	CRM Marketing Project Campaign
BUS2010022	CRM Marketing Project Campaign Element
BUS2010030	CRM Marketing Trade Promotion
BUS2010040	Marketing Project Deal
BUS2010050	CRM Marketing Project MDF Program
BUS2010060	CRM Marketing Project MDF Special Program
BUS1185	Target Group

Table 26.2 Business Object Types of Marketing

Business Object Type	Description
BUS1006	Business Partner
BUS1006002	Business Partner Contact Person
BUS1006003	Business Partner Employee
BUS1178	Product
BUS2300	Product Catalog

Table 26.3 Business Object Type of Master Data Management

Most of the SAP CRM standard workflows are based on business object types that are defined in BOR. However, some workflows are based on ABAP classes that implement the corresponding workflow interface. Because they are supported by the SAP CRM Worklist, ABAP classes are also used for some dialog tasks with user interaction. The enabling of dialog tasks that are based on ABAP classes is described in Section 26.4.4, Specifics of Dialog Tasks Based on Workflow ABAP Classes. For details on workflow ABAP classes, refer to Chapter 11, ABAP Classes.

26.1.3 Transaction History

When a follow-up document for a SAP CRM document is created, a link between the succeeding and the preceding document is written into the *transaction history* of the documents. This guarantees an access from one document to the other and gives a good overview of the complete transaction history. It can provide an overview of the whole process loop from marketing to billing:

▸ Execute an email campaign that has a questionnaire attached to emails.

▸ Collect questionnaire response, and create leads from response.

▸ Create an opportunity after the lead fulfills certain requirements and the sales department accepts the lead.

▸ Create a quotation for the opportunity.

▸ Create an order after the customer accepts the quotation.

▸ Trigger the billing.

All documents of the complete business process are linked to each other via the transaction history. The transaction history of the order displays the preceding quotation and vice versa. The same applies for the quotation and the lead and so forth. This enables you to easily trace the complete process. Besides the transaction history, the *change history* is also available, which traces the changes on field level that have been made on a document.

However, not all transactions are displayed in the transaction history as such anymore. This feature has been enhanced by adding several *assignment blocks* relating to different areas. These areas are specific to the type of transaction and have been removed from the transaction history and assigned to the appropriate assignment block instead, such as shipping, billing, and so on. This was done to provide a quicker and better overview of the documents contained in the transaction history.

Workflows can be used to automatically create follow-up documents or obtain approval for the creation of a follow-up document; for example, after a lead has reached a certain status, an opportunity can be created as a follow-up document. Section 26.5.2, Sales — Lead to Opportunity, explains such a standard scenario, and the corresponding workflow template can be used as a starting point for your own workflow implementation.

26.1.4 SAP CRM UI Framework

The SAP CRM UI framework basically consists of the following three components:

▶ **Generic Interaction Layer (GenIL Layer)**
This layer represents the connection between the framework and the API (usually function modules) of the respective business application. It handles the *interaction* between the framework and API. Each business application has its own implementation of the GenIL layer. This implementation is called *GenIL component*. Several GenIL components are combined into a *GenIL component set*.

GenIL components and component sets are published to the framework under the following IMG activity: Customer Relationship Management • CRM Cross-Application Components • Generic Interaction Layer/Object Layer • Basic Settings.

Each component has standard methods to publish its object model to the framework. These objects are used to build UI components and can be modified by the user. Changes on the objects are forwarded to the respective GenIL implementation class, which transforms the changes into calls of the underlying API.

▶ **Business Object Layer (BOL) framework**
The BOL framework handles the interaction between the UI when data is changed, read, and so on and the respective GenIL implementation class. It also contains its own buffer and handles relations between objects of the GenIL components.

The objects of a GenIL component are represented by *BOL entities* at runtime. They are instances of the objects of a GenIL component, and their instance attributes contain the object data. The BOL entities are kept in the BOL entity buffer of the framework and can be reread from the API when necessary (e.g., after changes).

A GenIL component usually contains an object hierarchy of *root objects* and *dependent objects*. A root object has no superior objects and is linked to its transactional context. It can have dependent objects assigned that do not have their own transactional context but depend on the root object and are also handled in the transactional context of the root object.

▶ **UI layer**

Transaction BSP_WD_CMPWB is the Component Workbench that enables you to build and configure *UI components*. A UI component can run on its own and embed other UI components. Common data that is used across various business transaction types is a very good example for the implementation of reuse UI components, for example, pricing data in business transactions.

You can create views, define navigation between views and other components, and so forth. Usually, an application displays and changes the data of objects of a certain GenIL component set. The objects' attributes and relations are used to easily generate and configure your UI component. At runtime, the attribute values of the according BOL entities represent the data that is used, displayed, and changed on the UI level. For configuration and navigation purposes, UI object types can be used.

The configuration of standard and custom UI components in the Component Workbench offers the following features:

▶ Fields and table columns can be added or removed.

▶ Captions of fields and table columns can be changed.

▶ Whole assignment blocks can be added or removed.

All of this can be done without any coding changes or modifications of the standard or custom UI components. Based on the configuration of a UI component, the user can also still personalize the UI to his needs.

UI object types can link BOL objects to BOR object types or workflow ABAP classes, which is essential in the workflow context. This is explained in detail in Section 26.4.2, Dynamic Navigation and the Workflow Inbox.

> **Note**
>
> The concept of *enhancement sets* allows you to add customer-specific behavior to standard UI components without modification. An enhancement set can be assigned per UI component. The usage of enhancement sets provides great flexibility in adopting standard UI components to your requirements. At the same time, they offer a convenient way to reuse the functionality of standard UI components and to just add specific functionality. Certain scenarios that require a specific UI component and functionality (e.g., a workflow process), however, can make it necessary to build your own UI component. An example for such a workflow-specific UI component is provided later in this chapter.

> **Tip**
>
> The SAP CRM Wiki of the SAP Community Network has information and provides a how-to guide about the enhancement of SAP CRM UI components at *https://www.sdn.sap.com/irj/scn/wiki*.

The different layers and their interaction are illustrated in Figure 26.1.

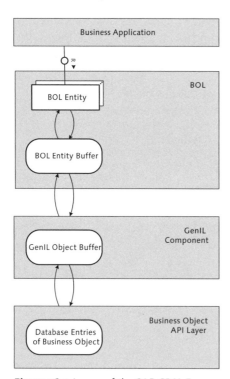

Figure 26.1 Layers of the SAP CRM Framework

26.1.5 Portal Integration

The SAP CRM framework is independent of the SAP NetWeaver Portal. This means that a SAP CRM system can be installed and run without having the SAP NetWeaver Portal in place. However, it can, of course, be integrated into SAP NetWeaver Portal, and users can access the SAP CRM system from the SAP NetWeaver Portal.

26.2 Customizing and Workflow Administration

There are no special techniques or frameworks used in SAP CRM for the integration of workflows into your business processes. Workflows can be integrated via methods such as status changes or actions.

26.2.1 Workflow Customizing

To be able to use workflows, the basic workflow customizing has to be set up. Chapter 3, Configuring the System, explains in detail the setup of the general workflow customizing. Before the SAP CRM standard workflows can be used, the usual activities have to be performed:

- Activate the event linkages.
- Set up the Organizational Management and rule integration for the agent determination.
- Perform maintenance of workflow start conditions where necessary.

Almost all of the SAP CRM standard workflows are integrated via start and terminating events of the respective BOR object.

26.2.2 Workflow Administration

There is no SAP CRM-specific workflow administration or monitoring required. The standard administration tools explained in Chapter 6, Workflow Administration, are sufficient. These tools are available in SAP GUI as part of the administrative functions.

26.3   Integrating Your Own Workflows

Business applications in SAP CRM reuse standard components of the SAP NetWeaver Application Server. This includes the reuse of standard workflow components to build your own workflows in SAP CRM.

26.3.1 Status Management

You can create subtypes of the SAP CRM standard object types and implement your own events on these. If you delegate your own BOR object type to a standard BOR object type, the status management allows you to assign your own events to *status changes*. They are then automatically raised by the system. This can be done in Transaction BSVW. This applies to system as well as user status changes. Most events of SAP CRM standard object types are configured and raised this way.

> **Hint**
>
> Linking events to status management is also discussed in Chapter 13, Using Events and Other Business Interfaces.

26.3.2 Actions

Actions are a common technique in SAP CRM to trigger and execute follow-up activities. You can use actions to configure and start predefined processes. You can assign start conditions (similar to the workflow start conditions) and configure the execution time and type of actions to adapt the system behavior to your own requirements.

Standard actions are used for the following purposes:

- ► Creation of follow-up documents
- ► Creation of line items in business transactions
- ► Print and output management
- ► Notification of partners

SAP CRM actions use the *Post Processing Framework (PPF)* of the SAP NetWeaver Application Server as a common interface for the various processing methods. The processing of actions can be configured for:

- Methods of Business Add-Ins (BAdIs)
- Start of workflow template
- SAP Smart Forms

An action that is configured for processing through a BAdI implementation can of course be used to trigger workflows as well. The respective business object event can be raised by calling function module SAP_WAPI_CREATE_EVENT. Raising the event this way is more flexible than configuring the action to directly trigger an individual workflow template. Processing actions by using a BAdI method allows you to perform additional, more complex checks than you can with an action's start condition.

Actions can be configured and assigned to various business applications in the IMG under CUSTOMER RELATIONSHIP MANAGEMENT • BASIC FUNCTIONS • ACTIONS. There is also further documentation available in the IMG. Configuring an action to call a BAdI is discussed in Section 26.6.6, Action to Automatically Set the Status "Accepted by Sales".

26.3.3 Agent Determination

SAP CRM uses the concept of *partner processing* to determine which business partners take part in a certain process. If possible, the partner processing determines the partners automatically and adds them to the process. The user can also manually enter one or more partners, and the other partners are automatically added by the system. The *partner determination procedure* that is derived from the customizing controls the partner processing.

Usually, it is advisable to keep the agent determination for SAP Business Workflow consistent to the result of the partner processing. To do so, you can use *agent determination rules* that determine the partners that are assigned to a document. A common example is the partner role Employee Responsible that has to be informed via a workflow task about further actions that need to be taken for a certain document.

The partners of business transactions can be read via function module CRM_ORDER_READ. For marketing documents, they can be read via class CL_CRM_MKTPL_APPL_BASE. After reading the partners, the required partner, such as the Employee Responsible, can be identified by the corresponding partner function category and can be used as the agent for a workflow task.

The Employee Responsible needs to be informed about changes on a business transaction. Listing 26.1 demonstrates a sample for an agent determination rule of type F Function to be Executed.

```
INCLUDE: <cntn01>, crm_object_names_con. "ObjectNames in 1Order
DATA: lv_header_guid         TYPE crmt_object_guid,
      lv_user                TYPE syuname,
      ls_actor               TYPE swhactor,
      lt_header_guids        TYPE crmt_object_guid_tab,
      lt_req_obj             TYPE crmt_object_name_tab,
      ls_partner             TYPE crmt_partner_external_wrk,
      lt_partner             TYPE crmt_partner_external_wrkt.
swc_get_element ac_container 'OrderGUID' lv_header_guid.
APPEND lv_header_guid TO lt_header_guids.
APPEND gc_object_name-partner TO lt_req_obj."only read Partners
* Get partners from business transaction
CALL FUNCTION 'CRM_ORDER_READ'
  EXPORTING
    it_header_guid      = lt_header_guids
    it_requested_objects = lt_req_obj
  IMPORTING
    et_partner          = lt_partner
  EXCEPTIONS
    OTHERS              = 99.
IF sy-subrc <> 0. RAISE order_not_found. ENDIF.
READ TABLE lt_partner INTO ls_partner WITH KEY mainpartner ='X'
              partner_pft = '0008'."Part.FunctionCategory
IF sy-subrc <> 0. RAISE partner_not_found. ENDIF.
* ALTERNATIVE: if partner function can be derived
READ TABLE lt_partner INTO ls_partner WITH KEY mainpartner ='X'
              partner_fct = '00000014'."Part.Function
  IF sy-subrc <> 0. RAISE partner_not_found. ENDIF.
CALL FUNCTION 'BP_CENTRALPERSON_GET'
  EXPORTING
    iv_bu_partner_guid = ls_partner-bp_partner_guid
  IMPORTING
    ev_username        = lv_user
  EXCEPTIONS
    OTHERS             = 99.
IF sy-subrc <> 0. RAISE bp_not_found. ENDIF.
ls_actor-objid = lv_user.
```

```
ls_actor-otype = 'US'.
APPEND ls_actor TO actor_tab.
```
Listing 26.1 Employee Responsible of a Business Transaction

Listing 26.1 shows that there are:

▶ **Partner function categories**
Partner function categories are system settings and cannot be modified. The available partner function categories can be found in system Table CRMC_PARTNER_PFT.

▶ **Partner functions**
Partner functions are customizing and can be modified as needed. A partner function is assigned to a partner function category. Numerous partner functions are part of the standard delivery. The partner functions can be found in customizing Table CRMC_PARTNER_FCT.

For further details, refer to the IMG documentation under CUSTOMER RELATIONSHIP MANAGEMENT • BASIC FUNCTIONS • PARTNER PROCESSING and the SAP Help Portal (*http://help.sap.com*).

26.4   SAP CRM Worklist

The *SAP CRM Worklist* provides central access to various inboxes that support the user in his daily work and help him keep track of his tasks:

▶ **Workflow Inbox**
The Workflow Inbox displays the workflow tasks that are currently assigned to the user. It enables the user to complete his workflow tasks, to forward them to another user, or to execute multiple decision tasks with one click.

▶ **Alerts inbox**
The Alerts inbox displays the alerts that are currently assigned to the user. It enables the user to complete the alerts or forward them to another user.

▶ **Business Transactions inbox**
The Business Transactions inbox enables the user to search for SAP CRM objects that are relevant for him. The user can search for business transactions that are assigned to him as the Employee Responsible or to his sales organization as a result of the partner processing. Thus, the search is typically based on

the result of the partner processing in the business transactions (refer to Section 26.3.3, Agent Determination).

Figure 26.2 shows the SAP CRM Home page for a sales professional, used to access workflow tasks, alerts, appointments, and other activities needed to perform daily tasks in SAP CRM.

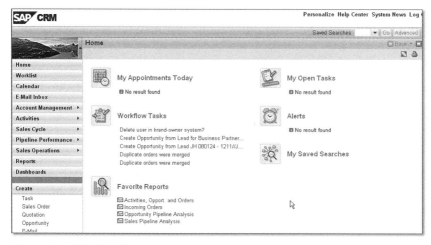

Figure 26.2 SAP CRM Home

The standard configuration of the SAP CRM Worklist contains the inboxes for alerts, business transactions, and workflow tasks (see Figure 26.3).

Figure 26.3 SAP CRM Worklist

The SAP CRM Workflow Inbox, its functionalities, and customizing are explained in detail in this chapter.

26.4.1 Basics About the Workflow Inbox

The Workflow Inbox of SAP CRM is basically a UI component like any other UI component in SAP CRM as of release 2007 (6.0):

▶ It comprises GenIL component WFI and a corresponding implementation class that handles the interaction between the Workflow Inbox, the BOL framework, and the Workflow Engine. GenIL component WFI contains the BOL root object WFRoot, which represents a single workflow task.

▶ Several UI components implement the views to display the workflow task list, workflow task details, and so on.

When a dialog workflow task is executed in the Business Workplace of the SAP GUI, the coding of the underlying BOR object method or of the underlying workflow ABAP class method is executed. Usually, a transaction or report is called, for example. The user interaction for dialog tasks is implemented differently in the SAP CRM Workflow Inbox because it is web-based.

The code of the BOR object or workflow ABAP class method is not executed when the user executes the workflow task in the Workflow Inbox. Instead, the method is mapped to a corresponding UI component that offers the required functionality. The Workflow Inbox determines this dynamic mapping and supplies the required data to the respective UI component. You will find a detailed explanation of this mapping in the succeeding sections.

26.4.2 Dynamic Navigation and the Workflow Inbox

As explained in Section 26.4.1, Basics About the Workflow Inbox, a dynamic mapping to a corresponding application is necessary for the execution of workflow tasks. This mapping is achieved by executing a *dynamic navigation* to the respective UI component. Dynamic navigation is a standard feature of the SAP CRM Web UI and is used by other components as well as the Workflow Inbox. It enables any UI component to navigate and display an object that belongs to another UI component without knowing what the other UI component is.

Example

A sales order always has a business partner assigned, which represents the sold-to-party. The UI component to create and maintain the sales order offers a hyperlink that enables you to navigate into the UI component for display and maintenance of the business partner of the sold-to-party.

To call the business partner component, it does not have to know the business partner component but triggers a dynamic navigation for the respective business partner instance (BOL entity) and the action to be executed for the business partner (action DIS-PLAY in this case).

An in-depth example of how to set up dynamic navigation in the workflow context is given in Section 26.6, Sample Implementation of a Customer Workflow in SAP CRM.

To use dynamic navigation for a certain object, the following *prerequisites* have to be fulfilled (for further details, refer to the corresponding IMG documentation):

▶ **UI object type**
  A corresponding UI object type needs to be available. UI object types can be maintained in the IMG under CUSTOMER RELATIONSHIP MANAGEMENT • UI FRAMEWORK • UI FRAMEWORK DEFINITION • DEFINE UI OBJECT TYPES. To use the UI object type for dynamic navigation, it has to be assigned to a BOL root object. If possible, it can also be assigned to a BOR object type. Standard UI object types are maintained in system Table BSP_DLC_OBJ_TYPE and cannot be modified.

▶ **Mapping class**
  A mapping class needs to be available for the BOL root object that is assigned to the UI object type. Mapping classes can be maintained in the IMG under CUSTOMER RELATIONSHIP MANAGEMENT • UI FRAMEWORK • TECHNICAL ROLE DEFI-NITION • DEFINE OBJECT MAPPING. The mapping class has to implement the interface IF_CRM_UI_OBJ_MAPPER. During the execution of a dynamic navigation, the BOL framework calls the respective mapping class (e.g., to retrieve the BOL entity). Standard mapping classes can be replaced by your own mapping classes.

▶ **UI component**
  The corresponding UI component needs to be assigned to a target ID. Target IDs can be maintained in the IMG under CUSTOMER RELATIONSHIP MANAGEMENT • UI FRAMEWORK • TECHNICAL ROLE DEFINITION • DEFINE WORK AREA COMPONENT REPOSITORY. The assignment of a target ID makes the inbound plugs of a UI component available for dynamic navigation.

▶ **Target ID**

The target ID needs to be available for the corresponding business roles. Target IDs can be assigned to the navigation bar profile of business roles in the IMG under Customer Relationship Management • UI Framework • Technical Role Definition • Define Navigation Bar Profile. The maintenance view under Define Profile • Define Generic OP Mapping allows the assignment of target IDs.

You can use every standard BOR object type that is enabled for dynamic navigation for your own workflows without further customizing and implementation effort. The Workflow Inbox automatically triggers a corresponding dynamic navigation to display the BOR object instance. The standard BOR object types are assigned to standard UI object types in system Table BSP_DLC_OBJ_TYPE.

If specific actions are required in your workflow, such as opening an object straight in edit mode or in your own UI component, a specific Workflow Inbox customizing is available. Further details about this customizing are given in the following sections.

26.4.3 Navigational Customizing of the Workflow Inbox

The Workflow Inbox provides additional customizing for dynamic navigation in the workflow context. This customizing allows additional functionality to integrate your workflows into the SAP CRM Web UI. It can be maintained object-specifically or task-specifically.

Object-Specific Navigation

Specific UI object types and actions can be assigned to BOR object types and methods in this IMG activity. It offers the following functionality:

▶ BOR object methods that are used in workflow tasks can be assigned directly to specific UI objects types and actions. For example, this opens an object directly in Edit mode when executing the workflow task

▶ Standard and custom BOR objects can be assigned per method to their own UI object types and their own UI components in the workflow context. These UI components may provide workflow-specific functionality, which is enhanced or reduced compared to the SAP standard UI component.

▶ Your own subtypes of standard BOR objects can be assigned to standard UI object types, and the mapping of the standard BOR object can be reused for your own BOR objects to launch the standard UI component.

▶ Workflow ABAP classes can be customized for dialog tasks

▶ The workflow task can be provided as a BOL entity to the UI component if supported by the UI component.

The object-specific navigational customizing of the Workflow Inbox can be maintained in the IMG under CUSTOMER RELATIONSHIP MANAGEMENT • BASIC FUNCTIONS • WORKLIST • DEFINE ALERT INBOX AND WORKFLOW INBOX • DEFINE OBJECT-SPECIFIC NAVIGATION. If there is an entry maintained for an object that does not specify an object method, it is considered the default entry by the Workflow Inbox for this object.

Hint

If the flag SET TO COMPLETED BY APPLICATION is set, the Workflow Inbox includes a BOL entity of the runtime instance of the workflow task in the dynamic navigation. This means that the UI component that is called up can retrieve this BOL entity of the workflow task in its inbound plug. It can then use this BOL entity to get additional data about the workflow task. If the data of the BOL entity and its dependent objects is not sufficient, the SAP_WAPIxxx interface can provide additional data.

This flag also implies that the inbox does not complete synchronous workflow tasks automatically, but that the workflow task has to be completed by the UI component (e.g., by the workflow API to complete the task). Standard UI components are not designed to retrieve a BOL entity of a workflow task in their inbound plugs. Setting this flag for a standard BOR and UI object type and thus, for a standard UI component, will lead to an error. If you only want to achieve that the workflow task is not immediately completed and closed on execution, then you should just set the flag CONFIRM END OF PROCESSING in the definition of your standard task.

ABAP classes used for workflow are workflow specific and thus not known to the SAP CRM UI framework. This is why an object-specific customizing *has to be maintained* in the case of dialog tasks for ABAP classes. The specifics for ABAP classes are explained in detail in Section 26.4.4, Specifics of Dialog Tasks Based on Workflow ABAP Classes. The IMG documentation provides further details.

Task-Specific Navigation

In some cases, it may be necessary to overwrite the object-specific customizing by a task-specific customizing. For example:

▶ BOR object type BUS2000116 and method ChangeWithDialog are assigned to UI object BT116_SRVO and action Edit. This customizing is sufficient for most of the respective workflow tasks.

▶ A certain task provides additional data for the maintenance of the service order, such as business partner data. It requires returning parameters after the maintenance of the service order because the returning parameters are required later on in your workflow.

▶ You do not want to create your own subtype of BUS2000116.

You can overwrite the object-specific customizing by assigning a specific standard task to your own UI object type and to your own UI component. By setting the flag WORKFLOW TASK SET TO 'COMPLETED' BY APPLICATION, the BOL entity of the workflow task is provided to your UI component. It can then react accordingly to the workflow task.

26.4.4 Specifics of Dialog Tasks Based on Workflow ABAP Classes

As already explained, workflow ABAP classes are not known to the SAP CRM UI framework. This is why they always have to be assigned to a UI object type in the object-specific navigation customizing. Via the assigned BOL root object (see Section 26.4.2, Dynamic Navigation and the Workflow Inbox), the UI object type is assigned to a mapping class.

Besides the usual interface IF_CRM_UI_OBJ_MAPPER of the framework, the mapping class can implement the Workflow Inbox interface IF_CRM_CT_IB_WF_UI_OBJ_MAPPER. If this interface is implemented by the mapping class, the Workflow Inbox calls methods of this interface to get the necessary data for the dynamic navigation.

If the mapping class does not implement interface IF_CRM_CT_IB_WF_UI_OBJ_MAPPER, then the key attribute of the workflow ABAP class has to suit the key attribute that is expected by the mapping class. Usually, this is according to the key attribute of the respective BOR object type (e.g., the order GUID of BUS20001).

26.4.5 Additional Customizing and Personalization

There is an additional customizing available for the integration of partner channel management under Customer Relationship Management • Basic Functions • Worklist • Define Alert Inbox and Workflow Inbox • Define Forwarding and Substitution. This customizing allows you to set up per business role if a user can forward workflow tasks only to internal, only to external, or to all business partners in the system. It might be necessary, for example, to restrict internal employees from forwarding workflow tasks to external partners because of confidential information.

The SAP CRM Workflow Inbox also provides functionality of personalization for the user by maintaining *substitutes*. The same logic for the maintenance of internal and external business partners as substitutes of a user applies here. Because the organizational management of the SAP CRM system is based on business partners, the maintenance of substitutes and the forwarding of workflow tasks are also based on business partners in the SAP CRM system. However, only those business partners can be maintained as substitute and recipient of a workflow task that have an SAP user ID assigned.

Apart from the required assignments between business partner and user ID, the substitute maintenance is the same functionality that is explained in Chapter 5, Agents.

> **Note**
>
> As will be explained in Section 26.4.6, SAP ERP Integration, it is possible to integrate SAP ERP workflows into the Workflow Inbox. In this scenario, the maintenance of substitutes in the SAP CRM system should be consistent with the maintenance of substitutes in the integrated SAP ERP system. The system always maintains the substitutes of a user in the integrated systems as well when the user changes his substitutes. Some prerequisites need to be fulfilled for consistent substitute maintenance:
>
> ► The user ID of the user in the SAP CRM system needs to be identical in the integrated system.
>
> ► The users ID of the substitutes need to be identical in the integrated system.
>
> ► If substitute profiles are used, the profile IDs need to be identical in all systems.

26.4.6 SAP ERP Integration

The Transaction Launcher of the SAP CRM UI framework provides functionality to integrate non-SAP CRM Web UIs into the SAP CRM UI framework. This includes in particular the web-based SAP GUI for SAP ERP documents that are integrated with SAP CRM documents. Details about the functionality and customizing of the Transaction Launcher can be found in the IMG under CUSTOMER RELATIONSHIP MANAGEMENT • UI FRAMEWORK • TECHNICAL ROLE DEFINITION • TRANSACTION LAUNCHER.

Usually, there is no SAP CRM web UI available for non-SAP CRM workflows. This is why it is necessary in most cases to use the web-based SAP GUI. To integrate other SAP systems, the corresponding logical systems have to be maintained in the IMG under CUSTOMER RELATIONSHIP MANAGEMENT • BASIC FUNCTION • WORKLIST • INTEGRATE OTHER SAP SYSTEMS IN WORKFLOW INBOX. The logical systems need to be set up for the Transaction Launcher as well.

> **Note**
>
> It is a prerequisite that users who have non-SAP CRM workflow tasks assigned must have the same user ID in the remote SAP system. For further details, refer to the IMG documentation of the Workflow Inbox and the Transaction Launcher.

Figure 26.4 shows an example of an SAP ERP workflow task in the Workflow Inbox.

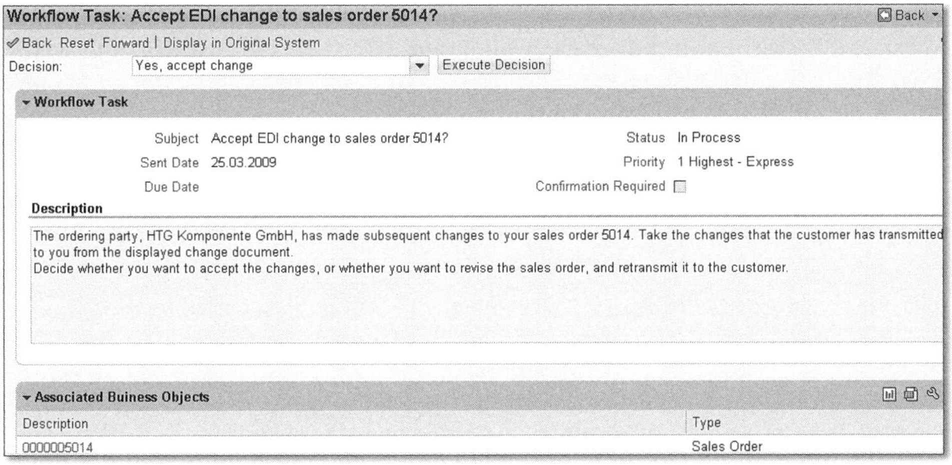

Figure 26.4 SAP ERP Workflow Task in the Workflow Inbox

Usually, there is no SAP CRM web UI available for BOR objects that originate from the SAP ERP system. This is why common SAP ERP objects that are linked to SAP CRM documents are assigned to specific UI object types in the SAP CRM system. These UI object types can be identified by the naming convention `WRAPPED_*` as UI object type name (refer to system table `BSP_DLC_OBJ_TYPE`). The user can then click on the link for the SAP ERP object under Associated Business Objects and directly navigate into the web-based SAP GUI to display and edit the objects.

However, there might be SAP ERP workflows for customer BOR objects, for example, that are not set up for direct navigation into the web-based SAP GUI via the Transaction Launcher. Then the button Display in Original System enables the user to display the workflow task in the web-based SAP GUI and from there on to navigate into the respective object. Additionally, it offers the possibility to access the standard SAP GUI functionality for workflow tasks.

For details about how to set up a direct navigation into the web-based SAP GUI for SAP ERP objects, refer to the documentation of the Transaction Launcher under Customer Relationship Management • UI Framework • Technical Role Definition • Transaction Launcher. The standard SAP CRM business roles already contain a mapping for UI object types `WRAPPED_*` to enable navigation into an SAP ERP object. You can use the customizing under Customer Relationship Management • UI Framework • Technical Role Definition • Define Navigation Bar Profile • view Define Profile – Define Generic OP Mapping as a template to customize further objects.

When the user executes an SAP ERP workflow task via the Execute button, the workflow task is executed in the web-based SAP GUI. Because UI object type `WORKITEM_IB_EXT` is required for this navigation, it *has to be maintained* for every business role that is used for SAP ERP integration under Customer Relationship Management • UI Framework • Technical Role Definition • Define Navigation Bar Profile • view Define Profile – Define Generic OP Mapping. Standard business roles can serve as a template for this.

Tip

An SAP ERP workflow task is always executed in the web-based SAP GUI, unless a specific navigation customizing is set up for the workflow task under Customer Relationship Management • Basic Functions • Worklist • Define Alert Inbox and Workflow Inbox.

To ensure a safe transactional behavior, the flag CONFIRM END OF PROCESSING should be set for synchronous SAP ERP workflow tasks that are integrated into SAP CRM.

Figure 26.5 shows the same workflow as in Figure 26.4 in the web-based SAP GUI after the user clicked on DISPLAY IN ORIGINAL SYSTEM.

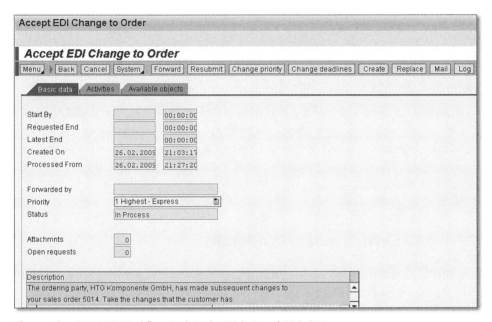

Figure 26.5 SAP ERP Workflow Task in the Web-Based SAP GUI

26.4.7 Universal Worklist Integration

The SAP CRM system and the Workflow Inbox can also be integrated into the Universal Worklist (UWL). As usual with UWL integration, the workflow visualization metadata needs to be maintained in Transaction SWFVISU. The entries for BOR object types BUS2000272 and BUS2000311 can serve as an example if you need further SAP CRM object types to be integrated into UWL. These two objects are default entries in Transaction SWFVISU.

The basic concept of the UWL integration in SAP CRM is the *object-based navigation*. The corresponding and common object type for UWL integration is the SAP CRM UI object type WI_BOR. The common UI object type WI_BOR is used, so the Workflow Inbox is always called first before the navigation into the actual object and SAP CRM UI component is executed. This approach ensures that a Workflow Inbox customizing is considered in the context of UWL integration as well (refer to Section 26.4.3, Navigational Customizing of the Workflow Inbox for details).

26.4.8 Administrative Standard Workflows

Standard workflows that are intended for system administrators need to be executed in the Business Workplace of the SAP GUI. The reason for this is that administrative transactions and functions also have to be executed in SAP GUI. Thus, it has to be ensured that such administrative workflows are assigned to corresponding users who also work in SAP GUI.

An example for such a workflow is standard task TS00007989 that handles errors in the IDoc processing. The IDoc customizing needs to be maintained, so the workflow tasks are assigned to the corresponding administrator and do not come up in the Workflow Inbox of other users. Otherwise, an error message is displayed that the workflow task cannot be processed.

26.5 SAP CRM Standard Workflows

This section explains some examples of SAP CRM standard workflows in SAP CRM scenarios and processes.

Hint
The workflows provided by SAP are discussed in the SAP Help Portal. If you do a search for SAP CRM workflow at *http://help.sap.com*, you will find a link to the workflow area in the SAP CRM documentation. This lists the provided workflows for business transactions, service process, lead management, marketing, interaction center, and grants management. The documentation provides information on the workflow, tasks, object types, and rules to find the selected agents at runtime.
To use a standard SAP CRM workflow, you just need to assign agents to the possible tasks, activate the event linkage, and do any additional IMG configuration that may be required per the template (the required IMG configuration is discussed in the SAP Help Portal as well).

26.5.1 Marketing: Campaign Automation

Campaign automation is designed to deal with multichannel, multiwave, and real-time campaigns, providing direct reactions to customer responses. Setting up a fully automated campaign means that employees can access the campaign automation tool directly from the campaign screen, improving planning and increasing transparency. Campaign automation allows you to model a campaign, and after the process model is triggered, no further manual intervention is necessary.

Workflow is the technique used to ensure an automatic campaign process that does not require any further manual action after it is executed. The campaign automation process is a chain of workflows where the next workflow is triggered or scheduled as soon as the preceding one has finished. SAP provides standard workflows that belong to the campaign automation task set. They can be directly assigned to a campaign element when you are modeling the campaign. You can enhance them to meet customer-specific requirements.

As usual, they are defined in the Workflow Builder. All those workflows are set up for BOR object type `BUS2010022` (Campaign Element). Each workflow has input parameters, which are retrieved from the campaign element. After starting the campaign (Start button in Campaign Automation), the workflows are scheduled or executed automatically. For this reason, no type linkages need to be maintained for this workflow sample. Figure 26.6 shows the campaign modeling.

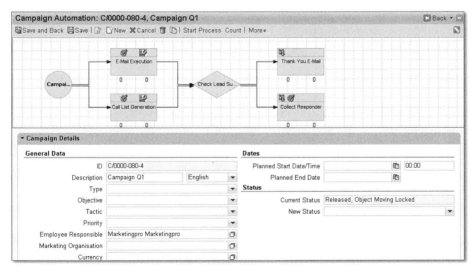

Figure 26.6 Campaign Automation

After successfully executing the corresponding workflow, the program exit `CL_CRM_MKTCA_WF_DESTRUCTOR_CPT` is called to ensure that the next workflow is scheduled on time.

In campaign automation, responses to a marketing campaign are created and evaluated, and, if necessary, additional campaign steps are planned and executed. In the standard version, a customer response is defined as an inbound contact. If a preceding campaign element is assigned to this business activity, then campaign automation rule evaluation is started via an action, and additional subsequent steps are scheduled.

For further details, refer to the IMG activity under CUSTOMER RELATIONSHIP MANAGEMENT • MARKETING • MARKETING PLANNING AND CAMPAIGN MANAGEMENT • CAMPAIGN AUTOMATION. The SAP Help Portal (*http://help.sap.com*) also provides a detailed description under SAP CUSTOMER RELATIONSHIP MANAGEMENT • COMPONENTS AND FUNCTIONS • BASIC FUNCTIONS • SAP BUSINESS WORKFLOW • SAP BUSINESS WORKFLOW IN MARKETING • SAP BUSINESS WORKFLOW IN CAMPAIGN AUTOMATION.

26.5.2 Sales — Lead to Opportunity

You can use the lead to opportunity business scenario to control your marketing and sales processes transparently. With this business scenario, you can process and analyze leads and opportunities, and process activities. It describes the individual processes and also demonstrates the entire cycle, from first interest when a lead is created, through to presales, when an opportunity is created, and finally to activity processing.

A *lead* is a business transaction that describes, stores, updates, and manages the potential interest of (and interaction with) a business partner over a certain timeframe. Leads are used to qualify a business partner's interest in a particular product or in making a purchase, with the aim of both establishing and then subsequently influencing this interest. After a lead has reached a certain status, it can be passed on to "sales" as decision support for creating an opportunity. This transformation from one business object lead (BUS2000108) into another business object opportunity (BUS2000111) can be achieved via the SAP CRM standard workflow WS10001011 (SAP CRM: Generate Opportunity from Lead). This workflow is started when a lead is saved with a QUALIFICATION LEVEL of HOT and a STATUS of ERROR-FREE.

If the lead-specific attributes priority and lead group fulfill specific criteria, the workflow automatically generates an opportunity. Otherwise, the workflow sends a work item to the sales employee responsible for creating the opportunity manually. The sales representative who entered in the lead is first taken as the sales employee whose task it is to create the opportunity based on the information in the lead. This person can be determined using partner determination in SAP CRM. The determination can depend on the prospect in the lead or be a manager of a sales area.

After checking the data in the lead, the sales employee can either reject this lead or create an opportunity from it (see Figure 26.7).

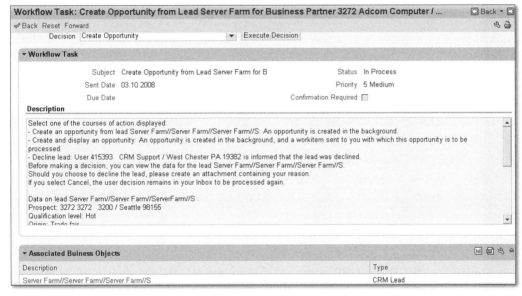

Figure 26.7 Decision Task for Manual Creation of Opportunity Out of Lead

If the sales employee decides that an opportunity can be created, the lead STATUS is set to ACCEPTED BY SALES, and an opportunity is created by a background workflow task (see Figure 26.8). After the opportunity has been created automatically or manually from the lead, the TRANSACTION HISTORY provides the link between the objects.

If the sales employee rejects the lead, the lead STATUS is set to REJECTED BY SALES by a background workflow task, and the initiator is informed by email.

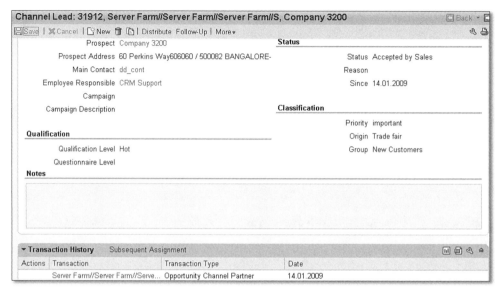

Figure 26.8 Transaction History of Lead and Opportunity

For further details, refer to the IMG activity under CUSTOMER RELATIONSHIP MANAGEMENT • TRANSACTIONS • SETTINGS FOR LEADS. The SAP Help Portal (*http://help.sap.com*) also provides details under SAP CUSTOMER RELATIONSHIP MANAGEMENT • COMPONENTS AND FUNCTIONS • BASIC FUNCTIONS • SAP BUSINESS WORKFLOW • SAP BUSINESS WORKFLOW IN LEAD MANAGEMENT • CREATE SAP BUSINESS WORKFLOW FOR OPPORTUNITY FROM LEAD.

26.6 Sample Implementation of a Customer Workflow in SAP CRM

The previous sections explained the SAP CRM UI framework, the one order concept, and how workflows can be integrated into SAP CRM, as well as provided examples of SAP CRM standard workflows. This section combines the previous explanations about SAP CRM and the given examples of standard SAP CRM workflows and explains how to set up your own custom-built SAP CRM workflows with your own SAP CRM UI component.

Attention

This section does not provide everything you need to know for working with the SAP CRM UI components; however, it shows the steps that must be taken for the SAP CRM UI to work with SAP Business Workflow.

26.6.1 Scenario and Requirements for the Custom Workflow

Section 26.5.2, Sales — Lead to Opportunity, gave an overview of the standard workflow scenario to create an opportunity as a follow-up transaction of a lead and how the responsible sales employees can accept or reject the lead. This process should be enhanced as follows:

▶ A workflow-specific application should be implemented to accept or reject the lead as a step in the workflow. As in the standard scenario, the workflow sets the corresponding status for the lead transaction and creates an opportunity in the background if the lead has been accepted.

▶ Additionally, the new application should allow the user to create the follow-up opportunity online. The user can still do manual adaptations of the opportunity before saving it.

▶ Whenever a follow-up opportunity is created, the preceding lead should be set into status ACCEPTED BY SALES. The status should be set irrespective of whether the opportunity was created out of the workflow context or not.

▶ Because the new functionality is considered to be workflow specific and to provide a self-contained example to demonstrate the usage of dynamic navigation in the workflow context, a custom UI component will be created. In reality, the enhancement of standard UI components is often sufficient.

26.6.2 Implementing the Workflow

In this section, we discuss how to implement the workflow for the custom workflow.

New BOR Object Type and Method

A new BOR object method is needed to provide the new functionality. For this purpose, subtype Z2000108 of the standard BOR object type BUS2000108 is created (Transaction SWO1). The new synchronous dialog method Zcreate_FollowUp_

`Oppt_Dialogue` is used for the new dialog standard task (TS). Because this method will be mapped to the corresponding UI component at runtime, the method implementation can stay empty. (The method will have only `BEGIN` method and `END` method with no coding.) Figure 26.9 shows the custom BOR object `Z2000108` and the new method `Zcreate_FollowUp_Oppt_Dialogue`.

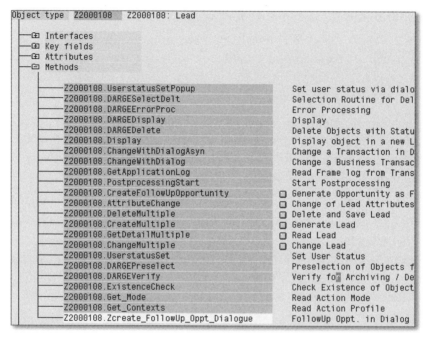

Figure 26.9 Custom BOR Object with Empty Method

Of course, you can also define this method as asynchronous and assign a terminating event in the task definition. But this requires more adaptations with regard to the SAP CRM standard workflow template because there is no standard BOR event provided for the status ACCEPTED/REJECTED BY SALES. By using a synchronous dialog method, the logic of the standard SAP CRM workflow of when to terminate can be reused.

After creating the new BOR object type and method, you need to create a standard task definition (TS). After adding the object `Z2000108` and method `Zcreate_FollowUp_Oppt_Dialogue`, be sure to set the flag CONFIRM END OF PROCESSING. This flag needs to be set because the task is synchronous, and the user might cancel the execution of the workflow task. As usual, an agent assignment needs to be maintained for the new task definition (you can make it a general task).

New Workflow Template

Because the scenario is very similar to the standard scenario, the standard workflow WS10001011 can simply be copied over to your own workflow template in the Workflow Builder (Transaction SWDD). The new workflow template then needs to be adapted as follows:

1. Create new container element Z2000108 of type Z2000108.

2. Insert a background step to retrieve the instance of Z2000108 according to the existing container element LEAD of type BUS2000108. This step should be inserted before the standard User Decision step.

> **Hint**
>
> This can be easily done by creating a task based on object type SYSTEM, method GENERICINSTANTIATE. The method receives a value for a key and the name of the object, and the method returns the instantiated object. This is discussed in Appendix A, Tips and Tricks.

3. Create a new step in the workflow for the new (TS) standard task of Z2000108. This step should be inserted after the new background step.

4. Copy over the user assignment from the existing User Decision step, and set the flag PROCESSING CAN BE REJECTED in the step details.

5. Cut the (background) workflow steps of the user decision branch Decline Lead, and paste them into the branch Processing Rejected of the new dialog step.

6. DELETE the old workflow step for the user decision, including all of its branches. SAVE and ACTIVATE the workflow template.

7. Adapt the condition of the LOOP (UNTIL) branch after event step WAIT FOR ATTRIBUTECHANGED as shown in Figure 26.10.

8. The adapted sections of the workflow template look like Figure 26.11.

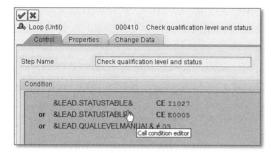

Figure 26.10 Loop Condition of Custom Lead Workflow

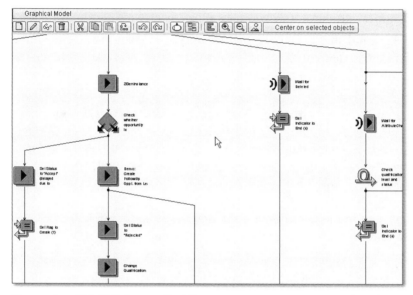

Figure 26.11 SAP CRM Custom Workflow to Create Opportunity Out of Lead

Now that the workflow template has been created, you need to build the new UI component. This basically replaces the implementation of the new BOR method where you would call a transaction, function module, report, and so forth for user interaction in SAP GUI.

26.6.3 Creating a BOL Model for Your SAP CRM Workflows

As already explained, usually a GenIL component (Generic Interaction Layer) and corresponding GenIL implementation is needed to build a SAP CRM UI component. A GenIL component and BOL model is especially required to enable dynamic navigation. Because your workflow mainly reuses standard functionality and a BOL model, implementing the GenIL component is fairly easy, assuming you have previous experience with the SAP CRM UI.

Tip

Building UI components is what makes workflow on SAP CRM different from traditional workflow. It is recommended that you already have experience with the SAP CRM UI before developing new workflows. The Business Process Expert community (BPX) in the SAP Community Network has information on the SAP CRM Web Client UI Framework. You can find it by searching for "CRM Web Client UI Framework" on *http://sdn.sap.com*. Additionally, a master list of SAP CRM articles is maintained on SDN at *https://www.sdn.sap.com/irj/scn/articles-crm-all*.

GenIL Implementation Class

The GenIL implementation class is always a subclass of the standard framework class CL_CRM_GENIL_ABSTR_COMPONENT2. In our example, this class is named ZCL_WF_FOR_BT_GENIL. The class and the corresponding GenIL component can be reused for any other of your workflow implementations in the one order context. BT is a common acronym for objects in the one order context and stands for *business transaction*.

Class ZCL_WF_FOR_BT_GENIL needs to redefine method IF_GENIL_APPL_MODEL~GET_OBJECT_PROPS. This method publishes all BOL objects of a single GenIL component to the framework:

1. Because your workflow reuses standard objects, your GenIL implementation class only needs to provide a single BOL root object, which will be used for the dynamic navigation customizing and the mapping of BOR object type Z2000108. The method implementation looks like Listing 26.2.

```
DATA: ls_crmt_obj_properties TYPE crmt_obj_properties,
      ls_key_struct           TYPE zst_wf4bt_root_key,
      ls_att_struct           TYPE zst_wf4bt_root_att.
* Root Object for WF Handling
ls_crmt_obj_properties-object_name =
c_root_obj_name."ObjectName
ls_crmt_obj_properties-object_kind =
  if_genil_obj_model=>root_object. "ObjectType: RootObject
ls_crmt_obj_properties-key_struct  = c_key_struct.
```

```
                                          "DDIC Structure for the ObjectKey
ls_crmt_obj_properties-attr_struct =
c_att_struct. "DDIC Structure for The ObjectAttributes
ls_crmt_obj_properties-root_object =
c_root_obj_name. "ObjectName of the RootObject
APPEND ls_crmt_obj_properties TO rt_obj_props.
```

Listing 26.2 Definition of the BOL Model for Custom Workflows

2. After activating the preceding GenIL implementation class, it can be maintained in the customizing for GenIL components under Customer Relationship Management • CRM Cross-Application Components • Generic Interaction Layer / Object Layer • Basic Settings (see Figure 26.12).

Dialog Structure	Component Definition			
🗀 Component Definition				
▽ 🗀 Component Set Definitio	Comp. Na	Description		Implementation Class
🗀 Component Assignm	ZWF4BT	Demo: WF Handling for Bus. Transactions		ZCL_WF_FOR_BT_GENIL

Figure 26.12 Customizing for GenIL Component of Custom Workflows

3. After your GenIL component has been defined, an accompanying component set ZWF4BT should be maintained. This component set can comprise various other GenIL components. Because your workflow application will handle leads and opportunities, you should include the GenIL component BT for business transactions (see Figure 26.13).

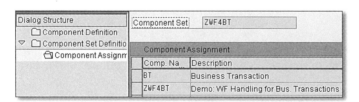

Dialog Structure	Component Set:	ZWF4BT	
🗀 Component Definition			
▽ 🗀 Component Set Definitio	Component Assignment		
🗀 Component Assignm	Comp. Na	Description	
	BT	Business Transaction	
	ZWF4BT	Demo: WF Handling for Bus. Transactions	

Figure 26.13 Customizing for GenIL Component Set of Custom Workflows

4. After maintaining the preceding customizing, you can display your GenIL component set and the corresponding model in the model browser (Transaction GENIL_MODEL_BROWSER), which may look like Figure 26.14. This means that you can reuse any BOL object of the standard GenIL component BT in the UI components that you implement for your workflow GenIL component set. You will see in Figure 26.14 that your GenIL component set comprises the standard BOL root object BTOrder.

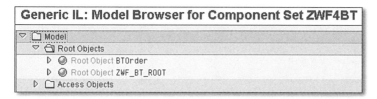

Generic IL: Model Browser for Component Set ZWF4BT

▽ ☐ Model
   ▽ ⬡ Root Objects
      ▷ ◉ Root Object BTOrder
      ▷ ◉ Root Object ZWF_BT_ROOT
   ▷ ☐ Access Objects

Figure 26.14 Model Browser for GenIL Component Set of Custom Workflows

26.6.4 Implementation of the Workflow Application

A detailed description of how to implement your own UI component is beyond the scope of this chapter. Thus, a brief summary is provided, and the major functionality specific to this application is described with the help of code samples. After you have familiarized yourself with the SAP CRM UI framework, you will be able to build UI components for your workflows and other purposes.

> **Tip**
>
> All SAP CRM UI components that deal with business transactions follow the same naming convention: BTxxxY_zzzz. xxx represents the standard subtype of BOR object type BUS20001 (e.g., BUS2000115 for sales orders). zzzz identifies the standard transaction type (e.g., SLSO for sales orders and SLSQ for sales order quotations, which are both implemented by BUS2000115). Y stands for the type of application, M identifies the main component that embeds all other components for an object, H is the header component, S is the search component, and so forth. Accordingly, the main standard UI components for the lead and opportunity example in this chapter are BT108M_LEA and BT111M_OPPT.

The concept of how to build SAP CRM UI components is similar to Web Dynpro applications. SAP CRM UI components also comprise the concept of *view controller, view layout,* and *context nodes* that contain the business data.

After starting Transaction BSP_WD_CMPWB, you can enter the name for your UI component and click CREATE (see Figure 26.15). The system then creates the UI component with a component controller, main window and XML Runtime Repository. To reuse the BOL objects of your GenIL component set, you need to assign the corresponding model in the Runtime Repository of the UI component. Figure 26.16 shows the node COMPONENTUSAGES in the Runtime Repository of the UI component. COMPONENTUSAGES define usages of other UI components.

Access BSP WD Workbench

Component	zbt108_approval
Test Application	

Display	Create	Test

Figure 26.15 Creation of Workflow UI Component

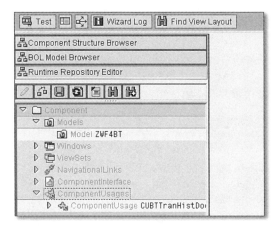

Figure 26.16 Runtime Repository of UI Component for Custom Workflow

Necessary Views

Views are created with the help of wizards of the UI component workbench. While creating a view, you can enter the BOL objects that are needed for the view and the system automatically creates the context nodes for these BOL objects. The UI component should at least comprise the following two views (see Figure 26.17):

- The view DETAILS contains context nodes to display basic data about the lead transaction, for example, description, ID, or status.

- The view OVERVIEW is a configurable overview page that contains the view DETAILS as an assignment block. The view DETAILS has to be assigned in the Runtime Repository Editor as an assignment block and can then be configured for the overview page under the CONFIGURATION tab.

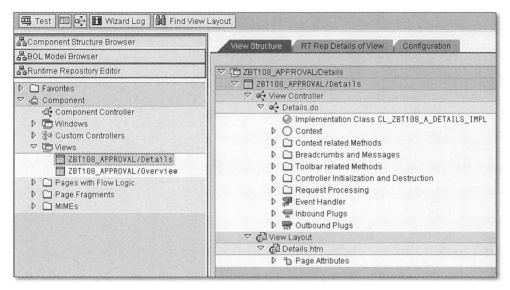

Figure 26.17 Views of UI Component for SAP CRM Custom Workflow

Window Plugs to Navigate In to and Out of the UI Component

As explained in Section 26.4.2, Dynamic Navigation and the Workflow Inbox, *inbound plugs* have to be defined to enable cross-component navigation into one UI component from another UI component. *Outbound plugs* represent the counterpart and are used to enable cross-component navigation from one UI component into another UI component. Your workflow application needs to provide the following inbound and outbound plugs (see Figure 26.18):

► Inbound plug IP_CREATE_FOLLOWUP_OPPT is called when starting up the UI component after the workflow task has been executed.

► Outbound plug OP_FOLLOWUP is fired by the UI component to trigger the navigation into the standard UI component for opportunities.

► Outbound plug OP_TO_LEAD is triggered by the UI component to trigger the navigation into the standard UI component for leads.

The inbound plug IP_CREATE_FOLLOWUP_OPPT (see Listing 26.3) retrieves the lead as a BOL entity and keeps it in the corresponding context node of the component controller. The views of the UI component can bind their respective context node against the context node of the component controller and thereby have access to the lead BOL entity.

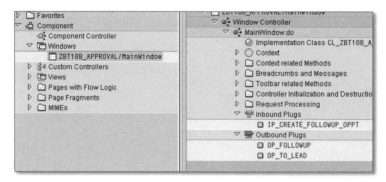

Figure 26.18 Inbound and Outbound Plugs of Workflow Application

```
DATA:
lr_comp_controller TYPE REF TO cl_zbt108_a_bspwdcomponen_impl,
lr_lead_entity     TYPE REF TO if_bol_bo_property_access.
lr_my_comp_controller ?= me->comp_controller.
CHECK iv_collection IS BOUND.
lr_my_comp_controller->typed_context->btorder->
  collection_wrapper->clear( ).
lr_lead_entity = iv_collection->get_current( ).
IF lr_lead_entity IS BOUND.
lr_my_comp_controller->typed_context->btorder->
  collection_wrapper->add(
    iv_entity    = lr_lead_entity
    iv_set_focus = abap_true ).
ENDIF.
```

Listing 26.3 Inbound Plug of Workflow UI Component

The window needs to be set up as an interface view of the UI component. Because window plugs can also be used only for component internal navigation from one view to the other, they still need to be set up as plugs of the component interface. Figure 26.19 shows the interface view of the workflow UI component.

Figure 26.19 Interface View of the Workflow UI Component

Providing the Required Actions

The actions are implemented as four buttons of the OVERVIEW view to reject or accept the lead, display all details of the lead, and to accept and create a follow-up opportunity (see Figure 26.20):

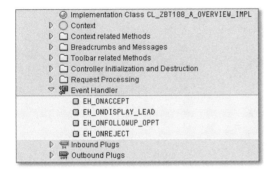

Figure 26.20 Actions/Buttons of the Workflow UI Component

▶ **Accept or reject the Lead**

The event handler of the ACCEPT button looks like Listing 25.4. The implementation of the REJECT button is the same besides the status ID.

```
DATA: lr_entity_coll    TYPE REF TO if_bol_entity_col,
      lr_entity         TYPE REF TO cl_crm_bol_entity,
      lr_trx_context    TYPE REF TO if_bol_transaction_context.
* The MethodCalls below (get_related_entities) evaluate BOL
* Relationships that are already provided by the CRM Standard
* Context Nodes like BTAdmminH are generated by the Workbench
* Get HeaderEntity
lr_entity ?= me->typed_context->btadminh->collection_wrapper->
  get_current( ).
CHECK lr_entity IS BOUND.
* Lock the transaction to be able to change it
CHECK lr_entity->lock( ) = abap_true.
* Get BOL entity for StatusSet of header
lr_entity_coll = lr_entity->get_related_entities(
  iv_relation_name = 'BTHeaderStatusSet' ).
lr_entity ?= lr_entity_coll->get_current( ).
CHECK lr_entity IS BOUND.
* Get BOL entity of current HeaderStatus
lr_entity_coll = lr_entity->get_related_entities(
  iv_relation_name = 'BTStatusHCurrent' ).
```

```
lr_entity ?= lr_entity_coll->get_current( ).
CHECK lr_entity IS BOUND.
* Set Status 'Accepted by Sales'
lr_entity->set_property(
  iv_attr_name = 'ACT_STATUS' " AttributeName of Status
  iv_value     = 'E0005' ).   "We know the value hardcoded here
lr_trx_context = lr_entity->get_transaction( ).
IF lr_trx_context->check_save_needed( ) = abap_false OR
   lr_trx_context->check_save_possible( ) = abap_false.
*  Changes were not accepted or Save is not possible
   lr_trx_context->revert( ).
   RETURN.
ENDIF.
IF lr_trx_context->save( ) = abap_false.
*   Save failed: Rollback & Revert
    lr_trx_context->rollback( ).
    lr_trx_context->revert( ).
    RETURN.
  ELSE.
*   Save successful: Commit Changes
    lr_trx_context->commit( ).
  ENDIF.
* We are finished because a final status has been set:
* => trigger DefaultNavigation back into Inbox
me->op_default_back( ). "Default OP of the Framework: We don't
                       "have to do anything here
```

Listing 26.4 Set Status for Lead Entity

▶ **Display the lead**

This button triggers the cross component navigation into the standard UI component for lead transactions. Listing 26.5 shows the event handler needed to trigger the dynamic navigation to the lead transaction.

```
DATA: lr_lead_entity       TYPE REF TO cl_crm_bol_entity,
      lr_entity_collection  TYPE REF TO if_bol_entity_col.
      lr_lead_entity ?= me->typed_context->btorder->
collection_wrapper->get_current( ).
CHECK lr_lead_entity IS BOUND.
CREATE OBJECT lr_entity_collection
    TYPE cl_crm_bol_entity_col.
lr_entity_collection->add( lr_lead_entity ).
```

```
* Navigate to follow-up UI component
  op_to_lead( lr_entity_collection ).
```
Listing 26.5 Event Handler to Trigger Navigation into Lead

The corresponding outbound plug of the view looks like Listing 26.6.

```
DATA lr_window TYPE REF TO cl_bsp_wd_window.
lr_window = me->view_manager->get_window_controller( ).
lr_window->call_outbound_plug( iv_outbound_plug  = 'TO_LEAD'
                iv_data_collection = iv_data_collection ).
```
Listing 26.6 View Outbound Plug to Trigger Navigation into Lead

▸ **Create follow-up opportunity**

This button creates the follow-up opportunity and triggers the navigation into the standard UI component for opportunities where it still needs to be saved by the user (see Listing 26.7).

```
DATA: lv_msgv             TYPE symsgv,
      lv_msg_dummy         TYPE string.
DATA: lt_method_param      TYPE crmt_name_value_pair_tab,
      ls_method_param      TYPE crmt_name_value_pair.
DATA: lr_lead_entity       TYPE REF TO cl_crm_bol_entity,
      lr_oppt_entity       TYPE REF TO cl_crm_bol_entity,
      lr_entity_collection TYPE REF TO cl_crm_bol_entity_col,
      lr_msg_srv       TYPE REF TO cl_bsp_wd_message_service.
      lr_lead_entity ?= me->typed_context->btadminh->
        collection_wrapper->get_current( ).
  CHECK lr_lead_entity IS BOUND.
* Get MethodParameters to create the opportunity as a FollowUp
* ProcessType for opportunity
ls_method_param-name = 'PROCESS_TYPE'.
ls_method_param-value = 'ZOPP'."Hard coded here
APPEND ls_method_param TO lt_method_param.
* Technical type of FollowUp document
ls_method_param-name  = 'VONA_KIND'.
ls_method_param-value = 'A'."Interlinkage with data transfer
"and update: transfer the Lead Data to the Opportunity
APPEND ls_method_param TO lt_method_param.
* Technical RelationshipType between the 2 documents
ls_method_param-name  = 'RELTYPE'.
ls_method_param-value = 'VONA'. "Predecessor-/Successor
```

```
"RelationshipType
 APPEND ls_method_param TO lt_method_param.
* Create BOL entity for opportunity as FollowUp TRx. of lead
* This is done via BOL method on AdminH BOL entity of lead
TRY.
  lr_entity_collection = lr_lead_entity->execute(
      iv_method_name = 'createFollowUp' "Standard BOL Method
                                        "for FollowUp Transaction
    it_param       = lt_method_param ).
  CATCH cx_crm_bol_meth_exec_failed.
* Locking of lead could have failed for example
  RETURN.
ENDTRY.
IF lr_entity_collection IS NOT BOUND.
* Error occurred during creation of opportunity
  lv_msgv = lr_lead_entity->get_property_as_string(
    iv_attr_name = 'OBJECT_ID' )."TransactionNumber
  lr_msg_srv = me->view_manager->get_message_service( ).
  MESSAGE e051(crm_copy) WITH lv_msgv INTO lv_msg_dummy.
  lr_msg_srv->add_message( iv_msg_type   = sy-msgty
                           iv_msg_id     = sy-msgid
                           iv_msg_number = sy-msgno
                           iv_msg_v1     = sy-msgv1
                           iv_important_info = abap_true ).
  RETURN.
ENDIF.
lr_oppt_entity = lr_entity_collection->get_current( ).
CHECK lr_oppt_entity IS BOUND.
CREATE OBJECT lr_entity_collection.
lr_entity_collection->add( lr_oppt_entity ).
* Navigate to follow-up UI component
op_followup( lr_entity_collection ).
```

Listing 26.7 Create Follow-Up Opportunity for Lead

Note

The BOL entity that is created in Listing 26.7 has not been saved and persisted yet. After the navigation into the UI component for opportunities has been executed, the user has to decide when to save the opportunity. Status ACCEPTED BY SALES has not yet been set either. This is done automatically by the action that is also explained in Section 26.6.6, Action to Automatically Set the Status "Accepted by Sales"

26.6.5 Setting Up Dynamic Navigation

After implementing your workflow UI component and publishing, its inbound and outbound plugs, the component can be set up in the customizing for dynamic navigation.

Definition of UI Object Type

The UI object type can be set up in the IMG under CUSTOMER RELATIONSHIP MANAGEMENT • UI FRAMEWORK • UI FRAMEWORK DEFINITION • DEFINE UI OBJECT TYPES. The customizing of the UI object type for the workflow UI component will look like Figure 26.21.

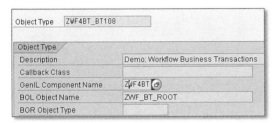

Object Type	ZWF4BT_BT108	
Object Type		
Description	Demo: Workflow Business Transactions	
Callback Class		
GenIL Component Name	ZWF4BT	
BOL Object Name	ZWF_BT_ROOT	
BOR Object Type		

Figure 26.21 UI Object Type for Workflow UI Component

Definition of Target IDs

Target IDs need to be defined for a UI component to assign the UI component to a UI object type. The corresponding IMG activity is available under CUSTOMER RELATIONSHIP MANAGEMENT • UI FRAMEWORK • TECHNICAL ROLE DEFINITION • DEFINE WORK AREA COMPONENT REPOSITORY. The target ID for the inbound navigation looks like Figure 26.22. Accordingly, the target IDs for the outbound navigation look like Figure 26.23.

Dialog Structure	Component Name	ZBT108_APPROVAL			
▽ ☐ Component Definition	Window Name	ZBT108_APPROVAL/MainWindow			
☐ Inbound Plug Definiti					
☐ Outbound Plug Defin	**Inbound Plug Definition**				
	Target ID	Inbound Plug		Object Type	Obj.Action
	ZFUPOPP	CREATE_FOLLOWUP_OPPT		F4BT_BT108	F Execute

Figure 26.22 Inbound Target ID for Workflow UI Component

Figure 26.23 Outbound Target IDs for Workflow UI Component

Make UI Object Type Accessible for Business Roles

The UI object type needs to be assigned to the navigation bar profile of all of the respective business roles that possibly execute the workflow task (see Figure 26.24). The corresponding IMG activity is available under CUSTOMER RELATIONSHIP MANAGEMENT • UI FRAMEWORK • TECHNICAL ROLE DEFINITION • DEFINE NAVIGATION BAR PROFILE.

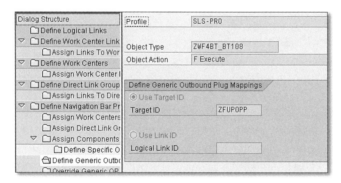

Figure 26.24 Assign UI Object Type to Business Role

Definition of Object Mapping

As already mentioned, an *object mapping class* needs to be defined if you create your own UI object types. This class needs to implement interface IF_CRM_UI_OBJ_MAPPER. In case of the workflow UI component, the only method that needs to be implemented is GET_ENTITY_FROM_BOR, which may look like Listing 26.8.

```
DATA: lv_order_guid       TYPE crmt_object_guid,
      lv_genil_id         TYPE crmt_genil_object_id.
```

```
  DATA: lr_bol_core            TYPE REF TO cl_crm_bol_core.
* Ensure that 1Order BOL/GenIL is loaded
  lr_bol_core = cl_crm_bol_core=>get_instance( ).
  lr_bol_core->load_component( 'BT' ).
* Convert the OrderGUID into KeyValue in Framework
lv_order_guid = iv_bor_object_key.
lv_genil_id = cl_crm_genil_container_tools=>build_object_id(
  is_object_key = lv_order_guid ).
IF iv_bor_object_type = 'Z2000108'.
*    Our SubType of Standard BOR Object BUS2000108
*    Get BOL Root Entity of Business Transaction
     rv_result = lr_bol_core->get_root_entity(
         iv_object_name = 'BTOrder'
         iv_object_guid = lv_order_guid ).
  ELSE.
    CLEAR rv_result.
  ENDIF.
```

Listing 26.8 Map Z-BOR Object Type to BOL Entity

This object mapping class needs to be assigned to your BOL model under Customer Relationship Management • UI Framework • Technical Role Definition •
Define Object Mapping (see Figure 26.25).

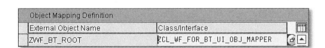

Figure 26.25 Assign Object Mapping Class

Define Method-Specific Navigation for SAP CRM Inbox

The last step that needs to be done for the UI part is to define the method specific
navigation for your own BOR object type in the Workflow Inbox under Customer Relationship Management • Basic Functions • Worklist • Define Alert
Inbox and Workflow Inbox • Define Object-Specific Navigation.

Figure 26.26 shows that Z200018 is mapped to the standard UI object for any
other BOR method besides ZCREATE_FOLLOWUP_OPPT_DIALOGUE (e.g., if the user
clicks on it under Associated Business Objects in the Workflow Inbox, the standard UI component for the lead transaction is started).

UIU WF Inbox Object (Method) specific Customizing						
External Sy	Obj. Cat.	Object Ty	Method	Object Type	Obj. Act.	
	0 BOR Object	Z2000108		BT108_LEA	B Display	▲
	0 BOR Object	Z2000108	ZCREATE_F	ZWF4BT_BT108	F Execute	▼

Figure 26.26 Inbox Customizing for Z2000108

26.6.6 Action to Automatically Set the Status "Accepted by Sales"

The last open requirement is to set the status ACCEPTED BY SALES every time a new opportunity is created for the lead. This requirement is supposed to be implemented in such a way that it is independent of a possible workflow (e.g., a user might create a follow-up opportunity without triggering the workflow because the lead is not in the required state to trigger the workflow). This can be achieved by an action that is executed every time an opportunity is created.

Set Up of the Action Definition and Profile

The customizing to set up and configure actions and action profiles for business transactions is available in the IMG under CUSTOMER RELATIONSHIP MANAGEMENT • BASIC FUNCTIONS • ACTIONS • ACTIONS IN TRANSACTION • CHANGE ACTIONS AND CONDITIONS. The action needs to be customized as shown in Figure 26.27. The important points to note are that the processing time is set to immediate processing and is scheduled automatically.

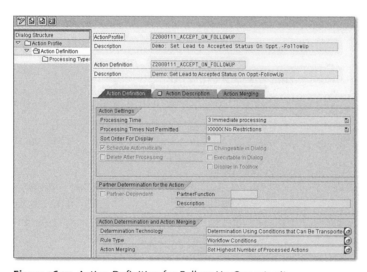

Figure 26.27 Action Definition for Follow-Up Opportunity

The next step is to define the PROCESSING TYPE of the action as METHOD CALL (see Figure 26.28). This processing type means that a BAdI method is called on the execution of the action. The BAdI implementation is automatically created by the system for the filter value that is entered under METHOD. The BAdI implementation contains method EXECUTE, which needs to be implemented and looks like Listing 26.9.

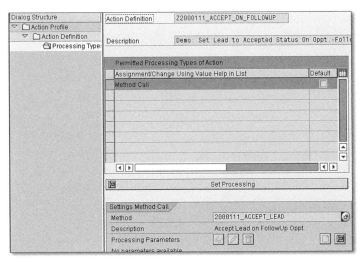

Figure 26.28 Processing Type of Follow-Up Action

```
DATA: lv_oppt_guid          TYPE crmt_object_guid,
      lv_lead_guid          TYPE crmt_object_guid,
      lv_status_profile     TYPE j_stsma.
DATA: lt_header_guid        TYPE crmt_object_guid_tab,
      lt_doc_flow           TYPE crmt_doc_flow_wrkt,
      ls_doc_flow           TYPE crmt_doc_flow_wrk,
      lt_status_current     TYPE TABLE OF jstat,
      lt_status             TYPE crmt_status_comt,
      ls_status             TYPE crmt_status_com,
      lt_input_fields       TYPE crmt_input_field_tab,
      ls_input_fields       TYPE crmt_input_field,
      ls_field_names        TYPE crmt_input_field_names.
DATA: lr_action             TYPE REF TO cl_action_execute.
* Set ActionStatus for sucessful execution (Reset if nec.)
rp_status = sppf_status_processed.
* Reference on action to get RunTimeData
CREATE OBJECT lr_action.
```

```
* HeaderGUID of Oppt.Transaction
CALL METHOD lr_action->get_ref_object
    EXPORTING
       io_appl_object = io_appl_object
       ip_action      = ip_action
       ip_preview     = ip_preview
       ii_container   = ii_container
    IMPORTING
       ev_guid_ref    = lv_oppt_guid.
* Get DocFlow (=TransactionHistory) of opportunity
APPEND lv_oppt_guid TO lt_header_guid.
CALL FUNCTION 'CRM_ORDER_READ'
    EXPORTING
     it_header_guid    = lt_header_guid
     iv_only_spec_items = abap_true
    IMPORTING
     et_doc_flow       = lt_doc_flow
    EXCEPTIONS
     OTHERS            = 99.
  CHECK sy-subrc = 0.
* Look for opportunity (HeaderGUID) in DocFlow
READ TABLE lt_doc_flow INTO ls_doc_flow TRANSPORTING objkey_a
  WITH KEY ref_guid  = lv_oppt_guid  " Read DocFlow for Oppt.
          objtype_a = 'BUS2000108' "Predecessor: Lead
          objkey_b  = lv_oppt_guid "SuccesorGUID: Oppt.GUID
          objtype_b = 'BUS2000111' "Successor: Opportunity
          reltype   = 'VONA'.       "Prede-/Successor RelShipType
CHECK sy-subrc = 0."No Lead as Predecessor otherwise

  lv_lead_guid = ls_doc_flow-objkey_a.
* Which status set on lead?(this depends on UserStat(schema)!!)
  CALL FUNCTION 'CRM_STATUS_READ'
    EXPORTING
     objnr             = lv_lead_guid
    IMPORTING
     stsma             = lv_status_profile
    TABLES
     status            = lt_status_current
    EXCEPTIONS
     OTHERS            = 99.
CHECK sy-subrc = 0.
CHECK lv_status_profile ='CRMLEAD'. "Wrong StatSchema otherwise
```

```
LOOP AT lt_status_current TRANSPORTING NO FIELDS WHERE
                 inact = abap_false AND
                 ( stat = 'E0005' OR  "Accepted by Sales
                   stat = 'I1027' ).  "Won
   EXIT.
ENDLOOP.
CHECK sy-subrc <> 0."One of the Status active otherwise
* Prepare StatusData for OrderMaintain
ls_status-activate = abap_true.
ls_status-ref_guid = lv_lead_guid."Status of Lead
ls_status-ref_kind = 'A'."Header: set Status on Header
ls_status-status = 'E0005'."UserStatus AcceptedBySales
ls_status-user_stat_proc = 'CRMLEAD'."UserStatusProcedure
APPEND ls_status TO lt_status.
* Prepare InputFields for OrderMaintain
ls_input_fields-objectname = 'STATUS'."Change StatusObj of Lead
ls_input_fields-ref_guid = lv_lead_guid."Input4Lead
ls_input_fields-ref_kind = 'A'."InputField for Header
ls_input_fields-logical_key = 'E0005CRMLEAD'."UserStat&Proc.
ls_field_names-fieldname = 'ACTIVATE'.
APPEND ls_field_names TO ls_input_fields-field_names.
APPEND ls_input_fields TO lt_input_fields.
* Maintain lead to set status
CALL FUNCTION 'CRM_ORDER_MAINTAIN'
   EXPORTING
     it_status      = lt_status
   CHANGING
     ct_input_fields = lt_input_fields
   EXCEPTIONS
     OTHERS         = 99.
  IF sy-subrc = 0.
*    Register lead to be saved with opportunity
*    Note: if the oppt. is not saved successfully, then
*    the changes on the lead won't be saved either
     lr_action->register_for_save(
         EXPORTING
           iv_source_header_guid = lv_oppt_guid
           iv_additional_header_guid = lv_lead_guid
           ip_application_log = ip_application_log
         IMPORTING
           rp_status = rp_status ).
ENDIF.
```

Listing 26.9 Action to Create Follow-Up Transaction

Action Conditions

After you have defined the action and the action profile, you need to customize the start conditions of the action. In this example, the condition is set to SCHEDULE AUTOMATICALLY when the document is saved (see Figure 26.29).

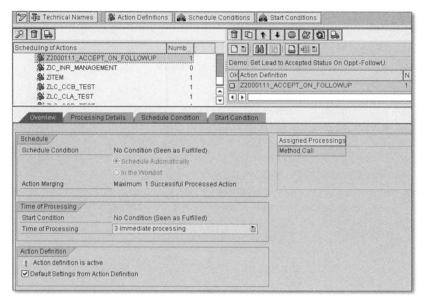

Figure 26.29 Conditions for Follow-Up Action

26.6.7 General Settings for Follow-Up Process

This section discusses the general settings required for the follow-up process.

Copy Control

Irrespective of possible workflow integration, a corresponding *copy control customizing* for the transaction types of lead and opportunity needs to be set up. This is a general customizing that needs to be set up if one transaction type represents possible follow-up transactions of another transaction type. This customizing is available under CUSTOMER RELATIONSHIP MANAGEMENT • TRANSACTIONS • BASIC SETTINGS • COPYING CONTROL FOR BUSINESS TRANSACTIONS • DEFINE COPYING CONTROL FOR TRANSACTION TYPES (see Figure 26.30). For further details about how to set up the copy control customizing between transaction types and item types, refer to the IMG documentation.

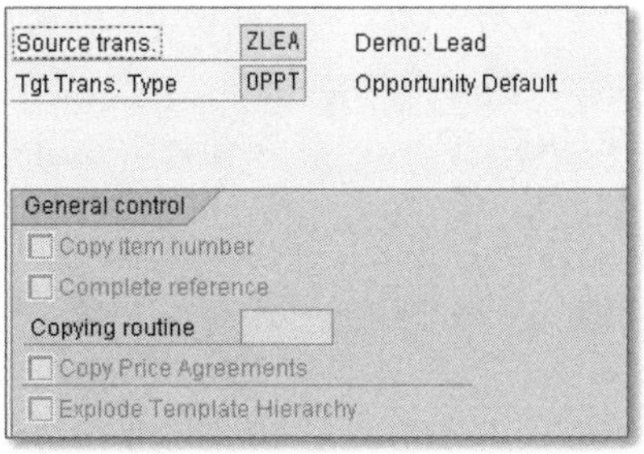

Figure 26.30 Copy Control for Follow-Up Opportunity

Action Profile in Transaction Type

The action profile to update the LEAD status needs to be assigned to the transaction type of the opportunity under CUSTOMER RELATIONSHIP MANAGEMENT • TRANSACTIONS • BASIC SETTINGS • DEFINE TRANSACTION TYPES (see Figure 26.31).

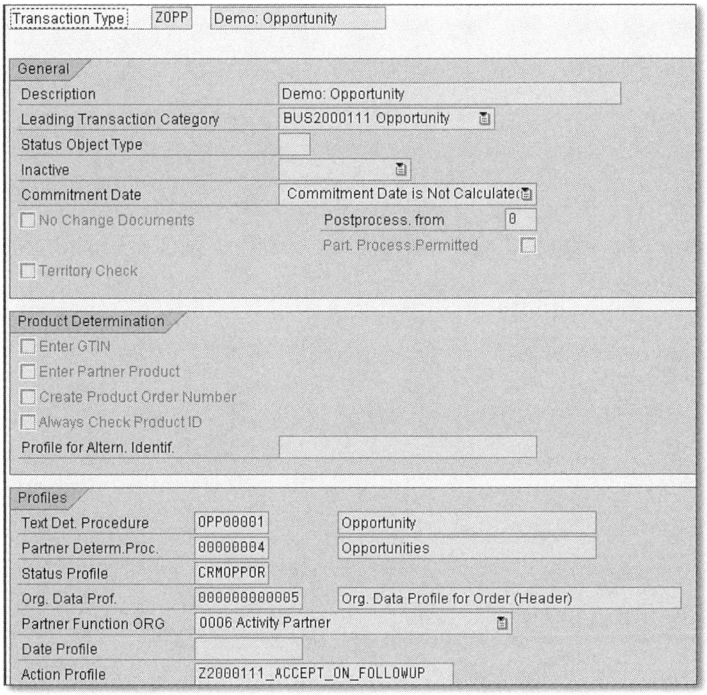

Figure 26.31 Transaction Type Customizing for Opportunity

26.6.8 Executing the Workflow

When the lead has reached a status as described in Section 26.5.2, Sales — Lead to Opportunity, your workflow is started. The corresponding workflow task looks like Figure 26.32 in the Workflow Inbox.

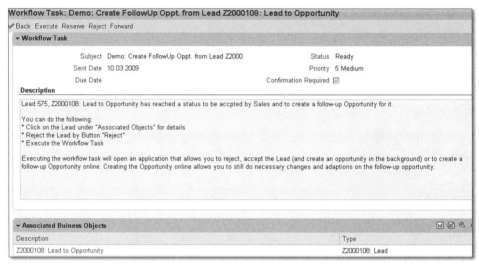

Figure 26.32 Custom Workflow Task for Follow-Up Opportunity

When the user clicks on the hyperlink under Associated Business Objects, the standard lead UI component is started. Executing the workflow task opens up the workflow-specific UI component (see Figure 26.33).

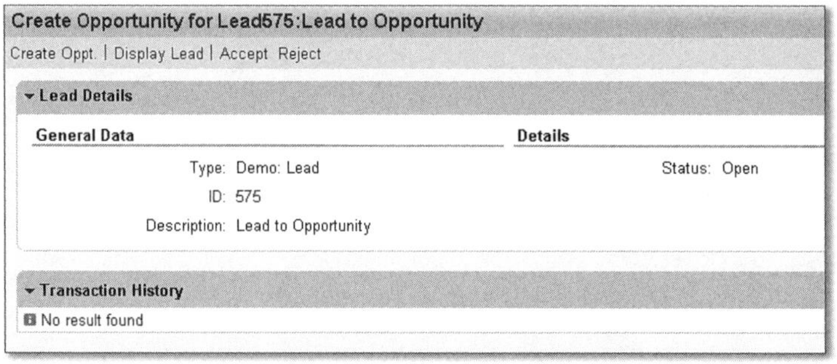

Figure 26.33 Workflow-Specific Lead UI Component

When the user clicks Create Opp., a follow-up opportunity is generated (see Figure 26.34) that the user can still adapt before saving it.

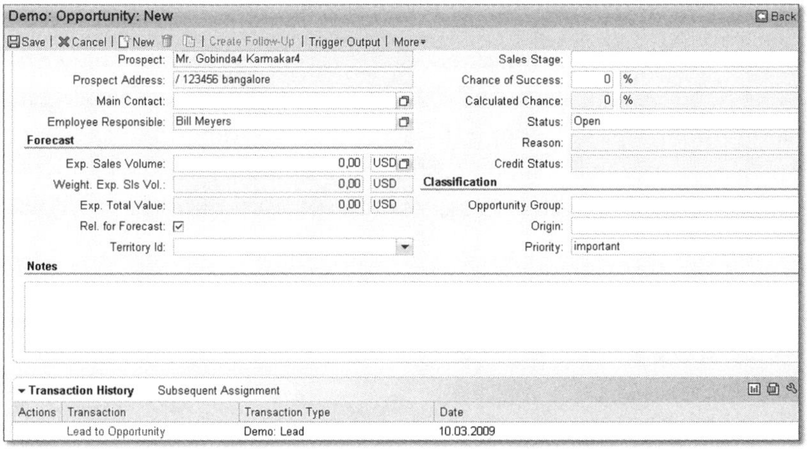

Figure 26.34 Follow-Up Opportunity Out of Custom Workflow Task

---

Note

The preceding lead transaction is already displayed in the assignment block for the TRANSACTION HISTORY. However, this assignment is only persisted together with the opportunity when the user saves the opportunity.

If the user chooses to CANCEL, the new opportunity is reverted, and the workflow task stays in process (see Figure 26.35).

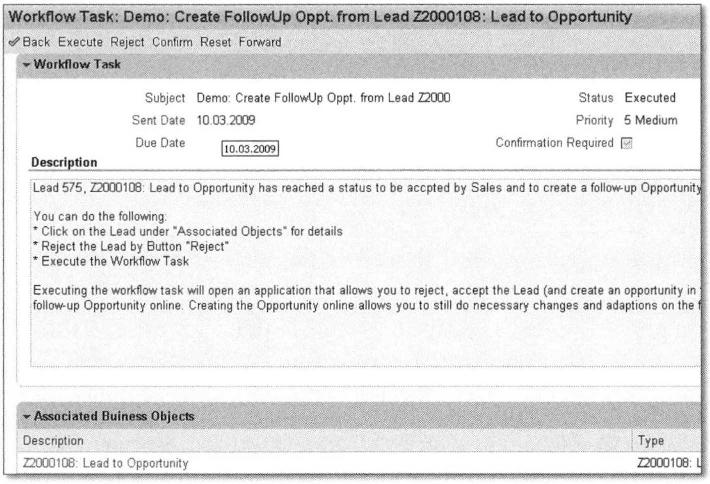

Figure 26.35 Custom Workflow Task for Follow-Up Opportunity After Cancellation by User

26.6.9 Optional Enhancement

Sometimes, data from the workflow task is needed for the processing of a workflow UI component. To read the necessary data, the workflow task has to be available for the application. This can simply be achieved by setting the flag Set to 'Completed' by Application in the inbox customizing under Customer Relationship Management • Basic Functions • Worklist • Define Alert Inbox and Workflow Inbox • Define Object-Specific Navigation (see Figure 26.36).

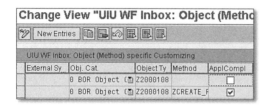

Figure 26.36 Inbox Customizing to Retrieve Workflow Task

Setting this flag for synchronous workflow tasks implies that the workflow task is not automatically completed, but your component has to complete the workflow task via the well-known `SAP_WAPI` interface.

You can add GenIL component `WFI` to your own GenIL component set. By doing this, the BOL root object `WFRoot` can be reused in your own BOL model, and you can easily generate context nodes for it to keep the BOL entity of the workflow task (see Figure 26.37).

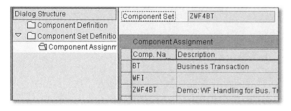

Figure 26.37 Include WFI GenIL Component

The according inbound plug of your UI component needs to be adapted as shown in Listing 26.10 to be able to handle both BOL object types (`BTOrder` and `WFRoot`).

```
DATA:
lr_comp_controller TYPE REF TO cl_zbt108_a_bspwdcomponen_impl,
lr_entity          TYPE REF TO cl_crm_bol_entity.
```

```
lr_comp_controller ?= me->comp_controller.
lr_comp_controller->typed_context->btorder->
  collection_wrapper->clear( ).
lr_comp_controller->typed_context->wfroot->
  collection_wrapper->clear( ).
CHECK iv_collection IS BOUND.
lr_entity ?= iv_collection->get_first( ).
WHILE lr_entity IS BOUND.
    CASE lr_entity->get_name( ).
        WHEN 'BTOrder'.
          lr_comp_controller->typed_context->btorder->
            collection_wrapper->add( iv_entity    = lr_entity
                            iv_set_focus = abap_true ).
        WHEN 'WFRoot'.
          lr_comp_controller->typed_context->wfroot->
            collection_wrapper->add( iv_entity    = lr_entity
                            iv_set_focus = abap_true ).
        WHEN OTHERS.
    ENDCASE.
    lr_entity ?= iv_collection->get_next( ).
ENDWHILE.
```

Listing 26.10 Retrieve Different BOL Object Types in Inbound Plug

Tip
As already mentioned, standard UI components do not expect to retrieve the BOL entity of a workflow task in their inbound plugs. You can enhance a standard UI component and then create an extra inbound plug that handles the BOL entity of workflow tasks similar to Listing 26.10. Information about the enhancement of UI components is available in the CRM Wiki of the SAP Community Network on *https://www.sdn.sap.com/irj/scn/wiki*.

HCM Processes and Forms is not only a good example of forms-based workflows, but it also demonstrates how to call SAP web-based applications, use program exits to extend workflow functionality, and adjust UWL configuration to suit your specific requirements. This chapter discusses how SAP Business Workflow is used as a critical component of HCM Processes and Forms.

27 SAP ERP Human Capital Management — Processes and Forms

Many organizations need system data to be entered by occasional or non-expert system users. Interactive forms are excellent for this business scenario because they provide a simplified user interface and give the opportunity for proposed system data to be validated, completed and approved by other personnel prior to database update. Workflow, of course, is an excellent tool for managing the communication among the form author, form processors, form approvers, and automated system updates.

HCM Processes and Forms is a solution available as part of business function set *HR Administrative Services* in SAP ECC 6.0 EhP1 and above, which brings together forms technology (i.e., SAP Interactive Forms by Adobe), application-specific logic in SAP ERP HCM, and workflow into a cohesive framework where users submit and track forms via links in the SAP NetWeaver Portal and access forms for approval or completion using the UWL (UWL).

This chapter looks at the part workflow plays in this framework and the special workflow techniques that are used to support this framework, including the following:

- Calling web-based applications by using Transaction SWFVISU
- Program exits to update workflow containers and create entries in tracking logs
- UWL configuration to create custom views (filters) and navigation

27.1 Business Overview

Before you can use HCM Processes and Forms, you need to understand how the solution works from a business perspective, what benefits its features provide, and its limitations. This is not the only forms-and-workflow framework available in SAP, but it is a particularly good framework because it provides a wide range of business features and is technically robust and scalable.

To a large extent, HCM Processes and Forms supersedes earlier forms-and-workflow frameworks such as Personnel Change Requests, Internet Service Requests, ITS (Internet Transaction Server) HTML-based Form Tasks, and Workflow Form Steps. Figure 27.1 shows a user's view when completing a form.

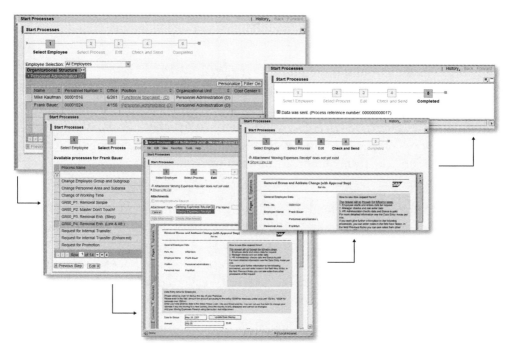

Figure 27.1 HCM Processes and Forms: A User's View of Form Submission

27.1.1 SAP ERP HCM Processes

A SAP ERP HCM Process represents a single end-to-end business process from initial form submission to final database update. A single instance of a process may include the following:

▶ **Several roles**

For example, form author, form approvers, and other form processors who might provide additional data, attachments, or comments.

▶ **Several forms and attachments**

For example, an employee Transfer process might include a Transfer form and a Change in Working Time form. When moving from one form to another, data and attachments can be automatically mapped from source to target form according to the process configuration, for example, the value of a field EFFEC-TIVE DATE passed from the Transfer form to the Change Salary form.

▶ **Several tables to be updated in the database**

For example, HR PA (Personnel Administration Data), HR PT (Time Data), HR PD (Organizational Management Data with EhP4), and custom HR infotypes or tables. These updates may even be staggered throughout the process, rather than all performed at the end.

Figure 27.2 shows typical steps and components used in a Single Form Process.

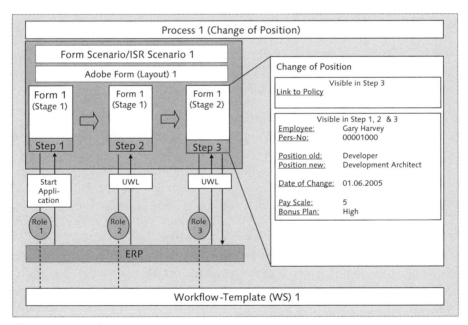

Figure 27.2 Sample HCM Process

Each HCM Process is linked to a single instance of a top-level workflow template that controls the process as soon as a form is submitted. When the user chooses to submit a form, the user chooses which process to start, rather than which form to enter. This enables forms to be reused in multiple processes; for example, a Change in Working Time process might include the same Change Salary form that is used in the Transfer process.

Each instance of the HCM Process is assigned a process object on submission of the initial form. The process object is the persistence layer of runtime data, that is, the reference to where the form data, attachments, and process/step instance information are kept in XML format in the Case Management component. The process object has a technical GUID (Globally Unique ID) to identify it to technical components, such as workflow, and is also given a more user-friendly process reference number for tracking by the user.

> **Note**
>
> Draft forms that have not been submitted are not assigned a process reference number but still have a process object.

27.1.2 Form Submission

SAP ERP HCM Processes are started via a link in the SAP NetWeaver Portal. The link may be directly on a portal page or configured via the ESS/MSS homepage framework (Employee/Manager Self-Services).

A number of views are presented when starting a process. The placement of the link in the SAP NetWeaver Portal and the parameters preset in the link determine which views are required. Most delivered HCM Processes use five different views in five sequential steps for new form submission as follows (see also Figure 27.3).

1. **Object Selection** (e.g., Select Employee)

   For an employee-based process, the employee must be selected. If the link is started via the ESS Homepage Framework, then the employee is preset to the user's own employee number. If the link is started via the MSS Homepage Framework, then the manager is presented with TEAMVIEWER type searches to find a subordinate employee in the manager's team. Otherwise, a generic employee search is presented.

   For an Organizational Management process, the type of organizational object (position, organizational unit, or job) and the object ID are selected via keyword and hierarchical structure searches.

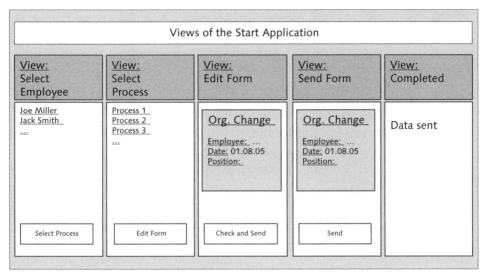

Figure 27.3 Views Used When Submitting Forms

2. **Process Selection**

This view can be skipped by presetting the PROCESS parameter. Otherwise, the list of processes that can be selected depends on the values in the parameters INITIATOR_ROLE (i.e., what type of processor is starting the process) and PROCESS_GROUP (i.e., related processes can be combined into a group specific to this link).

3. **Edit the Form**

The process automatically selects and presents the initial form of the process. As the user edits the form, default values are proposed, dropdown lists and other searches are available, and validations are performed dynamically against the backend system. The user may also be permitted to save the form as a draft or send the form to experts for assistance. The user may add comments for subsequent approvers/processors, add attachments, and use links to access related information such as intranet policy documents and Internet registration sites (e.g., DUNS numbers, Bank codes, etc.).

4. **Review and Send the Form**

So the user can perform a final check, the form and attachments are displayed in read-only mode along with any warnings. This view can only be reached if there are no errors returned during validation.

Note

Forms may be saved as a draft or sent to experts even if there are currently validation errors.

5. **Form Submission Completed**
   On submission of the form, the process object is created in the background, which saves the process and form data and triggers the workflow. A process reference number is issued to the user to help track the progress of the process. The user is given the option of immediately starting another process.

There are many variants of the form submission process, especially from SAP ERP HCM EhP4 onward. Common variants include the following:

▶ **No Start Object**
Processes may also be marked as not requiring a start object — in which case, the initial object selection step is completely skipped. A New Hire process where the employee number is not created until the end of the process is an example.

▶ **Mass Start for Multiple Employees**
As of EhP4, a process can be started for multiple employees. The list of employees is entered in a table, the user enters the form data as columns of the table, and a separate process instance is created for each employee. In this variant, the Adobe form layout is not used until after form submission.

▶ **Fast Data Entry**
This is similar to the Mass Start process but does not require any workflow or subsequent processing. The form author just enters the form data in columns, and the database is updated as a single step.

▶ **Deferred Employee Selection**
Processes may also be marked as not requiring an employee number at the start of the process, deferring the employee selection until later in the process.

27.1.3　Form Approval

If form approval is required, the form approver accesses the form via a work item in his UWL inbox. Form approval consists of two views: the Approve/Reject form view and the Approval Completed view (which simply confirms that the approval decision has been recorded). Figure 27.4 shows views used when creating forms.

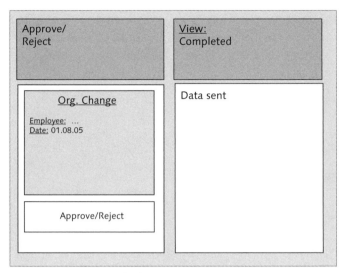

Figure 27.4 Views Used When Approving Forms

In the Approve/Reject Form view, the form is displayed with all of the data to be approved and the relevant buttons for approval. Usually all fields on the form are protected except the new comments area. The approver can add comments to the form and click the relevant button to APPROVE or REJECT the form. An option can also be provided for the approver to send the form BACK TO AUTHOR for revision. The chosen option is returned to the workflow, which then takes the appropriate action.

> **Note**
>
> By passing the option back to the workflow, an HCM Process can support many different business scenarios, such as no approval, multi-approval (sequential or parallel voting-style approval), and completion/review of the form before and/or after the approval.

The approver may be permitted to view and/or change attachments and use links.

27.1.4 Process Form (Revision or Completion)

If the form author or other form processors are required to revise or complete (i.e., provide further data) the form, the form processor accesses the form via a work item in his UWL inbox. The Process Form consists of three views: Edit form, Review and Send form, and Send Completed (see Figure 27.5)

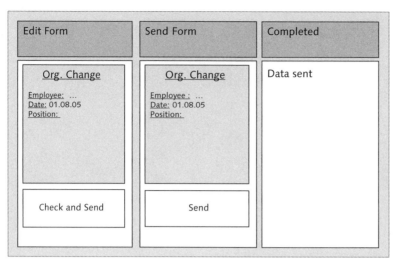

Figure 27.5 Views Used When Processing (e.g., Revising, Completing) Forms

In the Edit Form view, the form is displayed with the form data entered and ready for revision or completion. Which fields are open for editing or protected depend on the `FORM_SCENARIO_STAGE` parameter passed by the workflow, and the configuration of the form scenario stage in the form.

The form scenario stage (i.e., the step type) can be used to modify the form layout at different stages of the process. For example, when an employee's current manager submits a Transfer form, only the date of transfer and the new manager may be available, but when the workflow sends the form subsequently to the new manager, the form scenario stage can be used to protect data entered by the sending manager and reveal additional information for completion, such as the new position the employee will occupy.

The processor can edit and review the form similar to initial form submission. When the form changes are complete, the processor sends the form to indicate that the changes are complete. The form is then sent on to the next step of the process. That is, the workflow controls what happens next — whether the form is resubmitted for approval, sent to another person, or used to trigger database updates. An option can also be provided for the processor to withdraw the process, that is, to cancel all further processing. The option to withdraw can be prevented if some data has already been updated in the database by the process. The processor may be permitted to view and/or change attachments and use links.

27.1.5   Tracking Forms

Users can view processes they have started or have processed and that are not yet finished via the OPEN PROCESSES list. This is provided on a portal page and can be placed alongside the FORM SUBMISSION link or placed centrally, for example, near the UWL inbox.

From the OPEN PROCESSES list, the user can view other processors, the current processor(s), and the form as it appeared at the completion of each step of the process. The user may also opt to withdraw the process. The option to withdraw can be prevented if some data has already been updated by the process. A more extensive SEARCH PROCESSES list is provided for expert users.

27.1.6   Other Features

The following are some but not all of the other notable features of SAP ERP HCM Processes and Forms:

▶ Individual form fields and other form elements (such as buttons) can be protected or hidden depending on the type of process step, the type of processor, and the data entered into the form so far; for example, by default, all data fields other than comments are protected during approval.

▶ Dynamic validations often involve simulating database updates in the system. These can return messages that are only understandable to expert users. HCM Processes and Forms includes an option to map such messages to more user-friendly equivalents or to hide certain messages altogether.

▶ User events can be used to process parts of the form in isolation. In other words, a form has an initial entry area that is completed by the first processor, and then only when the second processor receives the forms are fields in the second entry area available and validated. For example, in a Transfer process, the sending manager nominates the date of transfer and the receiving manager, and then in a subsequent step, the receiving manager nominates the new position the employee will hold.

▶ Multiform processes can map data and attachments to be passed from one form to the next. For example, in a Change in Working Time process, a business justification attachment may be passed from the Change in Working Time form to the Change Salary form. In multiform processes, the workflow controls when and whether subsequent forms are made available.

- Database updates can be applied directly from the form — as processors submit or send the completed form — or as a defined background step of the workflow. Database updates can be staggered throughout the process; for example, in a multiform process, updates relating to each form can be applied as they are approved or altogether at the end of the process.

- Attachments and links are freely definable. This enables many different types of attachments to be handled, and links can be to Internet as well as intranet sites.

- Completed employee-based forms can be saved into the employee's digital personnel file as a permanent record.

- Users can print or save a copy of the form via the Adobe toolbar. They access the toolbar by pressing [F8] in any Adobe Reader window that displays the form.

27.1.7 Limitations

SAP ERP HCM Processes and Forms does not provide any capability for submitting forms or processing forms offline; that is, there is no option to upload an existing form from a user's machine. There is no capability for emailing a form directly out to an email inbox, or uploading a form from an email inbox. However, from EhP4 on, an email can be sent with a direct link to the work item, effectively allowing processors to bypass the UWL inbox and execute the work item directly via the hyperlink in the mail. This is particularly useful for occasional users who need to participate in form processes.

If either offline or direct email capability is required, you should consider using a custom forms-and-workflow framework based on SAP Interactive Forms by Adobe. A Closed Processes list is not provided as standard, although this has been added as a minor custom development at a number of sites following the same approach as OPEN PROCESSES.

27.2 Technical Overview of HCM Processes and Forms

SAP ERP HCM Processes and Forms brings together several technical components into a cohesive framework. The most important technical components, above and beyond standard components required for portal applications, are:

- Adobe Document Services
- Business function set
- SAP ERP HCM Processes and Forms Design Time
- Adobe LiveCycle Designer
- Adobe Reader
- Workflow Template
- SAP Case Management
- Certain SAP-provided Web Dynpro ABAP applications

27.2.1 Adobe Document Services

Adobe Document Services (ADS) allow SAP applications (either ABAP or Java) to take advantage of the full range of capabilities in Adobe Acrobat Professional, Adobe Acrobat Standard, and Adobe Reader. These capabilities enable the HCM Processes and Forms solution to:

- Create and deploy interactive forms that look exactly like their paper counterparts
- Capture data using forms and import that data directly into the SAP system
- Generate dynamic PDF documents from data contained in the SAP system
- Work with forms in online scenarios
- Embed other file formats inside PDF documents as attachments

ADS also provides other capabilities not used by HCM Processes and Forms but available to custom forms-and-workflow frameworks, such as:

- Work with forms in offline scenarios.
- Annotate PDF documents and collaborate on PDF document reviews.
- Allow users to digitally sign PDF documents.

ADS, by default, is configured for print forms only. For HCM Processes and Forms, ADS must be configured for interactive forms as detailed in the *Adobe Document Services Configuration Guide*, which can be found at the SAP Service Marketplace (*http://service.sap.com/instguides*). In particular, the Reader Rights credential must be installed. This enables users to save data into an Adobe form so that it can be passed to subsequent users and workflow steps. The *Visual Administrator* is used to apply licensing, monitor and adjust the ADS EJB (Enterprise JavaBean), and view logs and traces.

27.2.2 Business Function Set

A business function set is a self-contained industry-independent application that is provided as a component of SAP ERP. HCM Processes and Forms is available in SAP ERP EhP1 and above as part of the business function set *HR Administrative Services*. Example forms and workflow templates are provided as updates in enhancement packages. If you want to create forms based on Organizational Management objects such as position, organizational unit, or job, these are available as of EhP4.

The business function set contains a number of technical components such as application code in SAP ERP, analytic content for SAP NetWeaver BW, and portal business packages. When you plan to use HCM Processes and Forms, activating the business function (to make application code, configuration, and utilities available), and applying the portal business packages are mandatory. Use of the SAP NetWeaver BW content is optional. Certain forms scenarios may also make use of SAP NetWeaver Process Integration (SAP NetWeaver PI) for communication purposes, such as hiring employees via SAP E-Recruiting.

27.2.3 SAP ERP HCM Processes and Forms Design Time

The Design Time tool (Transaction HRASR_DT) is a central application for configuring your processes, forms, and related objects such as the form template and workflow template. You nominate:

▶ Who can start the process and what object, if any, must be selected to start the process.

▶ The features and options relevant to the form and process, such as what attachments and links are available, and whether any messages are mapped. The overall list of attachment types and links is defined outside of the Design Time tool as Cross Form Scenario settings.

▶ The form template.

▶ The workflow template and its event linkage.

▸ The different types of steps through which the form may pass (these can be used to control tracking information and which fields are hidden/protected).

▸ The fields to be held in the form and whether any defaults or dropdown lists are to be provided.

▸ Map fields to backend services that can provide dynamic defaults and dropdown lists, perform validations, and update the database.

A number of backend services are provided as standard:

▸ SAP_PA

All standard Personnel Administration infotypes that support the HR infotype framework (this includes custom infotypes that support the HR infotype framework).

▸ SAP_PT

Standard time management infotypes.

▸ SAP_PD

Standard Organizational Management objects, relationships, and related infotypes (as of EhP4).

Custom generic services can also be provided by using the Enhancement Spot HRASR00GENERIC_SERVICES for defaults, dropdown lists, or validations that are form-specific; or via extension of the HR infotype framework, for example, using Enhancement Spot HRPAD00INFTYUI for defaults, dropdown lists, and validations that are infotype-specific.

> **Note**
>
> Extending the HR infotype framework is useful when you need changes to be applied centrally throughout all HR functions, such as Transaction PA30 (Maintain HR Master Data), as well as in forms.

27.2.4 Adobe LiveCycle Designer

You develop the Adobe form templates using the Adobe LiveCycle Designer. The designer must be installed on the local machine of the form template developer. You can install the designer by selecting the appropriate options when installing SAP GUI for Windows.

> **Note**
>
> It's important to have the correct designer version to match your system's SAP NetWeaver release/support pack level, and you should check the SAP Service Marketplace for any release restrictions (e.g., for Adobe LiveCycle Designer 8.1, see SAP Note 1176858).

The form developer can access the designer via the FORMS subarea of the HCM Processes and Design Time (Transaction HRASR_DT) or via the LAYOUT tab in Transaction SFP.

> **Note**
>
> You should at least use Transaction HRASR_DT to generate the form interface and form context initially and to update the interface and context whenever you add or remove form fields from your form.

The form layout must have the form type set to ZCI (ZERO CLIENT INSTALLATION). This means that there is no footprint needed on the user's client machine to execute the forms. The user simply needs the correct Internet browser and Adobe Reader versions installed on his client machine and, of course, the relevant security/authorizations to access form applications and the UWL inbox via SAP NetWeaver Portal.

The Adobe form template converts to an XML document (suffix .XDP), which must include a special JavaScript for communicating with SAP via ADS. This JavaScript is named ContainerFoundation_JS, and it is critical that the correct version of this JavaScript for your release/support pack level is applied to your form templates.

> **Note**
>
> Each time you upgrade your support pack level, you must check the Release Notes to see if a new version of the JavaScript needs to be applied. Using the wrong version can result in unexpected behaviors such as form freezing or hanging.

The quickest and safest mechanism for applying the JavaScript and adjusting existing form fields to meet the requirements of the JavaScript is to use Transaction SFP_ZCI_UPDATE as described in SAP Note 1042394.

27.2.5 Adobe Reader

Every user who may need to submit, edit, or view a form must have Adobe Reader installed on his local machine. Adobe Reader is such commonly used software that often it is already included in the organization's SOE (Standard Operating Environment). However, making sure that users have the correct Adobe Reader version installed on their client machine is essential for good performance and for all features to work correctly. To execute ZCI (Zero Client Installation) interactive forms, as a minimum, Adobe Reader 8.1 must be installed according to SAP Note 1055911. ZCI means that there is no footprint needed on the user's client machine to execute the forms.

27.2.6 Workflow Template

Usually each SAP ERP HCM Process is linked to a single workflow template in the HCM Processes and Forms Design Time tool (Transaction HRASR_DT). The workflow template must fulfill certain requirements to be used with HCM Processes and Forms:

▶ The linkage between the event `CL_HRASR00_PROCESS_OBJECT.TRIGGERED` and the workflow must support the check function module `HR_ASR_CHECK_EVENT`. This is best done automatically by activating the event linkage in the workflow section of the HCM Process in Transaction HRASR_DT.

▶ The workflow should terminate if the event `CL_HRASR00_PROCESS_OBJECT.WITHDRAWN` is raised. Usually this event and response are set in the basic data of the workflow template.

▶ The workflow template's main container must include a container element `PROCESS_OBJECT` of data type reference to ABAP class `CL_HRASR00_PROCESS_OBJECT`.

▶ The program exit `CL_HRASR00_POBJ_WF_EXIT` must be applied to each dialog step that displays the form and any other steps that are to be shown in the tracking application when viewing the progress of the process. The program exits must also be applied to the basic data of the workflow template itself as the starting point of the process for the tracking application.

▶ The workflow must use tasks from task group `TG17900001`, or custom copies of these tasks, to access the form.

▶ Bindings of these tasks must be correct, for example, Form Scenario Id, Form Scenario Stage, and Processor Role.

- Each dialog task that a processor uses to access the form must have a Task Visualization entry in Transaction SWFVISU (or an equivalent launch mechanism specified for the relevant `ItemType` in the UWL configuration XML) to call the Web Dynpro ABAP application that presents the form.

Apart from these requirements, the workflow is a normal workflow that controls the progress of the process. The number of process steps is not fixed and can be freely designed. Loops and branches are possible. The workflow can send out emails or trigger additional background updates at the end of the process.

27.2.7 SAP Case Management

SAP Case Management is used to store the process object. The process object contains process information, information for each process step triggered so far, the form data relevant to each process step, and attachments as linked XML documents (see Figure 27.6).

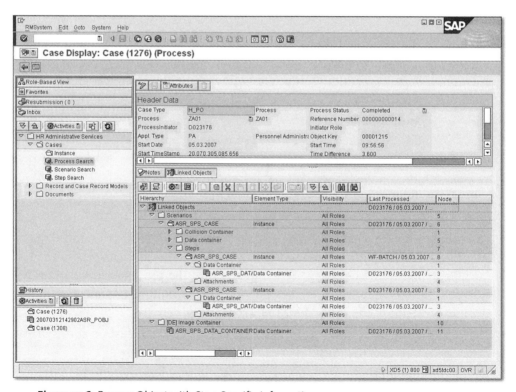

Figure 27.6 Process Object with Step-Specific Information

By holding so much information, tracking applications such as Open Processes and Search Processes are able to display not only what has happened to the process and form but also the form as it appeared at each step of the process. SAP Case Management is also used to store the Digital Personnel File if that feature is used.

Transaction SCASE can be used to access the XML-formatted data for analytics or troubleshooting using RMS ID `ASR_POBJ` (Records Management System).

27.2.8 Web Dynpro ABAP Applications

SAP provides a suite of standard Web Dynpro ABAP applications for handling forms. All of the relevant Web Dynpro ABAP applications are held in package `PAOC_ASR_WD`, which can be accessed using Transaction SE80).

The most important applications include the following:

▶ `ASR_PROCESS_EXECUTE`
Used to start "employee object" or "no start object" processes, or access forms of these processes from UWL.

▶ `ASR_PD_PROCESS_EXECUTE`
Used to start Organizational Management object-based forms, or access forms of these processes from UWL.

▶ `ASR_PROCESSES_DISPLAY`
Used by Open Processes and Search Processes to display a list of processes.

▶ `ASR_FORM_DISPLAY`
Used to display the form as it appeared at the completion of a step from the detail level of Open Processes and Search Processes.

The look and feel of these applications can be adjusted by making appropriate settings in the relevant portal roles/worksets/iViews, and by using Web Dynpro ABAP configuration, for example, to make the Process reference number a top-level column in the Open Processes list.

27.3   Standard Workflows in HCM Processes and Forms

All current workflows in SAP ERP HCM Processes and Forms can be found in the workflow explorer (Transaction SWDM) by using the search range application component `PA-AS`. A wide range of processes are delivered:

- Create, change, reassign, and delete Organizational Management objects (jobs, positions, and organization units)
- Hire and rehire employees
- Apply for maternity leave
- Apply for a company loan
- Pay membership fees
- Notify of birth of child
- Notify of change of permanent address
- Change the working time of an employee
- Change the salary of an employee
- Terminate an employee
- Transfer employee (i.e., move to a new position or organization unit)
- Make special payments (including payments to multiple employees)

The workflow templates provided may be used as is if the implemented scenario matches your requirements, or they may be used as working examples for creating your own workflow templates.

Some workflows are delivered to support particular form features such as the ones shown in Table 27.1. These workflow templates may be used as is. You only need to activate the event linkage for workflows that support form features you plan to use.

Workflow Template	Purpose
WS17900404	Handle drafts created during process start
WS17900418	Forward to experts a process started with errors
WS17900260	Save form with error handling
WS17900024	Exception handling: asynchronous
WS61000037	Subsequent activities to be performed when a process is withdrawn (enhanced)
WS17900396	Subsequent activities to be performed when a process is withdrawn (simple)

Table 27.1 SAP-Provided Workflow Templates Supporting Special Features of HCM Processes and Forms

Workflow Template	Purpose
WS17900415	Start process for SAP NetWeaver PI data: Start a process initiated by SAP E-Recruiting via SAP NetWeaver PI
WS17900015	Follow up after process with SAP NetWeaver PI scenario

Table 27.1 SAP-Provided Workflow Templates Supporting Special Features of HCM Processes and Forms (cont.)

27.4 Workflow Techniques

SAP ERP HCM Processes and Forms uses some specific workflow techniques that you can readily apply to other workflow templates to achieve similar benefits. The most notable are:

▶ Calling web-based SAP applications using Transaction SWFVISU

▶ Using program exits to update workflow containers and custom logs

▶ Using UWL configuration to create special filters (subviews) and additional inbox features

27.4.1 Calling Web-Based SAP Applications Using Transaction SWFVISU

In the HCM Processes and Form framework, each work item in UWL launches a form for revision, completion, or approval. That is, the work item must launch the Web Dynpro ABAP application ASR_PROCESS_EXECUTE (or ASR_PD_PROCESS_EXECUTE) with the relevant parameters to ensure the form is displayed in the correct mode and with the appropriate processing options available. This is achieved by using a simple but powerful technique — *Task Visualization* — maintained in Transaction SWFVISU. You can do this in your own workflows by:

▶ Including a step in your workflow that calls a dialog task. Many of the SAP-delivered HCM Processes and Forms workflow templates call tasks TS17900100 (Process Form) and/or TS17900101 (Approve Form), which are dialog tasks calling ABAP class CL_HRASR00_WF_COMPONENTS method WI_EXECUTION_VIA_R3_INBOX. This method performs no processing other than simply returning an error message in case the method is ever called directly in SAP GUI for Windows or SAP GUI for HTML instead of via the Task Visualization.

▶ Creating a Task Visualization entry in Transaction SWFVISU that links the task to the Visualization Type, that is, type of web-based SAP application to be started. Figure 27.7 shows the visualization in Transaction SWFVISU.

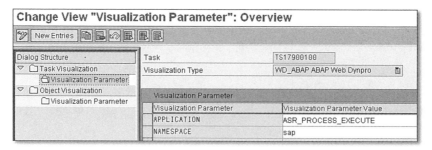

Figure 27.7 SWFVISU Task Visualization

Tasks TS17900100 (Process Form) and TS17900101 (Approve Form) are linked to Visualization Type Web Dynpro ABAP.

> **Note**
>
> If you see a link to Visualization Type Web Dynpro Java, this is a superseded entry from an earlier release of HCM Processes and Forms.

▶ Depending on the type of web-based SAP application, adding the relevant parameters to the Task Visualization entry such as the application ID. Tasks TS17900100 (Process Form) and TS17900101 (Approve Form) have the following parameters/values:

  ▶ APPLICATION: ASR_PROCESS_EXECUTE

  ▶ NAMESPACE: sap

These are the only parameters needed because, by default, UWL always passes the parameter WI_ID (work item ID) to any launch mechanism. The work item ID is sufficient because the called application can then use the work item ID and workflow APIs to retrieve additional information.

For example, when ASR_PROCESS_EXECUTE is launched with the parameter WI_ID, it reads additional information from the work item container such as the form step type (Form Scenario Stage), the processor role, and the process reference number. This approach is an alternative to passing additional dynamic parameters in the Task Visualization entry (via the parameter DYN-PARAM) or the UWL configuration XML.

▶ Re-registering the relevant system in the UWL Administration iView of the portal, and clearing the cache.

The end result is that the UWL configuration XML generated for the relevant system is updated with the appropriate launch mechanism so that the correct web application is launched when the user executes the work item in their UWL inbox.

If you want even greater control, you can change the Task Visualization entry or the UWL configuration XML file to call a portal iView, which in turn calls the relevant Web Dynpro application. This enables you to control other features through the portal content directory entries, such as window height and width. You can see an example of this in the HRAdmin UWL configuration file provided with the portal business package for HR Administrative Services, for example, for task TS17900113.

> **Note**
>
> If you have custom UWL configuration XML for the same system and item type (i.e., task), that will override the generated XML. So make sure that you copy the XML fragment for the launch mechanism from the generated file into your custom file.

Transaction SWFVISU (see Figure 27.8) can also be used to avoid users seeing technical objects as work item object attachments. For work items in HCM Processes and Forms, by default, an object attachment is automatically created referring to the main object of the work item, that is, ABAP class CL_HRASR00_WF_COMPONENTS, which is a purely technical object. By entering the object category CL (ABAP Class), the OBJECT TYPE CL_HRASR00_WF_COMPONENTS and the VISUALIZATION TYPE NONE (Object Not Represented) in the OBJECT VISUALIZATION section of Transaction SWFVISU, all technical object attachments of that ABAP class can be hidden for all work items in the UWL inbox.

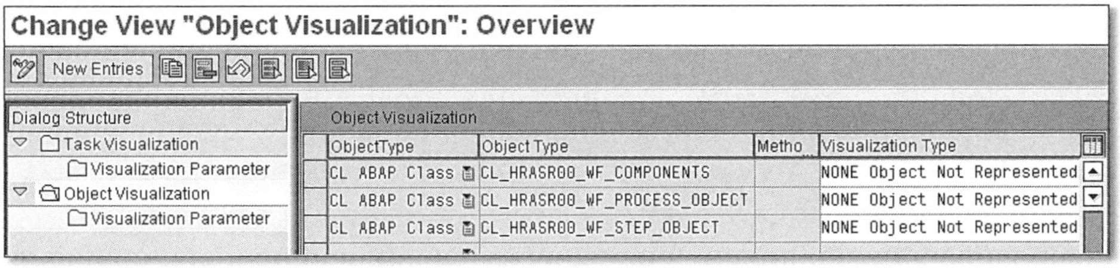

Figure 27.8 SWFVISU Object Visualization

> **Note**
>
> Similar to TASK VISUALIZATION, to make the OBJECT VISUALIZATION (see Figure 27.8) changes take affect, you must re-register the relevant system in the UWL Administration iView of the portal and clear the cache.

27.4.2 Program Exits

In the SAP ERP HCM Processes and Form framework, when the initial form of each process is submitted, a new process object is created. The creation of the process object triggers a new workflow instance. The program exit writes a new entry to the process object. As each step of the process is started, that is, on work item creation, or completed, that is, on work item completion, the process object is updated.

The log entries are created and maintained by a program exit, which must be specified in the Basic Data of the Workflow and in each dialog step that is to be shown in the log. The OPEN PROCESSES and SEARCH PROCESSES lists use the information written to the process object to build a user-relevant view of the progress of the process and its form(s). Figure 27.9 shows a program exit as it appears in workflow basic data.

Figure 27.9 Program Exit as It Appears in Workflow Basic Data

The program exit has a second function on the dialog steps, in that it generates some additional work item container elements such as STEP_OBJECT_GUID. The GUID is used by the Web Dynpro ABAP application ASR_PROCESS_EXECUTE (or ASR_PD_PROCESS_EXECUTE) when the work item is launched to identify the specific combination of the process, form step and work item. The GUID is used to cross-reference the form data in SAP Case Management, where the form data is stored in XML format, so that the correct data is shown when executing that step and when tracking the progress of the form; that is, a user can use OPEN PROCESSES or SEARCH PROCESSES to view the form as it appeared at the completion of each work item.

Because it is used as a workflow program exit, ABAP class CL_HRASR00_POBJ_WF_ EXIT supports the ABAP interface IF_SWF_IFS_WORKITEM_EXIT and implements method IF_SWF_IFS_WORKITEM_EXIT~EVENT_RAISED. When the workflow instance or a work item instance is created, executed, or completed, this method is called passing the work item context and a code indicating the status (e.g., BEFORE CREATION, AFTER CREATION, BEFORE EXECUTION, AFTER AN ACTION, etc.). The program exit uses this code and container element values derived from the work item context to trigger private methods that update the tracking log and work item containers.

If you develop workflow templates for your own HCM Processes and Forms, you simply use this program exit as is. However, when you develop workflow templates for other applications and non-form processes, you can develop your own program exits to write entries to your own custom logs or to manipulate container element values.

27.4.3 XML File for Universal Worklist Configuration

SAP ERP HCM Processes and Forms includes a UWL configuration XML file — HRAdmin — as part of the portal business package for HR Administrative Services. This UWL Configuration XML provides the following features:

▶ A variant of the UWL inbox that presents only HCM Processes and Forms work items by using the <NavigationNode> tag

▶ Filters (subviews) that show only certain groups of HCM Processes and Forms work items by using the <View> tag

▶ An additional inbox level button that redirects the user to the Portal Page HR Admin WorkCenter by using the <Action> tag and associating the action with the relevant view

You can optionally use this delivered UWL configuration XML file as is or create your alternative. It is common to create your own alternative if, for example, you want to include subviews for work items belonging to specific HCM Processes.

27.5 Creating Your Own Workflows

If you create your own custom SAP ERP HCM Process or want to adjust the processing of a SAP-delivered HCM Process, you need to create a suitable workflow template. Apart from satisfying the technical requirements specified in Section 27.2.6, Workflow Template, HCM Processes and Forms provide a suite of tasks in task group TG17900001 (Components for HCM Processes and Forms) that can be used directly or copied for use in your own workflows for your own HCM Processes.

The many delivered SAP workflow templates provide working examples of how these components are used, and you should use these as a guide for creating your own workflows. You can also add additional steps to your workflow templates (such as send mail steps, loops, forks) as you would with any other workflow template. Agents for executing dialog steps can be chosen freely using the same agent determination options as any other workflow template, for example, responsibility rules, function module rules, and evaluation path rules (i.e., using function module RH_GET_STRUCTURE).

However, the HCM Processes and Forms framework does provide a selection of simple rules for immediate use, including those in Table 27.2. There is also an excellent tutorial in the HR ADMINISTRATIVE SERVICES (PA-AS) • HCM PROCESSES AND FORMS section of the SAP Help Portal that demonstrates how to configure a process, form, and related workflow template.

ID	Purpose
AC17900013	Employee of organizational object
AC17900014	Manager of person
AC17900015	Administrator group of person
AC17900016	Personnel administrator of person
AC17900017	Time recording administrator of person
AC17900018	Payroll administrator of person

Table 27.2 SAP-Provided Agent Determination Rules for HCM Processes and Forms

27.5.1 Interactive Components

All interactive (i.e., dialog) tasks and subworkflows are held in the subtask group TG17900002. Tables 27.3 shows example SAP-provided interactive tasks and subworkflows for HCM Processes and Forms.

ID	Purpose
TS04000018	Process PD form
TS04000019	Approve PD form
TS04000020	PD form is edited again by author
TS17900100	Process form
TS17900101	Approve form
TS17900102	Form is edited again by author
WS17900260	Save form with error handling

Table 27.3 SAP-Provided Interactive Tasks and Subworkflows for HCM Processes and Forms

All of the tasks are used in much the same way; that is, they include container elements that are effectively parameters read by Web Dynpro ABAP application ASR_PROCESS_EXECUTE (or ASR_PD_PROCESS_EXECUTE for PD forms), which is linked to the task via the Task Visualization in Transaction SWFVISU or in the UWL configuration XML. Although you can use these tasks directly in your own workflows for your own HCM Processes, you may prefer to copy these tasks so that you can adjust work item texts, and combine tasks for particular processes and forms into your own subviews in your own UWL configuration XML.

Particular container elements that impact the behavior of the Web Dynpro ABAP application include those shown in Table 27.4.

Element ID	Purpose
Send_Variation	Indicates whether form data should be saved to the database at the end of the dialog. Blank indicates No SAVE, A indicates NORMAL SAVE, and B indicates No SAVE BUT TOLERATE ERRORS

Table 27.4 Standard Container Elements Used in HCM Processes and Forms Tasks

Element ID	Purpose
PROCSTATE	Exports the final status of the step, that is, for a form approval step whether APPROVE, REJECT, or BACK TO AUTHOR was chosen
Form_Scenario_Stage	Indicates form step type as specified in HRASR_DT (mandatory)
Save_Draft_Button_Visible	Indicates whether the user is allowed to save the form as a draft
Withdraw_Process_Button_Visible	Indicates whether the user is allowed to WITHDRAW the Process
Back_Button_Visible	Indicates whether the BACK TO AUTHOR option is allowed
Form	Form scenario ID (mandatory)
STEP_OBJECT	Value generated via the program exit
SEND_EXPERT_IF_INCONSISTENT_DATA	Indicates whether the FORWARD TO EXPERT option is allowed
ACTIVITY	Indicates the technical step type for authorization (mandatory), for example, APPROVE FORM, PROCESS FORM, START PROCESS
PROCESSOR_ROLE	Identifies the processor role to be shown on the tracking log
step_type	Indicates the technical step type for determining default form processing options (mandatory), for example, APPROVE, PROCESS, RE-PROCESS
Business_Status	Possible PROCSTATE values allowed (from EhP4)
notify_via_mail	Indicates whether an email notification of the work item should be created (from EhP4)
Assign_Object	Indicates whether the ASSIGN OBJECT option is allowed (from EhP4)

Table 27.4 Standard Container Elements Used in HCM Processes and Forms Tasks (cont.)

The WS17900260 subflow can be used if you allow the option to send the form to experts in the event of an error; that is, the subflow handles the process of the form being reviewed by experts and updates being retried.

27.5.2 Background Components

All background tasks are held in the subtask group TG17900003, as shown in Table 27.5.

ID	Purpose
TS17900106	Check existence of PA infotype.
	This can be used to determine whether a particular path should be taken in the workflow based on whether the employee already has data maintained in a specific infotype, for example, whether the employee has a contractual end date maintained in infotype 0016.
TS17900107	Check form data.
	Validates the form data as a background step, for example, to check that form data is still valid before saving the data to the database if there is a significant time gap between the last dialog step and saving of the data.
TS17900108	Save form data.
	Saves the form data to the database. The form data must already have been prepared for update by the backend services.
TS17900110	Import form container to workflow container.
	Reads up to three form fields into the workflow container fields.

Table 27.5 SAP-Provided Background Tasks for HCM Processes and Forms

All of these tasks can be used as is in your own workflows for HCM Processes and Forms. However, because task TS17900110 only imports three form fields at a time, this can become cumbersome if you have a large number of fields that you want to import for workflow use, for example, in work item texts. If you need to import more fields, you can create your own equivalent of this task, which calls your own method to read multiple fields very simply by calling ABAP class CL_HRASR00_WF_COMPONENTS method DATAMAPPING multiple times. You can also use this method to update the form with data values calculated in the workflow, although this is less common.

27.5.3 Troubleshooting

The most common error when creating your own workflow templates is not providing sufficient data for the container element `STEP_OBJECT_GUID` to be calculated by the program exit on dialog steps. Check that you have provided all mandatory container elements for dialog steps, and check that the program exit has been correctly assigned to the workflow step.

It is also important to check the process object itself using Transaction SCASE to make sure that it has been created correctly and that relevant step information is being updated as the workflow instance progresses.

Otherwise, troubleshooting HCM Process workflow templates is similar to any other workflow template. The HCM Processes and Forms framework also includes a powerful test tool, Transaction HRASR_TEST_PROCESS, which enables you to test the form configuration and overall workflow progress without direct use of the form layout or SAP NetWeaver Portal.

27.6 Universal Worklist Configuration

If you create your own custom HCM Process or want to adjust the processing of a SAP-delivered HCM Process, you may also want to create your own UWL configuration XML file, for example, to create filters (subview) that group process work items by process or add your own buttons to launch specific portal pages. Filters are particularly useful when users receive many work items from multiple workflow templates because they enable processors to quickly focus on specific tasks, such as a particular form or group of forms.

For example, you can create filters to temporarily restrict the UWL inbox list to groups such as:

▶ Draft forms

▶ Employee forms

▶ Hiring forms

▶ Organizational Management forms

▶ Forms requiring approval

Note

Although HCM Processes and Forms UWL configuration creates a UWL inbox variant that only presents HCM Processes and Forms work items, best practice is to handle all work items in one centralized UWL inbox to avoid users having to access multiple inbox variants. Using filters (subviews) is an effective way to handle specific solution requirements within the one centralized UWL inbox.

27.6.1 Subviews

The simplest way to create a filter (subview) for specific work items is to create specific tasks from which the work items will be generated and then group those tasks together. If you want to do this for your own HCM Process, you need to:

1. Copy the standard task that you want to use (e.g., TS17900100) to create your own task number, for example, TS90000001. Make sure you also copy the matching Task Visualization entry in Transaction SWFVISU.

2. Change your workflow template to use your new task instead of the original task.

3. In the UWL Administration iView, re-register the relevant system to update the generated UWL configuration XML file, that is, uwl.webflow.<YourSystem-Alias>.

4. Into your own XML file, copy just the relevant <ItemType> tag for your task for example, TS90000001, and the <View> tag for the DefaultView from the delivered UWL configuration XML file uwl.standard. If you prefer, you can copy the <View> tag from the HRAdmin file.

Note

This file is a delta file with only your <ItemType> and <View> tag, but you must still make sure you obey the format requirements as specified in the *uwl_configuration.dtd* file, which is also delivered by SAP and can be accessed from the UWL Administration iView.

5. In the <View> tag itself, use the name property to rename the view. In the <View> </View> block, add a <Descriptions> tag that the user will select in the UWL inbox to bring up the subview. Change the supportedItemTypes property to restrict the view to item types (work items) based on your task only, for example, uwl.webflow.TS90000001.

> **Note**
>
> If you want to group multiple item types (work items), simply separate them with commas in the supportedItemTypes list.

6. In the <ItemType> tag, change the property defaultView to the name of your new view.

7. Use the UWL Administration iView to upload your UWL configuration XML file, and clear the cache to make it take immediate effect.

If the user has work items generated from your task in his UWL inbox, the subview automatically appears as an option. The user can then select the subview to temporarily filter the list (see Figure 27.10). The user can choose the option No SUBVIEW… to return to the full list.

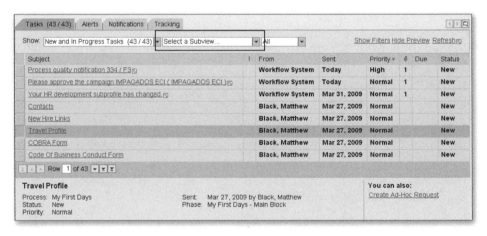

Figure 27.10 Filter (Subview) as It Appears in the Universal Worklist Inbox

After you have created a filter (subview), you can enhance it further by:

▶ Changing column order or sort order

▶ Adding or removing columns

▶ Adding custom attributes based on work item container elements, for example, for use as additional columns

▶ Renaming buttons or adding instruction texts to them, for example, renaming the standard LAUNCH WEB DYNPRO button to OPEN FORM

▶ Adding special buttons to your filter, for example, to launch special features

> **Note**
>
> If you create a number of filters, you may need to adjust the portal content directory setting for UWL that restricts the number of subviews that can appear together in any one inbox.

27.6.2 Buttons (Actions)

Often after you have a filter, you want to add buttons to provide filter-specific features, or you want to adjust buttons to add descriptions to clarify their purpose. Buttons are controlled by the `<Action>` tag in UWL configuration XML files. Where the button appears in the inbox depends on the association of the `<Action>` tag with a higher-level tag and some specific properties of the `<Action>` tag itself.

If you want to add your own button to redirect the user to a particular portal page, similar to the HR Admin Work Center button delivered in the `HRAdmin` XML file, you need to:

1. Add your `<Action>` tag in the `<Actions>` tag toward the top of your previous UWL configuration XML file, that is, before all item types and views. The action tag must include the `handler` property that indicates what type of application it will call; set other properties appropriate to that handler type to indicate how to call the application, such as the application ID.

2. Add a `<Descriptions>` tag to label the button for the user.

3. Adjust other properties as needed to control the placement of the button. For example, `display_order_priority` is used for the left to right preference order of the buttons, and `groupAction` determines in which content area the button should appear (e.g., if it should appear in the YOU CAN ALSO DO section of a work item)

4. Associate the action with the relevant `ItemType` (for work item level access) or view (for filter level access) by placing a reference to the action in the relevant `<ItemType></ItemType>` or `<View></View>` block.

5. Use the UWL Administration iView to upload your UWL configuration XML file, and clear the cache to make it take immediate effect.

The button will then appear whenever that work item or filter is used.

This chapter describes how to activate one SAP-provided workflow template in SAP ERP. Even if you do not require this particular scenario, this chapter gives you an idea of the time and effort involved. SAP workflows are delivered in many application areas.

28 Setting Up an SAP-Provided SAP ERP Workflow

In this chapter, you will learn how to activate workflow definitions delivered by SAP. The chapter is short because activating an SAP workflow is simple. This should, at the very least, convince you that it is worth activating an SAP workflow to demonstrate to colleagues what workflow is all about, even if you intend to create your own workflow later.

Of course, you may well decide to use the SAP workflow as is. Do not feel guilty about this. SAP application developers have spent a lot of time in the following activities:

▶ Blueprinting the best business process

▶ Developing the workflow definition

▶ Adjusting the application transactions so that they leverage the workflow benefits as tightly as possible

▶ Documenting the workflow and its customizing

The value gained when you activate a supplied workflow can be immense, which is the whole purpose of the exercise. There are two levels of workflow activation:

▶ You use the workflow without any enhancement whatsoever. All you have to do is assign agents to the different steps, activate the triggering events, and perform any IMG activities related to the process.

▶ You add your own simple enhancements, such as deadline handling, and your own task descriptions to make it easier for your users to use the workflow. These activities are not modifications, so if you go live with the workflow, your improvements are retained, even if SAP development enhances the next release of the workflow definition.

The example we have chosen is the *release of a blocked vendor*. You will find detailed notes about this in the online documentation in the SAP ERP Logistics (Materials Management) module or the catalog of workflows in the workflow tool section of the online documentation.

28.1 How Can You Find Workflows Delivered by SAP

Before we look at this scenario, let's start by discussing how you can find workflows provided by SAP.

28.1.1 Using SAP Help Portal to Find SAP Documented Workflows

The SAP Help Portal does provide documentation on provided workflows. It should be the first place you start. If you can find it in the SAP Help Portal, then the documentation can save you some time and provide guidance on configuring the workflow. However, sometimes finding the documentation can be a bit tricky. Start with the following:

1. Go to *http://help.sap.com*.
2. Select SAP ERP, and then select the link to the most recent release.
3. Select SAP ERP CROSS-APPLICATION FUNCTIONS. Workflow is normally mentioned as a cross area.
4. Select SCENARIOS IN APPLICATIONS, and then choose SAP BUSINESS WORKFLOW.
5. Another option is to do a search on "scenarios in applications" within SAP Help Portal. After you do this, you will see a list of the various applications. The workflow discussed in this chapter is under the LO-GENERAL LOGISTICS WORKFLOW SCENARIOS area.
6. After you find an area, the documentation normally lists the scenario, and then provides the technical realization (providing the object types, tasks, and workflow numbers involved), preparation and customizing (normally discusses required agent assignment for tasks and any IMG steps that may be required), and another area that might be specific to the application or the workflow.

28.1.2 Finding Workflows Within Workflow Builder

Finding workflows in SAP Help Portal is always a good first start because it includes helpful information. However, there could be other workflows that are not documented but do exist. These workflows need to be investigated because they might be helpful in your workflow journey.

1. Navigate to the Workflow Builder (Transaction SWDD or by menu path TOOLS • BUSINESS WORKFLOW • DEVELOPMENT • DEFINITION TOOLS • WORKFLOW BUILDER • WORKFLOW BUILDER).

2. Select WORKFLOW • OTHER WORKFLOW/VERSION.

3. Select the dropdown, STRUCTURE SEARCH.

4. Drill through the structure and search by application area.

5. Figure 28.1 shows the navigation when looking at LOGISTICS – GENERAL.

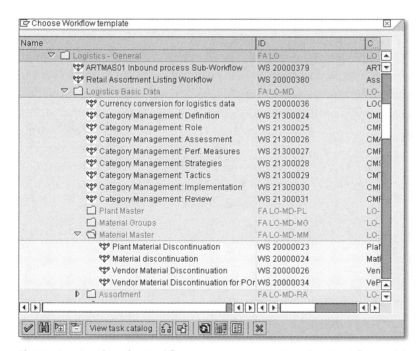

Figure 28.1 Searching for Workflows Using a Structure Search in Workflow Builder

If you find a workflow using this method, you should search for the workflow in SAP Help Portal.

Regardless of how you find the workflow, you always need to address the following:

▶ What is the triggering event that starts the workflow?

▶ Who should do each of the tasks? What is the role resolution provided in the template?

28.1.3 Technical Workflows

Even though it was mentioned in Chapter 9, Advanced Workflow Design Techniques, it's worth a quick mention that when researching SAP provided workflows, SAP provides technical workflows as well to learn how to use certain workflow features. These workflows start with WF_VER*. Most are WF_VERIFYxxx, with the xxx indicating the number of the technical workflow.

28.2 What Is the Business Scenario

The workflow we are going to activate in this example deals with the following common scenario. For various reasons, a company may need to prevent orders from being placed with a particular vendor. For example, vendors can be locked as a matter of course when a new vendor record is created or when an existing vendor record is changed. This is simply a procedural action to ensure the data quality of the vendor record or to provide a chance to perform background checks, such as a credit check, on the vendor. Existing vendors can also be blocked when they deliver substandard goods too often.

Many companies activate additional quality management workflows, which deal with quality checks on delivered goods, and some companies have created custom workflows to assess vendors that supply services. These are beyond the scope of this chapter, but thinking about the possibilities may give you an idea of how one workflow process can easily engender others.

A vendor that has been blocked unnecessarily or for too long is just as bad for business as a vendor block that has been released without the necessary checks. By driving the process with a workflow, you are adding control to the business process. This part of the process then becomes transparent, and SAP's Business Workflow Engine drives it faster and reliably. You can see from Figure 28.2 that the next step in improving efficiency and cutting costs is to automate other parts of this process, such as the liquidity check or the quality management of received goods.

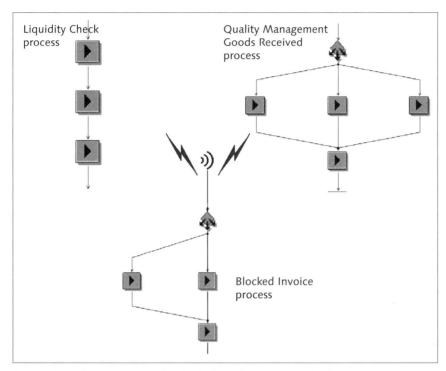

Figure 28.2 Relation Between the Blocked Vendor Process and Other Processes

When the vendor's record is blocked, the vendor maintenance transaction raises an event, which in turn triggers the workflow. The workflow alerts the responsible agent, who checks the vendor's record (and anything else that needs to be checked) before releasing the block.

28.3   Which SAP Workflows Are Involved

From the documentation, you can see at a glance which workflows are involved. In the case of the blocked vendor, it is a single workflow, WS20000001. In more complex scenarios involving several workflows, the documentation may refer to a task group, which is simply a package of workflows.

In this case, the documentation shows the tasks that are involved, but you can easily view this catalog by:

- Inspecting the workflow in the Workflow Builder
- Executing the IMG activity TASK SPECIFIC CUSTOMIZING
- Viewing the main workflow in the diagnosis Transaction SWUD

These are the tasks involved:

- Workflow WS20000001, which encompasses the complete process and can be started by three different events
- Task TS00300025, which is used to decide whether or not the vendor data will be displayed
- Three tasks (TS20000002, TS30000034, and TS00300028), which can be used to inspect the block, depending on which type of block is set
- Task TS00300034, which is used to decide whether or not to release the block
- Tasks TS20000003 and TS00300029, which are used to release the block, depending on what type of block has been set

28.4   How Is the Workflow Started

The three possible triggers for this workflow are shown in Table 28.1.

Technical Triggering Event	Meaning
Event BlockedForPurchasing from the business object LFA1	The vendor has been blocked completely.
Event BlockedForPurchOrg from the business object LFM1	This vendor has been blocked for a particular purchasing organization.
Event BlockedForVSROrPlan from the business object LFM1	One particular subrange or plant belonging to this vendor has been blocked for one particular purchasing organization.

Table 28.1 Triggers for the Process

When one of these events is raised in the background, the workflow is started. The data that the workflow needs depends on the type of block that is set. This data is passed from the transaction to the event and from the event to the workflow. Notice workflow WS20000001 in your system to view the triggers and the tasks.

28.5   How Do I Activate This Scenario

To activate this scenario, first check if the workflow system has been customized. To do this, call the workflow customizing transaction (SWU3). Check that the runtime system has a green check mark showing that it has been set up properly. If this is not the case, click the GENERATE icon (⬤), as described in Chapter 3, Configuring the System.

> **Note**
>
> The event linkage for every workflow in the system is inactive by default until you decide to activate it. This is true of workflows that you create yourself as well as the workflows delivered by SAP. The workflows will not trigger until you activate this linkage. It is not essential that workflows are triggered by events, but this is nearly always best practice because it allows the workflows to be activated, deactivated, or substituted by other workflow definitions easily. The blocked vendor workflow is no exception.

Before you activate the event linkage, you need to assign possible agents to the tasks. When a task is created or delivered by SAP, it has no agents assigned to it, so you must do this as part of the customizing activity.

In a production environment, you want to be restrictive about who may perform the task. You probably want to create an organizational module using the Organization Management part of the SAP NetWeaver Application Server and assign a job to the task. By doing this, you simplify authorization, organization, user management, and role management in addition to indirect benefits such as substitution management and reporting. This topic is covered in detail in Chapter 5, Agents. In this example, we will simply make all users in the system possible agents by declaring the tasks to be *general tasks*. In this particular workflow, the agent that performs the first step is automatically assigned to the following steps of the workflow.

1. Navigate to the IMG activity task-specific customizing of SAP Business Workflow: SAP NETWEAVER • APPLICATION SERVER • BUSINESS MANAGEMENT • SAP BUSINESS WORKFLOW • PERFORM TASK-SPECIFIC CUSTOMIZING.

2. Expand the tree to the branch Logistics – General • Logistics Basic Data • Business Partner • Vendor Master. Here you can assign the agents to the tasks and activate the event linkage.

3. Select Assign agents to task. You will see the following dialog tasks (ignore the background tasks) as shown in Table 28.2.

Task ID	Name	Possible Agents
TS20000002	Check general vendor data	General task.
TS20000034	Check the vendor's purchasing organization data	General task.
TS00300028	Check the vendor's sub-range or plant data	General task.
TS00300034	Decision to release vendor data	General task.
TS20000003	Lift central vendor purchasing block	General task.
TS00300029	Lift detailed purchasing block for vendor	General task.
TS00300025	Check vendor data decision	Assign yourself and anyone else in the system who wants to be involved in the scenario. Normally, this is assigned to the job responsible for vendor data maintenance.

Table 28.2 Tasks Used in the Process

Tasks that are classified as general tasks can be executed by everyone in the system. In practice, the workflow makes sure that the correct user is selected. The first step in the workflow appears to all of the agents assigned to the Check vendor data decision task. The agent executing the task is assigned to all subsequent work items in the workflow. So only assign the task Check vendor data decision to users that are responsible for the vendor data maintenance. In a production environment, you probably do this by assigning the task to a job, but to demonstrate the workflow, you can assign users directly.

4. Select Activate event linkage. When you expand the workflow WS20000001 branch, you see all three possible triggering events. Activate all of them.

This SAP-provided workflow will now be started every time a vendor is blocked. All of the users that you have assigned to the first step will receive a work item in their inbox. After an agent executes the work item, this agent must decide whether or not to display the vendor data (this depends on how familiar they are with the vendor). Finally, they can release the vendor block, which they can do themselves.

Congratulations! You have configured and activated your first workflow. If you are feeling adventurous, you can go to the workflow configuration transaction (Transaction SWDD_CONFIG or menu path TOOLS • BUSINESS WORKFLOW • DEVELOPMENT • DEFINITION TOOLS • WORKFLOW CONFIGURATION) and assign a deadline to the first step by specifying a time limit and activating the deadline.

28.6   Commonly Used SAP ERP Workflows

SAP Business Workflow has been used by customers for many years, and many workflows are provided. So, there are many workflows that are "heavy hitters" used by many customers. Probably one of the most used workflows provided by SAP is WS00000038 (Release requisition). There is some IMG configuration required for the release statuses, but it is a very common workflow to get you started. Another common workflow is WS98000001 (Parked invoices). The following lists some of the well-known SAP provided workflows in SAP ERP:

▶ Incoming IDocs for EDI. These are unique because they normally only execute if the inbound IDoc has an error. They are normally a TS single task only, not a WS, workflow task. They are configured in the inbound processing for the IDoc (TS00008068).

▶ Parked documents (WS20001004), contracts (WS20000079), complete invoices for posting (WS20001003).

▶ Approve travel expense (WS12500022).

▶ Engineering change orders and change requests (WS20000989).

▶ Release purchase requisition (WS00000038), purchase order (WS20000075), scheduling agreement (WS20000078), and locked vendor data (WS20000001).

▶ Quality notifications (WS24500047) and inspections (WS00200067).

▶ Plant maintenance notifications (WS20000317), maintenance orders (TS20000650), and service notifications (WS20000318).

Recommendation

Use the online help path mentioned in Section 28.1.1, Using SAP Help Portal to Find SAP Documented Workflows, to get the details on each of these workflows. In some cases, multiple workflow templates are provided, so it is critical that you use online help to ensure you research the correct workflow.

ArchiveLink provides the necessary infrastructure to make document information directly available to every authorized user. Workflow is used to coordinate the storage of digitized documents and how they are linked to the business objects in the SAP Business Suite. From here, workflow is used to accelerate the subsequent business processing. This chapter describes ArchiveLink and how it works with SAP Business Workflow.

29   ArchiveLink

Documents are carriers of business information exchanged between companies, initiating business processes or providing data for processes that are already in progress. The timely knowledge of business document contents and the course of their subsequent processing provide necessary information for the correct processing and evaluation of a company's procedures. Whether authorization or release procedures, procedures for purchasing, sales or requests, or decision processes, all processes require the availability, transparency, and legal certainty of business information, which can be achieved most efficiently by integrating the documents electronically.

Regardless of the original media, all business documents such as letters, faxes, and emails can be digitized upon arrival in the company. Then, in electronic form, they can be stored, distributed, and assigned to existing business objects or to business objects that have yet to be created. As a result, time-consuming procedures such as the duplication of these documents, the search for procedure-related information, and many other core activities in paper-based research are avoided. Documents can be displayed at any time and in any place to provide business information with no delay. ArchiveLink is the technology needed to integrate business documents in electronic procedures.

29.1 What Is ArchiveLink?

ArchiveLink has to be viewed from two perspectives: the functional business perspective and the technical perspective.

29.1.1 The Technical View of ArchiveLink

On the technical side, ArchiveLink can be understood by looking at its components. ArchiveLink provides the SAP application components with a bundle of interfaces, services, and scenarios, with which documents and business processes can be easily integrated. In addition, ArchiveLink has a certified interface to the storage systems (content servers) that enables features of the storage system to be called within the SAP component. To access documents stored externally, ArchiveLink includes an integrated, extendable user interface for complex search queries (*Document Finder*) and a flexible set of routines related to displaying documents, together with its own *Document Viewer*.

A typical ArchiveLink constellation consists of SAP components in conjunction with a content server for the storage of documents that cannot be changed, and possibly an SAP Content Server for the storage of documents that are being processed (i.e., can be changed). On the client-side, you can use centralized or local work centers for scanning and storing documents (see Figure 29.1). Local entry can be important for sensitive documents, such as HR documents, which you do not want left lying around. The document images can then be accessed from every client that has the necessary display components installed, when the user has the correct authorization.

Different display programs can be selected depending on the storage formats of the documents, the IT requirements, or the user roles. Examples of these are:

▸ An ECL (Engineering Client Viewer) display program for the display of incoming documents with the SAP GUI for Windows.

▸ An integrated Internet browser (HTML Control) for all SAP user interfaces. This HTML Control lets plugins be called for MIME-compatible external display programs in the web browser, but there are no restrictions for the display of different formats.

The ArchiveLink interface is an open interface to content servers that is implemented by SAP. Every system provider of content servers that are functionally compatible with the ArchiveLink interface can be certified by SAP. This comprises a comprehensive technical evaluation of the interface between SAP and the third-party software.

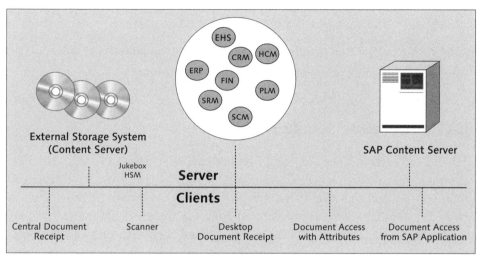

Figure 29.1 Example Configuration of an ArchiveLink System

29.1.2 The Business View of ArchiveLink

The central task of ArchiveLink is the integration of documents in business processes and the linking of business objects with documents (see Figure 29.2).

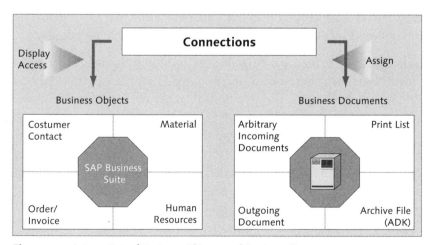

Figure 29.2 Integration of Business Objects and Business Documents

837

In this context, ArchiveLink supports displaying, storing, and retrieving documents and thus enables the intelligent organization and distribution of business documents. The advantages of this type of processing include the following:

▸ From an application record, all relevant image documents can be searched for and displayed (from any client worldwide).

▸ The authorization concept of ArchiveLink prevents unauthorized access.

▸ Documents can be integrated in processes from the start by using workflow.

29.2 ArchiveLink Standard Scenarios

ArchiveLink supports the storage of documents that arrive in your company (incoming documents), such as invoices, orders, credit memos, complaints, inquiries, or contracts. These initiate processes or are assigned processors to extract the content of the document and continue the processing. For example, suppose the contents of an incoming invoice have been extracted and posted as an electronic record of the invoice, and this has to be matched to the original purchase order. Linking the electronic image of the invoice to the invoice record is important for auditing and correcting mistakes. Similarly, the SAP component generates outgoing documents, such as order confirmations, purchase orders, invoices, and dunning notices. These are also taken care of by ArchiveLink. The image of the electronic document is important when, for example, a customer calls the customer interaction center to query an invoice. That customer has the paper invoice in front of him, and the control center agent needs to see both the image of the invoice as well as the electronic record to help with the enquiry.

ArchiveLink can also archive print lists (i.e., report output) such as account update journals in finance or warehouse stocks in materials management. This is either done simultaneously with the printing or as an alternative to printing. Using indices and freely definable search functions, you can also find the required list records on an ad-hoc basis. Hyperlinks are used so that when a row in an archived report is selected, the original document is displayed. In special cases, content servers (external storage systems) can also include archive files that were created with the *Archive Development Kit* (ADK) as part of a data archiving project. In this scenario, the content server is used purely as a storage system because all access to the stored data is controlled using the component ADK.

29.2.1 How SAP Business Workflow Integrates ArchiveLink

Workflow is used for streamlining the processing of incoming documents. There are two subprocesses (phases) involved:

▶ Phase one is the creation of the electronic document.

▶ Phase two is the subsequent processing of this document, such as the release of payment for an invoice.

We will only look at the first phase of processing in this chapter because the second phase is more or less a standard workflow scenario with very little ArchiveLink specifics.

Consider the typical case of how an incoming paper invoice is processed. The process begins when an invoice arrives in your company. Legal considerations require the invoice to be archived, and in some countries, there is a legal requirement to archive electronically, so the invoice is scanned and archived in an electronic storage system. This invoice must also be registered in the SAP component. These two steps must be integrated together efficiently, and there are two possible ways of doing this: integration using barcodes or the workflow-based procedure. Only the workflow-based procedure is described here.

Workflow-Based Documents Scenario: Storage for Later Entry (Previously Early Archiving)

The document is digitized and stored as soon as possible. This is most likely to be performed at a central scanning workplace (see Figure 29.3) to reduce the total cost of the hardware as well as the cost of training and office space.

After the document has been stored in the content server, a workflow is started that generates a work item for the responsible agents. When an agent executes the work item, he is presented with the digitized document displayed in a viewer. Simultaneously, the work item starts the data-entry transaction so that the agent can enter data directly into the transaction, based on what appears in the Document Viewer. Some companies use Optical Character Recognition (OCR) techniques to reduce the amount of human interaction necessary. After the data has been posted, the workflow links the electronic image to the newly created application document. This allows a user to view the posted document and to display the electronic image of the original invoice at any time and without any additional research.

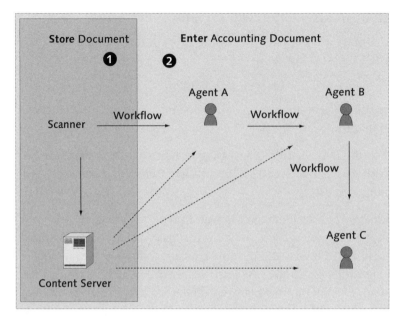

Figure 29.3 Workflow-Based Documents Scenario

If, for example, the vendor needs to follow this up with a letter (e.g., dispute the discount offered), the same workflow scenarios are available to assign the image of the letter to the existing application document. The advantage of document-based workflows is the ability to improve and accelerate the incoming document process. The following example of an incoming invoice demonstrates the advantages well.

Payment of an invoice can be made within a cash discount period, leading to a discount if the payment is made on time. To benefit from discount agreements, invoices have to be posted and released for payment as quickly as possible. In conventional financial accounting, it takes several days to process an invoice. In large enterprises, it takes several weeks because it has to go through various processing stages that involve offices in different geographic locations. The scenario described here considerably speeds up this procedure because the original documents were already scanned and archived when they arrived. From this point, they are available electronically and can be processed directly.

The storage of the document described in this scenario can take place in three ways:

▶ **Control by the SAP system**
The invoice is stored under the control of an SAP transaction.

▶ **Fax inbox**
If the invoice enters the SAP component by fax (e.g., via SAPconnect), the fax can automatically trigger a workflow that deals with the archiving and processing of the document. The customizing is performed using Transaction SO28.

▶ **Upstream storage**
It is possible to completely separate the digitization process from the business processing so that digitization (and storage) is completed upstream of the SAP component. The link to the archived document, referred to as the *unique document identifier*, is passed to the SAP component, and this triggers the business process. For this purpose, ArchiveLink specifies an interface for incoming documents that an external system can use to register the unique document identifier and document attributes to the SAP component. More sophisticated digitization mechanisms can be employed without losing the advantages of workflow. Examples of such mechanisms are offline scanning, web scanning, OCR, and classification.

Figure 29.4 shows the flow of what happens when a document is scanned to the creation of the work item.

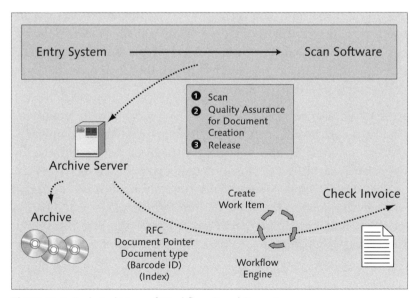

Figure 29.4 Technical View of Workflow-Based Scenarios

> **Caution**
>
> This ArchiveLink interface is not part of the ArchiveLink certification procedure, so you have to verify with the storage system vendor that they support this interface if you intend to use it.

29.3   Business Object Types

To use ArchiveLink, the business object types concerned must support the interface IFARCH21. This interface contains the method ShowAllDocuments that displays the documents related to a business object. The interface also defines the event assigned, including the parameters passed with the event. This event is used as a terminating event to confirm that the digitized document has been assigned to the application record posted in the SAP system. In other words, the work item that a user receives to enter the data for the posting is an asynchronous task.

The terminating event has two purposes:

▶ It confirms that the application record has been created and committed to the database.

▶ It returns the ID of the freshly created application record (i.e., the key of the new business object instance) to the workflow so that the workflow can continue processing it. This second part of the workflow is the business side of the process (not covered by this chapter), where, for example, a manager releases the invoice for payment. To do this, he has to be able to inspect both the ArchiveLink document and the SAP invoice.

The assigned event can also be used to trigger a new workflow to handle the business processing, the ArchiveLink document ID being passed as a parameter of the event. This is an example of how a single event can be both a terminating event and a triggering event. This also illustrates the power of BOR interfaces and how they contribute to software economy. This same mechanism is used for all business object types that support the IFARCH21 interface. So the technical part of document processing is identical, irrespective of whether the document is an invoice, goods-received document, or even a customer complaint.

Appendices

A Tips and Tricks

This appendix contains a collection of useful tips and tricks. You might not use them in every workflow, but they have great value for resolving some fairly common but potentially tricky workflow situations.

A.1 Working with Wizards

Wizards make your workflow development easier by helping to create workflows using tried and trusted templates. They range from generating whole workflows almost ready to use as is, to adding just a few steps to your existing workflows. When you use a wizard, it guides you through a series of questions and answers. Be sure to read the instructions carefully. Most wizards help build the pattern of steps needed to perform the required procedure, but you still need to check the steps created and adjust the agent assignment.

Most wizards assist you in searching for or creating any new tasks needed by the wizard on the fly. Even if you decide not to use the wizards, it is worthwhile running them just to get some ideas on good techniques to use in your own workflows.

Wizards can be found in the WIZARDS tray in the STEPS THAT CAN BE INSERTED frame in the Workflow Builder as discussed in Chapter 8, Creating a Workflow.

The available wizards at time of going to press include the following:

- **Modeling Support wizards**
  - Ad-Hoc: Include "Select Editor"
  - Ad-Hoc: Include "Exchange Task"
  - Model Deadline Monitoring
- **Approval Procedure wizards**
  - Parallel Approval
  - Hierarchical Approval

> ▸ Ad-Hoc Dynamic Hierarchical Approval

> ▸ Ad-Hoc Dynamic Parallel Authorization

These wizards create complex approval procedures in minimum time. Check that the business object you want to use as the basis for approval has implemented the interface IFAPPROVE, so that approval methods and results are consistently coded.

▸ **Circular Distribution wizards**

> ▸ Circular

> ▸ Parallel Circular

> ▸ Ad-Hoc Dynamic Circular

> ▸ Ad-Hoc Dynamic Parallel Circular

These wizards create circular distribution procedures in minimum time.

▸ **Generic Workflow Enhancers**

The following are items that can be useful when building a workflow:

> ▸ **Simplified workflow definition**
> Adds a series of steps based on one business object.

> ▸ **Creation of customizing workflows**
> Adds a series of steps to lead the agent through related customizing transactions.

> ▸ **Choose agent**
> Adds steps to your workflow to enable an agent to dynamically pick the appropriate agent for a subsequent step.

> ▸ **Model deadline monitoring**
> Adds steps that can cancel a work item and start alternative processing if a deadline is exceeded.

> ▸ **Create object reference**
> Adds a SYSTEM.GenericInstantiate step to instantiate an object of whatever business object you specify. In other words, a container element referencing a flat data field can be converted to a business object to give you access to attributes.

> ▸ **Execute report/job**
> Adds steps to execute an ABAP report or background job or send the results to a user.

Tip

The first time you use one of these wizards, it is worthwhile running it against an other-wise empty workflow first so you can see the impact the wizard will have on your work-flow before using it in your own workflow.

A.2 Working with Email

In most workflows, at some point, you will want to send an email to an interested party. The email recipient does not need to be an agent of the workflow, an employee of your company, or even a person at all because you can email to an Internet email address or to a fax number (i.e., *auto-faxing*).

Tip

Of course, if you do want to send mails externally (e.g., via the Internet or to a fax machine), you first need to check that an appropriate mail interface (such as SMTP, SAP-connect, auto-faxing, etc.) to your mail server has been implemented in your SAP com-ponent.

To email someone, you create a document, possibly with other documents attached, and send it to recipients via your existing mail servers. All of this can be done as a background task using object `SelfItem` and method `SendTaskDescrip-tion`.

You can create your own task for `SelfItem.SendTaskDescription` and include it in your workflow in an Activity step, or use the Send Mail step to generate a task for you. The result is similar; however, the advantage of using a Send Mail step is that a MAIL STEP icon appears in the flowchart, giving you greater clarity when using the flowchart to review or explain the process to business process owners and workflow users. If you have an existing task you want to reuse in a Send Mail step rather than generate a new task, attach your task by entering the task ID in the CONTROL tab of the Send Mail step definition.

A.2.1 The Send Mail Step

The advantage of using the send mail task is that the task description is transmit-ted so it is easy to include variables in the text. The Send Mail step is another task type that you can select when designing your workflow in the Workflow Builder. The minimum you need to provide to a Send Mail step is:

- **A subject text**
  You can use expressions based on container elements to provide dynamic values in your texts.

- **A body text**
  You can use expressions based on container elements (single, multiline, or object attributes) to provide dynamic values in your texts.

- **A recipient type**
  Note that you can only send to one type of recipient at a time. Possible types include but are not limited to SAP user, SAPoffice distribution list, Internet email address, fax number, telex number, or organizational object (e.g., send to everyone in a particular organizational unit).

- **A container element (single or multiline)**
  Holding the recipient addresses in the format appropriate for the recipient type. For example, if the type is SAP USER, then the address strings hold user IDs; if the type is INTERNET EMAIL ADDRESS, then the address strings hold Internet email addresses; if the type is FAX, then address strings holds fax numbers. You can enter as many recipients as you like but be careful that the data used matches the recipient type.

The Send Mail step details are used to generate a `SelfItem.SendTaskDescription` task and the binding from the workflow to the task. Via the CONTROL tab, you can change the binding, for example, to pass attachments to the email.

Note that any recipient types you use must be permitted in your system. For instance, if you want to send email to HR organizational objects (jobs, positions, etc.), the relevant configuration must be done in BUSINESS COMMUNICATION • ADMINISTRATION • SHARED OFFICE SETTINGS (Transaction SO16). If you want to send emails to Internet email addresses, then a connection to an external mail server (e.g., via SMTP, SAPconnect, etc.) must be available.

If you want to change the binding, you may find it helpful to know that the basic components of any `SelfItem.SendTaskDescription` task include the following:

- **Work item text**
  This becomes the subject line text of the email to be sent.

- **Long description**
  This becomes the body of the email.

- **Address strings**
  The address strings for the recipients in the format appropriate for the recipient type.

- **Receivers**
  This holds recipients as instances of the ADDRESS object type. Normally, you leave this empty because method SendTaskDescription converts all of the address strings into appropriate address objects based on the recipient type. However, it can be used to pass in a list of recipients of a previous email.

- **Type ID**
  This is the recipient type.

- **Express**
  This flag indicates whether the email is to be sent express. The actual effect of setting the express flag depends on the mail interface used. For instance, if sent to a user in an SAP component, an express pop-up box appears notifying the recipient of the incoming mail.

- **Language**
  If you have translated your texts into several languages, this identifies which language is to be used on the email. This is useful if, for example, your system language is Spanish, but you want to send the email in English.

- **Attachments**
  Multiple attachments can be passed in any format accepted by SAPoffice. This can include but is not limited to SAPscript documents, ABAP report lists, optically archived documents, binary documents (such as multimedia files), Microsoft Office documents such as Word and Excel files, graphics files, URLs, or even another work item. Each format needs to be activated in your system, and, if you wish, additional formats can be configured.

Tip

Remember that both the creator and the recipient of the attachment need the appropriate editors and viewers to read the attachment, and that not all attachment types are available from all inboxes. You might want to restrict the workflow participants to attachments valid from all inboxes, or at least tell them which formats they can safely use in their environment.

▶ **Line width**

If you want to send a long unbroken text in the body of your email, it can be helpful to increase the line width. Normal line width is 75 characters; maximum line width is 132 characters.

You can also add your own container elements to the task if, for example, you want to use them to add dynamic values to the email texts. For instance, you might create a `Customer` container element to hold a customer object instance, passed in the binding of the workflow step, so that you can display the customer name and address in your email text.

A.2.2 Working with Attachments

Because creating and viewing attachments are standard features of both work items and emails, it is useful to pass an attachment created for a work item to a subsequent email. For instance, take the scenario where a manager receives a work item requesting approval. As part of rejecting the request, the manager creates an attachment to the work item explaining why the request was rejected. In a subsequent step, you send a "Your request was rejected" email to the requestor along with the manager's attachment.

Every attachment created against a work item is automatically passed to the standard workflow container element `Attachments` (technical ID `_ATTACH_OBJECTS`) via automatic binding. Each dialog work item is automatically passed attachments from all previous work items in the workflow, and it automatically passes any created attachments back to the workflow.

If you want to pass all attachments created throughout the workflow to an email step, you need to bind the workflow container element `Attachments` to the `Attachments` container element of the send mail task via the CONTROL tab of the Send Mail step definition.

If you only want to pass attachments from a particular work item, change the binding of the matching workflow step to store any attachments created in your own workflow container element, which refers to object type SOFM (Office Document). You can then pass your own workflow container element to the `Attachments` container element of the send mail task in the same way.

A.2.3   Determining Recipients Via Rule Resolution

One of the few options you do not have available in a Send Mail step or `Self-Item.SendTaskDescription` task is the option to send to a list of recipients determined via a rule resolution. Therefore, if you want to send an email to a list of recipients based on a rule, you need to calculate the recipients in advance. There are a number of ways this can be done, but a few common options include the following:

▶ If you are using Release 6.10 or above, and the rule has already been used in a prior step, bind the `_RULE_RESULT` container element from the rule back to a workflow container element. You can then use an expression to assign the `Agents` attribute of the rule result held in your workflow container element as the recipients of the Send Mail step.

▶ If the criteria for the rule are based on an object, for example, rule "Vendor master owner" based on the city and country of the Vendor object, then create a virtual, multiline attribute against that object, based on data type `SWHACTOR`, that calls the rule using function module `RH_GET_ACTORS` and returns the list of agents. You can then use an expression to assign the object attribute, for example, `Vendor.MasterDataOwner`, as the recipient(s) of the Send Mail step.

▶ If the criteria for the rule are based on values that will not be known until runtime, for example, approver for authorization level (which will not be known until runtime), create a background method based on the most appropriate business object that accepts the criteria via method parameters. Then call the rule using module `RH_GET_ACTORS`, and return a list of agents. You can then add an Activity step to your workflow, prior to the Send Mail step, to call a task based on your new method, bind the criteria from the workflow to the task, and bind the result from the task back to a workflow container element. You can then use an expression to assign your workflow container element as the recipient(s) of the Send Mail step.

Tip

Remember when calling function module `RH_GET_ACTORS` that you need to pass the technical ID for your rule, for example, `AC90000001` where `90000001` is the rule number. Also, if multiple agents may be found, remember to make sure the container elements you use in your method, task, and workflow are multiline.

A.2.4 Customizing Considerations

Mail sending takes place in the background and is therefore executed by the WF-BATCH user, unless you specify another user (e.g., as an import parameter for the office API or method that sends the mail). This user must have a valid email address (i.e., a sender address) and the necessary authorization. Whenever the system sends mails, there is a very good chance that users will reply to WF-BATCH directly. Try to reduce the number of replies by including a notice to this effect in all of the emails that are sent. Giving WF-BATCH an email address along the lines of *DoNotReply@mycompany.com* will also help cut down the replies, but most effective of all is to mention an alternative feedback channel, such as a web site or a help desk number.

WF-BATCH also receives auto-response mails when a recipient is on vacation or the mail demon cannot locate an email address. The most important rule to observe here is not to reply to such mails automatically. Although it is tempting to send an auto-reply yourself, saying "Please do not send me any mails," this can start an avalanche of mails between both systems as they auto-respond to each other. Only auto-respond if you have implemented a counter that limits the number of responses (easily accomplished with a workflow).

The best way of dealing with replies of this sort is to configure an administrator as a mail substitute for WF-BATCH who can periodically go in and check the incoming mails. The administrator can delete mails and correct erroneous email addresses in the system.

> **Note**
>
> Whenever WF-BATCH sends a mail, it creates a copy in its outbox (unless the NO OUTBOX COPY flag is set in the function call). The easiest way of deleting these mails is by configuring a periodic batch job to do this for you.

Here is a summary of the steps that need to be performed before the workflow can transmit emails:

1. The SAP NetWeaver Application Server must be configured to send emails (check with your system administrator for more details on this topic).

2. Configure the email address for WF-BATCH using Transaction SU01.

3. Make sure that WF-BATCH has sufficient authorization to send mails (if you have not changed the authorizations given to WF-BATCH, it will have the relevant

authorization because `WF-BATCH` is assigned the authorization profile `SAP_ALL` as a default).

4. The `WF-BATCH` user's default login language should be set to the desired email language.

A.3   Showing the Decision Maker in a Follow-On Step

Showing the decision maker in a follow-on step is very handy for email notifications and rejections. It lets you suggest that the user contact the decision maker if the user needs more information about why the decision was made, especially if the decision maker has neglected to include an explanation in an attachment.

In the Decision step, you capture the actual agent (technical ID `_WI_ACTUAL_AGENT`) in the binding from task to workflow. Place the value in a workflow container element, for example, `ZActualAgent`, of ABAP Dictionary type `WFSYST-AGENT`.

However, if you want to use the agent's attributes as well (e.g., title, telephone number, or full name), then you need an object reference to the agent. The simplest way of doing this is to capture a reference to the decision work item itself in the workflow container. The work item object has an attribute `ExecutedByUser`, which is based on the object type `USR01`. This is exactly what you need, and it does not cost any extra storage space or performance because you are only capturing a reference.

To implement this, create a workflow container element (e.g., `DecisionStep`) based on the object type `WORKINGWI`. All dialog work items are of this type. In the workflow step that you need to capture, create an exporting binding from the `_Workitem` element to the newly created workflow container element.

> **Tip**
>
> Show the lines of the exporting binding definition first to make the `_Workitem` element visible.

You can then pass `DecisionStep.ExecutedByUser` to follow-on steps. For instance, you might want to display the decision maker's name in a subsequent email. So in your send mail task, you would:

- Include a task container element referring to object type USR01 to hold the user object instance, for example, ZDecisionMaker.

- Bind DecisionStep.ExecutedByUser to ZDecisionMaker in the matching workflow step.

- Refer to attributes of ZDecisionMaker in your work item text, for example "Unfortunately, your request has been rejected by &ZDecisionMaker.Name&. Please contact &ZDecisionMaker.Name& at &ZDecisionMaker.Telephone& if you require further details."

An additional bonus of capturing in this way is that there are other useful attributes of DecisionStep that you can also use, such as DecisionStep.Actual-EndDate, which is the day the decision was made.

A.4   Creating Your Own User Decision Template

Sometimes, it is useful to create your own user decision task, especially when you need to restrict the agent assignment for the decision (because the standard user decision task is a general task) or change the text instructions presented during execution. The standard user decision task is TS00008267. Before you create your own user decision task, make sure you familiarize yourself with the standard task.

To create your own user decision task, create a new task based on object DECISION and method PROCESS, or just copy TS00008267 as a starting point. The easiest way to do this is to create a standard User Decision step, and then use the COPY FROM TEMPLATE button on the CONTROL tab page of the workflow step definition. Then, enter your own texts and agent assignment for your new task. You can also add new container elements if you wish, especially if you want to add dynamic values to your instructions. Make sure you check any bindings.

> **Tip**
>
> If you do not want your user decision to appear in a pop-up screen, remove the standard work item display, overriding settings from the WI DISPLAY tab page in the step definition.

A.5 Using Secondary, Before, and After Methods

This section discusses how to use secondary methods.

A.5.1 Secondary Methods

If you want to help an agent make a decision by bringing extra assistance to the agent, that is, more than just text instructions, you can use *secondary methods*. For instance, if an agent has been asked to approve or reject the vacation request of a subordinate, it might be helpful to see a report showing who else on the team is going to be on leave at the same time. You can do this by defining a secondary method *Display team vacation schedule* against the Approve Vacation Request workflow step.

When the agent executes the work item, a second session window is opened, and the secondary method is executed there. For example, the agent might see the vacation request and the APPROVE/REJECT options in the first session window and the team vacation schedule in the second session window. While making the decision, the agent can switch between the two session windows, checking the vacation request details and comparing them with the team vacation schedule before making a final decision and completing the work item. When the work item is completed, the system automatically closes the secondary method session. If the agent cancels the work item execution and later re-executes it, the secondary method is restarted each time the work item is executed.

The secondary method session runs asynchronously to the work item execution session; that is, it is not aware of what is happening in the work item execution session.

> **Note**
>
> Because a second session window must be opened, this technique depends heavily on how the work items are delivered to an agent. If the work item is presented using SAP GUI for Windows, then the second session window can be created. However, other work item delivery mechanisms, such as the web inbox or external inboxes as in Microsoft Outlook or Lotus Notes, may not have the facility to open a second session window, in which case, the secondary method is ignored.
>
> Because secondary methods are not part of the main workflow and not included in the workflow log, they are primarily designed for display methods, for example, for showing extra data or statistics or a report.

To use secondary methods, in the METHODS tab of your Activity or User Decision workflow step, you specify in the SECONDARY METHODS section, your container element holding the relevant object instance and the method to be executed. Only automated binding is possible; that is, the method container of the step's main task-based method is passed to the secondary method. Of course, only import parameters can be used for the secondary method because the secondary method session runs asynchronously and therefore never returns results to the workflow. You can specify multiple secondary methods if you wish. An alternative is to append the report in the form of a business object to the work item (an attachment) so that the users can launch it from the work item when they need it.

A.5.2 Before and After Methods

Before methods and after methods are a type of secondary method that executes either *before* the work item launches, or *after* it completes. Before and after methods are similar to secondary methods in that:

- They are specified in the METHODS tab of the workflow step.
- They require you to specify a container element holding the object instance, and the method to be executed.
- You can only use automated binding; that is, the method container of the step's task-based method is passed to the before and after methods.
- You can specify multiple before and after methods if you wish.
- They are executed every time the work item is executed. In particular, the after method is *always* executed after the synchronous part of the work item execution is complete, regardless of whether the work item is waiting on a terminating event or has ended in error.
- They have no effect on the execution of the work item itself.

However, before and after methods are called modally, that is, as if they were extra steps in the same session as the work item. This means they can be used to manipulate the method container if you wish, or to influence the main task-based method or subsequent steps in the workflow.

Whereas secondary methods are best for displaying additional information to the agent, before and after methods are best for background tasks you want to call each time the work item is executed. You might want to use before and after methods for such activities as:

▸ Collecting additional statistics on the workflow into your own database tables for later analysis.

▸ Converting values returned by the work item in an after method.

▸ Notifying someone that the work item has been started in a before method, for example, in the vacation request scenario, to let an employee know that the approving agent has at least seen their vacation request form.

▸ Notifying someone of the work item result in an after method. Of course, this could also be done as part of the main workflow; however, it may be expedient to use an after method to avoid complicating the main workflow.

▸ Starting and stopping the ArchiveLink viewer.

Note that the object instance being used in a before or after method must exist before the work item is executed; for example, you cannot use a before method to create an object instance.

A.6   Looping Through a Multiline List

If you have a list of values in the workflow container, that is, as a multiline element, you may want to perform a series of steps on the individual items of the list. One option is to use table-driven dynamic parallel processing as described in Chapter 9, Advanced Workflow Design Techniques.

Table-driven processing creates parallel-processed work items, one work item per row, for the same task or subworkflow. However, if you need to split the list into individual rows and loop over them one after another when the processing of one row is dependent on the processing of a prior row, you may need to take a different approach.

One example of how to split a list into individual rows is provided using the object type SYSTEM methods DescribeAgents and LoopAtAgents, which allow you to take a list of agents and separate out each individual agent for processing. This works as follows:

1. Use an Activity step to call a task based on method SYSTEM.DescribeAgents.

2. Pass the list of agents to the method. The number of agents in the list is returned.

3. Store the number of agents in a workflow container element, for example, NumOfAgents.

4. Use a Loop step (Loop Until or Loop While) to keep looping while `NumOfAgents` has a value greater than zero.

5. Within the loop, use another Activity step to call a task based on method `SYSTEM.LoopAtAgents`. Pass it the list and the `NumOfAgents` value. The method returns the n-th value of the list where n = `NumOfAgents`.

6. You can then do whatever processing you need to do on the agent returned, for example, get his email address and send him an email.

7. As the final step within the loop, decrement the `NumOfAgents` value by one.

This process reads a list from highest value to lowest. The implementation of the `DescribeAgents` and `LoopAtAgents` methods is simple enough to reproduce in your own methods so that you can easily deal with any list of any data type, whether ABAP Dictionary or object reference.

A.7   Creating Object References Dynamically

Object references are very useful throughout workflow because you can use them to access all sorts of data, methods, and events. For instance, because business object types can contain attributes pointing to other business object types, you can refer to object-referencing attributes of business objects, for example, `SalesOrder.Customer.Name`, in container bindings and expressions such as in work item texts, the logical expressions in Loop steps, or in start conditions.

For those situations where you can find the key data defining an object instance but do not actually have access to the object instance in your workflow, object `SYSTEM` method `GenericInstantiate` can be used to create a new object reference dynamically. All you need to provide is the object key and the object type of the instance you want to access.

This is particularly useful when using utility objects such as the deadline object in Section A.9, Making the Most of Modeled Deadlines. Or you might want to create an object instance based on attributes from two or more different object instances you are using in your workflow. Usually, you need to calculate the key itself in a prior step (e.g., by using a container operation), or use an alternative binding (mentioned in Chapter 8, Creating a Workflow) to pass it to `SYSTEM.GenericInstantiate`.

A.8 Deadlines Based on the Factory Calendar

Deadlines are based on a reference date/time plus an absolute offset period. That is, deadline date/time is calculated simply by adding the offset period to the reference date/time. Weekends and holidays are not taken into account. If you want to ensure that your deadline is escalated on a working day, you need to use factory calendars, which hold the relevant weekends and holidays. Factory calendars can be maintained using Transaction SCAL.

To calculate the deadline date/time based on factory calendars, you need to:

▶ Create a deadline object that calculates the next working date/time based on the current work item creation, date/time.

▶ Set up a workflow container element based on your deadline object.

▶ Instantiate the deadline object in your workflow prior to the step with the deadline.

▶ Use the deadline object as the reference date/time in your deadline.

A.8.1 Creating the Deadline Object

This section describes the use of a custom business object to calculate a deadline for the factory calendar. Chapter 11, ABAP Classes, discussed how to use an ABAP class for a factory calendar deadline.

The custom deadline business object described in this section is essentially a utility to calculate a date and time based on a factory calendar and the current system date and time. At runtime, when the deadline object is referenced from the workflow step, the current system date and time would be equivalent to the work item creation date and time. The custom deadline object has no supertype.

The key for the custom business object is:

▶ **Offset**
A numerical offset relating to work item creation time.

▶ **Unit**
The time unit for the offset.

▶ **Calid**
Factory calendar ID, which must be active in the system.

The attributes for the custom business object are:

▶ **Date**

The calculated factory calendar date, based on data type SY-DATUM. This is a virtual attribute that calls function module END_TIME_DETERMINE to calculate the date.

▶ **Time**

The calculated factory calendar time, based on data type SY-UZEIT. This is a virtual attribute that calls function module END_TIME_DETERMINE to calculate the time.

Note that there is no buffering of the date and time attributes, so that even though you may instantiate the deadline object early in your workflow, when it is used to calculate a deadline, it always uses the current system date and time, that is, the work item creation time, as its starting point. If you need to pass in a specific date/time, you can make the starting date/time method parameters or part of the object key. Listing A.1 shows how to calculate a deadline based on the factory calendar.

```
PROGRAM ZDEADLINE.
*---------------------------------------------------------------
*---------------------------------------------------------------
INCLUDE <OBJECT>.
BEGIN_DATA OBJECT. " Do not change. DATA is generated
* only private members may be inserted into structure private
DATA:
" begin of private,
"    to declare private attributes remove comments and
"    insert private attributes here ...
" end of private,
  BEGIN OF KEY,
      OFFSET LIKE SY-MSGNO,
      UNIT LIKE SWD_SDYNP-LATE_END_U,
      CALID LIKE SCAL-FCALID,
  END OF KEY,
      DATE LIKE SY-DATUM,
      TIME LIKE SY-UZEIT.
END_DATA OBJECT. " Do not change.. DATA is generated
*---------------------------------------------------------------
GET_PROPERTY DATE CHANGING CONTAINER.
  DATA: DEADLINE_DATE LIKE SY-DATUM,
```

```
        DEADLINE_TIME LIKE SY-UZEIT.
* Calculate deadline end date and end time using SY-DATUM /
* SY-UZEIT as work item creation date and time
* Use object-key-values as defaults for offset, unit, and calid
  PERFORM CALCULATE_DEADLINE
      USING SY-DATUM SY-UZEIT
            OBJECT-KEY-OFFSET OBJECT-KEY-UNIT OBJECT-KEY-CALID
            DEADLINE_DATE DEADLINE_TIME.
* Put the calculated date into the container, skip the time
  SWC_SET_ELEMENT CONTAINER 'Date' DEADLINE_DATE .
END_PROPERTY.
*-------------------------------------------------------------
GET_PROPERTY TIME CHANGING CONTAINER.
  DATA: DEADLINE_DATE LIKE SY-DATUM,
        DEADLINE_TIME LIKE SY-UZEIT.
* Calculate deadline end date and end time  just like above
  PERFORM CALCULATE_DEADLINE
      USING SY-DATUM SY-UZEIT
            OBJECT-KEY-OFFSET OBJECT-KEY-UNIT OBJECT-KEY-CALID
            DEADLINE_DATE DEADLINE_TIME.
* Put the calculated time into the container, skip the date
  SWC_SET_ELEMENT CONTAINER 'Time' DEADLINE_TIME.
END_PROPERTY.
*-------------------------------------------------------------
FORM CALCULATE_DEADLINE USING VALUE(I_DATE) LIKE SY-DATUM
                              VALUE(I_TIME) LIKE SY-UZEIT
                              VALUE(I_OFFSET) VALUE(I_UNIT)
                              VALUE(I_CALID)
                              E_DATE LIKE SY-DATUM
                              E_TIME LIKE SY-UZEIT.
  DATA: OFFSET(10) TYPE N, UNIT(3), CALID LIKE SCAL-FCALID.
* Calculate deadline date/time based on factory calendar
  CALL FUNCTION 'END_TIME_DETERMINE'
      EXPORTING
          DURATION                = I_OFFSET
          UNIT                    = I_UNIT
          FACTORY_CALENDAR        = I_CALID
      IMPORTING
          END_DATE                = E_DATE
          END_TIME                = E_TIME
      CHANGING
          START_DATE              = I_DATE
```

```
                START_TIME              = I_TIME
          EXCEPTIONS
                OTHERS                  = 1.
   IF SY-SUBRC <> 0.
*      If there are any problems, provide a default date and time,
*      e.g. by calling END_TIME_DETERMINE without parameter
*      FACTORY_CALENDAR.
   CALL FUNCTION 'END_TIME_DETERMINE'
        EXPORTING
                DURATION                = I_OFFSET
                UNIT                    = I_UNIT
        IMPORTING
                END_DATE                = E_DATE
                END_TIME                = E_TIME
        CHANGING
                START_DATE              = I_DATE
                START_TIME              = I_TIME
          EXCEPTIONS
                OTHERS                  = 1.
   ENDIF.
ENDFORM.
```

Listing A.1 Using Factory Calendar for Deadlines

A.8.2   Using the Deadline Object in Your Workflow

To use the deadline object in your workflow, create a workflow container element, for example, ZFactoryDeadline referencing object type ZDEADLINE. In the workflow step to be monitored, turn on the relevant deadline (requested start, latest start, requested end, or latest end), and set the reference date/time to the following expression so it can be used to compare against the factory calendar:

```
Date = ZFactoryDeadline.DATE
Time = ZFactoryDeadline.TIME
```

You can also set the offset if you wish.

The deadline object must be instantiated before it is used at runtime. There are a number of ways to do this:

▶ Use the INITIAL VALUES option of the workflow container to set a default offset, unit, and factory calendar ID for ZFactoryDeadline.

▶ In a prior workflow step, use a task based on object `SYSTEM` method `GENERIC-INSTANTIATE` to instantiate `ZFactoryDeadline` using the appropriate offset, unit, and factory calendar ID.

The result is a deadline date/time created based on a factory calendar. Note that the reference date/time gives the date/time based on the factory calendar, but any offset is simply added to the reference date/time as normal.

A.9   Making the Most of Modeled Deadlines

This section provides recommendations when using modeled deadlines.

A.9.1   Taking Alternative Action

One of the most useful workflow techniques is a modeled deadline. This makes it possible to take an alternative action when a deadline is exceeded. If you have not used this technique before, using the MODEL DEADLINE MONITORING wizard will help. The basic process is:

▶ On the APPROPRIATE DEADLINE tab of the step to be monitored, you enter the deadline reference date/time, offset period, and your deadline exceeded outcome.

▶ On the step to be monitored, you activate the processing obsolete outcome.

The step to be monitored now has two additional outcomes as well as its usual outcomes, deadline exceeded and processing obsolete. Under the deadline exceeded outcome, you can then add a number of steps; for example, you might want to insert a step to notify someone that the deadline has been exceeded. The last step under the deadline exceeded outcome should be a Process Control step. You use the Process Control step to make the monitored work item obsolete, thus triggering the processing obsolete outcome. You can now add your alternative actions after the processing obsolete outcome.

Why have separate outcomes for deadline exceeded versus processing obsolete? Consider the following scenarios as a couple of examples that make this separation very useful:

▶ You want to notify several different groups of people, or the same people of when a deadline is exceeded rather than take alternative action, and you want this to repeat until the work is done. Using the deadline outcome on its own lets you do this without upsetting the normal operation and outcome of the monitored step.

▶ You want to take the same alternative actions if the deadline was exceeded or if the original agent rejects the work item. Having the alternative actions in one place, under the processing obsolete outcome, enables you to trigger it from either the deadline exceeded outcome or the processing rejected outcome.

A.9.2 Modeled Deadlines for (Repeated) Notifications

You do not have to use the modeled deadline pattern as is. It is quite useful to modify it to notify people via email when a deadline is exceeded. For instance, you can add a Send Mail step after your deadline exceeded outcome.

You might even want to send more than one notification, for instance, to notify someone that a work item is late every day until it is completed. To do this, create a Loop Until step after your deadline exceeded outcome checking a CONTAINER ELEMENT flag to see whether the main step has completed. You need to make sure that after the main work item has been completed, you fill this flag via a Container Operation step. In the loop, you send your mail; a requested start deadline can be used to ensure it is not sent until the next day. You can use a Process Control step to clear up any remaining waiting send mail work items after the main work item is complete.

A.10 Ad-Hoc Anchor Step

The Ad-Hoc Anchor step enables a workflow to add an additional workflow at runtime. The workflow designer adds the step as an Ad-Hoc step. At runtime, a user invokes the workflow through the graphical workflow log. The container for both workflows must be the same.

To set up a test to see how it works, do the following:

1. Create a workflow called WS_123.

2. Add the FORMABSENC to the workflow container. For testing, add an initial value in the workflow container (or provide initial value when testing, whichever you prefer).

3. Insert task TS3000017 into your workflow. It is an SAP-provided task to update the FORMABSENC object. Have the agent be an INITIATOR.

4. Create a second workflow. Add the `FORMABSENC` and an initial value to the container, just as you did for `WS_123`.

5. Add a User Decision step to the second workflow, with outcomes of YES and NO.

6. Add an Anchor step to the second workflow, after the User Decision step. In the Anchor step, add `WS_123`.

7. Test the second workflow. Start the workflow, for the User Decision step, select CANCEL AND KEEP IN THE INBOX.

8. Navigate to the workflow log, and from there to the graphical workflow log.

9. Select the ANCHOR icon ( ) in the graphical workflow log.

10. You will receive a dialog asking you to choose a task. Select the `WS_123` task, and the anchor graphic in the workflow log is replaced with the `WS_123`.

A.11   Review Workflows

You can define a review workflow (R) for a workflow (A). This review workflow can be started by an authorized user from the graphical workflow display of a workflow that is running (A). Here, all data of workflow A is transferred to the review workflow. In the review workflow, you can create attachments that can be seen in workflow A. You can start the review workflow multiple times for a workflow. You can see an example of this in task group `TG745000040`. The following are the general steps you need to do.

The task group includes two workflows: `WS971000308`, which serves as the main workflow (A), and `WS745000908`, which is the reviewer workflow (R). You can test the workflow `WS971000308` to understand how it works. The review is started from the graphical workflow log. The following are the major items that must be done:

1. Define a workflow (A) according to your own requirements.

2. Insert a step into this workflow (A) to start the review workflow.

3. Define a workflow (R) that should be the review workflow. Add this workflow to the REVIEWER tab of workflow A. This tab is in the VERSION-DEPENDENT tab under BASIC DATA.

4. Workflow R must have possible agents assigned to the workflow in the BASIC DATA tab.

B   Step-by-Step Troubleshooting Guide

This appendix provides a practical guide to troubleshooting some of the thornier problems that you may run into in the development environment. It does not make interesting reading, but it may nevertheless be useful to you when you develop your own workflows. When investigating a problem, your first point of attack is Transaction SWUD, Diagnosis. Start by selecting the most appropriate item from the list menu.

B.1   A Workflow That Does Not Start

The source of a workflow's triggering problems is straightforward to locate when you select the second item from the new list menu: PROBLEM: TASK DOES NOT START from Transaction SWUD. The first check is to see whether the workflow really did not start, or whether it was started but did not create a work item in the correct inbox.

B.1.1   Did It Really Fail to Start

Choose the first item in the new list menu (DETERMINE INSTANCES FOR TASK) to determine whether or not the list of instances is empty. The new list shows you all of the workflow work items created on that day for the particular workflow definition that you are investigating. If you want to view the work items created on another day, change the date in the preceding screen. If you want to search over a date range, then call up a work item list report (such as Transaction SWI1) directly.

An empty list shows clearly that your workflow really did not start, so you should proceed with the next test (see next Section B.1.2, Is the Triggering Event Set Up Correctly). However, if a workflow work item was created, then you can examine the log of the workflow to see if the first work item was created and to whom it was assigned. This being the case, you can skip this section and move to Section B.2, A Workflow That Stops in Mid-Track.

B.1.2   Is the Triggering Event Set Up Correctly

So your workflow really did *not* start. You are now a significant step closer to finding the solution. If the flow is started by an event, then you need to follow the list of checks relating to events. If this is *not* the case, jump to Section B.1.6, What Is Preventing the Workflow from Starting.

You will verify in the following tests:

▶ **Whether the event was raised correctly**

  ▷ Check whether the event was raised.

  ▷ Check whether there is a `COMMIT WORK` statement in the code following the event creation (this only needs to be checked if you are investigating a homemade event-creation).

  ▷ Check whether the event is not released until after the application object has been committed to the database.

▶ **Whether the event to workflow linkage occurred as expected**

  ▷ Check whether the event linkage is correct.

  ▷ Check whether any start conditions or check function modules used returned the correct result.

  ▷ Check whether the mandatory data required by the workflow is being passed by the event.

▶ **If the event is okay, but the first work item has failed to appear**

  ▷ Check whether an agent has been assigned to the first step in the workflow.

The event checks are relatively straightforward. These are presented to you in the menu. The only thing that you need to do is choose from the list the event that should trigger the workflow (if more than one event is possible). Now perform the checks one after another.

B.1.3   Check the RFC Queue to See if the Event Raising Has Aborted Midway

Check the RFC queue to verify that it is empty. This is a simple check that usually returns a positive result allowing you to move swiftly to the next test. When you perform this check, make sure that the "started by" user ID is that of the person who called the transaction that should have raised this event (usually your own). If there is an entry, take a look at the timestamp, and estimate whether or not it came from your test. An entry in this queue implies that the failure is either due to an incorrectly customized system (but you did check this earlier, didn't you?), an incorrect binding between the event and the workflow, or mandatory data missing in the event container.

Check the event trace to see if the event really was raised and that the start condition or check function module (if any) did not return an exception. Remember that, technically, start conditions are also implemented as a check function module, so if your start conditions have failed, this also shows up as a check function module exception. If the event is not found, make sure that the event trace is switched on and repeat the test if necessary.

> **Tip**
>
> You can use the workflow trace to investigate problems with the start condition definitions.

If the event still does not appear in the log, it has not been raised. The most likely cause is:

- Incorrect application customizing or lack of a call to the ABAP statement COMMIT WORK after the call to function module SWE_CREATE_EVENT (custom transaction).
- The SWE_CREATE_EVENT call is not being reached by the transaction (verify this with the ABAP Debugger). If the event occurs twice, the application customizing is incorrect. This happens if you have configured the event to be raised upon a status change, but the application is raising the event directly, too.

The error *Object does not exist* (message OL826) shows that the event is failing because the object does not yet exist in the database. This is most likely to happen when an object is created for the first time, and the CREATED event is triggered by incorrect program code. In other words, the event is triggered before the object has been committed to the database because it is still in the update task queue at the time the event is raised.

Refer to Chapter 14, Custom Programs, to find out how to raise such events correctly.

> **Note**
>
> In an incorrectly programmed custom transaction, an event can be raised when the user has canceled the transaction; that is, the status change that the event is reporting did not actually happen. This is most likely to happen if the event is raised without due regard to the logical unit of work (LUW) in the transaction; for example, if it was raised in the dialog task instead of the update task.

B.1.4   Check the Consistency of the Workflow Definition

This consistency check is worth performing next because it is so simple to perform but sometimes identifies the root problem very quickly. If the results of the test show that your workflow definition is correct, then you can jump straight to the next test.

The test makes sure that your workflow definition is correct, that agents have been assigned to the tasks in the workflow, and that the event bindings are defined properly. In early releases, if no agent has been assigned to the dialog task used in the first step in the workflow, the event fails to trigger the workflow. Similarly, a workflow definition that contains errors also fails to start.

B.1.5   Simulate the Event

Simulate the event to check the event linkage, using the menu in the diagnosis program. This shows you all of the workflows that are linked to the event and reason codes explaining why any of the workflows cannot be triggered. The reasons for failure vary from release to release (the workflow system has become more fault tolerant), but you will see at a glance if everything is okay. More often than not, if you reach this test, you may find that the event linkage has been automatically disabled by the workflow system.

When event queues are *not* used (prior to Release 4.6C), if a fatal error prevented a workflow from triggering, the event linkage is disabled by the system to prevent the RFC queue from choking. This means that after you have enabled the event linkage, you should always raise the event again and make sure that the workflow starts correctly. If the event linkage is deactivated again by the system, then you should look deeper for the cause of the problem. This is most likely to be a missing obligatory element in the event container or an inactive workflow definition.

To avoid event linkages being disabled, activate event queues as described in Chapter 13, Using Events and Other Business Interfaces. Event queues are also particularly useful when a lot of events fail before you can fix the error because they collect all failed events and give you an easy way to restart them en masse.

If none of these tests finds anything, the next step is to start the workflow directly and follow the checks described in the next section.

B.1.6 What Is Preventing the Workflow from Starting

By now, you have established that the event customizing is correct (or that no triggering events are involved). Now start the workflow directly from the test environment of the diagnosis transaction or from the Workflow Builder.

This has the advantage that any error messages that occur while the workflow is starting are displayed directly on the screen. If the workflow starts correctly and does not display any error messages on the screen, then the most likely source of the problem is that the parameters passed to the workflow in the test scenario are different from those passed from the triggering transaction. There are two ways of investigating the parameters that are passed by an event:

▶ Use the workflow trace, as described in Chapter 16, Advanced Diagnostics.

▶ Use the function module SWE_EVENT_MAIL.

If you want to be notified of an event being raised, regardless of whether a workflow is started, then function module SWE_EVENT_MAIL can be used to send a mail whenever the event occurs. Simply create an event linkage (Transaction SWE-TYPV) for your event, listing your user ID as the receiver type and SWE_EVENT_MAIL as the receiver function module.

When the event is raised, an SAPoffice mail is sent to you in your inbox. This mail includes a list of the event's container elements. Check that these elements include all of the mandatory elements required by the workflow. Check, too, that the elements have the correct format as expected by the workflow. For example, check that the leading zeros match and that the key of the object is complete. You may find it useful to consult Section B.3.2, Business Object Does Not Exist, if you find that the key is correct, but the workflow cannot find the object.

B.2   A Workflow That Stops in Mid-Track

Troubleshooting a workflow to find out why it has stopped is the trickiest part of workflow diagnostics, due in part to the fact that it can be difficult to reproduce the problem. For this reason, it is well worth investing effort in making a workflow robust from the outset rather than trying to track the errors down later.

Most problems are caused by hastily built background methods. Bear in mind that a background method that does not trap exceptions will terminate with an error message displayed on a virtual screen with no one there to view it. If the exception is not trapped, all clues simply evaporate into space and not even Sherlock Holmes can solve the mystery. However, if the exception is trapped via an exception defined in the method definition, this is logged in the workflow log when the exception occurs and you can see at a glance where the trouble lies.

When you select the PROBLEM: WORKFLOW IS HANGING suggestion in the diagnosis transaction, the first suggestion that you are presented with is the option to see the list of workflows running (DETERMINE INSTANCES FOR TASK) so that you can inspect the workflow's technical log. Make sure you have selected the technical view. The error messages are marked clearly with red traffic lights to help you pick them out. Choosing the red light will bring up the error message. Usually the long text of the error message describes exactly what has gone wrong. Choosing the very first red light in a workflow brings up an analysis of the relevant errors. For simple problems, this is a great help, but for more complex problems, you need to take the analysis with a pinch of salt because it may have been oversimplified. As a rule of thumb, check the suggested analysis first, but as soon as you suspect that this is not the solution, do not dwell on it any longer; follow your own nose instead.

If the work item has stopped with an error, the parent workflow work item goes into the ERROR status, too, and a new message (WL394) is logged against the parent workflow's work item. This message simply tells you which step caused the fatal error. Having located this step (usually the last step executed) you should put all your attention into investigating the error logged against this delinquent work item.

There are four types of error messages:

- ▶ Workflow system errors (Message ID WL).

- ▶ Errors that occur in business objects when expression evaluation fails, such as during a binding (Message ID OL).

- ▶ Errors that occur during agent determination (Message ID 5W).

- ▶ Exceptions from the business object methods called within the tasks. (Message IDs other than these usually come from the application your method is calling.)

It is sometimes a little tricky distinguishing knock-on errors from those that clearly point to the root of the problem. The best method is to view the technical display of the work item itself. You can view the actual error message that caused the work item to abort by clicking DISPLAYED to the right of the work item's status. In normal circumstances (no error), the button is not displayed at all or displays a temporary error message such as *Cancelled by user*. However, an erroneous work item shows the exception generated within the method, such as *Invoice locked*, *Master record does not exist* or *No authorization to perform this task*. It is now child's play to solve the problem.

Of course, if no exception has been defined in the method, no message is logged, and you have to continue the search by trying to reproduce the problem. It is often simpler to change the method to capture exceptions and then rerun the failed scenario than try to guess what went wrong.

B.3   The Most Likely Causes (and How to Avoid Them)

This section covers common problems and how to avoid them.

B.3.1   Background Work Items Aborting in the Middle

Background work items that abort in the middle (without an exception) do not return a result to the workflow system so they remain in the status STARTED. There is a background job, SWWERRE, which periodically searches for such work items and switches them to ERROR status with the appropriate WL message in the error log. Because the error message does not tell you much, the best course of action here is to test the method directly and try to reproduce the error.

A common cause of background method failure is incorrect or insufficient data passed to the method. You can use the workflow trace to determine exactly which parameters are being passed to the method. Another common cause of background method failure is a method that unexpectedly requires dialog input to continue. It can also occur when the preferences (e.g., for date and decimal format) of WF-BATCH are different from what the user used to create and test the background method. Usually, you need to correct the method's code to make it more robust.

Methods can be tested using Transaction SWO1, the Business Object Builder. This allows you to vary the parameters being passed to the method. One thing that you cannot test with this is whether the workflow agent or workflow batch user (WF-BATCH) has enough authorization to execute the method. This can only be checked before going live using real agents, or test agents having strict production security. If you have SAP ERP HCM implemented in your SAP component, watch out for HR structural authorizations to workflow here because these are often forgotten.

The diagnosis transaction also checks for short dumps under the WF-BATCH user caused by errant background methods. If it finds any, you will usually have to correct the method's program code to correct the problem.

B.3.2 Business Object Does Not Exist

When the workflow tries to execute a method or evaluate an obligatory expression based on an object that does not exist, you will see an OL826 message in the log. The most probable cause is one of the following:

- The binding is incorrect in the workflow definition.
- The object does not yet exist in the database.

The latter is the case when the workflow has been hastily modeled, and a race between the update task and the workflow system sporadically causes this effect (shown in Figure B.1). The read operation (marked with the number ❷ in diagram) occurs before the write operation (marked with the number ❶).

This problem is most likely to appear following a release change. The workflow system performance has improved in every new release, making the chances of the workflow system winning the race higher with each new release. The answer to the problem is to ensure that the workflow is in fact modeled correctly. Table B.1 shows the advantages and disadvantages of these methods. Any one of the three suggestions in Table B.1 can be followed, but they are listed in order of preference.

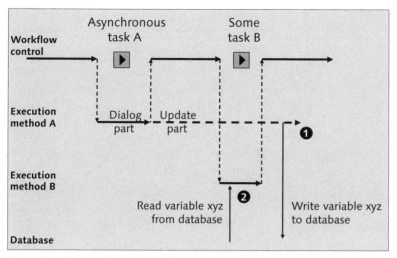

Figure B.1 Diagram Showing Update Task Race

Note

All of these approaches imply some additional performance cost, either in event creation, in background job execution, or in additional method execution, so it is up to you to ensure you use best practice options, such as event queues, to minimize system impact. Remember that the cost of business process failure is always higher than any performance cost. Read the sections on this in Chapter 10, Business Objects, Chapter 13, Using Events and Other Business Interfaces, and Chapter 14, Custom Programs, for how to set up asynchronous tasks and terminating events.

Method	Advantage	Disadvantage
Make the update task an asynchronous task so that it is completed by an event coming from the update task, which confirms that the data has been successfully committed to the database, for example, object CREATED or status CHANGED.	Workflow continues as soon as the data is ready. This solution always works.	Tricky for beginners to set up (but worth learning). You have to establish a suitable event creation mechanism if there is no standard event raised by the application.

Table B.1 Advantages and Disadvantages of Methods

Method	Advantage	Disadvantage
Complete the Execution condition in the workflow step. The workflow step is completed only after the condition object EXISTS is true.	Simple to set up. The solution always works.	The periodic evaluation of conditions means that the workflow will take several minutes before it continues with the next step. Create work item conditions for the next workflow step can be used instead.
Set a requested start deadline in the next step so that the workflow always waits, say five minutes, before the next step is started.	Simple to set up.	This is not a watertight solution. If the update task takes longer than five minutes or fails, then the next step will fail.

Table B.1 Advantages and Disadvantages of Methods (cont.)

B.3.3 Inconsistent Definition

The workflow runtime system determines the path to follow on the fly. This is an essential ingredient of the workflow system, allowing it to support ad-hoc workflow processing and versioning. If the system arrives at a point where it cannot determine the next step or where it expects to call a task that no longer exists, the workflow has no choice but to put the workflow work item into status ERROR with the error ID W8.

If this happens, first verify that the version on the workflow work item really is the latest active version. You can find the version by running the workflow list report (SWI1) with the ADDITIONAL DATA flag set so that the version of each workflow work item is displayed in a separate column, or you can examine the attributes of the workflow work item in the workflow container via the technical log. If the workflow is following the current version, then the most likely source of the problem is a corrupted or incompletely generated workflow runtime definition. This is occasionally caused by transport problems.

You can regenerate the workflow runtime version from the Workflow Builder in display mode or activate it again. The next time the workflow runs, it will follow the correct path.

B.3.4 Workflow Step Must Be Confirmed Manually

Occasionally in the production environment, new users may report that the work item does not disappear even when it has been executed. Check that the workflow step does not require manual confirmation. Users can chose to select CONFIRM END OF PROCESSING when defining a task for that step. If the workflow step does require manual confirmation, make sure that the agent is confirming after executing it.

B.3.5 Condition Set Up Incorrectly

If the workflow contains complex conditions, which appear to yield incorrect results, and the simulation of the condition in the condition editor fails to find the source of the problem, use the workflow trace to capture the results (and the analysis) of the conditions as the workflow executes.

B.4 Binding Problems with the Workflow Trace

The symptoms of binding problems are not easy to spot straight away. Usually, you are faced with another problem, such as the work item refusing to execute or the wrong agents receiving the work item. However, in such cases, you will often be confronted with the fact that data is not being passed through the workflow correctly. Either the data is being lost along the way, or the wrong data is being passed to the next step.

The cure is simply to correct the workflow definition so that the correct data is passed to the relevant step, but how do you locate the part of the workflow that is wrongly defined? There are two approaches: Either inspect the workflow definition checking every binding definition that has been made, or monitor each binding as it passes through the workflow instance. Even though the Workflow Builder offers a very useful cross-reference for container elements in the workflow definition, you will often find it simpler to monitor the data as it is passed through the workflow at runtime. This is because the bindings often use expressions, such as the attributes of an object (or the attributes of attributes), so it is not simply a question of which container element is used where. The Workflow Trace described in Section B.1.3, Check the RFC Queue to See if the Event Raising Has Aborted Midway, is the tool used to monitor the bindings.

Bear in mind that there is usually no binding between a task and a method (and vice versa) because this particular binding defaults to copying the task container straight to the method container (and vice versa). So you should concentrate on the WORKFLOW • TASK, and TASK • WORKFLOW BINDINGS when you are having problems with the execution of a workflow. If you are having problems with agent determination, then you need to start with the WORKFLOW • RULE BINDINGS and may need to extend your investigation to the other types of bindings after you have determined that the workflow container is incorrect at the time of the rule binding.

B.5   Why Duplicate or Multiple Workflows Are Triggered

If the workflow is being started twice, or more than one workflow is being started by the same event, the application configuration is probably incorrect. Bear in mind that some applications (e.g., Engineering Change) trigger the workflow directly from customizing tables and not from events. So if you have configured the workflow to be triggered by an event, too, the workflow is triggered once by your event and once again by the application directly! Check the online documentation of the application to determine how the workflow should be triggered.

To begin, look at the list of workflows started (Transaction SWI1). By examining the list of workflows started and checking the TASK ID column, you can see if the problem results from one workflow definition that is being triggered twice or two separate workflows.

Use the PROBLEM: TASK DOES NOT START suggestion of the diagnosis transaction to examine the event trace (are two events being triggered?) and to check the event simulation to determine whether or not two workflows are being configured to trigger from the same event. Possible causes are shown in Table B.2.

Cause	Solution
Two workflows are triggered by the same event.	Disable one of the event linkages.

Table B.2 Common Causes for Two Workflows Starting from an Event

Cause	Solution
Start conditions are used to determine which workflow should be triggered by a particular event, but the start conditions overlap.	Correct the start conditions.
One workflow is triggered by a subtype event, and the other workflow is triggered by the supertype event.	Use delegation so that just one event is raised, or disable one of the event linkages, or use start conditions (or a check function module) to decide which workflow should be started.
Workflow is triggered directly by a customizing table and also by an event.	Check the online documentation for this workflow, and, if necessary, disable the event linkage.

Table B.2 Common Causes for Two Workflows Starting from an Event (cont.)

B.6 Why an Agent Does Not Receive a Work Item

In a production system, the reason an agent does not receive a work item is likely to differ from that of a development system, but the administrator must be trained for all eventualities. While investigating why the user has not received the work item in his inbox, bear in mind the prerequisites for receiving a work item:

▶ The user has been assigned to the task as a possible agent (or it is a general task).

▶ The workflow step's agent determination technique (expression, rule resolution, etc.) has found this user, assuming an agent determination technique is defined.

▶ The default agent determination rule on the task level has found this user, assuming a default resolution is defined. The default agent determination rule is only called if no step agent determination rule has been defined or if the step agent determination rule fails to find a user.

▶ The agent is not on the list of excluded agents.

▶ The work item has not been reserved by anybody else and has not been forwarded to anybody else.

▶ The Organizational Management buffers are up-to-date with respect to this user; otherwise, the agent will be displayed as an actual agent but will not see the work item in his inbox.

▶ The user has sufficient security authorization to view and execute work items. Especially be careful of HR structural authorizations because they are often forgotten.

▶ The user is not locked in the system.

B.6.1 Check That the Agent Is Assigned to the Work Item

In the workflow log, view the list of actual agents, and make sure that the user's name is included in this list. To be doubly sure, switch to the user ID view (sometimes several users exist in the system with the same name but different user IDs).

If the agent is displayed, but the user does not see the work item in his inbox, then this user's buffered information is not up-to-date. In a production system, the user can refresh the buffer from the Business Workplace via the WORKFLOW SETTINGS menu, or the workflow administrator can refresh it for him by using Transaction SWU_OBUF. If the work item does not appear, he may need to log off and log on again, depending on the release of the SAP component.

In a development system, you can refresh the buffer for all users from the diagnosis transaction (PROBLEM: TASK DOES NOT START). Try to avoid this in the production system because it makes the inbox slower the first time a user calls it (subsequent calls are not affected).

B.6.2 Check That the Agent Is Assigned to the Task

In the technical workflow log, view the list of possible agents, and check that the agent's name is included in the list. You may need to expand the list to show the user view, rather than the view of Organizational Management objects. If the agent is not a possible agent, check that the task is a general task. If this is not the case, then the problem is that the agent has not been assigned to the task. The administrator needs to correct this.

B.6.3 Check That the Agent Has Not Been Excluded from This Work Item

This is not very likely, but it is very quick and easy to check. Look at the list of excluded agents for this work item (from the workflow log), and verify that this agent is not one of those excluded.

B.6.4 Check That the Agent Determination Rule Has Selected an Agent

Agent determination rule resolution is easy to check by calling the test facility in the agent determination rule definition tool. In a development system, you may want to use the workflow trace to make sure that the rule container is being filled with the correct data.

B.7 Why the Wrong Agent Receives the Work Item

When a user receives a work item that he should not have received, the tests that you need to perform are the same as when an agent fails to receive a work item (described previously). However, there is one important distinction: Because the agent has actually received something in the inbox, you can give him access to information about how to solve the problem himself or how to accelerate the procedure for getting it solved. This is important because the faster the problems are solved, the faster the workflow executes.

In other words, if the work item contains information on how the agent may have been chosen (e.g., "You have received this work item because you have been identified as the manager of cost center 9999") and the contact details for getting this corrected ("If you are not the manager of cost center 9999, please contact the help desk on extension 1111") in the long text of the work item, the agent can see at a glance if something has gone wrong. Further, a proactive environment for the user encourages him to understand the process rather than just react to it.

This improves when the agent has access to an FAQ list, which might even allow him to solve the problem himself. For example:

- **Buffers need refreshing**
  Can be solved by the agent.

- **Organizational Management not up to date**
  Must be solved by the administrator.

- **Security settings not up to date**
  Must be solved by the administrator.

B.8   Why the Work Item Follows the Wrong Route

That the work item follows the wrong route could be caused by an incorrect expression in a branch or the wrong workflow version being used, or the container element data evaluated in the branch being wrong. The solution is simple: Correct the workflow definition.

C   The Administrator's First Aid Guide

This appendix offers suggestions for repairing rare problems that may occur in the production system. Use the troubleshooting guide in Appendix B, Step-by-Step Troubleshooting Guide, to locate the cause.

C.1   Resolving Work Item Errors

Good workflow design and thorough testing of the workflow in a development environment can prevent most work item errors. These errors come in two broad categories:

▶ **Work items in Error status**
These work items are easy to find, and the messages in the work item display and workflow log are helpful when diagnosing the problem.

▶ **Work items that don't behave as expected**
These can be very difficult to track down, especially if the problem is not discovered until after the work item is completed. You cannot reactivate a completed work item, so you may need to fix the problem manually. If many work items have been affected, it may be worthwhile to create a program specifically to fix the problem. However, this is the worst case. If the work item is still active (e.g., in READY or STARTED status), you can usually resolve the problem readily.

Watch out for work items that take an unusually long time to complete because this can indicate an error situation. For instance, the delay may be caused by terminating events or escalation procedures (deadlines) that have failed, a background process that has started but not completed correctly, or the lack of an assigned agent. Of course, it could also be that the assigned agent has simply been slow to act. Common problems with work items include the following:

▶ **Work item in Error status with the message object does not exist**
This could be the result of binding problems (i.e., object was not passed correctly), sequencing problems (i.e., the object did not exist when the work item was first created/executed), or inadequate process design (e.g., the workflow did not take into account the fact that the object may occasionally be deleted manually).

▶ **Work item in Error status with the message mail could not be sent**
This is usually due to missing configuration information. It could be that the office settings do not allow for mails to be sent to the given mail type (e.g., HR objects). Or, if you are sending mails externally via a mail server, there could be a problem in the configuration between the SAP NetWeaver Application Server and the mail server. This can be a considerable nuisance because if the workflow runs frequently, a lot of workflows will be stopping with this error. If most emails are working, and just a particular instance of a workflow is not working, the problem may be simply a binding error.

▶ **Work item in Error status with an application message, that is, the underlying object method has failed**
This type of error occurs when the object method executes the underlying applications and routines. There are many possible causes for this such as changes in configuration, changes in the data used, underlying transactions executed in an unexpected way, or changes in user exits or BAdIs. Usually the problem is not the workflow itself, but you still need to coordinate problem resolution and restart the workflow after the error has been fixed.

▶ **A dialog work item that never completes because a terminating event did not occur**
This may be due to an agent who has not completed the work correctly; that is, because the work has not been done, the terminating event is not raised. It may also be an event linkage problem.

▶ **Background work items that start but never complete**
If the background work item is waiting on a terminating event, this could be an event linkage problem. The background work item may have failed because of a severe error in the underlying method. It is worthwhile checking for matching ABAP short dumps to see if this is the case. Fix the problem, and re-execute.

If the background work item is trying to execute a dialog step, execute the failed routine from the transactional RFC monitor and process the dialog step.

Most other problems can be resolved by using the option to re-execute the background item. However, if that fails, another option is to do the work manually, and then manually complete the background work item. Table C.1 shows common problems with work items and how to resolve them.

Problem	Repair
Work item deadline has not been escalated even though the deadline has expired.	▶ This may simply be a timing issue. Remember that deadlines are not escalated immediately when the deadline time is exceeded but only when the next deadline job runs. This means the timing of the deadline job is dependent on whether the deadline job is scheduled on a case-specific or periodic basis and the efficiency of the background queue.
	▶ If the deadline-monitoring job (background job SWWDHEX) has already been scheduled and released but is being held up, you may need to discuss this with the system administrators. For instance, you may need to increase the job priority, or more background queues may need to be added to cope with the background job load.
	▶ If you find that there are too many deadline-monitoring jobs (background job SWWDHEX) in the background queue, and they are blocking each other, you may need to reassess the scheduling of this job. In particular, if the job is being scheduled on a case-specific basis, you may need to switch to periodic monitoring. Because every deadline job assesses all exceeded deadlines on all work items being monitored, you can cancel the unnecessary deadline jobs to allow the currently active job to complete.
	▶ If the deadline job has not been scheduled at all, it is usually sufficient to restart the deadline-monitoring job (background job SWWDHEX) using workflow customizing (Transaction SWU3). However, you should be aware of any workflows that are awaiting a deadline. After you execute the SWWDHEX, they will all stop waiting, and this can have unintended consequences.

Table C.1 Common Problems with Work Items and How to Resolve Them

Problem	Repair
Work item has completed successfully even though an error occurred; that is, the object method did not report the error. These cases can be extremely difficult to diagnose, in part because it can be some time before anyone realizes that an apparently successful workflow process has failed to achieve the business result. If the data used is temporary and is deleted at the end of the workflow, this can be a real problem.	▶ If the workflow is still in progress, you may be able to manually correct the data, then change the containers of any failed work items, and restart the failed workflows. ▶ If the workflow has finished, you may be able to manually correct the data. If it was some time before the problem was detected, you may need a developer to write a program to fix the data en masse.

Table C.1 Common Problems with Work Items and How to Resolve Them (cont.)

C.1.1 Preventing Work Item Problems from Reoccurring

After you are confident the immediate problem is solved, you need to ensure that it does not reappear. This may mean:

▶ Initiating changes to the workflow design (e.g., to cope with the object being manually deleted while the workflow is still running) to fix binding errors, or to better handle common application errors.

▶ Improving quality assurance checklists to catch more problems. For example, check that every workflow design considers the impact of non-workflow activity on the workflow.

▶ Making sure that all workflows using temporary objects or deleting objects as part of the workflow include enough information in work item texts or container elements to give you a starting point for fixing problems after the workflow has completed. It can even be worthwhile putting redundant container elements in the workflow to hold this extra information.

▶ Re-examining the deadline job to see if it should have a higher job priority or be switched from case-specific to periodic monitoring.

C.1.2   Support Tools for Work Item Problems

In this section, we provide more reports and functions that you may find useful in dealing with work item errors.

Diagnosis of Workflows with Errors

ADMINISTRATION • WORKFLOW RUNTIME • DIAGNOSIS OF WORKFLOWS WITH ERRORS (Transaction SWI2_DIAG)

This function displays all workflows with errors and groups them according to error cause (agent, deadlines, binding, or other). This report helps you to assess whether particular types of errors are reoccurring across many workflows, or whether the problem is specific to just a particular work item. You can also fix and restart the workflow from this report.

> **Tip**
>
> The system determines the highest-level work items with errors; that is, if a work item is in ERROR status, the work item shown will belong to the highest workflow in error hierarchically above it.

Workflow Restart After Error

ADMINISTRATION • WORKFLOW RUNTIME • WORKFLOW RESTART AFTER ERROR (Transaction SWPR)

This report can be used to display a list of workflows with errors for a particular selection period, and then restart them. The benefit of this report is that it allows you to perform a mass restart of workflows.

Deadline Monitoring for Work Items

ADMINISTRATION • WORKFLOW RUNTIME • WORK ITEM DEADLINE MONITORING (Transaction SWI2_DEAD)

Tasks with deadlines also have deadline monitoring based on a background job. You can change the period duration of the background job, schedule it, display it, or execute it manually.

Work Item Rule Monitoring

ADMINISTRATION • WORKFLOW RUNTIME • WORK ITEM RULE MONITORING (Transaction RSWWCOND)

If conditions are defined for the work item start or work item end for steps in the workflow, these conditions must be regularly checked. This task is performed by a report that is controlled by a background job (SWWCOND). You can schedule or display the background job. You can also start the report manually using EXECUTE WORK ITEM RULE MONITORING.

C.2 Resolving Workflow Instance Errors

Usually errors in workflows are simply due to errors in work items. To resolve these, you usually fix the work items, and then restart the workflow (see the previous Section C.1, Resolving Work Item Errors, for more details).

> **Note**
>
> Make sure you distinguish workflow instance errors from work item errors. When a work item is in ERROR status, the system also puts the workflow instance into ERROR status, but the cause of the error is at the work item level. You know you have a *workflow instance error* when only the workflow instance is in error, and the underlying work items are okay.

There are a few problems that are specific to the workflow itself:

▶ Wrong version is active.

▶ No workflow definition is active.

▶ Workflow failed due to binding errors.

▶ Workflow appears to be successful but the work has not been done.

The majority of workflow instance errors are preventable if new and changed workflows are adequately designed and thoroughly tested prior to being moved to a production environment.

C.2.1 Fixing Workflow Instances in Error

Diagnosing why a workflow instance has failed is a topic in itself. Use the troubleshooting guide in Appendix B, Step-by-Step Troubleshooting Guide, to locate the cause. Knowing the cause will help you solve the problem. Table C.2 shows common workflow errors and how to repair them.

Cause	Repair
Wrong version of workflow is active.	▶ Verify that the production environment contains the correct version of the workflow definition. It may be that the workflow was not transported correctly or at all, or only part of the workflow was transported. ▶ If necessary, manually activate the correct workflow definition. In either case, all current workflows will be using the old version. You need to decide with the business process owner whether that is okay, or whether you should stop those workflows and trigger new versions of the workflows, for example, via GENERATE EVENT (Transaction SWUE). Obviously, this depends on what the difference is between the versions and how far the workflow has progressed. If the workflow is still in the initial stages, it is usually easier to stop and retrigger it, but if agents have already taken several actions, it may not be practical to stop the existing workflow.
Workflow has failed due to binding errors.	Because the workflow instance has its own work item (type F), you can change the workflow container via the work item technical display. Then restart the workflow.

Table C.2 Common Workflow Errors and How to Resolve Them

C.2.2 Preventing Workflow Instance Problems from Reoccurring

After you are confident the immediate problem is solved, you need to ensure that this does not happen again. This may mean:

▶ Ensuring transport logs are checked carefully after transporting workflows, and after transport, ensuring the version, activation of the workflow definition, event linkage activation and start conditions are checked.

► Improving quality assurance checklists, for example, to make sure the workflow has been thoroughly tested.

C.2.3 Support Tools for Workflow Instance Errors

In addition to the support tools listed in Section C.1.2, Support Tools for Work Item Problems, the following transactions are also useful.

Continue Workflow After System Crash

ADMINISTRATION • WORKFLOW RUNTIME • CONTINUE WORKFLOW AFTER SYSTEMCRASH (Transaction SWPC)

You can use this report to select and continue workflows that have had the status STARTED for longer than a day. This means that workflows that have come to a halt after system errors can be continued.

Workflow Restart After Error

ADMINISTRATION • WORKFLOW RUNTIME • WORKFLOW RESTART AFTER ERROR (Transaction SWPR)

You can use this report to select and continue workflows that have been in ERROR status, when you know that the root cause (i.e., bad data) has been corrected.

Restart Suspended Workflow Callbacks

ADMINISTRATION • WORKFLOW RUNTIME • RESTART SUSPENDED WORKFLOW CALLBACKS (Transaction SWF_ADM_SUSPEND)

This job can be run when you have evidence of workflows that were suspended (perhaps due to an incorrectly modeled queue). Entries that are suspended are in Table SWP_SUSPEN. This report repairs the suspended workflow callbacks. This condition can also be identified by messages.

Restart Suspended Workflow Callbacks

ADMINISTRATION • WORKFLOW RUNTIME • RESTART SUSPENDED WORKFLOW CALLBACKS (Transaction SWF_ADM_SWWWIDH)

This transaction displays the suspended deadline actions, that is, all SWWWIDH entries with the value 02 in component STATUS. Use the function EDIT • REACTIVATE to restart the deadline action. This function ensures that selected entries are processed during the next run of the batch job.

C.3   Finding Workflows That Appear to Have Disappeared

Finding workflows that appear to have disappeared is a common complaint soon after a workflow goes live, but it becomes less and less frequent as the users become familiar with the Workflow Engine.

C.3.1   Cause

The complaint arises when a user expects to receive a work item but does not. In nearly all cases, this is simply because the agent has not been assigned to the task, or another user who is also assigned to the task has processed it instead.

From the user's point of view, if one agent processes his work item so that it disappears from his inbox, but the next work item does not appear in the next user's inbox, he will claim that the "workflow has disappeared."

C.3.2   Repair

As an administrator, after the problem is reported to you, you can sort this out easily by checking the workflow log and work item display, but it is more efficient to have a description of what users should do (e.g., how to report the problem, how to find out where the workflow went) in the intranet support site. Bear in mind that the agents may not be familiar with workflow technology, so your FAQ section should include a section along the lines "What to do if the workflow disappears!"

Useful pointers for self-help are descriptions of how to locate the workflow (e.g., the outbox of the first agent or Generic Object Services [GOS] for the object) and how to establish who has received the work item by checking the workflow log.

C.4   Resolving Event Linkage Errors

Event linkage problems prevent workflows from being started or work items from being completed (assuming the work item is waiting on a terminating event). Be careful not to confuse event linkage errors with workflow instance errors where the workflow has started but has hung because these problems have very different solutions. The majority of event linkage errors are preventable if new and changed event linkages are thoroughly tested prior to being moved to a production environment.

In production environments, the most common problems are:

▶ The application that is supposed to raise the event has failed to do so because the workflow environment configuration or the application configuration is missing or incorrect.

▶ The event linkage has not been activated. Do not forget that events need to be "switched on."

▶ The event object does not satisfy the start conditions (if used), or the start condition is incorrect.

▶ The object instance does not satisfy the check function modules (if used).

▶ The event linkage binding contains errors.

You can counteract most of these problems by raising the event again manually, for example, by using Transaction SWUE (Generate Event). However, you need to be careful that you raise the event with all of the necessary data, including a designated workflow initiator.

Another related problem might be delays in event processing. This can result from impaired system performance or can be deliberate if the events have been placed in an event queue. Event queues are an advanced technique used to spread the workload of raising events over time. Check with the developer if you suspect an event queue has been used. Note that via the event linkage configuration (Transaction SWE2) and the event queue configuration (Transaction SWEQADM), you can also opt to send failed events to an event queue, rather than have the system deactivate the event linkage (refer to Chapter 13, Using Events and Other Business Interfaces). You can then redeliver the event (with all of the original data used during event creation) via the event queue.

> **Tip**
>
> Don't forget that if you have set up workflow error monitoring, event linkages that fail due to binding problems or are automatically deactivated by the system are reported to you (as the workflow administrator) via your inbox. You should make sure that you check your inbox regularly.

After the immediate problem has been solved, don't forget to make sure the problem doesn't happen again.

C.4.1 Fixing Workflows That Didn't Start

Table C.3 shows common causes for workflows that do not start and how to repair them.

Cause	Repair
Event was not raised at all.	▶ If nothing is found on the event log or in the transactional RFC monitor, check that workflow customizing has been done for the current client, and the workflow logical destination is working. If necessary, complete the workflow customizing, or change the workflow logical destination, and then use GENERATE EVENT to raise the event manually.
	▶ If the configuration for raising the event is not correct, complete the configuration. Then use GENERATE EVENT to raise the event manually.
	When you use GENERATE EVENT (Transaction SWUE) to raise the event manually, be careful to fill in all necessary data. Take care when doing this because the person raising the event will then be the event initiator. This variable may be referred to later in the workflow (e.g., to determine agents). If necessary, you may need to ask the real initiator to log on and generate the event using his user ID.
Event linkage was deactivated.	▶ The linkage can be reactivated using the SIMULATE EVENT function (Transaction SWU0). However, if the event has a start condition, the linkage should be reactivated from the START CONDITION function (Transaction SWB_COND).

Table C.3 Common Reasons for a Workflow to Not Start

Cause	Repair
Event linkage was deactivated. (Cont.)	▶ Then, if you can, raise the event again using the application. ▶ If this is not possible, use GENERATE EVENT (Transaction SWUE) to raise the event again manually, being careful to fill in all necessary data.
A start condition disqualified the event linkage.	▶ If the logical expression is incorrect, use the START CONDITION function (Transaction SWB_COND) to correct it. ▶ Then, if you can, raise the event again using the application. ▶ If this is not possible, use GENERATE EVENT (Transaction SWUE) to raise the event again manually, being careful to fill in all necessary data.
A check function module disqualified the event linkage.	Check and, if necessary, correct the underlying event data. Then use GENERATE EVENT (Transaction SWUE) to raise the event again manually, being careful to fill in all necessary data.
The event linkage failed due to binding errors.	▶ If the event binding is incorrect, and it is a triggering event for a workflow, do not use GENERATE EVENT to trigger a missing workflow. Instead, use TEST WORKFLOW (Transaction SWUS) to manually start the workflow, being careful to fill in all necessary data, including the workflow initiator. ▶ If the event binding is incorrect, and it is a terminating event, you may be able to use the work item display to fill the container with the correct return values, and manually complete the work item. However, this particular problem is rare for terminating events.

Table C.3 Common Reasons for a Workflow to Not Start (cont.)

Tip
When dealing with event-related issues, always take care when generating the event because the person raising the event will then be made the event initiator, which may be used later in the workflow, for example, to determine agents. If necessary, you may need to ask the real initiator to log on and raise the event using his user ID.

C.4.2 Preventing Error Linkage Problems from Reoccurring

After you are confident the immediate problem is solved, you need to ensure that this does not happen again. This may require you to ensure that:

▶ Binding problems, or failed check function modules, are fixed by the workflow developers, and quality assurance checklists are improved for new and changed workflows.

▶ Any failures in the transactional RFC (tRFC) monitor are resolved in the system. These may be due to configuration changes in the application or changes to the event linkage configuration.

▶ All event-raising configuration has been done prior to the workflow being started.

▶ Transport logs are checked carefully for workflows, and after transport, the version, activation of the workflow definition version, event linkage activation, and start conditions are correct.

C.4.3 Support Tools for Event Linkage Problems

ADMINISTRATION • WORKFLOW RUNTIME • WORKFLOW RFC MONITOR (Transaction SWU2)

You can use this function to display the log file of the tRFC. The log entries are displayed with the target system (logical destination) `WORKFLOW_LOCAL_<client>`. Use this report to follow up errors that have occurred in connection with the feedback from work items to the workflow runtime system after their execution.

D   Workflow Macros

Whenever workflow programming is involved, workflow macros are required to define and access object references, attributes, methods, and containers. There are a few macros specific to object type programming, but most macros are available for all workflow programs whether object type programs, agent determination rules, check function modules, receiver type function modules, or custom programs for monitoring and reporting on workflows.

D.1   Macros Specific to Object Type Programs

All the macros needed for general workflow programming are defined in the include program <OBJECT> (note the <> brackets are part of the name). This is automatically included in the object type program using the statement.

▶ INCLUDE <OBJECT>.

The following macros are specific to the object type program.

   ▶ BEGIN_DATA Object.
   Start of the object declaration.

   ▶ END_DATA.
   End of the object declaration.

   ▶ GET_PROPERTY <Attribute> CHANGING CONTAINER.
   Start of a virtual attribute implementation.

   ▶ GET_TABLE_PROPERTY <TableName>.
   Start of a database attribute implementation.

   ▶ END_PROPERTY.
   End of an attribute implementation.

   ▶ BEGIN_METHOD <Method> CHANGING CONTANER.
   Start of a method implementation.

   ▶ END_METHOD.
   End of a method implementation.

▶ SWC_SET_OBJECTKEY <ObjectKey>.

Sets the object key of the current object. Usually only instance-independent methods use this to return a reference to an object instance of the current object.

The following macros are used for method exceptions:

▶ EXIT_OBJECT_NOT_FOUND
Tells workflow that an object does not exist.

▶ EXIT_CANCELLED
Tells workflow that the user canceled execution of a method.

▶ EXIT_RETURN <Exception> <MessageVariable1> <MessageVariable2>
<MessageVariable3> <MessageVariable4>
Tells workflow that an error has occurred.

▶ EXIT_NOT_IMPLEMENTED
Tells workflow that a method is not implemented.

▶ EXIT_PARAMETER_NOT_FOUND
Tells workflow that a mandatory parameter of a method is missing.

D.2 Macros for General Workflow Programming

All of the macros needed for general workflow programming are defined in the include program <CNTN01> (note the <> brackets are part of the name). Apart from the object type program, which already includes this program as part of the include program <OBJECT>, you must add the include program to your own workflow program using the following statement:

INCLUDE <CNTN01>.

D.2.1 Macros to Process a Container as a Whole

These are the macros used to process a whole container:

▶ SWC_CONTAINER <Container>.
Declares a container.

▶ SWC_CREATE_CONTAINER <Container>.
Initializes a container. The macros SWC_RELEASE_CONTAINER and SWC_CLEAR_CONTAINER have the same functions.

D.2.2   Runtime Versus Persistent Containers

A runtime container only exists within the environment of the current program, for example, the object container. A persistent container can be passed to another program, for example, if you want to change the event container within a check function module or receiver type function module, or you want to pass the container to a function module such as a WAPI (refer to Chapter 14, Custom Programs) or `SWE_EVENT_CREATE`:

▶ `SWC_CONTAINER_TO_PERSISTENT <Container>.`
Makes a runtime container persistent.

▶ `SWC_CONTAINER_TO_RUNTIME <Container>.`
Makes a persistent container runtime.

D.2.3   Macros to Process Elements from the Container

These are the macros used to process elements from a container:

▶ `SWC_GET_ELEMENT <Container> <ContainerElement> <Variable>.`
Reads single value element from the container into a variable.

▶ `SWC_SET_ELEMENT <Container> <ContainerElement> <Variable>.`
Writes single value element from a variable to the container.

▶ `SWC_SET_TABLE <Container> <ContainerElement> <InternalTable>.`
Reads multiline element from the container into an internal table.

▶ `SWC_GET_TABLE <Container> <ContainerElement> <InternalTable>.`
Writes multiline element from an internal table to the container.

▶ `SWC_COPY_ELEMENT <SourceContainer> <SourceContainerElement> <TargetContainer> <TargetContainerElement>.`
Copies a container element from a source container to a target container.

▶ `SWC_DELETE_ELEMENT <Container> <ContainerElement>.`
Deletes a container element.

D.2.4   Macros for Processing Object References

These macros are used to process object references:

▶ `SWC_CREATE_OBJECT <Object> <ObjectType> <ObjectKey>.`
Creates an object reference from an object type and object key.

▶ SWC_REFRESH_OBJECT <Object>.
Invalidates the object reference buffer so that all attributes will be recalculated when they are next called.

▶ SWC_GET_OBJECT_KEY <Object> <ObjectKey>.
Returns the object key of an object reference; used in generic object programming.

▶ SWC_GET_OBJECT_TYPE <Object> <ObjectType>.
Returns the object type of an object reference; used in a generic object programming.

▶ SWC_OBJECT_FROM_PERSISTENT <Variable> <Object>.
Converts a persistent object reference to a runtime reference.

D.2.5 Macros for Retrieving Object Attributes

These macros enable you to get attribute values from objects:

▶ SWC_GET_PROPERTY <Object> <Attribute> <Variable>.
Retrieves a single value attribute of an object into a variable.

▶ SWC_GET_TABLE_PROPERTY <Object> <Attribute> <InternalVariable>.
Retrieves a multiline attribute of an object into an internal table.

D.2.6 Macros for Calling Object Methods

These macros are used to call methods of an object:

▶ SWC_CALL_METHOD <Object> <Method> <Container>.
Calls the method of an object. All parameters are passed to/from the method as contents of the container.

E   Preparation for Java Development

This chapter shows the required configuration that must be done before using the SAP NetWeaver Developer Studio (NWDS) on your local SAP NetWeaver Application Server (J2EE server) to create Web Dynpro applications. Web Dynpro Java development might be quite challenging in the beginning if you are new to this area. Specially, Web Dynpro Java development requires several system setups and configurations in the Java EE 5 side. Typically, you may want to install the J2EE engine in your own desktop so that you can deploy Web Dynpro Java to your local J2EE engine to perform unit testing. Testing would be very difficult without your local J2EE. After you finish your unit testing within your local J2EE, you can transport it to a central server for integration testing.

Several other prerequisites are involved: The JCo destination must be configured in the J2EE runtime system so that Web Dynpro Java can find out the target ABAP backend during runtime to use the adaptive RFC model.

> **Note**
>
> Because Web Dynpro is based on the MVC paradigm, the business logic is separate from the presentation logic. The business logic is handled by Web Dynpro models. One of the Web Dynpro models is the Adaptive RFC model. This RFC model is supposed to call RFC-enabled function modules, so Web Dynpro Java must know the target ABAP backend. The JCo destination points the target ABAP system to run the RFC-enabled function modules.

When you develop a Web Dynpro Java application, you are required to enter the JCo destination name. Two JCo destinations are needed:

- One for dictionary meta data
- The other for application data

JCo destination must be configured for each J2EE runtime system. The names of the JCo destination must be identical to the ones entered into Web Dynpro application. However, the corresponding physical ABAP backend is different, depending on whether the ABAP application was in a development or production environment. For example, let's say that you created a JCo destination named ECC_META, and you developed a Web Dynpro Java application using this JCo destination. When you run the Web Dynpro Java application in the development landscape, the ECC_META destination points to the development ABAP backend. However, when you run it in the production landscape, the ECC_META destination should point to the production ABAP backend.

Figure E.1 shows the JCo destination setup. This menu is available from the Web Dynpro Content Administrator screen. You can call the Web Dynpro Content Administrator screen by selecting CONTENT ADMINISTRATOR on the welcome page of the J2EE Engine (*http://<Host Name>:<Port Number>/webdynpro/welcome*).

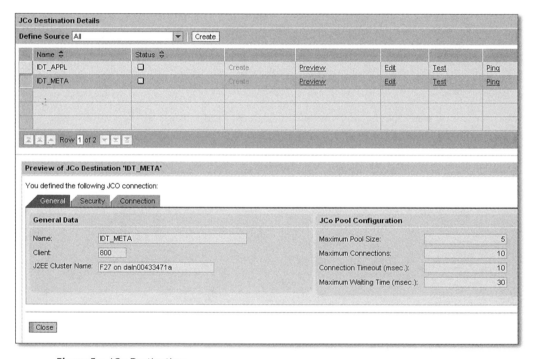

Figure E.1 JCo Destination

The System Landscape Directory (SLD) server is also required:

▶ The JCo destination setup requires the SLD up and running as a prerequisite. SLD manages all of the relevant information about software products and components. SLD also has information on all of the technical systems, including

Java and ABAP systems, in your system landscape. Therefore, the connection to SLD is required to set up the JCo destination.

▶ The SLD is also required if you use the SAP NetWeaver Development Infrastructure (NWDI) for Web Dynpro Java development. SLD is a starting point for the NWDI installation and configuration.

Figure E.2 shows the screen of the SLD server. In your system, to enter the SLD, use the URL *http://<host>:<port>/sld*.

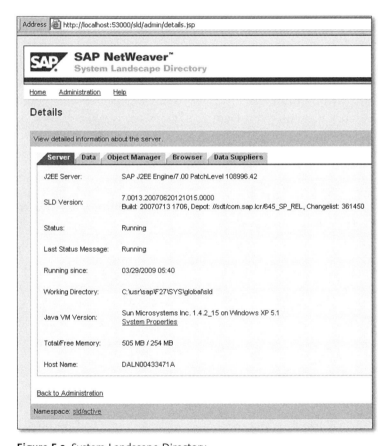

Figure E.2 System Landscape Directory

You need to consider NWDI because enterprise-level Java development should be development component (DC) development. DC was introduced mainly from SAP NetWeaver 6.40, and it is now considered standard for development of any Java-related SAP product. For example, SAP CRM Internet Sales is DC-based from version 5.0. Employee Self-Service (ESS) and Manager Self-Service (MSS) are also DC based.

Mainly a DC can be considered as a reusable unit. A DC can be reused and can be linked to and called by other DCs, which will build a software component (SC). This is represented as a *component model*. To develop a Java application as a DC-based Java application, the NWDI is mandatory. Mainly the NWDI takes care of three things:

▶ The source code control (with the Design Time Repository)

▶ The central build (with the Central Build Service)

▶ The transport management (with the Change Management Service)

In this appendix, however, we will develop a Web Dynpro Java application as the local object, (not DC based) because the DC is beyond the scope of this book. However, if you are working with Web Dynpro Java in real projects, keep in mind that it is highly recommended to develop it as DC based.

Table E.1 shows a typical cycle of DC-based development.

Job	Performed By	Description
1. SLD installation/configuration	Admin	Install/configure SLD
2. NWDI installation	Admin	NWDI installation
3. Create JCo destination on each J2EE runtime	Admin	JCo destination to connect from J2EE runtime to ABAP backend
4. Setup of Java Development Environment – local	Developer	Local NWDS installation/ configuration with J2EE and SLD information
5. (If custom SC) custom product and software component creation in SLD	Admin	Custom software component to be used by NWDI
6. Track creation and configuration	Admin	NWDI main configuration
7. Download DC from track to local NWDS	Developer	Track download to local NWDS
8. Develop or enhancement	Developer	J2EE, Web Dynpro development

Table E.1 Typical Cycle of DC-Based Development

Job	Performed By	Description
9. Check in, activate, and release via NWDS	Developer	Check in after successful unit testing
10. Assembly, transport to production	Admin	Transport via CMS
11. Preparation for new release development after go-live	For new development after Go-Live	

Table E.1 Typical Cycle of DC-Based Development (cont.)

Regardless of whether it is the development with NWDI or not, individual developers must install the SAP NetWeaver Developer Studio (NWDS) on their local client. NWDS is the SAP development environment based on the Eclipse platform. It is a robust platform for developing and running large-scale enterprise applications based on both standard (Java EE 5, J2EE, J2SE) and SAP-proprietary (e.g., Web Dynpro) Java models.

NWDS should know which J2EE server the Java development should be deployed to. Figure E.3 shows how to point the J2EE from NWDS. This menu can be accessed from NWDS via WINDOW • PREFERENCES • SAP J2EE ENGINE.

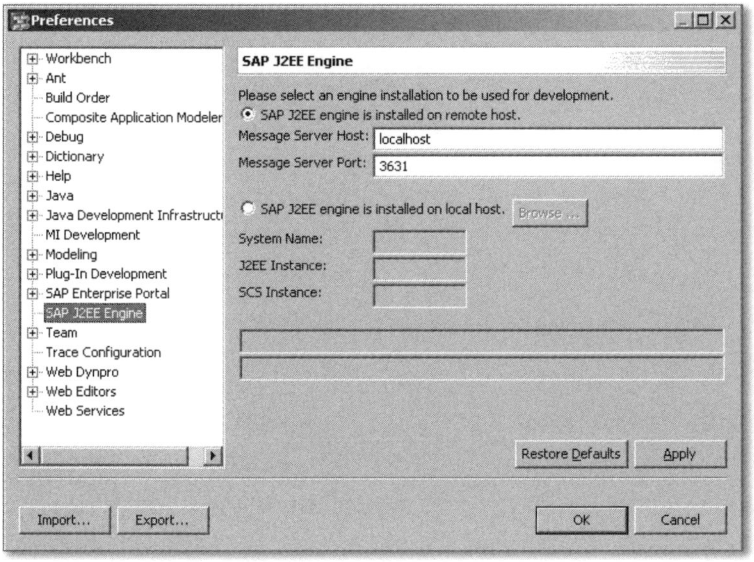

Figure E.3 NWDS Pointing Target J2EE for Deployment

After the J2EE is registered in NWDS, its running status is shows in the view of J2EE ENGINE. This menu is available from NWDS via WINDOW • SHOW VIEW • J2EE ENGINE. Figure E.4 shows the running status of the J2EE engine. Green means that the J2EE is up and running. If you see this screen, then you are ready to start Web Dynpro Java development.

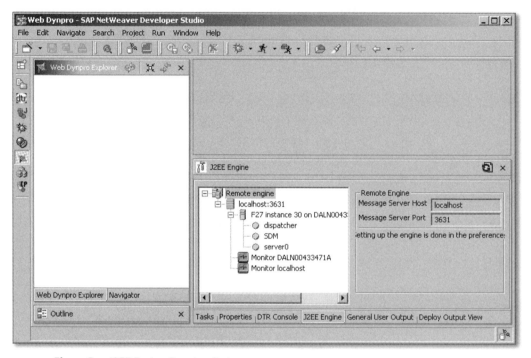

Figure E.4 J2EE Engine Running Status

F   Additional Information for SAP SRM

This appendix has additional information for SAP SRM, including Business Configuration Sets (BC Sets), Business Add-Ins (BAdIs), and troubleshooting tips.

F.1   Available Business Configuration Sets

Business Configuration Sets (BC Sets) that configure processes without approval use the naming convention /SAPSRM/C_<BO>_600_000_SP04:

- The /SAPSRM/ is the used namespace for SAP SRM.
- Letter C is used to point out that this BC Set is intended for customer usage.
- <BO> is the placeholder for the business object type.
- The next number specifies the SAP SRM Release when the BC Set was created.
- The next one is 000 in case of zero step approval and 001 in case of one step approval.
- The next letters specify the Support Package when the BC Set was created.

Table F.1 shows the BC Sets currently available.

Business Object	BC Set	Process Schema	Description
Shopping cart	/SAPSRM/ C_SC_600_000_SP04	9C_SC_600_000_SP04	Without approval
	/SAPSRM/ C_SC_600_001_SP04	9C_SC_600_001_SP04	One-step manager approval
Purchase order	SAPSRM/ C_PO_600_000_SP04	9C_PO_600_000_SP04	Without approval
	/SAPSRM/ C_PO_600_001_SP04	9C_PO_600_001_SP04	One-step manager approval

Table F.1 Available BC Sets for Business Objects

Business Object	BC Set	Process Schema	Description
Confirmation	/SAPSRM/ C_CO_600_000_SP04	9C_CO_600_000_SP04	Without approval
	/SAPSRM/ C_CO_600_001_SP04	9C_CO_600_001_SP04	One-step manager approval
Invoice	/SAPSRM/ C_IN_600_000_SP04	9C_IN_600_000_SP04	Without approval
	/SAPSRM/ C_IN_600_001_SP04	9C_IN_600_001_SP04	One-step manager approval
Contract	/SAPSRM/ C_CT_600_000_SP04	9C_CT_600_000_SP04	Without approval
	/SAPSRM/ C_CT_600_001_SP04	9C_CT_600_001_SP04	One-step manager approval
Quote	/SAPSRM/ C_QT_600_000_SP04	9C_QT_600_000_SP04	Without approval
	/SAPSRM/ C_QT_600_001_SP04	9C_QT_600_001_SP04	One-step manager approval
RFx	/SAPSRM/ C_RQ_600_000_SP04	9C_RQ_600_000_SP04	Without approval
	/SAPSRM/ C_RQ_600_001_SP04	9C_RQ_600_001_SP04	One-step manager approval

Table F.1 Available BC Sets for Business Objects (cont.)

F.2 BAdI Implementations for Agent Determination

A basic set of agent determination functionality is delivered as BAdI implementations for the BAdI definition /SAPSRM/BD_WF_RESP_RESOLVER. This enables a high flexibility because the customer can easily implement and use its own specific agent determination. Depending on the business object, the basic agent determination strategies shown in Table F.2 are delivered.

Business Object	Filter Values	BAdI Implementation		Description
	Document Type	Responsibility Resolver Name		
Shopping Cart	BUS2121	RR_EMPLOYEE	/SAPSRM/ BD_WF_SC_RR_ EMPLOYEE	Returns an employee (business partner) as responsible agent for shopping cart approval in the relevant process level. The document is not split into decision sets; that is, all items are assigned to the same agent.
	BUS2121	RR_MANAGER	/SAPSRM/ BD_WF_SC_RR_ MANAGER	Returns all managers of the shopping cart's requester of the previous level as responsible agents for shopping cart approval in the relevant process level. The document is not split into decision sets; that is, all items are assigned to the same agents.
	BUS2121	RR_MANAGER_ OF_MANAGER	/SAPSRM/ BD_WF_SC_RR_ MANOFMA	Returns all managers of approvers of the previous level as responsible agents for shopping cart approval in the relevant process level. The method assigns all items of a decision set to the same area, thus respecting the existing decision sets for the document.
	BUS2121	RR_ PURCHASING_ GROUP	/SAPSRM/ BD_WF_SC_RR_ PGRP	Returns all purchasers of an item's purchasing group as responsible agents for shopping cart approval in the relevant process level. The document is split into decision sets according to the assigned purchasing group.

Table F.2 BAdIs for Agent Determination

Business Object	Filter Values	BAdI Implementation		Description
	Document Type	Responsibility Resolver Name		
	BUS2121	RR_REPORTING_ LINE_UNIT	/SAPSRM/ BD_WF_SC_RR_ RLUNIT	Returns all employees of a specific reporting line unit as responsible agents for shopping cart approval in the relevant process level. The document is not split into decision sets; that is, all items are assigned to the same agents.
	BUS2121	RR_ROLE	/SAPSRM/ BD_WF_SC_RR_ ROLE	Returns all user accounts of a specific user role as responsible agents for shopping cart approval in the relevant process level. The document is not split into decision sets; that is, all items are assigned to the same agents
	BUS2121	RR_SPENDING_ LIMIT_ APPROVER	/SAPSRM/ BD_WF_SC_RR_ SL	Returns all spending-limit approvers (as defined in the PPOMA_BBP attribute "Approver for Value Limit", abbreviation SLAPPROVAL) of the shopping cart's requester for approval. The selected process level is representing a placeholder for a process-level sequence that will be calculated during process start by the BAdI implementation /SAPSRM/BD_WF_CONFIG_SC_ SL. The sequence (defined by the PPOMA_BBP attribute SLAP- PROVER) ends when the approver has an approval limit that exceeds the document's total value.

Table F.2 BAdIs for Agent Determination (cont.)

Business Object	Filter Values	BAdI Implementation		Description
	Document Type	Responsibility Resolver Name		
Purchase order	BUS2201	RR_EMPLOYEE	/SAPSRM/BD_WF_ PO_RR_EMPLOYEE	Returns an employee (business partner) as responsible agent for approval in the relevant process level. The document is not split into decision sets; that is, all items are assigned to the same agent.
	BUS2201	RR_MANAGER	/SAPSRM/BD_WF_ PO_RR_MANAGER	Returns all managers of the document's requester of the previous level as responsible agents for approval in the relevant process level. The document is not split into decision sets; that is, all items are assigned to the same agent.
	BUS2201	RR_MANAGER_ OF_MANAGER	/SAPSRM/BD_WF_ PO_RR_MANOFMA	Returns all managers of approvers of the previous level as responsible agents for approval in the relevant process level. The method assigns all items of a decision set to the same area, thus respecting the existing decision sets for the document.
	BUS2201	RR_ PURCHASING_ MANAGER	/SAPSRM/BD_WF_ PO_RR_PURMGR	Returns all managers of the document's purchasing group as responsible agents for approval in the relevant process level. The document is not split into decision sets; that is, all items are assigned to the same agents.

Table F.2 BAdIs for Agent Determination (cont.)

Business Object	Filter Values	BAdI Implementation	Description
	Document Type	Responsibility Resolver Name	
	BUS2201	RR_REPORTING_ LINE_UNIT /SAPSRM/BD_WF_ PO_RR_RLUNIT	Returns all employees of a specific reporting line unit as responsible agents for approval in the relevant process level. The document is not split into decision sets; that is, all items are assigned to the same agents.
	BUS2201	RR_ROLE /SAPSRM/BD_WF_ PO_RR_ROLE	Returns all user accounts of a specific user role as responsible agents for approval in the relevant process level. The document is not split into decision sets; that is, all items are assigned to the same agents.
	BUS2201	RR_SPENDING_ LIMIT_ APPROVER /SAPSRM/BD_WF_ PO_RR_SL	Returns all spending-limit approvers (as defined in the PPOMA_BBP attribute "Approver for Value Limit", abbreviation SLAPPROVAL) of the document's requester for approval. The selected process level is representing a placeholder for a process-level sequence that will be calculated during process start by BAdI implementation /SAPSRM/BD_WF_CONFIG_ PO_SL. The sequence (defined by the PPOMA_BBP attribute SLAPPROVER) ends when the approver has an approval limit that exceeds the document's total value.

Table F.2 BAdIs for Agent Determination (cont.)

Business Object	Filter Values	BAdI Implementation	Description
	Document Type	Responsibility Resolver Name	
Contract	BUS2000113	RR_EMPLOYEE	/SAPSRM/BD_WF_CTR_RR_EMPLOYEE	Returns an employee (business partner) as responsible agent for approval in the relevant process level. The document is not split into decision sets; that is, all items are assigned to the same agent.
	BUS2000113	RR_MANAGER	/SAPSRM/BD_WF_CTR_RR_MANAGER	Returns all managers of the document's requester of the previous level as responsible agents for approval in the relevant process level. The document is not split into decision sets; that is, all items are assigned to the same agent.
	BUS2000113	RR_MANAGER_OF_MANAGER	/SAPSRM/BD_WF_CTR_RR_MANOFMA	Returns all managers of approvers of the previous level as responsible agents for approval in the relevant process level. The method assigns all items of a decision set to the same area, thus respecting the existing decision sets for the document.
	BUS2000113	RR_PURCHASING_MANAGER	/SAPSRM/BD_WF_CTR_RR_PURMGR	Returns all managers of the document's purchasing group as responsible agents for approval in the relevant process level. The document is not split into decision sets; that is, all items are assigned to the same agents.

Table F.2 BAdIs for Agent Determination (cont.)

Business Object	Filter Values	BAdI Implementation		Description
	Document Type	Responsibility Resolver Name		
	BUS2000113	RR_REPORTING_ LINE_UNIT	/SAPSRM/BD_WF_ CTR_RR_RLUNIT	Returns all employees of a specific reporting-line unit as responsible agent for approval in the relevant process level. The document is not split into decision sets; that is, all items are assigned to the same agents.
	BUS2000113	RR_ROLE	/SAPSRM/BD_WF_ CTR_RR_ROLE	Returns all user accounts of a specific user role as responsible agents for approval in the relevant process level. The document is not split into decision sets; that is, all items are assigned to the same agents.
Confirmation	BUS2203	RR_EMPLOYEE	/SAPSRM/BD_WF_ CONF_RR_ EMPLOYEE	Returns an employee (business partner) as responsible agent for approval in the relevant process level. The document is not split into decision sets; that is, all items are assigned to the same agent.
	BUS2203	RR_MANAGER	/SAPSRM/BD_WF_ CONF_RR_ MANAGER	Returns all managers of the document's requester of the previous level as responsible agents for approval in the relevant process level. The document is not split into decision sets; that is, all items are assigned to the same agent.

Table F.2 BAdIs for Agent Determination (cont.)

Business Object	Filter Values	BAdI Implementation		Description
	Document Type	Responsibility Resolver Name		
	BUS2203	RR_MANAGER_ OF_MANAGER	/SAPSRM/BD_WF_ CONF_RR_ MANOFMA	Returns all managers of approvers of the previous level as responsible agents for approval in the relevant process level. The method assigns all items of a decision set to the same area, thus respecting the existing decision sets for the document.
	BUS2203	RR_ PURCHASING_ MANAGER	/SAPSRM/BD_WF_ CONF_RR_PURMGR	Returns all managers of the document's purchasing group as responsible agents for approval in the relevant process level. The document is not split into decision sets; that is, all items are assigned to the same agents.
	BUS2203	CONF_RR_ SOURCE_ DOCUMENT_ OWNER	/SAPSRM/BD_WF_ CONF_RR_P_ OWNER	Returns the document owner of the source document as responsible agents for approval in the relevant process level. The document is not split into decision sets.
	BUS2203	RR_REPORTING_ LINE_UNIT	/SAPSRM/BD_WF_ CONF_RR_RLUNIT	Returns all employees of a specific reporting-line unit as responsible agents for approval in the relevant process level. The document is not split into decision sets; that is, all items are assigned to the same agents.

Table F.2 BAdIs for Agent Determination (cont.)

Business Object	Filter Values	BAdI Implementation		Description
	Document Type	Responsibility Resolver Name		
	BUS2203	RR_ROLE	/SAPSRM/ BD_WF_CONF_RR_ ROLE	Returns all user accounts of a specific user role as responsible agents for approval in the relevant process level. The document is not split into decision sets; that is, all items are assigned to the same agents.
Invoice	BUS2205	RR_EMPLOYEE	/SAPSRM/BD_WF_ INV_RR_ EMPLOYEE	Returns an employee (business partner) as responsible agents for approval in the relevant process level. The document is not split into decision sets; that is, all items are assigned to the same agent.
	BUS2205	RR_MANAGER	/SAPSRM/BD_WF_ INV_RR_MANAGER	Returns all managers of the document's requester of the previous level as responsible agents for approval in the relevant process level. The document is not split into decision sets; that is, all items are assigned to the same agent.
	BUS2205	RR_MANAGER_ OF_ MANAGER	/SAPSRM/BD_WF_ INV_RR_MANOFMA	Returns all managers of approvers of the previous level as responsible agents for approval in the relevant process level. The method assigns all items of a decision set to the same area, thus respecting the existing decision sets for the document.

Table F.2 BAdIs for Agent Determination (cont.)

| Business Object | Filter Values | | BAdI Implementation | Description |
	Document Type	Responsibility Resolver Name		
	BUS2205	RR_PURCHASING_MANAGER	/SAPSRM/BD_WF_INV_RR_PURMGR	Returns all managers of the document's purchasing group as responsible agents for approval in the relevant process level. The document is not split into decision sets; that is, all items are assigned to the same agents.
	BUS2205	INV_RR_SOURCE_DOCUMENT_OWNER	/SAPSRM/BD_WF_INV_RR_P_OWNER	Returns the document owner of the source document as responsible agents for approval in the relevant process level.
	BUS2205	RR_REPORTING_LINE_UNIT	/SAPSRM/BD_WF_INV_RR_RLUNIT	Returns all employees of a specific reporting line unit as responsible agents for approval in the relevant process level. The document is not split into decision sets; that is, all items are assigned to the same agents.
	BUS2205	RR_ROLE	/SAPSRM/BD_WF_INV_RR_ROLE	Returns all user accounts of a specific user role as responsible agents for approval in the relevant process level. The document is not split into decision sets; that is, all items are assigned to the same agents.
Quote	BUS2202	RR_EMPLOYEE	/SAPSRM/BD_WF_QTE_RR_EMPLOYEE	Returns an employee (business partner) as responsible agent for approval in the relevant process level. The document is not split into decision sets; that is, all items are assigned to the same agent.

Table F.2 BAdIs for Agent Determination (cont.)

Business Object	Filter Values	BAdI Implementation	Description
	Document Type	Responsibility Resolver Name	
	BUS2202	RR_MANAGER_ OF_ MANAGER /SAPSRM/BD_WF_ QTE_RR_MANOFMA	Returns all managers of approvers of the previous level as responsible agents for approval in the relevant process level. The method assigns all items of a decision set to the same area, thus respecting the existing decision sets for the document.
	BUS2202	RR_ PURCHASING_ MANAGER /SAPSRM/BD_WF_ QTE_RR_PURMGR	Returns all managers of the document's purchasing group as responsible agents for approval in the relevant process level.
	BUS2202	RR_REPORTING_ LINE_UNIT /SAPSRM/BD_WF_ QTE_RR_RLUNIT	Returns all employees of a specific reporting-line unit as responsible agents for approval in the relevant process level. The document is not split into decision sets; that is, all items are assigned to the same agents.
	BUS2202	RR_ROLE /SAPSRM/BD_WF_ QTE_RR_ROLE	Returns all user accounts of a specific user role as responsible agents for approval in the relevant process level. The document is not split into decision sets; that is, all items are assigned to the same agents.

Table F.2 BAdIs for Agent Determination (cont.)

Business Object	Filter Values	BAdI Implementation		Description
	Document Type	Responsibility Resolver Name		
RFx	BUS2200	RR_EMPLOYEE	/SAPSRM/BD_WF_RFQ_RR_EMPLOYEE	Returns an employee (business partner) as responsible agent for approval in the relevant process level. The document is not split into decision sets, that is, all items are assigned to the same agent.
	BUS2200	RR_MANAGER	/SAPSRM/BD_WF_RFQ_RR_MANAGER	Returns all managers of the document's requester of the previous level as responsible agents for approval in the relevant process level. The document is not split into decision sets; that is, all items are assigned to the same agent.
	BUS2200	RR_MANAGER_OF_MANAGER	/SAPSRM/BD_WF_RFQ_RR_MANOFMA	Returns all managers of approvers of the previous level as responsible agents for approval in the relevant process level. The method assigns all items of a decision set to the same area, thus respecting the existing decision sets for the document.
	BUS2200	RR_PURCHASING_MANAGER	/SAPSRM/BD_WF_RFQ_RR_PURMGR	Returns all managers of the document's purchasing group as responsible agents for approval in the relevant process level. The document is not split into decision sets; that is, all items are assigned to the same agents.

Table F.2 BAdIs for Agent Determination (cont.)

Business Object	Filter Values		BAdI Implementation		Description
	Document Type	Responsibility Resolver Name			
	BUS2200	RR_REPORTING_LINE_UNIT	/SAPSRM/BD_WF_RFQ_RR_RLUNIT		Returns all employees of a specific reporting-line unit as responsible agents for approval in the relevant process level. The document is not split into decision sets; that is, all items are assigned to the same agents.
	BUS2200	RR_ROLE	/SAPSRM/BD_WF_RFQ_RR_ROLE		Returns all user accounts of a specific user role as responsible agents for approval in the relevant process level. The document is not split into decision sets; that is, all items are assigned to the same agents.

Table F.2 BAdIs for Agent Determination (cont.)

F.3   Process-Controlled Workflow Advanced Troubleshooting

There are a few problems that you might encounter, which are listed here. For more detailed guidelines, refer to Chapter 16, Advanced Diagnostics.

F.3.1   The Workflow Did Not Start at All

The workflow not starting at all usually happens because of two reasons:

▶ The event linkage is not activated for events READY_FOR_RELEASE or READY_FOR_WORKFLOW. This can be corrected in the IMG via SAP SUPPLIER RELATIONSHIP MANAGEMENT • SRM SERVER • CROSS-APPLICATION BASIC SETTINGS • BUSINESS WORKFLOW • PROCESS-CONTROLLED WORKFLOW • TECHNICAL CONFIGURATION • CHECK EVENT TYPE LINKAGE.

▶ System user WF-BATCH is not configured correctly, for example, because of a wrong password. For correcting this automatic workflow, configuration has to be executed again in the IMG via SAP Supplier Relationship Management • SRM Server • Cross-Application Basic Settings • Business Workflow • Process-Controlled Workflow • Technical Configuration • Customize SAP Business Workflow Automatically.

F.3.2 The Workflow Ran to Completion, But the Shopping Cart Is Still in Awaiting Approval Status

If the workflow ran to completion, but the shopping cart is still in Awaiting Approval status, this normally is not a workflow-related problem. At the end of an approval process, the control is handed back over from the SAP SRM workflow framework to the SAP SRM application. For this purpose, the /SAPSRM/ IF_PDO_ADV_BASE~HANDLE_PROCESS_FINISHED method of a business object (class SAPSRM/CL_PDO_BO_<BO>_ADV) is called. This method processes closing actions, for example, changing the status of a document to APPROVED or REJECTED. At this point in time, the workflow process is already finished. If the processing of this method fails, for example, due to an inconsistency within the document, the status of the document remains AWAITING APPROVAL.

You can check whether the described problem is the reason for the behavior in the workflow log. The name of the failed process step is Handle Process Finish. For further problem analysis, we recommend that you

▶ Check Transaction ST22. An exception (dump) might be listed describing the reason for failure.

▶ Check customer modifications made in this area.

▶ Search for available notes solving this issue, and debug the issue.

For debugging, you should do the following:

▶ Check in Transaction SWI6 to see if there is already a message that indicates what caused the failure. If the overall workflow status is in Error, then the background step Handle Process Finish will also be in status Error.

▶ Navigate to the background step, and check the Message tab in the Technical View for any message. If you don't have a message in the workflow or don't understand the message, you can also try to debug the final call.

To debug the call, you should do the following:

- Start Transaction SE24.

- Create an instance of `/SAPSRM/CL_WF_PDO_<BO>`, where `<BO>` denotes the concrete business object.

- Debug the message handle process finish. Change the `sy-uname` variable from your debug user to `WF-BATCH` to also consider authorization problems for the technical workflow user.

F.3.3   The Approval Work Item Was Not Sent Properly

If the approval work item was created but was not sent to anyone or was sent to the workflow administrator, it might have happened because of the following reasons:

- The tasks are not general tasks. The workflow log will show that there is no agent assigned to the actual workflow step. However, no error is logged. If the workflow tasks are not generalized, no one is allowed to execute the tasks.

    Whether the tasks are generalized or not can be checked and corrected in IMG via SAP SUPPLIER RELATIONSHIP MANAGEMENT • SRM SERVER • CROSS-APPLICATION BASIC SETTINGS • BUSINESS WORKFLOW • PROCESS-CONTROLLED WORKFLOW • TECHNICAL CONFIGURATION • GENERALIZE TASKS for all tasks of the task groups `40000003` (SRM Approval Process Decision Tasks) and `40000007` (SRM Approval Process User Tasks).

- The implementation for agent determination returns nothing or an agent who is excluded. The workflow log will show that there is no agent assigned to the actual workflow step. However, an error should be displayed, and the administrator should receive a CCMS entry.

- The UWL connector is not switched on or the connection fails. If the workflow log shows a correct agent assignment, and the user received a work item in his SAP Business Workplace, there must be a connection failure to UWL. This can be checked and corrected in the UWL administration area.

F.3.4   The Approval Display Is Wrong or Empty

The information visualized by the approval process overview is prepared data provided by SAP SRM approval frameworks. Therefore, erroneous preparation of the data or the supply of erroneous data can be the origin of an erroneous process visualization.

A link for downloading process data as an XML file is provided in the approval process overview. This downloaded file should be checked to determine whether the data provided for the approval process overview are correct or not. If the visualization of the data is wrong, the method /SAPSRM/IF_PDO_DO_APV_EXT~INI-TIALIZE of class /SAPSRM/CL_PDO_DO_APV_EXT should be debugged for further error analysis.

If the wrong data was provided, the executed approval process should be checked in Transaction SLG1. Therefore, you should use the parameter /SAPSRM/ as OBJECT and the SRM document GUID as EXTERNAL ID (see Figure F.1). The search result is a listing of the Business Rules Framework (BRF) evaluation results. You can read which process schema was found for the current SAP SRM document and which process levels are active.

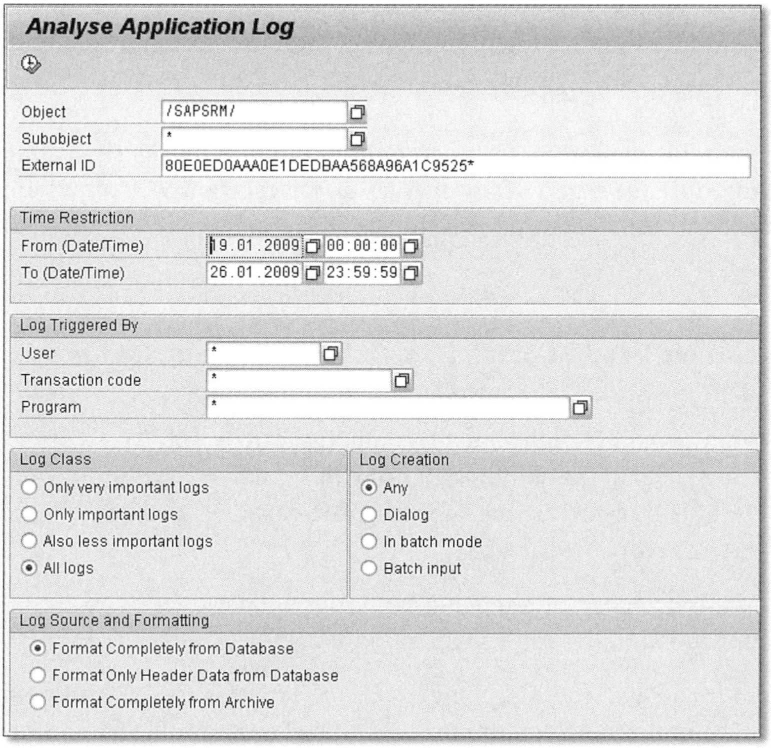

Figure F.1 Parameters for Relevant Logs

F.4 Application-Controlled Workflow Advanced Trouble-shooting

There are a few problems that you might encounter, which are listed here. For more detailed guidelines, refer to Chapter 16, Advanced Diagnostics.

F.4.1 The Workflow Did Not Start at All

The workflow not starting at all usually happens when you have defined incorrect start conditions (such as forgetting a NOT or using AND instead of OR). Track this by turning on the event log (Transaction SWELS), raising the event manually (Transaction SWUE), and looking at the log (Transaction SWEL) to verify that the events were successful.

> **Note**
>
> Keep in mind this is a troubleshooting tip to raise the event manually. At runtime, the workflows are started programmatically, and the events are not actually raised; however, they are all read programmatically. This means when troubleshooting, you can raise events manually to ensure everything is set up correctly.

Check that the logical expressions in the start conditions are correct by simulating them in the condition editor, and verify that all of the relevant workflows are active. The workflow trace shows you exactly how the condition is evaluated at runtime.

F.4.2 The Workflow Ran to Completion, But the Shopping Cart Is Still in "Awaiting Approval" Status

If the workflow ran to completion, but the shopping cart is still in AWAITING APPROVAL status, this actually has nothing to do with workflow. The problem is that the mechanism for transferring the shopping cart details to backend objects has failed to report an error correctly.

If errors are reported correctly, the shopping cart is put into CONTAINS ERRORS status, and entries are added to the application monitors.

If errors are not reported, the shopping cart simply remains in AWAITING APPROVAL status. The best way to determine the source of these problems is to use the function module TEST option (in Transaction SE37) to rerun and verify the behavior of the appropriate `SPOOL_*_CREATE_DO` function module, especially if you are using BAdIs to manipulate the data being transferred.

F.4.3 The Approval Work Item Was Created But Was Not Sent Properly

Both these scenarios, if the approval work item was created but was not sent to anyone, or if it was sent to the workflow administrator, indicate an agent assignment problem. Either no one was assigned to the relevant task on which the work item is based, or the approvers found do not have access to execute the relevant work item.

Remember that agent assignment starts with all possible agents, a then is narrowed to the subset of selected agents, and then narrowed again by removing any excluded agents. If the selected agents are not a subset of possible agents, they are ignored and the work item is — usually — sent to the workflow administrator (see SAP Note 491804).

If all possible/selected agents are also excluded agents, the work item will be in limbo without any valid agents. Your workflow administrator then needs to forward the work item to a more appropriate agent.

F.4.4 The Approval Display Is Wrong or Empty

The approval display is a tailored representation of the graphical workflow log. Usually, problems in the display are related to new steps being included in the graphical workflow log that the display program is not expecting. The problem can often be fixed by making sure that, if you add extra steps to a shopping cart workflow, all non-approval steps are marked as STEP NOT IN WORKFLOW LOG.

G   The Authors

Jocelyn Dart is an SAP employee and has a number of specialties, including SAP Business Workflow, SAP Interactive Forms by Adobe, and HCM Processes and Forms. She has been involved with SAP products since 1990 on various customer sites. In 1994, she joined SAP Australia as a help desk support consultant. Later, she became an instructor giving courses in ABAP, Internet Transaction Server, SAP Business Workflow, SAP SRM, and SAP Interactive Forms by Adobe. She is currently a SAP Field Services consultant advising various major Australian and New Zealand customers. She is acknowledged as a global expert in SAP Business Workflow and regional expert in HCM Processes and Forms. Jocelyn Dart has a bachelor's degree in applied science. (Computing Science) from the University of Technology, Sydney.

Erik Dick started his professional career as an independent software developer for personal computers. He did basic studies in computer science at TU of Kaiserslautern until 1997. He then joined the Fraunhofer Institute for Experimental Software Engineering as a professional software developer to support scientific projects (C++/Java SE). In 2001, he continued his career as a JEE expert at SAP Markets in the area of Content Integrator (Master Data Management). He then transitioned to SAP AG, working in the SRM development organization as an architecture developer for the SRM workflow framework (ABAP). Since 2008, he has worked as senior developer for the architecture group of SAP NetWeaver Business Process and Event Management.

Ginger Gatling is a senior product manager with SAP NetWeaver Management. She joined SAP in 1997 and spent her first seven years within Educational Services at SAP America. She taught more than 30 classes, including SAP Business Workflow, security, SAP CRM Middleware, integration, and administration courses. Additionally, she authored classes on SAP NetWeaver Business Warehouse security and system auditing. In 2004, she joined the SAP NetWeaver organization, working for SAP Labs, where she has served as product manager for BPM topics (including SAP Business Workflow, Universal Worklist, SAP NetWeaver Business Process Management), integration topics (SAP NetWeaver Process Integration), and other SAP NetWeaver topics as required. She is an active member in the Americas SAP User Group, serving on the board of her local North Texas ASUG Chapter, and she is a big fan and contributor to SDN and business process expert communities. Ginger has a master's degree in music theory from Northwestern University.

Oliver Hilss is a senior developer equally experienced in Java and ABAP technologies. He has been with SAP since 2001. After working as a Java developer in the area of Master Data Management he joined the SRM development team within the SAP Business Suite organization. During the past four years, Oliver was in charge of workflow-related development within the SAP SRM application and contributed significantly to corresponding architecture and design decisions. Oliver graduated in computer science at the University of Applied Sciences, Furtwangen.

Somya Kapoor is a product manager within Information Worker Solutions concentrating on Duet. She joined SAP in 2005 and had the opportunity to work on new and exciting SAP emerging solutions such as xApps (Resource Planning and Management [xRPM], Product Definition [xPD]), Enterprise Search, and Duet. She is an active contributor to the online communities SDN, BPX, and Microsoft TechNet. Somya has a bachelor's degree in computer science and master's degree in software engineering from San Jose State University.

Silvana Kempf studied civil engineering at Bauhaus University Weimar and BTU Cottbus. After graduating, she started her career as a Java developer at SAP Markets in 2001 in the area of Content Integrator (Master Data Management). She then transitioned to SAP AG, working in the SRM development organization. She started as an ABAP developer, and then became the project lead for workflow. In this context, she achieved the Project Management Professional (PMP) certificate by PMI®. After working within SAP SRM for three years, she became a project manager for the SAP NetWeaver organization. She currently works as a project manager for Java Server and Infrastructure development.

Susan Keohan is a senior application developer at MIT Lincoln Laboratory. She has worked with SAP since 1995, when MIT began its implementation. She has been designing and implementing processes with SAP Business Workflow since 1997, starting with SAP R/3 release 3.1C. She was instrumental in founding the ASUG Workflow and BPM Special Interest Group as well as the SAP-WUG mailing list. In 2002, Susan transferred to MIT Lincoln Laboratory to begin a new SAP implementation there — with many workflow applications to develop and maintain. She has presented various workflow-related topics at ASUG conferences and continues to serve as the Program Chair for the Workflow and BPM SIG. In 2008, Susan achieved one of her highest professional honors — to be named an SAP Mentor.

Thomas Kosog has been with SAP America since 1994 and in software development since 1986. As a Platinum Workflow Consultant, Thomas has designed and implemented SAP Business Workflows on several customer projects in almost all SAP applications and releases, especially in the SRM, HR organizational charts, Finance, and Master Data areas. Thomas has also given many workflow trainings and has been a speaker for workflow presentations at SAP TechEd and ASUG. Most recently, Thomas has been focused on the integration of Web Dynpro ABAP applications and SAP Interactive Forms by Adobe into custom built workflows as well as performing customization of work items in the Universal Worklist of the SAP NetWeaver Portal.

Paul Médaille is well known in the SAP technical community for his conference presentations, webinars, and contributions to SDN. Paul has been with SAP for more than 10 years as a consultant, educator, and product manager, with deep knowledge of Basis, SOA, and SAP NetWeaver Process Integration. He has a degree in mathematics from the University of California at Davis, and lives in Eugene, Oregon, with his wife Jessica and two greyhounds.

Mike Pokraka is an independent consultant who started working with SAP in 1997. His previous background was in both business and technical areas, having just left a data processing and high-volume laser printing bureau, which he co-founded five years prior in 1992. Upon joining the SAP world, he worked in various diverse areas ranging from database administration to MM/SD, ABAP development, and EDI, before finally discovering SAP Business Workflow in 2000 and working with it ever since. He is also a regular speaker at conferences such as ASUG and SAP TechEd and was nominated as an SAP Mentor for 2009.

Alan Rickayzen is the product manager of Alloy, the first joint software product between IBM and SAP. This integrates IBM Lotus Notes with SAP and includes workflow decision management. He has been with SAP since 1992 and in data processing since 1988. In 1995, he joined the SAP Business Workflow group performing development work as well as consulting for various major U.S. customers. During this time, he amassed a good technical knowledge of the product before moving in 1998 to workflow product management where he was the principal liaison for the SAP workflow user groups. He has written regularly for SAP journals and was an author of the first edition of *Practical Workflow for SAP*. In his pursuit of Interoperability he became one of the original authors of the Web standard BPEL4People and WS-HumanTask, which have now been taken to Oasis. Alan Rickayzen graduated from Kings College, London with a bachelor of science degree in physics.

Shalini Sabnani is a senior developer specializing in workflow and ABAP. She has been working with Innovapost since the company formed in 2001 developing and supporting one of the largest SAP implementations in North America. Since her original SAP implementation in the 1990s, Shalini has acquired many years of hands-on, real-world, client experience implementing and managing large SAP systems. She is currently part of Innovapost's Application Management team performing development work on various critical client projects within Canada. Prior to joining Innovapost, Shalini spent several years consulting to clients on various IS/IT matters with a particular expertise in data architecture. Shalini holds an honors degree in computer science and a bachelor of commerce degree from Pune University, India.

Jörn Sedlmayr joined SAP AG in 2005 and is a senior software developer. He studied industrial engineering at the university (TH) of Karlsruhe. After graduating, Jörn joined BASF IT Services GmbH as a custom developer for various modules of SAP R/3 and for SAP SRM, with a major focus on SAP Business Workflow design, development, and administration in these areas. Since he joined SAP, he has been working as a developer on various topics within SAP CRM, namely CRM Service, Resource Planning, and CRM Worklist integration for workflow.

Ted Sohn has developed numerous workflow applications for SAP internal and major U.S. customers. He is a Platinum consultant in the area of SAP NetWeaver development. He is unique because his expertise covers both ABAP and Java. His expertise includes SAP Business Workflow, Universal Worklist, Web Dynpro ABAP, Web Dynpro Java, Development Component based Java development, and so on. He also has solid experience in SAP NetWeaver Development Infrastructure (NWDI) administration. His current projects focus on SOA and SAP NetWeaver Business Process Management.

All authors have chosen to donate their royalties to Doctors Without Borders/ Médecins Sans Frontières.

Doctors Without Borders/Médecins Sans Frontières (MSF) is an international medical humanitarian organization that delivers emergency aid in nearly 60 countries to victims of armed conflict, medical catastrophe, natural disasters, and malnutrition. The organization was founded in 1971 by doctors and journalists in France and today is an international organization made up of 19 sections. The work of Doctors Without Borders is based on the humanitarian principles of medical ethics and impartiality. The organization is committed to bringing quality medical care to people caught in crisis regardless of race, religion, or political affiliation and operates independently of any political, military, or religious agendas. The organization received the Nobel Peace Prize in 1999.

Index

X

- Understand how to process all of your service, problem, and change requests

- Get step-by-step configuration instructions for ChaRM and Application Incident Management

- Find practical advice and best practices

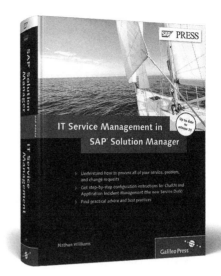

Nathan Williams

IT Service Management in SAP Solution Manager

Stay ahead of the curve with IT Service Management (ITSM)! This is the comprehensive guide to the new and improved functionalities in SAP Solution Manager. Find everything you need to work with the 7.1 versions of ChaRM and Application Incident Management (the new Service Desk): the important concepts, instructions for configuration and functionality, and expert tips and best practices.

903 pp., 2013, 79,95 Euro / US$ 79.95
ISBN 978-1-59229-440-4
www.sap-press.com

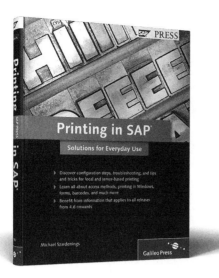

■ Discover configuration steps, troubleshooting, and tips and tricks for local and server-based printing

■ Learn all about access methods, printing in Windows, forms, barcodes, and much more

■ Benefit from information that applies to all releases from 4.6 onwards

Michael Szardenings

Printing in SAP

Solutions for Everyday Use

Become a printing expert after learning all of the answers to the most frequently asked questions for output management in SAP systems! This book teaches you the basic knowledge you need to configure printing setup (software and hardware) and describes the ways in which data from the SAP system can be converted in different print formats. You will also find screenshots and detailed descriptions of configuration parameters that will help you in your daily work.

286 pp., 2011, 69,95 Euro / US$ 69.95
ISBN 978-1-59229-396-4
www.sap-press.com

- Provides a complete overview of the solution for the management of business applications

- Explains the processes and functions in release 7.1 clearly

- Shows all tools in day-to-day use

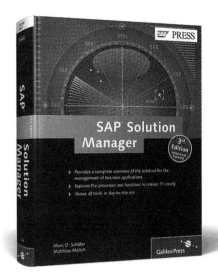

Marc O. Schäfer, Matthias Melich

SAP Solution Manager

Hardly any SAP product in recent years is as important or complex as the SAP Solution Manager. However, its scope is so vast that it can be difficult to understand how it can help you, or what has been updated since the prior release.

This book answers all of your questions regarding the Solution Manager, whether you are interested in implementation and documentation; maintenance and testing; or monitoring, technical operation, and management problems.

724 pp., 3. edition 2012, 69,95 Euro / US$ 69.95

ISBN 978-1-59229-388-9

www.sap-press.com

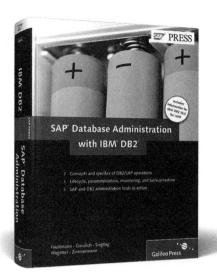

■ Concepts and specifics of
DB2/SAP operations

■ Lifecycle, parameterization,
monitoring, and backup/restore

■ SAP and DB2 administration tools
in action

■ Includes information for IBM DB2
10.5 for LUW

André Faustmann, Michael Greulich, André Siegling, Benjamin Wegener, Ronny
Zimmermann

SAP Database Administration with IBM DB2

When you're working with IBM DB2, you're maintaining the Rolls Royce
of the SAP-certified database systems. This book is your companion in
your daily tasks, from setup to decommissioning. Learn how SAP and
DB2 work together, see all administration tools in action, discover
strategies for troubleshooting, and acquire key skills for backup and
restore. Your non-stop guide to a safe ride!

approx. 753 pp., 89,95 Euro / US$ 89.95
ISBN 978-1-59229-449-7, June 2013
www.sap-press.com

■ Use SAP Solution Manager to monitor the amount and efficiency of custom code in your system

■ Learn how to take advantage of tools such as CCLM, SCOV, SAP Clone Finder, and more

■ Explore custom code best practices and reporting techniques

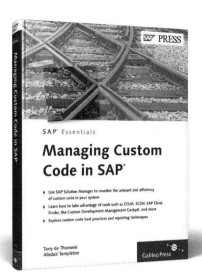

Alisdair Templeton, Tony de Thomasis

Managing Custom Code in SAP

Don't let custom code negatively affect your business—this book will help you create a lean and mean SAP system landscape! You'll learn what tools help determine when custom code is unnecessary, and how to assess the amount, quality, and efficiency of existing code. With the practical instructions in this book, you'll be able to use the tools you need in no time flat!

351 pp., 2013, 69,95 Euro / US$ 84.95
ISBN 978-1-59229-436-7
www.sap-press.com

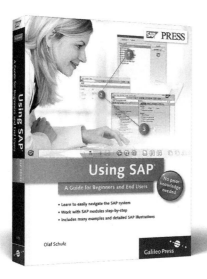

- Learn to easily navigate the SAP system

- Work with SAP modules step-by-step

- Includes many examples and detailed SAP illustrations

Olaf Schulz

Using SAP

A Guide for Beginners and End Users

This book helps end users and beginners get started in SAP ERP and provides readers with the basic knowledge they need for their daily work. Readers will get to know the essentials of working with the SAP system, learn about the SAP systems' structures and functions, and discover how SAP connects to critical business processes. Whether this book is used as an exercise book or as a reference book, readers will find what they need to help them become more comfortable with SAP ERP.

388 pp., 2012, 39,95 Euro / US$ 39.95
ISBN 978-1-59229-408-4
www.sap-press.com

Interested in reading more?

Please visit our website for all new
book and e-book releases from SAP PRESS.

www.sap-press.com